UNIVERSITY CASEBOOK SERIES®

PROFESSIONAL RESPONSIBILITY

PROBLEMS AND MATERIALS

CONCISE TWELFTH EDITION

by

THOMAS D. MORGAN
Oppenheim Professor of Law Emeritus
The George Washington University

RONALD D. ROTUNDA
The Doy & Dee Henly Chair and
Distinguished Professor of Jurisprudence
The Dale E. Fowler School of Law
Chapman University

JOHN S. DZIENKOWSKI
Dean John F. Sutton, Jr. Chair in
Lawyering and the Legal Process
The University of Texas

FOUNDATION
PRESS

© 1976, 1981, 1984, 1987, 1991, 1995, 2000, 2003 FOUNDATION PRESS
© 2006, 2008, 2011 THOMSON REUTERS/FOUNDATION PRESS
© 2014 LEG, Inc. d/b/a West Academic
    444 Cedar Street, Suite 700
    St. Paul, MN 55101
    1-877-888-1330

Printed in the United States of America

ISBN: 978-1-60930-324-2

Mat #41406002

To Kathryn, Nora, and Karla

PREFACE

The three years since the publication of our Eleventh Edition have seen a transformation in the lives of many American lawyers and students. Several thousand lawyers have lost their jobs entirely, many of them partners who thought they had lifetime tenure. Law students who imagined they would enter a highly-compensated, busy profession, now frequently find their entry deferred until an often-unspecified future date.

Some of the changes in the realities of practice can be attributed to the current economic recession, but at least part of the transformation may be traced to fundamental changes in the demand for legal services and to alternative ways of providing legal assistance. This book will explore many such changes and examine whether some of the traditional rules regulating lawyer conduct may now lack the moral and practical justification they once had.

This Twelfth Edition tries to acknowledge the profession's changes without losing the qualities that have made the book successful. Problems are still followed by questions designed to provoke discussion. Questions are followed by case and opinion summaries designed to give examples of ways courts and rule makers have approached the issues raised.

This Concise Edition differs from the unabridged Twelfth Edition primarily in length. It is designed for two-credit or shorter classes that cannot complete the full book. As in earlier editions, black letter fundamental questions are followed by references relevant to the issues those questions raise. Each problem continues to group questions under one of four issues, again to more clearly structure student preparation, discussion and understanding. For the Concise Edition, we have omitted six problems entirely and shortened others by deleting cases or topics. But we have also added text and note material that should allow classes to cover some of the omitted issues and minimize the loss of coverage. We have not, however, reduced the rigor required to wrestle with the questions raised.

References to the ABA Model Rules of Professional Conduct are to the Model Rules, as amended through 2013. References to the ABA Model Code of Judicial Conduct are to the 2007 version. Restatement references are to the Restatement Third, The Law Governing Lawyers, published by the American Law Institute in 2000.

This edition's three authors thank the authors and publishers cited, in particular the American Bar Association and American Law Institute, for permission to reprint their copyrighted material. We thank our research assistants, Alison Bollbach and William Gottfried, and our faculty assistants, Ms. Maria Sanchez and Penny Tillman. We also thank the many professors and practitioners who have offered thoughtful comments and suggestions on our materials. We listen to those comments and we hope you will find the Twelfth Edition an up-to-date and useful successor to its predecessors.

T.D.M

R.D.R

J.S.D.

Washington, D.C.
Orange, CA
Austin, TX

February 2014

SUMMARY OF CONTENTS

TABLE OF CONTENTS

TABLE OF CASES

The principal cases are in bold type.

TABLE OF STATUTES

TABLE OF AUTHORITIES

PROFESSIONAL RESPONSIBILITY

PROBLEMS AND MATERIALS

CONCISE TWELFTH EDITION

CHAPTER I

THE LEGAL PROFESSION: BACKGROUND AND FUNDAMENTAL ISSUES

A. INTRODUCTION

DOONESBURY   by Garry Trudeau

The Doonesbury humor is still biting after almost 40 years, but in this case, Garry Trudeau proved a poor prophet. The study of professional responsibility has proved to be more than "just another defunct fad." It has survived and prospered and seems likely to continue to do so. At least three reasons may account for the continuing interest.

First, the subject of the course in professional responsibility is the legal profession itself. As a lawyer, you may use the substance of your torts course periodically, but you will use the substance of professional responsibility daily. This course is about lawyers as they engage in the practice of law. Whatever the theoretical interest of the subject matter, its practical content is extremely high.

Second, at the time Trudeau produced the Doonesbury cartoon, the ABA Model Code of Professional Responsibility was only five years old. Many people believed that the Code, the product of several years' work by a distinguished commission, had resolved all questions that were worth considering.

Almost as soon as significant numbers of people began to look seriously at the Code, however, they realized it had answered many questions badly and left others unresolved altogether. The debate on the appropriate content of the standards, and the work of articulating them in enforceable rules, has continued to this day.

Third, while much of the work in professional responsibility has focused on the legal rules applicable to an attorney's behavior, it has become increasingly clear that the course in "legal ethics" offers an unusually good opportunity to apply the insights of history, sociology, economics, and philosophy to fundamental legal questions.

What such study reveals is that, far from being a unitary profession with a long and consistent tradition grounded in fundamental philosophical ideals, the legal profession is a rich, complex, and often perverse mixture of traditions, roles, and standards. Understanding the insights and distinctions suggested by history and philosophy will not automatically resolve practical problems, but it may help a lawyer better understand the questions presented and better see relationships between issues that otherwise might be obscured.

B. WHAT IS A LAWYER?

The subject of this course is the law governing the practice of law. A lawyer is someone legally authorized by a jurisdiction's highest court to engage in the practice of law. If that strikes you as circular and not very helpful, congratulations, you are paying attention.

Defining the "practice of law" is critical to understanding what only a lawyer is licensed to do. That definition, in turn has been maddeningly "vague or conclusory" and "jurisdictions have differed significantly" in describing what the definition includes.[1]

Perhaps the best single definition is the one that the ABA Model Code of Professional Responsibility, EC 3–5, offered in 1970: "[T]he practice of law relates to the rendition of services for others that call for the professional judgment of the lawyer * * * [which means the lawyer's] educated ability to relate the general body and philosophy of law to a specific legal problem of the client."

That definition tells us at least two things.

First, lawyers act for others. People do not have to be lawyers to write documents affecting themselves or even to appear in court on their own behalf. However, only lawyers may do those things on behalf of someone else.

Second, lawyers relate law to a client's specific fact situation. Your law professor, for example, does not have to be a licensed lawyer to write a book or even to teach you contracts or torts. Writing and talking about the law in general—even as the law might relate to hypothetical fact patterns—is not the practice of law because it does not address an actual problem facing the writer's or teacher's particular client.

Does it make sense to say that only lawyers may engage in the practice of law? Can you imagine a civilized society that does not regulate the delivery of legal services in that way? Whatever your answers to these questions, it is clear that the legal profession and the role of the lawyer in our society are significantly different today than at most times in the nation's history. The following two excerpts help put today's legal profession into context.

––––––––

[1]   Restatement Third, The Law Governing Lawyers § 4, Comment c. ABA Model Rule 5.5, Comment 2, simply says: "The definition of the practice of law is established by law and varies from one jurisdiction to another." Not much help there!

Richard B. Morris,* The Legal Profession in America on
the Eve of the Revolution, in Harry W. Jones, Ed.,
Political Separation and Legal Continuity
4–11, 18–19 (1976).**

If the Revolutionary era was a legal-and constitution-minded age dominated by lawyers, the period of seventeenth-century settlement was the miraculous era of law without lawyers, a time when law was shaped by theologians, politicians, farmers, fishermen, and merchants. This generalization applies to all the colonies settled before the Stuart Restoration, but it is conspicuously appropriate to the Puritan colonies wherein the clergy played an exceptional role in lawmaking and where laymen universally acted as judges. Not a single lawyer came to Plymouth on the *Mayflower*. Massachusetts Bay, settled a decade later, did have some legally-trained men among its first arrivals, but not one among them had then been practicing law in England. The first educated attorney venturing to practice in that colony was Thomas Lechford, whose activities dating from 1637 or thereabouts, were limited, since he was disbarred shortly thereafter for tampering with a jury. While lawyers were not technically prevented from practice, Article XXVI of the Body of Liberties, the initial law code adopted in 1641, while permitting attorneys to plead causes other than their own, disallowed all fees or rewards, thus, for a time at least, withholding inducements to practice as a respectable means of livelihood. Indeed, many of John Cotton's fellow Puritans, both in England and in America at that time, would have agreed with his characterization of lawyers as unconscionable advocates who "bolster out a bad case by quirks of writ and tricks and quillets of law."

Early hostility to the profession of the law was by no means confined to reformist New England. It was manifest as well in the tobacco colonies. A Maryland act of 1674 recited the allegation that the "good people of this Province are much burthened" by lawyers taking and exacting "excessive fees." Curbs continued into the eighteenth century. In 1707, Maryland's legislature set rules for controlling the admission of attorneys on the basis of the alleged "corruption, ignorance and extortion" of several of them and set such ceilings on fees that leading attorneys withdrew in protest from practice for a short time. The limitation on fees continued in force as late as 1729. In Virginia so deep-seated was anti-lawyer prejudice that a statute of 1645 virtually disbarred paid attorneys. Its repeal a decade later failed to end discrimination against the legal profession. In 1657 the court heavily fined a lawyer for appearing in court on behalf of a client, and the situation was not stabilized until 1680, when attorneys were permitted to practice under rigid restrictions and after obtaining a license from the governor. * * *

* * * In short, courts dominated by laymen informed by a few basic lawbooks such as Dalton's *Country Justice*, as in the contemporary English county seats, and litigated by attorneys in fact, who were

---

* When the author wrote this article, he was Gouverneur Morris Professor of History Emeritus at Columbia University.

** Copyright © 1976 by the American Bar Association. Reprinted by permission.

agents with powers of attorney (including among them numerous wives of absent litigants), provided the substance of justice without the benefit of a professional bar. * * *

* * * Somewhere between the Stuart Restoration and that systematic imperial machinery set up following the Glorious Revolution, one finds that the socio-economic structure of the colonies underwent a transformation. In the North a merchant-capitalist system was evolving based upon rapidly expanding transatlantic and intercolonial trade. In the South, a plantation economy emerged, based on the production for export of the great staples, tobacco and rice, and spawning a slave-holding and property-conscious society. That emergent business society was less egalitarian than at the time of settlement and determined to protect its interests against a variety of threats—whether from the constrictive trade laws of Parliament, from challenges to land titles, or from depreciating currencies. Everywhere the propertied class now exerted an influence toward security and stability, while the rapid expansion of business and the utilization of more sophisticated instruments in transatlantic trade necessitated a resort to the more technical legal system of the mother country.

Somewhere, then, around 1690 we find the legal profession establishing a foothold in the colonies. While the roster of trained legal specialists expanded dramatically over the next three decades, nonspecialists without professional training were descending on the courts in hordes. A host of parasitic pettifoggers, encouraged by the practice of filing writs by sheriffs and their deputies, easily outnumbered the trained members of the bar. Shoemakers, wigmakers, and masons procured deputations from the sheriffs and stirred up petty and contemptible litigation. It seems almost incredible that the colonial folk of the eighteenth century would manifest a litigious spirit even more intense than their forbears, but the theologian-statesman Cotton Mather was prompted in 1719 to found, in addition to a variety of organizations for effective lobbying and for suppressing vice, a Society of Peacemakers, which aimed to "divert Law-suits" and promote arbitration. If Mather achieved any success, it was not perceptible to the later generation of lawyers which claimed John Adams. Rather did Adams, whose own town attained such notoriety that "as litigious as Braintree" became proverbial, feel impelled to declaim against "the dirty dabblers in the law" who were taking bread out of the mouths of respectable lawyers.

Efforts to limit the legal profession to qualified attorneys mark the entire pre-Revolutionary era, along with enjoining sheriffs and their deputies from filing writs or giving legal advice. Even earlier, in the first few decades of the eighteenth century we find the legal profession asserting its claims to a monopoly over litigation. In New York a bar association has been unearthed as early as 1710, and one scholar insists that it functioned continuously thereafter, certainly in a rather formal sense by the year 1756. In Massachusetts an embryo bar association can be traced back at least to the year 1759. Even John Adams found its meeting "delightful." Aside from affording their members a chance for sociability, such associations, in effect guilds, were concerned about limiting the number of practitioners, restricting clerkships, barring the disqualified and, in later years, proposing legislative reforms.

To a rising and ambitious lawyer like Adams, the restrictive measures that had been taken by the bar of his province did not seem a sufficient deterrent, and he was led to bemoan the threatening number of his juniors seeking admission to practice. "They swarm and multiply," he complained with characteristic exaggeration. Still, the standards that were drawn up in Massachusetts were rather rigid. The Essex County bar in 1769 prescribed three years of clerking before admission to the inferior courts, another two years of practice in the lower courts before being admitted to the Superior Court as an attorney, and another two years more in practice before the Superior Court as a prerequisite to the status of barrister that they were desperately intent on establishing. Not only did they attempt to transplant those distinctions in the legal profession found in contemporary England, but in 1762 they further introduced the pageantry of the common law courts by requiring judges and lawyers to wear austere judicial gowns and wigs, a practice emulated in New York two years later.

In New York also, the lawyers raised the bars. An agreement entered into in 1756 by the "gentlemen of the Law" provided that they would cease taking any clerks for a period of fourteen years, the only exception being that each subscriber could take one of his own sons. Furthermore, at the end of that period, when clerkships were reopened, the lawyers stipulated that clerks must possess college degrees and that attorneys could take only one clerk at a time. The lawyer was to exact a £200 fee from his clerk, who would be required to serve for a minimum of five years. It was this monopolistic agreement which stood in the way of young John Jay's plans to study law. His father, a prosperous New York merchant, considered sending his son to London or Bristol to clerk in a law office there. He found out that in Bristol a five-year clerkship was required and the payment of a fee of from £200 to £300. If there was no alternative, Jay's father even thought of enrolling his son at the Inns of Court. Fortunately for Jay, in January of 1764 the members of the New York City bar relaxed their rules. Under the new agreement, an attorney could take a second clerk, but only after his first clerk had served for three years, thus insuring that no attorney would have more than two clerks at one time. Benjamin Kissam agreed to take John Jay on under these terms, but in fact Kissam had taken Lindley Murray as his clerk only a year before. Strictly speaking, Kissam should have waited until the end of 1764 before admitting another clerk to his office. Somehow these technicalities were waived; no one seems to have protested, and the first Chief Justice of the United States Supreme Court finally won his chance to climb the ladder of the legal profession.

———

Robert Stevens,[*] Democracy and the Legal Profession: Cautionary Notes
3 Learning and the Law 18 (No. 3, 1976).[**]

Law was not a profession [then] open to the masses, and during the 1780s and 1790s in most states an effort was made to keep it as narrow as possible. Each state except for Virginia—and that for peculiar reasons—retained a period of apprenticeship. This period was reduced if the young lawyer attended college, but there were still only half a dozen colleges in the new states. (For instance, Massachusetts had a five-year apprenticeship at that time, but only three years for Harvard or Yale graduates.)

* * * We still don't know what happened to lawyers [from 1820 to 1860] * * *. But what we can say, categorically, is that if the profession was heavily anglicized until 1820, after 1820 the old English notions of the professions slowly collapsed.

* * * In America, there was an obvious decline of formal structures; the bar associations had largely evaporated, as had the apprenticeship system. Legal education in the United States had fallen into a decline. The legal profession was "wide open." Such training as there was in law was almost invariably picked up on the job.

What appear[s] to have emerged from the impact of these forces is that, by the mid-nineteenth century, the lawyer had a different function in America from his counterpart in England. He became the man who greased the wheels of society—what today might be referred to, depending on one's perspective, as the "leading citizen," "hired gun," or "the multi-purpose social science decision maker." Whichever perspective you have, however, there is no question that the concept of the lawyer and the function he served in America after the Civil War bore little resemblance to his English counterparts.

What happened after 1870, both in the society as a whole and in the legal profession, was a process of institutionalization. It followed the years of Civil War, of rapid growth in population and of westward expansion. It was a time when great corporations were born, when great law firms grew and when universities came of age.

Significantly, the development of legal education—or, more accurately, of the resurgence of law schools—preceded that of the legal profession. Dwight at Columbia in the late 1860s, and Langdell, who became dean of Harvard Law School in 1870, were the two who set the pattern for the kind of legal education which we think of today.

What Langdell did was to take the erratic law training as it was being practiced in the law offices and systematize it. Building on the earlier work of Story at Harvard, he completed the process of taking law training out of the law offices and placed it firmly inside the universities. Academic law became respectable, as it never had been under the English system—or during the Jacksonian period. * * *

Langdell had a vision of academic respectability, and he was remarkably successful as a role model. Other universities began

---

[*]   When the author wrote this article, he was Provost at Tulane University.

[**]   Copyright © 1976 by the American Bar Association. Reprinted by permission.

developing law schools, as did various private entrepreneurs. At the same time, under pressure from the ABA, states gradually reintroduced a period of apprenticeship.

Indeed, by 1900 most states had returned to the three-year apprenticeship requirement, and bar exams had begun to reappear in the 1890s. Yet legal education still remained voluntary. "The principle of supply and demand works" remarked the Englishman Bryce upon his visit to Harvard during this time. "No one is obliged to attend these courses to obtain admission and the [bar] examinations are generally too lax to require elaborate preparation. But the instruction is found so valuable, so helpful for professional success, that young men throng the lecture halls, willingly spending two or three years in the scientific study of law, which they might have spent in the chambers of a practicing lawyer."

Basically, anyone who wanted to be a lawyer could hang out his shingle, and there were very few requirements for doing so, except limited apprenticeship in some states. So the vast majority of lawyers at the turn of the century—80 to 90 percent—never saw the inside of a university, whether it was a law school or a college. Most of them had to take a bar exam, but, unlike the situation today, the market was the primary determinant of whether they would be successful.

Meanwhile, Harvard Law School continued to grow and to train the elite lawyers—at least those whose parents had money. In 1900 a young man went to Harvard Law School if he wanted to practice with one of the large Boston or New York firms. But in addition, there were a plethora of other law schools—part-time and full-time, one year, two year and three year—while apprenticeship remained the normal method of entry to the profession.

In the last 70 years, we have seen the apprenticeship method go the way of the dodo and formal, institutionalized legal education become compulsory.

What happened was not really the academic lawyer's fault. It was the American Bar Association's. I don't mean to say that the academic lawyer was entirely innocent in the implementation of this retrograde step, but it was the ABA which was the primary mover in making law school compulsory. It wanted to make law school compulsory because it wanted to contribute to "raising standards."

"Raising standards" is purposely vague. What it meant in this case undoubtedly included concern over the large number of illiterate and dishonest lawyers. A significant number of lawyers in 1900 had not finished high school and heretofore the ABA's effort to raise standards was in part a genuine effort to protect the public.

The developments, however, also represented an effort on the part of many practitioners to restrict numbers. The move was, to some extent, an anticompetitive device, and it was also undoubtedly— although I think that some recent studies overstate this—an effort to discriminate against certain groups. It was an effort to keep blacks and immigrant groups—especially Jews—out of the legal profession.

The first state to make law school compulsory was West Virginia which, in 1928, required one year of law school. It was not difficult to see where these pressures were coming from. West Virginia argued the need to inculcate "The Spirit of American Government." A New York delegate to the ABA put it more bluntly: "The need to have lawyers able to read, write and talk the English language—not Bohemian, not Gaelic, not Yiddish, but English." That was the beginning of compulsory legal education and prior college training in the United States—the debates of the House of Delegates in the 1930s and 1940s make it clear that the same sentiment motivated the ABA when it tried to drive out some law schools—and the depression provided a powerful stimulus to "raising standards."

Gradually, between 1929 and 1942 each state, partly for anticompetitive reasons and partly in a genuine effort to raise standards, followed the lead of West Virginia—and the suggestions of the American Bar Association. In 1920 there had still been a certain flexibility: many law schools only had two-year programs and only two or three law schools required an undergraduate degree. Increasingly, lawyers had gone to law school and most of the leading universities had law schools—but not because they were required to. At that time virtually every state allowed, as an alternative, three years of apprenticeship; and the majority of American lawyers had still not been to law school.

By 1950 attendance at law school was compulsory, and during the 1950s law school entrance requirements included two, and later three years of college. It was all part of the movement to "improve standards," although for reasons both good and bad. Moreover, in the post-Second World War years, the number of lawyers who had attended law school for the first time outran the number who had not.

The transition from compulsory apprenticeship to compulsory legal education was accomplished in three steps. First, law schools had become an alternative to apprenticeship; second, they had gradually driven out apprenticeship, and finally, they had become anxious to tighten standards and cut back on the number of accredited schools, thereby further limiting access to a legal education. * * *

The question of access to the legal profession, especially for minorities, is directly tied to the accreditation process. For example, when a new, small, low cost law school opens which has a sizable minority student population, is that school serving a minority group or exploiting it? The line between serving and exploiting is an extremely difficult one, but, in effect, there is always an inherent danger in a self-regulating profession to reproduce itself in the same colors and tones.

C. HOW THE PRACTICE OF LAW HAS CHANGED OVER THE LAST HALF-CENTURY

History lets us see that what it means to be a lawyer and the standards for becoming a lawyer have changed across time. But most lawyers and law students want to know what standards apply to them today, and many wonder what is happening to the profession in which they hope to succeed.

Since about the 1950s—largely because of work by the American Bar Association (ABA)—law has seemed a remarkably stable profession. In most states, the practice of law has been limited to people licensed after completing four years of college, three years at an ABA-accredited law school, and passing a bar exam. Once licensed, a lawyer is legally entitled to do whatever constitutes the practice of law in any substantive field without any experience or renewed showing of competence.

Yet all of us know that our 21st Century world is radically different in most other respects from the world of the 1950s. And just beneath the patina of familiarity about law practice, the world of the American lawyer has been changing as well. The changes became painfully evident about 2008, at the same time the housing crisis and economic recession hit hard. But many of the changes were not linked to the recession and many appear unlikely to dissipate when economic recovery returns. We will group changes in a U.S. lawyer's world under six headings.

1. Growth in the Number of Lawyers

First and most obvious, the number of U.S. lawyers has exploded over the last almost 45 years. In 1970, the United States had about 300,000 lawyers.[2] Then law school applications soared—in part inspired by the central role law had played in social change such as the civil rights revolution and in part fueled by the number of women who became lawyers. New law schools opened and existing schools grew. Today, there are at least 1,200,000 persons trained as lawyers, of whom about 1,000,000 have law-related jobs.[3]

Even early in the profession's growth, not everyone took a sanguine view of it. In the 1980s, then Harvard President (and former law school dean) Derek Bok, for example, asserted:

> The net result of these trends is a massive diversion of exceptional talent into pursuits that often add little to the growth of the economy, the pursuit of culture, or the enhancement of the human spirit. I cannot press this point too strongly. * * * [T]he supply of exceptional people is limited. Yet far too many of these rare individuals are becoming lawyers at a time when the country cries out for more talented business executives, more enlightened public servants, more inventive engineers, more able high-school principals and teachers.

> * * * A nation's values and problems are mirrored in the ways in which it uses its ablest people. In Japan, a country only half our size, 30 percent more engineers graduate each year than in all the United States. But Japan boasts a total of less than 15,000 lawyers, while American universities graduate 35,000 *every year*. It would be hard to claim that these differences have no practical consequences. As the

---

[2]   Barbara A. Curran, et al., The Lawyer Statistical Report: A Statistical Profile of the U.S. Legal Profession in the 1980s (1985).

[3]   The actual number of lawyers in active practice is surprisingly hard to determine, but U.S. Census Bureau, Statistical Abstract of the United States 2010, Table 603, put the number of lawyers at 1,014,000, while the American Bar Association says the number with active law licenses in 2008 was 1,180,386. One problem in getting an accurate count is the practical difficulty knowing how many licensed lawyers are still engaged in a law-related activity.

Japanese put it, "Engineers make the pie grow larger; lawyers only decide how to carve it up."[4]

For many years, lawyers did well economically even as their numbers increased. By the turn of the 21st Century, graduates could earn as much as $160,000 in their first year out of law school and partners in successful firms had annual incomes over $1 million. In such an environment, it was hard to lose sleep over the number of lawyers. But all that changed in 2007–2009 as several thousand lawyers lost jobs, many from major firms, and up to half of law schools' graduates found no law-related jobs at all.

Some of the hiring issues are closely related to the economy. Over 40,000 graduates are admitted to the bar each year from ABA-accredited schools. Traditionally, the nation's demand for new lawyers most closely tracks the rate of increase in the nation's gross domestic product.[5] About 25 years of robust economic growth from the early 1980s to the 2008 financial crisis largely absorbed all the lawyers the nation produced.

When the economy slows but law schools keep producing the same number of new lawyers, however, we create a lawyer surplus that will not go away quickly. In 2008–09 alone, for example, law schools produced 4% more lawyers at a time when economic activity contracted almost 6%. It doesn't take great math skills to see that, in that short period alone, the nation created a large group of lawyers competing with new graduates for available jobs. Current annual economic growth continues to be around 2%, and the number of lawyers continues to increase at twice that level, but the business model of most law schools makes cutting enrollment very costly.

But a deeper question about these numbers is whether—apart from current lawyers' and law students' obvious economic interest in slowing the increasing number of professional competitors—can one objectively say that there are too many lawyers? For example, is it true that all persons with a need for a lawyer can get help at prices they can afford? And while the range of lawyer incomes is quite wide, the average American lawyer continues to earn about $130,000 per year.[6] Is that income characteristic of a profession that is overcrowded?

2. The Significant Loss of Lawyer Self-Regulation

It might seem tempting to assert that the ABA and state bar associations should try to manage the profession's structure and

---

[4] Derek Bok, "A Flawed System": Report to the [Harvard] Board of Overseers, 85 HARVARD Magazine 38, 41 (May–June 1983). Ironically, in recent years, 74 new law schools opened in Japan and the allowed bar exam pass rate has been raised from 3% to 33%. There are still many fewer lawyers per capita in Japan than in the United States, but Japan now recognizes that lawyers have a lot to contribute in business dealings and the Japanese legal profession is starting to look more like that of the United States rather than the other way around. See, e.g., Ronald D. Rotunda, Teaching Professional Responsibility and Ethics, 51 St. Louis U. L.J. 1223, 1230–33 (2007).

[5] See, e.g., Thomas D. Morgan, Economic Reality Facing Twenty–First Century Lawyers, 69 U. Washington L. Rev. 625 (1994), citing B. Peter Pashigian, The Market for Lawyers: The Determinants of the Demand for and Supply of Lawyers, 20 J. Law & Economics 53 (1977); Thomas D. Morgan, Practicing Law in the Interests of Justice in the Twenty–First Century, 70 Fordham L. Rev. 1793 (2002).

[6] Bureau of Labor Statistics, 2012 National Occupational Employment and Wage Estimates, http://www.bls.gov/oes/current/oes_nat.htm#23-0000.

growth. Lawyers sometimes speak admiringly of the medical profession, which seems to regulate its growth more successfully. But the second big change in the legal profession since the 1950s is that it is no longer entirely self-regulating. In the 1950s, lawyers largely wrote the rules by which they were governed and largely tended to write them in ways that favored themselves.[7]

But that began to change in the mid-1960s. *NAACP v. Button*[8] and a series of related cases struck down ethics rules that said lawyers could not cooperate with public interest groups and labor unions who sought to have panels of lawyers that their members could consult. In *Goldfarb v. Virginia State Bar,*[9] the Supreme Court then declared that lawyer professional standards are subject to federal antitrust challenge and that a bar association's minimum fee schedule constituted illegal price fixing. *Bates v. State Bar of Arizona*[10] soon followed and held that a state supreme court's prohibition of lawyer advertising violated the First Amendment to the U.S. Constitution.

Then, as the United States experienced crises and frauds in the savings and loan industry, in corporate mergers and public offerings, in the marketing of tax shelters with little or no economic substance, and Ponzi schemes and corporate mismanagement, federal agencies in banking, tax, and securities began to regulate the conduct of lawyers. One can expect an even greater federal regulatory presence in the control over lawyer conduct in the future.

In large part, this is because the ABA and other drafters of state ethics rules have failed to confront fundamental changes in the legal profession. In 2009, the ABA created an Ethics 20/20 Commission to consider fundamental changes in the practice of law in the United States and around the world, but in 2013, the Commission announced the completion of its work after two minor rounds of amendments to the ABA Model Rules. Thus, states seeking to regulate the conduct of lawyers who confront new challenges can often no longer count upon the ABA for reliable guidance. We will talk about the substance of such developments later and see how they led to specific changes in standards governing lawyers. But the fact that federal and other external law now governs lawyers has unsettled the relatively quiet life that self-regulation had created in the 1950s.

3. The Impact of Globalization on Lawyers

Lawyers, like others engaged in economic activity, are profoundly affected by increased competition and related forces at work in our 21st century world. Globalization is one of the economic forces that has had a profound effect on clients' personal and business lives and thus that has transformed many lawyers' practices. Instead of a client operating

---

[7] See, e.g., Thomas D. Morgan, The Evolving Concept of Professional Responsibility, 90 Harvard L. Rev. 702 (1977).

[8] 371 U.S. 415(1963). The related cases include Brotherhood of R.R. Trainmen v. Virginia ex rel. Virginia State Bar, 377 U.S. 1 (1964); United Mine Workers v. Illinois State Bar Ass'n; 389 U.S. 217 (1967); United Transportation Union v. State Bar of Michigan, 401 U.S. 576 (1971).

[9] 421 U.S. 773 (1975).

[10] 433 U.S. 350 (1977).

only under a variety of state laws, multiple different legal systems often govern a client's business and personal dealings. [11]

More generally, the legal complexity created by globalization and a changing regulatory environment has now made it nearly impossible for any single lawyer to take on all kinds of legal problems. Many lawyers in the 1950s hoped to see themselves as someone like Atticus Finch, an admired citizen who was willing to step in where the need was greatest. Today, for many legal problems, such an approach would be malpractice per se. As a result, many in the practice of law identify more with their fellow trial lawyers, immigration lawyers, corporate lawyers, and the like, than they do with the legal profession itself.[12]

Finally, and perhaps most important for students of legal ethics, in today's globalized world, American lawyers find themselves in competition with legal service providers all over the globe who operate under different ethical standards than some of those you will study here. As a result of the Legal Services Act of 2007, for example, UK lawyers now can practice in firms that have non-lawyer principals, and UK law firms can sell stock to the public.

Competition, in short, is not intense only because of the new U.S. lawyers who graduate each year. If American lawyers face direct competitors who operate under different professional rules that let them deliver services that clients find attractive, they should not be surprised if their clients seek the same or better service at lower cost elsewhere in the world.

4. The Technological Revolution in Law

Technological changes throughout society over the last 40 years—from personal computers to the Internet to smartphones—have transformed a lawyer's practice as well. Every law student knows the changes in legal research that electronic developments have created. However, advances in the use of electronic discovery may become even more significant in reducing the cost of litigation. We also know that technology has made lawyers' lives more hectic; clients can reach their lawyers from anywhere in the world and at any time of the day or night.

But most importantly, technology promises to transform lawyer work that used to be seen as complex, unique, and worthy of substantial fees into a series of commodities: simple, repetitive operations that will be sold to clients by the lowest bidder. Technology available on the simplest personal computer today can allow a lawyer to copy a 500-page document used in one transaction and change the names and terms for use in the next. The result must be made relevant to the new situation, of course, and the malpractice risk created by easy copying can be enormous, but the benefits of standardizing forms in transactions promises to reduce much of what lawyers used to think of as creative work.

Likewise, and in some ways even more frustrating for lawyers, is the fact that much of the information lawyers have traditionally sold is

[11] See, e.g., Laurel S. Terry, The Legal World is Flat: Globalization and Its Effect on Lawyers Practicing in Non–Global Law Firms, 28 Northwestern J. International Law & Business 527 (2008).

[12] This is part of the insight behind the title of Thomas D. Morgan, The Vanishing American Lawyer (2010).

now freely available on the Internet. Books about law have been around for years, but technology now makes the information ubiquitous. Free insights may be found in places ranging from Wikipedia to blogs, and the effect has been to make a great deal of formerly exotic legal information broadly accessible. Clearly, lawyers tend to be able to understand and apply such information more quickly and accurately than many clients can, but the breakthrough is that a lawyer's knowledge is no longer a black box that clients cannot penetrate. A client, whether a corporation or individual, can be expected to seek assistance from multiple sources ready to provide information rather than buy assistance in a proprietary form created and sold by lawyers alone.

Further, technology has facilitated the ability to break down legal matters into component parts and to manage large projects using service providers from all over the world. Thus, we no longer must see a lawsuit as a single activity. We can see it as consisting of steps such as document review, witness interviews, depositions, motions, negotiation, and sometimes even a trial and appeal. Not all of those steps need to be done by the same people and not all need to be done by lawyers. Specialists in finding relevant documents in an electronic database, for example, often need to know more about programming and search techniques than about civil procedure or the legal theories being asserted in a case. Comparable situations arise in many types of regulatory practice, real estate transactions and the like, so that even after U.S. economic recovery picks up, it seems unlikely that all the work we used to call the practice of law will once again be assigned to lawyers.

5. Transformation of the Hemispheres of the Bar

Yet another key development of the last 40 years has been the transformation of what scholars call the "hemispheres" of the bar. Sociologist Jerome Carlin reported that in New York in the 1960s, business lawyers made up 45% of the bar, while individual-oriented work such as personal injury, criminal, divorce, wills, and real estate made up the other 55%. "People" lawyers represented the public face of the law.

Just fifteen years later, Jack Heinz & Edward Laumann documented the individual/ business distinction in the Chicago bar and showed that the lawyers who populated each differed in terms of social class, where they went to law school, how much money they made, their status as leaders of the bar, and the like. They concluded that by 1975, 53% of lawyers worked on business issues, while only 40% of lawyers still did work for individuals.

After another two decades, in 1995, the authors concluded that the proportion of corporate lawyers had increased from 53% to 64%, while lawyers for individuals had fallen from 40% to 29%. That should not surprise us. Remember that the rapid growth in the number of lawyers tracked growth in the gross domestic product, not the growth in population. But the fact remains that—completely contrary to the 1950s and to many law students' original expectations—less than one-third of the legal talent in this country now focuses on trying to meet the needs of individual clients. The majority of American lawyers now do their primary work for business and government.

6. The Central Role of In-House Counsel

The shift of law practice toward corporate and institutional work has led in turn to the rising power of in-house counsel. Forty years ago, and in many cases much more recently, lawyers in private firms saw their role as providing wise advice to lay officers or employees of corporate clients. That is less true today. The people most lawyers now have to please are other lawyers, this time acting in the role of general counsel to corporations, government agencies, and other organizations. It is the in-house lawyers—who number about 10 percent of all lawyers—that tend to decide what services the client requires and why.

Companies began recruiting in-house lawyers rather than depending exclusively on outside firms as a way to avoid high law firm billing rates. But a strong internal lawyer staff also helps assure that legal service decisions are made by people who understand the client's business, know the type of legal work that is required, and are able to help managers think about the non-legal issues inherent in important business decisions.

Law firms have responded to these developments. One response has been a growth of the organizations in which many lawyers now practice. In 1960, fewer than 20 U.S. law firms employed more than 50 lawyers each. Even by 1968, only 20 firms in the country had over 100 lawyers. Now, Baker & McKenzie and DLA Piper each has over 4,000 lawyers, and 22 U.S. firms have crossed the 1,000–lawyer mark.[13]

Law firms get bigger because larger firms provide teams of lawyers and non-lawyers that can handle and coordinate the elements of matters sent to them by even the largest corporate clients. They can also provide a local name and face anywhere in the world in support of their clients' business activities. On the other hand, the continued growth of law firms is not inevitable and technology now makes it possible for in-house counsel to assemble virtual teams to handle matters on an as-needed basis.

Private law firms are familiar with the practice of hiring contract lawyers, i.e., lawyers hired to do particular tasks when the firm is especially busy on a case or a regulatory filing but who the firm will not need in the long run. Today, private law firms can perhaps best be seen as inside counsel's version of contract lawyers. It hurts for lawyers in private firms to realize that their practice has come to that. The firms they spent their lives building have now become the functional equivalent of temp agencies. And it hurts even more when they are beaten out for commodity work on which they used to train associates but that now can be done less expensively by firms elsewhere in the world.

Law firms have long used paralegal and other support personnel nominally working under the lawyer supervision that ethical standards require. Now, corporations also use non-lawyers to help deliver the total package of services needed to complete the project. Negotiating contracts, troubleshooting discrimination claims, and even writing

---

[13] The American Lawyer (May 2013), p. 137.

pleadings can all be done by non-lawyers who receive a level of lawyer supervision and training to which practice rules cannot effectively speak. Current legal ethics rules require a lawyer in a private law firm to supervise and take responsibility for the non-lawyer's work, but that requirement is easily met, and the non-lawyers are often accountants or lobbyists, economists or nurses, statisticians, or business specialists who are more than capable of acting on their own.

D. THE DEVELOPMENT OF STANDARDS OF PROFESSIONAL CONDUCT

In this course in legal ethics, you will learn some detailed, authoritative rules regulating lawyer conduct. That approach to lawyer regulation is relatively recent. In the United States before the 1970s, and in much of the rest of the world even today, lawyers learned only general principles of proper professional behavior.

The earliest efforts to prescribe such behavior were offered as moral principles with no legal effect. Throughout most of the 19th century, such principles were developed and published by lawyers who were also teaching law.

In 1836, for example, Baltimore lawyer David Hoffman closed his two-volume *A Course of Legal Study* with "Fifty Resolutions" to which he urged lawyers to adhere. Those resolutions, in turn, seem to have influenced the writing of George Sharswood, who published his *A Compend of Lectures on the Aims and Duties of the Profession of the Law* in Philadelphia in 1854. Sharswood's standards are usually cited as the source of the Code of Ethics adopted by the State of Alabama in 1887, and the Alabama Code then formed the basis for the American Bar Association's first statement of ethical principles, the Canons of Professional Ethics, published in 1908.

The ABA Canons were very general but they remained the national professional model for over sixty years. You will find the ABA Canons in the Standards Supplement to this book. In many states, however, lawyers were subject to professional discipline for offenses not much more specific than "conduct unbecoming a lawyer."

Then, in 1969, the ABA adopted its Model Code of Professional Responsibility. In part, the goal was to help standardize what it means to be a lawyer, and in part, it was to give lawyers fair warning of the conduct that would subject them to discipline. The Model Code, adopted almost universally by state supreme courts to govern lawyers subject to their jurisdiction, became "law" in the same sense that the Rules of Civil Procedure become law when a court adopts them.

The nine "Canons" in the Model Code were "axiomatic norms," i.e., general propositions serving as little more than chapter headings for the rest of the text. The "Disciplinary Rules" were "mandatory in character;" violations would subject the attorney to discipline up to and including disbarment. The Ethical Considerations, by contrast, were said to be "aspirational in character" and to offer an unenforceable but hopeful statement of the profession's consensus about proper lawyer conduct.

The decade of the 1970s was, also the decade in which President Richard Nixon made "Watergate" a household word and the ABA responded by requiring that all law schools teach courses in legal ethics. A new generation of lawyers and law teachers looked at the answers the Model Code offered to questions of professional conduct and soon found the Model Code inadequate.

Thus, the ABA created another commission. The work of the ABA Commission on Evaluation of Professional Standards, commonly called the Kutak Commission after its chair, the late Robert J. Kutak, produced the ABA Model Rules of Professional Conduct in 1983. The new Model Rules were structured in a "Restatement" format. They have black-letter rules that are followed by explanatory "Comments." It is those Model Rules, as amended over the last 30 years, that are likely to be central to your study of legal ethics.

But even the first version of the Model Rules was not satisfactory to everyone. Thus, in 1986, the American Law Institute (ALI) undertook work on Restatement Third, The Law Governing Lawyers.[14] Like other ALI Restatements, courts do not adopt it as legally binding, but it describes the law, influences its development, and organizes it in a way that shows that it is consistent with standards governing all agents who have fiduciary duties to others.

The ALI published the Restatement in 2000. It goes beyond subjects of lawyer discipline to cover issues such as the attorney-client privilege, lawyer malpractice, liens to secure legal fees, and the like. This book will often refer to the Restatement to articulate a particular legal rule, to explain the rationale for a principle of law set forth in the Model Rules, or to suggest the body of tort or agency law on which some provision of the Model Rules is based.[15]

The ABA has undertaken two major revisions of the Model Rules and made many more limited changes to the document, The ABA House of Delegates adopted proposals of its Ethics 2000 Commission in August 2001 and February 2002.[16] The changes reflect the most significant revision of the Model Rules to date. They incorporated many principles that are in the Restatement but were not in the original Model Rules, such as Model Rule 1.18 on prospective clients. The revisions expressly excluded consideration of proposed amendments to Model Rules 5.5 and 8.5 on multijurisdictional practice and Model Rules 1.13 and 1.6 on confidentiality and lawyer involvement in corporate misconduct, but after significant additional study and debate, the ABA amended those provisions as well in 2002 and 2003. Finally, the work of the ABA Ethics 20/20 Commission work led to the adoption of changes to the Model Rules in 2012 and 2013.

---

[14] Geoffrey C. Hazard, Jr., the Reporter for the 1983 Model Rules, became Director of the American Law Institute and initiated the Restatement effort. There is no Restatement, First or Second, of The Law Governing Lawyers. The ALI calls this Restatement "Third" because it was drafting the third wave of Restatements on various subjects. Although we do not normally think of a "third" unless there is a "second," there are exceptions. Napoleon III was Emperor of France although there was never an Emperor Napoleon II.

[15] The Model Rules and Restatement treatment of over two hundred topics are compared in Thomas D. Morgan, Lawyer Law: Comparing the ABA Model Rules of Professional Conduct with the ALI Restatement (Third) of the Law Governing Lawyers (ABA 2005).

[16] In November 2002, the ABA amended Rule 7.2 to permit reciprocal referral agreements between lawyers and other lawyers and nonlawyers under certain circumstances.

All references to Rule or Comment numbers in these materials are to the ABA Model Rules, as amended. The ABA Model Rules, whenever issued, are only *proposed* law. They are a "model," and the ABA must lobby state and federal courts to enact the Rules as positive law before they have any legal effect. The ABA has been quite successful in its lobbying efforts, but one finds more nonuniform versions of the Model Rules today than existed during the heyday of the Model Code. As of January 2014, forty-six jurisdictions have revised their rules to follow the 2002–03 amendments to the Model Rules in substantial part. Even if a state court has not adopted a version of the ABA Model Rules, state courts often cite them as evidence of the law. Progress on adopting later amendments is much slower, although most state supreme courts are likely to consider many of the changes in due course.[17]

You will find the current ABA Model Rules, the 1983 Model Rules, as amended, the 1970 ABA Model Code of Professional Responsibility, and the original 1908 ABA Canons of Ethics reprinted in the Standards Supplement to this book. In this text, we ask primarily how the Model Rules address the ethical issues that lawyers confront. Keep in mind, however, that the "code of ethics" that will be legally binding on you will be the one adopted by the supreme court of the state or states in which you are licensed.[18] It may not correspond exactly to the ABA Model Rules.[19]

At least three other sources of authority and advice are also important to your analysis of legal ethics issues. First are court decisions, whether in cases seeking discipline of lawyers, malpractice damages, disqualification motions, contempt sanctions, criminal convictions, or the like.

Second, the ABA and state and local bar associations often issue ethics opinions. These advisory opinions respond to a specific question or an assumed state of facts. Although such opinions usually are not formally binding on lawyers, they are influential with the courts, which often cite them as evidence of the law.

Finally, federal agencies have begun to issue regulations that regulate the work of lawyers who appear before them. They have always had rules governing practice before the agencies, but early in 2003, for example, in response to a series of corporate scandals, the Securities and Exchange Commission issued important new regulations dictating how lawyers for publicly-held companies must respond to possible wrongdoing by or within those companies.[20]

---

[17] The ABA reports changes in state rules at http://www.abanet.org/cpr/pic/ethics_2000_status_chart.pdf. See also, Lucian T. Pera, Grading ABA leadership: State Adoption of the Revised ABA Model Rules of Professional Conduct, 30 Oklahoma City U.L. Rev. 637 (2005).

[18] Lawyers licensed in more than one state are subject to discipline in each of them and may face problems of conflicting professional standards. Situations where one state requires disclose but another state prohibits it are particularly difficult. At least in principle, a state supreme court may impose discipline on lawyers it has licensed wherever the conduct takes place. ABA Model Rule 8.5(b), discussed in Problem 2 *infra*, tries to establish a common choice of law rule with which to deal with this problem.

[19] Appendices A, B, & C to the Model Rules in the Standards Supplement consist of charts that map out the important variations among state ethics rules that govern client confidences, lawyer screening, and when fee agreements must be in writing.

[20] For the SEC regulations, see 17 CFR Part 205, issued Jan. 29, 2003. The IRS has an Office of Professional Responsibility that regulates lawyers, accountants and others who

E. A WORD ON THE ORGANIZATION OF THIS BOOK

This book is organized as a series of problems. We adapted most of them from actual cases collected from ethics opinions, disciplinary proceedings, news articles, and the authors' professional experiences. Of course, all names are hypothetical and facts have been altered to protect the persons involved or to make a question more interesting. Yet real people confronted most of these problems. They should suggest that an attorney in a concrete situation must sometimes act when no course is wholly satisfactory.

They should also suggest that some situations may present professional dilemmas that are not at first apparent. Professor of psychiatry and law Andrew Watson properly accused law schools of developing analytic barriers to students' reliance on their personal moral reactions to situations.[21] But you will see that the courts also discipline lawyers for conduct that may trigger little righteous indignation; developing *sensitivity* to ethical ambiguity is an important objective of these materials.

We design each of the problems to require you to think. Initially, many may seem to set you adrift on a sea of ambiguity. To help you stay afloat, each problem begins with an introduction that puts it in context. After presentation of the facts of each problem, the remaining materials present four main topics in legal ethics that the problem raises. Each topic asks a series of black-letter questions that are intended to provide the structure for a logically-ordered discussion. The cases, ethics opinions, and other questions that follow each black-letter question are designed to help you answer the questions, but also to help you see why some of those questions have puzzled so many lawyers for so long.

As you read the problems in this book, consider questions such as the following:

1. Is the conduct in question a violation of one or more standards of the ABA Model Rules? What should be the penalty, if any, for the misconduct?

2. Have the relevant Model Rules kept up with changes in the profession and in the needs of clients? Do we sometimes hold lawyers to standards that do more harm than good?

3. Is the lawyer conduct in question properly subject to criticism even if it is consistent with the Model Rules? By what standard do you judge the moral character of the conduct?

4. Should the lawyer in a given situation have taken particular action even though the failure to take action would not subject the lawyer to discipline?

5. How could the lawyer whose conduct you are evaluating serve the client well and still be professionally responsible?

---

practice in the tax field. E.g., Treasury Department Circular 230, 31 CFR Part 10 (Sept. 26, 2007). The United States Patent & Trademark Office also has ethics regulations that govern lawyers and others whom it authorizes to practice before it. E.g., 37 CFR Part 11 (Aug. 14, 2008).

[21] Andrew Watson, The Watergate Lawyer Syndrome: An Educational Deficiency Disease, 26 J. Legal Ed. 441, 442 (1974).

A separate supplement of Selected Standards on Professional Responsibility that goes with this book is updated annually. That Supplement includes not only the ABA Model Rules of Professional Conduct and its predecessors, but the ABA Model Code of Judicial Conduct (which has also been adopted by many state supreme courts), and other statutes and guides to professional conduct that have proved influential in determining the legal profession's standards. You should begin an analysis of each problem by looking at the ABA Model Rules, but do not assume that they are the only sources of relevant authority.

After you have completed this course, you should be in a better position to evaluate the comments expressed at the outset of this Chapter by the Doonesbury characters. Is a course in professional responsibility a naive attempt to teach "right and wrong" to adults with fixed moral views? More cynically, is it only "trendy lip service to our better selves"? Or, is the study of professional responsibility based on a recognition that (1) ethical issues are as important to a lawyer as any other aspect of his or her professional life; (2) like any other area of law, the law of professional responsibility must be learned; and (3) professional responsibility questions present analytic problems as challenging and difficult as any a law student or lawyer will face?

CHAPTER II

REGULATION OF THE LEGAL PROFESSION

Traditionally, the highest court of each state regulates both entry into the legal profession and the conduct of lawyers once admitted. Most state supreme courts hold that they have *exclusive* power to govern the legal profession, although a few have ceded limited authority over lawyers to their state legislatures.

To exercise their authority, the courts establish admission and disciplinary offices that operate as government agencies only loosely related to voluntary bar associations. Some jurisdictions, however, require lawyers to join an official bar organization, an approach that is called an "integrated" or "unified" bar. The responsibilities of such an official bar association may include a role in bar admission and enforcement of conduct standards. Even in states that have no official bar association, courts often turn to lawyers to staff parts of the admission and disciplinary systems. Regardless of the formal approach a state takes, courts often fund the disciplinary system by taxing lawyers in the form of mandatory dues and fees.[*]

State supreme courts regulate the right to practice law even if the lawyer is solely an office counselor and never appears in court. Federal courts separately regulate admission to practice before them, but lawyers do not need to be admitted to a federal court unless they will be litigating there. Federal courts usually defer to state admission standards, and admission before a federal court is often close to automatic, although some federal courts have been interested in asserting a more active role.

In the problems that follow, consider questions such as:

    a.   Why do courts regulate admission to the bar and the professional behavior of attorneys? Should they be concerned about specific conduct, discerning a lawyer's moral character, or both?

    b.   What should be the relative roles of the courts, both state and federal, legislatures, bar associations, individual lawyers, and even lay persons in these processes?

    c.   What is the range of sanctions that lawyers face for a violation of professional standards? Are public sanctions such as disbarment necessarily of more concern to lawyers than private sanctions such as malpractice liability?

---

    [*]   Lathrop v. Donohue, 367 U.S. 820 (1961), with no majority opinion, upheld mandatory bar membership against an attack based on freedom of association. Keller v. State Bar of California, 496 U.S. 1 (1990) considered the uses to which the bar may spend mandatory dues. The Court held that state bars may only use mandatory dues to finance activities of common benefit to bar members because there would be a risk of "free riders" if all lawyers did not share the burden. Such activities include recommending bar admission standards, conducting bar discipline, and recommending changes in bar codes of conduct, but they may not include taking positions on broader public questions.

———

PROBLEM 1

ADMISSION TO THE BAR

Your first "case" as a law graduate will be your application for admission to the bar. In effect, you will file it as an original action before your state's supreme court. The remedy you seek will be an order placing you on the roll of attorneys licensed to appear before that supreme court and all the state's inferior courts. Typically, the state supreme court will delegate to bar examiners the task of reviewing the applications, the character and fitness reports, and the examination results. The examiners will then submit a list of approved candidates to the court for ratification. Your approval will get you a license that will allow you to give legal advice and engage in whatever other acts the state defines as the practice of law. This problem examines what you will be required to demonstrate to the state supreme court to justify the grant of that license. In particular, it considers the "character and fitness" requirement and your duty of candor in representations that you make in seeking bar admission.

FACTS

You have been in practice for a few years in the city where you went to law school. Gerry Smith, a third year law student, has come to you for help. "I have been accused of cheating on the final exam in my advanced tax class," he tells you. "I did it. I did not have time to study, and I wanted to get a good grade. The exam proctor will testify that he thought he saw me cheat, but I have denied everything. I'm afraid of what this could do to my chances of being admitted to the bar. Please help me."

In addition, Smith told you, "I changed my name when I was a freshman in college. My name then was Patrick Saville. Under that name, the court convicted me of a misdemeanor for possession of marijuana. Do I have to report something like that? Will the bar ever catch me?"

You are an old friend of the law school dean. The dean has offered not to charge Smith and force him to a hearing on the charge of cheating if Smith agrees to accept a failing grade in the course. He can make up the course in summer school (for which he will have to pay tuition), and that will let him graduate in time to take the bar with the rest of his class. The dean also offers to agree not to disclose the incident to the character and fitness committee of the bar. Smith is happy to be able to get off so lightly.

QUESTIONS

A. CHARACTER AND FITNESS FOR ADMISSION TO THE BAR

1. Every American jurisdiction requires that applicants for admission to the bar sustain the burden of proof that they have the necessary "character and fitness" to practice law. Why should bar admission authorities in your state concern themselves with Smith's character?

a. Restatement Third, The Law Governing Lawyers § 2, Comment *d*, explains the requirement this way:

> "A license to practice law confers great power on lawyers to do good or wrong. Lawyers practice an occupation that is complex and often, particularly to nonlawyers, mysterious. Clients and others are vulnerable to wrongdoing by corrupt lawyers. Hence, as far back as the first bars in medieval England efforts have been made to screen candidates for the bar with respect to their character. * * * The central inquiry concerns the present ability and disposition of the applicant to practice law competently and honestly."

b. Professor Deborah Rhode goes on:

> "The first [purpose] is shielding clients from potential abuses, such as misrepresentation, misappropriation of funds, or betrayal of confidences. * * * A second concern involves safeguarding the administration of justice from those who might subvert it through subornation of perjury, misrepresentation, bribery, or the like.
>
> "* * * [A] less frequently articulated rationale for character screening rests on the bar's own interest in maintaining a professional community and public image. * * * An overriding objective of any organized profession is to enhance its members' social standing, and the bar is scarcely an exception."[1]

2. Does Smith's cheating in law school demonstrate that he lacks "good moral character"?

a. Does cheating involve "dishonesty, fraud, deceit, or misrepresentation" so as to justify disciplining a licensed lawyer for violation of Model Rule 8.4(c)? Should we be as concerned about the subsequent denial of guilt as about the original act of cheating?

b. Should Smith's earlier drug conviction be conclusive evidence of a lack of "character and fitness"? Would your answer be different if the court convicted him of a drug-related *felony*?[2]

c. Is marijuana possession "a criminal act that reflects adversely on the lawyer's honesty, trustworthiness, or fitness as a lawyer in other respects"? See Model Rule 8.4(b) and Comment 2.

---

[1] Deborah L. Rhode, Moral Character as a Professional Credential, 94 Yale L.J. 491, 508–10 (1985).

[2] Current practice in most states does not automatically deny bar admission to convicted felons. See, e.g., In re Polin, 630 A.2d 1140 (D.C.1993) (applicant admitted to the bar after serving time for conspiracy to distribute cocaine).

d.   In re Glass, 2014 WL 280612 (Cal. 2014), involved Stephen Glass, a reporter for the New Republic from 1996 to 1998, who resigned when the New Republic learned that he fabricated many of his articles. He was a law student at the time and graduated from Georgetown Law in 2000. He passed the New York bar exam but withdrew his application for admission after he was notified that it would be denied. He began clerking for a California firm in 2004, passed the California bar exam in 2006 and faced a character and fitness hearing in 2007. Georgetown professors, his treating psychiatrist, and his current employer spoke on his behalf. The California Supreme Court, however, denied him admission. In his New York bar application, "he exaggerated his cooperation with the journals that had published his work and failed to supply a complete list of the fabricated articles that had injured others." Later, in "the California proceedings, Glass was not forthright in acknowledging the defects in his New York bar application." The court concluded Glass' efforts to show rehabilitation were less than sincere. "[M]anifest dishonesty ... provides a reasonable basis for the conclusion that the applicant ... cannot be relied upon to fulfill the moral obligations incumbent upon members of the legal profession." Is this case a sign of admirably high judicial standards? An example of insensitivity to the possibility people can change?

e.   If discipline authorities would not suspend or disbar a practicing lawyer in your state after conviction of marijuana possession, should bar admission authorities necessarily admit Smith to practice? Hallinan v. Committee of Bar Examiners, 421 P.2d 76 (Cal.1966), said the test for discipline and bar admission is the same, namely whether the individual "is a fit and proper person to be permitted to practice law." Most observers agree, however, that, in practice, the bar admissions authorities are more likely to deny a person a license to practice law than discipline authorities are to take it away later for identical conduct.

3.   Should dishonesty in the handling of money defeat a person's bar admission?

a.   In re Mustafa, 631 A.2d 45 (D.C.1993), involved the chief justice of a law school's moot court program who embezzled over $2000 from the moot court account to pay the emergency expenses of his sister. He repaid the money and the school fully supported his bar admission, but only a year had passed since the misconduct, so the court denied admission. See also, Application of Majorek, 508 N.W.2d 275 (Neb.1993), denying admission of an applicant who embezzled $300 of law student association funds and shoplifted a pack of cigarettes, among other offenses.

b.   Should the bar authorities deny admission to an applicant to the bar for borrowing money for his education and then filing for bankruptcy three days before law school graduation? Does such action show a lack of sensitivity to his "moral responsibility to his creditors * * * [and] a lack of the moral values" required of a lawyer? Some states have held that it does, while acknowledging the applicants' legal right to file bankruptcy.[3]

---

[3]   Florida Board of Bar Examiners v. G.W.L., 364 So.2d 454 (Fla.1978) (court denied admission of applicant because "he exercised his legal right to be freed of debt by bankruptcy

c.   Why might financial issues be of particular concern to bar admission authorities? Are lawyers so frequently entrusted with the handling of client funds that honesty in the handling of money should be a significant concern?

4.   Should there be a statute of limitations on how long prior incidents can affect current bar admission decisions?

a.   Note that some of Smith's problems occurred when he was a freshman in college, years before his graduation from law school. Should that make a difference? Hallinan v. Committee of Bar Examiners, supra, said that "adolescent misbehavior" was not sufficient to disqualify the applicant.[4] Would you want to know how old Smith was at the time of the alleged college incidents before you turned him in? Should you ask, or should you leave seeking such information up to others? Look at ABA Model Rule 8.1.

b.   Matter of Prager, 661 N.E.2d 84 (Mass.1996), involved an applicant who was in his late 40s. For about six years in the 1970s, he headed a "large-scale international marijuana smuggling operation." After indictment for his crimes, he fled the country and lived as a fugitive for several years in England and the Caribbean. He pled guilty when he returned to the country, and as a condition of his probation, he provided care in his home to terminal AIDS patients. He also attended the University of Maine law school, served on the law review, and after graduating summa cum laude, clerked for a justice of the Maine Supreme Court. The question was whether the applicant was sufficiently rehabilitated to sit for the Massachusetts bar examination. The court held he was not. His flight to avoid prosecution "undermined the integrity of the judicial process" and his admission without the passage of at least five more years, "would reflect poorly on the integrity of the bar." Do you agree?[5]

---

well before the first installments on his debt became due, with absolutely no regard for his moral responsibility to his creditors."); In re C.R.W., 481 S.E.2d 511 (Ga.1997) (applicant must show a good faith effort to meet financial obligations); In re Gahan, 279 N.W.2d 826 (Minn.1979); Application of Taylor, 647 P.2d 462 (Or.1982). But see, Matter of Anonymous, 549 N.E.2d 472 (N.Y.1989).

[4]   An interesting analogy can be drawn to the problem of an attorney's reinstatement after disbarment. As a general rule, almost no matter how serious the original offense, the attorney may be reinstated upon a showing of rehabilitation and present fitness. See, e.g., In re Hiss, 333 N.E.2d 429 (Mass.1975); In re Wigoda, 395 N.E.2d 571 (Ill.1979).

[5]   See also, In re Dortch, 860 A.2d 346 (D.C.2004) (same result where applicant planned and executed a bank robbery in 1974 in which his associate killed a police officer; applicant was a model prisoner and law-abiding citizen before and during law school).

Frasher v. West Virginia Bd. of Law Examiners, 408 S.E.2d 675 (W.Va.1991), even held that a record of three convictions for driving under the influence, along with other driving offenses, was enough to deny an applicant admission to the bar. The result initially seems harsh, but it represents an important part of a continuing struggle with the problem of lawyer alcoholism and drug abuse that we will see in Problem 2.

5. **Historically, the principal concern about the character and fitness requirement has been its potential to deny bar admission based on political beliefs rather than character. In the 1950s, for example, it was the principal basis for denying members of the Communist Party admission to the bar.[6] Is there a risk of that misuse of the requirement today?**

a. In re Converse, 602 N.W.2d 500 (Neb.1999), involved an applicant who engaged in bizarre but non-criminal behavior while in law school. The student wrote to the state supreme court and prominent federal judges to criticize his appellate advocacy teacher. When he got in trouble for displaying a photograph of a "nude female's backside" on his law school carrel, he raised a First Amendment charge. Later, he sold T-shirts with a "nude caricature of [his law school Dean] shown sitting astride * * * a very large hot dog" with a caption "Astride the Peter Principle." The court denied him admission to the bar, saying the "threshold question we must answer is whether conduct arguably protected by the First Amendment can be considered by the Commission during an investigation into an applicant's moral character and fitness to practice law. We answer this question in the affirmative." The court declared: "abusive, disruptive, hostile, intemperate, intimidating, irresponsible, threatening, or turbulent behavior is a proper basis for the denial of admission to the bar." Do you agree?

b. In re Hale, 723 N.E.2d 206 (Ill.1999), cert. denied sub nom. Hale v. Committee on Character and Fitness of the Illinois Bar, 530 U.S. 1261 (2000), involved Matthew Hale, an outspoken white supremacist who founded a "church" to espouse his beliefs. The Illinois character and fitness panel held that, in lawyer regulation, "'fundamental truths' of equality and nondiscrimination 'must be preferred over the values found in the First Amendment.'" Thus, the panel asserted, if Hale were admitted to the Bar, he would be "on a collision course with the Rules of Professional Conduct." The Illinois Supreme Court refused to review the character and fitness panel's opinion, thus affirming its denial of admission. In dissent, Justice Heiple argued: "The Committee seems to hold that it may deny petitioner's application for admission to the bar without finding that petitioner has engaged in any specific conduct that would have violated a disciplinary rule if petitioner were already a lawyer."

c. Do you agree with the results in these cases? Are courts likely to be reliable predictors of which people have sufficient character to be a lawyer? A grand jury later indicted Hale in Chicago for "plotting to kill

---

[6] Important constitutional cases on bar admissions include, Konigsberg v. State Bar, 353 U.S. 252 (1957) (Konigsberg I); Schware v. Board of Bar Examiners, 353 U.S. 232 (1957) (one cannot be denied admission merely because he is a member of the Communist Party); Konigsberg v. State Bar (Konigsberg II), 366 U.S. 36 (1961) (court may refuse admission because applicant obstructs the investigation—e.g., refuses to say whether he is or is not a knowing member of the Communist Party); In re Anastaplo, 366 U.S. 82 (1961); Baird v. State Bar of Arizona, 401 U.S. 1 (1971) (applicant may not be denied bar admission for failure to state whether she has ever been a member of an organization that "advocates overthrow of the United States by force or violence"); Application of Stolar, 401 U.S. 23 (1971); Law Students Civil Rights Research Council, Inc. v. Wadmond, 401 U.S. 154 (1971) (one can be refused admission if, with scienter, he is a knowing member of the Communist Party with intent to further its illegal goals). See generally, 5 Ronald D. Rotunda & John E. Nowak, Treatise on Constitutional Law: Substance and Procedure § 20.44 (15th ed.2013). John E. Nowak & Ronald D. Rotunda, Constitutional Law § 16.44 (8th ed.2010).

a federal judge and obstructing justice." Washington Post, Jan. 9, 2003, p. A–2. The jury found him guilty and he is now serving a 40–year sentence. Does that confirm the wisdom of earlier denying him admission to the bar?[7]

B.   CANDOR IN THE BAR APPLICATION PROCESS

1.   How candid must bar applicants like Smith and their supporters be in the application process?

a.   Authorities may be more likely to deny an applicant admission for covering up his or her past than for what that past contains. Attorney Grievance Comm'n v. Myers, 635 A.2d 1315 (Md.1994), for example, disbarred a lawyer for lying on his bar application about the number of traffic tickets he received, even though the driving record itself would not justify denial of admission. Cf. Model Rule 8.1. Is such an approach by admission authorities reasonable? Is it likely to be inevitable?

b.   In re Zbiegien, 433 N.W.2d 871 (Minn.1988), rewarded honesty. A bar applicant admitted he plagiarized several pages of a paper in a products liability seminar, but said that he was under great stress because of work pressures and injuries that his wife had suffered. Petitioner received an "F" in the course but permitted to graduate. He reported the incident in his application for admission to the bar. Although the court held that a single incident of misconduct could result in denial of bar admission, this applicant received enough punishment for the misconduct and now showed remorse. Thus, the court admitted him to the bar.

c.   But candor is not always rewarded. Application of Taylor, 647 P.2d 462 (Or.1982), involved an applicant arrested for shoplifting. The trial court dismissed the charges when the defendant denied he intended to steal the item. Before the bar committee, however, the applicant made a clean breast of things and admitted that he really had intended to steal. Rather than commend his current honesty, the committee denied him admission for his misleading testimony in the criminal case. Are you troubled by the result in Taylor? Are you relieved that the dishonesty came out in time? What is its message to bar applicants about how safe it is to volunteer incriminating information?

d.   Take a close look at Rule 8.1(b). Is honesty all it demands? What does the rule mean when it requires bar applicants to "correct a misapprehension known by the person to have arisen in the matter"? Assuming you have tried to be completely honest, are you likely in most cases to know whether bar admission authorities have misunderstood what you told them? Should you read communications that you get from those authorities very carefully to be sure to avoid letting misapprehensions go uncorrected?

---

[7]   Should a lawyer who violated no law but preached racial hatred after bar admission be subject to disbarment? Look at Rule 8.4, Comment 3. Does it address that question at all?

2.   How much information should a state supreme court be able to obtain from a candidate for bar admission about his or her history of mental illness?

a.   Is a mental illness a "disability" within the meaning of the Americans with Disabilities Act? Litigants have filed suits challenging such questions, and the ABA, being concerned that fear of such inquiries may prevent law students from getting mental health assistance, has urged states to limit inquiry to "specific, targeted questions about the applicant's behavior, conduct or any current impairment of the applicant's ability to practice law."

b.   Questions 25, 26, and 27 in the Character and Fitness questionnaire prepared by the National Conference of Bar Examiners now ask:

"25. Within the past five years, have you been diagnosed with or have you been treated for bi-polar disorder, schizophrenia, paranoia, or any other psychotic disorder?

"If you answered yes, complete Forms 7 and 8. * * *

"26. A. Do you currently have any condition or impairment (including, but not limited to, substance abuse, alcohol abuse, or a mental, emotional, or nervous disorder or condition) which in any way currently affects, or if untreated could affect, your ability to practice law in a competent and professional manner?

"B. If your answer to Question 26(A) is yes, are the limitations caused by your mental health condition or substance abuse problem reduced or ameliorated because you receive ongoing treatment (with or without medication) or because you participate in a monitoring program?

"If your answer to Question 26(A) or (B) is yes, complete Forms 7 and 8. * * * As used in Question 26, 'currently' means recently enough so that the condition could reasonably have an impact on your ability to function as a lawyer.

"27. Within the past five years, have you ever raised the issue of consumption of drugs or alcohol or the issue of a mental, emotional, nervous, or behavioral disorder or condition as a defense, mitigation, or explanation for your actions in the course of any administrative or judicial proceeding or investigation; any inquiry or other proceeding; or any proposed termination by an educational institution, employer, government agency, professional organization, or licensing authority?

"If you answered yes, furnish a thorough explanation * * *."

c. Are these questions inappropriately intrusive? Do they inquire into information that bar admission authorities need to know? Might the need to answer these questions deter law students from getting mental health treatment that they need?

3. Would you favor a policy that grants only conditional admission to persons who have recently undergone treatment for chemical dependency or mental illness?

a.   In February 2008, the ABA House of Delegates approved a model rule for states to use in creating a system of conditional admission for persons "whose rehabilitation or treatment is sufficiently recent that protection of the public requires monitoring of the applicant for a specified period." The rule only applies to persons with a "chemical dependency, mental or other illness" that previously made that person unable to "meet the functional requirements necessary to practice law." Having the option of conditional admission available would not preclude unconditional admission where rehabilitation was successful for a sustained period, nor would it preclude outright denial of admission in appropriate cases.

b.   If you were part of the bar admission process, what conditions might you consider imposing on a lawyer? If you were a client, would you want to know that your lawyer was only conditionally admitted to the bar? Would letting clients know a lawyer's mental history be too great an invasion of the lawyer's right to privacy? Whether or not to require disclosure proved so controversial that the ABA House of Delegates voted to leave the issue of disclosure up to each state.

4. If you are Smith's lawyer (or just his friend who happens to be a lawyer), what are your own obligations to the bar admission authorities in connection with Smith's bar application?

a.   Look at Model Rule 8.1(b). Must you report what Smith admitted to you about his guilt in the cheating case? Must you report what you know about Smith's change of name and past criminal record?

b.   Look at Model Rule 8.1, Comment 3. Why should your responsibilities change when you undertake to represent Smith? Is the public interest in having all the facts before bar admission authorities any less?

c.   What obligations should law schools and individual professors have in making reports to bar admission authorities? If they fail to be candid, might that damage future clients? Absolute immunity would encourage law school personnel to be candid, but would it also encourage them to make uninformed or idiosyncratic comments?

A FEW MORE ISSUES RELATING TO BAR ADMISSION

1.   A state may not require a bar applicant to be a U.S. citizen. In re Griffiths, 413 U.S. 717 (1973), held that such a requirement denies non-citizens the Fourteenth Amendment guarantee of equal protection of the law.

2.   The U.S. Supreme Court has also limited states' efforts to limit bar admission to the state's own residents. Supreme Court of New Hampshire v. Piper, 470 U.S. 274 (1985). *Piper* held that the practice of law is a fundamental right that deserves protection under the privileges and immunities clause. Thus, states may not discriminate against nonresidents unless they demonstrate a substantial state purpose and a narrowly drawn restriction to advance that purpose. See also, Supreme

Court of Virginia v. Friedman, 487 U.S. 59 (1988) (Virginia may not require nonresident lawyers to take its bar exam but admit its own residents to the bar without doing so).

3.   In re Sergio C. Garcia, 315 P.3d 117 (Cal. 2014), considered whether an otherwise-qualified undocumented immigrant may be admitted to the California bar. Garcia came to the United States at age 17 with his father who had permanent resident status and is now a citizen, but dependent children must receive their own immigrant visas and, because of the long line of applicants, Garcia still is undocumented 19-years after his application. A federal statute denies undocumented persons certain "public benefits," among them a "professional license." But state law may override that limitation and California passed such a law in 2013, shortly after the oral argument in *Garcia*. The court concluded that an undocumented immigrant's continued presence in the United States does not itself involve moral turpitude, that there is no California public policy against licensing such persons and thus that Garcia can be admitted to the bar.

4.   The courts of all states will permit graduates of ABA-accredited law schools to take their bar exam, but several states—most prominently California—also have accreditation regimes of their own. Graduates of state-accredited law schools may take those states' bar exams, and Wisconsin admits graduates from either of the state's two ABA-accredited law schools to its bar without taking any bar exam at all.

5.   Before graduates of a foreign law school may take a state's bar exam, they usually must show that they received an education that is "substantially equivalent" to that of an ABA-accredited law school. On the other hand, legal services are increasingly among the subjects countries consider in trade negotiations, to the admission of foreign lawyers to U.S. federal and state courts seems likely in the not-too-distant future.

6.   As a practical matter, admission to the highest court of a state will ordinarily be sufficient to qualify for admission to the federal courts of that state. See, e.g., United States District Courts for the Southern and Eastern Districts of New York, Local Civil Rule 1.3, contained in the Standards Supplement.

But a federal district court may not require a lawyer seeking admission to practice before it to either reside or maintain an office in the state where the federal court sits. Frazier v. Heebe, 482 U.S. 641 (1987).

––––––––

PROBLEM 2

LAWYER DISCIPLINE AND THE DISABLED LAWYER

Admitting an applicant to the bar is only the first time a state supreme court evaluates that person's conduct. For as long as the lawyer is a member of its bar, the court retains jurisdiction to sanction that lawyer for violations of the court's rules of professional conduct. This problem examines professional discipline in the context of the requirement that a lawyer represent each client competently and diligently. It then considers the serious problem of lawyer disability, primarily in the context of alcohol and drug abuse. Next, it asks which courts have jurisdiction to discipline a lawyer for misconduct, and what jurisdiction's law they will apply to evaluate conduct. Finally, it looks at each lawyer's duty to report the misconduct of other lawyers.

FACTS

Morris Andrews has been watching his peer and good friend Harold Black slowly lose his battle with a drinking problem. Andrews knows from long association that Black was once an able lawyer but that a series of personal crises have stimulated a case of alcoholism that has greatly reduced his effectiveness. In a recent case, Andrews' client had a less-than-even chance of winning, but won easily because Black seemed unable to represent his own client effectively.

Andrews resolved to go to Black and encourage him to withdraw from practice until he addressed his substance abuse problem. Black took the suggestion as an officious insult. "I represent my clients better than you do," Black said. "At least I don't take on more work than I can handle. You never finish anything. All your cases are on the back burner and you only appear in court to get continuances. I lay off the bottle when I have a big case, and as for that recent one when you beat me, you were just lucky."

Andrews did not consider Black's outburst responsive to the main issue, but he did have to admit that Black was right about his caseload. Indeed, Andrews made a mental note to settle some of his minor cases so as to spend more time on the rest. But he was still left uncertain about what, if anything, to do about Black.

QUESTIONS

A.   CONDUCT THAT CAN SUBJECT A LAWYER TO PROFESSIONAL DISCIPLINE

1.   Where does a lawyer look to see what can justify professional discipline?

a.   In a state that has adopted the ABA Model Rules, professional discipline is imposed for violation of Rule 8.4. Rule 8.4(a) incorporates by reference the other Model Rules.

b.   The remaining parts of Rule 8.4 are what Restatement Third, The Law Governing Lawyers § 5, Comment *c*, calls the "catch all" provisions. Notice that the term "appearance of impropriety" as a ground for discipline does not appear in the Model Rules, although some courts and commentators sometimes still use that phrase in justifying discipline.

2.   What should be the purposes and functions of the lawyer discipline process? Should we only punish dishonesty and other "serious" wrongdoing? Should the purposes of the process include responding to what clients see to be problems with their lawyers, even if the concerns seem minor to lawyers themselves?

a.   Two American Bar Foundation researchers have suggested that the process has three functions: "(1) to identify and remove from the profession all seriously deviant members (the 'cleansing' function), (2) to deter normative deviance and maximize compliance with norms among attorneys (the deterrence function), and (3) to maintain a level of response to deviance sufficient to forestall public dissatisfaction (the public image function)."[8]

b.   Restatement Third, The Law Governing Lawyers § 5, Comment *b*, explains that

> "Professional duties defined in lawyer codes are mainly concerned with lawyer functions performed by a lawyer in the course of representing a client and causing harm to the client, to a legal institution such as a court, or to a third person. Those duties extend further, however, and include some lawyer acts that, even if not directly involving the practice of law, draw into question the ability or willingness of the lawyer to abide by professional responsibilities."

c.   Do you agree with these analyses and explanations? How many lawyers do you think would have to be disciplined before the bar could completely "cleanse" itself of deviant members? Does the effectiveness of "deterrence" depend in part on the likelihood of getting caught?

d.   Would "public image" be improved by highly publicized discipline in cases that come to public attention but confidential treatment of other lawyer misconduct? Does enhancing lawyers' public image seem to you to be an appropriate *purpose* of professional discipline, as opposed to being a consequence of any effective system?

3.   Applying these ideas to the facts of this problem, does using the discipline process to pursue Andrews and Black seem desirable?

a.   Are Andrews and Black "bad people"? Indeed, is Andrews' problem that too many people think he is a good lawyer? As a practical matter, does Andrews have the luxury of determining the amount of work in the office at any one time? Might turning a client away today cause that client (and perhaps a friend of that client) not to come back tomorrow?

b.   Surely, however, representing clients "competently" and "diligently" are among the most important ethical responsibilities of a lawyer. See Model Rules 1.1 and 1.3. Has Andrews violated those rules by taking on more work than he can handle expeditiously and effectively?

---

[8]   Eric Steele & Raymond Nimmer, Lawyers, Clients and Professional Regulation, 1976 American Bar Foundation Research J. 917, 999–1014.

c.   Do we have evidence that Andrews has "neglected" his clients' work? ABA Informal Opinion 1273 (Nov. 20, 1973) asserted that:

> "Neglect involves indifference and a consistent failure to carry out the obligations which the lawyer has assumed to his client or a conscious disregard for the responsibility owed to the client. * * * Neglect usually involves more than a single act or omission. Neglect cannot be found if the acts or omissions complained of were inadvertent or the result of an error of judgment made in good faith."

Is that definition appropriate for interpreting Model Rule 1.3? Do you suppose clients care how many other cases a lawyer has neglected? May Andrews rely on Opinion 1273 to continue with business as usual or has Model Rule 1.3 effectively overruled that Opinion?

d.   Disciplinary authorities have pursued incompetence, negligence and neglect as violations of both Model Rules 1.1 and 1.3. Iowa Supreme Court Bd. of Professional Ethics & Conduct v. Hill, 576 N.W.2d 91 (Iowa 1998), for example, revoked the license of a lawyer who tried to handle an interstate adoption when he knew or should have known he was incompetent to do it. He said that he had "heard of" the interstate compact governing such adoptions but did not know its provisions and did not comply with it. Nor did he know that he had engaged in the unauthorized practice of law in Missouri as part of the adoption process. The Iowa Supreme Court found that a lawyer this incapable of competent practice "does not possess the attributes required of a lawyer licensed to practice in this state."

4.   Under Model Rule 8.4(b), what criminal acts "reflect adversely on the lawyer's honesty, trustworthiness or fitness as a lawyer in other respects"?

a.   Some of the conduct sanctioned under that rule borders on the unbelievable. In Attorney Grievance Comm'n v. Protokowicz, 619 A.2d 100 (Md.1993), a divorce lawyer was convicted of helping his former client break into the home of the client's estranged wife. When a feline resident of the home came into the kitchen, the lawyer put it into the microwave oven. You can guess the rest. The Maryland Court of Appeals suspended the lawyer for not less than one year for both breaking into the house and cooking the cat.

b.   In People v. Musick, 960 P.2d 89 (Colo.1998), the court suspended the lawyer for a year and a day on the basis of three incidents of physical assault against his live-in companion. The hearing board concluded that he was a good lawyer and that his temper was unlikely to affect dealings with his clients, but on review, the Colorado Supreme Court held that even though the prosecutor had declined to bring criminal charges against the lawyer, the conduct was malum in se and reflected adversely on his ability to practice law.[9]

c.   In The Florida Bar v. Brown, 790 So.2d 1081 (Fla.2001), an attorney assisted his corporate client to make illegal political contributions by soliciting $500 contributions from law firm employees that were to be reimbursed through billing inflated hours in the client's

---

[9]   See also, Lawyer Disciplinary Bd. v. Robinson, 736 S.E.2d 18 (W.Va. 2012) (lawyer disbarred for criminally beating his client with a baseball bat and then following the client down the street to continue the beating while the client lay on the ground).

legal matters. The client's officers were convicted of felony violations of state campaign finance laws, but the attorney claimed that he did not know the law banned his conduct. "Our legal system depends on attorneys who appropriately question requests from clients that should arouse suspicion," the court wrote. Even if the lawyer did not purposefully evade the law, his acts assisted a client in conduct the lawyer "should have known was criminal or fraudulent." The court suspended the lawyer for 90 days.

d.   In re Diaz, 288 P.3d 486 (Kan. 2012), involved a Navy Judge Advocate who unlawfully released the names of hundreds of Guantanamo detainees to a human rights lawyer. In Rasul v. Bush, 542 U.S. 466 (2004), the Supreme Court held that the detainees were entitled to challenge the validity of their detention. The Navy refused to release the names of all detainees to outside groups, and Diaz believed this violated the spirit of *Rasul*, so he sent one of the human rights lawyers a Valentine's Day card along with the classified list of names cut into strips. The military court martialed Diaz, sentenced him to six months confinement, and dismissed him from the Navy. The Kansas Supreme Court held that Diaz ignored the process described in Rule 1.13 for correcting a problem within an organization and released confidential client information in violation of Rule 1.6. He said he did so hoping that he could avoid detection and not hurt his naval career. The court disbarred Diaz.

5.   Should attorneys be subject to professional discipline for behavior not in their capacity as attorneys? Why should state supreme courts sanction lawyer misconduct even when the lawyer was not acting as a lawyer at the time?

a.   In re Boudreau, 815 So.2d 76 (La.2002), involved a lawyer importing sexually explicit child pornography from Europe, a crime for which he served 21 months in prison. The state supreme court disbarred Boudreau under Model Rule 8.4(b) even though he had no prior disciplinary record. The court found that the purchase of magazines constituted participation in the sexual exploitation of children, and analogized the conduct to making unwanted sexual demands on clients. Regardless of revulsion at the content of the magazines, do you agree that buying them reflects adversely on the lawyer's "honesty, trustworthiness or fitness as a lawyer in other respects"?

b.   Model Rule 8.4(c) also prohibits a lawyer's engaging "in conduct involving dishonesty, fraud, deceit or misrepresentation," whether or not in a representational setting. In re Fornari, 599 N.Y.S.2d 545 (N.Y.App.Div.1993), suspended a lawyer for one year for filing fraudulent documents in making a claim with his homeowner's insurer. For example, he submitted bills for work other than that caused by a storm, and he altered the figures on other bills, allegedly to speed up payment he claimed was legally was due. See also, In re Bikman, 760 N.Y.S.2d 5 (N.Y.App.Div.2003) (attorney moved into her sister's rent-controlled apartment after the sister passed away and forged her sister's signature on rent checks, thus taking advantage of the controlled rent).

c.   In re Scruggs, 475 N.W.2d 160 (Wis.1991), suspended a lawyer for resume fraud. He took another student's transcript and inserted his own name and biographical information on it. He also said he attended American University when he had actually attended American Technological University. Do you agree that these kinds of misrepresentations should cost a lawyer his or her license? Why or why not? See also In re Lamberis, 443 N.E.2d 549 (Ill.1982) (censure imposed for lawyer's plagiarism in work on an LL.M. degree); In re Lamb, 776 P.2d 765 (Cal.1989) (lawyer disbarred for five years for taking the bar exam for her husband).

   d.   Matter of Diggs, 544 S.E.2d 628 (S.C.2001), suspended a lawyer for 90 days for filing a form saying he attended a CLE seminar when, in fact, he arrived near the end of the program. Does this case send an important message to lawyers? You too may find that you don't like some of your CLE courses, but remember that if you lie to bar regulatory authorities you may be inviting a disciplinary complaint that you will like even less.

   6.   What conduct should be sufficient to violate the Model Rule 8.4(d) prohibition of "conduct that is prejudicial to the administration of justice"?

   a.   Matter of Karahalis, 706 N.E.2d 655 (Mass.1999), involved a lawyer whose uncle was housed in a federal prison far from his family. Relatives of a congressman told the lawyer that the congressman could get the uncle moved nearer to him if the lawyer paid $12,000 to the congressman, so the lawyer made the payment. He cooperated with the prosecution of the congressman, but the bribery was a serious enough offense that the court suspended the lawyer for four years.[10]

   b.   In Iowa Supreme Court Bd. of Professional Ethics & Conduct v. Lane, 642 N.W.2d 296 (Iowa 2002), Lane represented a client in a federal suit under the Americans with Disabilities Act. He submitted a lengthy post-trial brief to the court, and he certified in his fee application that he spent 80 hours writing the brief. The district judge noticed style oddities in the brief and made several requests for Lane to submit a list of sources that he used. Lane eventually provided a list of over 200 sources, but failed to call attention to any one of the sources. Through independent research, the district judge discovered that Lane copied over 18 pages of his brief verbatim, with footnotes, from a treatise on employment discrimination law. The Iowa Supreme Court suspended Lane for six months, finding that his billing for plagiarized work and repeated evasion of the court's inquiries constituted a deliberate attempt to perpetrate a fraud upon the court.

   c.   In Attorney Grievance Comm'n of Maryland v. Sheinbein, 812 A.2d 981 (Md.2002), the attorney's son was wanted for the murder of a neighbor. Attorney Sheinbein assured a police detective that he would contact her once he heard from his son or learned his whereabouts. Instead, Sheinbein encouraged his son to flee the country, drove from Maryland to New York to deliver his son's passport, and purchased his plane ticket to Israel. He never relayed the promised information to the detective. Even though the suspect was his son, the court held, "a lawyer's ensuring that a police investigation is thwarted by sending a main suspect known by him to be the killer in a murder case to a

---

   [10]   Cf. The Florida Bar v. Karahalis, 780 So.2d 27 (Fla.2001) (Florida gave the Massachusetts disciplinary findings preclusive effect and disbarred the respondent as well).

distant country necessarily reflects adversely on that lawyer's trustworthiness." The court disbarred Sheinbein. Two dissenting justices argued that it was neither illegal nor unethical for Sheinbein to send his son abroad before the state filed any criminal charges against him. What do you think? Is it relevant that Sheinbein assured a police detective that he would contact her once he heard from his son?

d.   If Harold Black asserts his privilege against self-incrimination in a discipline proceeding against him, is that assertion "prejudicial to the administration of justice" under Rule 8.4(d)? Spevack v. Klein, 385 U.S. 511 (1967), said no, holding that a state may not disbar an attorney for taking the Fifth Amendment.

B.   AGGRAVATING AND MITIGATING FACTORS IN DISCIPLINE CASES; THE PROBLEM OF ALCOHOL AND DRUG ABUSE, PSYCHOLOGICAL DISORDERS, AND MENTAL DISEASE

1.   Think about yourself and your law school colleagues. Are alcoholism and drug abuse serious problems among lawyers?

a.   There is evidence suggesting that the problem of lawyers' drug and alcohol abuse is significant. A state of Washington study, for example, reported that 18% of all lawyers and 25% of those in practice over 20 years have a problem with drugs or alcohol. See Wall Street J., Nov. 30, 1991, at B1.

b.   A study by the Association of American Law Schools Special Committee on Problems of Substance Abuse in the Law Schools, 44 J. Legal Educ. 35, 41 (1994), found that nearly two-thirds of law students admitted using at least one illegal drug during their lifetime. Over 20% used marijuana, and nearly 5% used cocaine during the previous year.

c.   Today, we often think of alcoholism as a disease, not a character flaw. Should the Bar discipline Harold Black for conduct resulting from a medical condition over which he lacked full control? Can we justify the discipline as a way to prevent future misconduct arising from such a condition? If we follow that logic to its conclusion, could bar admissions authorities require all lawyers to pass psychological predisposition tests before admission to practice?[11]

2.   Should Black's alcoholism be a factor that affects the nature of his discipline?

a.   In re Kelley, 801 P.2d 1126 (Cal.1990), involved a lawyer who was brought into the discipline system after her second conviction for drunken driving. She had violated the probation imposed in the first drunken driving case, but it seems bar discipline authorities became involved as part of California's effort to identify lawyers with an alcohol problem *before* they injure a client. Her professional discipline in this case consisted primarily of three years' probation on condition that she abstain from alcohol and participate in the State Bar alcohol abuse program. Three justices were troubled at what could become an arbitrary use of discipline to coerce behavior that only *might* get worse. Indeed, might sanctions imposed to try to prevent harm rather than punish actual conduct constitute a violation of the Americans with

---

[11]   Cf. Alan M. Dershowitz, Preventive Disbarment: The Numbers Are Against It, 58 A.B.A.J. 815 (1972).

Disabilities Act? Recall the relation of that law to bar admission issues discussed in Problem 1.

b.   Courts have sometimes cited alcoholism as mitigation of the sanction for lawyer misconduct. In Matter of Walker, 254 N.W.2d 452 (S.D.1977), for example, there was proof that alcoholism led to the lawyer's conduct. Proof the lawyer was now a recovering alcoholic, although not excusing the misconduct, led the court to allow the lawyer to keep his license. Cf. Petition of Johnson, 322 N.W.2d 616 (Minn.1982) (suggests criteria for when proof of recovery should lead to that result).

c.   Rule 23 of the ABA Model Rules for Lawyer Disciplinary Enforcement (2002) provides for placing lawyers in a "disability inactive status" for an indefinite period during their mental or physical incapacity. Proceedings are conducted in the manner of a discipline case, but they are confidential. Provisions are made to notify clients and the public if the lawyer is placed on disability status. Is such a procedure and disposition too severe for a condition such as alcoholism? Is it both necessary for protection of the public and more humane than disbarment? Is it necessary to have the leverage of tough sanctions, if only as a threat to coerce the lawyer into getting help?[12]

3.   Should psychological disorders and mental disease similarly affect a lawyer's level of discipline?

a.   In re Conduct of Loew, 642 P.2d 1171 (Or.1982), the lawyer's defense was that he was a victim of "burn-out syndrome." His psychiatrist testified that professionals commonly take on too much work and then psychologically evade it by "procrastination and self-denial." Should this be a good defense? Would recognition of such a defense give adequate protection to the lawyer's clients? This court was sufficiently impressed by the defense that it did not disbar the lawyer, although it did suspend him for 30 days.

b.   People v. Lujan, 890 P.2d 109 (Colo.1995), involved a lawyer who received a head injury four years earlier that she said gave her a "compulsion to shop." The manifestation of that compulsion was that she charged her personal expenses to her firm's credit card and fabricated justifications for the charges. The court accepted her story in mitigation and noted she was on medication for her condition. Because the lawyer was already on disability inactive status, however, she would have to apply to the court before resuming the active practice of law.

c.   The Florida Bar v. Clement, 662 So.2d 690 (Fla.1995), raised the issue whether the Americans with Disabilities Act (ADA) protects a lawyer with bipolar disorder (often called manic depression) against disbarment. The lawyer engaged in complex financial deals with little attention to whether he was using client funds improperly. The psychiatric testimony was that the disease kept him from knowing right from wrong. The court held that, even if that were true, the ADA did not void the requirement that an impaired individual must be

---

[12]   The impaired attorney has been one of the particular concerns of the ABA in recent years, and Model Rule 8.3 was amended in August 1991 to provide that lawyers need not report to discipline authorities any information they learn as part of a lawyers' assistance program (often called an "L.A.P.") designed to help lawyer-abusers recover from addiction.

"qualified" to practice his profession. Thus, the ADA did not prevent the lawyer's disbarment.

d. How would you have treated the lawyers' claims in these cases? Is there any way to find an appropriate accommodation of the lawyer's mental condition and the clients' legitimate expectation that their lawyers will be able to represent them effectively?

C. INTERSTATE DISCIPLINE: JURISDICTIONS THAT MAY SANCTION AND THE LAW THEY APPLY

1. What jurisdictions may impose professional discipline on a lawyer?

a. In our problem, Black and Andrews are practicing in the same jurisdiction. Does the analysis change if Black were admitted in State #1 but lost his case against Andrews in State #2? Assume that the court admitted Black in State #2 only for that particular case. Look at Model Rule 8.5(a). Notice that, basically, any state in which the lawyer is licensed may discipline a lawyer for misconduct wherever it occurs, and even a state where the lawyer travels for temporary practice may try the lawyer for conduct occurring there.

b. In the Matter of Spraker, 744 N.E.2d 415 (Ind.2001), shows the operation of Rule 8.5. The court imposed discipline on an Indiana lawyer for conduct that occurred in Illinois but was illegal in both states. Spraker represented clients attempting to obtain permanent residency in the United States. There was evidence that he had failed to properly submit forms to the INS on more than 50 occasions. Indeed, several forms contained misstatements and lies about the clients. However, Spraker's clients all resided in Illinois where the alleged misconduct took place. The Supreme Court of Indiana found it had jurisdiction over Spraker's discipline because of his Indiana license. The court even allowed the hearing to take place in Illinois, given the sensitivity of many of Spraker's former clients to crossing state lines while they were still undocumented residents. The court suspended Spraker from practice in Indiana for two years.

2. Does each jurisdiction simply apply its own standards to evaluate the conduct? Which ethics rule governs a lawyer licensed in one state who negotiates a contract in another?

a. Look at Model Rule 8.5(b). Suppose a lawyer licensed in Florida negotiates a commercial transaction with a New Jersey resident and learns that the lawyer's client has lied about certain important facts. New Jersey ethics rules require its lawyers to disclose facts necessary to prevent a fraud and New Jersey clients may have come to expect such conduct from lawyers with whom they deal. Florida ethics law, in contrast, requires its lawyers *not* to disclose such facts. The lawyer's principal office is in Miami but the negotiations occurred in Newark. What is the lawyer to do about disclosure?

b. Must the lawyer assume the risk that a court will later say she followed the rules of the wrong state? How would a lawyer prove he or she complied with Rule 8.5(b)(2)'s safe harbor for "reasonable belief" that the "predominant effect of the conduct" will be in a particular jurisdiction? Does Model Rule 8.5, Comment 5, answer that question?

3. What is the effect of lawyer discipline in one state on a lawyer's status in other states where the lawyer is admitted to practice?

a. Should the sanction is imposed by the first state to discipline a lawyer be binding in all other states? Does Model Rule 8.5, Comment 1, speak to that question?

b. In Matter of Iulo, 766 A.2d 335 (Pa.2001), New Jersey permanently disbarred a lawyer in 1989 for misapplying client funds. In 1996, Pennsylvania allowed the lawyer to sit for its bar exam, and later admitted him, even after it learned of the New Jersey action. In 1999, the Pennsylvania Office of Disciplinary Counsel sought to have the lawyer subjected to reciprocal disbarment based on the New Jersey action. The Pennsylvania Supreme Court said no. Pennsylvania seeks to rehabilitate lawyers, the court said, while New Jersey seeks to exclude them from practice. Principles of reciprocal discipline may require honoring factual findings made elsewhere but they do not require identical sanctions. The court said, "imposition of reciprocal discipline in this instance would be a grave injustice." Do you agree? Would the court decide this case the same way under the current version of Model Rule 8.5?

4. Should federal courts create their own disciplinary standards or apply the state disciplinary standards of the state in which they are sitting?

a. United States v. Walsh, 699 F.Supp. 469 (D.N.J.1988), considered New Jersey amendments to Model Rule 1.11 on disqualification of former government lawyers. In practice, many federal courts adopt, as a matter of "dynamic conformity," the ethics rules of the states in which they sit; a few courts adopt their own ethics rules. In this case, the court held that the Model Rules as adopted by the ABA were controlling in that federal court, not the Rules as adopted by New Jersey, the state in which the court is located.

b. In re Hoare, 155 F.3d 937 (8th Cir.1998), dealt with reciprocal discipline in a federal court based on state discipline. The federal court required that a lawyer disciplined in state court show by clear and convincing evidence why the federal system should not impose identical discipline. The Eighth Circuit upheld that standard and the disbarment of the lawyer for driving while intoxicated, killing another driver in a collision, and refusing a blood alcohol test. See also, In re Kramer, 282 F.3d 721 (9th Cir.2002) (applies the multi-factored test of Selling v. Radford, 243 U.S. 46 (1917), to federal court imposition of reciprocal discipline).

c. Surrick v. Killion, 449 F.3d 520 (3d Cir.2006), addressed whether a lawyer barred from practice in state court may maintain a law office in that state to conduct a federal practice. The Pennsylvania Supreme Court suspended attorney Surrick for five years, but the federal district court before which Surrick was admitted to practice imposed a shorter punishment. Thus, the federal court reinstated Surrick to practice while the state court suspension was still in place. He refrained from opening a law office in Pennsylvania for fear of prosecution,[13] but he filed a complaint challenging the state's policy of denying attorneys in his position the right to open an office. The federal district court held that, although a state's disciplinary sanction is entitled to respect, it does not bind the federal courts. Even when a matter of important state concern is involved, if state law conflicts with federal law, the federal law must prevail. Office space is necessary for the "effective representation of [federal-law] clients," the district court noted, so denial of Surrick's right to operate such an office would give the state the power to second-guess a federal court's determination of Surrick's fitness to practice. The Third Circuit affirmed.

D. THE DUTY TO REPORT ANOTHER LAWYER'S MISCONDUCT

1. Should the courts discipline a lawyer for failure to report another lawyer?

a.   Model Rule 8.3 addresses a lawyer's duty to report misconduct of another lawyer or judge. This requirement tends to be one of the most under-enforced rules of professional conduct, although it is often the subject of bar association opinions. See, e.g., ABA Formal Opinion 03–431 (Aug. 8, 2003) (duty to report another lawyer suspected of suffering from alcoholism, drug addiction or other mental impairment); ABA Formal Opinion 04–433 (Aug. 25, 2004) (duty to report misconduct that raises a substantial question of an admitted but nonpracticing lawyer's honesty, trustworthiness or fitness).

b.   The first case to discipline a lawyer *solely* for the failure to report was In re Himmel, 533 N.E.2d 790 (Ill.1988). Himmel represented Tammy Forsberg, a client injured in a motorcycle accident. Earlier, Forsberg retained a different lawyer (Casey) to represent her in her personal injury action. Casey negotiated a settlement of $35,000 on Forsberg's behalf, received the settlement check, endorsed it, and converted the funds. Forsberg then retained Himmel to get her share back. He negotiated an arrangement whereby Casey would pay Forsberg $75,000 if she would not report him to the authorities for possible criminal or disciplinary sanction. Casey never paid the $75,000, and "Forsberg told respondent that she simply wanted her money back and specifically instructed respondent to take no other action." Himmel followed Forsberg's direction, recovered a total of $10,400 and took no fee for his work on the case.

The court said that "the client had contacted the [Illinois Attorney Registration and Disciplinary] Commission [ARDC] prior to retaining respondent and, therefore, the Commission did have knowledge of the alleged misconduct," And the Illinois Supreme Court disbarred Casey in 1985. The ARDC then pursued Himmel for his failure to report Casey, and the Illinois Supreme Court suspended Himmel from practice for a year. The court asserted:

---

[13] Surrick's concern was well based. In Office of Disciplinary Counsel v. Marcone, 855 A.2d 654 (Pa.2004), the court expressly held that an attorney suspended from the practice of law in Pennsylvania may not maintain an office to conduct a federal practice. The court held that while federal courts may regulate practice before them, state courts control who may operate law offices within their states.

"Common sense would dictate that if a lawyer has a duty * * * [to report], the actions of a client would not relieve the attorney of his own duty. * * *

"As to respondent's argument that he did not report Casey's misconduct because his client directed him not to do so, we again note respondent's failure to suggest any legal support for such a defense. A lawyer, as an officer of the court, is duty-bound to uphold the rules in the Code. * * * A lawyer may not choose to circumvent the rules by simply asserting that his client asked him to do so. * * * "14

c. If the court decided *Himmel* under today's Model Rules, would it reach the same result? Does Rule 1.6 give a client the right to put other clients at risk by telling her lawyer not to disclose an earlier lawyer's misconduct to the disciplinary commission?

d. In our problem, is Andrews' knowledge about Black "confidential" and thereby protected against disclosure by Rule 8.3(c) and Rule 1.6? Would Andrews' client want it known that he won largely because Black was an alcoholic? Is that the kind of information Rule 1.6 was meant to protect? Should the courts construe confidentiality broadly or narrowly for this purpose?

2. How soon must the lawyer make a report against a fellow lawyer? How sure should a lawyer be before reporting?

a. If there is a civil or criminal action pending involving the same conduct, disciplinary authorities often prefer that the lawyer wait until that action is completed. If the information comes in earlier, disciplinary authorities often suspend or abate their own inquiry so as to be able to work with a complete record and avoid duplicative investigation.

b. Would a delay allow the lawyer to use the threat of discipline as leverage in the civil case? See ABA Formal Opinion 94–383 (July 5, 1994), expressing a concern that the lawyer may use the threat to file a discipline charge to secure an advantage in a civil case. It urged the lawyer to postpone reporting until the conclusion of that case. Do you agree? Do the dynamics work the other way? Would the coercive power of a threatened charge exist *before* reporting and not exist thereafter?15

c. New York State Bar Ass'n Comm. on Prof. Ethics, Opinion 854 (Mar. 11, 2011), discusses when a law firm associate must report a firm partner's misconduct. The opinion says reporting is mandatory when four conditions are all met: (1) Associate has "actual knowledge" or a "clear belief" about the pertinent facts, (2) the conduct violates one or more rules of professional conduct, (3) the violation raises a "substantial question" about Partner's "honesty, trustworthiness or fitness as a lawyer," and (4) none of the information is protected by Rule 1.6 or was

---

14 At the time of the *Himmel* case, Illinois was operating under the Code of Professional Responsibility, which required disclosure of "unprivileged" information. The court found that the attorney-client privilege did not protect the information because the client's mother and fiancé was present when the client talked to the lawyer. You will learn more about the attorney-client privilege and protection of confidential information in Problem 7.

15 Cf. ABA Formal Opinion 94–384 (July 5, 1994), advising that a lawyer who becomes the subject of a disciplinary charge filed by the opponent in connection with a pending case is not required to withdraw from representation of the client in that case.

gained while participating in a lawyer assistance program. Even if not all the criteria are met, Associate may report "reasonable suspicions of misconduct" unless the information is protected by Rule 1.6 or Associate's intent is to "gain a tactical advantage" in litigation, business or personal relationships.

d.   In re Riehlmann, 891 So.2d 1239 (La.2005) (per curiam), discussed a lawyer's duty to report the misconduct of another lawyer in a particularly dramatic situation. Riehlmann and his best friend, Deegan, were both former prosecutors. One night Deegan told Riehlmann that he was dying of cancer. During the same conversation, Deegan told Riehlmann that he had suppressed exculpatory blood evidence in one of the cases he prosecuted. He did not identify the case. Riehlmann urged Deegan to report what he had done, but Riehlmann did not report Deegan himself.

Five years after Deegan's death, Riehlmann heard about a case where the crime lab discovered that the perpetrator of a crime had a different blood type than the person now on death row. He realized that this case was probably the case to which Deegan had referred, so he told the defendant's attorney of his conversation with Deegan. He subsequently executed an affidavit attesting to the fact that Deegan had indeed suppressed the exculpatory evidence. The month after signing the affidavit, and five years after Deegan's confession, Riehlmann also reported Deegan's misconduct to the Office of Disciplinary Counsel. That office's response was to charge Riehlmann under Rule 8.3(a) for failing to report the information earlier.

The Louisiana Supreme Court found that a reporting requirement is triggered whenever the supporting evidence would allow a "reasonable lawyer under the circumstances" to form a "firm belief that the conduct in question had more likely than not occurred." The court held that the lawyer must promptly report the misconduct in order to ensure that someone can investigate the offense and adequately protect the public and the profession against the offending attorney's possible future wrongdoings. In Riehlmann's case, the court found that a reasonable attorney would have formed a firm belief at the time of Deegan's confession that the misconduct likely occurred. Do you agree with the court's analysis?

3.   If a judge observes Black's impaired state or Andrews' inability to keep up with his caseload, is the judge's obligation to report different from that of a lawyer?

a.   The Illinois Disciplinary Commission did not seek any discipline against the judge who presided in the case that Forsberg brought against Casey. Should the judge also be liable? See ABA Model Code of Judicial Conduct (2007), Rule 2.15(D), which parallels Model Rule 8.3. May a judge assume that an attorney will report all misconduct in a case? Should the lawyers, in turn, rely on the judge? Once we start looking for violators of Model Rule 8.3, will there be any easy place to stop?[16]

b.   Are lawyers required to report the misconduct of judges? Look at Model Rule 8.3(b).

---

[16]   See Ronald D. Rotunda, The Lawyer's Duty To Report Another Lawyer's Unethical Violations in the Wake of Himmel, 1988 U. Illinois L. Rev. 977.

HOW THE DISCIPLINARY PROCESS OPERATES

If someone files a complaint against a lawyer with a disciplinary agency, the procedures described in the ABA Model Rules for Lawyer Disciplinary Enforcement are representative of what happens. A state's "disciplinary counsel," operating under the authority of the state's highest court, evaluates all complaints filed by clients or others about a lawyer. If the conduct would not violate the state disciplinary rules even if true, the complaint is dismissed. This is the basis upon which fee disputes, for example, are often dismissed if they do not allege fraud or overreaching.

However, if the facts alleged would constitute a violation of the rules of professional conduct, the disciplinary counsel is required to investigate whether or not the facts are true. Ordinarily, at least by that point, the lawyer is offered a chance to respond to the complaint. If the disciplinary counsel finds (or the lawyer admits) a non-serious violation, disciplinary counsel may impose a private sanction such as an admonition and the case is closed. However, if the alleged violation is serious, or if the lawyer does not consent to the private sanction, the disciplinary counsel will likely file a formal charge that the lawyer must answer.

The matter is then set for trial before a hearing panel (usually, comprised of other lawyers, typically working as volunteers) which either dismisses the matter or recommends a sanction. The lawyer may then appeal the sanction to a review board comprised of fellow lawyers. If that board also recommends a sanction, the lawyer may appeal to the licensing court. It is the court decisions in such cases that you will read about throughout this book. (Some states provide that the hearing panels will include a nonlawyer).

In 1986, the ABA House of Delegates approved the "Standards for Imposing Lawyer Sanctions." Various courts have referred to these new Standards for guidance. The Standards (as amended in 1992) propose that a court, in imposing a sanction after a finding of lawyer misconduct, should consider four factors: (a) the duty violated; (b) the lawyer's mental state; (c) the actual or potential injury caused by the lawyer's misconduct; and (d) the existence of aggravating or mitigating factors.

If a lawyer "engages in a pattern of neglect with respect to client matters and causes serious or potentially serious injury to a client," the Standards state that disbarment is generally appropriate. Standard 4.41(c). If the lawyer's pattern of neglect causes injury or potential injury that is not serious, the Standards recommend suspension. Standard 4.42(b). If the lawyer is merely negligent, does not act with reasonable diligence, and causes injury or potential injury to a client, the Standards recommend only a reprimand. Standard 4.43. If such a lawyer causes little or no actual or potential injury, the Standards recommend admonition. Standard 4.44. A reprimand is a public censure and an admonition is private.[17]

In addition to the sanctions of disbarment, suspension, reprimand, admonition, or probation (which allows the lawyer to practice law under specified conditions), the Standards allow "restitution, assessment of costs, limitation upon practice, appointment of a receiver, requirement that the lawyer take the bar examination or professional responsibility examination, requirement that the lawyer attend continuing education courses," or other sanctions that the disciplinary authority consider appropriate.[18] Standard 2.8.

The ABA reports that in 1995 lawyer discipline agencies received over 116,000 complaints, about one for every nine lawyers in the country. Of those complaints, however, the Bar dismissed almost 50,000 for failure to allege a violation of the disciplinary rules. Of the 66,000 remaining complaints, it dismissed 49,000 more after investigation. Often in such cases, the Bar does not tell the complainant what happened as a result of the complaint.

Indeed, only about 5,700 complaints (under 5%) actually led to formal disciplinary charges, and only about half of those, 2,900, led to convictions after trial. Of lawyers convicted, about 25% were disbarred, 50% suspended, and 25% publicly reprimanded.[19]

Does this data suggest that lawyers in the discipline process are too forgiving? The ABA Model Rules for Lawyer Disciplinary Enforcement now provide for one-third public members on both the hearing panels and disciplinary board. Do you agree with that approach? Does it represent an undesirable decline in self-regulation by the bar?

———

PROBLEM 3

REGULATING LAWYERS OUTSIDE OF THE FORMAL DISCIPLINARY SYSTEM

We examined professional discipline in Problem 2. Here, we look at additional sanctions that lawyers may face. Actions for professional malpractice may seek damages against a lawyer for wrongs characterized in at least three ways—as a tort committed by the lawyer against the client, as a breach of the contract the client made for the lawyer's services, or as a breach of fiduciary duties that the lawyer owes to the client. Sometimes all of these theories work equally well; sometimes the theory matters, as when the statute of limitations may have run on one or more claims, or when the remedy affects the amount of damages, e.g., when the client may seek punitive damages in tort but not in contract. In this problem, we look first at the standard of care and conduct used in malpractice cases. Next, we examine what goes into determining whether a lawyer has violated that standard. Then we consider remedies for professional malpractice and attempts to contract away those remedies. Finally, we look at a range of sanctions other than professional malpractice that a lawyer may face for his or her professional misconduct.

FACTS

Sarah Field is a young lawyer with a great future. She has attracted several clients with a wide range of interests and problems. Her outstanding record before juries is the envy of the local bar. Sometimes, however, she is not as careful as she might be.

Field is active in local politics. At a party picnic, an acquaintance of hers, Mary Moore, took her aside and told Field, "My doctor really messed me up two years ago. He performed supposedly minor surgery but cut the wrong things and now I can never have children." Field put her arm around Moore and said, "That's terrible. I know how to handle doctors like that. Leave everything to me." When Field got back to her office, she wrote a nasty letter to the doctor demanding that he "fully compensate my client." By return mail, she received a settlement offer of $250,000. Moore, the client, said she was delighted and Field was impressed at how intimidated the doctor seemed to be by her letter. Field did not have Moore examined by an independent physician. Had she done so, both would have learned that Moore's injuries were much worse than she believed. Instead, Field recommended that Moore accept the settlement, which she did. Now, Moore has learned the full extent of her injuries, and she realizes the inadequacy of her settlement.

Field does very little tax work. One of her wealthy clients heard that she could arrange her affairs so that income is taxable to her children, instead of herself, by using certain trusts. She asked Field to see that the trusts were properly prepared. Field researched the problem as well as her small office library would permit and discussed the issues over coffee with a CPA from down the hall. The client later learned that Field's handiwork was not good enough to accomplish her objectives, and the IRS assessed a large tax deficiency. "Don't blame me," Field said defensively, "If you wanted tax advice you should have called a specialist. I told you I was not positive of the tax consequences."

In yet another incident, a judge appointed Field to represent a defendant in a criminal trial. However, Field went on vacation and failed to appear when the court called the case for trial. The judge reset the case for the following morning, and Field quickly returned. The next day, Field was physically present for the trial, but she was not prepared and did a terrible job. The jury convicted the client and the judge sentenced him to a long prison term.

QUESTIONS

A.   THE STANDARD OF CARE AND CONDUCT IN A MALPRACTICE ACTION

1.   What standard governs a lawyer in a malpractice case?

a.   A leading treatise on lawyer malpractice says:

"[T]he essential elements of a cause of action for professional negligence are:

"(1) The employment of the attorney or other basis for imposing a duty;

"(2) the failure of the attorney to exercise ordinary skill and knowledge; and

"(3) that such negligence was the proximate cause of damage to the plaintiff."

1 Ronald E. Mallen & Jeffrey M. Smith, Legal Malpractice § 8.13 (2010 ed.).

b.   Restatement Third, The Law Governing Lawyers § 52(1) is more succinct: "[A] lawyer who owes a duty of care must exercise the competence and diligence normally exercised by lawyers in similar circumstances."[20]

c.   Lawyers sometimes try to comfort themselves by citing Lucas v. Hamm, 364 P.2d 685 (Cal.1961), which said the rule against perpetuities is so difficult that a lawyer's violation of it is not necessarily malpractice. However, in reality, Lucas is of little help. Horne v. Peckham, 158 Cal.Rptr. 714 (Cal.Ct.App.1979), made clear that the Lucas situation was unusual if not unique. "An attorney's obligation is not satisfied by simply determining that the law on a particular subject is doubtful or debatable [because] an attorney has a duty to avoid involving his client in murky areas of law if research reveals alternative courses of conduct. At least he should inform his client of uncertainties and let the client make the decision."

d.   In L.D.G. Inc. v. Robinson, 290 P.3d 215 (Alaska 2012), the client company asked lawyer Robinson to defend it in a dram shop action alleging it sold liquor to a man who then left and murdered someone. Robinson failed to join the killer as a second defendant for purposes of allocating fault. As a result, the court held the client liable for 100% of the damages. The right to join the killer in such a case was uncertain, but the court said the fact the law was unsettled did not

---

[20]   Gunn v. Minton, 133 S.Ct. 1059 (2013), explored whether malpractice cases involving patent issues might only be triable in federal court. In the early 1990s, Minton patented a computer program to facilitate securities trading. When he sued the NASDAQ stock market for infringement, however, the court declared his patent invalid because the invention was on sale for more than a year prior to being patented. Minton then tried to sue his lawyer for malpractice, but the Texas Supreme Court held such a case properly belonged in the federal courts because of the substantial federal interest in uniform interpretation of the patent law. The U.S. Supreme Court unanimously reversed. A legal malpractice case arises under state law, the Chief Justice wrote. A federal question was actually raised and disputed in this case, but its resolution was not of "substantial" consequence for the development of federal patent law. The case raised a question of damages but it did not validate the underlying patent so only traditional malpractice issues were before the court.

excuse the lawyer from doing what a reasonable lawyer would do to protect the client.[21]

2.   Did Sarah Field commit malpractice by recommending the inadequate settlement to the victim of medical malpractice?

a.   Traditional doctrine used to say that a client could not sue for malpractice after agreeing to settle a case because she would not have settled unless she were happy with the result. Later cases, however, reason that clients tend to follow their lawyers' advice and do not have independent bases on which to evaluate a settlement. Therefore, recommending an inadequate settlement may indeed constitute malpractice.

b.   *Woodruff v. Tomlin*, 616 F.2d 924 (6th Cir.1980) (en banc), cert. denied, 449 U.S. 888 (1980), relied on the typical rule that there is no malpractice liability for an honest exercise of professional judgment as to whether to call a particular person as a witness. Nevertheless, *Woodruff* said that the rule does not protect a lawyer's decision not to interview a potentially material witness as Field failed to do in this case. Without interviewing the witness, the lawyer would have no basis on which to make a judgment about the witness' importance, so the failure to interview may indeed be malpractice.

c.   *Wood v. McGrath, North, Mullin & Kratz, P.C.*, 589 N.W.2d 103 (Neb.1999), upheld a claim against lawyers who allegedly failed to tell the wife in a divorce action that the law was unsettled but that she might be entitled to a share of her husband's unvested stock options, and capital gain taxes might not have to be deducted from the share to which she was entitled. The lawyers said their overall advice about the merits of the settlement was sound, but the court held the client could not decide whether to settle without adequate information about the particular legal questions presented.

3.   Was Field obliged to refer the tax case to a specialist?

a.   In *Horne v. Peckham*, supra, the client asked Attorney to draft a Clifford trust in order to shelter income from federal taxes. Attorney testified that he told the client: "I had no knowledge of tax matters. I had no expertise in tax matters; that if somebody else could figure out what needed to be done, I could draft the documents." Attorney consulted with the client's accountant and a two-volume set of American Jurisprudence on federal taxation. When the trust failed to qualify for favorable tax treatment, the client sued and the jury awarded damages of $64,983.31. The appellate court affirmed the judgment and upheld a jury instruction that said, it "is the duty of an attorney who is a general practitioner to refer his client to a specialist or recommend the assistance of a specialist if under the circumstances a reasonably careful and skillful practitioner would do so." If Attorney did not refer the case or seek a specialist's help, it was his duty to have the knowledge and skill possessed and used by specialists in the same locality and under the same circumstances.

b.   *Battle v. Thornton*, 646 A.2d 315 (D.C.1994), however, held that if the jurisdiction does not certify specialties, the malpractice

---

[21] But see, Biomet Inc. v. Finnegan Henderson LLP, 967 A.2d 662 (D.C. 2009) (not malpractice to make a tactical decision based upon a reasonable reading of unsettled law, even if that reading is proven ultimately to be wrong).

standard is the skill of an ordinary lawyer, not persons who concentrate their practice in a given area of the law and usually handle a given kind of case.

c.   Which rule do you prefer? Does the California rule encourage making legal services more expensive? Can most clients be expected to understand the significance of a lawyer's warning that she has "no knowledge of tax matters"? Compare Model Rule 1.8(h)(1) (advance waiver of malpractice liability).

4.   Should Field be liable to the criminal defendant whose defense she handled badly?

a.   The majority rule on this subject may surprise you. Ordinarily, an element of a suit for lawyer malpractice is that a convicted criminal defendant must prove himself actually innocent of the charges against him, not just that a better lawyer might have obtained a not guilty verdict. Wiley v. County of San Diego, 966 P.2d 983 (Cal.1998), for example, in finding that "the clear majority of courts that have considered the question * * * require proof of actual innocence," explained:

> "[A] guilty defendant's conviction and sentence are the direct consequence of his own perfidy. The fact that nonnegligent counsel 'could have done better' may warrant postconviction relief, but it does not translate into civil damages, which are intended to make the plaintiff whole. While a conviction predicated on incompetence may be erroneous, it is not unjust. * * * Only an innocent person wrongly convicted due to inadequate representation has suffered a compensable injury * * *."

b.   Restatement Third, The Law Governing Lawyers § 53, Comment *d*, acknowledged cases like *Wiley* but proposed a less restrictive rule, saying:

> "Although most jurisdictions addressing the issue have stricter rules, under this Section, it is not necessary to prove that the convicted defendant was in fact innocent. As required by most jurisdictions addressing the issue, it is necessary for a former criminal defendant seeking damages for malpractice causing a conviction to have had that conviction set aside, when process for that relief on the grounds asserted in the malpractice action was available."

c.   Do you agree that courts should be cautious about allowing malpractice actions after criminal cases? Is there a reason to treat criminal and civil clients differently with respect to attorney malpractice? Might it be harder to find lawyers willing to act as criminal defense counsel if the law permitted more such suits?[1]

---

[1]   Whether appointed counsel should ever be subject to a malpractice action has been a controversial issue. Dziubak v. Mott, 503 N.W.2d 771 (Minn.1993), held that a public defender is immune from suit; public defenders may not turn down cases, and the public treasury cannot afford to defend malpractice cases. Moreover, immunity may encourage private lawyers to accept court appointments. See also, Polk County v. Dodson, 454 U.S. 312 (1981) (state public defender does not act "under color of state law" so as to be liable for malpractice under 42 U.S.C. § 1983). However, Ferri v. Ackerman, 444 U.S. 193 (1979), said that federal law does not require immunity of appointed counsel in federal cases from state malpractice claim. See

d.   Even though the majority rule remains intact,[2] courts are chipping away at its edges. Levine v. Kling, 123 F.3d 580 (7th Cir.1997), for example, acknowledged the usual rule but, in dictum, distinguished a situation where a client did the prohibited act but might have a complete legal defense to the criminal charge.

"We used the awkward term 'guilty in law' to distinguish the case in which the defendant is guilty in fact but has a sound legal defense, such as double jeopardy, from a case in which he is both guilty in fact and has no sound legal defense yet might, because of the heavy burden of proof on the prosecution, have obtained an acquittal if he had had a skillful lawyer. Only in the second case is the malpractice suit against the less-than-skillful lawyer barred."

e.   In Stichting v. Schreiber, 327 F.3d 173 (2d Cir.2003), a Dutch company, Saybolt International, wanted to buy a parcel of land for its operations in Panama, but its lawyers advised that it would first have to make a $50,000 bribe to a Panamanian official. Saybolt believed that, based on this advice, it would not violate the Foreign Corrupt Practices Act (FCPA) if it paid the bribe as a Dutch company rather than through its U.S. subsidiary. When the government filed criminal charges, Saybolt America pled guilty and sued its lawyer for giving advice that the payment would be legal. The district court granted the lawyers' motion for summary judgment, but the Second Circuit disagreed. Because of the lawyers' bad advice, Saybolt did not know its conduct was criminal, so letting Saybolt sue for that bad advice would not allow it to profit from intentionally wrongful conduct. See also, Mrozek v. Intra Financial Corp., 699 N.W.2d 54 (Wis.2005) (guilty plea to securities fraud does not bar malpractice action for bad advice about what disclosures were required).

5.   May Field be held liable for professional malpractice to persons other than her clients?

a.   A lawyer's liability for malpractice to someone who is not her client is a controversial and evolving area of lawyer liability. Restatement Third, The Law Governing Lawyers § 51 suggests four situations in which liability may be found.

b.   FIRST, a lawyer may be liable to a prospective client for revealing confidential information communicated to the lawyer or, for example, if the lawyer fails to tell the prospective client that the statute of limitations on his claim will soon run out, e.g., Miller v. Metzinger, 154 Cal.Rptr. 22 (Cal.Ct.App.1979).

c.   SECOND, a lawyer may be liable to beneficiaries named in a client's will if, due to the lawyer's negligence, the will does not carry out the testator's intention. Blair v. Ing, 21 P.3d 452 (Haw. 2001), for example, held that beneficiaries of a trust had standing to sue the draftsman whose negligence cost the trust $200,000 in increased taxes.

---

also, Mossow v. United States, 987 F.2d 1365 (8th Cir.1993) (government can be sued for malpractice of military lawyer); Rowell v. Holt, 850 So.2d 474 (Fla.2003) (public defender liable where failed to point out that the conduct alleged was not a crime at all).

[2]   Not all states follow the rule requiring exoneration. Rantz v. Kaufman, 109 P.3d 132 (Colo.2005) rejects the exoneration requirement, although it agrees that denial of post-conviction relief could preclude litigation of some issues in the malpractice case.

The plaintiffs were the intended beneficiaries of the lawyer-client relationship, the court said, and they could make the lawyer restore the trust corpus to the level it would have been but for the negligence.[22]

d.   THIRD, a lawyer may be liable to a non-client if the lawyer expressly assumes an obligation to investigate facts and accurately report them to the non-client. See, e.g., Greycas, Inc. v. Proud, 826 F.2d 1560 (7th Cir.1987), cert. denied, 484 U.S. 1043 (1988) (lawyer who agreed to investigate the state of client's title to property being posted as security for loan is liable to the lender when the lawyer failed to investigate and inaccurately reported the state of the client's title).[23]

In Paradigm Insurance Co. v. Langerman Law Offices, P.A., 24 P.3d 593 (Ariz.2001), the issue was whether an insurance company that retains a lawyer to defend the insured may sue that lawyer for malpractice. The insurance company paid a settlement on behalf of the insured doctor after the defendant lawyer mistakenly concluded that the hospital's malpractice insurance did not cover the doctor. Relying on § 51(3) of the Restatement, the court held that the fact that the lawyer-defendant in this case earlier represented only the doctor (not the doctor's insurance company), did not defeat the insurance company's claims. When an insurance company hires a lawyer to represent the insured, the lawyer's obligation to the insured (to defeat the claim) and to the insurer is the same. It would be unjust, the court said, for the lawyer to have no malpractice liability to the insurer that retained him, assigned the case to him, and paid his fees.

e.   FOURTH, under Restatement § 51(4), and Comment *h*, a lawyer who aids a trustee-like fiduciary to breach an obligation to the intended beneficiary of the fiduciary's duty may be liable to that beneficiary. See, e.g., Fickett v. Superior Court, 558 P.2d 988 (Ariz.App.1976); Reynolds v. Schrock, 107 P.3d 52 (Or.Ct.App.2005).

In Guardianship of Karan, 38 P.3d 396 (Wash.Ct.App.2002), the plaintiff was the successor guardian of a minor, Amanda, who was the beneficiary of her father's life insurance policy. When Amanda's father died, her mother hired the defendant-lawyer to represent the mother in a petition in which she asked to be the guardian of Amanda's estate. The lawyer obtained an order for Amanda's mother to establish and manage an account in Amanda's name, but he failed to include statutorily-required safeguards requiring the mother to post a bond or to place the funds in a blocked account. By the time that the court substituted the plaintiff as Amanda's guardian, her mother was judgment-proof and had spent most of the $50,000 left to Amanda. When the plaintiff sued the lawyer for legal malpractice, the lawyer argued that only Amanda's mother, his client, could bring a malpractice claim. The court rejected that defense, pointing to several factors in the case: the lawyer performed the work for Amanda's benefit; it was reasonably foreseeable that a failure to obtain the required safeguards would make depletion of the estate more likely; Amanda suffered harm as a result; the failure to implement the safeguards caused Amanda's

---

[22] But see, Miller v. Mooney, 725 N.E.2d 545 (Mass.2000) (will beneficiaries cannot sue lawyer because they were neither clients of the lawyer, nor third-party beneficiaries of a contract with the lawyer, nor persons entitled to be told how the testator was leaving her money).

[23] You will see more about this role of the lawyer as "evaluator" in Problem 21, *infra*.

injury; if the court refused to impose a duty on lawyers to act in the interests of the beneficiaries who are minors, similarly situated individuals will be harmed in the future; and imposing such a duty will not create any undue burden on lawyers because the beneficiary's interest is not in conflict with any legitimate request of any guardian.

    f.   Some states, notably New York and Texas, significantly qualify the theory of liability to non-clients by requiring privity between lawyer and client in order to maintain a malpractice action. The leading case on the privity limitation is Ultramares v. Touche, 174 N.E. 441 (N.Y.1931), where Judge Cardozo, for the court, feared giving professionals unlimited liability to investors who relied on their opinions. Compare, e.g., Security Pacific Business Credit, Inc. v. Peat Marwick Main & Co., 597 N.E.2d 1080 (N.Y.1992) (continuing to follow *Ultramares*), with Vereins–Und Westbank, AG v. Carter, 691 F.Supp. 704 (S.D.N.Y.1988) (holding lawyer liable on opinion letter). Do you see any good reason to retain the privity requirement today?

B.   PROVING A MALPRACTICE CASE

    1.   How does the trier of fact know what skill and knowledge a lawyer would ordinarily employ in the circumstances presented in this problem?

    a.   A plaintiff must ordinarily present expert testimony about the duty of care in a suit for professional malpractice. This rule applies even in a bench trial because the plaintiff must prove the standard of care on the record with an opportunity for the adverse party to cross-examine the expert.

    b.   In some cases, the court excuses expert testimony, when the issue is so simple or the lack of skill so obvious as to be within the range of ordinary experience of lay people. In Schmitz v. Crotty, 528 N.W.2d 112 (Iowa 1995), for example, the lawyer was completing death tax returns that another lawyer had started. The successor lawyer did not recognize that the return was reporting the same land more than once, thus increasing the taxes due. The court found the negligence so obvious that it did not require an expert to explain it to the jury.

    2.   If a client sues Sarah Field for malpractice, should the state's rules of professional conduct determine the standards of care and conduct?

    a.   Should violations of professional conduct rules be like the violations of law underlying the tort doctrine of negligence per se? For example, if the speed limit is 40 m.p.h., and the driver is traveling at 50 m.p.h., the normal rule is that driver's speeding is negligent. He cannot argue he was not driving too fast; he can only argue causation and damages.

    b.   Scope ¶ 18 of the 1983 Model Rules disclaimed using professional standards in malpractice cases. It said in part, "Violation of a Rule should not give rise to a cause of action nor should it create any presumption that a legal duty has been breached. * * * [N]othing in the Rules should be deemed to augment any substantive legal duty of lawyers or the extra-disciplinary consequences of violating such a duty." What effect should a court have given to that disclaimer?

c. Most courts at least allowed expert witnesses to cite the professional rules as evidence of the standards to which most lawyers adhere in the situations they face. See, e.g., Woodruff v. Tomlin, 616 F.2d 924 (6th Cir.1980) (en banc), cert. denied, 449 U.S. 888 (1980) (Model Code is "some evidence of the standards required of lawyers"); Mirabito v. Liccardo, 5 Cal.Rptr.2d 571 (Ct.App.1992) (disciplinary standards may be the subject of experts' testimony and cited to the jury); Maritrans GP Inc. v. Pepper, Hamilton & Scheetz, 602 A.2d 1277 (Pa.1992) (violation of state disciplinary rule does not *preclude* finding of malpractice; the rule may state a principle of fiduciary duty, for example, that will be enforced in a malpractice case even if the rule is not itself enforced).

Hizey v. Carpenter, 830 P.2d 646 (Wash.1992), however, held that violation of a disciplinary rule is not only not enough to show malpractice, the language of the rule may not even form the basis of a jury instruction. See also, Lazy Seven Coal Sales, Inc. v. Stone & Hinds, P.C., 813 S.W.2d 400 (Tenn.1991); Mergler v. Crystal Properties Associates, Ltd., 583 N.Y.S.2d 229 (App.Div.1992).

d. Restatement Third, The Law Governing Lawyers § 52(2) concluded that proof of violation of a professional rule (a) "does not give rise to an implied cause of action" for negligence or breach of fiduciary duty, (b) "does not preclude other proof concerning the duty of care * * * or the fiduciary duty," but (c) "may be considered by a trier of fact as an aid in understanding and applying" the applicable standard of care or conduct.

Does this rule guarantee work for legal ethics experts? What does it mean to say that violation of a professional standard "may be considered by the trier of fact"? Should the jury take the violation seriously or not?

e. The drafters of the 2002 Model Rules, in what is now Scope ¶ 20, have deleted the earlier disclaimer and substituted: "Nevertheless, since the Rules do establish standards of conduct by lawyers, a lawyer's violation of a Rule may be evidence of breach of the applicable standard of conduct." Now is the relevance of the Rules clear?

3. How should courts deal with the problem of causation? Should a client recover damages if the client would have lost the case no matter what the lawyer did?

a. The traditional burden on plaintiff in a malpractice case is to prove by a preponderance of the evidence that, but for the defendant lawyer's misconduct, the plaintiff would have obtained and collected a more favorable judgment in the original action. Thus, there is a "trial within a trial" or a "suit-within-a-suit." Restatement Third, The Law Governing Lawyers § 53, Comment *b*, explains:

"All the issues that would have been litigated in the previous action are litigated between the plaintiff and the plaintiff's former lawyer, with the latter taking the place and bearing the burdens that properly would have fallen on the defendant in the original action. * * * Similar principles apply when a former civil defendant contends that, but for the misconduct of the defendant's former lawyer, the defendant would have secured a better result at trial."

b.   Applying the suit-within-a-suit requirement to this problem, Field might try to defend against Moore's malpractice claim by showing that Moore did not have a very strong case as to the doctor's negligence, or that Moore herself was negligent in waiting too long to seek medical help. What do you think of permitting such a defense?

c.   Should a lawyer be able to use a client's trust in the lawyer against the client to prove the client's contributory negligence? In Arnav Industries, Inc. Retirement Trust v. Brown, Raysman, Millstein, Felder & Steiner, LLP, 751 N.E.2d 936 (N.Y.2001), the defendant law firm revised a settlement agreement for the plaintiff client and represented that the revised version only corrected a typographical error in the original. In fact, the new version also misstated the total amount due, a mistake that was costly to the plaintiff. Given the firm's representation that there was only one change, the plaintiff signed the revised document without reading it. The court held that the plaintiff's failure to read the contract did not defeat a malpractice claim, reasoning that the plaintiff justifiably relied on its attorney's representations.

C. MALPRACTICE REMEDIES; ADVANCE WAIVERS OF A LAWYER'S MALPRACTICE

1. What remedies should be available to redress Sarah Field's professional malpractice?

a.   The range of possible remedies is substantial. Typically, the client's damages are what the client would have obtained by way of trial or settlement if the lawyer had handled the matter non-negligently. However, malpractice can take other forms; a lawyer who negligently discloses a client's trade secret, for example, might be liable for damage to the client's business resulting from the disclosure. See Restatement Third, The Law Governing Lawyers § 53, Comment *b*.

b.   Campagnola v. Mulholland, Minion & Roe, 555 N.E.2d 611 (N.Y.1990), added a wrinkle to the question of damages. Because the lawyer did not comply with the policy provisions, the client lost her $100,000 uninsured motorist coverage. The lawyer asserted that the court should reduce this sum by the portion of the judgment she would have had to pay to the lawyer as his contingent fee. In a sharply divided 4 to 3 decision, the New York Court of Appeals said her contract to pay fees to her first lawyer was not part of the measure of what she had lost. Judge Kaye wrote in a concurring opinion that the plaintiff would be required to pay fees to bring this malpractice case, so not deducting fees for the first case from the damage award was necessary to make her whole.

However, Horn v. Wooser, 165 P.3d 69 (Wyo.2007), explicitly rejected the result and analysis in *Campagnola*. The Wyoming court said that the plaintiff would have incurred legal fees to collect damages in the underlying case and that an accurate measure of the plaintiff's actual loss must reflect the amount of those fees. Further, Judge Kaye's approach requiring the lawyer malpractice defendant to pay in effect the client's fees for suing the lawyer would be inconsistent with the usual requirement that parties pay their own legal fees. With which decision do you agree?

2. Some cases involving breach of a lawyer's duty to a client involve more than simple negligence. They involve breach of a traditional fiduciary duty such as the duty of loyalty. In the case of a breach of fiduciary duty, should a court excuse the client from paying all or part of the lawyer's fee even if the client can show no actual damages?

a.   Hendry v. Pelland, 73 F.3d 397 (D.C.Cir.1996), is one of the increasing number of claims for fee forfeiture, even in the absence of economic harm to the client. The law firm represented all five members of a family selling a parcel of land. All the clients had somewhat different interests about the terms of sale. The court found no intentional misconduct that would support punitive damages, or even any actual damage suffered by family members. Still, the court found that the lawyer was guilty of a conflict of interest by representing all five. Because a conflict of interest is a breach of fiduciary duty, the court required the law firm to disgorge all fees it earned in the case.

What do you think of this result? Can a clever plaintiff plead almost every mistake that a lawyer makes as a breach of fiduciary duty? Does the punishment exceed the crime if the court imposes fee forfeiture when the lawyer's action caused no harm to the client?

b.   Restatement Third, The Law Governing Lawyers § 37, Comment *b*, acknowledges fee forfeiture as a theory of relief but it makes clear:

> "Forfeiture of fees * * * is not justified in each instance in which a lawyer violates a legal duty, nor is total forfeiture always appropriate. Some violations are inadvertent or do not significantly harm the client. Some can be adequately dealt with by [other remedies] or by a partial forfeiture. Denying the lawyer all compensation would sometimes be an excessive sanction, giving a windfall to the client. The remedy of this Section should hence be applied with discretion."

c.   Burrow v. Arce, 997 S.W.2d 229 (Tex.1999), agreed with § 37 of the Restatement that the remedy of fee forfeiture does not require proof that a client suffered actual damage from the lawyer's conduct. However, the court went on, the trial judge should set the amount of any forfeiture, not the jury.

3. In the future, in order to reduce her malpractice liability, should Field add a provision to her standard engagement letter providing that the client waives any malpractice claims against Field?

a.   Look at Model Rule 1.8(h)(1). Under what conditions, if any, might Field offer such an option to her client? DR 6–102 of the ABA Model Code of Professional Responsibility did not allow such a provision under any circumstances. Do you agree with Rule 1.8(h)(1) that clients should be able to consent to such a provision if another lawyer independently represents them in doing so?

b.   Why would any client agree to such an arrangement? Suppose that Field, in exchange for the client's wavier of malpractice, charges less per hour than a specialist. A client has a right to buy a Kia instead of a Mercedes. Should the client have the right to buy lower quality legal services?

c.   What client would seek independent legal counsel about whether to sign such a clause? In the case of a corporate client, could such independent advice come from the company's in-house lawyer? Why would a corporate client be willing to sign such a clause?

d.   Do you have similar concerns when a lawyer settles a fee dispute with a client and asks the client for a general release of any malpractice claims the client might assert? Look at Rule 1.8(h)(2).

State Bar of California, Standing Comm. on Prof'l Responsibility and Conduct, Formal Op. 2009–178 (2009), said that conflict rules are implicated when a fee dispute involves a potential claim for legal malpractice and the proposed release and waiver is broad enough to release the claim. In such a case, an attorney must abide by California Rule 3–400(B) (ABA Model Rule 1.8(h)(2)). When settlement of the fee dispute involves the release of such a claim, the Committee said, the attorney should not continue to represent the client unless he or she provides a written disclosure regarding his or her financial or professional interests surrounding the claim. Further, the attorney should advise the client that he cannot represent the client in connection with the proposed settlement. In determining whether to withdraw from the underlying representation, the attorney should evaluate the circumstances motivating the inclusion of the release, the level of antagonism between the attorney and the client, and the degree to which a decision to withdraw would prejudice the client.

4.   Does a lawyer have a duty to tell a client about the lawyer's own malpractice in the client's case?

a.   Matter of Tallon, 447 N.Y.S.2d 50 (N.Y.App.Div.1982), held that a lawyer must inform the client, withdraw, and advise the client to get independent legal advice about whether or not to sue. Cf. ABA Model Rule 1.8(h)(2) and California Rules of Professional Conduct Rule 3–400, discussed above.

b.   In re Blackwelder, 615 N.E.2d 106 (Ind.1993), involved a lawyer whose clients sought to reopen a default judgment entered against them. The lawyer missed the filing deadline for doing so, and he proposed to handle their bankruptcy free in exchange for a release from malpractice liability. The court found that the lawyer did not advise the clients in writing to get independent counsel before signing the malpractice release, so it publicly reprimanded the lawyer.

c.   New York State Bar Association Committee on Professional Ethics, Opinion 734 (2000) discussed whether the ethical duty of lawyers to disclose their malpractice to their clients also applies to the lawyers in a legal aid society The opinion states that the society is obliged to keep clients reasonably informed about their cases and therefore has a duty to disclose any significant error or omission. The society can then continue representing the client only after getting that client's informed consent and a showing that "a disinterested lawyer would believe that the representation of the client would not be adversely affected thereby."

d.   Should a lawyer have any duty to tell a client about the possible malpractice of the client's former lawyer? Suppose the current lawyer learned in the course of representing a client that the previous lawyer missed a statute of limitations, forfeiting the client's right to sue. Should there be a tacit understanding among lawyers that we will not speak negatively about a fellow professional? May the previous lawyer properly charge the second lawyer with barratry, i.e., stirring up litigation, if the current lawyer mentions the earlier malpractice? Should we take exactly the opposite view?

5.   Should the law allow law firms to shield each of the lawyers from vicarious liability for the malpractice of other lawyers in the firm?

a.   Traditionally, lawyers practiced in general partnerships, and each partner was jointly and severally liable for the torts of the other partners. Now, depending on state statute, the usual vehicle for trying to do that is the limited liability company (LLC) or the limited liability partnership (LLP). Each is a form of law firm organization that limits personal liability to those lawyers who commit the malpractice and those who supervise those lawyers.

b.   ABA Formal Opinion 96–401 (Aug. 2, 1996) ruled that it does not violate the Model Rules for a lawyer to be part of a limited liability partnership. Model Rule 1.8(h)(1) on limiting liability for one's own malpractice does not address vicarious liability, and no other Model Rule requires a lawyer to be liable for his or her partner's malpractice. However, limited liability companies, like other law firms, must comply with Model Rules 5.1 and 5.3 on the duty to supervise and Rule 5.4 on participation of non-lawyers in the organization.

c.   In Gosselin v. Webb, 242 F.3d 412 (1st Cir.2001), a group of lawyers shared office space but were not legally partners. The district court granted them summary judgment, holding the lawyers were not vicariously liable for each other's conduct. The First Circuit disagreed and remanded for a trial. The lawyers practiced under a common trade name, and the negligent lawyer represented that he was "with" a firm. A jury could find those acts (holding out as a partnership) sufficient to make the lawyers vicariously liable for each other's acts.

d.   Do you agree that lawyers should be able to limit their own liability for the malpractice of their partners? Might such limitations reduce partners' efforts to improve the culture of high professional standards in a firm? Does the fact that most law firms carry high levels of malpractice insurance tend to make questions of personal liability of less concern than they would otherwise be?

D.   OTHER CONSEQUENCES OF NEGLIGENCE OR MISCONDUCT
     BY LAWYERS

1.   Professional malpractice is the most common civil claim against a lawyer, but is far from the only one. Disqualification of the lawyer from participation in a case is a common remedy that we will see primarily in Chapter 4. Restatement Third, The Law Governing Lawyers § 6 lists thirteen remedies available to a client or non-client to redress a lawyer's conduct.

2.   In criminal cases, criminal defendants have a constitutional right to effective assistance of counsel and this inquiry serves as a basis for regulating the conduct of criminal defense counsel. The leading case on "ineffective assistance of counsel" is Strickland v. Washington, 466 U.S. 668 (1984). The Court upheld a guilty plea and death sentence even though the defense lawyer did not request a presentence report. The lawyer's decision not to present evidence concerning the defendant's character and emotional state reflected his reasonable effort to prevent the State from cross-examining defendant and from presenting its own psychiatric evidence. Even in a death penalty case, the Court held, for the defendant to secure a writ of habeas corpus, a court must find that the lawyer's acts or omissions were not only "outside the wide range of professionally competent assistance" but also that the ineffectiveness caused "actual prejudice." "It is not enough for the defendant to show that the errors had some conceivable effect on the outcome of the proceedings." 466 U.S. at 693. "The defendant must show that there is a reasonable probability that, but for counsel's unprofessional errors, the result of the proceeding would have been different. A reasonable probability is a probability sufficient to undermine confidence in the outcome."

3.   A court also may void transactions made in violation of the lawyer's professional obligations. See, e.g., Abstract & Title Corp. of Florida v. Cochran, 414 So.2d 284 (Fla.App.1982) (lawyer's right of first refusal on client's property set aside); Spaulding v. Zimmerman, 116 N.W.2d 704 (Minn.1962) (tort settlement with minor set aside where lawyer for defendant did not disclose what he knew of the seriousness of plaintiff's injury).

4.   Another context involves the application of statutes to lawyers' conduct. In Heintz v. Jenkins, 514 U.S. 291 (1995), a unanimous Supreme Court held that plaintiffs may sue lawyers who collect consumer debts through litigation under the Fair Debt Collection Practices Act for engaging in abusive and unfair practices. Depending on the nature of their practice, lawyers can come within the statutory description of persons who "regularly collect or attempt to collect [consumer] debts," and there is no basis to exclude them from the Act's coverage.

The Telephone Consumer Protection Act (TCPA), 47 U.S.C.A. § 227, exposed a lawyer to statutory damages of over $4 million in Holtzman v. Turza, 728 F.3d 682 (7th Cir. 2013). Every other week, the lawyer faxed a one-page "Daily Plan-It" to over 200 CPAs. Each fax included some "business advice," but Turza also prominently displayed his contact information. The TCPA imposes a $500 statutory penalty for each faxed "unsolicited advertisement," which the court found included Tursa's "Plan-It" fax. Lawyers should see the case as a warning that inattention to the law governing their own conduct can be very expensive.

5.   The conduct of lawyers on behalf of clients may subject them to criminal responsibility. Lawyers have been found to be criminal accomplices of their clients more often than lawyers like to think. See, e.g., United States v. Morris, 988 F.2d 1335 (4th Cir.1993), where the government charged a lawyer with conspiracy to distribute drugs based

in part on real estate work he did in closing the purchase of a house where crack cocaine was manufactured.

United States v. Cueto, 151 F.3d 620 (7th Cir.1998), affirmed an obstruction of justice conviction against a lawyer who (1) falsely charged an FBI investigator with soliciting a bribe, (2) filed false motions that attacked the operations of the FBI and U.S. attorney, and (3) urged the defendants to file several motions, including one to disqualify the district judge. The National Association of Criminal Defense Lawyers filed a brief on behalf of the defendant who said he was just doing his job and only committed, if anything, a victimless crime, but the court disagreed. "We refuse to accept the notion that lawyers may do anything, including violating the law, to zealously advocate their clients' interests and then avoid criminal prosecution by claiming that they were 'just doing their job'."

In United States v. Sattar, 314 F.Supp.2d 279 (S.D.N.Y.2004), the government alleged that attorney Lynne Stewart facilitated communication between her client, convicted terrorist Sheikh Abdel Rahman, and Sattar, his surrogate in Egypt. Stewart argued that lawyers should be exempt from charges of alleged conspiracy to commit terrorism, at least as they relate to communications with their clients. The court rejected any such "roving commission to flout the criminal law with immunity," and upheld Stewart's conviction.

6.   The bottom line of the cases in this problem is that being a lawyer is a risky business. The issues you will see in the remainder of this book raise not only questions about potential disciplinary sanctions, but also questions of civil liability and even whether you will be able to stay out of jail. Ethical issues raise important questions of right and wrong, but the law governing lawyers also has teeth.

CHAPTER III

FUNDAMENTALS OF THE LAWYER–CLIENT RELATIONSHIP

A good lawyer-client relationship works on many levels. Ideally, a lawyer and client like each other and trust that each will communicate with candor and act with integrity. Ideally, the lawyer acts as a client's friend, telling the hard truth when necessary but consistently providing reliable support. Ultimately, however, law governs the relationship between lawyer and client. Many of the legal elements of the relationship seem *sui generis*, but they are made up of familiar elements—agency law, contracts, and requirements of the ABA Model Rules.

We can best understand the lawyer-client legal relationship as a mixture of status and contract. That is, some elements of the relationship are the subject of a contract between lawyer and client that is like any other service contract. Other obligations, however, are inherent in the status of a lawyer as a fiduciary and are not entirely subject to amendment by lawyer and client.

Throughout this chapter, ask which obligations justify an absolute requirement or prohibition and which the informed consent of the client controls. Think about questions such as the following:

a. How do the parties form the lawyer-client relationship? At what point do preliminary discussions produce enforceable obligations? What does it mean to call the lawyer's relationship with a client a "fiduciary" relationship?

b. What is a lawyer required/authorized to do on behalf of a client? May lawyer and client define and limit the scope and objectives of the representation? What are the lawyer's rights and obligations if they fail to do so?

c. What is the impact of the financial relation between lawyer and client on the lawyer's obligations? May a lawyer refuse to provide legal services until client pays the fee? Does the lawyer's obligation to protect confidential information of the client continue if there is a fee dispute?

d. What are the lawyer's obligations to protect client property in the lawyer's possession? Should failure to keep accurate financial records be grounds for the lawyer's disbarment?

e. What protection does the law give to communications between lawyer and client? What obligations does that protection impose on the lawyer?

———

PROBLEM 4

UNDERTAKING TO REPRESENT A CLIENT

If you join a law firm, you will find, at first, that work for existing clients appears as if by magic on your desk. Each of the firm's clients, however, was once a prospective client. Both the potential client and the firm had to decide whether to commit to the relationship. Obviously, a firm cannot turn down all prospective clients and remain in operation, but neither is the decision to take on a client automatic. Once representation begins, a lawyer assumes duties not easily shed and cases sometimes assume a life of their own. This problem puts you first in the role of dealing with a prospective client. Then, you will make the decision whether to undertake a representation and work through the matter of documenting that relationship. Finally, you will consider decision making within the lawyer-client relationship.

FACTS

You are a lawyer in a private firm. Not long ago, Morris Cannell, an elderly man whom you had never met before, came to you complaining about the handling of his investment account by a local broker. Cannell told you that the broker invested over $200,000 of Cannell's pension money in speculative stocks, and losses have reduced the account's value to less than $20,000. Cannell claimed that the broker not only took excessive risks with his money, he also bought and sold the stocks frequently, with the result that the broker made a lot in commissions while the client's retirement savings almost vanished.

As Cannell talked, he became more animated and more candid. "I knew what he was doing," he said, "and I suppose I could have stopped him at any time. But I guess I got greedy and wanted to turn my nest egg into millions just like I thought all my friends were doing." Cannell was very bitter and told you in no uncertain terms, "I want you to throw the book at my broker. He showed me no mercy and I don't want you to show any to him."

In researching the problem before deciding whether to take the case, you concluded that your best arguments would be that the broker engaged in illegal churning (excessive buying and selling), and that he violated federal rules relating to an investor's suitability (what stocks are suitable to meet a given investor's objectives, here safety and income). With respect to both arguments, you planned to allude to Cannell's age and relative lack of sophistication.

When you told Cannell the results of your analysis, however, he was angry and wanted you to do more. "He must have a license," Cannell said. "Do everything you can to get him suspended. See what you can do to tie up his bank accounts. If you won't do it, show me what to do and I'll do it myself."

The statute of limitations was about to run on all state and federal claims, and you told Cannell you would represent him only if he agreed to raise no more than the churning and suitability issues. You refused to seek suspension of the broker's license or to try to harass him financially, and you refused to give Cannell the behind-the-scenes help to take those steps himself. Cannell reluctantly agreed to your terms and signed your engagement letter. You entered an appearance as Cannell's attorney and filed suit on his behalf.

After extensive discovery, the broker's lawyer made what to you seemed a fair settlement offer. Knowing that your client was still angry, you did not want to have him throw away the opportunity to conclude the case and you accepted the offer on the spot.

QUESTIONS

A. THE LAWYER'S DUTIES TO A PROSPECTIVE CLIENT

1. Before you had agreed to represent Mr. Cannell, did you have any obligations to him?

a. Lawyers often like to think that until they agree to represent a client, they owe no duties to the person across their desk. However, that is not true. Until the adoption of Model Rule 1.18, no professional rule described the relationship in detail, but as Restatement Third, The Law Governing Lawyers § 15 reports, the law has long been clear on at least three points:

(1) Communications from a prospective client are legally privileged and the lawyer's duty of confidentiality applies as if an actual client made the communications;

(2) If the lawyer takes possession of documents or other property of a prospective client, the lawyer must protect those items as if they were documents or property of a client; and

(3) If the lawyer gives advice to a prospective client, for example, by saying, "you have no claim and it is not worth your while to retain a lawyer," the lawyer may be liable to the prospective client for malpractice if that advice is wrong, because the lawyer owes a duty of reasonable care to the prospective client.

b. ABA Model Rule 1.18 confirms these principles; see especially, Comments 3 & 9. The term used to describe Mr. Cannell, both in Restatement § 15 and Model Rule 1.18, is "prospective client." As you see, such persons are legally far from strangers.

2. Suppose that shortly after Mr. Cannell left your office, you learned that someone else in your firm had already agreed to represent Mr. Cannell's broker in the matter. May you or your firm continue to represent the broker?

a. As you will learn from Model Rule 1.7 ("Conflict of Interest: Current Clients"), you clearly would have to decline to represent Mr. Cannell, because a law firm may not represent both sides in the same litigated case. As you will also learn in later problems, the fact that a lawyer has learned confidential information from an *actual* client typically means that neither that lawyer—nor anyone else in that lawyer's firm—may oppose that client in the same or a substantially related matter. See Model Rules 1.9 and 1.10.

b.   Because the prospective client, Mr. Cannell, gave you confidential information, under Model Rule 1.18(b), (c) & (d), you personally cannot be involved in the broker's defense. Do you suppose that on the facts in this problem, Mr. Cannell would be likely to consent to your involvement?

c.   Under what conditions may other lawyers in your firm represent the broker in the defense of Mr. Cannell's claim? What does it mean to avoid "exposure to more disqualifying information than was reasonably necessary to determine whether to represent the prospective client?" Model Rule 1.18, Comments 4 & 5, may be helpful in suggesting ways to conduct an initial interview to minimize the likelihood of later disqualification. See also, ABA Formal Opinion 90–358 (Sept. 13, 1990). As you study the prospective client rule, you quickly learn why law firms create intake systems for evaluating representation of new clients.

d.   Model Rule 1.18(d)(2)(i) would also require that you be "timely screened" from participation in the broker's defense. You will see screening possibilities in later problems as well. You will find "screened" defined in Model Rule 1.0(k) and Comments 8–10. See also, Model Rule 1.18, Comment 7.

Why are you required to notify Mr. Cannell about the fact you have been screened? Is he likely to be pleased to hear from you? What does "timely" notice require? Look at Model Rule 1.18, Comment 8. Must you give this notice before Mr. Cannell would normally learn which firm is going to represent the broker?

e.   Suppose you learn that Mr. Cannell met with four different business litigation attorneys about his claim in addition to your meeting. You discover that Cannell had read on the internet that it is good for plaintiffs to meet with the best lawyers in town in order to make sure they do not show up on the other side for the broker. Do you owe prospective client duties to a person who met with you for the purpose of seeking to disqualify you from representing his adversary? See Comment 2 to Model Rule 1.18. How easy would it be to prove Mr. Cannell's motive?

3.   Imagine that, instead of meeting Mr. Cannell in your office, you had talked to him while doing pro bono work at a local legal services agency. Suppose that Mr. Cannell did not want to hire you; he simply wanted some basic advice and asked you how to file a claim against the broker himself. Under those circumstances, would Mr. Cannell be a prospective client or an actual client?

a.   May you provide advice to Mr. Cannell in that context without your usual conflicts review? Look at Model Rule 6.5 and Comment 1.

b.   Suppose that when you get back to your office, you find that—although you did not know it earlier—your firm already represents the broker. Has your discussion with Mr. Cannell in the legal services context disqualified your firm from continuing that representation? Look at Model Rule 6.5, Comments 3 & 4.

c.   Does Model Rule 6.5 even prevent you from representing the broker yourself? At what time is the lawyer's "knowledge" of a conflict disqualifying under Model Rule 6.5(a)(1)? Whatever your answer is to that question, does Model Rule 6.5 require that the law firm screen you from future involvement in the matter?

d.   Does Model Rule 6.5 adequately protect legal services clients? The purpose of this Rule is to help assure that private lawyers will be available to staff "hot line" services. Should we be concerned that if we insist on giving middle class and poor clients "first class" service, we may deny them needed legal help altogether? Should we be more concerned that if we insist on giving such clients "second class" service, we may discourage them from seeking legal help at all?

4.   Now, imagine that your discussion with Mr. Cannell occurred online or in a chat room for people interested in investing. How does that affect your obligations to Mr. Cannell?

a.   D.C. Bar Association Opinion 316 (2002) deals with chat rooms where lawyers give real-time, online advice and invite inquirers to contact the lawyers for further help.[1] After reviewing the possible ineffectiveness of the lawyer disclaiming that these inquiries create no lawyer-client relationship, the opinion recognizes a tension between the desirability of educating the public about their legal rights and the danger of the inquirer relying on a lawyer-client relationship that the lawyer wants to avoid. The opinion advises lawyers to make clear from the outset that they are providing only legal "information," not legal advice. It also suggests running a conflicts check before agreeing to consider client-specific information. However, the opinion does not condemn chat rooms and notes that they may become useful ways to deliver legal services to poor and middle class persons who today often go unserved.

b.   Suppose your firm has a website with information about areas of practice, lawyers' credentials, and representative clients and cases. Each lawyer's page has an email address and telephone number. Mr. Cannell's sends an email to you with an attachment containing information about his case. Do you have an obligation to open the email? Do you have a duty to respond to the email? Is Mr. Cannell a prospective client? By having information about the firm and lawyers on your website, are you necessarily inviting prospective clients to inquire about possible representation?

c.   The ABA amended Model Rule 1.18, Comment 2, in 2012 to address the issue of client contact with a lawyer's website. It says that someone is likely to become a prospective client if a lawyer's web site "specifically requests or invites" people to submit information about a potential representation "without clear and reasonably understandable warnings and cautionary statements that limit the lawyer's obligations." However, a person who submits information to the lawyer in response to advertising "that merely describes the lawyer's education, experience, areas of practice, and contact information" would

---

[1]   We will explore the "solicitation" implications of doing so in Problem 31.

not necessarily become a prospective client to whom the lawyer owes duties. See also, ABA Formal Opinion 10–457 (Aug. 2010).

B. THE DECISION TO REPRESENT A CLIENT

1. What is the significance of accepting someone as your client? What obligations do you assume when you make that decision?

You will spend much of the rest of this course answering those questions. The short answer is that you become your client's agent and assume fiduciary duties to that client. Fiduciary duties require the lawyer to put each client's interest ahead of the lawyer's interest and the interests of third parties. Without being exhaustive here, watch for the following kinds of fiduciary duties:

a. The duties of care, competence and diligence, which we saw in Problems 2 & 3. Some cases call all three the duty of zealous representation.

b. The duty of communication. In this Problem, we see it as the duty to let the client determine the objectives of the representation and the duty to keep the client informed as events change the client's original understanding of the possible outcomes and available choices.

c. The duty of confidentiality that we will see in Problems 7 & 8. This duty is fundamental. It may help you to think of the client's information as client property that you will see the lawyer has an affirmative duty to protect.

d. The duty of loyalty that we will see in Chapter 4 under the label "conflict of interest." For example, if the lawyer must put each client's interest first in each client's matter, it will obviously be important not to assume an obligation to one client that will make it impossible to pursue a similar obligation on behalf of another client.

2. Given the significance of the decision to undertake a representation, did you have a professional obligation to accept Cannell as your client?

a. ABA Model Code of Professional Responsibility, EC 2–26, stated the traditional view that:

"A lawyer is under no obligation to act as advisor or advocate for every person who may wish to become his client; but in furtherance of the objective of the bar to make legal services fully available, a lawyer should not lightly decline proffered employment. The fulfillment of this objective requires acceptance by a lawyer of his share of tendered employment which may be unattractive both to him and the bar generally."

b. The Model Rules contain no comparable statement; the nearest analogue is Model Rule 6.2, Comment 1, dealing with the duty to accept court appointments to represent indigent clients. The fact the Rules need to state the duty there suggests that there is no general duty to agree to represent a client.

c.   Was Cannell someone whose representation would be "unattractive to . . . the bar generally"? If we can expect some lawyer to take Cannell's case, must you be the one who does so?

3.   Is it fair to say that a lawyer makes an implicit moral decision every time the lawyer undertakes to use his or her talent and training in support of a cause?

a.   Given the fact that every client's right to have a lawyer does not necessarily translate into a personal obligation on every lawyer to undertake every proffered representation, Professor Monroe Freedman says:

> "[A] lawyer's decision to represent a client may commit that lawyer to zealously furthering the interests of one whom the lawyer or others in the community believe to be morally repugnant. For that reason, the question of whether to represent a particular client can present the lawyer with an important moral decision—a decision for which the lawyer can properly be held morally accountable, in the sense of being under a burden of public justification.
>
> "That would not be so if each lawyer were ethically bound to represent every client seeking the lawyer's services. If there were no choice, there would be no responsibility. Under both rule and practice, however, lawyers have always been free to choose whether to represent particular clients. * * * [Indeed,] the Comment to Rule 6.2 of the ABA Model Rules of Professional Conduct says * * * that a lawyer ordinarily is 'not obliged to accept a client whose character or cause the lawyer regards as repugnant.' "[2]

b.   Do you agree with Professor Freedman's conclusion? Does that make Model Rule 1.2(b) somewhat disingenuous when it says that in accepting a representation, a lawyer does not "endorse" the "client's political, economic, social or moral views or activities"?

4.   Even assuming that there is no obligation to accept every client, are there legal limits that restrain a lawyer's right to reject a particular case?

a.   Until recently, the lawyer's right to decline a case for any reason—or no reason—was virtually absolute, except perhaps when a court appointed the lawyer.

In Stropnicky v. Nathanson, 19 M.D.L.R. 39 (M.C.A.D.1997), however, the Massachusetts Commission Against Discrimination found that a law firm that specialized in representing women in divorce cases violated the state's antidiscrimination law by refusing to represent a man in such a case. The firm had a reputation for securing large awards for women who had put their husbands through professional school, and the prospective male client had done that for his wife.

Was *Stropnicky* correctly decided? Do lawyers have a right to devote their time and talent to representing only women, not men? Is that different from a lawyer deciding to represent only corporations? Suppose the law firm wanted to represent only abused women with

---

[2]   Monroe Freedman, Must You Be the Devil's Advocate?, Legal Times, Aug. 23, 1993, p. 19.

children? Would your answer be different if the lawyers wanted to represent only *white* women? Only men? What is the basis for any distinctions you would draw?

b. Wishnatsky v. Rovner, 433 F.3d 608 (8th Cir.2006), is another example of a limit on a lawyer's freedom to reject a case. The clinic at the University of North Dakota School of Law rejected a prospective client, Martin Wishnatsky, who had earlier objected to the fact that the clinic had filed a suit challenging public display of the Ten Commandments. Now, Wishnatsky wanted the clinic to file a suit on his behalf challenging the county's display of a statue of the goddess Themis on top of the county courthouse. The clinic declined his request for representation, and Wishnatsky filed this action *pro se* asserting that the clinic's refusal to represent him violated the First Amendment.

The district court dismissed the complaint, but the Eighth Circuit reversed. The First Amendment requires that a public law school clinic not deny representation to someone "simply because he has engaged in protected speech that the director of the program finds disagreeable," the Eighth Circuit said. "[W]hich cases and clients to accept in an academic environment should be entitled to substantial deference," but the reasons the clinic rejected this case raised questions of fact that the judge should not resolve on a motion to dismiss. The clinic had implicitly argued that "it may exclude persons from the program solely on the basis of their viewpoint," but the Eighth Circuit said no.

Do you agree? Was this a unique case? Must every law school clinic justify to a federal court its decision about whom the clinic represents?

5. Should you give weight to your client's anger at the broker in deciding whether to take the case?

a. Suppose you believe that your client's claim has modest merit, but that the main reason the client wants to sue is to make the broker's life miserable. Is your time and effort something you are willing to sell simply to help a client settle a grudge? Remember that Cannell admitted to you privately, "I knew what he was doing and I could have stopped him at any time, but I guess I got greedy."

b. Cannell has already shown himself willing to sue one professional—the broker. Are you worried that he would choose to sue you next if he becomes unhappy with the result in the case against the broker? Is that appropriate to consider when you decide whether to represent Cannell?

C. DOCUMENTING THE DECISION TO UNDERTAKE A REPRESENTATION

1. When did Mr. Cannell become your client?

a. The magic moment when someone becomes your client is an important issue in many cases seeking to define your obligations. Restatement Third, The Law Governing Lawyers § 14 says:

> "A relationship of client and lawyer arises when:
>
> "(1) a person manifests to a lawyer the person's intent that the lawyer provide legal services for the person; and either
>
> > "(a) the lawyer manifests to the person consent to do so; or

"(b) the lawyer fails to manifest lack of consent to do so, and the lawyer knows or reasonably should know that the person reasonably relies on the lawyer to provide the services * * *."

b.   ABA Formal Opinion 07–448 (Oct. 20, 2007) considered the obligations a court-appointed lawyer owes to a "client" who rejects the lawyer's representation. Once informally called the "Guantanamo question," the opinion notes that some states require that defendants have lawyers in some criminal cases when the defendant insists on representing himself. The lawyer may be required by the court to attend the proceedings and to be available as a stand-by, but a "lawyer whose would-be client has never accepted the client-lawyer relationship * * * has no such relationship." Thus, the lawyer has no obligation to protect confidential information or to avoid conflicts of interests with the purported client, the opinion asserts. "The lawyer's ethical duties are limited to complying with the Rules defining a lawyer's obligations to persons other than a client."

Do you agree that an appointed but unwanted lawyer's obligations should be this limited? What good is such a lawyer if she has a conflict of interest that would otherwise bar her participation in the matter?

2.   Who should bear the risk of ambiguity about whether the lawyer-client relationship exists?

a.   In Togstad v. Vesely, Otto, Miller & Keefe, 291 N.W.2d 686 (Minn.1980), Mrs. Togstad consulted an attorney about a possible medical malpractice claim. The attorney said he did not believe she had a case but that he would "discuss this with his partner." The attorney did not send a bill and Mrs. Togstad waited a full year before talking to another attorney. By then, the statute of limitations had run. The court held the first law firm liable to the Togstads for $649,500, the amount the jury found she would have won if the lawyers had timely filed the medical malpractice case. The informal advice the lawyer had given Mrs. Togstad about her lack of a case was both inaccurate and inadequate. At a minimum, the lawyer should have told Mrs. Togstad about the statute of limitations.

b.   In DeVaux v. American Home Assurance Co., 444 N.E.2d 355 (Mass.1983), a prospective client called the attorney's firm asking for legal help in connection with an accident at a store. The lawyer's secretary advised her to write a letter to the store and arranged a medical examination by the store's insurance company. Finally, the secretary asked the potential client to write to the attorney requesting legal assistance. The client did so but the secretary misfiled it when it arrived so the lawyer never saw it until after the statute of limitations had expired. The law firm asked for summary judgment but the court denied it, concluding that a jury could reasonably find that an attorney-client relationship existed. Does that help clarify that the test is whether a reasonable client would believe the relationship exists?

3.   What matters will you want to address in any engagement letter with your client?

a.   Because lawyers assume significant duties to their clients, in order to avoid ambiguity about the fact and nature of the relationship, at the outset of any representation, a lawyer should prepare an "engagement letter," transmit it to the client, and ask the client to countersigns it. At least the following items should typically appear in a good engagement letter.[3]

(1) Who the client is (and sometimes who the client is *not*). This is particularly important in the case of a corporation with multiple subsidiaries, but it can also be important where, for example, the law firm agrees to represent a husband in drafting a will but not also to represent the wife.

(2) The scope of the representation, i.e., what the lawyer is undertaking to do and not to do. See Model Rules 1.2(c) and 1.5(b). This problem illustrates the negotiation of these matters with a prospective client. The lawyer wants to avoid malpractice liability for matters the firm never thought it was supposed to undertake and it wants to establish the work covered by the fee.

(3) The fee for the representation, or the basis of the fee, and an outline of expenses for which the client will be responsible. See Model Rule 1.5(b) & (c). It is also helpful for the law firm to specify when it will send bills, how promptly the client must pay them, and whether the law firm will charge the client interest for late payments.

(4) Conflicts of interest the lawyer may have and sufficient information to let the client give informed consent if it is willing to waive the conflicts. See Model Rule 1.7 and 1.9.

(5) Any departures from the usual assumptions about handling confidential information, such as an agreement not to share information between spouses who come in for joint estate planning. See Model Rule 1.6.

(6) Specific obligations that the client will assume to the lawyer regarding the representation, such as a duty to cooperate with the lawyer and to be candid with the lawyer about the relevant facts.[4]

b.   If a lawyer decides not to represent a client, a wise lawyer will send a letter documenting that fact so as to avoid a later claim that the prospective client reasonably believed the lawyer had undertaken the representation.

4.   Why might you want to limit the scope of your representation of a client?

a.   Few issues are more basic to defining the lawyer-client relationship than the specific tasks that the client expects the lawyer to perform. Does the client with $50,000 in assets want the lawyer to do the same kind of estate planning the lawyer would do for a client worth $100 million? If the client is leaving for a trip later in the afternoon, does the client expect more than lawyer offering a standard form will today that will addresses no more than the client's basic testamentary wishes? Does a litigation client want the lawyer to research causes of action under the law of 50 states, or is the client's current objective much more modest, just filing one cause of action? In every representation, questions such as these help define the scope of the

---

[3]   We will take up the substantive content of various of these items in later problems.

[4]   More suggestions for engagement letters, file control, and the like, may be found in Ronald E. Mallen, Jeffrey M. Smith & Allison Rhodes, Legal Malpractice, Ch. 2 (2014 ed.).

lawyer's work. What do Model Rule 1.2(c), and Comments 6 to 8 say about when limitations on the scope of representation are appropriate?

b.   Amendments To Rules Regulating the Florida Bar * * * (Unbundled Legal Services), 860 So.2d 394 (Fla.2003), represents a developing approach to practice where a lawyer does not undertake complete representation of a client, but rather contracts to provide specific "unbundled" services. Pursuant to this approach, for example, the lawyer could draft pleadings for a limited-service client, but not accompany that client to court. The Florida Supreme Court believes that such limited services may make the legal system more accessible to persons who now represent themselves.[5]

c.   The lawyer may not treat limitations on the scope of representation as self-evident. A client may later file a malpractice charge against a lawyer who fails to secure consent to such a limitation. In Nichols v. Keller, 19 Cal.Rptr.2d 601 (Cal.Ct.App.1993), the client was a construction worker who had been hit in the head by a piece of steel while on the job. He signed a retainer asking the lawyer to file a worker's compensation claim on his behalf. Later, Nichols learned he could have filed a third-party claim as well, and he sued the lawyer for not telling him. The court held that when a lawyer takes on a case, the client might not know the range of remedies that is possible. It is not enough to present a retainer agreement for the worker's compensation case without discussing with the client what other remedies may be possible and either bringing those actions as well or advising the client that he may get other counsel to do so.[6]

d.   Is it wise to reach an agreement to limit the issues you will assert at the outset of the representation? Typically, the client may avoid an agreement between lawyer and client made after representation has begun unless the lawyer proves that both the substance of the agreement and the manner of reaching it are fair and reasonable to the client. Restatement Third, The Law Governing Lawyers § 18(1)(a); Terzis v. Estate of Whalen, 489 A.2d 608 (N.H.1985) (attempt to revise fee agreement).

D.   DECISION MAKING DURING REPRESENTATION—ISSUES THE LAWYER IS TO DECIDE AND ISSUES RESERVED TO THE CLIENT

1.   Should you have to get permission from your client to say what you plan to say in the pleading about his lack of financial sophistication?

a.   Look at Model Rules 1.4 and 1.6. Is your client reasonably entitled to be interested in what you say about him in a public document?

b.   Assume that you explain the pleading to Cannell and he says, "I'm paying you to represent me; I don't want you to say that." Your firm has a reputation as a tough litigator, and you are reluctant to abandon your best argument. May you, notwithstanding client

---

[5]   See, e.g., Rachel Brill & Rochelle Sparko, Limited Legal Services and Conflicts of Interest: Unbundling in the Public Interest, 16 Georgetown J. Legal Ethics 553 (2003).

[6]   See AmBase Corp. v. Davis Polk & Wardwell, 866 N.E.2d 1033 (N.Y.2007) (firm that undertook only to resolve tax issues with the IRS not guilty of malpractice for failing also to recommend allocating tax burden to another corporation).

objection, make the argument? Are Model Rule 1.2(a), and its Comments 1 & 2, helpful on this issue?

2. May the client require you to make an argument that, although not frivolous, is likely to be a loser that will weaken the case?

a.   Suppose Mr. Cannell has a theory that the broker's firm had registered its name incorrectly. You explain the weakness of that argument, but the client insists that you use it anyway and you have to admit that doing so would not violate Model Rule 3.1. If you may make the argument, must you do so?[7]

b.   Is making such an argument a matter of "objectives" or "means" under Model Rule 1.2? Does Rule 1.2, Comment 2, provide much help about how such disagreements are to be resolved?

c.   Notice that Rule 1.2 expects that the "communication" required by Rule 1.4 will ordinarily be sufficient for the lawyer and client to reach agreement about most important issues. Look at Rule 1.4(a)(2) and Comment 3. What is the lawyer supposed to do if the disagreement about use of the argument cannot be resolved?

3. Is the lawyer the one who makes the decision whether to accept what he or she thinks is a good settlement of a civil case?

a.   Look at Model Rule 1.2(a). Who has the authority to decide whether or not to settle a civil case? If the client has not authorized the lawyer to accept the settlement, can the lawyer bind the client? Put another way, may the opposing party assume that the lawyer making the settlement has the actual and apparent authority to do so?

b.   The law's answer may surprise you. Restatement § 27, Comment *d*, says:

> "Generally, a client is not bound by a settlement that the client has not authorized a lawyer to make by express, implied, or apparent authority (and that is not validated by later ratification under § 26(3)). * * * When a lawyer purports to enter a settlement binding on the client but lacks authority to do so, the burden of inconvenience resulting if the client repudiates the settlement is properly with the opposing party, who should know that settlements are normally subject to approval by the client and who has no manifested contrary indication from the client. The opposing party can protect itself by obtaining clarification of the lawyer's authority."

See also, Restatement Third, The Law Governing Lawyers § 22 (authority reserved to client); § 26 (lawyer's actual authority); § 30(3) (lawyer's liability to third person for [unauthorized] conduct on behalf of client).

---

[7]   We will see this issue in Problem 29 when we consider possible limits on the proper zeal of a prosecutor. Cf. Bill Johnson's Restaurants, Inc. v. NLRB, 461 U.S. 731, 742–43 (1983) (In light of "the First Amendment right of access to the courts," the "filing and prosecution of a well-founded lawsuit may not be enjoined as an unfair labor practice, even if it would not have been commenced but for plaintiff's desire to retaliate against the defendant for exercising rights protected by the [National Labor Relations] Act.").

c.   In Luethke v. Suhr, 650 N.W.2d 220 (Neb.2002), the parties' lawyers thought they had reached a settlement agreement, but when the defendants tried to enforce it, the plaintiff said he had not authorized his lawyer to settle. The plaintiff was developmentally disabled, and his lawyer was not able to reach him before agreeing to the settlement. The defense lawyer knew of those circumstances but the plaintiff's lawyer assured him that there would be no problem getting the plaintiff's agreement. The court affirmed a finding that the plaintiff's lawyer could not bind her client. "The ordinary employment or retainer of a lawyer * * * does not of itself give the lawyer the implied or apparent authority to bind the client by a settlement or compromise of the claim; and, in the absence of express authority, knowledge, or consent, the lawyer cannot do so."[8]

d.   In Makins v. District of Columbia, 861 A.2d 590 (D.C. 2004) (en banc), Makins hired attorney Harrison to represent her in a Title VII sex discrimination and retaliatory firing case she brought against her employer, the D.C. Department of Corrections (District). At a pre-trial conference, the judge referred the case to a magistrate for settlement purposes. The judge ordered the District to send someone "with full settlement authority" to each settlement meeting, but failed to say the same thing to Makins and Harrison. At the settlement conference, Harrison negotiated a deal with the District, then left the room, ostensibly to call Makins. He returned, shook hands with opposing counsel, and reduced the deal to writing. However, when Harrison gave Makins a copy to sign, she refused. The District filed a motion to enforce the settlement, and, represented by new counsel, Makins testified that she did not give Harrison the authority to settle the case on the terms Harrison had accepted. The trial court found for the District on an alternative ground that Harrison was acting under apparent authority to bind Makins in settlement negotiations. Makins appealed.

The D.C. Court of Appeals said first that apparent authority exists only when the principal places her agent "in a position which causes a third person to reasonably believe the principal has consented to the exercise of authority the agent purports to hold." Under agency law, the principal's conduct—not that of the attorney—determines whether the third party reasonably believed the principal consented to the agent's authority. Relying on both D.C. Rule of Professional Conduct 1.2(a) and Restatement Third, The Law Governing Lawyers §§ 22 & 27, the court acknowledged the well-accepted principle that "the decision to settle belongs to the client," not the attorney. The District's evidence was replete with instances where Harrison manifested his authority to bind Makins, but it did not contain a single instance where Makins' conduct should have led the District's attorneys to believe she had given Harrison authority to finalize a settlement agreement on her behalf. Settlement talks were properly in Harrison's domain, but the court held that absent representations made by Makins, the District was

---

[8]   A lawyer who affirmatively misrepresents his or her settlement authority to a non-client is subject to liability for damages proximately caused by that misrepresentation. Restatement Third, The Law Governing Lawyers § 30. Many of these issues are also discussed in a useful report of the ABA Section of Litigation, Ethical Guidelines for Settlement Negotiations (2002).

unreasonable in believing that Harrison had the authority to execute the settlement.

4.   Is Model Rule 1.2(a) wise to give the client the exclusive authority to decide what plea to enter in a criminal case?

a.   People v. Bloom, 774 P.2d 698 (Cal.1989), gives many people pause about giving a criminal defendant authority to make key decisions about the representation. By the time of the penalty phase of his murder trial, Bloom demanded to address the jury directly and ask that they sentence him to death. Both the trial judge and the defense counsel tried to talk Bloom out of his decision, but he insisted and the jury gave him his wish. Ultimately, so did the Supreme Court of California, which said:

> "Given the importance which the decisions of both this court and the United States Supreme Court have attached to an accused's ability to control his or her own destiny and to make fundamental decisions affecting trial of the action, and given this court's recognition that it is not irrational to prefer the death penalty to life imprisonment without parole, it would be incongruous to hold that a trial court lacked power to grant a mid-trial motion for self-representation in a capital case merely because the accused stated an intention to seek a death verdict. While we do not suggest that trial courts must or even should grant such mid-trial motions, we do not find the trial court's ruling on the motion in this case to be violative of defendant's rights or contrary to any fundamental public policy."

Do you agree? Does this decision take deference to client wishes beyond all reasonable limits? Is it allowing the client to choose death with what to him may seem relative dignity?

b.   In People v. Colville, 979 N.E.2d 1125 (N.Y. 2012), the state charged defendant with murder, which has several lesser-included offenses. At the close of the evidence, defense counsel asserted, and the trial judge agreed, that the court should offer the jury the full range of verdicts from which to choose. However, the defendant objected and the trial judge acceded to his views. The jury found him guilty of murder but the New York Court of Appeals reversed. The court, citing Commentary to the 1993 ABA Standards for Criminal Justice, Defense Function, said, "whether or not to ask the trial judge to instruct the jury on lesser-included offenses is a matter of strategy and tactics ceded by the defendant to his lawyer." The choice is "a complicated one involving legal expertise and trial strategy." See also, Commonwealth v. Lavoie, 981 N.E.2d 192 (Mass. 2013) (decision to exclude defendant's family from the courtroom during jury selection is for the lawyer alone).

Do you agree? What happened to the idea that the client is the principal and the lawyer only the client's agent?

5.   What values are at stake in the question of who controls the litigation?

a.   Do you agree with the commentator who argued: "Unless the client chooses to delegate decision-making authority to the lawyer, the client should be presumed to have control over all aspects of his case. [Client control increases] the moral force and acceptability of the decisions made by the system, in that each party has had the opportunity 'to choose his strategy, plot his fate, and rise or fall by his own choices.' * * * When the lawyer, as a representative, acts without authority, he violates the client's integrity by presenting the client falsely to others."[9] If the client must make all the key decisions, what is the professional role of the lawyer?

b.   Does it follow that the client should be able to control decisions about trial strategy? What about decisions to show common courtesy? Suppose that, after you file the complaint, defense counsel asks you for a short delay to allow him extra time to file an answer. May the client forbid you to grant any delays on the ground that he is anxious to speed resolution of the case? Look at the last sentence of Rule 1.3, Comment 3: "A lawyer's duty to act with reasonable promptness * * * does not preclude the lawyer from agreeing to a reasonable request for a postponement that will not prejudice the client." Who gets to decide what will "prejudice" the client? Suppose the client is so angry with the broker that he does not want to give any quarter?

c.   Restatement Third, The Law Governing Lawyers § 23 identifies only two matters that are beyond the reach of client direction. The lawyer may alone decide "to refuse to * * * [act in a way] that the lawyer reasonably believes to be unlawful," and "to take actions * * * that the lawyer reasonably believes to be required by law or an order of a tribunal." Do you agree that lawyers require no more inherent discretion than that?

d.   Suppose Mr. Cannell had been investing the $200,000 as trustee for his grandchildren. Would that change your obligation to follow the client's directions? Suppose a trustee asked you to settle a case on terms that would enrich trustee, but not benefit the trust?

The point is that a client's authority to direct a lawyer depends in part on restrictions the law imposes on the client's conduct. If in your own practice, you knowingly accept a direction the client does not have legal authority to give, you may be liable to the party to whom the client owed duties. As you will see later in Problem 22, many lawyers paid substantial sums in damages to the receivers of their failed financial institution clients for accepting direction from officers of those clients to do things that the law did not authorize the officers to direct.

———————

PROBLEM 5

BILLING FOR LEGAL SERVICES

Noble as it might seem to pretend otherwise, the ability to earn a substantial fee is a major part of many lawyers' decisions to take some cases and reject others. How lawyers bill their clients, however, has varied over the years. For a long time, lawyers charged fixed fees for routine work. Indeed, not that many years ago, local bar associations

---

[9]   Mark Spiegel, Lawyering and Client Decision–Making: Informed Consent and the Legal Profession, 128 U. Pennsylvania L. Rev. 41, 73–76 (1979).

published schedules of minimum fees for particular services and lawyers in that area adhered to them.

Goldfarb v. Virginia State Bar, 421 U.S. 773 (1975), changed all that. The Supreme Court of the United States intervened in the world of the previously state-regulated legal profession and held that such "minimum fee schedules" violate federal antitrust laws. Since *Goldfarb,* other bases for setting fees have assumed more importance. Fees based on hourly rates, for example, have dominated life in most firms in recent years, while contingent fees continue to predominate in personal injury cases. This problem first asks when the lawyer and client must reach a fee agreement and what limit the law imposes on the size of a lawyer's fee. It then considers specialized rules applicable to contingent fees, and issues surrounding hourly rate fees as well.

FACTS

A well-known local psychiatrist has a contract claim for about $100,000 against a local company. The matter appears to be of average complexity. She has brought her case to attorney Paul T. Novak. "I'll take your case," Novak says. "My fee will be only 44% of the amount recovered." Shocked, the psychiatrist says that she has never heard of even psychiatrists charging such high fees. "One-third is average," Novak tells her. "I am giving you a bargain. I am only charging you one-third more than the going rate and I am at least twice as good as the average lawyer."

Novak also has agreed to represent a plaintiff in a personal injury suit for a "discount" contingent fee of one-third of the amount recovered. The other side has offered, before Novak begins work, to pay his client $15,000. Based on what he knows about the case, Novak believes the actual damages that a jury would award would be more like $60,000, but it would take him about 200 hours of work to recover that amount, and, of course, the client might not recover anything at all. Novak has concluded that it is best to recommend to the client that he accept the $15,000 immediately so that Novak can pocket a $5,000 fee with little effort and go on to the next case.

When a prospective client asked Novak about his willingness to charge a fee on an hourly-rate basis, Novak simply laughed and said he would never agree to charge fees on any basis other than one that let him share in any good result. Novak added that other lawyers charge hourly fees and the prospective client could always go there.

QUESTIONS

A. THE FEE AGREEMENT BETWEEN LAWYER AND CLIENT

1. Must a lawyer's fee agreement be in writing?

a. Notice that Model Rule 1.5(c) requires a written agreement in the case of a contingent fee but Model Rule 1.5(b) declares only that a written agreement is "preferable." Does that distinction make sense to you?

Starkey, Kelly, Blaney & White v. Estate of Nicolaysen, 796 A.2d 238 (N.J.2002), dealt with the Rule 1.5(c) requirement that a contingent fee agreement be in writing. The law firm represented an elderly couple who were attempting to sell their farm. The firm represented the couple over several years, and the parties initially entered into an oral contingent fee agreement that entitled the attorney to 30% of any purchase price obtained in excess of the price in an earlier contract. However, the firm did not reduce the agreement to writing for two-and-a-half years, and when it did, the agreement reduced the law firm's percentage to 20%. The couple died, and when the attorneys sought payment from the couple's estate, the beneficiaries refused to recognize the fee agreement. They argued it was invalid because the attorneys waited too long to formalize it. The Supreme Court of New Jersey agreed, and refused to uphold the contract. The court found, however, that the attorneys satisfied the requirements for *quantum meruit* recovery by showing that (1) the lawyer performed legal services in good faith, (2) the clients accepted the services, (3) the clients expected to pay for the services, (4) and the court could ascertain the value of the services.[10]

b.   We talked in Problem 4 about the desirability of using an engagement letter to define a lawyer-client relationship, including the fee to be paid, but should the law require that all fee agreements be in writing? D.C. Rule of Professional Conduct 1.5(b), for example, requires a writing in all cases where the lawyer has not regularly represented the client before.

c.   Should the requirement turn on how large the bill is likely to be? California Business & Professions Code § 6148 requires a writing when it is "reasonably foreseeable" that fees and expenses in a matter will exceed $1000.

d.   Quite apart from any formal requirement, would you be wise to rely on an oral agreement to be paid an hourly fee? Would you want to put the agreement in writing for your own protection and possible use in later efforts to collect the fee?

2.   The 2002 revision of Model Rule 1.5(b) added a requirement that the lawyer communicate to the client, "preferably in writing," the expenses for which the client will be responsible. Why is it important to spell out responsibility for those expenses?

a.   Would it shock you to know that some lawyers view their copy machine as a profit center in their practice, charging 50 cents or more per page copied? One lawyer once called the firm's photocopy machine a "silent partner." Should a firm be able to charge the client $2 per page faxed, even for local calls? Can you think of other ways in which a client

---

[10]   See also, Mullens v. Hansel–Henderson, 65 P.3d 992 (Colo.2002) ("When an attorney completes the legal services for which he was retained, the fact that the underlying fee agreement was unenforceable does not itself preclude the attorney from being paid the reasonable value of his services. When a contract fails, equity steps in to prevent one party from taking advantage of the other.")

might feel cheated if not told in advance how a lawyer planned to bill expenses?

b. Does this requirement in Model Rule 1.5(a) now make it potentially unreasonable for a lawyer to fly first class? Assuming that the bill to the client accurately lists all expenses, is it inherently unreasonable for a lawyer to order an expensive wine with dinner?

In short, what constitutes an "unreasonable amount for expenses" in violation of Model Rule 1.5(a)? Do the eight factors listed in Model Rule 1.5(a) help you answer that question? The Rules originally intended these factors to define what constitutes an unreasonable fee; one can argue they are not of much help with respect to expenses.

c. Columbus Bar Association v. Brooks, 721 N.E.2d 23 (Ohio 1999), suspended a lawyer for two years, all but six months stayed, for various violations, including collecting a one-third contingent fee but then also charging an hourly rate for the lawyer's secretary and paralegal as additional expenses. The court found that, unless clearly agreed otherwise in writing, secretarial and legal assistant expenses are general overhead, not separately billable. "[B]y collecting for secretarial and law clerk expenses, in addition to filing fees, deposition fees, and his thirty-three percent of the settlement, respondent did not adhere to his written contract with the Jacksons and thereby charged a clearly excessive fee in violation of DR 2–106(A)."

d. Does Rule 1.5, Comment 1, give more help in understanding what costs are reasonable? Does it limit the lawyer to simply passing through out-of-pocket costs? Should it be limited in that way? ABA Formal Opinion 00–420 (Nov. 29, 2000) considered whether a firm may add a surcharge in billing for the services of a contract attorney that it hires to work on a case. Absent a separate agreement, the opinion says, if the firm treats the work as an expense item (over and above its fee), the firm must bill only what it actually paid for the contract lawyer's services. However, if the firm bills a contract lawyer as just another lawyer whose work makes up the fee for the matter, the firm may bill any reasonable rate for the services, as it does for the services of its associates.

3. May a lawyer charge a client a "nonrefundable retainer"? That is, may the lawyer say that her entire fee is payable before any work is begun and is not refundable even if the work turns out to take little time or if the client later fires the lawyer?

a. Matter of Cooperman, 633 N.E.2d 1069 (N.Y.1994), said that many nonrefundable fees are invalid. Cooperman in effect told his clients, "Once I enter an appearance in this case, even if you fire me, I will not have to return any part of the fee." In at least three cases, the clients fired him before he did much work. Nonrefundable fees violate the fiduciary relationship between lawyer and client, the New York Court of Appeals said; they inhibit the client's right to terminate the lawyer. Thus, the court affirmed the lawyer's two-year suspension from practice.[11] However, the court said: "Minimum fee arrangements and

---

[11] Kelly v. MD Buyline, Inc., 2 F.Supp.2d 420 (S.D.N.Y.1998), distinguished *Cooperman* as only involving single-case, or "special" retainers; a non-refundable retainer is permissible if it is for a fixed amount to be available for a defined period. "[G]eneral retainer agreements

general retainers that provide for fees, not laden with the nonrefundability impediment irrespective of any services, will continue to be valid and not subject in and of themselves to professional discipline."

b.   Do you agree that the issue is that simple? Suppose a lawyer incurs real opportunity costs by taking a case? What if the client tells the lawyer he wants her to set aside the month of May to try a matter. She agrees to do so for a "nonrefundable" fee of $25,000, her typical monthly billing, and turns down work she would otherwise do in May. On April 30, the client fires the lawyer. Is it clear the lawyer should not be able to keep all or most of the fee?

4.   Should a lawyer be able to increase her fees during the course of the representation?

a.   Severson & Werson v. Bolinger, 1 Cal.Rptr.2d 531 (Cal.Ct.App.1991), says the issue turns on the understanding of a reasonable client. The firm's standard contract said the client would pay the firm's "regular hourly rates." The firm told the client orally what those rates were. The court held that under these circumstances, the firm could not increase the rates it charged the client "without notice." The court left open the option of giving notice of an increase and then imposing it if the client did not object. However, what if the client objects? Should a client have a right to insist that a lawyer freeze its rates for the many years it may take to complete a matter?

b.   ABA Formal Opinion 11–458 (Aug. 4, 2011) recognizes that a fee agreement is a contract that an attorney may not modify unilaterally. Further, under Restatement § 18, if the proposed modification is "beyond a reasonable time after the lawyer has begun to represent the client in the matter," the burden is on the attorney to demonstrate that the modification was "fair and reasonable to the client." Rule 1.4 gives the attorney an affirmative duty to inform the client promptly about developments relevant to the case, which would include any proposed change in the fee. Rule 1.5(a) outlines the criteria used to assess the reasonableness of a fee arrangement. It assesses reasonableness as of the time the client and lawyer make the arrangement. Rule 1.8(a) governs a business arrangement with a client, which "ordinarily" will apply when the revised fee arrangement concerns more than cash, e.g., a security interest in property. The Opinion concludes that a lawyer may make "periodic, incremental increases in a lawyer's regular hourly billing rates" if the lawyer clearly communicates that right when the client-lawyer relationship begins. However, changes "sought by a lawyer that change the basic nature of a fee arrangement or significantly increase the lawyer's compensation absent an unanticipated change in circumstances ordinarily will be unreasonable."

provide that the attorney will be available for a period of time, whereas in 'special' retainer agreements the attorney is hired to handle a specific case or matter." The court concluded that a three-year retainer agreement was a *general* retainer agreement and thus was enforceable.

B. THE REQUIREMENT THAT A LAWYER CHARGE ONLY A "REASONABLE" FEE

1. Is the fee Novak proposes to charge the psychiatrist unreasonable? Are all fees reasonable if a lawyer and competent client negotiate them at arm's length?

a. Is the case likely to take extraordinary skill? Has the doctor set unusual time limitations on the lawyer's work? Do Novak's reputation and experience justify a higher-than-normal fee?

b. In King v. Fox, 851 N.E.2d 1184 (N.Y.2006), the plaintiff alleged that it was "unconscionable" for the lawyer to charge a musician a share of future royalties. The Second Circuit certified to the New York Court of Appeals the question whether the client's ratification of an unconscionable fee renders it valid and enforceable. The New York court said yes, although it will be a "rare case," that "a fully informed client with equal bargaining power knowingly and voluntarily affirms" a fee arrangement otherwise voidable as unconscionable.

c. In re Fordham, 668 N.E.2d 816 (Mass.1996), involved a prominent lawyer who charged a client $50,000 to defend the client's son's drunk driving case. The evidence showed that other lawyers would have taken the case for between $3,000 and $10,000, but this lawyer billed at his large firm's regular hourly rates. The jury acquitted the son, but the father balked at paying such a large amount. The court found the hours the firm spent on the case were disproportionate to its difficulty, and it imposed a public censure.

d. Do all fee arrangements present an inherent conflict of interest between lawyer and client because they create a way for a lawyer to put his or her interest ahead of the client's interest? Should we consider the process of agreeing upon a fee itself inherently "unethical" because it is a time in the lawyer-client relationship that the lawyer and client are adversaries? Could lawyers ever get paid if that were the law?

2. Are there situations in which it is important to limit freedom of contract between lawyer and client?

a. In American Home Assurance Co. v. Golomb, 606 N.E.2d 793 (Ill.App.1992), a lawyer in a medical malpractice case had his clients sign an agreement purporting to pay a contingent fee of 40% and to "hold the lawyer harmless" from any reduction of fees required by an Illinois statute limiting fees in such cases. The court held the fee contract void for encouraging an illegal act and it denied the lawyer all fees for the representation, even on a *quantum meruit* basis.

b. In Matter of Hanna, 362 S.E.2d 632 (S.C.1987), the lawyer charged 40% to collect the no-fault benefits under a client's auto policy. The benefits were "no-fault," so there really was no contingency. The court found the fee excessive, publicly reprimanded the lawyer, and required him to make restitution.

c. White v. McBride, 937 S.W.2d 796 (Tenn.1996), involved a contract to charge a one-third contingent fee to help a surviving spouse collect what was due to him from his wife's estate. The client had an inventory of the wife's assets and there was very little to do. The court held that the lawyer's continuing effort to collect the unreasonable fee showed his conduct was not inadvertent, and he thus lost his right to collect a fee on a *quantum meruit* basis as well.

d.   In re Green, 11 P.3d 1078 (Colo.2000), found a fee excessive when it was based on time the lawyer spent faxing documents, calling the clerk's office, and other tasks that would usually be done by an assistant. "There is no reason or excuse for charging a client," the court said, "for one's own inefficiencies."[12]

3.   May a local bar association simply adopt a schedule of fees that lawyers must charge for particular services?

a.   As discussed in the introduction to this problem, Goldfarb v. Virginia State Bar, 421 U.S. 773 (1975), established that such a fee schedule would violate the antitrust law. The *Goldfarb* plaintiffs needed a title examination to secure title insurance and only a member of the Virginia State Bar could legally perform that service. Their lawyer "quoted them the precise fee suggested in a minimum fee schedule published by respondent Fairfax County Bar Association," and no other lawyer would charge them less than that rate. The bar association was "a purely voluntary association of attorneys" with "no formal enforcement powers." In principle, the state disciplinary agency could charge lawyers with improperly soliciting clients if they regularly charged less than the prescribed fee, but it had never done so. Petitioners argued that the use of such a minimum fee schedule constituted price fixing in violation of § 1 of the Sherman Act, and the Supreme Court unanimously agreed.

The County Bar argued that lawyers were members of a "learned profession," not engaged in "trade or commerce," and thus not subject to the Sherman Act. The Court responded that the "public service aspect of professional practice [is not] controlling in determining whether § 1 includes professions. * * * Whatever else it may be, the examination of a land title is a service; the exchange of such a service for money is 'commerce' in the most common usage of that word. It is no disparagement of the practice of law as a profession to acknowledge that it has this business aspect * * *."

The Court acknowledged that a "purely advisory fee schedule issued to provide guidelines, or an exchange of price information without a showing of an actual restraint on trade, would present us with a different question." However, in this case, the lawyers desired "to comply with announced professional norms," and their motivation to do so "was reinforced by the assurance that other lawyers would not compete by underbidding."

b.   Should *Goldfarb* also prohibit lawyers from agreeing to maximum fees? For example, might a local voluntary bar association, in an effort to deal with complaints that lawyers make too much money, publish a schedule of maximum fees in routine cases? See, e.g., Arizona v. Maricopa County Med. Soc'y, 457 U.S. 332 (1982) (schedule of doctors' maximum rates to be reimbursed by insurance companies held per se illegal).

---

[12] See also, In re Guste, 118 So.3d 1023 (La.2012) (lawyer for severely disabled client could not charge usual legal fee for time spent driving client to appointments and doing errands).

c.   After *Goldfarb*, could lawyers seek to take advantage of the antitrust "state action" exemption by lobbying their state supreme court or legislature to enact into law the minimum fee schedule that *Goldfarb* held violated the Sherman Act?[13] Lawyers did not respond to *Goldfarb* in that way. Why would lawyers be reluctant to do so?

4.   At what point in the case should one judge the reasonableness of a fee?

a.   If a case turns out to be resolved more easily than expected, should a client be able to have a large fee reduced? Restatement Third, The Law Governing Lawyers § 34, Comment *c*, says:

> "Although reasonableness is usually assessed as of the time the contract was entered into, later events might be relevant. * * * [E]vents not known or contemplated when the contract was made can render the contract unreasonably favorable to the lawyer or, occasionally, to the client. Compare Restatement Second, Contracts §§ 152–154 and 261–265 (doctrines of mistake, supervening impracticality, supervening frustration). To determine what events client and lawyer contemplated, their contract must be construed in light of its goals and circumstances and in light of the possibilities discussed with the client * * *. Events within [the contemplated] range of risks, such as a high recovery, do not make unreasonable a contract that was reasonable when made."

Do you agree that this standard captures the proper considerations a court should use for evaluating a fee after the lawyer completes the work? Do you believe the standard will be easy to apply in concrete cases?

b.   In Holmes v. Loveless, 94 P.3d 338 (Wash.Ct.App.2004), retired attorneys sued their former client for a fee. The former client was still making payments to the attorneys thirty years after parties negotiated the fee agreement. In 1972, attorneys Holmes and Kruger agreed to provide legal services to Loveless and Barclay, two real estate developers, to develop a shopping mall. The fee agreement said that the law firm would provide discounted legal services for two-and-a-half years, but after that, the client would pay the full rate. In exchange for the initial reduced rates, the developers agreed to pay the attorneys' firm 5% of cash distributions that the shopping mall produced. The mall turned out to be a great success, and by 2001, the developers had paid over $380,000 to the law firm, although the discounted value of legal services rendered in the 1970s was only about $8,000. The developers argued that the fee agreement violated Rule 1.8(a) as an unreasonable business transaction with a client and Rule 1.5 as an unreasonable fee. The attorneys argued that the fee was reasonable, but the court agreed

---

[13] *Goldfarb* distinguished situations where a state agency sets the prices for services: "In Parker v. Brown, 317 U.S. 341 (1943), the Court held that an anticompetitive marketing program 'which derived its authority and efficacy from the legislative command of the state' was not a violation of the Sherman Act because the Act was intended to regulate private practices and not to prohibit a State from imposing a restraint as an act of government. * * * [But h]ere we need not inquire further into the state action question because it cannot fairly be said that the State of Virginia through its Supreme Court Rules required the anticompetitive activities of either respondent."

with the developers. A fee agreement is not a typical "business transaction" with a client, the court said, but it found that this one was directly linked to the success of the shopping mall. Consistent with Restatement § 34, the court said that a seemingly fair agreement at the time of its execution must be reevaluated "when subsequent events alter the circumstances of the relationship." Given the combination of a limited initial period of fee discount, the payments already made, and the lack of any end date, the court held that the fee agreement was unreasonable and therefore no longer enforceable.[14]

C.   SPECIAL RULES APPLICABLE TO CONTINGENT FEES

1. In England, the contingent fee was traditionally considered inherently unethical as a violation of the rule against champerty, which prohibits a lawyer financially supporting a lawsuit in exchange for a share in the expected recovery.[15] Should the same be true in this country?

a.   The contingent fee is sometimes called a "poor person's fee." Should a contingent fee be improper if the client can afford to pay an hourly rate? Why would a corporation or wealthy individual prefer a contingent fee in some cases?

b.   The Chicago Council of Lawyers has suggested "that the contingent fee 'problem' is a symptom, rather than a cause of a much wider problem—the unequal access to the courts for the poor and near poor."[16] Thus, the Council favors dealing with that "wider problem." Do you agree? In what ways could prepaid legal insurance radically change the calculation as to the proper time to charge a contingent fee? Would that be a change for the better? Should that affect the bar's position on prepaid insurance?[17]

c.   Does a lawyer have to advise a client that he or she may choose between a contingent fee and a non-contingent fee? What is now Model Rule 1.5, Comment 5, used to say:

> "When there is doubt whether a contingent fee is consistent with the client's best interest, the lawyer should offer the client alternative bases for the fee and explain their implications."

The 2002 revisions deleted that sentence. Does that mean that lawyers may insist on contingent fees even if they are not in their client's best interests? Would a lawyer who did so be breaching his or her fiduciary obligations to the client?

d.   Drafters of the change were told that some lawyers—like Novak in our problem—only charge contingent fees. Does that justify the deletion? In such a situation, would it simply make sense for the lawyer to say: "In this circumstance, where there is strict liability and only a minor dispute over damages, it may make more sense for you to

---

[14]   See also, Lawrence v. Miller, 901 N.E.2d 1268 (N.Y. 2008) (court should examine the fee for unconscionability both at the time the parties made it and at the end of the case).

[15]   England no longer prohibits all contingent fees, although their use is still less frequent than in the United States.

[16]   Chicago Council of Lawyers, Report on Code of Professional Responsibility 20 (1972).

[17]   Issues relating to prepaid legal insurance are in Problem 34 of these materials.

pay a lawyer an hourly fee. I only work for contingent fees, but I can recommend others who charge hourly or fixed fees."?

2.   May Novak claim a $5,000 fee in the personal injury suit if the parties settle the case before he begins work?

a.   What if Novak says that the reason the defendant quickly offered to settle is because he knew that Novak now represented the plaintiff?

b.   Is it enough to say that Novak needs to make a few easy fees, as here, to make up for the losing cases on which he works long hours but realizes nothing? Judge John Grady takes that argument head on:[18]

> "What causes me to question the propriety of the ever-increasing fee in proportion to the size of the verdict is this: there is little, if any, relationship between the efforts of the lawyer and the size of the verdict, once we assume a verdict in favor of the plaintiff. The size of the verdict is determined by the nature and extent of the plaintiff's injury and resulting damages. Conceding that some lawyers are more brilliant and more eloquent than others, we flatter ourselves unduly if we think the performance of counsel is a large factor in the size of the verdict. * * * To illustrate the point, the identical collision can cause a whiplash injury or result in an amputation of a leg. * * * But even though the same amount of work is involved, the whiplash verdict might be $4,500, for a fee of $50 per hour, while the amputation verdict might be $200,000, providing a fee of more than $6,000 per hour. * * *

> "Another fortuitous circumstance affecting the fee is the number of claimants the lawyer represents in a particular case. Assume that a father, mother and two children are struck at an intersection and all of them sustain injuries. The liability evidence is the same for all. Frequently, they will have the same doctor, who simply brings four sets of records to court instead of one. His testimony takes longer, and I admit that there is some additional work required of the lawyer. However, in the typical case of four plaintiffs, the additional work is not at all proportionate to the additional fees the lawyer will realize when he charges each of the plaintiffs the same percentage, which—make no mistake about it—is what he ordinarily does. * * *

> * * *

> "One sometimes hears the argument that the attorney is entitled to collect his 'third' in easy cases to make up for all the 'losers' he handles. This explanation does not withstand analysis. Putting aside for a moment the question of whether one client can properly be surcharged to compensate for the deficiencies in another client's case, the fact of the matter is that there just are not very many 'losers.' * * * [A]t least 95 percent of the total claims handled by lawyers are settled before trial, and [generate at least some fee]. * * *

---

[18] John F. Grady, Some Ethical Questions About Percentage Fees, 2 Litigation 20 (Summer, 1976). Copyright 1976 by the American Bar Association. Used with permission.

c.   Do you agree with Judge Grady?[19] Should clients simply shop around for the best lawyer at the lowest price? When we discuss lawyer advertising in Problem 31, you will see that it is easier to shop around now than when Judge Grady wrote his article. Based on what you have observed about law practice, however, do you think that lawyers are likely to offer their clients a wide range of contingent fee percentages?

d.   Suppose the law required personal injury lawyers to ask the defendant to make an offer of settlement very early. If plaintiff accepted that offer, the plaintiff's lawyer would have to bill based on hours worked and the total fee could be no more than 10% of the recovery. However, if the plaintiff rejected the initial offer, the lawyer could charge a contingent fee on only as much of the ultimate recovery that exceeded the initial offer.

Would you favor such a plan? What would it do to the dynamics of settlement negotiations? Would it reduce the number of lawyers who serve injured clients? Would it tend to reduce the amount of lawyer advertising as the expected return to the lawyer from getting each new client into the office decreased? See Lester Brickman, Michael Horowitz & Jeffrey O'Connell, Rethinking Contingency Fees (1994).[20]

3.   Are there kinds of cases in which a contingent fee should not be proper?

a.   May a lawyer charge a contingent fee in a domestic relations case? Look at Model Rule 1.5(d)(1). What is the basis for such a prohibition? Is Model Rule 1.5, Comment 6, helpful in explaining the rationale?

Connecticut Bar Ethics Opinion 87–17 (1988) takes the position that a lawyer may charge a contingent fee in an action to partition ownership of a house owned by an unmarried couple. The court said that the rule against charging a contingent fee in domestic relations matters does not apply where the couple is not married. Do you agree with the distinction? In a time when unmarried relationships are common, might one ask whether the policies behind the rule, e.g., not discouraging parties from reconciling, should apply to such cases too?

b.   Should the law allow a contingent fee in a criminal case? Look at Rule 1.5(d)(2). What reasons support such a prohibition? What kinds of clients would benefit from allowing contingent fees in criminal cases?

Winkler v. Keane, 7 F.3d 304 (2d Cir.1993), considered whether a defense lawyer's charging a contingent fee in a criminal case should be per se grounds for reversal of the conviction. The state accused the

---

[19] The ABA Standing Committee on Ethics and Professional Responsibility has said only that "the charging of a contingent fee * * * does not violate ethical standards as long as the fee is appropriate in the circumstances and reasonable in amount, and as long as the client has been fully advised of the availability of alternative fee arrangements." ABA Formal Opinion 94–389 (Dec. 5, 1994).

[20] In this connection, see Committee on Legal Ethics of the W. Va. State Bar v. Gallaher, 376 S.E.2d 346 (W.Va.1988). The court found that a 50% contingent fee was excessive for recovering personal injury damages where the lawyer advised acceptance of the first real offer the insurance company made: "If an attorney's fee is grossly disproportionate to the services rendered and is charged to a client who lacks full information about all of the relevant circumstances, the fee is 'clearly excessive' within the meaning of Disciplinary Rule 2–106(A), even though the client has consented to such fee." The court ordered restitution to the personal injury plaintiff of an amount sufficient to reduce the fee to one-third.

defendant of killing his father. The fee agreement provided that if the lawyer secured an acquittal so that the defendant could inherit from his father, the lawyer would get an extra $25,000. The New York Court of Appeals accepted the defendant's contention that allowing contingent fees in criminal cases may discourage the lawyer from working out a guilty plea in an appropriate case, seeking a charge on a lesser-included offense, or the like. However, the court held that, although charging the contingent fee is grounds for professional discipline of the lawyer, it was not per se grounds for reversing the criminal conviction. For that, the defendant must show actual prejudice, and, in this case, the Second Circuit found none.

4.   Should the law prohibit contingent fees in other kinds of cases?

a.   Should the ethics rules ban contingent fees for defense counsel in civil cases? Wunschel Law Firm, P. C. v. Clabaugh, 291 N.W.2d 331 (Iowa 1980), was a defamation action. The defendant agreed with defense counsel that the law firm would defend him for a fee that would be one-third of the difference between the prayer in the petition and the amount actually awarded. The lawyer offered the defendant the alternative of paying a fee of $50 per hour. The court held that such a contingent defense fee is void and unenforceable as a matter of public policy. The court reasoned that such a fee is based on "pure speculation" because "it provides for determination of the fee by factors having no logical relationship to the value of the services." Do you agree?

b.   ABA Formal Opinion 93–373 (Apr. 16, 1993), expressly rejected that view and said that contingent fees for defense counsel in civil cases do not violate the Model Rules if the amount saved is "reasonably ascertainable," the total amount of the fee is reasonable, and the client's consent to the arrangement was "fully informed." See also, D.C. Bar Opinion 347 (Mar. 2009), adopting the view of Formal Opinion 93–373 when the lawyer is dealing with a sophisticated client and when the lawyer describes, preferably in writing, the base from which savings will be calculated and the percentage to be applied to the savings.

c.   May lawyers in takeover fights receive a "premium" if they successfully pursue or defeat the takeover attempt? Does the practice sound better if a lawyer calls it "value billing" and consistently sets the fee on the basis of how much the client has benefited from the lawyer's efforts? See, e.g., ABA Commission on Billable Hours Report (2002).

D.   THE ALTERNATIVE OF THE HOURLY-RATE FEE

1.   At least a generation of lawyers experienced the hourly rate fee as dominant in the life at most law firms. Does hourly rate billing harmonize the interests of lawyers and clients?

a.   What abuses are inherent in hourly billing? Does hourly billing give firms the wrong incentives, such as the incentive to take more time than if they were billing on a contingent fee basis? Might hourly billing encourage a firm to file every possible motion and to have associates research tangential legal theories?

b.   In re Myers, 127 P.3d 325 (Kan.2006), involved an attorney, Myers, who charged a client for 43.5 hours of work in closing an estate.

In all but one instance, he billed services in one-hour increments, i.e., not six-minute or even quarter-hour units. Myers freely acknowledged that if he had spent only 45 minutes on a project, he billed it as a whole hour, although he insisted that if he worked on something for less than 15 minutes, he usually would not bill at all. The Kansas Supreme Court agreed with its hearing panel that "billing in one-hour increments when one-hour is not spent working on a matter is an improper billing practice and is in violation of [Rule] 1.5." It publicly censured Mr. Myers.

c.   What about billing twice for the same time if the lawyer is doing two different things? Suppose a lawyer has to fly to a meeting for Client A, but works on the airplane on a matter for Client B. May the lawyer bill the same hour twice, once to each client? ABA Formal Opinion 93–379 (Dec. 6, 1993) addressed the issue as follows:

> " * * * [I]t is helpful to consider these questions, not from the perspective of what a client could be forced to pay, but rather from the perspective of what the lawyer actually earned. A lawyer who spends four hours of time on behalf of three clients has not earned twelve billable hours. A lawyer who flies for six hours for one client, while working for five hours on behalf of another, has not earned eleven billable hours. A lawyer who is able to reuse old work product has not re-earned the hours previously billed and compensated when the work product was first generated. * * * [If] it turns out that the lawyer is particularly efficient in accomplishing a given result, it nonetheless will not be permissible to charge the client for more hours than were actually expended on the matter. * * * [T]he economies associated with the result must inure to the benefit of the client, not give rise to an opportunity to bill a client for phantom hours."

Not all lawyers and firms have taken the ABA's directions to heart. See Lisa G. Lerman, Lying to Clients, 138 U. Pennsylvania L. Rev. 659 (1990), and Lisa G. Lerman, Unethical Billing Practices, 50 Rutgers L. Rev. 2151 (1998).

d.   In re Siderits, 824 N.W.2d 812 (Wis. 2013), emphasizes that hourly rate billing requires honest reporting of hours. The lawyer's firm gave a bonus to lawyers who billed over 1,800 hours in a year. Mr. Siderits was short hours one year, so he padded his time charges to get himself over the magic 1,800 hours. The next year, he reduced the time he billed affected clients, thinking that eliminated any net harm to them. The court found that, regardless of harm, the lawyer's manipulation of his time records was conduct involving dishonesty, fraud, deceit and misrepresentation designed to get him almost $47,000 in bonuses. Because Siderits lost his job and had to repay the firm, the court limited his suspension to 1 year.

2.   Are there alternatives to hourly rate and contingent fees that would better align the lawyer's incentives with client's interests while still producing an appropriate return for the lawyer's efforts?

a.   The ABA Commission on Billable Hours Report (2002) found a move toward fixed fees for recurring, routine tasks (sometimes-called "commodity" work) because clients want the burden of doing the work efficiently placed entirely on the law firm. Billable Hours Report at 25. Can you see any collateral effects to such a development?

b.   The report also suggests that lawyers should measure productivity in terms of revenue generated for the firm, in whatever form, and not on hours worked. Billable Hours Report at 28. Would you prefer to work under such a system?

c.   Fixed fees make it easier for corporate counsel to conduct auctions in which firms compete to offer the lowest prices for the right to do defined packages of work, say defense of sets of 100 personal injury cases. Billable Hours Report at 33. Does that represent a move in a direction you would favor?

d.   Does the move toward fixed fees seem appropriate for services that are not routine and that require work by experienced experts? Are fees ultimately likely to be set at some combination of fixed fee for routine services, hourly rate where complexity of the case is hard to predict, and a contingent element where intensity of the lawyer's efforts may make a difference?[21]

PROBLEM 6

HANDLING CLIENT PROPERTY AND WITHDRAWING FROM A REPRESENTATION

Issues of the relationship between lawyer and client are in some ways best seen when the going gets tough. The client may be unhappy because things are going more slowly or less well than hoped. The lawyer may be unhappy because the client demands more services than expected and pays less promptly than promised. Some clients are "high maintenance." This problem examines some of the issues that can arise in such contexts. It first considers the lawyer's duty to protect and account for a client's property. It then examines the circumstances under which a lawyer may withdraw from representing the client. Then, it considers how lawyers should deal with clients who fail to pay the lawyer's fee. Finally, it considers the lawyer's possible right to a lien on client property and papers.

FACTS

In a recent suit to recover a valuable ring that the defendant had wrongfully withheld, a jury awarded Elizabeth Jackson's client the ring and $100,000 punitive damages. The fee contract between Jackson and her client provided that Jackson would get 40% of all punitive damages. "That was because we thought the punitive damages would be low," the client complained after the jury verdict announced the verdict. "On a big recovery such as this, 40% is unfair," the client said. "I'll pay you 25% and not a penny more." The defendant satisfied the judgment by giving Jackson the ring and a check

21   See, e.g., Ronald D. Rotunda, Moving from Billable Hours to Fixed–Fees: Task–Based Fees and Legal Ethics, 47 U. Kansas L. Rev. 819 (1999).

for $100,000 payable to Jackson and the client. Jackson promptly deposited the full amount of the check into her client trust account and put the ring on her finger. She told the client, "Until we get this fee dispute worked out, I'm not giving you a nickel."

Jackson is a well-known and very busy litigator and she doesn't have time for difficult clients. When one client told her that she was not returning his phone calls quickly enough, she told him to get another lawyer, filed a notice of withdrawal with the court before which the matter was pending, and did no more work on the matter.

In another case, Jackson represented a local businessperson in a dispute over title to real estate. She anticipated a hard time collecting her fee, so she took a security interest in the real estate that was the subject of the suit. When the case was over and the client was slow to pay, Jackson sued to collect her fee out of the proceeds of an involuntary sale of the real estate. She also refused to send her client a copy of the judgment entered in the underlying case that the client needed to obtain a bank loan.

QUESTIONS

A. HANDLING CLIENT PROPERTY

1. Why is it important that lawyers pay attention to their handling of client property?

a. A lawyer has a fiduciary relationship with a client. "Fiduciary" is a title also applied to trustees and guardians, i.e., people who manage the property of others. In that sense, the trustworthy management of a client's property is one of the most fundamental duties of a lawyer.

b. Violation of fiduciary standards with respect to client property is also one of the most certain ways for a lawyer to be disbarred. That is only partly because of the seriousness of the offense. It is also in part because proof of a violation of accounting rules is typically much more straightforward than proof of a failure to be forthcoming in disclosing information, proof of less-than-competent representation of a client, or even proof of a conflict of interest. Disciplinary authorities have limited resources and tend to use them in cases where the results will be most certain.

c. It is thus critically important that you as a lawyer know the rules for management of client property. Large firms will have a whole staff devoted to preserving and accounting for such property, but ultimately the ones with their licenses on the line will be the lawyers for whom the staff work. Those lawyers need to know the rules as well.

d. Ethics opinions have considered what client property a lawyer must keep and what the lawyer may destroy. Arizona State Bar Opinion 08–02 (Dec. 2008), said that a client is entitled to most of the contents of its closed file and the lawyer must retain such files. A lawyer may adopt a file retention policy that destroys files after a given period, but the lawyer must tell the client the lawyer's policy at the outset of the relationship and act only in accordance with it. If the lawyer has no policy, the lawyer ordinarily must notify the client before destruction of a client's file.

Advisory Comm. of the Supreme Court of Missouri Formal Opinion 127 (2009) said that after the conclusion of a representation, a law firm may destroy the paper copy of a client's file without the client's consent, but only if the firm maintains a scanned, electronic copy. The law firm must keep in paper form only items with intrinsic value, and wills and documents with legal significance. Electronic storage media must be of archive quality integrity for the entire maintenance period. In this regard, the firm may need to periodically transfer the data to new forms of media to protect its integrity. The firm must maintain the proper hardware and software to be able to access the file, and this may require the lawyer or firm to stay abreast of technological developments, and perhaps consult with individuals with technological expertise.

Do you see how protecting a client's property can get to be challenging?

2.   Was it proper for Jackson to wear the client's ring while it was in her possession?

a.   Restatement Third, The Law Governing Lawyers § 44, Comment *e*, makes clear:

> "This Section requires a lawyer to use reasonable measures for safekeeping such objects, for example, by placing them in a safe-deposit box or office safe. The reasonableness of measures depends on the circumstances, including the market value of the property, its special value to the client * * *, and special difficulties that would be required to replace it if known to the lawyer * * *."

b.   The Florida Bar v. Grosso, 760 So.2d 940 (Fla.2000) (per curiam), illustrates how a lawyer can unintentionally fail to protect client property. When the court sentenced the lawyer's client to probation, it provided that he could not have a gun. The lawyer agreed to keep the client's gun collection for him and put the guns in his garage. Florida weather being humid, when the lawyer returned the guns one year later, the client discovered that they were rusty and pitted, with parts missing. The court suspended the lawyer for 90 days because he did not act reasonably in caring for the client's guns.

3.   How must an attorney keep his or her office accounts?

a.   A lawyer need not deposit each client's funds into a separate account, but the lawyer must keep individual records of each client's funds. In August 2010, the ABA House of Delegates adopted the Model Rules for Client Trust Account Records. They are not officially part of the Model Rules of Professional Conduct, but they may be influential in the states. These detailed rules require a lawyer to maintain records for at least five years of — (a) all deposits to and withdrawals from client trust accounts, "as well as the date, payee and purpose of each disbursement;" (b) ledger records that show, for each beneficiary, the source and disbursement of all funds, (c) copies of all retainer and compensation agreements with clients, (d) copies of all accountings made to clients, (e) copies of all bills for fees and expenses, (f) copies of all records showing disbursements on behalf of clients, and (g) "physical or electronic equivalents of all checkbook registers, bank statements, records of deposit, pre-numbered cancelled checks, and substitute checks provided by a financial institution."

b.   Columbus Bar Association v. Zauderer, 687 N.E.2d 410 (Ohio 1997), involved a lawyer who collected a lot of money for his clients. His problem arose when he started to allocate expenses of the cases. Without prior agreement with his clients, he accrued many of his litigation-related expenses in a "general" category and then created a formula to assign them to individual cases. Some claimants complained, and the bar charged him with failure to keep adequate records. The Ohio Supreme Court agreed and suspended Zauderer for a year.

4.   Did Jackson violate Model Rule 1.15 by depositing the $100,000 settlement check into her trust account?

a.   A lawyer may sign the lawyer's own name on a settlement check made out to the lawyer, but the lawyer may sign the client's name on a settlement check only if she has actual authority to do so. Sometimes the client gives this authority, but too often, the lawyer overlooks it. A lawyer who, without such authority, signs the client's name on a check may not only commit a disciplinary violation, but also the crime of conversion. See, e.g., Sampson v. State Bar, 524 P.2d 139 (Cal.1974) (endorsement of clients' names to checks without authorization of clients, accepting false acknowledgments, and failing to secure clients' authorization for payment of settlement funds to doctor is conduct subject to disciplinary action).

b.   Matter of Advisory Committee on Professional Ethics Docket No. 22–95, 677 A.2d 1100 (N.J.1996), held that a lawyer doing debt collection work for an institutional creditor may accept the creditor's suggestion that the lawyer endorse checks as they arrive, deduct the lawyer's contingent fee, and transmit the balance to the creditor. The court found that it was reasonable for the client to give this authority because debt collection is a big business with many small transactions; any other system would be unnecessarily complex.

c.   Bazinet v. Kluge, 764 N.Y.S.2d 320 (N.Y.Sup.Ct.2003), presented a lawyer's worst nightmare. Lawyer Reiser received an escrow deposit of 10% of the value of Kluge's property in connection with its sale. When the initial contract failed to close, Reiser received another 10% escrow deposit related to a second contract. The combined deposits totaled $2.73 million, which Reiser deposited in a small bank. When the second sales transaction closed, and his client sought the money, Reiser learned that the FDIC had closed the bank and was now the receiver. The FDIC only insured each account up to $100,000, so the other $2.53 million was apparently lost. In a claim for malpractice, the court said: "[A]n attorney is not held to the rule of infallibility and is not liable for an honest mistake of judgment where the proper course is open to reasonable doubt." The client had raised a sufficient claim of negligence, however, to withstand a motion to dismiss.

5.   When the client asked for his money, should lawyer Jackson have paid over the full $75,000 that the client thought was due? Would it be proper for Jackson to pay the client only what Jackson thought was due?

a.   Look at Model Rule 1.15(d). How much is Jackson required to pay over to the client?

b.   What should she do with the portion of the fee that the client agrees Jackson is due? May she keep it in the trust account? Would that be consistent with Model Rule 1.15(a) and (b)? What must she do with the amount of the fee that remains in dispute?

c.   Suppose a creditor of the client asserts a lien on the client's share of the judgment. May the lawyer ignore that lien? Look at Model Rule 1.15(e). A lawyer who pays settlement proceeds to the client in knowing disregard of a creditor's lien may become directly liable to the lienholder. The lawyer must pay twice. Kaiser Foundation Health Plan, Inc. v. Aguiluz, 54 Cal.Rptr.2d 665 (Cal.Ct.App.1996).

d.   In re Martin, 67 A.3d 1032 (D.C. 2013), involved a client who objected to a fee calculation. Martin represented a client, originally on an hourly basis, but the lawyer and client later substituted a contingent fee. The parties settled the underlying claim and agreed to collect it from brokerage accounts on which the United States also had a claim. Martin agreed to charge an hourly fee for the fight with the government. The litigation finally ended and Martin sent the client a statement consisting partly of a contingent fee and partly an hourly rate. The client disputed the amount of the fee and the way it was calculated, but the lawyer distributed the money to himself and other lawyers pursuant to his original bill rather than putting the disputed portion into his trust account. The DC Bar Attorney-Client Arbitration Board agreed with the client's view of the proper fee, but Martin resisted repayment by trying to remove the dispute to federal court and did not put the disputed sum into a trust account until 9 months after the client complained. The court found that Martin violated Rule 1.15(a) & (c). While the court acknowledged that Martin had a right to contest the arbitration award, it held that by "litigating [it] to the death" Martin also violated Rule 1.16(d), which requires a lawyer to return money to the client to which the client is entitled.

6.   Should the law subject a lawyer to discipline if her office staff or associated lawyers engage in dishonesty? Have no doubt; it happens.

a.   In Office of Disciplinary Counsel v. Ball, 618 N.E.2d 159 (Ohio 1993), a lawyer gave responsibility for most of his probate practice to his secretary. She took in money and wrote checks on his trust accounts. Ultimately, she diverted funds from some accounts to others. The lawyer said he knew nothing about this. Even if that were true, the court said, the lawyer failed in his duty of supervision, see Model Rule 5.3. The court suspended the lawyer from practice for six months.

b.   In Florida Bar v. Rousso, 117 So.3d 756 (Fla. 2013), Rousso's non-lawyer bookkeeper embezzled $4.38 million from the law firm's trust account over a period of several years. After discovering the deficiency in 2008, Rousso took steps to protect his clients against loss, but the Florida Supreme Court found that the lawyer would have caught the loss much earlier if he had followed the state's trust accounting rules. "A lawyer's responsibility for safekeeping of trust account funds cannot be delegated to a non-lawyer employee of the firm," the court said. "Misappropriation by office staff does not relieve the lawyer from the requirements of the minimum standards requiring a trust account." The court disbarred Mr. Rousso.

7. Should a lawyer's trust account be subject to random audits by disciplinary authorities? Should lawyers collectively have to reimburse clients victimized by the acts of other lawyers?

a.   Traditional doctrine requires that there can be no audit unless there is probable cause to believe that the lawyer has not properly maintained the accounts. In February 1992, the ABA House of Delegates approved proposals for disciplinary reform that called for random audits, but states have not adopted the proposals. Proponents believe that such audits would catch some lawyers who commingle funds and deter others from doing so.

b.   Some lawyers have tried to resist audit of their trust accounts, citing attorney-client privilege or their own expectation of privacy. Those defenses have generally not prevailed, e.g., In re Kennedy, 442 A.2d 79 (Del.1982) (spot check system), cert. denied, 467 U.S. 1205 (1984); Doyle v. State Bar of California, 648 P.2d 942 (Cal.1982) (subpoena system).

c.   Even where the audit shows that the lawyer stole from his or her law firm instead of from a client, the lawyer can suffer disbarment, because the lawyer still acted dishonestly. See, e.g., In re Busby, 855 P.2d 156 (Or.1993) (lawyer suspended for four months for lying to his firm about the fees he was paid and pocketing the difference).

d.   Suppose the lawyer who converted client funds is now judgment-proof. What remedies, if any, should you pursue on the client's behalf? Most states have established a client security fund to reimburse clients victimized by their attorneys.[22] Should the Court assess all members of the bar to fund the corpus of such a fund? Should the Bar keep the existence of the fund quiet to prevent the lawyers' assessments from becoming as high as doctors' malpractice premiums?

B.   LAWYER WITHDRAWAL WITHOUT CONSENT OF THE CLIENT

1.   Should a lawyer ever be *required* to terminate a representation?

a.   Model Rule 1.16(a)(1) requires withdrawal if the lawyer's continued representation will violate another Model Rule. As you go through this course, watch for situations that might trigger such a requirement. Conflicts of interest create such situations, for example. Also, watch for situations involving uncorrected client fraud.

---

[22] See, e.g., Murray T. Bloom, The Trouble With Lawyers 1–35 (1969). Beard v. North Carolina State Bar, 357 S.E.2d 694 (N.C.1987), upheld a system by which the state supreme court requires each lawyer to pay $50 each year into the client security fund. See also, Clients' Security Fund of State v. Grandeau, 526 N.E.2d 270 (N.Y.1988) (upheld suit by New York Fund against the partner of defaulting lawyer on a theory of vicarious liability).

b.   Model Rule 1.16(a)(2) makes withdrawal mandatory where "the lawyer's physical or mental condition materially impairs the lawyer's ability to represent the client." How should that rule apply to aging lawyers? Where should we draw the line between "he's not what he once was" and a situation requiring withdrawal?

c.   Model Rule 1.16(a)(3) requires withdrawal when the client discharges the lawyer. Ordinarily the client may discharge the lawyer at any time and for any reason, having an obligation only to pay for work done up to that time. Restatement Third, The Law Governing Lawyers § 32(1), Comment b, says bluntly: "A client may always discharge a lawyer, regardless of cause and regardless of any agreement between them." Why should a client have more right than a lawyer to walk away from what is otherwise a binding contract between them? Are Model Rule 1.16, Comments 4–6, helpful in answering that question?[23]

d.   In the absence of an agreement, what rights should a lawyer have if the client terminates the relationship the day before trial, or under other circumstances where the lawyer has invested significant time but not achieved any results on which to calculate a contingent or percentage fee? The usual rule permits the lawyer a quantum meruit recovery. However, in the case of a contingent fee, the first lawyer can usually recover only if the second lawyer wins the case, i.e., if the plaintiff ultimately prevails, e.g., Plaza Shoe Store, Inc. v. Hermel, Inc., 636 S.W.2d 53 (Mo.1982) (en banc).

2.   We know a lawyer has significant discretion whether to undertake representation of a client, but once having done so, does the lawyer have less ability to terminate that representation over the client's objection?

a.   Model Rule 1.16(b)(1) authorizes a lawyer to withdraw from representation at any time if the withdrawal affects no material interests of the client adversely. If the client does not want the lawyer to withdraw, are the client's material interests *always* adversely affected?

b.   Is withdrawal a breach of the lawyer's duty of loyalty to the client unless the lawyer has a reason for withdrawal other than being tired of the client's personality? If the lawyer does withdraw, who should pay for the cost of bringing a new lawyer up to speed?

c.   B. Dahlenburg Bonar, P.S.C. v. Waite, Schneider, Bayless & Chesley, 373 S.W.3d 419 (Ky. 2012), shows withdrawal may be costly. The lawyer, a former bar president, was co-counsel in a class action against the local Catholic diocese for sex abuse and had a deal with her co-counsel to split any fees recovered. When co-counsel directed allegations at current programs of the diocese, however, the lawyer became uncomfortable and voluntarily withdrew because the allegations might jeopardize her relationship with "her client base." However, when time came to split the fee award, she sought to enforce

---

[23]   Kolschefsky v. Harris, 72 P.3d 1144 (Wyo.2003), presented an unexpected case of client discharge. The trial court held that "their voluntary bankruptcy petition constituted an anticipatory breach or repudiation of the contingent fee arrangement with their attorney, discharging him from any further performance as their attorney." The Wyoming Supreme Court affirmed.

the earlier agreement. A lawyer who withdraws from a contingency fee case without good cause forfeits any fee, the court said. Moreover, preserving a relationship with the defendants or others is not good cause. Ms. Bonar was not even entitled to a quantum meruit recovery. "When an attorney voluntarily withdraws from a contingency fee case without good cause, he or she forfeits any fee." Do you think this is a good result? Why or why not?

3. May a lawyer withdraw under Model Rule 1.16(b)(4) whenever the client insists on taking action "with which the lawyer has a fundamental disagreement"?

a.   Is it the lawyer or the client who has authority to define the objectives of representation under Model Rule 1.2(a)? Can that authority be real if a lawyer who disagrees with client decisions may simply resign?

b.   The "fundamental disagreement" language replaced a standard permitting a lawyer to withdraw in the face of any decision the lawyer found "imprudent." Was that ground even more favorable to lawyer withdrawal?

c.   Is the answer that Model Rule 1.16(d) requires a lawyer to take "reasonably practicable" steps "to protect a client's interest"? Are you satisfied that such a cautionary requirement overcomes the consequences of a lawyer's election to withdraw?

4. May a lawyer withdraw from a case that has become financially unprofitable for the lawyer to pursue?

a.   In Smith v. R.J. Reynolds, 630 A.2d 820 (N.J.Super.App.Div.1993), a firm agreed to charge a contingent fee to represent a smoker in a damage claim against R.J. Reynolds. As discovery went on, however, the firm had expended over $1 million in out-of-pocket costs and $5 million in lawyer time. The prospect of much more expense remained before the case would come to trial, but the plaintiffs wanted to go to trial to establish a "principle." The lawyers responded that "there comes a time when we can't afford to operate on the fuel of just principle * * * when the finances are such that it becomes an unreasonable burden."

Should the court let the lawyers off the hook? In this case, the appellate division concluded that if the party paid for litigation at hourly rates, all would agree the time had come to call it quits. Because a contingent fee contract gives the client no incentive to drop the matter, the court ordered the trial judge to determine the likelihood of success in the case, the likely recovery, if any, and then make the assessment that new Model Rule 1.16(b)(6) contemplates. But see Haines v. Liggett Group, 814 F.Supp. 414 (D.N.J.1993), a related case in which the court said the firm had made a deal with the client and had to live with it.

b.   Restatement Third, The Law Governing Lawyers § 32 identifies no ground comparable to Model Rule 1.16(b)(6). Should courts permit withdrawal on financial grounds? Would failure to do so harm future clients by making it hard to get lawyers to take cases with uncertain costs and outcomes? See, e.g., Fidelity Nat'l Title Ins. Co. v. Intercounty Nat'l Title Ins. Co., 310 F.3d 537 (7th Cir.2002) (business firms "have no right to free legal aid in civil suits").

5. What role should courts play in reviewing attempted withdrawal?

a. If a matter from which the lawyer seeks to withdraw is pending before a tribunal, the rules of that tribunal will ordinarily require the tribunal's permission to withdraw. See Model Rule 1.16(c).

b. Can you imagine circumstances in which a court will not permit a lawyer to withdraw even where withdrawal would be required under Model Rule 1.16(a)? Keep that question in mind when you look at Problem 27, for example, on what to do when a client lies in court testimony.

c. Maples v. Thomas, 132 S.Ct. 912 (2012), should remind young lawyers that it is critical to get court permission to withdraw where the lawyer has entered an appearance but can no longer continue working. Two associates at Sullivan & Cromwell, working pro bono, sought state habeas corpus for a defendant sentenced to death. A local Alabama lawyer moved their admission pro hac vice. He "made clear, however, that he would undertake no substantive involvement in the case." Later, the two associates left the firm and their "new employment disabled them from representing" the defendant (one became a prosecutor and one moved abroad). Neither associate sought the trial court's leave to withdraw (which Alabama law required), nor found anyone else to assume the representation. Moreover, no other Sullivan & Cromwell lawyer entered an appearance, moved to substitute counsel, or otherwise notified the court of a need to change the defendant's representation.

When the Alabama court denied the writ, it sent a notice addressed to the lawyers at the firm's address. The law firm mailroom returned the notice, unopened, to the sender, and trial court clerk attempted no further mailing. After the time for state appeal expired, an Alabama Assistant Attorney General sent a letter directly to the defendant informing him of the missed deadline. The defendant contacted his mother who called Sullivan & Cromwell. Three lawyers there tried to persuade the state court to excuse the delay, but it refused.

The defendant filed for habeas corpus relief in the federal district court, but that court held it could not grant the relief because the defendant failed to meet a state procedural requirement. The issue before the U.S. Supreme Court was whether the defendant showed sufficient "cause" to excuse his procedural default. Justice Ginsburg, for the Court, acknowledged that the usual rule is that even a negligent lawyer-agent binds the defendant. Here, however, the lawyers "abandoned" the client without notice, thus severing the lawyer-client relationship and ending the agency relationship. This made the failure to appeal an "extraordinary circumstance" beyond the client's control and excused the procedural default. Justices Scalia and Thomas dissented, arguing that the criminal justice system depends on a presumption that lawyers' actions bind their client-defendants.

C. LIMITATIONS ON A LAWYER'S EFFORTS TO COLLECT A FEE

1. Should the ethics rules permit a lawyer to sue a client to collect a fee?

a. ABA Formal Opinion 250 (1943) upheld suits against clients, but without enthusiasm. Do you agree with the committee's view that "ours is a learned profession, not a mere money-getting trade"? ABA Model Code of Professional Responsibility, EC 2–23 provided that "suits to collect fees should be avoided."

b. Any legal prohibition on suits to collect legal fees is now ancient history, see Restatement Third, The Law Governing Lawyers § 42(1), although such suits often backfire against lawyers when clients use them as an occasion to file a counterclaim alleging professional malpractice.

c. Matter of Simon, 20 A.3d 421 (N.J. 2011), holds that, although a lawyer may sue a client for a fee after a case is over, to do so while the case is still pending creates a prohibited conflict of interest. The lawyer agreed with a family to represent the defendant in a murder case for a fee of $325 per hour. After being paid about $20,000 and having unpaid time of $50,000 in the case, the client's brother told the lawyer there "was no more money" and the client should take a plea." The lawyer sought court permission to withdraw, but the court denied the motion. He then sued the family for the unpaid fees after family members engaged in fraudulent conveyances to try to become judgment proof. Although the lawyer remained willing to conduct the defense, the trial judge said suing the family created a conflict of interest that required new counsel. The judge also referred the matter for discipline. In this discipline action, the New Jersey Supreme Court (citing Restatement § 7), agreed that principles of fiduciary duty limit the ways a lawyer may collect a fee. Over the dissent of a justice who pointed out that a solo practice criminal lawyer could be ruined by being put in such a financial bind, the court made it a disciplinary violation to "sue a present or existing client during active representation." Because the rules were formerly unclear on the point, however, the court imposed only a formal reprimand.

2. Does the lawyer's obligation to preserve client confidences and secrets prohibit the lawyer from establishing the elements of the lawyer's claim?

a. As you will see in later problems, a lawyer's duty to keep information about a client confidential is very strict. However, look at Model Rule 1.6(b)(5). What principle, if any, would justify sacrificing the client's interest in confidentiality in favor of furthering the lawyer's interest in getting paid?[24]

b. Restatement Third, The Law Governing Lawyers § 65, Comment *b*, argues:

---

[24] Lawyers' claims of a right to do so are not new. ABA Opinion 250 (1943) concluded that Canon 4 of the former ABA Model Code of Professional Responsibility did not prevent a lawyer from disclosing confidential information in order to attach the client's property to collect his fee. See also, Nakasian v. Incontrade, Inc., 409 F.Supp. 1220, 1224 (S.D.N.Y.1976) (in order to collect fee, lawyer may attach the funds of his clients, even where the attachment is facilitated by confidential information possessed by the lawyer).

"Without this exception, a lawyer could be deprived of important evidence to prove a rightful claim. Clients would thus sometimes be immune from honest claims for legal fees. Moreover, at least some disclosures necessary to establish a fee will not involve information that a client would find embarrassing or prejudicial, other than in defeating the client's position in the dispute."

Does this argument convince you? By failing to pay the lawyer's fee, has the client breached the contract that underlies the lawyer's confidentiality obligation?[25]

3.   In order to "encourage" the client's payment, may the lawyer threaten to reveal more client confidences than necessary to prove the lawyer's case?

a.   In re Disciplinary Proceeding Against Boelter, 985 P.2d 328 (Wash.1999), suspended a lawyer for six months for telling his client that failure to pay means "you forego the attorney-client privilege and I would be forced to reveal that you lied on your statements to the IRS and to the bank as to your financial condition. This would entail disclosure of the tapes of our conversations about your hidden assets. There is a federal statute, 18 U.S.C. § 1001, which provides for up to one year in jail for such perjury. The choice is yours." Fair warning about the firm's limited ability to disclose confidential information is permissible, the court said, but the "tape" was a fabrication and the fees claimed were excessive. The threats justified the lawyer's six-month suspension.

b.   In State ex rel. Counsel for Discipline of Nebraska Supreme Court v. Lopez Wilson, 634 N.W.2d 467 (Neb.2001), the lawyer represented a client in obtaining a visa and in filing for a divorce. But when the lawyer learned that the client was engaged in an intimate relationship with the lawyer's ex-wife, he withdrew and threatened both to tell the INS that the client's job status had changed and to reopen the prior divorce proceedings unless the client paid him for services that the lawyer had theretofore provided free of charge. In upholding a two-year suspension, the court stated that Canon 4 of the Model Code of Professional Responsibility allowed limited disclosure of client confidences in a suit to collect a legal fee, but it did not permit "violent threats" to disclose such information more generally.

c.   Are these cases consistent with the Model Rules? Look at Model Rule 1.6, Comment 14.

4.   Should a fee dispute between attorney and client be subject to mandatory arbitration at the request of the client?

a.   Several states require fee arbitration if the client wants it. Anderson v. Elliott, 555 A.2d 1042 (Me.1989), cert. denied, 493 U.S. 978 (1989), upheld the Maine requirement. The lawyer argued that arbitration denied him his constitutional right to a jury trial, but the

---

[25]   D.C. Bar Legal Ethics Committee, Opinion No. 298 (2000) says that a lawyer may use a collection agency to collect legal fees as long as the ethical standards of the agency is consistent with the lawyer's ethical standards and the lawyer only discloses the minimal information about the representation necessary to collect the fee. The opinion advised that the ethics rules prohibit the outright sale of client accounts receivable to a collection agency.

court held that that it must interpret that right in the context of the court's supervisory power over attorneys.

b.   In Guralnick v. Supreme Court of New Jersey, 747 F.Supp. 1109 (D.N.J.1990), aff'd, 961 F.2d 209 (3d Cir.1992), lawyers argued that a New Jersey system of fee arbitration that only a client may initiate unconstitutionally denied them due process, violated their Thirteenth Amendment rights and violated the antitrust laws as well. In a thoughtful opinion, the court rejected all such challenges.

c.   A. Fred Miller, P.C. v. Purvis, 921 P.2d 610 (Alaska 1996), held that the lack of judicial review of an arbitration award did not deny due process. The court agreed that judicial review on the merits is desirable in an arbitration process, but part of the purpose of arbitration is to achieve a quick, binding review of a dispute. Judicial review would put a burden on clients that the Constitution does not require. See also, Nodvin v. State Bar of Georgia, 544 S.E.2d 142 (Ga.2001) (upholds fee arbitration procedure).

d.   May a lawyer's engagement letter specify that the client must submit non-fee complaints about the lawyer to arbitration? Remember that a lawyer's suit for unpaid fees will often trigger a malpractice claim from the client who hopes to reach a compromise of the fee amount. ABA Formal Opinion 02–425 (2002) said that an arbitration clause, by itself, does not violate Rule 1.8(h). The opinion acknowledged that an attorney has a fiduciary duty under Rule 1.4(b) "to advise clients of the possible adverse consequences as well as the benefits that may arise from the execution of an agreement." Because a client potentially waives significant rights by agreeing to mandatory arbitration, the lawyer has a duty to explain the potential consequences of that "to the extent reasonably necessary to permit the client to make [an] informed decision about the contract." However, the opinion reasoned, because the arbitration clause only defines the forum in which the disgruntled client must proceed, it does not limit the lawyer's liability for malpractice.

D.   ATTORNEYS' LIENS AND OTHER SECURITY INTERESTS

1.   May the lawyer retain a client's property and papers until the client pays the lawyer's fee?

a.   In Sage Realty Corp. v. Proskauer Rose Goetz & Mendelsohn L.L.P., 689 N.E.2d 879 (N.Y.1997), a client who had paid over a million dollars in fees in a large financing transaction decided to switch lawyers. It asked the firm for its file, now totaling so many volumes that the index alone ran 58 pages. The firm turned over the closing documents, client-supplied papers and correspondence with third parties, but not its own internal work product. The New York Court of Appeals cited what is now § 43 of the Restatement Third, The Law Governing Lawyers, and held that the client is presumptively entitled to all its papers, subject to several exceptions. The lawyer should not turn over documents that might violate the firm's duty of nondisclosure owed to a third party, or the firm's duties otherwise imposed by law. The law firm also does not have to turn over firm documents intended for internal law office review and use (such as "documents containing attorneys' general or other assessment of the client, or tentative preliminary impressions of the legal or factual issues presented in the representation, recorded primarily for the purpose of giving internal direction to facilitate performance of the legal services entailed in that representation."). The court said that the firm may ordinarily charge the client for the cost of assembling and delivering the documents to the client.

b.   In many states, (California is a major exception), an attorney has a "retaining lien" that gives the lawyer a possessory interest in the client's papers and funds in the attorney's possession.[26] Restatement Third, The Law Governing Lawyers § 43, however, rejected the general availability of such a lien on the ground that "[a] broad retaining lien could impose pressure on a client disproportionate to the size or validity of the lawyer's fee claim." Do you think lawyers should have a right to a retaining lien?

c.   The significance of the retaining lien is greatest when the client desperately needs the papers—for example, where new counsel needs the files to prepare for trial. Pomerantz v. Schandler, 704 F.2d 681 (2d Cir.1983) (per curiam), found an exception to the attorney's retaining lien when the client had an urgent need for papers to defend a criminal case and lacked the means to pay the lawyer's fee.

d.   However, that exception is not broad. The whole purpose of a retaining lien is to put pressure on the client to pay the lawyer's bill. An "attorney's lien cannot otherwise be disregarded merely because the pressure it is supposed to exert becomes effective." 704 F.2d 681, 683.

e.   Thus, even the Restatement recognizes that "[a] client who fails to pay for the lawyer's work in preparing particular documents * * * ordinarily is not entitled to receive those documents." Restatement Third, The Law Governing Lawyers § 43, Comment c.

2.   In order to guarantee payment of a lawyer's fee, may the lawyer assert a lien on sums recovered on behalf of the client?

a.   Most states give the lawyer a right to assert a "charging lien" that gives the lawyer a right to apply the recovery in a case to payment of his or her fees. Restatement Third, The Law Governing Lawyers § 43, Comment d, explains that many states "recognize a charging lien without a contract" between the lawyer and client, but Restatement § 43(2) provides that there should be a written contract in order to safeguard the client. See also, Fletcher v. Davis, 90 P.3d 1216 (Cal.2004), which refuses to enforce an oral charging lien.

b.   The attorney must give notice of the lien to the person paying the judgment or settlement. Once she gives such notice, the person paying the judgment or settlement is liable for the attorney's fees if that person pays the entire judgment or settlement directly to the attorney's client. See Restatement Third, The Law Governing Lawyers § 43, Comment e.

---

[26] The retaining lien does not apply to property simply given to the lawyer for safekeeping. See Akers v. Akers, 46 N.W.2d 87 (Minn.1951) (evidence sustained finding that property was originally left with attorney for purpose of placing it beyond reach of defendant Akers and not for security for payment of attorney's fees). Similarly, a lawyer may not take excess funds deposited by the client for payment of court reporter charges and apply them to payment of the lawyer's unpaid fees. See State ex rel. Oklahoma Bar Ass'n v. Cummings, 863 P.2d 1164 (Okl.1993).

3.   May the engagement letter with a client give the lawyer a security interest in the property that is the subject matter of the litigation?

a.   Look at Model Rule 1.8(i). Why might such a security interest be suspect? Restatement Third, The Law Governing Lawyers § 36, Comment *b*, traces the prohibition to common law fears of champerty and maintenance, i.e., that wealthy lawyers would buy claims and clog the courts with litigation. If that were the only rationale, would you favor repeal of Model Rule 1.8(i)?

b.   However, the same Comment continues:

> "The justification for the rule in its present form is that a lawyer's ownership gives the lawyer an economic basis for claiming to control the prosecution and settlement of the claim and provides an incentive for the lawyer to relegate the client to a subordinate position. * * * The rule also prevents a lawyer from disguising an unreasonably large fee, violative of § 34, by buying part of the claim for a low price."

Does that give you more confidence that Model Rule 1.8(i) has a place in modern law?[27]

4.   Is Model Rule 1.8(i) the only Rule that governs when the lawyer may take an interest in the client's property?

a.   Hawk v. State Bar of California, 754 P.2d 1096 (Cal.1988), says that when a lawyer takes any interest in property of the client as security for payment of the lawyer's fee, the arrangement is a business transaction with the client subject to the California equivalent of Model Rule 1.8(a). The court implies that in some cases the arrangement is a proper way of helping the client afford necessary legal services. If the lawyer ignores the conflict of interest concerns and does not comply with the safeguards of the cited rules, however, he or she will be subject to discipline. In this case, the court suspended attorney Hawk for six months and put him on probation for four years.

b.   ABA Formal Opinion 02–427 (May 31, 2002) also said that "there is nothing inherently unethical in a lawyer asking a client to provide security for payment of fees." Such a transaction is subject to the standards in Model Rule 1.8(a), however, and if the lawyer takes possession of the security, the lawyer must safeguard it as provided in Model Rule 1.15(a). Further, if the client transfers property to the lawyer as payment of the fee, the lawyer may retain only so much of the proceeds as represents a reasonable fee. The lawyer must treat any excess value as property belonging to the client. [28]

---

[27] The Comment continues: "The prohibition * * * is limited to matters in litigation. Thus, * * * a lawyer may acquire an ownership or other proprietary interest in a client's patent when retained to file a patent application, while * * * the lawyer could not acquire such an interest if retained to bring a patent-infringement suit. The difference in treatment is largely historical." In other words, in litigation, the lawyer cannot use the contingent fee to become part owner of the property such that he can prevent settlement. Assuming the fee is otherwise reasonable, he can become a 10% owner of a patent as a charge for filing the patent. If there is litigation, as long as the lawyer is not an owner of the patent, he can charge 10% of the value of the patent as his contingent fee, but he cannot become a 10% owner of the patent because that would make him a co-plaintiff and allow the laywer to prevent settlement.

[28] ABA Formal Opinion 02–427 (May 31, 2002) advises: "As indicated by Comment [16], it is the intent of Rule 1.8(i) to permit a contractual lien in the subject of litigation to be

PROBLEM 7

THE DUTY OF CONFIDENTIALITY

The ability to talk freely and confidentially is one of the central elements defining the relationship between lawyer and client. What lawyers can find confusing, however, is the fact that their confidentiality obligation derives from three different bodies of law:

1.   The attorney-client privilege is part of the law of evidence and allows a lawyer and client to refuse to testify about communications between them, made in confidence, for the purpose of giving or receiving legal advice.

2.   Work product immunity, which arises out of the law of civil procedure, protects a lawyer's work done in anticipation of litigation from otherwise applicable requirements to disclose relevant information, typically during pre-trial discovery.

3.   The professional duty of confidentiality, on the other hand, found in Model Rule 1.6, broadly forbids a lawyer from using or revealing information relating to the representation other than for the client's benefit. This duty grows out of fiduciary obligations of trustees and agents.

The first three topics in this problem try to help you keep those concepts straight. You will see that the scope and character of each of the protections can vary considerably in a given case. The fourth topic examines how privilege and confidentiality protection might be lost and suggests the care a lawyer must take against that eventuality.

FACTS

Your longtime client, John Carter, recently came to your office to tell you that he expects the person who bought his house will sue him. When the buyer expressly asked him, just before sale, if the house had a dry basement, he said yes. Now, he admits to you that, although the basement had never flooded in the five years he lived there, a prior owner had warned Carter that the basement regularly flooded after a heavy rain. There was such a rain this year, shortly after he sold the house, and some of the buyer's expensive electronic equipment suffered major damage.

You were able to interview the prior owner of the house shortly before his death. He confirmed to you what he had told Carter about the basement's tendency to flood. You have notes of that interview in which you comment on the former owner's likely credibility at trial. Later, at a party at a friend's home, Carter's banker casually mentions to you that Carter is in bad

---

acquired independently of Rule 1.8(a), as long as acquiring such a lien is not inconsistent with an applicable statute or rule. Rule 1.8(a) should not be regarded as a rule that is inconsistent with Rule 1.8(i) and we conclude that it does not apply to the acquisition by contract of a security interest in the subject of litigation for fees."

financial condition. You mentally filed that away as important to your settlement posture in case Carter is sued.

The buyer has now filed suit against Carter. The buyer has subpoenaed your notes of your interview with the prior owner. Someone else has asked you informally if the rumors that Carter has suffered financial reverses are true.

QUESTIONS

A. INFORMATION PROTECTED BY THE ATTORNEY-CLIENT PRIVILEGE

1. Protecting information covered by the attorney-client privilege is one of a lawyer's most basic obligations. How will you know such information when you see it?

a. Restatement Third, The Law Governing Lawyers § 68 says that the attorney-client privilege protects "(1) a communication, (2) made between privileged persons,[29] (3) in confidence, (4) for the purpose of obtaining or providing legal assistance for the client."

b. Proposed Federal Rule 503[30] goes into more detail about what the privilege protects and does not protect:

"(a) Definitions. As used in this rule:

"(1) A 'client' is a person, public officer, or corporation, association, or other organization or entity, either public or private, who is rendered professional legal services by a lawyer, or who consults a lawyer with a view to obtaining professional legal services from him.

"(2) A 'lawyer' is a person authorized, or reasonably believed by the client to be authorized, to practice law in any state or nation.

"(3) A 'representative of the lawyer' is one employed to assist the lawyer in the rendition of professional legal services.

"(4) A communication is 'confidential' if not intended to be disclosed to third persons other than those to whom disclosure is in furtherance of the rendition of professional legal services to the client or those reasonably necessary for the transmission of the communication.

"(b) General Rule of Privilege. A client has a privilege to refuse to disclose and to prevent any other person from disclosing confidential communications made for the purpose of facilitating the rendition of professional legal services to the client, (1) between himself or his representative and his lawyer or his lawyer's representative, or (2) between his lawyer and the lawyer's representative, or (3) by him or his lawyer to a

---

[29] "Privileged persons" are "the client (including a prospective client), the client's lawyer, agents of either who facilitate communication between them, and agents of the lawyer who facilitate the representation." Restatement Third, The Law Governing Lawyers § 70.

[30] When Congress approved the Federal Rules of Evidence, it did not enact any of the 13 rules dealing with privileges, including Proposed Rule 503, see Fed. Rules of Evidence, Pub.L. 93–595 (Jan. 2, 1975). The reasons for non-enactment did not reflect on the merits of Proposed Rule 503, which is, in general, a fair summary of the law of most states.

lawyer representing another in a matter of common interest, or (4) between representatives of the client or between the client and a representative of the client, or (5) between lawyers representing the client.

"(c) Who May Claim the Privilege. The privilege may be claimed by the client, his guardian or conservator, the personal representative of a deceased client, or the successor, trustee, or similar representative of a corporation, association, or other organization, whether or not in existence. The person who was the lawyer at the time of the communication may claim the privilege but only on behalf of the client. His authority to do so is presumed in the absence of evidence to the contrary.

"(d) Exceptions. There is no privilege under this rule:

"(1) Furtherance of crime or fraud. If the services of the lawyer were sought or obtained to enable or aid anyone to commit or plan to commit what the client knew or reasonably should have known to be a crime or fraud; or

"(2) Claimants through same deceased client. As to a communication relevant to an issue between parties who claim through the same deceased client, regardless of whether the claims are by testate or intestate succession or by *inter vivos* transactions; or

"(3) Breach of duty by lawyer or client. As to a communication relevant to an issue of breach of duty by the lawyer to his client or by the client to his lawyer; or

"(4) Document attested by lawyer. As to a communication relevant to an issue concerning an attested document to which the lawyer is an attesting witness; or

"(5) Joint clients. As to a communication relevant to a matter of common interest between two or more clients if the communication was made by any of them to a lawyer retained or consulted in common, when offered in an action between any of the clients."

2. Because the privilege applies only to certain communications, there is substantial litigation over when the client may assert it. Does the privilege apply in the following situations?

a. In Commonwealth v. Mrozek, 657 A.2d 997 (Pa.Super.Ct.1995), a potential client called the lawyer's office to ask the receptionist for an appointment because "I've just committed a homicide." The court held that statement to the receptionist (a non-lawyer) was privileged because she was an employee of the lawyer whose job it was to communicate with clients and potential clients.

b. In D'Alessio v. Gilberg, 617 N.Y.S.2d 484 (N.Y.App.Div.1994), the question was the privileged character of the client's identity. A man who caused a hit-and-run accident consulted a lawyer about the accident. The victim wanted to sue the man but did not know his name. The identity of a client is normally not privileged; it is the first thing the lawyer discloses when entering an appearance in a case. In this situation, however, the lawyer had not yet entered an appearance and revealing the client's identity could cause the client to be prosecuted criminally and to be sued civilly. Thus, the court held the identity privileged.

c.   In re Grand Jury Subpoenas Dated March 9, 2001, 179 F.Supp.2d 270 (S.D.N.Y.2001), sought production of documents related to the effort by lawyers for Marc Rich and Pincus Green to get them a presidential pardon. Since 1983, Rich and Green were living abroad. They refused to return to the United States to face criminal charges. Prosecutors in the Southern District of New York refused to drop the charges, so the defendants' lawyers developed a network of contacts with then-President Clinton who pardoned the two men in early 2001. In this case, the Justice Department sought production of documents as part of its investigation of circumstances surrounding the pardon. The court held that materials related to procuring Rich's pardon were not privileged because the lawyers were acting as lobbyists, not lawyers, once the client decided to seek a pardon. The court held that because nonlawyers can engage in lobbying, the lawyers' communications were not for the purpose of rendering legal assistance to Rich. Do you agree? Needless to say, this opinion has worried many lawyers who do things for clients, e.g., lobbying, that non-lawyers could also legally do.

d.   Al Odah v. United States, 346 F.Supp.2d 1 (D.D.C.2004), considered the scope of the privilege for communications between Guantanamo Bay detainees and lawyers working on their habeas corpus petitions. Pursuant to the September 14, 2001, Joint Resolution of Congress authorizing the president to use "all means necessary" to defeat terrorism, the FBI promulgated a set of monitoring procedures for "designated detainees" held at Guantanamo Bay. Under these procedures, a "privilege team"—one or more intelligence or law enforcement agents or Department of Defense attorneys screened from other aspects of the detainees' cases—would "monitor [and record] oral communications in real time between counsel and the detainee during any meetings," and conduct a "classification review" of all written materials brought in or out of any such meetings, including the attorney's notes. The petitioner, one of three "designated detainees" held at Guantanamo Bay, challenged the procedures as an impermissible infringement on the attorney-client privilege. The court recognized that the government had significant national security concerns with respect to certain detainees. In order to balance these concerns with the confidentiality required by the privilege, the court previously required detainees' counsel to obtain the necessary security clearances for access to the information the government believes that the detainee may have. Thereafter, information the attorney received from the detainee in confidence would fall under the protection of the privilege, but if the detainee disclosed information "involving future events that threaten national security or involve immediate violence," the attorney would be *required* to disclose the information. The government's attempt at more extensive monitoring, however, "fl[ies] in the face" of the principles behind the attorney-client privilege, so the court did not allow real-time monitoring of attorney-client meetings.

e.   In Stengart v. Loving Care Agency, Inc., 973 A.2d 390 (N.J. Super.Ct.App.Div. 2009), a company executive resigned her position and sued the company for violating anti-discrimination laws. Prior to resigning, the plaintiff communicated via email with her attorney regarding her case. She sent emails from her personal email account that she had accessed from a company-owned laptop. After her resignation, the company's counsel made a copy of the laptop hard drive and discovered the emails. The plaintiff objected, but the trial court refused to treat the communications as privileged, because the company had a policy giving it the right to intercept and monitor email. The appellate division agreed that employer handbooks can create unilateral contracts with employees, but the court must interpret them according to the reasonable expectations of employees and must be reasonable to be enforceable. The court found that the policy did not support the company's claim of ownership of the personal communications. Citing Thyroff v. Nationwide Mut. Ins. Co., 864 N.E.2d 1272 (N.Y. 2007), the court reasoned that a company computer used to send personal emails is analogous to a filing cabinet; the employer offends property rights when it searches and claims ownership of an employee's private papers or communications. In an electronic age, it can be difficult to segregate company from personal business, and employees have a reasonable expectation of privacy in their personal emails regarding attorney-client matters. Therefore, a policy where the company claims to own all personal communications because they own the computer that the employee used does *not* serve a "legitimate business interest."

3.   With all this in mind, go back to the facts in our problem. May the other lawyer force you, Carter's lawyer, to testify that your client, John Carter, admitted to you that he had lied to the buyer of his home about the tendency of the basement to flood?

a.   Why should the law protect communications with a lawyer that the lawyer and client used to help the client avoid the consequences of his wrongful conduct? Professor Wigmore says:

> "In order to promote freedom of consultation of legal advisers by clients, the apprehension of compelled disclosure by the legal advisers must be removed; hence the law must prohibit such disclosure except on the client's consent." 8 Wigmore, Evidence § 2291 at 545 (McNaughton rev. 1961).

Are you convinced?

b.   Because the exercise of the attorney-client privilege so clearly conflicts with the search for truth, commentators and courts have long held that the privilege "ought to be strictly confined within the narrowest possible limits consistent with the logic of its principle." 8 Wigmore, supra § 2291, at 554. Thus:

> (1) While the court will not force Carter to testify about the content of his conversation with you, the fact that he talked to you about what he knew will not prevent Carter himself from being compelled to testify about his knowledge of the house's tendency to flood.

(2) The attorney-client privilege will not prevent you from being compelled to produce your notes of the statement by the former owner. Do you see why?[31]

(3) Likewise, the privilege will not protect against your revealing what you heard about your client from the banker. When you look at the factors required before a statement is protected by the attorney-client privilege, you should see several reasons why this is so.

(4) If Carter told you that he planned to lie to the buyer *before* he did so, would that statement be privileged? Look at the crime-fraud exception in Proposed Federal Rule of Evidence 503(d)(1), supra.

c.   Lawyers often glibly cite the "privilege" either when it doesn't apply or when they are relying on some other doctrine. The attorney-client privilege would protect only one kind of material in this problem against testimony from the lawyer. If the lawyer is not to reveal other facts in the problem, it must be on the basis of some other principles.

B.   INFORMATION PROTECTED BY WORK PRODUCT IMMUNITY

1.   What constitutes a lawyer's "work product" and what are the consequences of so designating it?

a.   Restatement Third, The Law Governing Lawyers § 87 says:

"(1) Work product consists of tangible material or its intangible equivalent in unwritten or oral form, other than underlying facts, prepared by a lawyer for litigation then in progress or in reasonable anticipation of future litigation.

"(2) Opinion work product consists of the opinions or mental impressions of a lawyer; all other work product is ordinary work product.

"(3) Except for material which by applicable law is not so protected, work product is immune from discovery or other compelled disclosure * * *."

b.   Work product immunity is the legacy of Hickman v. Taylor, 329 U.S. 495 (1947). Construing the proper scope of discovery, the Court wrote: "Not even the most liberal of discovery theories can justify unwarranted inquiries into the files and the mental impressions of an attorney." The Court went on to say that where one side has information other than mental impressions that was "essential to the preparation of [the other side's] case," it could be discovered "and production might be justified where the witnesses are no longer available or can be reached only with difficulty." The doctrine is now codified in Federal Rules of Civil Procedure, Rule 26(b)(3).

c.   In re Cendant Corp. Securities Litigation, 343 F.3d 658 (3d Cir.2003), involved "Dr. Phil" McGraw in the role in which Oprah found him, that of a trial consultant who helped lawyers and witnesses

---

[31]   The work product doctrine may protect the notes against disclosure, but the attorney-client privilege will not. Because the attorney-client privilege provides absolute protection while the work product immunity is subject to a necessity exception, the distinction is important to understand.

prepare a master plan for their case. In deposition, a lawyer asked one of the witnesses how often Dr. Phil met with him and what they discussed. The Third Circuit sustained a claim that the information constituted protected work product. Work product protects an attorney's mental processes and tactical planning, the court said, and that includes the mental processes of the attorney's agents and consultants whose work was in anticipation of litigation. Moreover, the information constituted opinion work product, which would require exceptional circumstances before the court would order discovery. See also, In re Grand Jury Subpoenas, 265 F.Supp.2d 321 (S.D.N.Y.2003) (grants work product protection to suggestions of public relations consultant hired by lawyers for a potential criminal defendant).[32]

2. Is any of the information in this problem protected by work product immunity?

a. What about the interview with the former owner? Did you interview him in anticipation of litigation? Does it matter whether the anticipated litigation was this particular lawsuit?

b. Should the fact that the former owner is now dead mean that the notes you took will now be discoverable? A witness' death does not itself affect the character of the notes as work product. However, under Federal Rule 26(b)(3), a "party seeking discovery [may show it] has substantial need of the materials in preparation of the party's case and that the party is unable without undue hardship to obtain the substantial equivalent of the material by other means."

3. Is it relevant whether the notes of the discussion with the now-deceased former owner are "ordinary work product" or "opinion work product"?

a. Look at the language of Hickman v. Taylor quoted above; the party may discover "ordinary" work product after showing "substantial need." However, according to Restatement Third, The Law Governing Lawyers § 89:

> "[O]pinion work product is immune from discovery or other compelled disclosure unless * * * extraordinary circumstances justify disclosure."

b. Should the fact that the former owner is now dead constitute such "extraordinary circumstances" that compelled disclosure is justified? Restatement § 89, Comment *d*, says that "the concept of 'extraordinary circumstances' has never been intelligibly defined. It apparently signifies unwillingness on the part of tribunals to put the work-product immunity on quite the same footing as the attorney-client privilege."

c. In re Green Grand Jury Proceedings, 492 F.3d 976 (8th Cir.2007), drew another important distinction between ordinary and opinion work product. The defendant gave his lawyer a benign account of his plans but then used the lawyer's advice and documents to engage in illegal conduct. The government moved to compel the lawyer to

---

[32] In 2010, the Supreme Court approved a modification to Federal Rule of Civil Procedure Rule 26(b)(4) that expands work product protection of drafts of expert reports and communications between counsel and the expert. However, parties can still discover communications relating to expert compensation, assumptions the lawyer provided to (and relied upon by) the expert, and the facts the expert has considered.

testify before the grand jury and bring relevant documents, urging that the crime-fraud exception to work product immunity applied. The court held that the client's illegal conduct denied the client the right to assert work product protection for 36 of the documents. However, because the lawyer did not know the client's true plans, the lawyer had independent work product protection for the lawyer's opinion work product contained in the documents. The client's crime or fraud did not taint that protection.

d.   How should work product immunity apply in this problem? If you make sure to comment in your notes about the witness' credibility, should the notes be absolutely immune from discovery?

C.   THE LAWYER'S PROFESSIONAL OBLIGATION OF CONFIDENTIALITY

1.   May you respond to the informal inquiry about your client's financial situation? Is the chance information you learned at a party something you must keep confidential unless ordered by a court to disclose it?

a.   Is the information about your client's financial situation within either the attorney-client privilege or work product immunity? Why or why not?

b.   Look at Model Rule 1.6(a). Does the information you received from the Carter's banker qualify as "relating to the representation"? Remember, you have said to yourself that the information may affect your settlement posture.

c.   Look at ABA Model Code of Professional Responsibility, DR 4–101(A). Is the information you learned at the party a "confidence" of the client? Is it a "secret"? Would it tend to embarrass the client? Did you learn it as part of the "professional relationship"?

2.   What does it mean to say that Rule 1.6 protects the information against disclosure even if the evidentiary privilege does not apply? Does it only mean that the lawyer may not volunteer the information to others?

a.   If the opposing party calls you to testify about what you heard at the party about Carter's financial situation, will the court require you to reveal the information? It is important to see that one of the important distinctions between information that is "privileged" and information protected only by the obligation of "confidentiality" is that a court may require a lawyer to testify about the latter. See Model Rule 1.6(b)(6); Restatement Third, The Law Governing Lawyers § 63.

b.   In Matter of Goebel, 703 N.E.2d 1045 (Ind.1998), the lawyer represented a criminal defendant while the lawyer's partner was handling an unrelated guardianship. By chance, the husband of the guardianship client was to be a prosecution witness in the criminal case. The criminal client asked the guardianship client's address. To prove he didn't know, the lawyer showed the criminal client an envelope returned because it had the wrong address. However, even the wrong address was enough to help the criminal client find the prosecution witness and kill him. The court said that the incorrect address was "information relating to the representation" of the guardianship client. Thus, the court publicly reprimanded the lawyer for revealing it.

c.   Iowa Sup. Ct. Attorney Disciplinary Bd. v. Marzen, 779 N.W.2d 757 (Iowa 2010), found that a lawyer breached the duty of confidentiality even though the information was publicly available. The court appointed a lawyer to represent a woman in a hospitalization commitment proceeding. He later agreed to represent her in other matters, including a dispute with her mother and a child-custody proceeding. During an interview with a television news reporter, the lawyer revealed the fact that the woman had previously sued and received a settlement from a parole officer whom she claimed had engaged in sexual misconduct. The lawyer argued he had done nothing wrong because information about the prior suit was available from public sources, but the court disagreed. The ethical requirement of maintaining client confidentiality is broader than information protected by the attorney-client privilege. The lawyer intended his comments to defame his own client and the disclosure justified his suspension from practice. Notice that the information was available but not "generally known," the standard used in Rule 1.9(c)(1). If a lawyer may only disclose information that is generally known about a *former* client, surely a lawyer may not disclose more about a *current* client.

d.   Louisiana Crisis Assistance Center v. Marzano-Lesnevich, 2011 WL 5878159 (E.D.La.2011), makes clear that confidentiality obligations can apply to information you learn while a law student. A student served as an unpaid summer law clerk giving assistance to indigent capital defendants. After law school, she became a writer and published essays and fictional works about the death penalty and sex crimes. The director of the center where she had worked recognized confidential client information in her work, and after the lawyer refused to cease using what the center believed was confidential information, the center sued her for breach of contract and breach of fiduciary duty. The court found several incidents about which she wrote represented confidential client information, and a jury could find her contract with the center prohibited her from disclosing it.

3.   How much affirmative effort must a lawyer undertake to preserve the confidentiality of communications with clients and others?

a.   Lawyers must carefully maintain the confidentiality of their oral and written communications with clients. See Restatement Third, The Law Governing Lawyers § 60(1)(b): "[T]he lawyer must take steps reasonable in the circumstances to protect confidential client information against impermissible use or disclosure." That principle is now incorporated in Model Rule 1.6(c): "A lawyer shall make reasonable efforts to prevent the inadvertent or unauthorized disclosure of, or unauthorized access to, information relating to the representation of a client."

b.   Comment 18 makes clear that a lawyer who acts reasonably does not violate Rule 1.6(c) when inadvertent or unauthorized disclosures occur. The determination of reasonableness depends upon the following factors: "the sensitivity of the information, the likelihood of disclosure if additional safeguards are not employed, the costs of employing additional safeguards, the difficulty of implementing the safeguards, and the extent to which the safeguards adversely affect the lawyer's ability to represent clients." Model Rule 1.6(c), Comment 18.

Does this give lawyers too much leeway or does it impose different standards of conduct for different clients? How much do you know about the security of information transmitted on your phone or computer?

c.   ABA Formal Opinion 99–413 (Mar. 10, 1999) discussed sending unencrypted email and concluded that a failure to use encryption neither violates the duty of confidentiality nor waives the privilege unless the client insists on, or unusual circumstances require, heightened security. Statutes prohibit illegal interception of email communications, the opinion said, so lawyer and client have a reasonable expectation of privacy. Further, the risk of interception is no greater than that inherent in landline phones. Several state bar opinions come to the same conclusion. See ABA Model Rule 1.6, Comment 19: a lawyer need not "use special security measures if the method of communication affords a reasonable expectation of privacy."

Could lawyers effectively carry on their practice in modern times if the rule were different? Is the rule likely to change if problems of electronic spying make law firms' technology potential points of entry into client files?

d.   New York State Bar Opinion 782 (Dec. 8, 2004) looked at a lawyer's duty to avoid sending metadata in documents transmitted electronically. Metadata is hidden text generated and saved in computer-prepared documents that may contain privileged information, legal strategies, information embarrassing to clients, legal advice, and other protected information. The opinion first declared that New York law imposes a duty to use reasonable care to prevent inadvertent disclosures of client confidences and secrets, even those in documents transmitted over the Internet. Because computer technologies differ, the opinion could not lay down absolute rules, but it said that what constitutes reasonable care depends on the circumstances. Lawyers need to keep up to date on changing technologies. In determining what are reasonable precautions, lawyers should consider (1) the document's subject matter; (2) whether the lawyer created document from a template used in other clients' cases; (3) whether there are multiple drafts of the document with comments from multiple sources; (4) whether the document contains client confidences; and (5) the identity of the intended recipients of the document.[33] We return to metadata issues in Problem 24, *infra*.

e.   State Bar of California Standing Committee on Professional Responsibility and Conduct, Formal Opinion No. 2012-184 (2012), considered what special confidentiality obligations a lawyer with a "virtual" law practice might have. In such a practice, clients communicate with the lawyer through a secure portal that is password protected and encrypted. The Opinion says that the lawyer's ethical duties are the same in such a practice as in a more traditional one. The lawyer is not required to become a technology expert, but she must "have a basic understanding of the protections afforded by the technology she uses." As technology changes, security standards will also change. The lawyer must keep abreast of such changed standards,

---

[33] See also, ABA Formal Opinion 06–442 (Aug. 5, 2006) (describes ways to remove ("scrub") metadata from documents but "a lawyer must not alter a document when it would be unlawful or unethical to do so").

lest practices that are sufficient today might become outdated. See also, ABA Rule 1.1, Comment 8.

f.   Many traditional law firms have placed client files on servers accessible remotely by lawyers and clients. The storage of confidential client information on computer networks exposes those files to theft or destruction by cyber thieves and hackers. Arizona Bar Opinion 05–04 requires that lawyers take "competent and reasonable steps" to secure the client information from theft or destruction. Such steps may include the use of firewall, password, and encryption technology to prevent unauthorized access to the network. See also, N.Y. State Bar Ass'n Comm. on Professional Ethics, Opinion 842 (2010) (lawyer may store information in an online "cloud" computer system that the lawyer has taken reasonable care to assure is secure); Iowa State Bar Ass'n Committee on Ethics and Practice Guidelines, Ethics Opinion 11-01: Use of Software as a Service—Cloud Computing (Sept. 9, 2011); Mass. Bar Ass'n Committee on Professional Ethics, Opinion 12–03 (May 17, 2012) (approving storing client information with reliable third-party providers).

4.   What are the boundaries of a lawyer's duty of confidentiality? Is the lawyer required never to disclose information relating to representation of the client?

a.   Sandwiched between Rule 1.6(a) and (c) are seven situations where the Rule authorizes the lawyer to reveal otherwise confidential client information "to the extent the lawyer reasonably believes necessary." These exceptions will arise in many later problems, but they all involve disclosure to protect third parties, to allow a lawyer to operate her practice, and to comply with the lawyer's other ethical obligations.

b.   Before its amendment in 2002, Model Rule 1.6(b)(1) only let a lawyer disclose "to prevent the client from committing a criminal act that the lawyer believes is likely to result in imminent death or substantial bodily harm." Even before 2002, however, many states permittedᴄor even requiredᴄa lawyer to make disclosure to save the life of a third party.

Look at Model Rule 1.6(b)(1) today.[34] Does the rule require that what you are disclosing be an act of the client? Is your authority to disclose limited to criminal acts? Must the conduct occur in the future or only have future effects? Does the rule require that the adverse effects occur within any particular time period? Model Rule 1.6, Comment 6, makes clear that the drafters clearly intended these changes.[35]

c.   Until 2003, the ABA House of Delegates had consistently rejected any proposed authority for a lawyer to reveal information to prevent or rectify a fraudulent act of the client, even an act "that the

[34]   Current Model Rule 1.6(b)(1) comes directly from Restatement Third, The Law Governing Lawyers § 66(1): "A lawyer may use or disclose confidential client information when the lawyer reasonably believes such use or disclosure is necessary to prevent reasonably certain death or serious bodily harm to a person."

[35]   In 2004, California adopted its Rule 3–100. It is slightly less broad than Model Rule 1.6(b)(1), but it allows an attorney to disclose confidential client information if "necessary to prevent a criminal act that the member reasonably believes is likely to result in death of, or substantial bodily harm to, an individual."

lawyer reasonably believes is likely to result * * * in substantial injury to the financial interests or property of another."[36] Until 2003, the Model Rules had limited lawyers to "noisy withdrawal" in such cases. The idea was that, pursuant to Model Rule 1.16(b) & (c), a lawyer should withdraw and then send a notice to others with whom the lawyer had dealt in the matter, saying something like: "I have withdrawn from this matter for ethical reasons." Some lawyers objected that this withdrawal was "flying a red flag" and prejudiced their client's interests. However, the preʙ2003 Comments specifically approved a "noisy" notice of withdrawal, and the present Rules still refer to it.[37]

d.   What if you, the lawyer, want ethics advice from a lawyer in another firm about your own obligations in a particular matter? May you discuss the issues in the matter with the other lawyer without violating your duty of confidentiality and forfeiting the privilege? Look at Model Rule 1.6(b)(4) & Comment 9.

ABA Formal Opinion 98–411 (1998) acknowledged that such consultations, made typically without fee and without intending to create an additional lawyer-client relationship, are often useful and in the interest of the client. However, the opinion tells the lawyer to: (1) do so in hypothetical terms, (2) get permission from the client if the consultation might put the client at risk, (3) not consult a lawyer who might represent the adverse party, and (4) obtain assurances of confidentiality for the information.

e.   We considered Model Rule 1.6(b)(5) in Problem 5. Do you agree that without the ability to reveal at least some confidential client information, a lawyer would be unable to respond even to unfounded charges of misconduct?

f.   If a court orders the lawyer to testify about confidential information that the lawyer believes is protected by the attorney-client privilege or work product immunity, must the lawyer resist the order to testify? Is a lawyer required to go to jail for contempt of court rather than provide the testimony? Look at Model Rule 1.6(b)(6) and Comment 15. Does the approach outlined there make sense to you?

g.   Model Rule 1.6(b)(7) was added in 2012. Do you agree that it is a necessary and useful addition? You should be better able to answer that question when you study conflicts of interest in Chapter 4.

D. HOW LEGAL PROTECTION AGAINST DISCLOSURE CAN BE LOST

1. Should disclosure of privileged information outside the confidential relationship forfeit the attorney-client privilege?

a.   If the client, by mistake or otherwise, tells an outsider—even a trusted friend—the content of your confidential conversations with him, the attorney-client privilege as to those conversations will be lost for all time. Restatement Third, The Law Governing Lawyers § 79. If the

---

[36] But before 2003, Restatement Third, The Law Governing Lawyers § 67(1)(d), had said that lawyers had authority to disclose in such cases, at least if "the client has employed or is employing the lawyer's services in the matter in which the crime or fraud is committed." See also, state rules on this issue in Appendix A, "Ethics Rules on Client Confidences," that comes after the Model Rules in the Standards Supplement.

[37] Provisions that now allude to a notice of withdrawal are in Model Rule 1.2, Comment 10 and Model Rule 4.1, Comment 3.

client reveals some privileged information, the privilege often will be lost at least for all information needed to put the privileged material into context. Indeed, the court may construe the waiver even more broadly. See Restatement Third, The Law Governing Lawyers § 79, Comment f (subject matter waiver).

b. Suppose your revelation of privileged information is made in settlement negotiations, i.e., you say, "I have told my client to be willing to accept $50,000." Typically, such a revelation—whether by lawyer or client—will result in waiver of the privilege. See, e.g., United States v. Martin, 773 F.2d 579 (4th Cir.1985) (attempt to settle tax case).

c. Would revelation in a settlement discussion ordinarily violate your professional obligation of confidentiality? Look at Model Rule 1.6(a). A lawyer may make disclosures that are "impliedly authorized to carry out the representation." The fact that disclosure does not violate the obligation of confidentiality has no effect on whether it forfeits the attorney-client privilege.

d. In Center Partners, Ltd. v. Growth Head GP, LLC, 981 N.E.2d 845 (Ill. 2012), the parties (while negotiating the acquisition of a shopping center developer) disclosed to each other some of their lawyers' advice about the transaction. This case involved an alleged breach of duties that the buyers owed to the seller. The buyer used a non-traditional business entity to acquire some assets, and the seller wanted access to what the buyer's lawyer told them about the entity and their duties under it. The court acknowledged that the Reporters Notes to § 79 of Restatement (Third), The Law Governing Lawyers says that most courts find a subject matter waiver in such out-of-court disclosure cases, but the Illinois Supreme Court rejected that approach. The point of subject matter waiver in litigation, the court said, is to give the trier of fact the full context of what the person or entity disclosed. The fact that the parties to a business deal may talk about what their lawyers have told them as they negotiate the deal should not require them to disclose advice that the parties are not asserting as relevant in this litigation.

e. Mohawk Industries, Inc. v. Carpenter, 558 U.S. 100, 130 S.Ct. 599, 175 L.Ed.2d 458 (2009), decided the important practical question whether a party may take an interlocutory appeal of an order requiring disclosure of a communication arguably protected by the attorney-client privilege. The Supreme Court held that an order is only immediately reviewable under the collateral order doctrine if it "(1) conclusively determines the disputed question; (2) resolves an important issue completely separate from the merits of the action; and (3) is effectively unreviewable on appeal from a final judgment," citing Cohen v. Beneficial Industrial Loan Corp., 337 U.S. 541 (1949). This test focuses on the entire class of claims, and not the individualized order in a particular case. Under the test, the order did not meet the third prong because courts can review orders that are adverse to the attorney-client privilege following a final judgment. On appeal, a court could find an order regarding the privilege erroneous, vacate the judgment, and remand for a new trial where the court excludes the "privileged material and its fruits."

The Court asserted that the risk that a trial court may order disclosure probably will not reduce the incentives for lawyers and clients to communicate fully under the anticipated benefit of a broad attorney-client privilege. A litigant facing an injurious or novel privilege ruling may seek certification of the order for interlocutory appeal, seek a writ of mandamus, or refuse to comply, thereby having the trial court impose sanctions or hold the party in contempt so as to seek post-judgment review of the order. Even if the damage done to some litigants was "only imperfectly reparable" upon review of a final judgment, the Court said, it is inappropriate to make disclosure orders immediately appealable as of right. Do you agree?

2.   What should happen if a lawyer or client inadvertently reveals confidential client information? Suppose, for example, the lawyer's secretary mistakenly faxes a highly confidential memo to opposing counsel instead of to the client?

a.   Restatement Third, The Law Governing Lawyers § 79, Comment *h*, says that a privilege "waiver does not result if the client or other disclosing person took precautions reasonable in the circumstances to guard against such disclosure." See, e.g., In re Reorganization of Electric Mutual Liability Ins. Co. (Bermuda), 681 N.E.2d 838 (Mass.1997) (if the client could show that adequate protective steps were taken to preserve the confidentiality of the information, the disclosure would be presumed not to have been voluntary).

b.   However, the courts have often found waiver of the privilege or work product where a lawyer was insufficiently attentive to guarding information against disclosure. United States v. Gangi, 1 F.Supp.2d 256 (S.D.N.Y.1998), involved a government strategy memorandum in a securities and bank fraud case that was mistakenly handed to a magistrate judge in open court in Arizona in the belief it was a copy of the indictment. In fact, however, it contained highly confidential wiretap material and information about witnesses. It bore the legend "This Document Contains Grand Jury Material" but it was not otherwise marked confidential or privileged. The judge turned the document over to defense counsel, it got into the hands of other corporate officers, and it was in the public court file for three weeks. Only when the case was moved to New York did the government realize the mistake and ask for the return of all copies of the document. Under these circumstances, the court held the privilege was waived, although it did permit redacting a limited amount of sensitive information. See also, S.E.C. v. Cassano, 189 F.R.D. 83 (S.D.N.Y.1999) (erroneously disclosed 100–page trial memo cannot regain its attorney-client privilege and work product character).

c.   In Amgen v. Hoechst Marion Roussel, Inc., 190 F.R.D. 287 (D.Mass.2000), the defense counsel inadvertently produced a box of over 3200 pages of privileged material among boxes with 70,000 pages of unprivileged material. The opinion distinguishes three ways courts have approached such situations—the "never waived" rule that requires giving the documents back, the "strict accountability" rule that treats all such situations as waivers, and a third or middle ground that looks at (1) reasonableness of precautions taken, (2) time taken to discover the error, (3) scope of the production, (4) extent of the disclosure, and (5) the interests of fairness in the situation. In this case, the defendant did not realize what had happened until the plaintiff called the situation to its attention and, by then, counsel could do little to avoid damage. The court treated the privilege as waived, saying it would be unjust to reward counsel's "gross negligence."

d.   To try to minimize some of these consequences, especially in the context of high volume electronic discovery, Federal Rule of Civil Procedure 26(f) now provides for putting a "clawback" provision into a discovery plan pursuant to which the parties may assert privileges as to documents even after they initially turned them over. The effect of such agreements on the documents' privileged character in later state cases, however, remains to be determined.[38]

3.   Should a client's claim that a lawyer provided ineffective assistance of counsel waive the attorney client privilege and allow the lawyer to show the context of the lawyer's actions?

a.   A criminal defense client's assertion that his lawyer provided constitutionally ineffective assistance of counsel ordinarily waives the attorney-client privilege with respect to communications relevant to that contention. Restatement Third, The Law Governing Lawyers § 80(1)(b), Comment c.

b.   Does that waiver extend to the lawyer's Rule 1.6 obligation not to disclose information relating to the representation? ABA Formal Opinion 10–456 (July 2010) said no. If asked by the prosecutor for the defendant's file, defense counsel must raise all non-frivolous defenses to disclosure. The lawyer may be required by a court to testify in response to the defendant's charges, but until ordered to do so, the lawyer must remain silent. Some might believe that a claim of ineffective assistance falls within the "self-defense" exception of Rule 1.6(b)(5), the opinion said, but that exception only applies where a response from the lawyer is objectively necessary. "[I]t will be extremely difficult for defense counsel to conclude that there is a reasonable need in self-defense to disclose client confidences to the prosecutor outside any court-supervised setting."

c.   Virginia State Bar Opinion 1859 (June 6, 2012) considered the situation where a government lawyer called the former defense lawyer to get information to defeat the ineffective assistance claim brought in a habeas proceeding. The Opinion interpreted what corresponds to ABA Rule 1.6(b)(5). The lawyer may reveal enough information to defend herself against such claims, the opinion says, but the lawyer may not act before the court finds that a habeas corpus hearing is necessary. Normally, the lawyer should wait for the judge to order disclosure.

d.   D.C. Bar Opinion 364 (Jan. 2013), on the other hand, said that the DC rules permit disclosure even in the absence of a planned or actual case against the lawyer. A lawyer must disclose only as much as necessary, the Committee wrote, and be careful not to reveal information that could be used against the client in other ways. However, the lawyer need not wait for a court order or even judicial

---

[38] Further, the question for the *recipient* of the information is how to know whether the privilege has been lost. Look at Model Rule 4.4(b) and Comment 2: "Whether the lawyer is required to * * * [return a] document is a matter of law beyond the scope of these Rules, as is the question of whether the privileged status of a document has been waived." We return to the recipient's duties in Problem 24, *infra*.

approval before explaining his action or inaction as defense counsel. Recall that ABA Model Rule 1.6, Comment 10, says the "lawyer's right to respond arises when an assertion of such complicity has been made, and Rule 1.6(b)(5) does not require the lawyer to await the commencement of an action or proceeding that charges such complicity, so that the defense may be established by responding directly to a third party who has made such an assertion."[39]

4.   Should the attorney-client privilege, work product immunity, or the lawyer's duty of confidentiality be lost by the passage of time or by the client's death?

a.   Restatement Third, The Law Governing Lawyers § 77, after noting that lawyers may sometimes testify to privileged conversations in order to explain the terms of a will or otherwise carry out the wishes of the deceased client, says in Comment *d*:

> "It would be desirable that a tribunal be empowered to withhold the privilege of a person then deceased as to a communication that bears on a litigated issue of pivotal significance. The tribunal could balance the interest in confidentiality against any exceptional need for the communication. The tribunal also could consider limiting the proof or sealing the record to limit disclosure. Permitting such disclosure would do little to inhibit clients from confiding in their lawyers."

Do you agree with this attempt to balance the competing interests in cases where the confidential communications could help do justice in a pending matter? Do you agree that such a rule would have little effect on the willingness of clients to entrust information to their lawyers?

b.   Matter of John Doe Grand Jury Investigation, 562 N.E.2d 69 (Mass.1990), gave the usual answer on some tough facts. The case involved whether the late Charles Stuart was responsible for the deaths of Carol and Christopher Stuart. Charles Stuart talked with his lawyer for two hours on the day before his suicide, and the prosecutor guessed that he had admitted the crime to the lawyer. If so, the state could both stop looking for a suspect for the murders and be sure not to charge someone else for them. The court held, however, that the privilege did not end with Charles' death and no amount of interest in knowing the truth could justify making the lawyer testify. Do you agree? If the prosecutor gave Stuart criminal immunity, the court could force him to testify. Now, Stuart was dead. Should the court treat that as the functional equivalent of immunity in order to find the truth?

c.   What rule would you apply in a case like State v. Macumber, 544 P.2d 1084 (Ariz.1976)? The defendant was convicted of two murders and was serving a life term. At trial, his lawyer tried to call two other lawyers who were prepared to testify that their now-deceased client had confessed to them that he, not Macumber, had committed the murders. The court excluded the testimony. Communications with a lawyer are

---

[39] Cf., Los Angeles County Bar Ass'n Professional Responsibility and Ethics Comm., Opinion 525 (Dec. 6, 2012) (lawyer must be "proportionate and restrained" in responding to client criticism that is posted on a website); In re Skinner, 2013 WL 1092904 (Ga. 2013) (reprimand is insufficient sanction for revealing confidential client information in response to client's web criticism of the lawyer).

privileged, the court said, and that privilege does not end with death. Is the Restatement wrong to suggest that sometimes the need to do justice to the living should prevail over the interests of the dead?[40]

d.   Swidler & Berlin v. United States, 524 U.S. 399 (1998), was the celebrated case testing whether the Office of Independent Counsel could obtain notes of conversations between Vincent Foster (a White House lawyer) and his lawyer shortly before Mr. Foster's suicide. The D.C. Circuit found that, while cases often say the attorney-client privilege survives death, courts usually say that in the context of finding an exception to the rule to assist in construction of a will, the so-called testamentary exception. Thus, the court said, it is reasonable to make another exception for communications significant to a criminal prosecution since the client's own criminal liability obviously expires when he does. Further, the court held, post-death reputation is not sufficiently important to most people to make them not be candid with their lawyer even if the privilege would not survive them. In re Sealed Case, 124 F.3d 230 (D.C.Cir.1997).

The U.S. Supreme Court reversed by a vote of 6 to 3. Writing for the Court and upholding survival of the privilege, Chief Justice Rehnquist said:

> "While the arguments against the survival of the privilege are by no means frivolous, they are based in large part on speculation—thoughtful speculation, but speculation nonetheless—as to whether posthumous termination of the privilege would diminish a client's willingness to confide in an attorney. In an area where empirical information would be useful, it is scant and inconclusive."

Do you agree that the problem is a lack of empirical evidence? Commentators dispute whether there is solid evidence demonstrating the value of the attorney-client privilege in the first place. Do you base your views about the privilege on empirical studies, or on instinctive ideas of what justice requires?

————

PRIVILEGE AND WORK PRODUCT IN THE ORGANIZATION SETTING

Imagine now that your client is an organization, not an individual. Should corporations and other organizations have exactly the same attorney-client privilege and work product protection that individuals have? What individuals' communications with a lawyer should qualify as privileged communications of the organization?

Such questions were addressed in Upjohn Co. v. United States, 449 U.S. 383 (1981). The company learned that some of its subsidiaries probably had made payments to foreign governments in violation of U.S. law. It assigned lawyers to conduct an internal investigation of the situation. After it voluntarily reported the offense, the government asked for the internal investigative memos written by its lawyers. The

---

[40] We will see this issue later when we get to Problem 30, *infra*. At least part of the problem in *Macumber* may have been doubts about the truth of such confessions. One can give a relatively costless gift to a friend by making a deathbed confession to a crime the friend committed.

company claimed privilege and work product protection, and the Supreme Court agreed, saying: "Information, not available from upper-echelon management, was needed to supply a basis for legal advice concerning compliance with securities and tax laws, foreign laws, currency regulations, duties to shareholders, and potential litigation in each of these areas." The court held that "consistent with the underlying purposes of the attorney-client privilege, these communications must be protected against compelled disclosure."

Some states only give protection to communication from an organization's "control group" (its top-level management personnel). But most states follow *Upjohn* and say that even communications from middle-level and lower-level personnel are protected if they are "within the scope of the employees' corporate duties and the employees themselves were sufficiently aware that they were being questioned in order that the corporation could obtain legal advice." It is important to recognize, however, that the privilege belongs to the organization, not the individual organization employees who are talking to the lawyer. Thus, if an employee tells the corporate attorney, "Yes, I violated the law," the lawyer may report the admission to law enforcement authorities. See Restatement Third, The Law Governing Lawyers § 74. The fact that some corporate officials may not realize that the company lawyer does not represent them personally requires lawyers in such situations to make their role clear." See Model Rule 1.13(f).

The highest court in Europe has not embraced the U.S. Supreme Court's view of what communications are within the corporate privilege. In Australian Mining & Smelting Europe, Ltd. v. European Commission, [1982] 2 C.M.L.R. 264, 1982 WL 221208, the European Court of Justice held that in-house counsel are not sufficiently "independent" of their corporate colleagues to make communications with them legally privileged. The opinion was reaffirmed in Akzo Nobel Chemicals Ltd. v. European Commission, Case C–550/07 P, Celex No. 607J0550, 2010 ECJ EUR–Lex Lexis 807, 23–24 (ECJ EUR–Lex 2010). The European Court of Justice reasoned:

> "45. * * * An in-house lawyer, despite his enrolment[sic] with a Bar or Law Society and the professional ethical obligations to which he is, as a result, subject, does not enjoy the same degree of independence from his employer as a lawyer working in an external law firm does in relation to his client. Consequently, an in-house lawyer is less able to deal effectively with any conflicts between his professional obligations and the aims of his client.

> "48. * * * [U]nder the terms of his contract of employment, an in-house lawyer may be required to carry out other tasks, namely, as in the present case, the task of competition law coordinator, which may have an effect on the commercial policy of the undertaking. Such functions cannot but reinforce the close ties between the lawyer and his employer."

Do you agree that the corporate privilege should only apply to communications with outside counsel who are licensed in Europe? Lest you think such European decisions will have no effect on your practice, think about how conflicting approaches to privilege questions will affect internal investigations at multinational companies, for example, or how you as a U.S. lawyer will give advice to a U.S. company's European subsidiary.

Other issues can arise when the organization considers whether to waive the privilege. People who owned the company when privileged communications were made may not want people who bought the company to reveal earlier lawyer advice. The usual rule, however, is that whoever is in charge of the company at the time the company considers waiver makes the decision. For example, a trustee in bankruptcy may waive the privilege in the face of former management's opposition to revelation of their discussions with counsel. Commodity Futures Trading Commission v. Weintraub, 471 U.S. 343 (1985).

THE COMMON INTEREST PRIVILEGE AMONG MULTIPLE PARTIES

Suppose several individuals or companies are joint defendants in a case. May they share information as they work together to prepare a common defense? The common-interest privilege permits privileged discussions in such situations. Ordinarily, defendants with a common interest may hold joint discussions at which they and the various lawyers talk freely with each other about matters relevant to their common interest. Any client who is part of that discussion or similar information exchange may assert the privilege just as it could if the client had been talking to its lawyer alone.

If the parties later have a falling-out, or one decides to plead guilty and implicate the others, typically, any of the parties may disclose what it and its attorney said, but the privilege continues to apply to what all the others in the arrangement disclosed.

On the other hand, if, in the course of the discussions, one of the parties learns that it was injured by one of the common-interest parties, it may file a suit for damages and use against that other party whatever the other party may have been disclosed. Unless the parties have agreed otherwise in advance, the common interest privilege does not protect information disclosed by the participants in "subsequent adverse proceedings" between them. See Restatement Third, The Law Governing Lawyers § 76, Comment *f*.

Similarly, if a single lawyer represents two or more co-clients in the same matter, if the co-clients later have a falling out, the lawyer may be required to testify about what either or both clients have said. Indeed, traditionally, if one client tells the common lawyer something relevant to the other client[s] in the joint representation, unless the clients have agreed otherwise, the lawyer must disclose that information to the other clients even if the disclosing client would prefer that it remain confidential. See Restatement Third, The Law Governing Lawyers § 60, Comment *l*: "Sharing of information among the co-clients with respect to the matter involved in the representation is normal and typically expected."

Thus, before undertaking to represent two or more clients jointly and before entering into a common-interest arrangement, a lawyer should specifically address the effects on confidentiality with the client or clients, and if necessary, get an advance agreement from the client(s) about what to do if there is a falling out among them. See Model Rule 1.7, Comments 30–31; ABA Formal Opinion 08–450 (Apr. 9, 2008).

LIMITS ON CONFIDENTIALITY IN CASES OF RISK TO THIRD PARTIES

Before leaving issues of confidentiality, remember from Problem 7 that the privilege does not extend to discussions in furtherance of an intended, unlawful end. The traditional common law view was that a communication to a lawyer "for the purpose, later accomplished, of obtaining assistance to engage in a crime or fraud," is not protected by privilege. Restatement Third, The Law Governing Lawyers §82(a).

In addition, Model Rule 1.6(b)(1) permits a lawyer to disclose otherwise confidential client information, "to the extent the lawyer reasonably believes necessary to prevent reasonably certain death or substantial bodily injury. Notice that the rule does not require that what you are disclosing must be an act of the client. Nor is disclosure limited to future criminal acts. The conduct need only have future effects. Does the new rule require that the adverse effects occur with any particular time period. Look at Model Rule 1.6, Comment 6.

As you remember, the crime-fraud exception to the attorney-client privilege and work product immunity applies to fraud as well as crime. Non-disclosure may not always be fraudulent, but when it is, neither the privilege nor work product immunity will bar disclosure.

Look at Model Rule 4.1(b). Does that provision *mandate* disclosure in a case of client fraud? Would disclosure always be "prohibited by Rule 1.6"?

Until 2003, the ABA House of Delegates consistently rejected any proposed authority of a lawyer to reveal information to prevent or rectify a fraudulent act of the client, even an act "that the lawyer reasonably believes is likely to result * * * in substantial injury to the financial interests or property of another." However, the ABA adopted Model Rules 1.6(b)(2) & (b)(3) when the Enron and WorldCom collapses made some action inevitable. What is the effect of those provisions on your Rule 4.1(b) obligation?

Until 2003, the Model Rules limited lawyers to "noisy withdrawal" in such cases. The idea was that, pursuant to Model Rule 1.6(b) & (c), a lawyer should withdraw and then send a notice of withdrawal to others with whom the lawyer had dealt in the matter saying something like "I have withdrawn from this matter for ethical reasons." Some lawyers objected that this withdrawal was a "flying a red flag" and thus prejudiced their clients' interests. However, the pre-2003 Comments specifically approved of the noisy notice of the withdrawal, and the present rule still refers to it.

Assuming that you want to disclose the report and memorandum to the EPA voluntarily, is there anything you must to do before disclosure? Look at Model Rule 1.6, Comment 14. Do you agree that "Where practicable, the lawyer should first seek to persuade the client to take suitable action to obviate the need for disclosure"?[41]

Why does Rule 1.6 add this caveat? If the lawyer discusses the issue with the client and gets him focused on the problem, might that obviate the need for disclosure? Does this caveat tell us that it is better

---

[41] This comes directly from Restatement Third, The Law Governing Lawyers § 66(2).

that the client do the right thing than for its lawyer to tattle on the client?

Should the lawyer be subject to discipline—or liability—for a failure to disclose what Rule 1.6(b) merely permits the lawyer to disclose? What Rule 1.6, Comment 15 say about that? What is the rationale for this protection against civil liability? Is it that it is hard in many cases for a lawyer to assess the risks correctly before harm occurs and then impossible later for the lawyer to explain the ambiguity to a jury that is looking for deep pockets? Is that a complicated way of saying that the purpose of this rule against civil liability is to protect the lawyer's self-interest?

PROBLEM 8

CONFIDENTIALITY AND THE ORGANIZATION AS A CLIENT

OMITTED IN CONCISE EDITION

CHAPTER IV

THE REQUIREMENT OF LOYALTY TO THE CLIENT

The biblical injunction against serving inconsistent masters has long been a fundamental principle of fiduciary duty. Because lawyers have a fiduciary relationship with their clients, the principle applies with full force in the Model Rules. For a lawyer, interests possibly conflicting with the client's interest may be the interest of another client, a former client, a third party, or even the lawyer's own self-interest.

Each client of a lawyer expects full loyalty, yet it is as usual for a lawyer to represent many clients as for a doctor to treat many patients. Indeed, in some cases, several clients want a common attorney. Moreover, the lawyer's partners will all have clients, thus extending the possible conflicts, because the Model Rules typically impute the conflicts of one lawyer to others in the same firm.

Lawyers are usually not happy to discover a conflict of interest; they face economic pressures that discourage them from turning away business. However, the law of legal ethics sets limits beyond which lawyers may not go without client consent. Those limits are the subject of this chapter, and you are likely to find that the questions you examine here will be the ethical issues that most frequently arise in your practice. In the problems that follow, consider questions such as:

a. How can a lawyer recognize, anticipate, and avoid conflicts of interest?

b. When will your personal interests, as opposed to those of your other clients, raise questions about the zealousness of your representation?

c. Do rules about conflicts of interest ever serve to increase, unnecessarily, the cost of legal services? Might they prevent clients from legitimately choosing to save the cost of the extra lawyer?

d. If a lawyer determines that he or she is in a conflict situation, how should the lawyer deal with it? Is it enough to obtain consent of all the affected persons? When must the lawyer refuse to take the case? When must she withdraw?

e. To what extent do conflict of interest rules represent ends in themselves, and to what extent do they further other objectives such as the obligation to preserve client confidences?

———

PROBLEM 9

REPRESENTING MULTIPLE PARTIES DEALING WITH EACH OTHER

Probably the most basic kind of conflict of interest is that between two clients, simultaneously represented by a single lawyer, when everything gained by one of them will be at the other's expense. It might seem never appropriate to have a single lawyer represent both parties to such a "zero-sum game," but many real-life situations make such representation tempting, and starting our analysis of conflicts of interest there is helpful in identifying the factors that will be important throughout this chapter.

FACTS

Mr. and Mrs. Wilson have been married for 12 years. They have children ages 10, 8, and 6. They both realize that their marriage has not been going well for the past four years, and while they consider each other friends, they no longer wish to remain married. They have come to attorney Wayne Green's office and have asked Green to help them secure a divorce.

The Wilsons tell Green they have agreed that Mr. Wilson will be the custodial parent of the 8–year–old son and Mrs. Wilson will be custodial parent of the two daughters. Each will have liberal rights of contact with the children living with the other. Mrs. Wilson wants $1000 a month child support, and Mr. Wilson considers that a bargain.

Neither of the Wilsons wants a separate attorney called into the case because of the added expense. "We both trust you," they say. "Why create problems when there aren't any now?"

QUESTIONS

A. DETERMINING WHETHER A LAWYER HAS A CONFLICT OF INTEREST

1. Will the simultaneous representation of both Wilsons involve attorney Green in a conflict of interest?

a. The Wilsons have told Green that they have worked everything out. Do you agree that they have done so? Are there practical problems Green should foresee in helping two people achieve even an amicable dissolution of an unwanted legal relationship? What might be some of those practical problems?

b. Restatement Third, The Law Governing Lawyers § 121 describes the basic rule prohibiting a lawyer's conflict of interest.

> "Unless all affected [persons give informed consent] * * *, a lawyer may not represent a client if the representation would involve a conflict of interest. A conflict of interest is involved if there is substantial risk that the lawyer's representation of the client would be materially and adversely affected by the lawyer's own interests or by the lawyer's duties to another current client, a former client, or a third person."

c. The corresponding provision in the ABA Model Rules is Rule 1.7(a):

"Except [with informed consent] * * *, a lawyer shall not represent a client if the representation involves a concurrent conflict of interest. A concurrent conflict of interest exists if:

"(1) the representation of one client will be *directly adverse* to another client; or

"(2) there is a significant risk that the representation of one or more clients will be *materially limited* by the lawyer's responsibilities to another client, a former client or a third person or by a personal interest of the lawyer." [emphasis added]

d. Under these definitions, are the representations of Mr. Wilson and Mrs. Wilson each "directly adverse" to the other? The caption for this lawsuit for divorce will be *Wilson v. Wilson*. The lawyer cannot be on both sides of that lawsuit. Does "direct" only cover that example? Right now, they may only be asking the lawyer to advise them what to do and how to draw up the papers. Does that mean the representation is not "directly adverse," at least not yet?

e. What "material limits" on the representation of Mr. or Mrs. Wilson is Green likely to experience? Is "materially limited" a subjective test or an objective one? Is the problem that Green personally may have a subjective inability to diligently pursue the interest of each client? Alternatively, is the problem that no reasonable lawyer could argue for more child support for Mrs. Wilson while also arguing for less if Mr. Wilson prefers that?

2. What concerns underlie the rules governing conflicts of interest?

a. Model Rule 1.7, Comments 6 and 8, provide a start toward answering the question. Is the inability of Wayne Green to push hard for one client at the expense of the other a serious problem? If Mr. Wilson is willing to pay only $1000 a month, for example, may Green, on behalf of Mrs. Wilson, ask for $1500?

b. Both the Restatement and Model Rule provisions replaced ABA Model Code of Professional Responsibility DR 5–105(A) that provided:

"A lawyer shall decline proffered employment if the exercise of his independent professional judgment in behalf of a client will be or is likely to be adversely affected by the acceptance of the proffered employment, or if it would be likely to involve him in representing differing interests * * *."

c. Was the concept of "independent professional judgment" in DR 5–105(A) a useful one for defining the fundamental concern underlying conflict of interest regulation? On the other hand, is the effect on lawyer "judgment" the real concern?

3.   Should Green be able to avoid the conflict problem by representing Mr. Wilson himself while having his law partner represent Mrs. Wilson?

a.   It is important to understand that ABA Model Rule 1.10(a) usually "imputes" a single lawyer's conflicts to all other lawyers in the firm. That would be true even if Mrs. Wilson were to consult Green's partner who worked out of an office in another city. It would be true even if the two lawyers never talk to each other except with their clients present. It would be true even if Mr. and Mrs. Wilson have no material secrets to keep from each other about this matter.

b.   What concerns or assumptions about attorney behavior underlie such imputation? Do you agree with those assumptions? Does it follow that the imputation should be automatic?

c.   Whatever your view of imputation, it represents well-settled law that you should presume applies throughout most of the issues in the chapter. We will explore the most important implications of the concept later, primarily in Problem 15.

B.   WAIVER OF A CONFLICT OF INTEREST; THE REQUIREMENT OF INFORMED CONSENT

1.   Is the short answer to conflicts issues that clients may waive the conflicts whenever the rules get in the way of what the clients want to do?

a.   The conclusion that a conflict exists does not necessarily mean that Green cannot undertake the common representation. It simply means that whether he may do so is not for Green alone to decide.

b.   Restatement Third, The Law Governing Lawyers § 122(1) says:

"A lawyer may represent a client notwithstanding a conflict of interest prohibited by § 121 if each affected client or former client gives informed consent to the lawyer's representation. Informed consent requires that the client or former client have reasonably adequate information about the material risks of such representation to that client or former client."

The corresponding provision in the ABA Model Rules is Rule 1.7(b)(4).

2.   What kind of information should Green provide the Wilsons about the "material risks" of his representing them both?

a.   Does Model Rule 1.7, Comment 18, give a complete answer to that question? As you can see from that Comment, even discussion of the effects of the conflict on "loyalty, confidentiality and the attorney-client privilege and the advantages and risks involved" includes quite a list of topics.

b.   Look at Model Rule 1.0, the Terminology section. The need for "informed consent" appears throughout the Model Rules, so the definition is in Model Rule 1.0(e).

c.   What disadvantages should Green mention? May he contrast them with the potential cost saving if he represents them both? Do you suppose Green will be telling the Wilsons something they do not already know? If they already know or should know, for example, that Green will not keep any of Mr. Wilson's secrets from Mrs. Wilson, is Green's reminder still useful?

3.   Should the Model Rules require that any client consent to a conflict be in writing?

a.   California Rule of Professional Conduct 3–310 imposes such a requirement. Model Rule 1.7, prior to 2002, did not.

b.   Look at the requirement now imposed by Model Rule 1.7(b)(4). What does it mean to have consent "confirmed in writing"?

c.   Model Rule 1.7, Comment 20, provides the answer. Do you agree that it should be sufficient to send a client a letter that the client does not need to acknowledge? Will a failure to challenge the accuracy of the representations that the lawyer makes about consent constitute agreement with the representations?

d.   As a matter of prudence, of course, most lawyers will discuss conflicts in the engagement letter that they will have the client countersign. If they have fully memorialized the advice they gave about the advantages and disadvantages of waiving the conflict, any subsequent dispute will more likely be resolved in their favor. Of course, any advice they forget to mention in the letter may seem never to have been said.

4.   For how long should a conflict waiver be effective? Suppose that in the course of the representation, the lawyer learns facts that make the conflict more severe than first appeared. Must she secure a new waiver?

a.   In re Cohen, 853 P.2d 286 (Or.1993), illustrates how a relatively simple situation can quickly get out of hand. Wife accused Husband of beating their daughter. Husband faced criminal charges and both parents faced the possibility that a family judge would take the child from them. The lawyer agreed to represent Husband in the criminal case and to represent both parents in the custody matter. Later, Wife called the lawyer and told him that Husband was not going to counseling. A presentence report agreed and said that Wife was often calling the police about Husband. Wife said she still wanted lawyer to represent them jointly so they could "act as a team." In imposing discipline on the lawyer, the court found that he had neither adequately explained the potential conflict at the outset nor dealt with the actual conflict later.

b.   In re Houston, 985 P.2d 752 (N.M.1999), was another case of the lawyer going too far trying to represent everyone in a family. The wife went to the lawyer, who advised her to report to police that her husband had beaten her and molested her daughter. The lawyer then defended the husband against the wife's charges; the wife consented to this but the lawyer did not tell her that she would have to testify at the trial. He also represented both husband and wife in a divorce and secured a court decree giving the husband unsupervised visitation rights that the wife found unsatisfactory. For this web of conflicts, the court required the lawyer to submit to 18 months of supervised probation.

5.   May the client revoke consent and then require that the lawyer not represent either of the clients?

a.   Look at Model Rule 1.7, Comment 21. Clearly, either of the clients may terminate his or her own representation for any (or no) reason. The subject of this Comment is whether the client who terminates can thereby preclude the lawyer from representing the other client.

b.   Comment 21 is derived from Restatement Third, The Law Governing Lawyers § 122, Comment *f*. Two examples that the Restatement offers illustrate the distinction. Illustration 4 says:

> "Client A and Client B validly consent to be represented by Lawyer in operating a restaurant in a city. After a period of amicable and profitable collaboration, Client A reasonably concludes that Lawyer has begun to take positions against Client A and consistently favoring the interests of Client B in the business. Reasonably concerned that Lawyer is no longer properly serving the interests of both Clients, Client A withdraws consent. Withdrawal of consent is effective and justified. Lawyer may not thereafter continue representing either Client A or Client B in a matter adverse to the other and substantially related to Lawyer's former representation of the clients."

Contrast Illustration 6:

> "Clients A and B validly consent to Lawyer representing them jointly as co-defendants in a breach-of-contract action. On the eve of trial and after months of pretrial discovery on the part of all parties, Client A withdraws consent to the joint representation for reasons not justified by the conduct of Lawyer or Client B and insists that Lawyer cease representing Client B. At this point, it would be difficult and expensive for Client B to find separate representation for the impending trial. Client A's withdrawal of consent is ineffective to prevent the continuing representation of B in the absence of compelling considerations such as harmful disloyalty by Lawyer."

c.   Could a lawyer eliminate this issue by drafting the consent more carefully? For example, could the clients' consent provide that either Client A or Client B may revoke consent at any time, for any reason, but that if either A or B does that, the Lawyer may continue to represent the other client? Are there fiduciary obligations inherent in such situations that should override such private agreements?[1]

C.   CONFLICTS FOR WHICH CONSENT IS NOT EFFECTIVE

1.   Are there some conflicts that a client may not waive?

a.   Restatement Third, The Law Governing Lawyers § 122(2) says:

> "(2) Notwithstanding the informed consent of each affected client or former client, a lawyer may not represent a client if:
>
> > "(a) the representation is prohibited by law;

---

[1]   We will return to an issue much like this, the issue of advance consent, in Problem 10.

"(b) one client will assert a claim against the other in the same litigation; or

"(c) in the circumstances, it is not reasonably likely that the lawyer will be able to provide adequate representation to one or more of the clients."

The corresponding Model Rule provisions are Model Rules 1.7(b)(1)–(b)(3).

b.   The first two Restatement subsections are easy enough to understand. What about the third? When should the law provide that competent and fully informed adults may not waive a conflict?

c.   Is the rule really trying to identify situations in which a reasonable party would not grant consent if he or she were fully informed? Does the rule instead assume that the system of justice has an interest in who represents parties so that makes some conflicts not subject to waiver?

2.   When should Rule 1.7 prohibit a client from waiving a conflict?

a.   Matter of Michelman, 616 N.Y.S.2d 409 (N.Y.App.Div.1994), leave to appeal denied 84 N.Y.2d 811 (1994), considered the problem of representing both a biological mother and adoptive parents in a private adoption. The adoptive parents were already the lawyer's clients and a medical doctor referred the biological mother to the lawyer, who prepared the necessary papers and explained the process to her. Assuming that all the participants consented to the common representation, do you see any problem with it? What if a biological mother has a right to revoke consent to the adoption? Because it is easy to foresee that an effort to revoke consent might occur, ABA Informal Opinion 87–1523 (1987) concluded that the situation presented a nonconsentable conflict. This court agreed, and under the circumstances of the case, suspended the lawyer for three years.

b.   In Fiandaca v. Cunningham, 827 F.2d 825 (1st Cir.1987), New Hampshire Legal Assistance (NHLA) represented women prison inmates who claimed that their prison facilities were overcrowded. The state offered to move some of the female inmates to another facility that mentally retarded patients currently used as a hospital. The NHLA, which represented these patients in another case challenging conditions at that facility, rejected the state's offer because it would adversely affect the mentally retarded clients if the state converted that hospital into a women's prison. The court held that it was error for the trial court to certify NHLA as class counsel. When a lawyer must decline a settlement offer in one case in order to benefit the lawyer's clients in another case, there is a fatal conflict of interest requiring NHLA's disqualification from continuing to act for the prisoners.

c.   Baldasarre v. Butler, 625 A.2d 458 (N.J.1993), involved a lawyer who represented the sellers in a real estate transaction, while knowing that the buyer, his other client, already arranged to sell that property to someone else at a large profit. The sellers believed their lawyer should have told them that the ultimate buyer wanted the property and that he should have helped them get the higher price. The New Jersey Supreme Court said there was no way the lawyer could have acted loyally to both clients in such a situation and held that a lawyer may not represent both buyer and seller in a commercial real estate deal, even with the consent of each.

Do you agree with this result? Is this simply a case where there could be no valid consent because the lawyer could not fully inform the original sellers of the buyer's plans?

d.   Association of the Bar of the City of New York Committee on Professional and Judicial Ethics, Formal Opinion 2001–2 (Apr. 2001), was more sympathetic to joint representation. It concluded that, particularly if the lawyer regularly represents each of the parties, each client almost has a fundamental right not to be required to get new counsel. The key issue should be whether a "disinterested lawyer" would conclude that the lawyer cannot adequately represent each client. Such an analysis would require a focus on the nature of the conflict, the ability to preserve confidential information of each client, the ability of the lawyer to explain the conflict, the clients' ability to understand the foreseeable risks, and whether the lawyer has a closer relationship to one of the parties. The opinion suggests that, under the right facts, a law firm could even represent two clients negotiating a major merger.

e.   Are Comments 15–17 of Model Rule 1.7 helpful in determining whether the clients may waive a conflict? Do they persuade you whether the above cases and opinions are correct?

3.   Should courts and disciplinary authorities treat Green's representation of Mr. and Mrs. Wilson as a nonconsentable conflict?

a.   Even if the parties do not contest the divorce, in most cases they file the case in the form of litigation between the husband and wife. May a lawyer represent both the plaintiff and defendant in a litigated case? Does the fact that the court will have to approve the Wilsons' divorce mean that there could be no harm from Green's representing them both?

b.   The Reporter's Note to Restatement Third, The Law Governing Lawyers § 128, Comment *c* says:

"The question of representing opposing clients in hearings on uncontested marital dissolution has arisen frequently. Some courts have permitted use of only one lawyer in some of those situations. While the divorce proceeding is still a nominally contested litigation in most jurisdictions, in some remedial contexts, courts will confirm a negotiated property settlement where both parties consented to the simultaneous representation and the settlement appears fair. See, e.g., Klemm v. Superior Court, 142 Cal.Rptr. 509 (Cal.Ct.App.1977) (while parties may not waive conflict in contested litigation, they may do so in an uncontested dissolution); * * *. [However, s]everal jurisdictions treat joint representation of spouses in a dissolution action as a nonconsentable conflict in all instances."

c.   Might Green handle the representation jointly through negotiation of the property settlement, but have the Wilsons hire another lawyer to represent one of the parties at the divorce hearing while Mr. Green represents the other? Is there any public interest in requiring that the process be bifurcated in that way? If Mr. Green represents one of the parties, how will he choose which one? If a new lawyer represents the other party, is that lawyer required to accept the property settlement as given, or should he or she independently evaluate it?

4. Should consent be easier to secure in business planning matters and other nonlitigation settings that are less contentious than a divorce?

a. Assume, for example, that the parties who have come to Green are three individuals who wish to set up a close corporation. Green has met none of them before. Is it possible that he can represent them all effectively?

b. Before the ABA House of Delegates deleted Model Rule 2.2 in the 2002 revisions, that Rule addressed this situation. It called the lawyer an "intermediary between clients." Deleted Model Rule 2.2 permitted the lawyer to undertake such representation if:

"(1) the lawyer consults with each client concerning the implications of the common representation, including the advantages and risks involved, and the effect on the attorney-client privileges, and obtains each client's consent to the common representation;

"(2) the lawyer reasonably believes that the matter can be resolved on terms compatible with the clients' best interests, that each client will be able to make adequately informed decisions in the matter and that there is little risk of material prejudice to the interest of any of the clients if the contemplated resolution is unsuccessful; and

"(3) the lawyer reasonably believes that the common representation can be undertaken impartially and without improper effect on other responsibilities the lawyer has to any of the clients."

c. At the time the ABA Commission revised the Model Rules in 2002, the drafters concluded that these principles were already inherent in Model Rule 1.7. Do you agree?

d. Although the ABA repealed Model Rule 2.2, Rule 1.7, Comments 28–33 reflect some of its ideas. What would you conclude from those Comments about the ability of the parties to consent to using a single lawyer in establishing a business?

5. Could Green represent both Mr. and Mrs. Wilson if, instead of seeking a divorce, they came to Green for estate planning advice?

a. An ABA report analyzed the issue as follows:

"From an ethical standpoint, the risk is that, in counseling the couple as a unit for tax and planning purposes, neither individual will receive the representation a single individual might receive under the same circumstances. Yet family needs, tax incentives, and the very nature of marriage often make separate counseling unnecessary, and indeed, inappropriate."[2]

b.   Under that analysis, should a lawyer normally obtain a conflicts waiver before beginning estate planning for the couple? May the lawyer properly "view the couple as unified in goals and interests until shown otherwise"?[3]

c.   Restatement Third, The Law Governing Lawyers § 130, Comment *c*, cautions: "A lawyer is not required to suggest or assume discord where none exists, but when a conflict is reasonably apparent or foreseeable, the lawyer may proceed with multiple representation only after all affected clients have consented' as provided in § 122." Do you agree with the Restatement approach?

6.   What are Green's obligations to Mr. Wilson if, during estate planning, Mrs. Wilson privately discloses confidential information to Green but not to her spouse?

a.   Confronted with the choice between both hiring the same lawyer or each hiring a lawyer from separate law firms, which option do you believe most couples would choose, at least when they were together in a lawyer's office? However, what should Green do if, the day after Mr. and Mrs. Wilson sign both wills, Mrs. Wilson goes to the lawyer's office and says, "I want to change my will and don't want my husband to know"? Does your answer depend on whether Mr. Wilson is leaving all his property to his wife in the expectation that she is doing the same for him?

b.   A v. B. v. Hill Wallack, 726 A.2d 924 (N.J.1999), presented a very similar question. Husband and Wife sought estate-planning advice from Hill Wallack. Because of a mistake in conflicts checking, Hill Wallack did not discover until later that it had already accepted another woman's paternity action against Husband. Husband did not object to Hill Wallack's handling that case against him, and DNA tests showed he was the father of the woman's child. At that point, Hill Wallack wanted to tell Wife that, because she was leaving the residue of her estate to Husband, part of that estate could wind up going to his illegitimate child. Husband did not want the firm to tell Wife that he had fathered the child. The court said that a lawyer for co-clients should reach an agreement *in advance* about how to handle confidential information of each. Citing an earlier version of what is now Restatement Third, The Law Governing Lawyers § 60, Comment *l*, however, the court held that, in the absence of such an agreement, the lawyer has the "discretion" to tell each client the secrets of the other that may adversely affect that client's interest. It authorized the firm to tell Wife the existence but not the identity of the child.

c.   What does "discretion to tell" mean? The Restatement section on which the *Wallack* court relied makes clear that "[s]haring of information among the co-clients with respect to the matter involved in the representation is normal and typically expected. * * * Moreover, the common lawyer is required to keep each of the co-clients informed of all

---

[2]   Report of the Special Study Committee on Professional Responsibility, Comments and Recommendations on the Lawyer's Duties in Representing Husband and Wife, 28 Real Property, Probate & Trust Journal 765, 770 (1994).

[3]   Id. at 779.

information reasonably necessary for the co-client to make decisions in connection with the matter." When the lawyer receives information that one client wants to keep secret from the other, there is a conflict of interest that the lawyer cannot ignore. That is the context of the Restatement passage that the *Wallack* court quotes: "In the course of withdrawal [because of the conflict], the lawyer has discretion to warn the affected co-client that a matter seriously and adversely affecting that person's interests has come to light, which the other co-client refuses to permit the lawyer to disclose."

d.　D.C. Bar Legal Ethics Opinion 296 (2000) concluded that a lawyer may *not* reveal a secret of one joint client to another but must withdraw from the representation of both. A lawyer who undertakes dual representation has a duty to clarify, at the outset of the representation, "the impact of joint representation on the lawyer's duty to maintain client confidences and to keep each client reasonably informed, and obtain each client's informed consent to the arrangement." In the absence of such an agreement, when one joint client discloses confidential information that a lawyer would have a duty to disclose to the other in order to keep that client reasonably informed, the lawyer must seek consent to disclose such information from the disclosing client. According to the opinion, if the lawyer is unable to obtain consent, a conflict of interest arises and the lawyer must withdraw from the case. After withdrawal, the lawyer may not represent either client in the matter without the consent of the other.

e.　The Model Rules now address this issue in Rule 1.7, Comments 30 & 31. How do they direct Green to proceed? How should the lawyer have proceeded in the *Wallack* case?

f.　If the lawyer knows before undertaking the representation that one of the clients is withholding relevant information from the other, may the lawyer take the case at all? Look at Model Rule 1.7, Comment 19. May he take the case with the informed consent of the other client? Does the lawyer's inability to make full disclosure mean that it is impossible to secure *informed* consent?

7.　Are the Model Rules too quick to find conflicts and prohibit consent?

a.　In spite of the obvious problems associated with Mr. and Mrs. Wilson using the same lawyer for their divorce, is it nonetheless reasonable for them to desire that arrangement? Is their desire for a noncontentious resolution of the matter a legitimate concern? Should the ethics rules require two lawyers if one will do?

b.　Do you agree with the following view?

"[H]aving more than one lawyer to accomplish the parties' objectives may be an unnecessary and wasteful luxury. Individuals entering upon a contractual relationship, for example, might find it significantly less expensive and less disruptive to hire a single lawyer to draft a contract incorporating the business consensus of both sides than to have two lawyers, each trying to exact the marginal pound of flesh for his client. So, too, in many cases of uncontested divorce, the presence of combatant lawyers may reopen wounds better left closed and exacerbate problems rather than solve them.

"The response to this argument from many lawyers is that a situation which appears nonlitigious at the moment may develop into a contested situation in the future. This is not an unreasonable concern * * *. But having two lawyers from the outset in every case is expensive insurance against the unknown. Moreover, in many situations where things go badly, both sides can simply bring in separate counsel. The only person hurt by such a procedure would be the first lawyer who will now represent neither party. That the lawyer might not like this result is understandable. That his unhappiness should rise to the level of an ethical precept is less clear."[4]

c.   ABA Formal Opinion 07–447 (Aug. 9, 2007) addresses the growing practice of using collaborative lawyering in lieu of adversarial litigation in divorce. The opinion acknowledges the value of reaching agreement with minimal adversarial complications. A "collaborative law process" involves lawyers seeking to focus on the interests of both clients and to find a mutually acceptable divorce settlement that the parties jointly can submit to a court for approval. The parties must consent in advance to such a process, the opinion said, and if they cannot reach an agreement, both lawyers must withdraw and engage new lawyers to prepare the matter for trial. However, the opinion rejected the idea that the parties could never agree to a "limited scope" representation, and although the collaborative process discussed here involved a separate lawyer for each party, it may not be a long step from there to permitting a single lawyer to broker the agreement.

D. REMEDIES OTHER THAN PROFESSIONAL DISCIPLINE FOR A CONFLICT OF INTEREST VIOLATION

1. Should a judge enforce the rule against representing conflicting interests by ordering the representation terminated, or should judges leave enforcement to the lawyer discipline process?

a.   In litigated matters, a court faced with a conflict of interest will most often order the lawyer disqualified from representing any or all of the clients in the matter. Restatement Third, The Law Governing Lawyers § 6, Comment *i* explains:

"Disqualification draws on the inherent power of courts to regulate the conduct of lawyers * * * as well as the related inherent power of judges to regulate the course of proceedings before them * * *. Disqualification, where appropriate, ensures that the case is well presented in court, that confidential information of present or former clients is not misused, and that a client's substantial interest in a lawyer's loyalty is protected."[5]

---

[4] Thomas D. Morgan, The Evolving Concept of Professional Responsibility, 90 Harvard L. Rev. 702, 727–28 (1977). Copyright © 1977 by the Harvard Law Review Association.

[5] In federal courts, the denial of a disqualification motion in a civil case is *not* appealable as a final order under 28 U.S.C.A. § 1291. Firestone Tire & Rubber Co. v. Risjord, 449 U.S. 368 (1981). Similarly, the grant of a disqualification is not immediately appealable. Richardson–Merrell, Inc. v. Koller, 472 U.S. 424 (1985). The same rule applies in criminal

b.   In nonlitigation matters, some courts will issue an injunction against the continued representation and thereby achieve the practical effect of a disqualification. See Maritrans GP Inc. v. Pepper, Hamilton & Scheetz, 602 A.2d 1277 (Pa.1992).

c.   Yet, as Panduit Corp. v. All States Plastic Mfg. Co., Inc., 744 F.2d 1564, 1576–77 (Fed.Cir.1984), warns: "Judges must exercise caution not to paint with a broad brush under the misguided belief that coming down on the side of disqualification raises the standard of legal ethics and the public's respect. The opposite effects are just as likely— encouragement of vexatious tactics and increased cynicism by the public."

d.   Throughout this chapter, watch for this tension between rigorous enforcement of professional standards and the desire to prevent opportunistic efforts by the parties to impose additional costs on each other by seeking to disqualify their lawyers.

2.   What other remedies should be available to sanction a lawyer who represented conflicting interests?

a.   If a conflict disadvantages either of the clients, a malpractice remedy is often available. See, e.g., Hughes v. Consol–Pennsylvania Coal Co., 945 F.2d 594, 617 & n.3 (3d Cir.1991) (client called for advice whether transaction was fair; lawyer did not disclose he represented the other side; trial court erred by failing to uphold the jury verdict on malpractice); Milbank, Tweed, Hadley & McCloy v. Boon, 13 F.3d 537 (2d Cir.1994) ($2 million in damages awarded for acting adversely to client in same transaction).

b.   Even in the absence of economic harm to the clients, some courts deny lawyers part or all of their fees as a sanction for the breach of fiduciary duty inherent in a lawyer's conflict of interest.

In Hendry v. Pelland, 73 F.3d 397 (D.C.Cir.1996), for example, the law firm represented all five members of a family selling a parcel of land. Each of the clients had somewhat different views about acceptable terms for the sale. While finding no intentional misconduct that would support punitive damages, or even any actual damage suffered by family members, the court ruled that representation of all five family members was a conflict of interest that required the law firm to disgorge all fees it had earned in the case. See also, Burrow v. Arce, 997 S.W.2d 229, 240 (Tex.1999): "a client need not prove actual damages in order to obtain forfeiture of an attorney's fee for the attorney's breach of fiduciary duty to the client."

c.   United States v. Gellene, 182 F.3d 578 (7th Cir.1999), held that failure to disclose a conflict of interest can sometimes be a crime. Gellene, a partner in the New York firm Milbank, Tweed, Hadley &

---

cases. Flanagan v. United States, 465 U.S. 259 (1984) (granting disqualification motion not immediately appealable); United States v. White, 743 F.2d 488 (7th Cir.1984) (the denial of a motion to disqualify in a criminal case).

However, a few courts of appeal have agreed to review lower court decisions when the losing party has sought a writ of mandamus, e.g., In re American Airlines, Inc., 972 F.2d 605 (5th Cir.1992); Matter of Sandahl, 980 F.2d 1118 (7th Cir.1992). The Seventh Circuit has concluded that mandamus is appropriate if the trial judge applied an incorrect legal rule; it continues to defer to the trial judge on questions of fact. Do you think it is easy to apply the law/fact distinction in disqualification cases?

McCloy, represented the debtor in a Chapter 11 bankruptcy. He signed a sworn declaration identifying the firm's connection to all other parties in interest, but he failed to disclose that the firm also represented the senior secured creditor. He admitted bad judgment but denied a fraudulent intent. The jury found otherwise. The court sentenced Gellene to 15 months in the penitentiary and imposed a $15,000 fine. The court said it increased the sentence because Gellene, as a lawyer, abused a "position of trust."

e.   Should each of these remedies be exclusive, or should all be available simultaneously in appropriate cases?

———

PROBLEM 10

THE DUTY OF LOYALTY

Problem 9 involved representation of clients with opposing positions in the same case. More commonly, a client asks the lawyer to represent that client against another client whom the lawyer represents in a different case. Literally any of the clients that a lawyer represents in any matter might coincidentally become the opponent of another of the lawyer's clients. The growth of multistate and multinational law firms with hundreds of lawyers, each of whose conflicts is imputed to the other, means the possibility that one of a law firm's clients will oppose another is enormous. This problem explores (1) how firms deal with the problem of "direct adversity;" (2) how one determines who is "currently" a client of a law firm; (3) whether the firm may terminate the disfavored client to eliminate the conflict; and (4) how lawyers deal with situations where two clients, in two factually unrelated cases, differ on how they believe a court should rule on a point of law.

FACTS

You represent the First National Bank in its commercial lending work. The bank made a large mortgage loan to International Bolts Co., a parts manufacturer, for construction of a new plant. The loan has now gone into default, and the bank has directed you to commence foreclosure proceedings.

International Bolts has occasionally hired you over the last few years to write opinion letters on labor law matters. You are not now drafting any opinion for that company. You have never represented International Bolts in connection with this loan, but when you mention to the president of International Bolts that you will soon be handling the foreclosure of his plant, he is personally offended. "I really would not like you to be the one that does that to us," he says, "after all we've been through together."

Meanwhile, a neighbor has consulted you with respect to a "prepayment penalty" in the residential mortgage loan he has with the Second National Bank. Second National is not one of your clients, and you agree with the neighbor that prepayment penalties are not in consumers' best interests. Thus, as a favor to your neighbor, you have agreed to file a declaratory judgment action challenging the validity of such agreements under state and federal law.

You have informed the Second National Bank of the impending suit, and you later receive a call from the president of your client, the First National Bank, who says, "I've heard about your proposed law suit against the Second National Bank. We do not want the law of prepayment penalties changed." Then the president tells you: "You owe it to us to withdraw from representing the plaintiff in the pending suit." First National Bank has nothing to do with the proposed lawsuit against Second National Bank, which has never been your client, but First National Bank is concerned about the holding that may emerge from your prospective lawsuit.

QUESTIONS

A.   TAKING A CASE AGAINST A CURRENT CLIENT

1.   Is International Bolts' demand that you not represent the First National Bank in the foreclosure proceeding more than simply a question of keeping good relations with a sometimes client? Does International Bolts have a legal right to keep you out of the case?

a.   Look at Model Rule 1.7(a)(1). Must you take International Bolts' objection seriously?[6] As a matter of good business, you may not want to offend International Bolts. However, would you be acting "unethically" if you were willing to file the foreclosure case?

b.   What is the purpose of Model Rule 1.7(a)(1)? Does the concern about protecting clients' confidences help justify it? Remember that in many instances (like the one in this problem), there will be no substantive factual or legal relationship between the cases at all and thus no significant likelihood of misuse of any confidential information.

2.   Does the overarching concern go to the lawyer's loyalty to the client rather than protection of the client's confidences?

a.   Early cases like Grievance Committee v. Rottner, 203 A.2d 82 (Conn.1964), focused on loyalty. A law firm aggressively pursued an assault and battery case for O'Brien against Twible. When that case began, the firm was representing Twible in a collection matter against a third party. The cases were not at all related but the court explained:

> "When a client engages the services of a lawyer in a given piece of business he is entitled to feel that, until that business is finally disposed of in some manner, he has the undivided loyalty of the one upon whom he looks as his advocate and his champion. If, as in this case, he is sued and his home attached by his own attorney, who is representing him in another matter, all feeling of loyalty is necessarily destroyed, and the

---

[6]   In re Dresser Industries, Inc., 972 F.2d 540 (5th Cir.1992), holds that the principle against filing suit for one client against another current client is a national standard that federal courts must use in ruling on disqualification motions, even in the face of contrary state law.

profession is exposed to the charge that it is interested only in money."

b.   Cinema 5, Ltd. v. Cinerama, Inc., 528 F.2d 1384 (2d Cir.1976), applied this principle where attorney Fleischmann was a partner in two different law firms, one in New York City and one in Buffalo. Cinerama hired the Buffalo firm to represent it in an antitrust action that upstate New York theater operators filed. Later, several plaintiffs retained the New York City firm to sue several companies, including Cinerama, for alleged attempts to take over theater companies in New York City. Thus, one law firm was suing Cinerama while the other law firm was defending Cinerama. Because Fleischmann was the common partner in the two firms, the court treated the situation as a single law firm representing its client in one case while suing it in a different case.

The firm appealed the district court disqualification, saying that two different cases in completely different markets were involved. The Second Circuit assumed the two lawsuits were not related and responded:

"The 'substantial relationship' test is indeed the one that we have customarily applied in determining whether a lawyer may accept employment against a former client. * * * However, in this case, suit is not against a former client, but an existing one. One firm in which attorney Fleischmann is a partner is suing an actively represented client of another firm in which attorney Fleischmann is a partner. The propriety of this conduct must be measured not so much against the similarities in litigation, as against the duty of undivided loyalty which an attorney owes to each of his clients.

"A lawyer's duty to his client is that of a fiduciary or trustee. * * * When Cinerama retained Mr. Fleischmann as its attorney in the Western District litigation, it was entitled to feel that at least until that litigation was at an end, it had his undivided loyalty as its advocate and champion, * * * and could rely upon his 'undivided allegiance and faithful, devoted service.' * * * Because 'no man can serve two masters', Matthew 6:24; * * * it had the right to expect also that he would 'accept no retainer to do anything that might be adverse to his client's interests.' * * * Needless to say, when Mr. Fleischmann and his New York City partners undertook to represent Cinema 5, Ltd., they owed it the same fiduciary duty of undivided loyalty and allegiance. * * * "

"Whether such adverse representation, without more, requires disqualification in every case, is a matter we need not now decide. We do hold, however, that the 'substantial relationship' test does not set a sufficiently high standard by which the necessity for disqualification should be determined. That test may properly be applied only where the representation of a former client has been terminated and the parameters of such relationship have been fixed. Where the relationship is a continuing one, adverse representation is prima facie improper, * * * and the attorney must be prepared to show, at the very least, that there will be no actual or *apparent* conflict in loyalties or diminution in the vigor of his representation. We think that appellants have failed to meet this heavy burden * * *. [T]he record shows that after learning of the conflict which had developed, the Jaeckle firm, through Mr. Fleischmann, offered to withdraw its representation of Cinerama in the Western District actions. However, that offer was not accepted, and Mr. Fleischmann continued, albeit reluctantly, to have one foot in each camp."

Thus, the court affirmed the disqualification order.

3.   In addition to the issue of loyalty, should there be a concern that the lawyer might represent Client A less vigorously so as not to offend Client B?

a.   In Zuck v. Alabama, 588 F.2d 436 (5th Cir.1979), a law firm represented a defendant in a criminal case while also representing the prosecutor sued in his personal capacity in an unrelated civil matter. The prosecutor was not the real party in interest in the criminal case: he was not the state. Yet, "the defense attorneys were subject to the encumbrance that the prosecutor might take umbrage at a vigorous defense of Zuck and dispense with the services of their firm." In other words, the defense lawyer might be cautious about offending the prosecutor, his civil client, such as by charging prosecutorial misconduct. This constituted an actual conflict of interest rendering the criminal trial unfair in the absence of the criminal defendant's knowing and intelligent waiver. A witness informed the defendant that his lawyers were also representing the prosecutor, but that fact did not establish that the defendant waived his right to conflict-free representation. The state must show that the defendant was aware of the consequences of proceeding to trial with such counsel or that he knew that he had a right to have other counsel. See Rule 1.0(e) ("informed consent") and Rule 1.7, Comments 6 & 18.

b.   ABA Formal Opinion 97–406 (Apr. 19, 1997) considered the case where one lawyer (Lawyer 1) represents another lawyer (Lawyer 2). For example, Lawyer 2 might be a defendant in a malpractice case. At the same time, Lawyer 1 simultaneously represents clients who oppose parties that Lawyer 2 represents in different, unrelated cases. The opinion said that we should analyze this issue under what is now Model Rule 1.7(a)(2), not 1.7(a)(1). The opinion advised that there is a conflict if there is reason to believe that one or the other of the representations "may be materially limited" by duties the lawyer owes the other client. In the view of the opinion, six issues affect the determination of this issue: (1) the relative importance of the matters to the represented lawyer, (2) the relative sizes of the fees expected by the representing lawyer, (3) the relative importance of the clients' matters to each lawyer and client, (4) the sensitivity of each matter, (5) the similarity of the subject matter of the cases, and (6) the nature of the relationship of the lawyers with each other and with their clients.[7]

---

[7]   Association of the Bar of the City of New York Formal Opinion 1996–3 (Apr. 2, 1996) discusses concerns when one firm [Firm A] represents another law firm [Firm B] as a client while Firm B is also representing clients in other cases where Firm A opposes Firm B. One concern is that Firm A will learn things about Firm B that Firm A can use adversely to Firm B's clients in the other matters. Another concern is Firm A may pull its punches in the unrelated matters to preserve the good will of Firm B (which is also its client). The opinion concludes that there is no bright line test to determine when the representation represents a

4.   Should the concern about lawyer loyalty extend to more than instances of filing suit against another client?

a.   The ABA Standing Committee on Ethics and Professional Responsibility has explored the suit against a present client issue in several other contexts. For example, ABA Formal Opinion 97–407 (May 13, 1997) considered the situation where a lawyer serves as an expert witness in a matter. Does that lawyer have a lawyer-client relationship with the party for whom he or she testifies, which would prevent that lawyer from acting contrary to the interest of that party in another matter? The opinion said "no" if the lawyer is only testifying on the party's behalf (as either a fact witness or an expert), but "yes" if the lawyer is also consulting with lawyers for that party. If the lawyer's testimony affects his or her duty of confidentiality to other clients, however, the lawyer must secure consent of those other clients before the lawyer could act as an expert at all.

b.   May a lawyer cross-examine an opponent's expert witness whom the lawyer concurrently represents in unrelated matters? ABA Formal Opinion 92–367 (Oct. 16, 1992) concluded that the cross-examination would "ordinarily" present a conflict under what is now Rule 1.7(a)(1). The opinion reasoned that vigorous cross-examination would violate the lawyer's duty of loyalty to one client, the expert, while failure to cross-examine vigorously would violate the duty to represent zealously the lawyer's other client. Furthermore, the lawyer might know confidential information about the expert that would be relevant to the cross-examination but Rule 1.6 would forbid the lawyer to use that information. The opinion suggests that a lawyer from another firm could be retained to conduct the cross-examination, and that the first lawyer could continue to conduct the rest of the defense. Do you agree that such a solution should suffice? Cf. Rule 1.7, Comment 8.

c.   Is a lawyer who is also a public official (a member of the county council) liable for breach of fiduciary duty to a client because he voted in a way that was adverse to that client? Joe v. Two Thirty Nine Joint Venture, 145 S.W.3d 150 (Tex.2004), involved the firm of Jenkens & Gilchrist, which represented 239 Joint Venture in its sale of a tract of land designated for apartments. Prior to the sale's closing, the county council voted to place a moratorium on apartment construction in the county. Joe, who was both a partner in Jenkens & Gilchrist and a member of the county council, voted in favor of the moratorium. 239 Joint Venture sued Joe and Jenkens & Gilchrist claiming that Joe's vote constituted a breach of fiduciary duty to the client. The Texas Supreme Court held that official immunity shielded Joe from any conflict of interest arising from Joe's legitimate legislative functions. The court found that Joe's actions "involved personal deliberation, decision, and judgment characteristic of a discretionary act that was delegated to him as a public official."

---

conflict of interest. If a lawyer in a big firm closes a residential real estate transaction for a lawyer in another firm whose out-of-state office is litigating against a different office of the first firm, there may be no conflict at all. If a solo practitioner represents a small firm lawyer in a divorce case, taking even unrelated cases against each other might be a nonconsentable conflict. Somewhere between those extremes, the lawyers must notify the clients in the unrelated matters and give them the chance to consent or get other counsel.

d.   Rule 1.7(a)(1) speaks of a conflict if the lawyer's representation of one client is "directly adverse" to another client. What makes a representation "directly adverse," as opposed to "materially limited," which is the standard in Rule 1.7(a)(2)? "Directly adverse" suggests that the lawyer may be "indirectly adverse," so long as no "material limitation" is involved.

ABA Formal Opinion 05–434 (Dec. 8, 2004) said there is no "direct adversity" when a lawyer represents a testator who seeks to disinherit a person who is also one of the lawyer's clients. Obviously, no potential beneficiary wants to be disinherited, but such a person has only an expectancy interest—not a legal right—to a bequest. Therefore, unless the testator has contractual or quasi-contractual obligations to leave property to the person, the lawyer is not representing a client "directly adverse" to another client, under Rule 1.7(a)(1). Turning to the "materially limited representation" standard of Rule 1.7(a)(2), the opinion advised that, in most cases, preparing an instrument to disinherit a beneficiary is a "simple, straightforward, almost ministerial task." However, if the lawyer provides *advice* as to whether to disinherit one of the lawyer's other clients or drafts documents in violation of "previously agreed-upon family estate planning objectives," there is a "heightened risk" that representing a testator trying to disinherit one of the lawyer's other clients will be materially limited by the lawyer's obligations to the beneficiary.

ABA Formal Opinion 05–435 (Dec. 8, 2004) involved a lawyer who represents a liability insurer in various matters and represents a client who seeks to sue someone covered by a policy issued by that insurer. The opinion concludes that the lawyer in that case is not normally "directly adverse" to the insurer unless the lawyer names the liability insurer as a defendant or the attorney takes discovery of the insurer's representatives. However, the lawyer's representation of the plaintiff seeking recovery may have a "material limitation" conflict. The opinion says the critical issues are the "likelihood that a difference in interests will occur" and whether such differences "will materially interfere with the lawyer's independent professional judgment in considering alternatives or foreclose courses of action that reasonably should be pursued on behalf of the client." For example, if the lawyer learned information in connection with the representation of the liability insurer that would materially help the new client's case *against* the insured defendant, a conflict of interest would exist under Rule 1.7(a)(2).

5.   May a lawyer avoid conflicts by limiting the scope of the representation?

a.   In Sumitomo Corp v. J.P. Morgan & Co., Inc., 2000 WL 145747 (S.D.N.Y.2000), the Paul Weiss firm represented Sumitomo in investigating an employee who was responsible for losses from copper trading. Later, various banks demanded payments from Sumitomo with respect to transactions of which it was unaware. Paul Weiss realized that it represented some of those banks and told Sumitomo it could not evaluate or litigate the bank claims on Sumitomo's behalf. Paul Weiss represented Sumitomo in filing suit against J.P. Morgan, but Chase Manhattan, a Paul Weiss client in other matters, refused to waive the conflict, so Sumitomo had another firm represent it in filing suit against

Chase. Hence, Chase was not a party to the litigation where Paul Weiss was representing Sumitomo. However, the judge then consolidated the two cases for pretrial discovery, and Chase then moved to disqualify Paul Weiss from suing J.P. Morgan. The court refused. "Chase is a huge financial institution," the court said. It is not an individual who would feel a betrayal of trust. The court consolidated the two cases for discovery purposes only because the court granted Chase's motion to do that. Chase's lawyers acknowledged that there were no issues involving the use of confidences.[8]

b.   Association of the Bar of the City of New York Committee on Professional and Judicial Ethics, Formal Opinion 2001–3 (2001), also addressed this issue. The opinion approved having another firm bring the case against the client that the principal firm cannot sue. The opinion also referred to negotiations in multiparty business deals where the lawyers may use this technique. The disqualified law firm may not use this procedure as a sham (where the otherwise conflicted firm is a behind-the-scenes manager of the matter that it has undertaken not to pursue). The firm also may not take actions that hurt the firm's other client. With those caveats, however, the presence of one or two avoided areas of conflict does not mean the lawyer is disqualified altogether.

c.   Does this approach make sense to you? Can you think of other situations where the lawyer can use Rule 1.2(c) to limit the scope of representation so that the lawyer will avoid violating Model Rule 1.7(a)(1)?

6. Can concern about loyalty to the lawyer's current clients be so excessive that it leads to injustice to clients who are trying to find a capable lawyer to represent them?

a.   In Flatt v. Superior Court (Daniel), 885 P.2d 950 (Cal.1994), a prospective client asked a law firm to sue his former lawyer. The prospective client disclosed confidential information to a lawyer in this new firm who told him that he "definitely" had a good malpractice claim. A week later, the firm called the prospective client back and declined the representation because it was representing the prior lawyer in an unrelated matter. The firm did not tell the prospective client about the statute of limitations for his claim or recommend that he retain other counsel. The California Supreme Court declared that this handling of the conflict was proper because giving the prospective client information about protecting his interests would have been disloyal to the existing client. Do you agree?

b.   What is the relevance of Model Rule 4.3 to the situation presented in *Flatt*? Rule 4.3 says: "The lawyer shall not give legal advice to an unrepresented person, other than the advice to secure counsel, if the lawyer knows or should reasonably should know that the interests of such a person are or have a reasonable possibility of being in conflict with the interests of the client." Is a prospective client just like any other unrepresented person in terms of the application of Rule 4.3?

---

[8]   See discussion in Ronald D. Rotunda, Resolving Client Conflicts by Hiring "Conflicts Counsel," 62 Hastings L. J. 677 (2011).

B. ASCERTAINING WHO IS A CURRENT CLIENT

1.   Generally, a lawyer may not represent someone in litigation against a current client without both parties' consent. Is International Bolts a current client? At this moment, you are not doing any work for International Bolts, and the company may never call again.

a.   In IBM Corp. v. Levin, 579 F.2d 271 (3d Cir.1978), IBM sought to disqualify a law firm, CBM, for representing a client in a suit against IBM. The trial court disqualified CBM and the court of appeals affirmed. The trial court "found as a fact that at all relevant times CBM had an on-going attorney-client relationship with both IBM and the plaintiffs. This assessment of the relationship seems entirely reasonable to us. Although CBM had no specific assignment from IBM on hand on the day that [CBM filed] the antitrust complaint [against IBM] and even though CBM performed services for IBM on a fee-for-services basis rather than pursuant to a retainer arrangement, the pattern of repeated retainers, both before and after the filing of the complaint, supports the finding of a continuous relationship."

b.   In, Parallel Iron, LLC v. Adobe Systems, Inc., 2013 WL 789207 (D.Del.2013), the RAK law firm represented Parallel Iron in a suit alleging that Adobe infringed two Parallel Iron patents. Adobe moved to disqualify RAK because RAK earlier issued three opinion letters—in 2006–08, 2009 and 2010–11—to Adobe discussing whether Adobe was violating patents *unrelated* to those of Parallel Iron. There was a separate statement of work and fee agreement for each opinion, but Adobe said that it continued to think of RAK as its opinion counsel. The court said it must take a "client-centric" approach to the analysis and determine what Adobe could reasonably believe. "[T]he six year history between Adobe and RAK was sufficient to instill in Adobe a reasonable belief that it would not be sued by RAK, at least absent some sort of prior notice that RAK would no longer be available to serve as Adobe's opinion counsel." The role of opinion counsel is "limited," but "opinion counsel is still counsel, complete with fiduciary duties to clients and professional obligations under the Model Rules." RAK had never refused work from Adobe, and the fact it could do so in the future "does not mean it is free to sue its client prior to making it clear that the relationship is over." The court granted the motion to disqualify.

c.   Should a law firm avoid the inference of continued representation by writing a "letter of disengagement" to each client terminating the relationship at the end of a given matter? Why do you suppose firms are loath to do that? Is the approach in IBM v. Levin simply recognizing a relationship the firm hopes the client believes still exists? [9]

2.   Is every division and wholly-owned subsidiary of a current client a client of the lawyer for conflict purposes?

a.   Courts typically treat a division within one corporation as part of the client itself. In Image Technical Services, Inc. v. Eastman Kodak Co., 820 F.Supp. 1212 (N.D.Cal.1993), for example, the law firm

---

[9]   For more about the history of the rule and the desirability of tempering its application with a rule of reason, see Thomas D. Morgan, Suing a Current Client, 9 Georgetown J. Legal Ethics 1157 (1996).

prepared plaintiffs' briefs in a Supreme Court antitrust case against Kodak. At the same time, the firm's Hong Kong office represented a division of Kodak that was doing completely unrelated work in China and other international markets. The law firm obtained oral consent from the division representative with whom the firm worked, but it did not seek consent from the Kodak general counsel. The court disqualified the law firm from all further participation in the case. Later, when the plaintiff (using different counsel) won the case on remand to the trial court, the first law firm applied for statutory attorneys' fees due the prevailing plaintiff under the Clayton Act. The Ninth Circuit denied attorneys'' fees to the law firm for its representation of plaintiff prior to its disqualification. Image Technical Service v. Eastman Kodak Co., 136 F.3d 1354 (9th Cir.1998).

b.   ABA Formal Opinion 95–390 (Jan. 25, 1995), broadly analyzed conflicts of interest in the corporate family context. The opinion said that corporate family relationships are too varied to adopt a bright-line rule forbidding a law firm that represents a parent corporation, for example, from suing the parent's subsidiary. The lawyer must ask whether (1) the subsidiary and parent are in effect operated as one entity, (2) there has been an agreement to treat the whole corporate family as the client, or (3) the lawyer's obligations to the parent will materially limit pursuit of the claim against the subsidiary.[10] See also, Model Rule 1.7, Comment 34 & 35 ("Organizational Clients"); Association of the Bar of the City of New York Committee on Professional and Judicial Ethics, Formal Opinion 2007–3 (Sept. 2007) (consider law firm dealings with the affiliate during work for the current client, confidential information the firm may have learned, and any significant risk of material limitation on the firm's ability to act for either the current or adverse client).

c.   GSI Commerce Solutions, Inc. v. Babycenter, LLC, 618 F.3d 204 (2d Cir. 2010), relied on ABA Formal Opinion 95–390 and Model Rule 1.7, Comment 34, when it upheld the trial court's disqualification of a law firm. The law firm simultaneously represented a parent company (Johnson & Johnson) on various matters, while representing a party adverse to one of Johnson & Johnson's wholly-owned subsidiaries. The litigation involved a matter unrelated to the law firm's representation of Johnson & Johnson. The Second Circuit held that the district court did not abuse its discretion in granting the disqualification motion that the subsidiary filed because the operational relationship between the two companies was close and thus the representation reasonably could diminish "the level of confidence and trust in counsel" held by Johnson & Johnson. In determining whether the parent company and its subsidiary are effectively one entity for conflict-of-interest purposes, the court looked at (1) the entities' financial interdependence and (2) the operational commonality across multiple departments (e.g. accounting, audit, cash management, employee benefits, finance, human resources, information technology, insurance, payroll, and travel services and systems). The court

---

[10] See, e.g., Ronald D. Rotunda, Conflict Problems When Representing Members of Corporate Families, 72 Notre Dame L. Rev. 655 (1997); Robert C. Hacker & Ronald D. Rotunda, Representing the Corporate Client and the Proposed Rules of Professional Conduct, 6 Corporation L. Rev. 269 (1983).

emphasized that both entities relied on the same in-house legal department to handle their legal affairs. This counsel was involved in the underlying dispute since it first arose, including mediation efforts and obtaining outside counsel for the subsidiary. This combination of these factors called for disqualification of the firm.[11]

d.   ABA Formal Opinion 97–405 (Apr. 19, 1997) found it "fairly clear" that, under Model Rule 1.7(a)(1), a lawyer who currently represents a government entity in some kinds of work may not represent a private client against that entity, even in an unrelated matter. The question then became whether the lawyer for one government entity (say a school board) may represent a private client against a different government entity in the same jurisdiction (say the city government). The opinion said that the identity of a government client is "to some extent a matter of common sense and sensibility," and is a matter of functional considerations of how the government works. If the same city attorney represents both entities, the Rules are more likely to consider them a single client for purposes of Rule 1.7(a)(1). Ideally, lawyer and governmental client will reach agreement on that issue at the outset of the representation of the government entity.[12] See Model Rule 1.13, Comment 9 (Government Agency).

e.   Association of the Bar of the City of New York, Formal Opinion 2008–2 (Sept. 2008), examined when in-house counsel may represent both a parent and its corporate affiliates where the interests of the units are not identical, e.g., when the parent does not wholly own the subsidiary. Inside counsel must do the same kinds of conflicts checks that outside firms do, and sometimes handling the conflicts incorrectly may disqualify the whole legal department. Two ways that in-house counsel may deal with this issue are by seeking advance waivers or limiting the scope of representation.

3.   Is the lawyer for a business partnership or trade association the lawyer for each of the individual members?

a.   Most courts hold that it depends on the facts. Courts will ordinarily enforce a specific undertaking to represent the partnership and not to represent its individual members, whether the partnership (for purposes of state partnership law) is an "entity" or an "aggregate" of the individual partners. See, e.g., Greate Bay Hotel & Casino, Inc. v. Atlantic City, 624 A.2d 102 (N.J.Super.L.1993) (a lawyer for a business trust represents the trust as an "entity" and thus is not barred from suing a member of the trust in an unrelated matter); Responsible

---

[11]   See also, Discotrade Ltd. v. Wyeth–Ayerst Int'l Inc., 200 F.Supp.2d 355 (S.D.N.Y.2002) (Dorsey & Whitney disqualified from representing plaintiff because it also represented the defendant's sister corporation in unrelated matters. All of the directors of the sister companies were the same, they shared the same president, computer system, and financial management, and the same in-house legal department served them all.) Cases such as these are discussed in Ronald D. Rotunda, Conflict Problems When Representing Members of Corporate Families, 72 Notre Dame L. Rev. 655 (1997).

[12]   A particularly difficult form of conflict can arise in the patent field where a law firm has two clients seeking related patents. Under the rules of the Patent and Trademark Office, 37 C.F.R. § 1.56, a lawyer for an applicant must disclose all "prior art" in the applicant's field. At the time of consideration of the applications, however, they are each confidential and Rule 1.6 would protect information about each. Although the court acknowledged the impossible situation the law firm found itself in, it ruled that failure to disclose the application of one client in the application of the other was "inequitable conduct" that rendered the issued patent invalid and unenforceable. Molins PLC v. Textron, Inc., 48 F.3d 1172 (Fed.Cir.1995).

Citizens v. Superior Court (Askins), 20 Cal.Rptr.2d 756 (Cal.Ct.App.1993) (lawyer who represents partnership may sue individual partner in unrelated proceeding).

b. ABA Formal Opinion 91–361 (July 12, 1991) concludes that the Model Rules treat partnerships as entities and that Rule 1.13 governs their representation. One or more individual members of a partnership may separately retain the partnership lawyer, as provided in Rule 1.13(e), but representation of an individual partner is not automatic. The opinion concludes that lawyers should make clear to the individual partners at the outset of the representation whom the lawyers represent in order to avoid misunderstandings later. See Model Rule 1.7, Comment 34, and Model Rule 1.13, Comments 7 and 8.

c. In Westinghouse Electric Corp. v. Kerr–McGee Corp., 580 F.2d 1311 (7th Cir.1978), cert. denied 439 U.S. 955 (1978), Kirkland & Ellis filed an antitrust action on behalf of its client, Westinghouse, against various corporations alleging price fixing violations in the uranium industry. Meanwhile the American Petroleum Institute (API) retained Kirkland to oppose legislative proposals introduced in Congress to cause energy companies to divest uranium companies that they owned. On the same day that Kirkland's Chicago office filed the antitrust suit, Kirkland's Washington, D.C. office, representing API, released a report that developed the opposite thesis and took an affirmative position on the subject of competition in the oil-uranium industry. API was not a defendant in the antitrust suit, but three API *members* were defendants.

Individual members of API gave Kirkland & Ellis' Washington office confidential information on their uranium assets in order to aid the firm in opposing the threatened legislation. Moreover, the general counsel of API and Kirkland & Ellis promised the members that they would keep this information confidential. The Seventh Circuit held that API members "each entertained a reasonable belief that it was submitting confidential information regarding its involvement in the uranium industry to a law firm which had solicited the information upon a representation that the firm was acting in the undivided interest of each company." It disqualified Kirkland.

Do you agree? Does *Westinghouse* only hold that when parties supply information on a promise of confidentiality, a court will make them honor their promise? Could the lawyers have avoided this problem if they had not promised confidentiality and had clarified their role? Model Rule 1.13, Comment 10.

d. D.C. Bar Legal Ethics Opinion 305 (2001), concludes that a lawyer who represents a trade association as an entity does not thereby create an attorney-client relationship with the individual members of the association. However, there are circumstances where representing a client adverse to a member of the association can create a conflict of interest. If the member reasonably believes that the lawyer is representing him individually, the member is, regardless of an express agreement, a *de facto* client of the lawyer. Factors one looks at include whether the member of the association disclosed confidential information to the association's lawyer, whether the member has separate representation, whether the lawyer ever previously represented the member individually, and whether the member relied on the lawyer's representation of his individual interest.

See also, ABA Formal Opinion 92–365 (July 6, 1992) (law firm that represents a trade association ordinarily may file an unrelated action against a member of the association with whom the lawyer has formed no attorney-client relationship unless the representation would impair the lawyer's representation of the association itself).

Do these opinions reject *Westinghouse* or apply it?

e.   Jesse v. Danforth, 485 N.W.2d 63 (Wis. 1992), adopted a "retroactive entity" theory when a number of individuals hired a lawyer to form an entity. Under this theory, when the lawyer creates the entity, the court presumes that the only client of the lawyer is the entity and not the individuals that formed it. In *Jesse*, a law firm formed an entity for a group of 23 physicians. Later, a spouse of one of the physicians asked the law firm to represent her in a divorce. The physician moved to disqualify the law firm, but the court refused. The law firm had never had an attorney-client relationship with the individual physicians. Thus, no conflict arose and the law firm could represent the spouse.

Only a minority of jurisdictions apply this retroactive entity theory. Do you agree with the analysis in *Jesse*? Would your answer change if the law firm had met with the physicians and obtained significant and relevant confidential information from them in forming the entity?

f.   Some law firms seek to apply the retroactive entity rule to entity-formation representation by putting the rule in the attorney-client engagement agreement. If a jurisdiction does not ordinarily follow this rule, should lawyers be able to enforce it contractually against a client? Some scholars and large law firms have argued that the law of lawyering should have a contract component when such agreements do not violate public policy.[13] Do you agree?

C.   FIRING A CURRENT CLIENT; THE HOT POTATO RULE

1.   If you find that a conflict develops between two clients, may you avoid the problem by "firing" one of the clients and continuing to represent the other?

a.   At the end of *Cinema 5*, supra, the Second Circuit noted that attorney Fleischmann offered to withdraw from representation of Cinerama in the Western District actions, but Cinerama refused and pressed forward on its disqualification motion. The court did not treat Cinerama's refusal to permit withdrawal as a waiver of its conflict claim. Why not? We know that at least part of the justification for disqualification is the breach of fiduciary duty of loyalty inherent in a conflict of interest. If the court permitted Fleischmann to withdraw from further representation of Cinerama without penalty, would he be seeking to profit from his breach of loyalty?

b.   Unified Sewerage Agency of Washington County, Oregon v. Jelco Inc., 646 F.2d 1339, 1345 n.4 (9th Cir.1981), discussed the problem of the lawyer choosing to represent one client against another.

---

[13] See Richard W. Painter, Rules Lawyers Play By, 76 N.Y.U.L.Rev. 665 (2001); http://www.yalelawjournal.org/forum/in-defense-of-a-reasoned-dialogue-about-law-firms-and-their-sophisticated-clients.

It concluded that a lawyer may not convert a *current* client governed by Rule 1.7 into a *former* client governed by Rule 1.9 merely "by choosing when to cease to represent the disfavored client."

c.   In Picker International, Inc. v. Varian Associates, Inc., 670 F.Supp. 1363 (N.D.Ohio 1987), aff'd, 869 F.2d 578 (Fed.Cir.1989), a large national law firm merged with a firm in another city, and when the client lists were compared, it turned out that the merging firms represented clients who were opponents in current litigation. The merged firm was suing *B* on behalf of *A* (a longtime client of the acquiring firm), while representing *B* (the acquired firm's client) on various other matters. The firm sought to withdraw from representation of *B*, and to continue to represent the longtime client of the big firm. The court held that the firm could not do that without consent of all affected clients. Failing consent, the new firm must withdraw from *all* representation of all parties in the case of *A v. B*. The court said: "A firm may not drop a client like a hot potato, especially if it is in order to keep a far more lucrative client." The case law often calls this principle the "hot potato" rule. The law of conflicts develops from a metaphor of the kitchen.

2.   Should the "hot potato" rule recognize exceptions?

a.   The law of ethics does not have the certainty of Euclidian geometry, and courts do not always apply the hot potato rule inflexibly. In Pennwalt Corp. v. Plough, Inc., 85 F.R.D. 264 (D.Del.1980), the law firm represented Pennwalt for decades. In 1978, the firm began to defend Scholl against antitrust charges. In April 1979, Schering–Plough acquired Scholl as a wholly owned subsidiary. Because Plough was already a wholly owned subsidiary of Schering–Plough, Scholl and Plough became sister corporations. In May 1979, the law firm filed suit against Plough on behalf of its longtime client Pennwalt. Upon learning a week or two later that it represented Scholl in one case and simultaneously represented Pennwalt against Scholl's "sister," the firm sought to withdraw from representing Scholl. After the court granted that motion, Plough moved to disqualify the firm from the case against Plough. The court agreed that counsel may not eliminate a conflict "merely by choosing to represent the more favored client and withdrawing its representation of the other." However, in this case the firm's conflict was inadvertent: the merger activities of the client created the problem. "Scholl is a corporate entity distinct from Plough and Schering–Plough," and it was highly unlikely that as of the date of the law firm's representation there was any misuse of confidential information or adverse effect on its exercise of independent judgment. Thus, the court did not mandate disqualification. See Rule 1.7, Comment 5, which takes this case into account.

b.   In Gould, Inc. v. Mitsui Mining & Smelting Co., 738 F.Supp. 1121 (N.D.Ohio 1990), the Jones Day law firm was representing Gould in suing various defendants who allegedly misappropriated Gould trade secrets. One of these defendants was Pechiney. In 1989, Pechiney acquired IG Technologies (IGT), a company that Jones Day represented in an unrelated matter. Thus, Jones Day found itself in a conflict between Gould and IGT's parent. In response to a motion to disqualify Jones Day from representing Gould against Pechiney, the court reasoned that, because of the "explosion of merger activity by corporations during the past fifteen years" it is appropriate to adopt a "less mechanical approach" and "balanc[e] the various interests." In this case, there was "no demonstration that Pechiney has been prejudiced by the law firm's representation of Gould." Further, disqualification would cost Gould a great deal of time and money, and significantly delay progress in this case. Moreover, "the conflict was created by Pechiney's acquisition of IGT several years after the instant case was commenced, not by an affirmative act of Jones Day." However, the court held, the conflict "must not endure." Hence, the law firm must discontinue its representation of either Gould or IGT, and erect a "screen" around the lawyers who had worked for the party that the firm dropped.[14]

c.   In Pioneer–Standard Electronics, Inc. v. Cap Gemini America, Inc., 2002 WL 553460 (N.D.Ohio 2002), plaintiff Pioneer–Standard, moved to disqualify defendant's counsel, Shearman & Sterling, arguing that the firm currently represented it. Shearman & Sterling's relationship with Pioneer–Standard began when Shearman merged with a German law firm that was handling Pioneer–Standard regulatory matters before the European Commission. After the merger, Shearman & Sterling billed approximately ten hours to Pioneer–Standard on those matters. After Pioneer–Standard refused to waive the conflict, Shearman & Sterling withdrew from the European representation. Although the court found that Pioneer–Standard was a current client of Shearman & Sterling, it refused to disqualify. It acknowledged the hot potato rule but found that there should be no disqualification if the matters "were unrelated and posed no likelihood of passing confidential information." The European regulatory matters did not generate confidential information that could be used against Pioneer–Standard in this case; there was no other prejudice to Pioneer–Standard from the continued representation; the foreign matter was limited to registering a commercial transaction of plaintiff; it consumed few hours of counsel's time; and the case was wholly unrelated to the instant litigation.

The court refused to apply the hot potato rule but offered no bright-line test to replace it. Instead, it said the court would not disqualify a law firm "if the attorney can show that he can represent adverse clients concurrently with equal vigor, without conflict of loyalties and without using confidential information to the detriment of either client." Does the case simply acknowledge that a rule of reason is appropriate in a world of complex legal relationships? Or, does a vague rule give a competitive advantage to the least ethical firms—the ones most willing to test the limits of ethical conduct?

3.   **What about waivers of possible future conflicts? Should clients be able to agree at the outset of the representation that, if a conflict later arises, the lawyer may represent one of the clients against the other? Should law firms make an advance waiver of conflicts part of the boilerplate in their retainer agreements?**

a.   Restatement (Third) The Law Governing Lawyers § 122, Comment *d*, says:

> "A client's open-ended agreement to consent to all conflicts normally should be ineffective unless the client possesses

---

[14]   You will see more about "screening" in Problems 15 & 16, *infra*.

sophistication in the matter in question and has had the opportunity to receive independent legal advice about the consent. * * *

"On the other hand, particularly in a continuing client-lawyer relationship in which the lawyer is expected to act on behalf of the client without a new engagement for each matter, the gains to both lawyer and client from a system of advance consent to defined future conflicts might be substantial. A client might, for example, give informed consent in advance to types of conflicts that are familiar to the client. Such an agreement could effectively protect the client's interest while assuring that the lawyer did not undertake a potentially disqualifying representation."

b.   General Cigar Holdings, Inc. v. Altadis, S.A., 144 F.Supp.2d 1334 (S.D.Fla.2001), honored a broad advance waiver. Latham & Watkins, counsel to General Cigar in an antitrust suit against Altadis, continued to represent General Cigar, Altadis, and other tobacco companies in an action to challenge state advertising restrictions in Massachusetts. When the firm accepted the Massachusetts engagement, it secured a signed waiver from each client waiving any objection to current or future representation of one against the other in some other matter. None of the lawyers handling the antitrust suit worked on the Massachusetts case, nor did firm members have access to other confidential information about Altadis. The court concluded that Altadis' advance consent was valid. The parties were informed and sophisticated, and they knew of the firm's standing relationship with General Cigar, even though they did not know of the planned antitrust litigation. The antitrust/trademark claims in this suit were not substantially related to the free speech/advertising claims in the other case. The court concluded that representation of the plaintiff in this case would not impair the firm's substantive representation of Altadis in any other matter.

c.   Worldspan, L.P. v. Sabre Group Holdings, Inc., 5 F.Supp.2d 1356 (N.D.Ga.1998), however, was less friendly to advance waivers. The law firm was counsel to Worldspan in state tax matters in Georgia and Tennessee. In this case, it agreed to represent the defendants in an unrelated suit that Worldspan had filed. The firm relied on its standard engagement letter that Worldspan signed six years earlier on the advice of experienced, independent counsel. The letter stated, "we will not be precluded from representing clients who may have interests adverse to Worldspan" that are not substantially related and do not involve the use of adverse information. The court held that this six-year-old waiver did not constitute an informed prospective consent to the current representation; its language was not specific enough to cover representing an adverse party in a lawsuit filed by Worldspan, even where the letter expressly named that adverse party as an existing client of the law firm. The court also found the tax work was more closely related to the current litigation than the law firm had believed.

d.   ABA Formal Opinion 05–436 (May 11, 2005) advises that general and open-ended prospective consent is more likely valid when the client is an experienced user of legal services, "particularly if, for example, the client is independently represented by other counsel in giving consent and the consent is limited to future conflicts unrelated to the subject of the representation." The intent of the 2002 amendments to Rule 1.7 is to permit "a lawyer to obtain effective informed consent to a wider range of future conflicts than would have been possible under the Model Rules prior to their amendment."[15] Now, there is a new Comment 22, which specifically authorizes prospective consents to future conflicts. The term "waiver" in Comment 22, means "the same thing as the term 'informed consent,' as used in Rule 1.7 and elsewhere in the Comments."

Opinion 05–436 reminds lawyers that if a conflict is not consentable at all, it is not subject to advance consent. Further, the client's consent must be confirmed in writing, Rule 1.7(b)(4). In addition, "a client's informed consent to a future conflict, without more, does not constitute the client's informed consent to the disclosure or use of the client's confidential information against the client." Finally, the advance consent does not eliminate the lawyer's need to secure informed consent from the client the lawyer wants to represent in the later matter.

See also, D.C. Bar Legal Ethics Opinion 309 (2001); Association of the Bar of the City of New York, Committee on Professional and Judicial Ethics, Formal Op. 2006–1 (Feb. 17, 2006) (advance waivers permissible where given by sophisticated clients who have advice of counsel and where no confidential information of one client will be used to advantage another).

e.   Galderma Laboratories v. Actavis Mid Atlantic LLC, 927 F.Supp.2d 390 (N.D. Tex. 2013), held a sophisticated client to an advance waiver executed when the client was represented by its in-house counsel. Galderma is a worldwide leader in branded skin products. It retained Vinson & Elkins (V&E) to advise it on employee benefit plans. In the engagement letter that its in-house counsel approved, Galderma agreed that with the exception of matters that would put confidential information at risk, V&E was "free to represent other clients, including clients whose interests may conflict with [Galderma's] in litigation, business transactions, or other legal matters." Actavis, a long-time V&E client, then retained V&E to defend it in an intellectual property case filed by Galderma against Actavis. Galderma moved to disqualify V&E, but the court denied the motion. The issue is whether Galderma knew what it was doing when it gave its advanced consent. "The more experienced the client is in legal matters generally and in making decisions of the type involved, the less information and explanation is needed for the consent to be informed." A client who is advised by independent counsel in giving the advance consent "should be assumed to have given informed consent." The court specifically relied on the ABA Model Rules rather than the "less restrictive" Texas Disciplinary Rules of Professional Conduct. The Court relied on ABA Formal Opinion 05–436 (May 11, 2005).

f.   If you were the general counsel of a corporation, would you advise your client to sign an advance consent to a future conflict? What questions would you ask the outside law firm that seeks such advance

_____

[15] This opinion specifically withdrew (i.e., overruled) Formal Opinion 93–372 (Apr. 16, 1993) (Waiver of Future Conflicts of Interest).

consent? Would you be more likely to consent to a conflict that arose in a transactional matter rather than a litigation matter? What does your client receive in return for signing an advance consent?

D.   THE PROBLEM OF POSITIONAL CONFLICTS

1.   What duty of loyalty, if any, do you have not to take a legal position on prepayment penalties that is inconsistent with the interest of a regular client like the First National Bank? Is there a technical conflict of interest that would obligate you not to take this case?

a.   We know that lawyers often take inconsistent legal positions in the *same* case. A lawyer for an alleged debtor may plead, "My client did not borrow the money (it was a gift), but even if he did borrow it, he already has repaid the debt." Is the problem of inconsistency *between* cases different?

b.   Does the permissibility of positional conflicts depend on whether interpretations of fact or of law are involved? Might you represent Client Y in one case arguing that facts justify a finding of negligence, but defend Client Z in another case on identical facts saying that the conduct showed due care? Should the propriety of the conduct be different if, as in this problem, you plan to try to change a controlling legal standard?

2.   Should it matter whether you take inconsistent positions before the same court? What if your law firm takes inconsistent positions in different courts?

a.   Before the 2002 amendments, Model Rule 1.7, Comment 9, said:

> "[I]t is ordinarily not improper to assert such [inconsistent] positions in cases pending in different trial courts, but it may be improper to do so in cases pending at the same time in an appellate court."

Do you agree that the trial-appellate and different appellate court distinctions were useful ways to decide when a positional conflict is proper or improper?

b.   ABA Formal Opinion 93–377 (Oct. 16, 1993) cast doubt on the trial-appellate court distinction. It analyzed the so-called "positional conflicts" issue as follows:

> "[I]f the two matters are being litigated in the same jurisdiction, and there is a substantial risk that the law firm's representation of one client will create a legal precedent, even if not binding, which is likely materially to undercut the legal position being urged on behalf of the other client, the lawyer should either refuse to accept the second representation or (if otherwise permissible) withdraw from the first, unless both clients consent after full disclosure of the potential ramifications of the lawyer continuing to handle both matters. * * *

> "[Even if the matters are being litigated in different jurisdictions,] if the lawyer concludes that the issue is of such importance and that its determination in one case is likely to

have a significant impact on its determination in the second case, thus impairing the lawyer's effectiveness—or if the lawyer concludes that, because of the dual representation, there will be an inclination by the firm either to 'soft pedal' the issue or to alter the firm's arguments on behalf of one or both clients, thus again impairing the lawyer's effectiveness—the lawyer should not accept the second representation."

c.   Model Rule 1.7, Comment 24, takes a different approach to positional conflicts. The Comment suggests looking at various factors, such as whether the issue is procedural or substantive, where the cases are pending, the clients' "reasonable expectations," the "temporal relationship between the matters," and the importance of the issue to the short-and long-term interests of the clients. It posits two examples: First, advocating Client A's position that *"might* create precedent adverse to the interests" of Client B whom the lawyer represents in an unrelated matter is not a conflict. Second, if the lawyer has successfully advanced Client A's position, and the resulting decision *"will create* a precedent *likely* to seriously weaken the position" taken on behalf of Client B, the Comment advises that this does present a conflict of interest. Is this clear?

d.   Does Model Rule 1.7 provide good guidance to lawyers trying to conduct a complex practice in a manner consistent with appropriate professional standards? Is it too vague? Association of the Bar of the City of New York Committee on Professional and Judicial Ethics, Formal Opinion 2003–03 discussed how modern firms should run conflicts checks. Firms must keep written or electronic records and maintain them in such a form that the law firm can quickly and accurately search them. New York records must go back at least to 1996 when the rule first required these records. They must include client names, adverse party names, and a brief description of each engagement, and each office must consult those records before undertaking any new matter. Firms need not keep detailed lists of all corporate family relationships except for those they regularly represent. Would even such records let a law firm check for positional conflicts?

3.   Would Model Rule 6.3 impose different obligations if you were a member of a legal service organization's board of directors that wanted to take a position contrary to one of your paying clients?

a.   When the president appointed John Erlenborn, a former member of Congress, to the board of the Legal Services Corporation (LSC), he was also a partner in a major law firm that represented growers in disputes over farm workers' conditions. The LSC-funded lawyers often represented the farm workers. The American Farm Bureau Federation, a private lobbying group representing agricultural interests, was not one of the firm's clients. However, it began a campaign to persuade the firm's agricultural clients to object to what the Farm Bureau characterized as Erlenborn's conflict of interest, i.e., he took positions as an LSC board member that the Farm Bureau claimed were harmful to farm interests.

Erlenborn offered to recuse himself from any decisions of the LSC board that directly involved reform legislation that the Farm Bureau supported, or that involved agricultural activities that could have an impact on his firm's clients. However, the Farm Bureau's objections (including its objection to Erlenborn's proposed congressional testimony on the reform legislation) continued until Erlenborn resigned from the LSC board. The ABA president-elect said that there was no conflict of interest and that nothing required Erlenborn's resignation. Do you agree? Did the Rules require Erlenborn to resign from the LSC board, or was he simply bending over backwards to please some firm clients?

b.   Suppose that the legal services agency agrees with your bank client and opposes regulations prohibiting prepayment penalties because it believes such regulations will raise the cost of credit to unacceptable levels. May you lobby on the agency's behalf against the regulatory proposals? Must you inform the agency that you also represent the First National Bank, which supports the agency's position? Look at Model Rule 6.4.

c.   Assume that you fully inform the legal services agency and the bank of your representation of each. Does either Rule 3.9 or Rule 6.4 require you to voluntarily disclose to the regulatory body that in appearing on behalf of the legal services agency you also further the interests of the First National Bank?

4.   Even if the ethics rules allow you to represent the consumer against the bank, are there other problems you might face?

a.   Could your banking client force you out of the case indirectly? Could it insist that, although it is not now a party, it wants you to file an amicus brief on its behalf? If you agreed and withdrew from representing your neighbor, could your neighbor force you to withdraw from the case altogether? Of course, you could ask your regular client, the First National Bank, to relieve you of any further obligations to represent it in paying matters, but that would make your pro bono activities on behalf of your neighbor a lot more costly.

b.   If you take this case, must you warn your neighbor that one of your best clients is a bank that opposes to your attacking the prepayment penalty? Even if no technical conflict of interest exists, would the neighbor consider this information relevant? Remember that your consumer-client is not a repeat litigator, but the bank is.[16] In other words, the banks constantly face challenges to prepayment penalties and the issue may be worth millions of dollars to them over a twenty-year period. Should that affect your answer?

c.   Now, assure that the bank belongs to a banking-industry group that has confidential guidelines on how to oppose challenges to the prepayment penalties. If you had access to those guidelines it would help you craft the neighbor's attack on prepayment penalties because you would know the bank's "playbook," i.e., its general approach to settlement, litigation strategy, strengths, weaknesses, and attitudes. Must you disqualify yourself if you have access to that information even if you do not look at it?

------

[16] For further analysis, see John S. Dzienkowski, Positional Conflicts of Interest, 71 Texas L. Rev. 457 (1993).

CONFLICTS OF INTEREST IN CRIMINAL LITIGATION

Criminal cases present some of the most interesting conflicts of interest questions. The principles are the same as in the preceding problems, but in most civil cases, we assume there is little public stake in a decision whether to consent to a conflict of interest. In criminal cases, on the other hand, courts have a duty to protect defendants' constitutional right to a fair trial.

Holloway v. Arkansas, 435 U.S. 475 (1978), raised a lawyer's conflicts of interest to a constitutional dimension. It said that the court must reverse a state criminal conviction if a trial judge requires joint representation in a criminal case after a defendant's timely objection. The court, in this circumstance, must presumes the joint representation is prejudicial. "Joint representation of conflicting interests is suspect because of what it tends to prevent the attorney from doing."

In *Holloway,* the conflict may have precluded defense counsel "from exploring possible plea negotiations and the possibility of an agreement to testify for the prosecution, provided a lesser charge or a favorable sentencing recommendation would be acceptable. Generally speaking, a conflict may also prevent an attorney from challenging the admission of evidence prejudicial to one client but perhaps favorable to another, or from arguing at the sentencing hearing the relative involvement and culpability of his clients in order to minimize the culpability of one by emphasizing that of another."

Cuyler v. Sullivan, 446 U.S. 335 (1980), added that the court need not wait for the defendants to object to joint representation. If the court knows or reasonably should know that a particular conflict of interest exists, it must initiate an inquiry into the propriety of multiple representation. Even when the court did not know of the possible conflict, if "actual conflict of interest * * * adversely affected" the lawyer's performance, the court must reverse the defendant's conviction.

Indeed, the concern about conflict-free representation is so strong that a prosecutor sometimes may object to a conflict that the defendants are willing to waive. United States v. Locascio, 6 F.3d 924 (2d Cir.1993), cert. denied, 511 U.S. 1070 (1994), involved the prosecution of alleged mob boss John Gotti. Bruce Cutler had very effectively represented Gotti in previous criminal trials. The government did not want him to do so again. This time, the Government caught him on tapes of conversations with Gotti. The government intended to introduce these tapes at trial to show the planning of illegal acts. Thus, even if Cutler would not testify, he was in a position analogous to an "unsworn witness" who would be forced to defend his own conduct before the jury. Further, Cutler had once represented a Gotti associate, Michael Coiro, who would be government witness. Therefore, Cutler would be impaired in cross-examining Coiro. Over Gotti's objection, the court intervened to "protect" Gotti from Mr. Cutler's conflicts. The Second Circuit affirmed. Do you suppose that Mr. Gotti was pleased by the court's concern for his welfare? Was the Second Circuit right?

RULE 1.8(d) AND THE ISSUE OF PUBLICATION RIGHTS

Model Rule 1.8(d) says that, "prior to the conclusion of a representation of a client, a lawyer shall not make or negotiate an agreement giving the lawyer literary or media rights to a portrayal or account based in substantial part on information relating to the representation.

What purpose does the rule serve? Does Model Rule 1.8, Comment 9, help provide an answer?

In People v. Corona, 145 Cal.Rptr. 894 (Cal.Ct.App.1978), the court observed that by entering into a literary rights contract with the accused prior to trial, the lawyer "was forced to choose between his own pocketbook and the best interests of his client, the accused." The lawyer's financial stake in the literary rights encouraged him to insist on a lengthy and sensational trial, rather than invoke various defenses that might abort or change the nature of the trial.[17]

Should a client be able to waive the protection of Rule 1.8(d)?

Maxwell v. Superior Court, 639 P.2d 248 (Cal.1982), allowed a waiver by relying on a California provision, Rule 5–101, which allows lawyers to enter into business relations adverse to a client if the client consents. The defendant, charged with capital crimes, signed a contract with his lawyers. The lawyers promised to act competently and warned the defendant of the possible conflicts and prejudice that the publication agreement would create: "It declares that counsel may wish to (1) create damaging publicity to enhance exploitation value, (2) avoid mental defenses because, if successful, they might suggest petitioner's incapacity to make the contract, and (3) see him convicted and even sentenced to death for publicity value." The defendant filed a mandamus action against the trial judge for relying on the rule to disqualify his defense lawyer and the California Supreme Court ordered the disqualification overturned.

Do you agree with this result? Is there a systemic interest (an interest of justice) in seeing that defendants get a fair trial? If that interest is relevant, should it be improper for a court to accept the defendant's "waiver" of the conflict?

May a criminal defense lawyer secure literary rights *after* the conclusion of the legal matter? Why should we draw this distinction? If a lawyer publishes his memoirs, does that waive the attorney-client privilege of his clients regardless of when the client and lawyer sign any contract? See, e.g., In re von Bülow, 828 F.2d 94 (2d Cir.1987), where von Bülow acquiesced in his lawyer's publication of the book regarding details of the prior representation. He even joined with his lawyer in actively promoting sales of book. The court held that the client waived the privilege as to matters specifically revealed in the book, but there

---

[17] United States v. Hearst, 638 F.2d 1190 (9th Cir.1980), ordered a hearing Patty Hearst must show that the conflict in fact affected her lawyer's judgment whether to seek a continuance and a change of venue, and whether to have the defendant testify. It would not be necessary, however, for her to show that the conflict actually changed the result in the case.

was no broader subject matter waiver as to undisclosed communications not mentioned in the book.[18]

Rule 1.8(d) applies only to defense counsel. Should there be similar limits on prosecutors who write memoirs about their careers?

Problem 11

CONFLICTS OF INTEREST IN CRIMINAL LITIGATION

OMITTED IN CONCISE EDITION

———

Problem 12

CONFLICTS BETWEEN CLIENT INTERESTS AND THE LAWYER'S PERSONAL INTEREST

A lawyer who represents a client must put the client's interest ahead of the lawyer's own. That is easy to say, harder to assure, and proving that the requirement has been met can be harder still. This problem presents some situations in which a lawyer might profit as a result of a professional relationship in ways that go beyond collecting normal legal fees. We first ask under what conditions a lawyer may properly collect a fee in a form that makes the lawyer a business associate of the client. Next, we ask whether a lawyer may use confidential client information to engage in business transactions with third parties. Then we look at whether a lawyer may accept a client's gift, and at what happens when the lawyer and client fall in love.

FACTS

Attorney Joan Doe went to high school with James Johnson, a local engineer. Johnson asked Doe to help him set up a small business. He had very little money, and the capital he had raised from a few local investors was not enough to pay much of a legal fee. Johnson asked if he could pay the fee over an extended period, with interest. Instead, Doe suggested that Johnson pay her by giving her 10 percent of the stock in the new corporation as payment for all the work necessary to establish it and carry it through the first year. Doe thought the business looked like a good, relatively cheap investment opportunity, and after Johnson agreed to the arrangement, Doe drafted the articles of incorporation, bylaws, and a shareholders' agreement.

Johnson's company is doing very well. Doe has learned from him that the company will be building a new plant in an industrial park near town. The plans for the industrial park

---

[18] In that case, the state prosecuted Count von Bülow for attempting to kill his wife, Martha "Sunny" by allegedly injecting her with insulin causing her to lapse into an irreversible coma. The jury convicted von Bulow and the court sentenced him to 30 years. Professor Alan Dershowitz represented him on appeal and secured a reversal. At the second trial, the jury acquitted Von Bülow. That led to a movie, Reversal of Fortune (1990), adapted from Dershowitz's book, Reversal of Fortune: Inside the von Bülow Case (1985).

are a secret to all but a few people, and Doe realizes that property in proximity to the park is likely to increase in value. She knows of such a nearby parcel that is for sale, and, after concluding that Johnson probably does not plan to buy it, she bought it.

After his company made its first million dollars, Johnson was thrilled. "Joan," he said, "you have been my lawyer these three years and I could not have succeeded without you. Please draw up the papers to transfer the title to my year-old Mercedes Benz to yourself." The car is worth $75,000. Doe was stunned and does not know how to reply to Johnson's generous direction.

Now, Doe and Johnson have fallen in love. Marriage seems in their future, but meanwhile, they are together whenever they are not both at work.

QUESTIONS

A. ACCEPTING PAYMENT IN THE FORM OF STOCK; BUSINESS TRANSACTIONS WITH A CLIENT

1. Does the law prohibit lawyers from taking all or part of their fee in the form of stock in the client's business?

a.   Historically, lawyers have entered into business transactions with clients. For example, oil and gas lawyers have purchased interests in their client's oil wells and real estate lawyers have purchased client properties as investments. In some of those cases, the lawyers exchanged legal services for the investments. However, prior to 2000, lawyers generally did not invest in the stock of corporate clients. The notable exception to this was in California's Silicon Valley, where law firms took advantage of the more liberal California conflicts rules and often invested in client equity. With the dot.com boom of the late 1990s, law firms all over the United States sought to participate in the wealth generated through initial public offerings of client stock. These efforts led to a series of ethics opinions approving, with certain limitations, such investments and trading legal services for equity. Proponents of such arrangements argued that (1) clients want lawyers to take equity positions as a way of showing lawyer confidence in the client's business model, (2) lawyers' equity positions reduce the clients' need for capital and align the interests of lawyers and clients, (3) paying lawyers with equity makes legal fees lower than they otherwise would have been, (4) law firm equity investments create a compensation structure that allows firms to retain lawyers and promote innovative client fee structures, and (5) equity investments tend to keep the client loyal to the law firm and thus retain the client for future business.

b.   ABA Formal Opinion 00–418 (July 7, 2000) makes clear that Model Rule 1.8(a) treats fees paid in the form of stock as business transactions with a client. Such a fee is also subject to Rule 1.5(a)'s requirement that the total fee be reasonable. We value the stock at the time the lawyers acquire, it and we determine its reasonableness at that time. The opinion also notes other conflicts that can arise, e.g., problems under Rule 1.8(i) if the company's only asset is a cause of action, and under Rule 1.7(a)(2) if the stock is a major asset of the lawyer.

c.   Utah State Bar Advisory Opinion 98–13 (1998) agrees that Rules 1.5, 1.7(a)(2), and 1.8(a)   apply when a lawyer takes stock in payment of a fee. The lawyer should be especially concerned if the stock will be publicly traded or if the client might want restrictions on its trading. Both will affect determination of the stock's value and the latter could constitute a conflict of interest. In any event, Rule 1.8(a) requires that the terms of a stock transaction must be fair and reasonable and disclosed in writing to the client. The value of the stock must also be reasonable as required by Rule 1.5.

d.   The law firm of Wilson Sonsini has held equity investments in clients since the 1950s and has adopted several policies to minimize potential conflicts of interest. The firm never trades services for stock; it charges normal attorneys' fees and purchases stock with cash, not to exceed an investment of $100,000. The law firm holds the stock in a law firm investment partnership separate from the law firm, and the partners in the firm are partners in the investment vehicle. The management committee of the investment partnership makes the decisions to invest. Stock is held long term, and the partnership never votes stock to break a tie.[19]

Many law firms still refuse to invest in client equity because of the risks that such investments entail. Suppose Company's outside law firm invested in Company's stock and provided advice regarding Company's reporting obligations. What might happen to the law firm when Company's fraud leads to Company's bankruptcy?

2.   Why do the courts view business dealings with clients with suspicion? What are the ways in which the lawyer might take advantage of the client?

a.   In re Hibner, 897 N.Y.S.2d 489 (N.Y.App.Div. 2010), is a good example of overreaching a poor couple. The lawyer represented a couple in child neglect proceedings in family court. During the representation, lenders prepared to foreclose on the clients' home. To help avoid foreclosure, the lawyer advised the clients to deed the property to him— apparently in an attempt to defraud creditors. The lawyer paid the balance of the mortgage to the lender and leased the house back to the clients, who then missed several rent payments. Then the lawyer, while still representing the clients in the child neglect proceedings, sued his current clients and obtained a judgment for eviction. The clients sued the lawyer to vacate the deed and enjoin the eviction. The parties eventually settled that suit.

Because of his actions, the Grievance Committee brought disciplinary charges against the lawyer. He permitted his own interests to affect his professional judgment in the course of the representation. He entered into a business transaction with clients where they had differing interests without adequately disclosing the terms and obtaining the clients' informed consent to the transaction and conflict of interest, and he intentionally damaged the clients' during the course of

---

[19] John S. Dzienkowski & Robert J. Peroni, The Decline in Lawyer Independence: Lawyer Equity Investments in Clients, 81 Texas L. Rev. 405, 416 n.39 (2002).

the representation by attempting to evict them. The court sustained all charges and suspended the lawyer for four years.

b.   Cotton v. Kronenberg, 44 P.3d 878 (Wash.App.2002), involved the defense of Cotton against serious charges of child rape. Cotton signed two fee agreements with lawyer Kronenberg. The first provided that Cotton would pay Kronenberg an hourly fee of $140. The second, signed three days later, required Cotton to pay for the services upfront and estimated the cost at between $10,000 and $30,000. In satisfaction of the fee, Cotton deeded real property to Kronenberg, but before the trial even began, the court disqualified Kronenberg because he had improperly contacted some of the prosecution's witnesses. Nevertheless, Kronenberg kept Cotton's land, and eventually sold it for about $42,000. Cotton sought a full refund, arguing that the fee agreement was void because Kronenberg breached his fiduciary duty to Cotton. The court agreed. Taking the land in payment was a business transaction with the client under Rule 1.8(a), and the land-for-services transaction was not fair and reasonable to the client. The lawyer breached his fiduciary duty, which justified forfeiture of his entire fee.

c.   In Medina County Bar Ass'n v. Carlson, 797 N.E.2d 55 (Ohio 2003) (per curiam), the health department ordered a mentally ill client to clean up his property. Carlson represented the client, who offered to sell the land to the lawyer for $52,500 the day before another buyer offered $470,000 for the property. Carlson had the client sign a statement that gave the appearance that he fully understood the deal with Carlson, the conflict of interest that it presented, and that he had consulted independent counsel (who gave no substantive advice). When the client was about to go to discipline authorities, Carlson offered to unwind the deal, but the Ohio Supreme Court suspended Carlson for two years.

3.   Are all business transactions with clients suspect? Is Model Rule 1.8(a) a trap for the unwary?

a.   In Passante v. McWilliam, 62 Cal.Rptr.2d 298 (Cal.Ct.App.1997), a client invented baseball cards imprinted with a hologram to prevent counterfeiting. The company flourished, but early in its history, it lacked $100,000 to buy an order of paper without which it would have failed. The lawyer stepped up to the plate and went to bat for the client, lending it the desperately needed $100,000. In gratitude, the company orally promised to give him 3% of the common stock. The lawyer never sought repayment of the $100,000 loan, but when the 3% share became worth $33 million, he asked for the shares. The court, however, said he could not have them. If they were a gift from the company, he had no contractual right to the shares. Further, as a business deal, he had not complied with the professional rules. His apparent home run became simply a long out.

b.   In re Kirsh, 973 F.2d 1454 (9th Cir.1992), involved a lawyer who lent money to his client, a close friend. The lawyer knew the friend was in financial trouble, lent him $40,000, and took some real property as security. He took the client's word that the title was good. It was not, the client filed for bankruptcy, and the lawyer alleged that his client had defrauded him, and thus that the court should not discharge the debt. The court disagreed. While lawyers ordinarily should not engage in business transactions with clients, the court said, the purpose of that rule is to protect clients against overreaching. In this case, the terms of the loan were fair to the client, and the lawyer was the victim. The Rules of Professional Conduct "were not intended as a protection for clients who wrong their lawyers," but, because of his specialized knowledge and experience, this lawyer did not reasonably rely on his client's knowingly false representation about that title within the meaning of the bankruptcy law. Hence, the court discharged the client's debt.

c.   Do you agree with the results in these cases? Should the law allow the lawyer a complete defense if the transaction is fair? Restatement Third, The Law Governing Lawyers § 126, Comment *b*, says the rationale for the strict rule is that "[p]roving fraud or actual overreaching might be difficult." Do you agree? Might the law deal with that difficulty by putting the burden of proving fairness on the lawyer?

4.   Must a lawyer comply with the terms of Model Rule 1.8(a) when she buys a car from her car dealer client? Does a lawyer who owns a restaurant have to abide by Model Rule 1.8(a) whenever a client comes in for a meal?

a.   Look at Comment 1 to Model Rule 1.8. Does it resolve both questions? Restatement § 126 also makes clear that Rule 1.8(a) does not prohibit "standard commercial transactions in the regular course of business of the client, involving a product or service as to which the lawyer does not render legal services." Comment *c* explains that these are transactions "regularly entered into between the [lawyer or] client and the general public, typically in which the terms and conditions are the same for all customers."

b.   Comment *c* warns, however, that "where a lawyer engages in the sale of goods or services ancillary to the practice of law, for example, the sale of title insurance, the requirements of this Section do apply." Do you see a good reason for such an exception to the rule? Rule 5.7 deals with lawyers providing "law-related services," a topic considered in Problem 37.

c.   Comment *a* to Restatement § 126 says that "ordinary client-lawyer fee agreements providing, for example, for hourly, lump-sum, or contingent fees" are not business transactions with the client. Is that statement literally true? Does it make more sense to conclude that fee agreements are business transactions that that exist in almost every lawyer-client relationship, and that Model Rule 1.5 separately addresses that particular issue?

B.   USING   CONFIDENTIAL   CLIENT   INFORMATION   TO   MAKE PRIVATE INVESTMENTS

1.   May Doe, without Johnson's consent, invest in the parcel near the industrial park? As we have posed the problem, Johnson does not want to buy the property himself.

a.   ABA Canons of Professional Ethics (1908), Canon 11, made clear that: "The lawyer should refrain from any action whereby for his personal benefit or gain he abuses or takes advantage of the confidence reposed in him by his client." This provision prohibited a lawyer from using confidential client information for the lawyer's benefit, even if the lawyer did not reveal the information to third parties and even if the client did not suffer detriment. See, e.g., Healy v. Gray, 168 N.W. 222 (Iowa 1918). This secret information is property that belongs to the client, unless the client waives his rights.

b.   Model Code of Professional Responsibility DR 4–101(B)(3) was equally definitive that, absent informed client consent, a lawyer may not "knowingly * * * [u]se a confidence or secret of his client for the advantage *of himself* or of a third person." (emphasis added).

c.   Model Rule 1.8(b) instead says that, without the client's informed consent, a lawyer "shall not use information relating to representation of a client *to the disadvantage of the client*" unless the client consents. (emphasis added).

2.   Do you agree with the Model Rules' limitation of the prohibition? Is possible disadvantage of the client the only concern that underlies the rule?

a.   The source of the earlier ethics rule is agency law. A lawyer is an agent of the client; the client is the principal. The typical agency rule is that an agent (whether a lawyer, or other agent) may not use secret information of a principal without securing the principal's consent. The remedy in agency law is for the agent to disgorge the profit to the principal. See Restatement Second, Agency § 388, Comment *c*:

> "[If] a corporation has decided to operate an enterprise at a place where land values will be increased because of such operation, a corporate officer who takes advantage of his special knowledge to buy land in the vicinity is accountable for the profits he makes, even though such purchases have no adverse effect upon the enterprise."

b.   A draft of Restatement Third, The Law Governing Lawyers, Tentative Draft No. 3 (1990), followed Model Rule 1.8(b). However, following the law of agency, the final Restatement provides in § 60 that, unless the client consents, "a lawyer who uses confidential information of a client for the lawyer's pecuniary gain other than in the practice of law must account to the client for any profits made."

c.   Comment *j* to this section of the Restatement explains that this duty exists "regardless of lack of risk of prejudice to the affected client." The Comment goes on to say that the

> "sole remedy of the client for breach of duty is restitutionary relief in the form of disgorgement of profit (see Restatement, Second, Agency § 388, Comment *c*). The lawyer codes differ over whether such self-enriching use or disclosure constitutes a disciplinary violation in the absence of prejudice to the client."

3.   Is the only remedy for a violation of this principle a suit for disgorgement? Should professional discipline be a possible sanction?

a.   Look at ABA Model Rule 1.8, Comment 5. Does it give a satisfactory explanation of why discipline for use of the information should be unavailable? Indeed, does it attempt to give any explanation at all?

b.   United States v. O'Hagan, 521 U.S. 642 (1997), addressed the securities law consequences of insider trading in securities of a client. Grand Metropolitan PLC (Grand Met), a London corporation, retained

Dorsey & Whitney in Minneapolis, in an effort to acquire Pillsbury, a large publicly-traded company. O'Hagan, a Dorsey & Whitney partner not working on the matter, purchased call option contracts and shares of Pillsbury stock on the open market. When Grand Met announced its takeover plans, Pillsbury stock rose from $39 to $60 and O'Hagan made over $4.3 million. The SEC prosecuted him criminally for securities fraud under the so-called "misappropriation theory," i.e., it said he defrauded both his law firm and its client, persons to whom he owed a fiduciary duty, by taking their information and using it to benefit himself. Writing for a six-person majority, Justice Ginsburg sustained the application of the misappropriation theory to Rule 10b–5 cases. Use of the information is inherently "deceptive," the Court said, and the fraud is "consummated" when the confidential information is used "in connection with the purchase or sale of [a] security."

c.   Where does that ruling leave the lawyer for purposes of professional discipline? If a lawyer engages in illegal insider trading in a client's stock, but the trading does not directly injure the client, is the lawyer immune from professional discipline? Should Model Rule 8.4(b) trump Rule 1.8(b) in such a case?

C.   ACCEPTING UNSOLICITED GIFTS FROM HAPPY CLIENTS

1.   May Doe follow Johnson's direction to prepare the documents necessary to give herself title to the Mercedes Benz?

a.   Does your answer turn on fact that a Mercedes Benz is more valuable than a Hyundai? What does Model Rule 1.8(c) tell you are the relevant issues for Doe to consider?[20]

b.   Would all ethical questions vanish if Johnson had simply thrown Doe the keys to the car and no paperwork were involved? Of course, someone must transfer the car title for the gift to be effective, so Johnson cannot avoid the language of Rule 1.8(c) referring to an instrument. However, why should preparation of an instrument be relevant at all? Does it make sense that a gift without an instrument would present fewer ethical issues?

c.   Restatement Third, The Law Governing Lawyers § 127(2), tells lawyers that they "may not *accept*" (emphasis added) a substantial gift from a client, whether or not preparation of an instrument is required. Perhaps we can explain the different statement of the rule by referring to Model Rule 1.8, Comment 6; it says that a lawyer may accept a substantial gift, but the gift "may be voidable by the client under the doctrine of undue influence, which treats client gifts as presumptively fraudulent." In short, the Restatement is addressing a variety of sources of law, while the Model Rules only focus on when a lawyer will be subject to discipline if preparation of an instrument was involved.

---

[20] In re Barrick, 429 N.E.2d 842 (Ill.1981), decided before the prohibitory language of Model Rule 1.8(c), upheld a gift by an elderly widow to her lawyer. The widow was "adamant" that she did not want to consult independent counsel. The state supreme court said: "[A]lthough undue influence might [be] presumed, the evidence established that there was none. There was no overreaching by the respondent. On the contrary, he urged his client to employ another attorney until she would hear no more about it. Exactly how far to press the point was a matter of judgment, and we will not snipe at the respondent's." Do not rely on this case. Rule 1.8(c) does not embrace it.

d. Attorney Grievance Commission of Maryland v. Stein, 819 A.2d 372 (Md.2003), held that the attorney violated Maryland's Rule 1.8(c) when he drafted a will for his client providing a substantial gift to himself. The issue was the appropriate sanction. The court imposed an indefinite suspension upon Stein, because "[w]e consider a violation of Rule 1.8(c) to be most serious." However, the majority refused to require the lawyer to renounce any interest in his deceased client's estate as a condition of reinstatement. The majority believed there was no precedent for such a sanction. It acknowledged that there may be the potential for a "cost/benefit analysis" leading to a lawyer's violation of the rule, but it found no evidence that Stein had engaged in such an analysis. The dissent was troubled by the failure to implement "the one sanction that, more than any other, will assure that the Rule is followed." "If lawyers know that a violation of the Rule will bring them no financial gain, they will have no incentive to violate the Rule, and that, above all else, is what will protect the public." Given the Restatement treatment of gifts to clients, did the majority view the appropriate sanction too narrowly?

2. Would it be proper for Doe to admire the car and let Johnson know she would like to have it?

a. Before the 2002 amendments, Model Rule 1.8(c) did not prohibit Doe from "soliciting" a substantial gift. Do you agree the change to prohibit such solicitation was an improvement? Does Model Rule 1.8, Comment 6, supply a persuasive explanation of why solicitation of a substantial gift from a client should subject a lawyer to discipline?

b. Morrissey v. Virginia State Bar, 448 S.E.2d 615 (Va.1994), helps illustrate the concern, albeit in a very unusual situation. As part of a plea agreement in a rape case, the defendant agreed to pay the victim $25,000 damages and to give a $25,000 gift to charities selected by the prosecutor. (The prosecutor originally wanted the $25,000 to fund a "prosecutor's corner" show on a local TV station.) The prosecutor did not disclose the charitable gift portion of the agreement to the victim or the court. The court found that, in soliciting this arrangement, the prosecutor misled the victim of the crime into accepting this resolution of the case and concealed the terms of the gift from the court, both violating what are now Model Rules 8.4(c) and (d). The court suspended the prosecutor from practice for six months.

3. Why does Model Rule 1.8(c) have an exception for gifts to relatives and others in a "familial relationship" with the lawyer?

a. Is the exception self-evident? Would any other rule mean that if the lawyer's spouse is also a client, the spouse could never throw the lawyer a birthday party?

b. On the other hand, is it really a good idea for lawyers to represent their relatives as this rule clearly tolerates? What problems can you see if you draft your mother's will, for example, and she gives you a gift that is larger than the one she gives your sister? Restatement Third, The Law Governing Lawyers § 127(1) provides that the lawyer may not prepare an instrument effecting a gift unless the lawyer is a relative or in a similar position *and* the "gift is not significantly disproportionate to those given other donees similarly related to the donor." Do you think this is a more appropriate statement of the rule than that found in Model Rule 1.8(c)?

4.   Is a lawyer's appointment as a compensated executor of a client's estate, or to a similar fiduciary position, a "gift" from the client within the meaning of Model Rule 1.8(c)?

a.   The executor of an estate collects the decedent's assets and, after payment of bills owed by the estate, distributes the assets to the beneficiaries designated in the decedent's will. Being an executor takes work, and the estate typically pays the executor a fee. Sometimes, a statute sets the fee; sometimes, a court must approve it. In either case, the fee can be substantial. A family member who is designated executor, on the other hand, will often waive the fee and leave more to distribute to the beneficiaries.

b.   In addition, an executor ordinarily consults a lawyer who receives a fee as well. Sometimes, law firms try to secure appointment as executor of their clients' estates, lawyer for the executor, or both. Should the lawyer or law firm that drafts the will be able to accept such an appointment? Is an appointment the equivalent of receiving a substantial bequest from a client? Why or why not?

c.   Comment 8 to Model Rule 1.8 tries to give an authoritative answer to such questions. The first sentence is definitive. On the other hand, does the remainder of Comment 8 give adequate guidance to a lawyer about what the lawyer must tell a client about the client's options? Could a lawyer's appointment as executor ever *not* create a conflict of interest for the lawyer that requires her to secure client consent under Model Rule 1.7(b)? When does the possibility of a "lucrative fiduciary position" ever not "materially limit" the lawyer's likely advice?

d.   ABA Formal Opinion 02–426 (May 31, 2002) advises that the lawyer/fiduciary's law firm may represent the lawyer in administration of the estate, but the combined fee for acting as fiduciary and as lawyer must be reasonable under Model Rule 1.5(a). Now is your mind at ease? If the fee is "reasonable" under Model Rule 1.5(a), do the other ethics issues go away?

D.   INTIMATE RELATIONSHIPS BETWEEN LAWYERS AND CLIENTS

1.   Does Doe put her license to practice at risk if Doe and Johnson enter into a consensual relationship involving physical intimacy? Why might we be concerned about such a relationship between lawyer and client?

a.   ABA Formal Opinion 92–364 (July 6, 1992) wrestled with this issue. It concentrates on (1) potential abuse of the fiduciary relationship between the lawyer and a vulnerable client, (2) loss of emotional distance from the client required for good professional judgment, (3) potential conflicts of interest between lawyer and client, and (4) confusion between which communications were made in a professional relationship and which were personal. The opinion concludes:

> "[B]ecause of the danger of impairment to the lawyer's representation associated with a sexual relationship between lawyer and client, the lawyer would be well advised to refrain

from such a relationship. If such a sexual relationship occurs and the impairment is not avoided, the lawyer will have violated ethical obligations to the client. * * *

"The client's consent to sexual relations alone will rarely be sufficient to eliminate this danger. In many cases, the client's ability to give meaningful consent is vitiated by the lawyer's potential undue influence and/or the emotional vulnerability of the client."

b. How do those considerations apply to the facts of this problem? Look at Rule 1.8(j). Is James Johnson, the client, likely weak or vulnerable, for example? On the other hand, are Joan Doe's possible loss of emotional distance, potential conflicts of interest, and possible compromise of confidentiality legitimate concerns?

2. Did ethical standards prior to the adoption of Model Rule 1.8(j) prohibit sexual relationships between lawyers and clients?

a. Many reported cases involved sex with clients. The ABA adopted new Model Rule 1.8(j) in large part because the lack of specific prohibition in the Model Rules meant some courts exonerated lawyers in egregious situations. Some courts saw lawyers are fiduciaries who are required not to take advantage of their clients; other courts showed less concern about the seriousness of the issue.

b. Suppressed v. Suppressed, 565 N.E.2d 101 (Ill.App.Ct.1990), for example, involved a divorce client who testified that her lawyer had twice taken her to an apartment where he had her inhale something that disoriented her and then had sexual relations with her. She filed a charge with the Illinois Attorney Registration and Disciplinary Commission, but it dismissed the matter. The court also dismissed a malpractice action alleging breach of fiduciary duty. This Illinois appellate court said that a lawyer's only fiduciary obligation to a client is not to make sex a quid pro quo for legal services. The client felt coerced into sex, the court acknowledged, but that alone was not enough. Further, the client only suffered emotional harm, not "quantifiable" injury. (We are not making this up!) Does the result shock you?[21]

c. Drucker's Case, 577 A.2d 1198 (N.H.1990), in contrast to *Suppressed*, involved a lawyer who knew his divorce client was under psychiatric care and emotionally fragile. The lawyer initiated, then ended their affair, but the client had fallen in love with him and her husband found her diary describing her feelings, thus prejudicing her in the divorce case. In spite of the lack of a specific prohibition of the relationship, the court found that the lawyer had taken advantage of his client and suspended him for two years.

---

[21] In re Rinella, 677 N.E.2d 909 (Ill.1997), later agreed that such charges are serious even in Illinois. Even without a disciplinary rule specifically on pressuring a client into a sexual relationship, the Illinois Supreme Court held that it constituted a conflict of interest in that the women believed they had to submit to get quality legal representation. The conduct was also prejudicial to the administration of justice. The court suspended the lawyer for three years. Doe v. Roe, 681 N.E.2d 640 (Ill.App.Ct.1997), appeal denied, 686 N.E.2d 1160 (Ill.1997), went even farther. Rejecting much of the analysis in *Suppressed*, the court held that a lawyer in a divorce case who coerces the client into a sexual relationship breaches a fiduciary duty to the client and that the court may consider emotional distress as an element of damages.

d. In Lawyer Disciplinary Bd. v. Artimez, 540 S.E.2d 156 (W.Va.2000), a lawyer for the victim of an auto accident started a sexual relationship with the client's wife. She later left her husband and, at that point, the lawyer asked his partner to represent the husband in the accident case. Of course, he lied to both the client and his partner about the reason why. After the husband discovered the sexual relationship, he sued the lawyer for malpractice and threatened to file ethics charges against him. The lawyer agreed to take a lesser legal fee in exchange for the client's agreement not to tell the disciplinary authorities, but ultimately, the client went to the authorities anyway. The investigative panel found the sexual relationship violated Rule 1.7(b), while lying about it violated Rule 8.4(c). The West Virginia Supreme Court, however, found that no ethics rule specifically forbids a sexual relationship with the wife of a client, so the conduct could not lead to discipline. The court further concluded that the lawyer's initial lie about his inappropriate sexual relationship concerned a matter that did not constitute an ethical violation per se, and, thus, "we are hard-pressed to find that his failure to be forthcoming with his law partner about this matter violated Rule 8.4(c)." The court "appreciate[d] his recognition of his irreconcilable conflicting personal interests" in asking his partner to take over the case. Only the effort to get the husband not to file ethics charges resulted in discipline for the lawyer, and the court limited that discipline to a public reprimand.

e. Gaspard v. Beadle, 36 S.W.3d 229 (Tex.App.2001), involved a lawyer who undertook a real estate matter for a couple. The wife then filed for divorce and began a sexual relationship with the lawyer. The lawyer also represented her individually in a matter collateral to the divorce. He did not bill her while the relationship continued, but after it ended, he sent a bill for all the work done. A jury found him guilty of fraud and intentional infliction of emotional distress for his conduct, but this court reversed. A man giving the impression that he loves a woman is not actionable fraud, the court said. Further, failing to send a legal bill until a sexual relationship with a client ended amounted only to the kind of "occasional malicious and abusive" conduct that society must tolerate, not the "extreme and outrageous conduct" that could give rise to a cause of action.

Is it any wonder that the ABA thought a specific regulatory rule was required?

3. Does Model Rule 1.8(j) deal adequately with the issues that sexual relationships present?

a. Does Model Rule 1.8(j) reach relationships with clients' spouses of the kind found in *Artimez*, for example? In Hernandez v. State, 750 So.2d 50 (Fla.Ct.App.1999) (motion on rehearing en banc), a lawyer had an affair with his criminal defense client's wife. A panel of the court originally concluded this was per se ineffective assistance of counsel; the lawyer could not truly want the defendant acquitted so he could return home. The full court, however, saw the case differently. The conflict of interest was only "potential," not actual, the court said. The defendant's argument that this affair affected the defense was simply "informed speculation." In fact, the jury acquitted the defendant of the most serious charge against him.[22] Do you agree? Should the law of ethics prohibit such conduct? Do Comments 17–19 to Model Rule 1.8 explain the rule sufficiently and suggest appropriate areas of caution?

b.   Should the ethics rules only prohibit intercourse with a client? In re Heilprin, 482 N.W.2d 908 (Wis.1992), for example, disbarred the lawyer for asking women clients "sexually explicit and suggestive * * * questions." The court earlier suspended the lawyer after he exposed himself to clients! Should acts that fall short of intimate physical contact raise discipline issues? Should the court discipline a lawyer who makes explicit and suggestive remarks to his secretary or another person who is not a client or client's spouse?

c.   Is it important to create an exception for preexisting sexual relationships? Is that exception necessary so that a lawyer may represent his or her spouse? Should the rule not allow the exception because the spouse or paramour probably should have a different lawyer anyway? Note that even if the lawyer complies with Rule 1.8(j), Rule 1.7(a)(2) is still relevant. See Model Rule 1.8, Comment 18.

d.   Should the prohibition extend to relationships between lawyers and officials of the lawyers' corporate clients? Look at Model Rule 1.8, Comment 19. Are such relationships likely to present the same problems as those with individual clients? Think of issues of professional distance and confusion about what communications are confidential, for example. Does Comment 19 take the prohibition too far or are its boundaries appropriate?

e.   If one lawyer in a firm enters into a sexual relationship with a client, should the lawyer be able to refer the client to another lawyer in the firm? Notice that Model Rule 1.8(k), confirmed in Comment 20, expressly does not impute the Model Rule 1.8(j) prohibition throughout a law firm. Can you see any good reason for not doing so?

————

ISSUES WHEN A THIRD PARTY PAYS THE LAWYER'S FEE

At the beginning of this chapter, we mentioned four kinds of conflicts of interest. We have not looked at two of them—conflicts among current clients and conflicts between the interest of the client and that of the lawyer. The third kind of conflict arises when a third party proposed to pay a lawyer to represent a client, for example, when a parent retains a lawyer to represent her child, or an employee hires a lawyer for an employee.

When you think about it, the conflict here is a lot like the personal interest conflict. We tend to fear the "golden rule," for example, "the one who pays the money makes the rules." We may also fear that the lawyer's long-term loyalty and relationship will be with the party who pays her, not the immediate client.

---

[22] The defendant's unqualified endorsement of the results achieved by the same lawyer in a concurrent federal prosecution also undercut the defendant's argument. See also, Hernandez v. Spears, 2002 WL 1205058 (S.D.Fla.2002), denying habeas corpus and saying it would be possible for a lawyer to provide an effective defense even though his success would let the defendant possibly bring an end to the affair.

The situation arises frequently enough that the Model Rules single it out for special treatment in Rule 1.8(f). The rule is stated negatively, but stated affirmatively it says that before a lawyer accepts compensation from a third party for representing a client the lawyer must verify that: (1) the client gives informed consent, (2) the lawyer's professional judgment on the client's behalf will be unimpaired, and (3) the lawyer will protect the client's confidential information.

All three are unsurprising, but they are not always easy to honor. Suppose your long-time friend and client asks you to represent her son who is charged with drunk driving. What will you say when she asks you, "was my son drinking or wasn't he?" What will you do when she says, "Don't seek bail; I think a few days in jail will do him good."? You know the required answers, but will you have the courage to honor the requirements of Model Rule 1.8(f) when your friendship may be on the line?

SPECIAL ISSUES WHEN AN INSURANCE COMPANY PAYS A LAWYER TO REPRESENT ITS POLICYHOLDER

When an insured driver gets into an auto accident, he notifies his insurance company. The company then often retains a lawyer to represent the driver in any proceedings related to the accident.

Whom does the lawyer represent? At the very least, the lawyer represents the driver. The driver will be the person named in any lawsuit and the person on whose behalf the lawyer will enter her appearance in the case. However, does the lawyer also represent the insurance company that contacted her and will pay her fee, or is the insurance company only a third party paying for the representation and subject to only the restriction of Model Rule 1.8(f)?

You might be surprised to learn how controversial that question is in the insurance industry.

Restatement Third, The Law Governing Lawyers § 134, Comment *a*, takes the position that whether the lawyer has one client or two is a matter of insurance law, not the law governing lawyers. However, Comment *f* goes on to say that "it is clear in an insurance situation that a lawyer designated to defend the insured has a client-lawyer relationship with the insured. The insurer is not, simply by the fact that it designates the lawyer, a client of the lawyer."[23]

Insurance companies tend not to like that answer. First, the companies point out, if the verdict or settlement is within policy limits, only the company's dollars are at stake. Surely, the companies say, we should be seen as a client when the driver has little or nothing at stake.

Further, Rule 1.2(a) only gives clients the right to settle a case and to decide how much to expend in its defense. When our money is on the table, companies say, we should have those rights.

Finally, the insurance companies say, we need to know all confidential information about the case that is possessed by the lawyer.

---

[23] For a further development of these issues, see Thomas D. Morgan, Whose Lawyer Are You Anyway?, 23 Wm. Mitchell L. Rev. 11 (1997).

Unless we are at least a co-client with the driver, we cannot get that information and intelligently exercise our rights.

States differ as to whether a lawyer retained in such a case has one client or two. Some cases try to straddle both ideas by saying that the insurer-insured-lawyer relationship is "tripartite" or "triangular."

When you think about it, however, not much really turns on the characterization. Under either view, the lawyer is having her fee for representing the driver paid by the insurance company and thus Rule 1.8(f) does apply. Indeed, under the two-client view, the restrictive requirements of Rule 1.7 apply as well.

And even in the most "one-client" states, the lawyer owes duties to the insurance company, including a duty to keep it informed about developments, although not to disclose confidential personal information the lawyer learns about the insured. See, e.g., Parsons v. Continental National American Group, 550 P.2d 94 (Ariz.1976); ABA Formal Opinions 96-403 (Aug. 2, 1996) and 08-450 (Apr. 9, 2008); Restatement Third, The Law Governing Lawyers § 134, Comment *f*.

Problem 13

REPRESENTING THE INSURED AND THE INSURER

OMITTED IN CONCISE EDITION

——————

Problem 14

THE LAWYER AND HER FORMER CLIENT

So far, we have seen problems involving conflicts among prospective clients, current clients, conflicts with the lawyer's own interest, and conflicts created by the involvement of a third party. Now, we look at how a current representation may affect a lawyer's duties to a former client and present a threat to the former client, the current client, or both. Lawyers and law firms often have long lives. That means they have a great many former clients, and it would impossibly limit the choice of counsel available to current clients to say that lawyers are as prohibited from opposing a former client as they are from opposing a current one. We will ask, then, how broadly the prohibition of opposing a former client extends, what makes matters the same or substantially related, whether nonlawyers face similar prohibitions, and what lawyers may do with their work product if a court disqualifies them in a case.

FACTS

Martha Heath has a wide reputation for her success in handling medical malpractice cases for plaintiffs. She is in great demand and doctor rightfully fear her.

Recently, Linda Parker came to Heath with a claim against Dr. Charles Abraham. Heath investigated the facts, found they seemed sound, and proceeded to work on the matter. After she had worked on the case for about 90 days,

Heath recalled that, about five years earlier, she represented Dr. Abraham in the routine adoption of his wife's children.

Heath might have forgotten Dr. Abraham but he did not forget her. "How could you of all people—my own lawyer—sue me?" he said. More to the point, he had his malpractice defense counsel move to disqualify Martha Heath from handling Parker's claim.

QUESTIONS

A. MATTERS AS TO WHICH DISQUALIFICATION IS REQUIRED

1. Does a lawyer owe the same duty of loyalty to a former client as to a current one? What standard defines when a lawyer may undertake a matter that is contrary to the interest of a former client?

a. Judge Weinfeld developed the basic standard limiting such representation in the leading case of T. C. Theatre Corp. v. Warner Bros. Pictures, Inc., 113 F.Supp. 265, 268–69 (S.D.N.Y.1953):

> " * * * I hold that the former client need show no more than that matters embraced within the pending suit wherein his former attorney appears on behalf of his adversary are *substantially related* to the matters or cause of action wherein the attorney previously represented him, the former client. The Court will assume that during the course of the former representation confidences were disclosed to the attorney bearing on the subject matter of the representation. It will not inquire into their nature and extent. Only in this manner can the lawyer's duty of absolute fidelity be enforced and the spirit of the rule relating to privileged communications be maintained." (emphasis added.)

b. The Model Rules now incorporate Judge Weinfeld's test in ABA Model Rule 1.9(a). Lawyers look to Rule 1.9, not Rule 1.7(a), to determine their obligations to a former client.[24]

c. Restatement Third, The Law Governing Lawyers § 132, Comment *b*, says that the former client rule:

> "accommodates four policies. First, absent the rule, a lawyer's incentive to serve a present client might cause the lawyer to compromise the lawyer's continuing duties to the former client. Specifically, the lawyer might use confidential information of the former client contrary to that client's interest * * *. The second policy consideration is the converse of the first. The lawyer's obligations to the former client might constrain the lawyer in representing the present client effectively, for example, by limiting the questions the lawyer could ask the former client in testimony. Third, at the time the lawyer represented the former client, the lawyer should have no incentive to lay the basis for subsequent representation

---

[24] You will see a reference to "former client" in Model Rule 1.7(a)(2). That refers to the effect of the lawyer's obligations under Model Rule 1.9 to a former client on the interest of the lawyer's current client.

against that client, such as by drafting provisions in a contract that could later be construed against the former client. Fourth, and pointing the other way, because much law practice is transactional, clients often retain lawyers for services only on specific cases or issues. A rule that would transform each engagement into a lifetime commitment would make lawyers reluctant to take new, relatively modest matters."

Would those policies help a judge in deciding Dr. Abraham's motion to disqualify Martha Heath?

2. Does the term "matter" refer only to litigated cases?

a. Notice that Judge Weinfeld makes clear that "matters" are not limited to "causes of action." Model Rule 1.9, Comment 2 also makes clear that the term "matter" covers more than lawsuits. For example, should the ethics rules bar a lawyer from seeking to rescind a contract drafted for a former client? Is the rationale that the Restatement offers convincing in explaining why the rule extends that far?

b. In Berry v. Saline Memorial Hospital, 907 S.W.2d 736 (Ark.1995), a lawyer in the plaintiff's firm was also a director of the defendant hospital. He did not know confidential information about this case; but he knew generally the hospital's policies and practices that were at issue in this matter. Because the lawyer-director owed a continuing duty of loyalty to the hospital, the court disqualified his firm from taking the case.[25]

c. In Townsend v. Townsend, 474 S.E.2d 424 (S.C.1996), a lawyer tried to represent a father who was trying to reduce his child support payments. Earlier, the lawyer had served as guardian ad litem for the child. The court conceded that a guardian ad litem is an officer of the court and does not technically represent the child. However, as guardian, the lawyer needed to have the confidence of the child and the family and may have received confidential information that would justify invoking Rule 1.9's bar.

d. Fields–D'Arpino v. Restaurant Associates, Inc., 39 F.Supp.2d 412 (S.D.N.Y.1999), asked whether an act of "informal mediation" constituted a "matter" for purposes of Rule 1.9. The plaintiff complained that the defendant was discriminating against her because of her pregnancy. A lawyer from the outside law firm representing the defendant held a meeting of the parties to try to resolve the dispute short of litigation. Even after the filing of an administrative complaint, the lawyer tried to mediate the dispute. Now the question was whether that lawyer's firm could represent the defendant in the subsequent litigation. The court held it could not. All parties to a mediation must have the assurance it will be confidential. That assurance will not exist if the mediator's firm now represents one of the parties, so the court required disqualification.[26]

---

[25] Conflicts created by a lawyer's "fiduciary or other legal obligation to a nonclient" are the subject of Restatement Third, The Law Governing Lawyers § 135.

[26] See also, McKenzie Constr. v. St. Croix Storage Corp., 961 F.Supp. 857 (D.Virgin Islands 1997), holding that a lawyer who was an unsuccessful mediator in a case could not become of counsel to the firm representing one of the parties without disqualifying that firm from work on the case. The court cited Poly Software Int'l, Inc. v. Su, 880 F.Supp. 1487

B. DETERMINING WHEN MATTERS ARE THE "SAME OR SUBSTANTIALLY
    RELATED"

**1.   In the middle of her representation of Dr. Abraham in
the adoption matter, could Heath withdraw and take the side of
Mrs. Abraham's former husband in seeking to resist the doctor's
adoption of his and his former wife's children?**

a.   Something as blatant as a lawyer switching sides in the *same*
case rarely arises in practice. Far more often, what happens is that
Heath would resign from one firm and move to a new firm that has
been representing Mrs. Abraham's former husband. Remember, under
Rule 1.10(a), if a lawyer is disqualified and then changes law firms, her
disqualification is normally imputed to everyone at the new firm (unless
she is screened, an issue we discuss in Problem 15).

b.   The harder problem for lawyers is deciding when two matters
are "substantially related" within the meaning of Model Rule 1.9.
Restatement Third, The Law Governing Lawyers § 132 says:

> " * * * The current matter is substantially related to the
> earlier matter if:

>> "(1) the current matter involves the work the lawyer
>> performed for the former client; or

>> "(2) there is a substantial risk that representation of
>> the present client will involve the use of information
>> acquired in the course of representing the former client,
>> unless that information has become generally known."

Comment 3 to Model Rule 1.9 expands on this definition and provides
examples. Can you begin to identify some recurring types of issues
lawyers will face?

c.   One type of substantially related matter consists of later
developments in an earlier matter. In Damron v. Herzog, 67 F.3d 211
(9th Cir.1995), cert. denied, 516 U.S. 1117 (1996), Lawyer represented
Seller in sale of his business. Nine years later, Lawyer represented
Buyer and told him to stop making payments for the company because
Seller had not complied with the terms of the deal. The court held that
such advice breached Lawyer's continuing "ethical duty of loyalty to his
former client" and constituted a basis for a malpractice action even
though there was no showing that the lawyer used or disclosed
confidential information of the former client.

Sullivan County Regional Refuse Disposal Dist. v. Town of
Acworth, 686 A.2d 755 (N.H.1996), involved a lawyer who had
previously helped set up a multi-town garbage disposal district. The
court prohibited the lawyer from helping one of the member towns to
withdraw from that agreement. If there is a violation of Rule 1.9(a) the
court will disqualify. No confidential information of the district was at
issue, and the agreement was a public document, but the case involved
construction of language drafted while the lawyer was principal counsel
for the district. If the lawyer now advocated a particular interpretation
of the agreement, that would be contrary to his duty of loyalty to the

---

(D.Utah 1995), and Cho v. Superior Court, 45 Cal.Rptr.2d 863 (Cal.Ct.App.1995). We focus
more directly on limitations on former mediators in Problem 16.

rest of the towns in the district. Even "in the absence of any confidences, an attorney owes a duty of loyalty to a former client that prevents that attorney from attacking, or interpreting, work she performed, or supervised, for the former client."

2. Are the current medical malpractice case and the former adoption proceeding discussed in this problem "substantially related" matters?

a.   The touchstone in most cases is whether the lawyer received relevant confidential information in the prior representation. If use of confidential information is the key issue, of course, courts and lawyers have an inevitable dilemma. Restatement Third, The Law Governing Lawyers § 132, Comment *d(iii)*, explains:

> "A concern to protect a former client's confidential information would be self-defeating if, in order to obtain its protection, the former client were required to reveal in a public proceeding the particular communication or other confidential information that could be used in the subsequent representation. The interests of subsequent clients also militate against extensive inquiry into the precise nature of the lawyer's representation of the subsequent client and the nature of exchanges between them.

> "The substantial-relationship test avoids requiring disclosure of confidential information by focusing upon the general features of the matters involved and inferences as to the likelihood that confidences were imparted by the former client that could be used to adverse effect in the subsequent representation. The inquiry into the issues involved in the prior representation should be as specific as possible without thereby revealing the confidential client information itself or confidential information concerning the second client. When the prior matter involved litigation, it will be conclusively presumed that the lawyer obtained confidential information about the issues involved in the litigation. When the prior matter did not involve litigation, its scope is assessed by reference to the work that the lawyer undertook and the array of information that a lawyer ordinarily would have obtained to carry out that work. The information obtained by the lawyer might also be proved by inferences from redacted documents, for example."

b.   In making the substantial relationship determination, courts often apply factors such as those articulated in H.F. Ahmanson & Co. v. Salomon Bros., Inc., 280 Cal.Rptr. 614 (Cal.Ct.App.1991): (1) the factual similarity of the cases, (2) their legal similarity, and (3) the extent of the lawyers' involvement in the cases. The fact that firm members testify they do not presently remember anything about the prior representation is ordinarily *not* a relevant factor.

c.   Other courts use a two-step inquiry: (1) are the matters related, and if so, (2) did the law firm learn confidential information that would help the client in the second matter. Some states place a burden on the law firm to prove that it does not possess confidential information from the prior representation.

Analytica, Inc. v. NPD Research, Inc., 708 F.2d 1263 (7th Cir. 1983), asked whether, from an objective perspective, it was likely that the firm learned confidential information that would be helpful in the second case. However, the court refused to inquire into what actual information the law firm learned, lest the information thereby lose its confidential character. The Fifth Circuit, however, in In re American Airlines, 972 F.2d 605 (5th Cir.1992), read the substantial relationship test to focus more on law firm loyalty to former clients rather than on confidential information alone. Which approach do you believe is more consistent with the principles underlying Model Rule 1.9?

d.   National Medical Enterprises, Inc. v. Godbey, 924 S.W.2d 123 (Tex.1996), disqualified a law firm in a damage suit against a chain of psychiatric hospitals because one of its lateral hires had previously represented one of the hospitals' administrators in a criminal case arising out of the same facts. The lawyer in question had never represented the hospital itself, but he had expressly promised to keep confidential the corporate information he had learned while representing the administrator. In addition, the information turned up by the firm in the tort case could lead to the filing of new criminal charges against the administrator who was clearly a former client.

e.   Cardona v. General Motors Corp., 939 F.Supp. 351 and 942 F.Supp. 968 (D.N.J.1996), involved firms who specialized in so-called "lemon law" cases involving allegedly defective cars. The small firm that represented hundreds of lemon law plaintiffs hired a lawyer who had defended hundreds of lemon law cases on behalf of General Motors (GM). To GM, that disloyalty violated Rule 1.9 even though the plaintiffs in the cases the lawyer would work on now were all different from the parties in the cases he had defended. The court agreed that while every car and every "lemon" was different, there was a factual nexus running through the cases that made it very likely confidential knowledge of GM's approach to the cases would be important in the lawyer's new job. The court held that the cases were substantially related and it therefore ordered disqualification.

3.   Suppose Heath knows no crucial secrets (e.g., that Abraham operates while intoxicated), but she does have general impressions of Abraham's personality and specific knowledge of his financial situation. Could that make the cases "substantially related"?

a.   In Chugach Electric Ass'n v. United States Dist. Court, 370 F.2d 441 (9th Cir.1966), cert. denied, 389 U.S. 820 (1967), the attorney was general counsel and later a consultant to Chugach. The board of directors of the company was divided on many issues and when a minority of the board gained control and became a majority, the attorney resigned. The attorney later represented the trustee in bankruptcy of a coal company and sued Chugach, claiming an antitrust conspiracy because of alleged agreements and overt acts occurring after the attorney severed any connection with Chugach. The court disqualified the attorney. "The problem here is not limited to the question whether [the attorney] was connected with petitioner as its counsel at the time agreements were reached and overt acts taken, but includes the question whether, as attorney, he was in a position to acquire knowledge casting light on the purpose of later acts and agreements. * * * A likelihood here exists which cannot be disregarded that [the attorney's] knowledge of private matters gained in confidence would provide him with greater insight and understanding of the significance of subsequent events in an antitrust context and offer a promising source of discovery." 370 F.2d at 443.

b.   In Franzoni v. Hart Schaffner & Marx, 726 N.E.2d 719 (Ill.App.Ct.2000), plaintiff's counsel in an age discrimination and retaliatory discharge case served for 14 years as the defendant's in-house counsel. Some years earlier, on behalf of the company, the lawyer negotiated a settlement with the plaintiff in another case and had worked on over 580 employment-related matters for all divisions of the company. The court found the lawyer was "privy to the secrets and confidences of [the company]" as it related to cases like the current one. Further, executives he might be required to depose or cross-examine were persons with whom he had worked while at the company. Thus, the court disqualified the lawyer.

c.   In Mitchell v. Metropolitan Life Ins. Co., 2002 WL 441194 (S.D.N.Y.2002), plaintiffs sued their former employer for gender-based employment discrimination. Fleishman, a partner at one of two firms hired by the plaintiffs, had previously worked at a different firm and defended MetLife in a variety of products liability suits over a period of several years. The court disqualified Fleishman's current firm. First, the scope of Fleishman's prior representation of MetLife exposed her to matters that would be at issue in the instant case. For instance, Fleishman defended MetLife against claims for unfair selling practices and interviewed several employees in the company's sales division. The plaintiffs in this case worked in that division and lodged their discrimination complaints against supervisors whom Fleishman had interviewed. Thus, the matters were substantially related even though the legal issues were much different. Fleishman learned "confidential" information that is "substantially related to disputed factual issues material to the resolution of the present action."

d.   In State ex rel. Wal–Mart Stores v. Kortum, 559 N.W.2d 496 (Neb.1997), plaintiff sued for damages from a fall in the store's parking lot. The lawyer had previously defended the store in a claim for a fall inside the store and in so doing had received access to Wal–Mart's policies and general defense strategy. The court said the fact the pleadings in the two cases were similar was not controlling. Similarly, the Wal–Mart procedures were common knowledge and the policies manuals were discoverable. Thus, neither represented truly confidential information. The court concluded that the cases were not substantially related. See also, ABA Formal Opinion 99–415 (Sept. 8, 1999) ("general knowledge of the strategies, policies, or personnel of the former employer" is not sufficient to justify disqualification. Otherwise, a lawyer could never sue a former client).

4.   Are cases considered "substantially related" if the factual issues in two or more cases are closely related, but there is no confidentiality?

a.   Allegaert v. Perot, 565 F.2d 246 (2d Cir.1977), was a bankruptcy case. Law Firm earlier represented a joint venture consisting of Company A and Company B. Company B was now bankrupt. Law Firm wanted to represent Company A in the bankruptcy proceeding but the trustee for Company B objected. Law Firm was obviously closely involved with the factual issues relating to the joint venture, the court held, but Company B had no reasonable expectation that the Law Firm would keep confidential from Company B the facts that it learned from Company A. Thus, the Company B could not meet the "substantial relation" test. "[B]efore the substantial relationship test is even implicated, it must be shown that the attorney was in a position where he could have received information which his former client might reasonably have assumed the attorney would withhold from his present client."

b.   Restatement Third, The Law Governing Lawyers § 132, Comment *i*, created the concept of an "accommodation client" to deal with cases where the lawyer clearly represented one client but agreed to act for the benefit of another in a setting in which the clients did not expect to keep any confidences from each other. There is an "accommodation client" when the lawyer, as an accommodation to the existing client, will represent another client "typically for a limited purpose in order to avoid duplication of services and consequent higher fees." When the interests of the two later differ, the Comment says, the lawyer may not continue to represent both, but she may continue to represent the original client even contrary to the interest of the client that had been "accommodated." The typical circumstances that warrant the inference that the "accommodation client" understood and (at least impliedly) consented to the lawyer's continuing to represent the regular client are that "the lawyer has represented the regular client for a long period of time before undertaking representation of the other client, that the representation was to be of limited scope and duration, and that the lawyer was not expected to keep confidential from the regular client any information provided to the lawyer by the other client."

c.   In re Rite Aid Corp. Securities Litigation, 139 F.Supp.2d 649 (E.D.Pa.2001), applied the accommodation client principle in a securities action filed against the Rite Aid Corporation and some of its directors and officers. Ballard Spahr, long-time company counsel, represented all of the defendants, including Grass, the former CEO, from the time the suit commenced. Grass then resigned from Rite–Aid, and other director-defendants retained other lawyers to represent them, but Ballard Spahr continued to represent the corporation. When new corporate management directed the firm to attempt to settle with the plaintiffs, a settlement agreement allowed the plaintiffs to preserve their claims against Grass. In this motion, Grass sought to disqualify Ballard Spahr from settling with the rest of the defendants, arguing that the firm had taken a position adverse to his interests as a client without obtaining consent. The court denied the motion. First, the court said, from the beginning, the corporation was the primary client and Grass's interests were secondary. Furthermore, Grass left the company after the litigation had started; that act created the conflict of interest. Next, the court held that representing Grass was simply an accommodation and that Ballard Spahr had agreed with Rite–Aid that, if a conflict arose between Rite–Aid and Grass, it would continue to represent Rite–Aid. The court held that by using the corporation's counsel at all, Grass effectively consented to this provision of the engagement.

C. OTHER SITUATIONS WHERE MODEL RULE 1.9 MAY REQUIRE DISQUALIFICATION

1. Assume that Martha Heath did not represent Dr. Abraham in any earlier malpractice case, but she did represent a co-defendant in such a case. Should that bar her from taking the current case against Dr. Abraham?

a.   Does Rule 1.9 apply to the co-defendant situation? See Wilson P. Abraham Const. Corp. v. Armco Steel Corp., 559 F.2d 250 (5th Cir.1977), and Kevlik v. Goldstein, 724 F.2d 844 (1st Cir.1984), holding that, absent the consent of both clients, the lawyer must be disqualified because confidences are shared in such a common defense. The courts treat these cases as not involving a client who asks the lawyer to represent another client as an accommodation. Rather, two clients ask one lawyer to represent them and then there is a falling out.

b.   GTE North, Inc. v. Apache Products Co., 914 F.Supp. 1575 (N.D.Ill.1996), involved a "joint investigation agreement" (JIA) under which separately represented firms shared the costs of determining responsibility for waste at a Superfund site. Later, counsel for one potential defendant undertook representation of a claimant suing a different defendant who had been part of the JIA for the same site. The court found that each JIA member was an "implied client" of the firm and consequently ordered disqualification.

c.   ABA Ethics Opinion 95–395 (July 24, 1995) asked whether a lawyer who had once represented one member of a joint insurance-defense consortium might take on a related case against one of the other insurer-members. The lawyer could not disclose relevant confidential information learned from the prior client, the opinion said, and the lawyer could not act contrary to the interest of his own former client. Hence, if the lawyer knows no relevant confidences, and if the new case is not contrary to the interests of the prior client, or if the prior client waives its rights, there is no per se prohibition. However, the new client should know these limitations and the lawyer must tell him of any implications they may have for the lawyer's role in the present case.

d.   Colorpix Systems of America v. Broan Mfg. Co., 131 F.Supp.2d 331 (D.Conn.2001), applied a similar analysis to determine when representation of a parent company in a prior case would bar later representation against a subsidiary. The plaintiffs alleged that defective bathroom exhaust fans made by Broan caused two fires. The plaintiff's law firm represented Broan's parent company, Nortek, in an earlier case of the same kind. First, the court noted that Broan shared the same legal department with Nortek, and Broan and Nortek had developed a common strategy for defending cases such as these. Then, in order to determine whether Broan had been a "vicarious client" of the plaintiff's law firm in the prior case (and thus was a former client in this case), the court asked (1) whether the current litigation will have a financial impact on the former client, Nortek, (2) whether the former client attached great importance to the current litigation against its subsidiary in terms of supervision, and (3) whether the affiliated companies share an "identity of interest." In this case, Broan accounted for a substantial share of Nortek's business, Nortek's general counsel had supervised Broan's defense in the present action, and Broan and Nortek shared an "identity of interest" because they shared a legal department and business philosophy. Thus, the court required disqualification.

2.   Suppose that, while doing discovery in her earlier representation of Dr. Abraham's co-defendant, Heath learned something about a different patient of that doctor—the patient's tendency to alcoholism, for example. Could Heath use that information in a suit against that other patient on behalf of a current client?

a.   Look at Model Rule 1.9(c). Notice that, quite apart from whether two matters are the same or substantially related, a lawyer may not use or reveal information acquired in a prior representation contrary to the interest of the former client unless the information "has become generally known."

b.   The former client—the doctor—has a duty to protect the confidentiality of his patients' medical information. While defending him, Martha Heath learned information about his prior cases subject to that confidentiality obligation. Thus, it would be contrary to the interest and obligation of the former client to have the information used by Heath in a current case.

c.   Restatement Third, The Law Governing Lawyers § 132, Comment *g(ii)*, Illustration 7 explains:

> "Lawyer has represented Hospital in several medical-malpractice cases. In the course of preparing to defend one such case, Lawyer reviewed the confidential medical file of Patient who was not a party in the action. From the file, Lawyer learned that Patient had been convicted of a narcotics offense in another jurisdiction. Patient is now a material witness for the defense in an unrelated case that Lawyer has filed on behalf of Plaintiff. Adequate representation of Plaintiff would require Lawyer to cross-examine Patient about the narcotics conviction in an effort to undermine Patient's credibility. Lawyer may not reveal information about Patient that Hospital has an obligation to keep confidential. That limitation in turn may preclude effective representation of Plaintiff in the pending case."

Does recognition of this obligation make sense to you?

3.   Suppose Heath recently settled a class action on behalf of all the residents of her city against a local department store for systematically overcharging interest on past due accounts. May Heath now represent the department store suing a customer (who was a member of the former class) for failure to pay a department store bill?

a.   Because of the many members of a represented class and the lack of confidential information acquired by the class action lawyer about any one of them, typically the court will not bar a lawyer from proceeding in a later action against such a former class member. See ABA Model Rule 1.7, Comment 25.

b.   Fuchs v. Schick, 2002 WL 538842 (S.D.N.Y.2002), was an exception to that principle because the class action lawyer conferred confidentially with a particular member of the class. Fuchs sued Schick for selling partnership units in a Marriott hotel venture at a price that exceeded the market value for the units. The lawyer for Fuchs previously represented Schick when Schick was a plaintiff in a similar class action suit against Marriott. In that suit, Schick served as the head of a committee of plaintiffs and, as such, had conversations with lawyers for the class regarding the purchase and sale of the partnership units. Schick's prior relationship with those lawyers led the court to reject the motion of Fuchs' lawyer who sought admission pro hac vice. Because Schick was not a *passive* class member, it was fair to say that his former lawyer secured secret information from Schick in that earlier case and would now be appearing against him in a substantially related matter.

D.   ACCESS TO THE WORK PRODUCT OF DISQUALIFIED COUNSEL

1.   If the court granted Dr. Abraham's motion and disqualified Heath, should substituted counsel have access to Heath's work product?

a.   Should the answer depend on why the court disqualifies the lawyer? For example, if the court disqualifies the lawyer because the lawyer knew material confidences, and transferring the work product would transfer the confidences, then the rule should bar the transfer. However, if the work product was not tainted by the confidential information, why should the new counsel not be entitled to it?

b.   In First Wisconsin Mortgage Trust v. First Wisconsin Corp., 584 F.2d 201 (7th Cir.1978) (en banc), the majority held that there is no per se rule against subsequent counsel's use of work product developed by disqualified counsel. Thus, unless there is evidence of "improper advantage" having been secured, "such as the use of confidential information," it is an abuse of discretion for the trial court to prevent turning over of the work product. The work product at issue in that case was an analysis of loan files conducted by a team of 15 lawyers for more than a year prior to the ultimate disqualification of the firm. The majority thought the loan file summaries were "the result of routine lawyer work of a type which any competent lawyer, by spending the substantial time which would be required, could accomplish just as well as did [the disqualified counsel]." Accord, IBM Corp. v. Levin, 579 F.2d 271 (3d Cir.1978).

c.   In re EPIC Holdings, Inc., 28 S.W.3d 511 (Tex.2000), was a case in which the court had earlier disqualified the plaintiff's first firm. Some of that firm's members had been at the firm that had incorporated the defendant company and thus they could have received relevant confidential information. Now, the disqualified firm sought to prevent plaintiff's new counsel from using the former counsel's work product. The firm was afraid that defendant could later accuse it of turning over confidential information and wanted to assure it had a defense to that charge. The Texas Supreme Court refused to prohibit use of all such work product. First, "when an attorney is disqualified, successor counsel is presumptively entitled to obtain the pleadings, discovery, correspondence and all other materials in the public record or exchanged by the parties." As for other material, the court created a rebuttable presumption that the work product contained confidential information. There were three dissents.

2. How can the new lawyer demonstrate that no confidential information is included in the material he or she uses?

a.   Is the theoretical ability to use the work product merely a mirage? The dissent in *First Wisconsin* accused the majority of "attempting to draw fine ethical lines based upon the specific content of the objectionable material," an approach "which has been repeatedly condemned. * * * [T]he majority further compounds its error by intimating that once the defendants have disclaimed the use of confidential information, the former client is the one who must point to the confidences used in the work." *In camera* inspection of the work product, the dissenters argued, would be "both unworkable and a dangerous departure from long-accepted ethical guidelines." 584 F.2d at 211–13.

b.   The dissenters made similar arguments in *EPIC Holdings*. The majority, however, outlined standards for determining whether the material contained or reflected confidential information of the defendant. The subject matter of the work product is relevant, e.g., factual information or legal research, the court said. So is its nature, i.e., lawyer notes or deposition transcripts. The trial judge should inspect the materials *in camera* if the answer is not obvious.

c.   Who has the better of the argument on this issue? The right to such work product will not be worth fighting about if the litigation costs outweigh the cost of redoing the work. Thus, the client may wind up paying twice for discovery of the information.

———

Problem 15

IMPUTED DISQUALIFICATION

Ever since Problem 9, we have assumed that if one lawyer in a law firm has a conflict of interest, we treat every lawyer as having such a conflict. Thus, if one lawyer in a firm formerly represented the plaintiff in a lawsuit, another lawyer in the firm may not now represent the defendant even if the respective lawyers worked in offices in different cities. The law does not impute all conflicts,[27] but it imputes many, and that obviously creates a very important limit on the operation of law firms. In this problem, we look at particular issues that arise in administration of the principle. We first ask how the principle applies in firms and organizations other than traditional firms. Next, we ask to how many firms in any single case the reach of the rule might extend. We then ask whether the same principle should impute conflicts among

---

[27]   Note that the general imputation rule, Rule 1.10(a), imputes only Rules 1.7 and 1.9. Rule 1.8(k) makes clear that all of that Rule is imputed except Rule 1.8(j), dealing with sexual relations with a client. Rule 3.7(b) makes clear that the it does not impute the provisions of Rule 3.7(a) unless the lawyer is also covered under Rules 1.7 or 1.9. Rule 1.10(d) recognizes that Rule 1.11 has special rules for imputation involving former government lawyers.

family members who practice law in different firms, and whether "screening" the conflicted lawyer should be sufficient to overcome the force of the rule.

FACTS

Charles & Burls (C & B) is a prestigious, 200–person Wall Street firm with a national clientele. It represents World Wide Container Corp. (World Wide) in many matters, one of which is a suit by National Gasket Co. against World Wide for contribution in a products liability case. The lawyers will try the case in New Orleans, and C & B is cooperating with Willis & Xeres (W & X), the law firm that World Wide uses as local counsel in New Orleans.

Willis of W & X is the only lawyer in that firm actively working on the case. His only role is to file papers, motions, and other pleadings forwarded to him by C & B. National Gasket has now moved to disqualify both C & B and W & X from acting as World Wide's lawyers. Its reasoning is that Xeres (when he was in a solo practice prior to forming W & X) represented National Gasket in various product liability matters arising out of the same facts that led to the present suit. Xeres learned confidential information that, if disclosed, would be useful to World Wide's defense of the present suit. C & B has never represented National Gasket.

QUESTIONS

A.   IMPUTATION OF CONFLICTS THROUGHOUT A LAW FIRM

1.   May Willis continue to act as local counsel for World Wide?

a.   Look at Model Rule 1.10(a). We know from Problem 14 that Xeres could not represent World Wide because of his previous representation of National Gasket in a matter substantially related to the present matter. What reasons justify a sweeping disqualification of everyone in Xeres' firm?

b.   Should disqualification turn on whether Willis has learned any relevant confidential information from Xeres? Could Xeres properly disclose any such information to Willis, whether or not the firm was involved in this lawsuit? Remember that Xeres learned the information while working somewhere else. Why shouldn't the law simply assume that Xeres will comply with his duties of loyalty and confidentiality and let the other lawyers in W & X work on the case?

c.   W.E. Bassett Co. v. H.C. Cook Co., 201 F.Supp. 821 (D.Conn.1961), aff'd per curiam, 302 F.2d 268 (2d Cir.1962), was one of the early cases establishing the clear and sweeping imputation rule. Lawyer X represented the plaintiff in a lengthy case. X then joined a firm—one member of which had once represented and advised a corporate defendant on some important issues in the same controversy. The lawyers in X's new firm agreed that X would continue to represent the plaintiff corporation in the matter, but without any participation by X's new partners in either the work or the fees. However, when the district court learned of this plan, it sua sponte held a hearing on the disqualification of X. The court found X's partners and X "made every effort to comply with Canons 6 and 37 [of the 1908 ABA Canons of Ethics as amended] as they honestly interpreted them," but the circumstances "will inevitably lead to suspicion and distrust in them in the minds of the defendants and the opportunity for misunderstanding on the part of the public. * * * " Thus, the court required X to cease all further participation in the case.

2.   Should the law impute conflicts throughout the law firm that are "personal" to one lawyer?

a.   Look at ABA Model Rule 1.10(a) and Comment 3. Note that, ordinarily, the Rules do not impute "personal" interest conflicts. Assume that Lawyer A in a criminal defense firm objects to defending persons charged with rape because of strongly held moral or political beliefs. His objection is such that he could not do a competent job. Clearly, Lawyer A may not take that case because to do so would violate Rule 1.1. However, if the law firm excuses Lawyer A from working on such cases, should the law governing lawyers impute Lawyer A's repugnance to other members of the firm? If lawyer L, in the firm of A & B, is unable to represent fur companies because she is a member of PETA and objects strongly to wearing animal fur, should the entire law firm of A & B be disqualified?

b.   Restatement Third, The Law Governing Lawyers § 123 and § 125, Comment g, were written when Model Rule 1.10(a) did not have the "personal interest" exception. Thus, the ALI restated the law as imputing such conflicts but suggested that the rule should not apply where "the personal interest conflict [of Lawyer A] was not known to the [other] lawyer handling the matter and could not have been determined by use of a reasonable conflict-checking system." Comment g also says that one should not impute "idiosyncratic" personal interests. For example, if Lawyer A has "strong philosophical or political aversion" to the objectives of Landlord, Lawyer B in the same firm can represent Landlord "as long as Lawyer A has no part in the representation and no supervisory or other control over Lawyer B * * *." Restatement § 125, Comment g, Illustration 7.

c.   How should we define a personal conflict of interest? Examine Comments 10 through 12 to Model Rule 1.7. Why should the law treat personal conflicts differently from law firm business conflicts? If one lawyer in the law firm owns stock in a company that is sued by other lawyers in the firm on behalf of a firm client, should the law treat this "personal interest" conflict in a different way? Would the plaintiff client want to know about the lawyer's investment? Should it matter whether the lawyer with the strong beliefs is a new associate or the firm's influential senior partner?

3.   How should courts approach the question of imputation outside the traditional law firm setting?

a.   How should one define a "firm" for purposes of Rule 1.10? See Rule 1.10, Comment 1, and Rule 1.0(c). For example, should strict imputation be required if opposing parties are both clients of a legal aid office? That is, if one legal aid lawyer represents the plaintiff, may another represent the defendant? See Rule 1.10, Comment 1. Some argue that, unlike a private law firm, a "government-financed organization of lawyers does not receive any compensation directly from its clients; therefore, a legal aid attorney has no economic interest in a client represented by a colleague in the same office." Lawyers "in a legal aid service are not associated for the practice of law in the same sense that private law firm members are associated. Legal aid operates solely as a nonprofit, public benefit organization."[28]

b.   Should that distinction be controlling? What problems occur if the legal aid lawyers are part of a single office? Flores v. Flores, 598 P.2d 893 (Alaska 1979), said that a state must supply private counsel to one party where the legal services agency's internal procedures were inadequate to guarantee confidentiality to both. Restatement Third, The Law Governing Lawyers § 123, Comment *d(v)*, agrees.

Compare, In re Charlisse C., 194 P.3d 330 (Cal. 2008). The Juvenile Dependency Court appointed the L.A. Children's Law Center to represent Charlisse C, a minor, in a case to protect her from abuse due to mental health problems of her mother. Her mother moved to disqualify the Law Center because it had represented her in the past. The Law Center is a single agency, but it was organized into three units with separate offices and no contact with each other. The purpose of this organization was precisely to deal with such conflicts. The California Supreme Court held that, in a former client case, the question is not loyalty but rather protection of the former client's confidential information through screening and structural safeguards. The court would disqualify the Law Center unless it could prove that it would protect the mother's confidences

c.   Does the same analysis apply to dual representation by a public defender's office? A state's chief public defender asked for an ABA ethics opinion as to whether the public defender department could represent two criminal defendants in the same case if the defendants had conflicting interests. The public defender office in City 1 had 16 lawyers and public defender office in City 2 had five lawyers. The opinion ruled that if one public defender in City 1 is disqualified, all those in the City 1 office are disqualified, and because all offices of the public defender department are "subject to the common control" of the chief public defender, all the lawyers in the City 2 office are disqualified as well. The ethics committee offered no reason and merely cited DR 5–105(D). ABA Informal Opinion 1418 (1978). Accord, Commonwealth v. Westbrook, 400 A.2d 160 (Pa.1979) (members of public defender's office are members of the "same firm" for conflict of interest purposes); Duvall v. State, 923 A.2d 81 (Md.2007) (actual prejudice to defense is presumed when the defendant's lawyer would be trying to try to pin crime on another client of the public defender's office within a particular judicial district); State v. Veale, 919 A.2d 794 (N.H.2007) (state appellate defender has a conflict of interest in a case requiring it to argue that a local public defender provided inadequate assistance of counsel).

d.   In United States v. Reynoso, 6 F.Supp.2d 269 (S.D.N.Y.1998), the Federal Defender Division of the Legal Aid Society assigned Lawyer 1 to represent Reynoso. Four years earlier, Lawyer 2, while in private practice but now also in the Federal Defender Division, represented Vasquez in another trial. Vasquez was now a potential government

---

[28] Donald E. Woody, Note, Professional Responsibility—Conflicts of Interest Between Legal Aid Lawyers, 37 Missouri L. Rev. 346, 349 (1972).

witness against Reynoso. The government argued that the court should disqualify Lawyer 2 from cross-examining his former client about the matter that was the subject of the former representation, and the court agreed. The government then argued that the court should impute Lawyer 2's disqualification to Lawyer 1, but the court disagreed and refused to impute disqualification within the Federal Defender Division. The lawyers had no common financial interest in the cases, they did not talk about the cases, and the files in the earlier case had been sent to storage. The court held that it would not treat the Federal Defender Division as a private law firm.

Do you agree? Are there costs to imputing the disqualification of one public defender to other lawyers in the organization? How great are the costs of failing to do so?

4. Should there be imputation among private lawyers who share office space but not fees?

a.   In Great Britain, chambers of barristers are not partnerships. Each barrister is an independent lawyer, and it is possible for one barrister in the chambers to be prosecuting a case that another is defending. America has not copied the barrister model, but there are many instances of lawyers who are not partners but who share offices, share a library, and may even share secretarial staff. If one lawyer is disqualified, should another lawyer in the same office suite be disqualified, even though they are not partners?

b.   ABA Informal Opinion 1486 (1982) says it all depends. There should be no imputation if the lawyers "exercise reasonable care" to protect confidences of the clients. See also, Rule 1.0, Comment 2. Restatement Third, The Law Governing Lawyers § 123, Comment *e*, is to the same effect.

c.   How would you organize such an office protect confidential information? How should lawyers make clear to the world that they are in the same office but not in the same firm?

B. PERSONS AND FIRMS TO WHICH IMPUTATION WILL EXTEND

1. If the court disqualifies the firm of W & X and all of its partners and associates, may C & B simply get new local counsel? Will the disqualification of W & X require that C & B be disqualified as well?

a.   Should the law consider W & X and C & B one firm for purposes of the imputation rules? Rule 1.0, Comment 3 recognizes that some corporations are "affiliated" with other corporations. Should we treat a law firm as "affiliated" with another firm?

b.   ABA Formal Opinion 94–388 (Dec. 5, 1994) considered issues of "affiliations" between firms that are initiated and advertised to give a national scope to relatively small local firms. When firms suggest they are affiliated, they risk misleading a client into believing a small firm has more resources at its disposal than it really has. In addition, if two firms hold themselves out as a single firm (e.g., use a common name), the law treats them as one for conflict purposes. While the opinion refused to draw bright lines as to when relationships require firms to be treated as one, it said it should be relevant whether the law firms have a "close and regular, continuing and semi-permanent" relationship. See also, Mustang Enterprises, Inc. v. Plug–In Storage Systems, Inc., 874 F.Supp. 881 (N.D.Ill.1995) (firms in different cities who hold themselves out as "affiliated" will be held to be one firm for conflicts purposes).

c.   Traditionally, if lawyers are "of counsel" to a firm, the law imputes their conflicts to others in the firm. An "of counsel" designation normally indicates that the person will assist in the legal matter but is not a partner or an associate in the firm. ABA Formal Opinion 90–357 (May 10, 1990) said that the title "of counsel" on letterheads, law lists, professional cards, notices, office signs and the like is "a holding out to the world at large about some general and continuing relationship between the lawyers and the law firms in question. A different use of the same term occurs when a lawyer (or firm) is designated as of counsel in filings in a particular case: in such circumstances there is no general holding out as to a continuing relationship, or as to a relationship that applies to anything but the individual case." A lawyer may be "of counsel" to more than one firm, and a firm may be "of counsel" to another firm. The opinion concluded:

> "There can be no doubt that an of counsel lawyer (or firm) is 'associated in' and has an 'association with' the firm (or firms) to which the lawyer is of counsel, for purposes of both the general imputation of disqualification pursuant to Rule 1.10 of the Model Rules and the imputation of disqualifications resulting from former government service under Rules 1.11(a) and 1.12(c); and is a lawyer *in* the firm for purposes of Rule 3.7(b), regarding the circumstances in which, when a lawyer is to be a witness in a proceeding, the lawyer's colleague may nonetheless represent the client in that proceeding."

See also, Hempstead Video, Inc. v. Incorporated Village of Valley Stream, 409 F.3d 127 (2d Cir.2005) (where a lawyer was of counsel to firm for some purposes but a solo practitioner for others, the lawyer should be able to rebut the presumption that he had shared confidential information with the firm).

d.   Brown v. Florida Dep't of Highway Safety, 2012 WL 4758150 (N.D. Fla. 2012), involved Lawyer who personally worked on this very case for the defendant before she left the Florida attorney general's office. No one suggested she could work for the plaintiff in that case now. However, the job she took in private practice was working from home on various summary judgment motions in other cases that the plaintiff's firm sent her. Did her work in other cases mean that Lawyer was "associated" with that plaintiff's law firm, so that the court must disqualify that firm from this case? The District Court said no. "The meaning of 'associated' is not completely clear. But one thing is clear: not every lawyer who is paid by a law firm to do work of a legal nature is 'associated' with the firm. Thus, for example, a firm can outsource research . . . . * * * [A]n attorney who contracts to do research or draft pleadings from the attorney's own premises on the attorney's own schedule ordinarily is not an associate." The court refused to disqualify the plaintiff's firm.

2.   If Xeres' confidential knowledge about National Gasket is imputed to Sandra Jones, an associate at W & X, and then Jones leaves to join a second firm, what does Model Rule 1.9(b) say about whether her new firm will also be disqualified?

a.   American Can Co. v. Citrus Feed Co., 436 F.2d 1125 (5th Cir.1971), is the leading case on the point. The Fifth Circuit noted that: "All authorities agree that all members of a partnership are barred from participating in a case from which one partner is disqualified. * * * [O]nce a partner is thus vicariously disqualified for a particular case, the subsequent dissolution of the partnership cannot cure his ineligibility to act as counsel in that case. * * * However, new partners of a vicariously disqualified partner, to whom knowledge has been imputed during a former partnership, are not necessarily disqualified: they need show only that the vicariously disqualified partner's knowledge was imputed, not actual." The court was concerned that "imputation and consequent disqualification could continue *ad infinitum,*" and that such a result is not needed "to maintain public confidence in the bar."

Do you agree with this analysis? Is it consistent with Model Rule 1.9(b)? Dicta in *American Can* says that the subsequent dissolution of the partnership cannot cure the conflict of the *vicariously* disqualified lawyer. Does Rule 1.9(b) reject that conclusion? The Rules now impute a lawyer's knowledge, but do they impute the lawyer's imputed knowledge? Does Rule 1.9 reject "double imputation"?

b.   Essex Chemical Corp. v. Hartford Accident and Indemnity Co., 993 F.Supp. 241 (D.N.J.1998), involved an action filed by Essex seeking a declaration of insurance coverage for certain environmental claims. In 1988, Essex retained Skadden Arps to fight off a takeover, and in the course of that representation, Skadden learned confidential information about Essex. In this case, filed in 1993, Skadden appeared for Home Insurance, one of the defendants. The court found the confidences previously acquired were sufficient to disqualify Skadden, and in an earlier opinion, 975 F.Supp. 650 (D.N.J.1997), the magistrate judge also disqualified the firms representing the other defendants who were party to a joint defense agreement in the case. However, the district court found the last step went too far. Citing *American Can*, it said the court should not presume that the law firm was sharing confidences with other firms; it ordered a hearing on the real nature of the joint defense work.

c.   Adams v. Aerojet–General Corp., 104 Cal.Rptr.2d 116 (Cal.Ct.App.2001), confirms that California law reaches the same result as Model Rule 1.9(b). Plaintiff's lawyer in an environmental case had formerly been at a firm that represented the defendant on environmental issues. The trial court disqualified the lawyer, presuming that he had learned the confidential information the firm had received. The Court of Appeals rejected such an automatic rule: the court will not automatically disqualify a firm-switching attorney on the basis of imputed knowledge, from a case involving a client of a former law firm. The court remanded and concluded that the lawyer whose disqualification is sought should carry the burden of proving that he had no exposure to confidential information relevant to the current action while he was a member of the former firm. The trial court must review the lawyer's billing records or other evidence of what information he may have received.

3.   Now, suppose Xeres resigns from the firm of W & X. Will the law still disqualify Willis from representing World Wide?

a.   What factual determination does Rule 1.10(b) require be made? Who should have the burden of proof on the question of what information Xeres disclosed before he left the firm? Would a hearing on that question ever consist of more than testimony about who told what to whom at W & X, testimony that the other side could neither challenge nor rebut?

b.   Should the extent of imputation depend on how large a part the disqualified lawyer played in the earlier matter? In Silver Chrysler Plymouth, Inc. v. Chrysler Motors Corp., 518 F.2d 751 (2d Cir.1975), the court considered whether an attorney was disqualified from representing an automobile dealer by reason of once having been an associate in the firm that represented the manufacturer. At that firm, he conceded he had worked on Chrysler matters. The court concluded, however, that the "cases and the Canons on which they are based are intended to protect the confidences of former clients when an attorney has been in a position to learn them." The court held that the attorney had rebutted the presumption that he had received significant confidential material when he was associated with the 80–member firm. The attorney's involvement—

> "was, at most, limited to brief, informal discussions on a procedural matter or research on a specific point of law. * * * [W]e do not believe that there is any basis for distinguishing between partners and associates on the basis of title alone— both are members of the bar and bound by the same Code of Professional Responsibility. But there is reason to differentiate for disqualification purposes between lawyers who become heavily involved in the facts of a particular matter and those who enter briefly on the periphery for a limited and specific purpose related solely to legal questions. In large firms at least, the former are normally the more seasoned lawyers and the latter the more junior."

While purporting not to make a distinction between partners and associates, is the *Silver* case in effect making such a distinction? While neither the Model Rules nor the Model Code distinguishes between partners and associates, should they? Would a bright line test be appropriate?

c.   In deciding these cases, should courts give weight to the fact that lawyers' movement from one position to another is very common these days?

City of Cleveland v. Cleveland Elec. Illuminating Co., 440 F.Supp. 193, 211 (N.D.Ohio 1976), aff'd without published opinion, 573 F.2d 1310 (6th Cir.1977), noted: "Imputing to an attorney in the private practice all confidential information obtained, or presumed to have been obtained, by other members of his law firm may severely limit the scope of the private attorney's future career and the effective operation of his firm, as well as the individual's right to legal counsel of choice."[29]

What role do you think facilitation of lawyer mobility should play in conflicts analysis? Do you agree with Reardon v. Marlayne, 416 A.2d 852, 860 (N.J.1980), that "problems of the job market and mobility are not solved by loosening ethical standards required of the profession"?

4.   Suppose that the lawyer does not change firms, but the lawyer's nonlawyer assistant, e.g., a secretary or paralegal, does. Do Model Rules 1.9 or 1.10 have anything to say about that situation?

a.   Rule 1.9 only talks of lawyers, but Model Rule 1.10, Comment 4, says that law firms ordinarily must screen people like paralegals. The leading case on the issue is Herron v. Jones, 637 S.W.2d 569 (Ark.1982), requiring disqualification of the new firm unless the secretary is screened from work on the case for the new firm.[30]

b.   In re Complex Asbestos Litigation, 283 Cal.Rptr. 732 (Cal.Ct.App.1991), upheld the disqualification of a law firm representing plaintiffs in asbestos claims because it had hired a paralegal who had worked for one of the defense firms on similar cases. The danger of misuse of defense confidences was too great given the failure to screen the paralegal from participation in asbestos matters.

c.   In re American Home Products, 985 S.W.2d 68 (Tex.1998), concerned disqualification of a law firm that hired a legal assistant. This assistant earlier worked for a lawyer representing one of the defendants in the Norplant litigation. She billed 72.5 hours interviewing potential witnesses, meeting with counsel, investigating plaintiffs, and writing memoranda about witnesses. Then, the lawyers for the plaintiffs hired her, and the defendant moved to disqualify that firm. The Texas Supreme Court ordered disqualification. It was not improper to hire an opposing firm's legal assistant, but in this case, it was improper not to screen her. Indeed, the court must disqualify because her new law firm assigned to work on the very case she had researched for the other side. The court did not automatically disqualify plaintiffs' co-counsel, but it might have done so if co-counsel had jointly prepared the case for trial or otherwise shared the legal assistant's tainted information. Compare, Phoenix Founders, Inc. v. Marshall, 887 S.W.2d 831 (Tex.1994) (firm not disqualified where paralegal worked only 0.6 hours looking for a pleading and the new law firm screened her).

---

[29] The court also proposed a narrow, test that does not represent what the law now is. "The * * * rule in the private practice of law should therefore limit the imputation of confidential disclosures, actual or presumed, to only those lawyers practicing in the attorney's area of concentration. Absent direct proof to the contrary, the attorney would not be deemed to have shared confidential information relating to matters and services exclusively within the sphere of representation of another department or section of his firm. This * * * rule is more acutely dramatized in the large, departmentalized law firm characteristically more prevalent in an era of evolving legal specialization." Should modern courts apply this rule?

[30] Although requirements that someone be "screened" are usually apply to lawyers, and the ABA Model Rules' definition of "screened" speaks of the isolation of a "lawyer," the requirements for such a "screen" described in new ABA Model Rule 1.0(k) and Comments 8–10 would presumably apply to the screening of nonlawyers as well.

d.   However, Zimmerman v. Mahaska Bottling Co., 19 P.3d 784 (Kan.2001), rejected the usual rule that it is sufficient if a lawyer firm screens a secretary who moves from one law firm to another. In this case, the secretary had not worked for anyone connected with the case, although lawyers at the former firm talked about it in front of her. The court concluded that the secretary acquired material and confidential information regarding the personal injury suit while working for plaintiff's lawyers, and thus it disqualified the defendants' firm where the secretary began working after leaving plaintiff's firm. If the secretary had been a lawyer moving from one firm to the other, the court would have disqualified her in spite of screening, the court said, and there was no reason to treat nonlawyers differently. "[W]e decline to create a screening exception in this case. The need for confidentiality, the trust of the client, and the public's respect for the legal system all support the rule in Kansas prohibiting the use of screening devices."

5.   Bring the facts closer to home. Suppose you, a law student, worked on a case for Firm A between your first and second years in law school. Then you worked for opposing counsel, Firm B, during the next summer. Should that disqualify Firm B from continuing in the case? Must Firm B screen you from participation in the matter that you worked on at Firm A?

a.   Allen v. Academic Games Leagues of America, Inc., 831 F.Supp. 785 (C.D.Cal.1993), was a suit for trademark and copyright infringement that a maker of educational games filed. Wright (now the lawyer for the defendant) worked with the plaintiff when he was a law student. Wright also served on the plaintiff's advisory committee, and even tried to help settle this lawsuit. Once he became a lawyer, he went to work for the firm that represented the defendant and participated actively in that defense. Because Wright had been a law student at the earlier time, the plaintiff was not his "former client." Wright had a duty to protect the plaintiff's confidential information, however, because Wright was the common law agent of the plaintiff and assumed a fiduciary duty. To prevent a violation of that duty, the court disqualified Wright and his law firm from continuing to represent the defendant.

b.   In Actel Corp. v. Quicklogic Corp., 1996 WL 297045 (N.D.Cal.1996), an associate in the law firm representing the plaintiff worked a split-summer for the firm defending a case while he was in law school. When interviewed by the plaintiff's firm, he said he had no memory of working on the case. Later he said that he remembered nothing substantive about the case, but his time records showed he spent two hours working on a memorandum and "reading the case file." The court found these facts raised a presumption that the student, now a lawyer, had received and shared confidential information. Given that his new firm neither screened the lawyer nor overcame the presumption of shared confidential information, the court disqualified the plaintiff's firm.

c.   Do these cases give you pause? Why should law firms be able to screen law students and lawyers who obtained their disqualifying information before becoming lawyers? Notice that Model Rule 1.10, Comment 4, expressly adopts this rule.

Restatement Third, The Law Governing Lawyers § 123, Comment *f*, says that law clerks "typically have limited responsibilities and thus might acquire little sensitive information. Absent special circumstances, they should be considered nonlawyer employees for the purposes" of imputing their knowledge to others in the law firm. On the other hand, "[p]ersons who have completed their legal education and are awaiting admission to practice at the time of providing services to a client of a law firm typically have duties comparable to admitted lawyers and accordingly should ordinarily be treated as lawyers for purposes of imputation."

d.   Do you agree with this approach to law student conflicts? Would any other rule make it too risky for firms, particularly large firms, to hire students during law school? Should placement concerns be relevant where issues of ethical conduct are at stake?

6.   What about "lawyer-temporaries" engaged by a law firm for a limited period, either directly or through a placement agency? Should the law treat them like any other lawyers for purposes of imputing disqualification?

a.   Functionally, a "temp" looks a lot like a law student or other nonlawyer. Temps may work on a single matter or on several different matters. Sometimes, they may simultaneously work on different matters for two or more firms. Firms typically hire temporaries to meet short-term staffing needs or to supply special expertise on a particular matter. On the other hand, they are not nonlawyers; they are licensed to practice law.

b.   ABA Formal Opinion 88–356 (Dec. 16, 1988) said that Model Rules 1.7 and 1.9 govern such lawyers. For example, under Rule 1.7, a temporary lawyer may not personally work simultaneously on matters for clients of different firms if the work for each is directly adverse to the other.

c.   Are temporary lawyers "associated" with a firm for purposes of the *imputed* disqualification sections of Rule 1.10? ABA Opinion 88–356 concluded that it must employ a functional analysis of the facts and circumstances involved.

> "Ultimately, whether a temporary lawyer is treated as being 'associated with a firm' while working on a matter for the firm depends on whether the nature of the relationship is such that the temporary lawyer has access to information relating to the representation of firm clients other than the client on whose matters the lawyer is working and the consequent risk of improper disclosure or misuse of information relating to representation of other clients of the firm."

d.   D.C. Bar Association Ethics Opinion 352 (2010) came to a similar conclusion. Law Firm A hires a temporary lawyer (TL) to work on Case #1. Law Firm B represents the adverse party in Case #1. That case continues but TL has left Firm A. Now, Law Firm B wants to hire TL to work on unrelated matters in Case #2. Does TL have a conflict imputed to Law Firm B?

The D.C. Opinion advised that a fact-specific analysis governs whether to impute the conflict. The court will not impute TL's conflicts to Firm B if TL's new work would be for a limited duration, TL would work either at a separate location or at a segregated area in the firm's offices, and TL's access to confidential information would be limited to the issue upon which TL was working.

By contrast, TL is "associated" with the Firm B (and the conflict is imputed) if TL works in the Firm B's offices on multiple matters simultaneously, is listed on Firm B's website or materials (thus leaving the impression that he has full association with the law firm), and has access to Firm B's files and email. In short, Law Firm B should screen TL who still has an ethical obligation to preserve client confidences learned while employed by Firm A.

e.   What do these examples suggest to you about the general duty of a law firm to supervise the handling of confidential information by its professional and support employees? Look at Model Rules 5.1 and 5.3.

C.   IMPUTATION WITHIN LAWYERS' FAMILIES

1.   Assuming that Willis & Xeres may not represent World Wide in the case brought by National Gasket, may W & X suggest that World Wide go to the firm across the street where Xeres' wife practices?

a.   Is there any reason for concern if Xeres' wife represents a client that her husband may not represent? If we presume that lawyers in a firm may share confidential information, should we presume the same about lawyers in a marriage?

b.   ABA Formal Opinion 340 (Sept. 23, 1975) addressed such questions and concluded:

> "It is not necessarily improper for husband-and-wife lawyers who are practicing in different offices or firms to represent differing interests. No disciplinary rule expressly requires a lawyer to decline employment if a husband, wife, son, daughter, brother, father, or other close relative represents the opposing party in negotiation or litigation. Likewise, it is not necessarily improper for a law firm having a married partner or associate to represent clients whose interests are opposed to those of other clients represented by another law firm with which the married lawyer's spouse is associated as a lawyer.
>
> " * * * We cannot assume that a lawyer who is married to another lawyer necessarily will violate any particular disciplinary rule, such as those that protect a client's confidences, that proscribe neglect of a client's interest, and that forbid representation of differing interests. Yet it also must be recognized that the relationship of husband and wife is so close that the possibility of an inadvertent breach of a confidence or the unavoidable receipt of information concerning the client by the spouse other than the one who represents the client (for example, information contained in a telephoned message left for the lawyer at home) is substantial. * * *
>
> " * * * [T]he possibility of a violation of DR 5–101, in particular, is real and must be carefully considered in each

instance. If the interest of one of the marriage partners as attorney for an opposing party creates a financial or personal interest that reasonably might affect the ability of a lawyer to represent fully his or her client with undivided loyalty and free exercise of professional judgment, the employment must be declined. We cannot assume, however, that certain facts, such as a fee being contingent or varying according to results obtained, necessarily will involve a violation of DR 5–101(A). * * *

"In any event, * * * the lawyer should advise the client of all circumstances that might cause one to question the undivided loyalty of the law firm and let the client make the decision as to its employment. If the client prefers not to employ a law firm containing a lawyer whose spouse is associated with a firm representing an opposing party, that decision should be respected."

c. Do you agree with the analysis in this opinion? If the representation is not inherently improper, why does the opinion require disclosure to, and consent by, the client? Note that the end of this opinion says that "the lawyer should advise the client," who can then decide whether it wants to "employ a law firm containing a lawyer whose spouse is associated with a firm representing an opposing party." Do the Rules now contain such a requirement? Look at Model Rule 1.7, Comment 11.

2. Should we presume that Xeres' wife would share whatever relevant information she learned from Xeres with others in her firm?

a. Why should we assume she will treat this information differently from other relevant information she learns? If we assume such sharing as to all other information and thus disqualify law firms under Model Rule 1.10(a), must we disqualify all lawyers in the wife's firm as well?

b. Model Rule 1.7, Comment 11, says the conflict is "personal," and thus "ordinarily is not imputed." Restatement § 123, Comment g, agrees that "in general, the law does not impute conflicts" because of family relationships, but the husband and wife may not "personally represent" clients adverse to each other.

c. Is the problem one of knowing where we can arbitrarily terminate the logic of imputation? Should it be relevant that there are many two-lawyer marriages today and that without some limit on imputation, most couples could not get jobs in the same geographic area? See Restatement Third, The Law Governing Lawyers § 123, Comment g, offering this rationale for the failure to require broader imputation.

3. Does the concern that spouses might intentionally or inadvertently share confidential information apply with the same force to other relationships?

a. Are persons in familial relationships other than marriage likely to get each other's phone messages or share fees earned in a matter? How about a brother and a sister sharing an apartment? Or a child taking a phone message and leaving it with the wrong parent?

b.   What has caused the rules to lump all such relationships into the same rule? Are we concerned that a parent might pull her punches so as not to embarrass her child (an adult daughter) who is representing the other side? Does that same concern arise if siblings are opposing lawyers?

c.   Note that Model Rule 1.7, Comment 11, like the case law, refers to lawyers related by "blood or marriage." What if lawyers are living together but not joined by benefit of clergy? Does Model Rule 1.7(a)(2) ("a personal interest of the lawyer") clearly cover that situation? Suppose that, instead of being married, the opposing lawyers had gone to dinner together several times? Is it fair to have a strict rule governing those who marry and no rule for the rest?

d.   Restatement Third, The Law Governing Lawyers § 123, Comment *g*, says: "Conflicts arising out of relationships in which financial resources are pooled and living quarters shared in circumstances closely approximating marriage should be treated in the same way as spousal conflicts." Do you agree? Should lawyers in such relationships be required to inform their clients of their relationship and to obtain informed consent to continued representation of the parties? How much privacy must lawyers surrender to avoid a conflict of interest charge?

e.   State Bar of Arizona Opinion 2001–10 (2001), says that cohabiting couples who oppose each other in a criminal case should be subject to the same rules as married couples. The same problem of inadvertently getting confidential information can arise, the opinion says, as can the same loss of professional distance. Thus, where a prosecutor and public defender live together, the opinion holds, they may not work on cases against each other without the consent of their respective clients.[31]

D.   USING "SCREENING" TO AVOID IMPUTATION

1.   Does ABA Model Rule 1.10 recognize the availability of screening to avoid imputation in the case of lawyers like Xeres who have moved from one private firm to another?

a.   For many years, the ABA Model Rules rejected screening when lawyers moved from one private firm to another. Yet the Rules certainly recognize screening in other contexts. Rule 1.11 provides for screening the former government lawyer, Rule 1.12 permits screening of former judges and law clerks, and Rule 1.18 allows screening of the lawyer who talked to a prospective client. Proponents of modifying the imputation rules have argued that recognition of widespread lateral movement of lawyers from firm to firm today required that screening should be more widely available.

b.   Even before the recent amendment to Model Rule 1.10(a), some courts recognized screening as effective in a limited number of cases.

---

[31] See also, People v. Jackson, 213 Cal.Rptr. 521 (Cal.Ct.App.1985) (defendant's conviction set aside because neither the prosecutor nor the appointed defense counsel disclosed that they were dating each other before the trial and that they continued to meet on a "regular basis" for movie and dinner dates throughout duration of the criminal proceedings against the defendant).

Nemours Foundation v. Gilbane, Aetna, Federal Ins. Co., 632 F.Supp. 418 (D.Del.1986), upheld screening Lawyer, formerly an associate at Firm A, even though the ethics rule did not authorize a screen. Firm A represented Client. At the direction of lead counsel, Lawyer prepared books of documents to use in a "mini-trial," used as a part of settlement negotiations. After the mini-trial, Firm B (the firm that represented Opponent in the litigation) hired Lawyer to work on completely different matters. Firm B "screened" Lawyer from the ongoing litigation between Client and Opponent. No one at Firm B could talk to Lawyer about the case, and Lawyer had no access to Opponent's files. Because of what the court called the policies underlying Rule 1.6, it held that the "cone of silence" that Firm B created around Lawyer was sufficient to avoid disqualification. In addition, Lawyer had been an associate at Firm A and was not intimately involved in the case. The court refused to adopt a per se rule, arguing that, "Attorney mobility, especially among young associates, would be severely restricted if a per se rule against a 'cone of silence' were adopted."

In Cromley v. Board of Educ. of Lockport Tp. High School Dist. 205, 17 F.3d 1059 (7th Cir.1994), the law firm represented a teacher who said that she was improperly denied administrative positions. A lawyer in that firm moved to the law firm representing the school board. The court ruled that the same matter was involved and (citing *Schiessle v. Stephens*), it found that the law firm had established an effective screening procedure that promptly went into effect when the firm hired this lawyer. The screen denied the lawyer access to the relevant files (which were kept in a different city), instructed the lawyer not to discuss the case, and denied him any share in the fees derived from the case.[32]

c.   Restatement Third, The Law Governing Lawyers § 124(2), completed in 2000, rejected screening in most cases, but left the door open slightly. Even if a lawyer in a law firm has confidential information about a former client, the Restatement does not require the firm's disqualification when—

" * * * there is no substantial risk that confidential information of the former client will be used with material adverse effect on the former client because:

"(a) any confidential client information * * * is unlikely to be significant in the subsequent matter;

---

[32] Other cases were more restrictive. State ex rel. Freezer Services, Inc. v. Mullen, 458 N.W.2d 245 (Neb.1990), for example, involved a merger of the law firm representing the plaintiff with the firm representing the defendant. The new firm wished to continue to represent the defendant and to screen the lawyer who had handled the plaintiff's case. The court disqualified the firm. When a lawyer who has been "intimately involved" with one side of a case joins the firm on the other side, no amount of screening can give the first client a secure feeling that its confidential information will be safe. Courts have also rejected screening as a remedy in Lansing–Delaware Water Dist. v. Oak Lane Park, Inc., 808 P.2d 1369 (Kan.1991); United States v. Davis, 780 F.Supp. 21 (D.D.C.1991); and Henriksen v. Great Am. Savings & Loan, 14 Cal.Rptr.2d 184 (Cal.Ct.App.1992). See also, Kala v. Aluminum Smelting & Refining Co., 688 N.E.2d 258 (Ohio 1998) (screening imposed when lawyer arrived at firm, but lawyer's job negotiations with opposing counsel at the same time he was representing the client were so egregiously disloyal that the screen did not prevent the new firm's disqualification).

"(b) the personally prohibited lawyer is subject to screening measures adequate to eliminate participation by that lawyer in the representation; and

"(c) timely and adequate notice of the screening has been provided to all affected clients."

d.   What do you think of the Restatement approach? Do the standards appropriately balance the competing interests? Do they unwisely capitulate to the interests of large law firms who want to take on more cases? How should a court determine if the information is "unlikely to be significant" in the latter case without requiring the moving party to reveal its confidential information in open court?

e.   Proponents of change finally succeeded in 2008 when the ABA amended Rule 1.10(a). Now, pursuant to Rule 1.10(a)(2), if the court disqualifies a lawyer because of his association with a prior law firm, the new law firm can avoid disqualification by screening the disqualified lawyer. Many states now approve some form of screening. You can find these states in Appendix B, "Chart on Lawyer Screening," in the Standards Supplement.

2.   When should a court decide that the screen is sufficiently opaque and not translucent?

a.   Model Rule 1.0(k) defines screening by saying that " 'screened' denotes the isolation of a lawyer from any participation in a matter through the timely imposition of procedures within a firm that are reasonably adequate under the circumstances to protect information that the isolated lawyer is obligated to protect under these Rules or other law."

b.   Even before the change in Model Rule 1.10(a)(2), some courts considered what kind of screening would be sufficient. Schiessle v. Stephens, 717 F.2d 417 (7th Cir.1983), required that a "specific institutional mechanism" must be implemented to insulate effectively against confidential information flowing from the "infected" lawyer to any other member of his present firm.

> "Such a determination can be based on objective and verifiable evidence presented to the trial court and must be made on a case-by-case basis. Factors appropriate for consideration by the trial court might include, but are not limited to, the size and structural divisions of the law firm involved, the likelihood of contact between the 'infected' attorney and the specific attorneys responsible for the present representation, the existence of rules which prevent the 'infected' attorney from access to the present litigation or which prevent him from sharing in the fees derived from such litigation."

c.   In Manning v. Waring, Cox, James, Sklar & Allen, 849 F.2d 222 (6th Cir.1988), the court remanded for factual findings but held that the law firm can avoid imputed disqualification if it proves that there is an effective screen by "objective and verifiable evidence." The lower court should consider factors such as the "size and structural divisions" of the firm, rules that prevent the "infected" lawyer from having access to case files, and rules preventing the infected lawyer from sharing fees from the case.

d.   In Burgess–Lester v. Ford Motor Co., 643 F.Supp.2d 811 (N.D. W.Va. 2008), a lawyer who was representing Ford Motor in this case moved to the law firm representing plaintiff. The new firm said it restricted the lawyer's access to any computer files relating to the case, stored all case files in a location where the lawyer had no access, told the firm employees not to talk to the lawyer about it, and provided that the lawyer would share no fees in the case. However, the lawyer himself said he did "not know the precise details of the barrier," and the firm size was relatively small. Therefore, the court disqualified the firm. Would this case come out the same way under Rule 1.10(a)(2)?

e.   Kirk v. First American Title Ins. Co., 108 Cal. Rptr. 3d 620 (Cal. Ct. App. 2010), articulated what law firms must do to make the screen truly opaque (quoting an earlier California case):

> "The typical elements of an ethical wall are: [1] physical, geographic, and departmental separation of attorneys; [2] prohibitions against and sanctions for discussing confidential matters; [3] established rules and procedures preventing access to confidential information and files; [4] procedures preventing a disqualified attorney from sharing in the profits from the representation; and [5] continuing education in professional responsibility."

What does not "sharing in the profits" mean? See Rule 1.10, Comment 8.

3. Should the Model Rules permit screening in other conflict of interest situations?

a.   Was amending Rule 1.10(a)(2) a good idea? Should the Model Rules reject screening? One commentator has argued that imputed disqualification based on an irrebuttable presumption of shared confidential information "is required by three realities of life in the modern law firm."

> "First is the relative informality of information exchange within most law firms [because] people tend to specialize their work within firms and tend to consult others in the firm who can give them necessary help on areas outside their expertise.

> "Second is the powerful economic incentive to use information that will help the firm win a case on behalf of a current client. * * * Indeed, a highly-regarded American Bar Foundation study of Chicago lawyers suggests that the fear of losing clients creates the single most important pressure to engage in less-than-clearly ethical behavior today.

> "Third and perhaps most important is the fact that no one outside a firm—indeed often leadership inside a firm—can ever be sure what has transpired behind the law firm's closed doors."

The proper question, therefore, is "not whether one can screen the disqualified lawyer from contact with others in the firm—but whether the lawyer realistically should be said to have received enough of the former client's information that the court's protection is required."[33]

---

[33] Thomas D. Morgan, Screening the Disqualified Lawyer: The Wrong Solution to the Wrong Problem, 10 U. Arkansas Little Rock L. J.37, 48 (1987–88).

b.   The Ad Hoc Committee on Ethics 2000 of the ABA Section of Business Law unsuccessfully urged the ABA to allow screening for conflicts arising under Rule 1.7 and not simply Rule 1.9. Thus, one lawyer in a law firm could represent Client A in one matter while another lawyer in the same law firm could simultaneously represent Client B in a matter adverse to Client A. The Committee urged the ABA to allow such representation if (1) screening is in place, (2) the matters are not related, (3) each affected client is notified (but need not consent), and (4) there is no significant risk of diminution of the loyalty owed by any lawyer in the firm to its clients. The Committee argued that the law should not assume that lawyers would engage in improper conduct. As you see, the ABA ultimately did not recognize this type of screening in the current client situation.

c.   Although Rule 1.10(a)(2), as now written, limits disciplinary exposure when a law firm screens a lawyer subject to a former-client conflict as a result of changing firms. Should it prevent a court from disqualifying the firm from continuing to represent the client? Notice that Rule 1.10, Comment 7, expressly warns that courts might impose disqualification. If courts refuse to recognize the change to Rule 1.10 in disqualification cases, will the large firms who advocated the change have won a pyrrhic victory?

———

Problem 16

CONFLICT OF INTEREST ISSUES FOR GOVERNMENT LAWYERS AND JUDGES

Federal, state, and local governmental entities employ lawyers to represent them in various legal tasks including criminal and civil litigation, investigations, drafting and interpreting laws and regulations, and adjudicating disputes. Some of these lawyers spend their careers in government practice, but many lawyers, including at the highest levels of government practice, come from private practice and subsequently return there. The rules of professional responsibility apply to all lawyers, but the role of the lawyer in representing a government client presents special issues. Government lawyers have responsibilities beyond those of lawyers in private practice. Some people worry, for example, that the lawyers might use their public position to benefit a future private employer. Others fear that former private clients might get special treatment—whether favorable or unfavorable—from their former lawyer. Concerns such as these have produced the conflicts of interest rules governing government lawyers that this problem explores. First, we look at the limits on the conduct of former government lawyers under the Model Rules and the corresponding federal criminal statute. Then, we examine limits on the practice of former private lawyers while in government. Third, we consider the special screening rules applicable to government lawyers, and finally we look at the rules applicable to former judges, arbitrators, mediators, and analogous third-party neutrals.

FACTS

Harold Smithers was a commissioner with the Federal Trade Commission for several years until 10 months ago when his term expired. Prior to his appointment as a commissioner, he spent about 15 years—over half of his professional life—on the staff of the FTC.

Smithers retired from the government at the end of his term and became a partner in the well-respected firm of Able & Baker in Washington, D.C. Smithers became familiar with Able & Baker because it engages in a great deal of FTC work and has a reputation for excellence. In fact, for the last year, the firm has been representing the subject of a major investigation before the FTC. Although Smithers disagreed with the strategy that Able & Baker was using in that case, he carefully avoided discussing that case while he was quietly negotiating with Able & Baker about his future employment at the firm.

Now that Smithers has moved to Able & Baker, P. D. Quick, chief executive officer of Quick, Inc., has come from California to seek Able & Baker's help. The Commission staff has threatened to file an action in United States District Court seeking a preliminary injunction pending institution of a proceeding before the Commission alleging consumer fraud by Quick, Inc. The fraud is minor, but Quick is personally worried about it and wants to end the matter as soon as possible.

Neither Quick nor Quick, Inc., had ever before consulted with Able & Baker about this matter. P. D. Quick, during his initial conference with Smithers, mentioned in passing that the reason he decided to come to Able & Baker was because Smithers was there. Quick mentioned a recent article about Smithers in *Forbes* (published as he was leaving the FTC) that said that Smithers was one of the most influential and hardworking members in the history of the Commission. The article quoted one FTC staff member who said that "even today when Smithers calls me on the phone, I instinctively straighten my tie and call him 'Sir!' "

Another partner of Able & Baker will draft the papers filed with the Commission staff, but the client and the active partner have asked Smithers to give "a topside look" at the client's problems and to sign the important papers that the law firm will file with the Commission. Smithers also has agreed to call several staff members and a current commissioner or two who "owe their jobs to me." He made this last remark in an offhand way in the presence of P. D. Quick who appeared pleased.

QUESTIONS

A.   THE RULES APPLICABLE TO FORMER GOVERNMENT LAWYERS

1.   What legal standards govern Smithers' return to private life?

a.   Because Smithers is a lawyer, he is subject to ABA Model Rule 1.11, even though he was not acting as a lawyer when he was a

Commissioner. He is not subject to Model Rule 1.9, except as Model Rule 1.11(a)(1) expressly subjects him to Model Rule 1.9(c).[34]

b.   The content of Model Rule 1.11 derives from ABA Formal Opinion 342 (Nov. 24, 1975), which interpreted ABA Model Code of Professional Responsibility DR 9–101(B). This Opinion is old, but its rationale is still valid.

"The policy considerations underlying DR 9–101(B) have been thought to be the following: the treachery of switching sides; the safe-guarding of confidential governmental information from future use against the government; the need to discourage government lawyers from handling particular assignments in such a way as to encourage their own future employment in regard to those particular matters after leaving government service; and the professional benefit derived from avoiding the appearance of evil.

"There are, however, weighty policy considerations in support of the view that a special disciplinary rule relating only to former government lawyers should not broadly limit the lawyer's employment after he leaves government service. Some of the underlying considerations favoring a construction of the rule in a manner not to restrict unduly the lawyer's future employment are the following: the ability of government to recruit young professionals and competent lawyers should not be interfered with by imposition of harsh restraints upon future practice nor should too great a sacrifice be demanded of the lawyers willing to enter government service; the rule serves no worthwhile public interest if it becomes a mere tool enabling a litigant to improve his prospects by depriving his opponent of competent counsel; and the rule should not be permitted to interfere needlessly with the right of litigants to obtain competent counsel of their own choosing, particularly in specialized areas requiring special, technical training and experience. * * *

"As used in DR 9–101(B), 'substantial responsibility' envisages a much closer and more direct relationship than that of a mere perfunctory approval or disapproval of the matter in question. It contemplates a responsibility requiring the official to become personally involved to an important, material degree, in the investigative or deliberative processes regarding the transactions or facts in question. Thus, being the chief official in some vast office or organization does not *ipso facto* give that government official or employee the 'substantial responsibility' contemplated by the rule in regard to all the minutiae of facts lodged within that office. Yet it is not

---

[34]   Before the 2002 revisions of the Model Rules, there was some precedent for applying both Model Rules 1.9 and 1.11 to former government lawyers, e.g., Violet v. Brown, 9 Vet.App. 530 (Ct.Vet.App.1996). ABA Formal Opinion 97–409 (Aug. 2, 1997), on the other hand, said that Rule 1.11, not Rule 1.9, governs the conflict of interest obligations of a former government lawyer. Because Rule 1.9(c), prohibiting use and disclosure of a former client's confidential information, has no counterpart in Rule 1.11, however, the ABA Opinion said it was applicable to a former government lawyer as well. Now, Model Rule 1.11 alone governs the conduct of former government lawyers. See Comment 1 to Model Rule 1.9.

necessary that the public employee or official shall have personally and in a substantial manner investigated or passed upon the particular matter, for it is sufficient that he had such a heavy responsibility for the matter in question that it is unlikely he did not become personally and substantially involved in the investigative or deliberate processes regarding that matter. * * *

"The extension by DR 5–105(D) of disqualification to all affiliated lawyers is to prevent circumvention by a lawyer of the Disciplinary Rules. Past government employment creates an unusual situation in which inflexible application of DR 5–105(D) would actually thwart the policy considerations underlying DR 9–101(B). * * *

" * * * The purposes of limiting the mandate to matters in which the former public employee had a substantial responsibility are to inhibit government recruitment as little as possible and enhance the opportunity for all litigants to obtain competent counsel of their own choosing, particularly in specialized areas. An inflexible extension of disqualification throughout an entire firm would thwart those purposes. So long as the individual lawyer is held to be disqualified and is screened from any direct or indirect participation in the matter, the problem of his switching sides is not present; by contrast, an inflexible extension of disqualification throughout the firm often would result in real hardship to a client if complete withdrawal of representation was mandated, because substantial work may have been completed regarding specific litigation prior to the time the government employee joined the partnership, or the client may have relied in the past on representation by the firm."

2. How do these rules apply to someone like Smithers?

a. In re Sofaer, 728 A.2d 625 (D.C.1999), was a case where the disciplinary authorities accused a well-known lawyer, Abraham Sofaer, of violating Rule 1.11(a). While serving as legal advisor (functionally the general counsel) to the State Department, he took part in "legal activities flowing from the government's efforts to address" the Pan Am 103 bombing incident that the Libyan government had ordered. After leaving the State Department, Libya retained Sofaer at a fee of $250,000 per month to represent it in connection with civil and criminal litigation arising out of that incident. When charged with a violation of Rule 1.11(a), Sofaer responded that his involvement in the matter at the State Department had not been "personal and substantial." Indeed, while he was in the government, most of the suspicion focused on other possible perpetrators. Amici curiae added that if Sofaer were guilty, no lawyer could safely move in and out of government. However, the court found that there was a clear violation of Rule 1.11 and ordered an informal admonition.

b. D.C. Bar Legal Ethics Opinion 297 (2000) explored whether a former government lawyer may represent a private party in a negotiated rulemaking in which the lawyer had participated while in government. A special statute authorizes a negotiated rulemaking committee, which is "an advisory committee established by an agency" in order "to consider and discuss issues for the purpose of reaching a consensus in the development of a proposed rule." 5 U.S.C.A. § 562(7). The D.C. opinion said that there is no violation of Rule 1.11 because negotiated rulemaking does not involve specific participants. Instead, it deals with formation of general policy and thus is not the kind of "matter" involving particular parties to which conflicts rules apply.

    c.   *Outdoor Advertising Ass'n of Ga., Inc. v. Garden Club of Ga., Inc.*, 527 S.E.2d 856 (Ga.2000), involved a former state attorney general's subsequent employment. The client wanted to trim trees to make billboards easier to see from the highway. Earlier, Michael Bowers was Georgia attorney general while his office was counsel of record for the state Department of Transportation. The deputy attorney general who handled the litigation never consulted with Bowers, who made no court appearances. However, his office issued a legal opinion about some of the relevant legal issues. The court would not disqualify Bowers because he had no "substantial responsibility" for the earlier matters. Otherwise, he would be disqualified from all 16,000 cases that were in his office while he was attorney general.

    d.   In *E.E.O.C. v. Exxon Corp.*, 202 F.3d 755 (5th Cir.2000), the EEOC alleged that Exxon violated the Americans with Disabilities Act because it would not allow alcoholics to pilot oil tankers. Part of Exxon's defense was that its policy grew out of a requirement that the federal government placed on it as part of settling criminal charges arising out of a massive oil spill involving the Exxon Valdez, an oil tanker. In that earlier suit the government had charged that Exxon's failure to monitor an employee's alcoholism contributed to the accident. For its defense, Exxon hired two former Justice Department lawyers, now in private practice, as expert witnesses to testify about the events leading up to the earlier settlement. The Justice Department asserted that their testimony would violate federal ethics standards, but the court permitted the testimony insofar as it was limited to publicly-known information. Being an expert witness is not the same as representing a party, the court said, so the ABA Model Rules do not forbid it. For the same reasons, there was no violation of the Texas Ethics Rules (the jurisdiction where this action arose) or the D.C. Bar Rules (the jurisdiction where the lawyers were admitted).

    e.   *United States v. Philip Morris Inc.*, 312 F.Supp.2d 27 (D.D.C.2004), involved *confidential* government information. The court disqualified a former Justice Department lawyer and his law firm from defending certain cases involving tobacco companies. The lawyer had worked for the Justice Department for 28 years. He also worked on an FDA rulemaking that asserted the FDA's right to regulate tobacco; he worked on the litigation seeking to defend that rule; he worked on an analysis of the Master Settlement Agreement between the tobacco industry and the states; and he wrote a memorandum on obtaining access to internal tobacco company documents. After his retirement, Shearman & Sterling hired him. In this motion to disqualify Shearman & Sterling, the court found that the work the lawyer did on the earlier FDA cases constituted a "matter" and that work done on the rulemaking was closely related to it. It concluded the lawyer learned confidential government information that could be relevant to the current litigation and ordered Shearman & Sterling disqualified because it had not created a screen.

3. ABA Model Rule 1.9 only prohibits representation that is "materially adverse" to the former client. Is Rule 1.11 so limited?

a. Why should the ethics rules forbid a lawyer who has left government from taking a case that *furthers* the government's objectives? Is it because government lawyers might bring cases that they could later exploit, when they leave government? Do you agree that government lawyers have access to information that private lawyers would not have or could not obtain through discovery?

b. ABA Model Rule 1.11(a) and Comment 3 are derived from General Motors Corp. v. City of New York, 501 F.2d 639 (2d Cir.1974). While a lawyer for the U.S. Government in 1956, the lawyer filed and signed an antitrust complaint against General Motors. Subsequently, in 1972 while he was in private practice, he agreed to represent New York City in another, similar antitrust claim on a contingent fee basis.[35] The court disqualified the lawyer. It concluded that his prior responsibility for the case was "substantial;" that his contingent fee arrangement with the city constituted private employment; that the city's antitrust suit was sufficiently similar to the federal case so as to constitute the same "matter" for purposes of DR 9–101(B); that it was irrelevant that the lawyer had not "switched sides" but had continued to litigate against General Motors; and that the lawyer's representation of the City would constitute the "appearance of impropriety." Do you think the court reached the right result?

c. Suppose that while working at the FTC, Smithers learned some shocking information about the business practices of several companies. May he represent persons who were injured by the companies whose practices he had studied? Look at Model Rule 1.11(c). Why should the law prevent Smithers from working *on behalf of* companies whose injuries he is especially well suited to redress? Does Rule 1.11, Comment 4 explain the underlying policies to your satisfaction? Does the rule prohibiting Smithers' use of confidential government information give too much protection to wrongdoers whom the agency may lack the resources to pursue?

d. Iowa Supreme Court Attorney Disciplinary Board v. Johnson, 728 N.W.2d 199 (Iowa 2007), is a poignant reminder that this aspect of Rule 1.11 can be a trap for the unwary. Johnson was an assistant county attorney responsible for emergency removal and child-in-need petitions. She signed several such petitions and appeared in several such cases. Later, she became executive director of the Youth Law Center, an organization that employs lawyers whom the courts appoint guardians-ad-litem for children. She intended to screen herself from cases in which she had appeared earlier for the state, but eventually she made some mistakes. Even though she was clearly trying to act in the best interests of the children in both the earlier and later roles, the

---

[35] There is no statute of limitations on the bar to subsequent representation of a private party in such a case. For example, if Smithers had personally worked on a case 15 years ago (early in his career at the FTC), one might think that he should now be free to work on that matter in private practice. As the *General Motors* case shows, however, that is not the law.

court said, Rule 1.11 bars later involvement in any matter in which the lawyer had personal and substantial responsibility while in government. Seeing the big picture, however, the court limited its sanction to a public reprimand.

4. In the case involving Quick, Inc., do the Rules bar Smithers from all activity within his own law firm? May Smithers talk to Quick about what the FTC is likely to do? May he give tactical advice to his partners who are handling the Quick matter?

a. Model Rule 1.11(b) provides that the law firm can avoid imputation only by timely "screening" the former government lawyer.[36] The screened lawyer, Smithers, could not provide informal advice to his partners about the Quick matter.

b. Problem 15 discussed the debates over whether to permit screening when a lawyer moves from one private firm to another. Are there any different risks (either in degree or in kind) with screening in cases involving former government lawyers? Is it easier to keep track of cases on which a former SEC employee may not work, than to do so in the case of a private litigator whose cases may have involved many different clients? On the other hand, what dangers of intentional or inadvertent "breaches in the wall" can you see? Are there any different incentives to violate the screen?

B.   THE FORMER PRIVATE LAWYER WHO ENTERS GOVERNMENT SERVICE

1.   Consider the other direction of the revolving door. What must a lawyer consider when he or she enters government service?

a. Must a government official recuse herself every time something comes up involving a former private client? Does the lawyer continue to owe the former client duties under ABA Model Rules 1.6 and 1.9(a)? In what ways does Model Rule 1.11(d) differ from Rule 1.9(a)?

b. Model Rule 1.11(d) is based on ABA Formal Opinion 342, supra, which said:

"When the Disciplinary Rules of Canons 4 and 5 mandate the disqualification of a government lawyer who has come from private practice, his governmental department or division cannot practicably be rendered incapable of handling even the specific matter. Clearly, if DR 5–105(D) were so construed, the government's ability to function would be unreasonably impaired. * * * The relationships among lawyers within a government agency are different from those among partners and associates of a law firm. The salaried government employee does not have the financial interest in the success of departmental representation that is inherent in private practice. * * * The channeling of advocacy toward a just result as opposed to vindication of a particular claim [also] lessens the temptation to circumvent the disciplinary rules through the action of associates. Accordingly, we construe DR 5–105(D)

---

[36] Remember, the requirements for an effective screen are set forth in ABA Model Rule 1.0(k) and Model Rule 1.0, Comments 8–10.

to be inapplicable to other government lawyers associated with a particular government lawyer who is himself disqualified * * *. Although vicarious disqualification of a government department is not necessary or wise, the individual lawyer should be screened from any direct or indirect participation in the matter, and discussion with his colleagues concerning the relevant transaction or set of transactions is prohibited by those rules."

c.   In analyzing these issues, D.C. Bar Legal Ethics Opinion 308 (2001), concluded that the lawyer's first constraint stems from the duty of confidentiality. Rule 1.6 says that (1) the lawyer must be vigilant not to reveal any protected information obtained from the former client, and (2) the lawyer may not knowingly "use" protected information "to the disadvantage of the client." Thus, even though not all uses of a former client's confidences involve revealing them to others, the second part of Rule 1.6 does not allow use either.

The second constraint stems from Rule 1.9. The test to determine if a lawyer may work on a matter while in government, the opinion says, is "whether the lawyer was so involved in the matter that the subsequent representation can be justly regarded as a changing of sides in the matter in question." If the answer is yes, the lawyer may not continue without written consent from both sides. If lawyer cannot secure written consent, the lawyer may not work for the government in the matter.

d.   For the reasons stated in ABA Formal Opinion 342, the principles of imputed disqualification do not apply to lawyers who practice in a government agency with the lawyer who is personally disqualified. However, D.C. Opinion 308, supra, says that the agency should consider voluntary screening measures. See also, ABA Model Rule 1.11, Comment 2.

2.   Should the law impute disqualification within a prosecutor's office when a prosecutor is hired from private practice?

a.   Restatement Third, The Law Governing Lawyers § 123, Comment *d(iii)*, concludes that imputation should not be inevitable "if the [prosecutor's] office is operated so as to avoid material risk that confidential information will be inadequately safeguarded."

b.   State ex rel. Romley v. Superior Court In and For the County of Maricopa, 908 P.2d 37 (Ariz.App.1995), held that if the government screens the disqualified prosecutor from participation in a matter, the court need not disqualify the whole Maricopa County prosecutor's office. Are courts justifiably concerned that states not wind up in a situation in which no persons will be available to prosecute criminal defendants if courts impose strict imputation?

c.   In City & County of San Francisco v. Cobra Solutions, Inc., 135 P.3d 20 (Cal.2006), however, the California Supreme Court (5 to 2) disqualified the whole San Francisco city attorney's office because the elected city attorney formerly represented a company that the city was now charging with fraud in its dealings with the city. The city attorney did not assist the client with the alleged fraudulent transactions, but he had worked on substantially related matters. Further, when the fraud investigation began, the city attorney did not know it would lead to his former client, but when it did, his office immediately screened him from involvement in the matter. The court recognized that Model Rule 1.11(d)(2) would allow a prosecutor's office to continue to handle the case, but "California has not adopted the ABA Model Rules," although "they may serve as guidelines absent on-point California authority or a conflicting state public policy." In this case, the court was concerned that a city attorney has such policymaking and supervisory duties that his staff in the office may do what they think the screened city attorney would want done. For individual attorneys coming into the office, screening should be enough; for supervisory attorneys, the office should conduct a factual investigation. However, to protect public confidence in the city's decisions, even screening could not avoid imputing the city attorney's own conflicts to others in the office.

3. What conflicts might arise when a government lawyer advises multiple agency clients?

a.   State Bar of California Formal Opinion No. 2001–156 (2001), discusses when a conflict of interest arises under California Rule 3–310(C) where a city attorney offers legal advice to different constituent sub-entities or to officials of a city whose positions differ on a subject.

The opinion recognizes that application of the Rules of Professional Conduct must consider factors peculiar to the governmental context. It says the courts have developed a two-part test to determine potential conflicts of interest arising from an attorney advising different bodies or officials within a city government: (1) An attorney for a governmental entity such as a city usually has only one client, the entity itself, and (2) A constituent sub-entity or official may become an independent client of the entity's attorney only if the sub-entity or official possesses authority to act independently of the main entity and if the entity's attorney is asked to represent the constituent sub-entity or official in its independent capacity.

Therefore, no conflict of interest arises when there is a disagreement between a government entity and its subordinate constituents, or between subordinate constituents of the entity. However, a conflict of interest may arise if a constituent or official has an independent right of action that would require the attorney to choose between conflicting duties. In the case of a city council and a mayor seeking legal advice from the city attorney, but taking different positions, no conflict of interest exists because the attorney represents neither the city council nor the mayor; the lawyer represents only the municipal corporation as an indivisible unit. Further, because neither of these sub-entities of the municipal corporation can function independently, the attorney may not represent either in its independent capacity. See ABA Model Rule 1.13, Comment 9.

b.   Military legal offices regularly also represent multiple clients and multiple interests. Except in cases of military necessity, the ABA Standing Committee on Ethics and Professional Responsibility says, "representation of opposing sides by lawyers working in the same military office and sharing common secretarial and filing facilities should be avoided." ABA Informal Opinion 1474 (1982) (citing Formal Opinion 343 and Informal Opinion 1309).

C. NEGOTIATING FOR POST-GOVERNMENT EMPLOYMENT WHILE STILL
    IN GOVERNMENT

1. Was it proper for Smithers to negotiate for employment prior to his retirement from the FTC? How may a lawyer in government service look for a job on the outside?

a. May the government lawyer seeking employment contact firms that regularly deal with the lawyer's agency? Look at ABA Model Rule 1.11(d)(2)(ii). Are those firms the ones most likely to find the lawyer's experience valuable?

b. Federal employees are also subject to 18 U.S.C. § 208(a) that provides:

> "[W]hoever, being an officer or employee of the executive branch of the United States Government * * * participates personally and substantially as a Government officer or employee * * * in a * * * particular matter in which to his knowledge, * * * any person or organization with whom he is negotiating or has any arrangement concerning prospective employment, has a financial interest [may be imprisoned up to 5 years, pay a $50,000 fine, or both]."

c. Section 208 creates an exception where the government employee makes a full advance disclosure of all relevant facts to the "Government official responsible for appointment to his or her position" and then receives a written determination "that the interest is not so substantial as to be likely to affect the integrity of the services" that the employee will render in the matter.

To whom would Smithers write such a letter? Do you suppose the President of the United States spends a lot of time making the determinations required by such notifications?

2. Smithers told P.D. Quick that several commissioners "owe their jobs to me." Is there anything wrong with saying that? How about saying it to law firms with whom he is negotiating employment?

a. Assuming that this statement is factually correct and well known, what is the comment trying to imply? Does the comment violate Model Rule 8.4(e)? Consider P.D. Quick's view of the situation. If Smithers cannot work on the matter, why should Quick travel all the way from California to hire Smithers when there are plenty of good lawyers in California? Does Model Rule 8.4(e) have any effect on what Smithers can say about his ability to help Quick?

b. Is it be unrealistic to require people like Smithers never to use the access they obtained while working for the government? President Truman—

> "had strong feelings about using one's official position, *past or present*, for gain. He was extremely fond of General Omar Bradley, the fellow Missourian who at one time during Mr. Truman's administration was Chief of Staff. After Bradley retired, he took a job as chairman of the board of the Bulova Watch Company, and one day in discussing General Bradley Mr. Truman said, 'I hold it against him, taking that job. They weren't hiring him; what they thought they were doing was

buying some influence in the Pentagon, and I don't care at all for that sort of thing, and I can't understand how General Bradley could bring himself to do it.' Being an admirer of General Bradley, I said, no doubt apologetically, 'He probably felt he needed the money.' And Mr. Truman said, 'Nobody ever needs money that bad.' "[37]

c.   When President Kennedy appointed Arthur Goldberg to the cabinet as secretary of labor, Goldberg promised never to practice labor law again, although that field of law had been his specialty. Goldberg always kept that promise. Would such a prophylactic rule—preventing a former government employee from using the benefits of his former position while in private practice—tend to discourage many good persons from entering government service?

D.   CONFLICTS OF THE FORMER JUDGE OR THIRD PARTY NEUTRAL

1.   Where does one find the limits on the activities of a former judge?

a.   Notice that former government officials who have served as judges are subject, not to ABA Model Rule 1.11, but to Model Rule 1.12. That rule also governs judges' law clerks, private arbitrators, mediators and other third-party neutrals.

b.   What values are we trying to protect by imposing limits on later private work by judges and other neutrals? None of the former adjudicators governed by Model Rule 1.12(a) "represented" anyone in their prior role. None of them has any duty of "loyalty" to the parties who appeared before them. Nor is information that comes out at trial "confidential" in any meaningful sense. What, if anything, should we worry about?

c.   Model Rule 1.12, Comment 1, says that Model Rule 1.12 generally parallels Model Rule 1.11, as well as corresponding provisions in the ABA Model Code of Judicial Conduct. Look at Comment 3. Does it provide an independent rationale for the rule?

d.   In James v. Mississippi Bar, 962 So.2d 528 (Miss.2007), James, a judge, presided in a case alleging that Husband had abused his wife and child. She ordered that Husband not have unsupervised visitation of the child. Now, James (no longer a judge) sought to represent Wife in a proceeding to modify the child custody provisions of the couple's divorce decree that a different judge had entered. The court acknowledged that the abuse case and the current one were not the same, but both involved the "same party or parties." Further, the allegations of physical abuse were at the heart of both proceedings, and James had earlier ruled on an issue of child custody. Thus, the court found a violation of Rule 1.12, but limited the sanction to a public reprimand.

e.   Comparato v. Schait, 848 A.2d 770 (N.J.2004), is one of the relatively few cases that deals with the disqualification of a judge's former law clerk and her firm. While Priscilla Miller was working as a law clerk for Judge Convery, a divorce case was before that judge. A few

---

[37] Merle Miller, Plain Speaking: An Oral Biography of Harry S. Truman 201–02, n. † (1974) (emphasis added).

months before her clerkship ended, Miller interviewed for a position with the firm representing Schait, the defendant in the case. She took the position, informed the judge that she had done so, and began working at the firm shortly after her clerkship ended. At the law firm, Miller worked on defendant Schait's case. She reviewed the plaintiff's motion for leave to appeal, drafted an appellate brief for defendant Schait, and met with Schait. When plaintiff's counsel became aware that Miller had been Judge Convery's law clerk while the case was before him, the counsel moved to disqualify defendant's law firm in the case. The New Jersey Supreme Court noted that N.J. Rule 1.12(a) forbids an attorney from representing a client where the lawyer "participated personally and substantially as a . . . law clerk" in connection with a matter involving that client unless all parties consent to the representation after full disclosure. The court warned that a law clerk's involvement could be "personal and substantial" if the clerk's role was substantive, such as recommending a certain disposition to the judge. However, while Miller was a clerk, any contact she may have had was non-substantive: she certified that her responsibilities had consisted mainly of calendaring motions filed during her tenure and performing other related ministerial tasks. Furthermore, she was not privy to confidential information regarding the case. Thus, Miller's involvement in the case was not sufficient to require disqualification. As a precautionary matter, however, Miller's firm screened her from further participation in the case, and the court made screening a part of its order.

2. What does Model Rule 1.12(b) tell us about how judges should accomplish a transition back to practice?

a.   Isn't it likely that almost *all* the major firms in a given area are likely to be counsel, or potentially counsel, in cases before the judge while she is looking for post-judicial employment? Does Model Rule 1.12(b) mean that the judge may not talk to any of them?

b.   Comment 3 to Model Rule 1.11 states that the purpose of Model Rule 1.11(d)(2) is to "prevent a lawyer from exploiting public office for the advantage of another client." That is not literally applicable to the judge, but does the same concern underlie Model Rule 1.12(b)?

c.   Boumediene v. Bush, 476 F.3d 934 (D.C.Cir.2006), involved a group of former judges who filed an amicus brief. These former federal judges sought leave to file an amicus brief in a case challenging the Military Commissions Act of 2006. The court denied the motion because the former judges all used the title "judge" to describe themselves in their brief. The court relied on Advisory Opinion No. 72 of the Committee on Codes of Conduct of the U.S. Judicial Conference: "Judges should insure that the title 'judge' is not used in the courtroom or in papers involved in litigation before them to designate a former judge, unless the designation is necessary to describe accurately a person's status at a time pertinent to the lawsuit." As the opinion noted, there used to be very few former federal judges. Now there are many, and they are more active in litigation. The opinion said that it is unfair for a party to have to oppose persons who can call themselves "judge" while other lawyers are not able to do so. Do you agree?

3.   If the judge does not comply with the requirements of Model Rule 1.12, what remedies or sanctions should the judge expect?

a.   Pepsico, Inc. v. McMillen, 764 F.2d 458 (7th Cir.1985), involved a judge who became eligible to take senior status. He contacted a "head hunter" who agreed to contact Chicago firms to see if any would want the judge to become affiliated with them. Inadvertently, and contrary to the judge's instructions, the headhunter contacted firms representing both the plaintiff and defendant in a pending antitrust case. Neither expressed an interest in hiring the judge, although the plaintiff's firm left the matter a bit more open than did the other. The judge did not go to work for either firm. Defendants sought a writ of mandamus to disqualify the judge. The Court of Appeals was careful to stress that the judge committed no intentional impropriety in the case, but it ordered the judge recused to avoid any "appearance of partiality" in the matter before him. See Model Rule 1.12(b).

b.   Kentucky Bar Ass'n v. Bates, 26 S.W.3d 788 (Ky.2000), is part of the "what was he thinking" line of cases. A part-time judge also practiced law as permitted by the state's code of judicial conduct. On behalf of one of his private divorce clients, he filed a petition seeking a divorce; five days later, he filed another petition, also on behalf of this client, seeking an emergency protective order against the wife, alleging an immediate danger of domestic violence. Purportedly because no other judge was handy, the lawyer not only drafted the order on behalf of his client but also signed it in his capacity as a judge. The next day, another judge signed the protective order. The court found a violation of Rule 1.12(a) because the lawyer had acted as counsel in a matter on which he had acted as a judge. It issued a public reprimand.

4.   Are the rationales for Model Rules 1.12(a) and 1.12(b) the same?

a.   One can readily understand why under Model Rule 1.12(b) a judge may not negotiate for employment with law firms representing parties whose cases he has not yet decided; the opportunity for bribery is obvious.

b.   Does a similar opportunity for dishonesty exist where a former judge, who decided a case long ago, represents the winner in seeking to get the loser to comply with the earlier order? Model Rule 1.12(a) clearly prohibits that representation. Why? Is it realistic to expect that the other party would consent to such representation? Why should the other party be concerned about the former judge's involvement?

c.   Does the screening authorized by Model Rule 1.12(c) provide adequate protection for the values implicit in Model Rule 1.12? If one is concerned that a party might reward a judge who grants a favorable verdict by later hiring the law firm where the judge now works, does the prohibition on the judge's directly collecting a fee for the matter remove all concern?

5.   Is it wise to try to deal with all forms of third-party neutrals in a single rule? For example, is our concern about later involvement by a mediator different from our concern about a former arbitrator or judge?

a.   Mediators often necessarily learn each side's bargaining positions that would never come out at a trial. See ABA Model Code of Judicial Conduct, Rule 2.9(A)(4). Should the rule treat persons who have obtained such confidential information differently from those who have not?

b.   Cho v. Superior Court, 45 Cal.Rptr.2d 863 (Cal.Ct.App.1995), involved a judge who presided over settlement discussions in a case and then left the bench and joined the defendant's law firm while the case was still pending. The court ordered the former judge's entire firm disqualified: "[A]lthough mediators function in some ways as neutral coordinators of dispute resolution, they also assume the role of a confidant, and it is that aspect of their role that distinguishes them from adjudicators."

c.   *Cho* said that screening under Model Rule 1.12 is proper for former adjudicators who only see what each side shows the other, but in the case of judges acting as mediators, disqualification of the entire firm is required. Do you agree? Does the current version of Model Rule 1.12 draw this distinction? Should it do so?

––––––––

THE FEDERAL STATUTORY COUNTERPART TO MODEL RULE 1.11

The federal statutory counterpart to Model Rule 1.11 is 18 U.S.C. § 207, found in the Standards Supplement. It is an extraordinarily long, complicated statute. Basically, it (i) applies to nonlawyers as well as lawyers, and (ii) applies to representation consistent with the former employee's work while in government as well as representation adverse to the government's position.

One of the important differences, of course, is that 18 U.S.C. § 207 is a *criminal* provision whose violation exposes the former federal employee to five years in prison, a fine, or both. Section 207 has at least three important parts.

1.   Section 207(a)(1) is a lifetime bar. It prohibits all former federal officials from making "any communication to or appearance before any officer or employee of [the United States] in connection with a particular matter" in connection with "a particular matter [involving a specific party or specific parties] in which the United States * * * is a party or has a direct and substantial interest" and in which the former official "participated personally and substantially" while in government.

2.   Section 207(a)(2) is a two-year bar from any "communication or appearance" in connection with any matter "which such person knows or reasonably should know was actually pending under his or her official responsibility [as a federal official] within a period of 1 year before" he or she left government.

3.   Section 207(c) is a one-year bar that prevents certain "senior personnel" from communicating with or appearing before their former

agency with an intent to influence any matter, whether or not he or she worked on it while in government.

Notice that, consistent with § 207, the former official may talk to clients about what their former agency is likely to do. He or she may also give tactical advice to partners who are handling the matter before the agency. The federal statute only forbids Smithers from talking with current agency officials. The legislative history of § 207 shows that Congress meant to have questions about imputation with a law firm, and any right of the government to waive the disqualification, governed by the bar's own rules of ethics, not federal statutes. The federal government seems more concerned about abuse of personal relationships within federal agencies than about exchange of information within law firms.

———

CHAPTER V

ADVISING CLIENTS

A news story reported a class discussion in a business school:

> "What should your role as a manager be when a subordinate comes to you reporting a product safety defect?" [Professor James Wilson of the University of Pittsburgh] asks. "Is your primary motivation to make a good widget or a good profit?"
>
> "I'd get another opinion," ventures one candidate for a master's in business administration.[*]

The lawyer for this widget producer should not be surprised if the manager comes to her for the other opinion. What should the lawyer say?

Lawyers usually spend more time counseling and trying to stay out of court than they do litigating cases. At least two different kinds of issues arise in trying to help clients solve their own problems rather than leaving the solution up to courts. First, how should you interact with your client and react to his or her assessment of the problem? Second, how should you deal with others on behalf of your client in settings such as negotiation or investigation? More specifically, consider questions such as these:

a.   What is the standard for determining the best interest of the client? Is the client by definition the best judge of his or her interest? Does the lawyer have a right—an obligation—to offer an opinion about what course of action would be in the client's best interest? Should a lawyer ever try to pressure a client into taking one course of action rather than another?

b.   What special questions exist when the client is not an individual, e.g., when the client is a partnership or a corporation? When the client is a corporation, who really speaks for the client? Is it the board of directors? The managers? The common stockholders? If the client is the fictional corporate entity, what does that mean when the flesh and blood persons are at odds and the lawyer is in the middle?

c.   Does a lawyer ever owe obligations to persons or entities other than the client? Does the lawyer owe the same obligation to a third party that the client owes to that party? Are there circumstances when the lawyer voluntarily assumes an obligation to report accurate information on which third parties may rely? Why would a lawyer assume that obligation even where the report does not reflect entirely favorably on the lawyer's client?

d.   Does a lawyer have a right—an obligation—to warn third parties about potential wrongdoing by the lawyer's client? On what theory would such a right or obligation rest? Should the lawyer with

---

[*]   Victor Zonana, Bribery & Slush Spur Ethics Courses at Business Schools: Would You Have Gone Along With Equity Funding Deal? Many Students Say Yes, Wall Street J., July 8, 1975, p. 1, col. 4.

knowledge of potential wrongdoing have a different right or obligation of disclosure than a nonlawyer would have?

PROBLEM 17

THE LAWYER FOR AN INDIVIDUAL CLIENT

Clients have the almost infinite range of characteristics human beings can have. Some seek to protect their wealth, others hope to expand their influence, and still others want to avoid being hurt by someone else. As we introduce you to the lawyer's advisor role, we focus on how you deal with your own client. Your new client is confused and frustrated by a legal system that she believes has not served her or her family well. This problem first asks the difference between a lawyer acting as an advisor and acting as an advocate; indeed, it asks whether a lawyer may have both roles in the same matter. Then, it explores what limits exist on the advice a lawyer may give and the projects a lawyer may assist. Next, it examines how the lawyer's role differs if the lawyer concludes that the client lacks normal mental ability. Finally, it asks the lawyer's options if the client's conduct seems likely to endanger others.

FACTS

Marilyn Anderson came to you for legal help. "They have taken away my children," she told you bitterly. "I have a right to them, don't I? I am a good mother, but the welfare department has put my babies in a foster home."

You were moved by Anderson's sincerity and agreed to take the case. In the course of your subsequent investigation, however, you discovered that Anderson had not told you all the facts. Family Services removed the children, Mary, age 7, and Billy, age 3, from the home after the Family Law Judge found both neglect and abuse. Social workers at Mary's school became suspicious when the little girl appeared bruised and malnourished after several days' absence. The social workers' questioning of Mary revealed that Anderson sometimes hit the children and sent them to bed hungry. Anderson also often left the home for hours at a time leaving no adult to care for them.

But that was only the beginning of the story. Anderson herself told you that her husband, John, has frequent violent episodes during which Anderson sometimes leaves the house and the children because she literally fears for her life. John has a job, but he is paid in cash and the family cannot rely on how much will be left in the pay envelope after he gets home. Anderson worked as a hospital aide before Mary was born, but she has enjoyed staying home with her children.

Anderson tells you that her elderly mother has been a particular irritant in the Andersons' relationship. Her mother is alert and lives in her own house, but she is lonely. Anderson wants to invite her to come to live with the family, but whenever she suggests it, John flies into a violent rage.

You wonder whether Marilyn Anderson should win the upcoming custody hearing. Although you sympathize with her situation, you hesitate to use all the skill and resources at your command to overwhelm the overworked counsel for the Department of Children and Family Services. If you do restore custody to Anderson, you worry about the children's future.[1]

QUESTIONS

A. THE DIFFERENCE BETWEEN ADVICE AND ADVOCACY

1. In this problem, is Marilyn Anderson asking you only to advocate for the return of her children? Is she also seeking your experience and judgment about how to deal with her situation?

a. In 1952, the ABA and the Association of American Law Schools established a Joint Conference on Professional Responsibility. Among its conclusions were:

"The most effective realization of the law's aims often takes place in the attorney's office, where litigation is forestalled by anticipating its outcome, where the lawyer's quiet counsel takes the place of public force. Contrary to popular belief, the compliance with the law thus brought about is not generally lip serving and narrow, for by reminding him of its long-run costs the lawyer often deters his client from a course of conduct technically permissible under existing law, though inconsistent with its underlying spirit and purpose.

"Although the lawyer serves the administration of justice indispensably both as an advocate and as office counselor, the demands imposed on him by these two roles must be sharply distinguished. * * * [R]esolution of doubts in one direction [in favor of the client] becomes inappropriate when the lawyer acts as counselor. * * * "[2]

b. Later, Model Code of Professional Responsibility Ethical Consideration 7–3 picked up that theme, saying:

"A lawyer may serve simultaneously as both advocate and adviser, but the two roles are essentially different. In asserting a position on behalf of his client, an advocate for the most part deals with past conduct and must take the facts as he finds them. By contrast, a lawyer serving as adviser primarily assists his client in determining the course of future conduct and relationships. While serving as advocate, a lawyer should resolve in favor of his client doubts as to the bounds of the law. In serving a client as adviser, a lawyer in appropriate circumstances should give his professional opinion as to what the ultimate decisions of the courts would likely be as to the applicable law."

---

[1] This problem is adapted with permission from one discussed in Murray Teigh Bloom (ed.), Lawyers, Clients & Ethics 1–5 (Council on Legal Education for Professional Responsibility, Inc. 1974).

[2] Professional Responsibility: Report of the Joint Conference, 44 A.B.A.J. 1159, 1161 (1958).

c.   Is this distinction between advice and advocacy self-righteous and naive? Is a client always entitled to a lawyer who makes a pit bull seem docile? What does Model Rule 2.1 tell you about your duty to Anderson? Does the distinction capture an important reality about how lawyers will best serve their clients' interests?

d.   Is there a difference between Anderson's short-term and long-term interests? Which should be more important as you decide how to proceed and what to advise her to do? Does the answer to that question vary from client to client?

2.   Are you confident that you know the dynamics of this family situation? Are you obliged to accept what your client tells you as true? Should you assume that most clients will lie about things that embarrass them, at least until they begin to trust you?

a.   Professor Naomi Cahn suggests that almost all events are likely to come to the lawyer in the form of "inconsistent stories."

"A woman, Darlene Adams, has come into my office, saying that she wants to leave the man she has been living with because he has beaten her up. In the initial interview, she states that the most recent time this happened was yesterday, when she was leaving the apartment with a female friend to go out to the movies. Mr. Ponds pleaded with her not to go; when she refused, he called her a whore and threatened to call Child Protective Services. He then slapped her face and pulled out a clump of hair. Her face stung for several hours, and her scalp still hurt when she came to see me. * * * She wants Mr. Ponds to leave the apartment and to stay away from her; she also wants custody of their child.

"At the interview, I take a picture of the bald spot on her head. Ms. Adams then tells me that the friend with whom she was going to the movies came with her to my office and would be happy to talk to me about what happened. When I interview the friend, Ms. Campbell, she tells me that she and Ms. Adams had talked to each other earlier in the day, and that Ms. Adams had told her that the situation at home was tense. When Ms. Campbell came over, the two of them decided to go to a movie, taking along young Ben. As they were leaving, Ms. Adams walked past Mr. Ponds, who then reached out towards her head. After Ms. Adams pulled away from him, he was left holding some hair. The friend did not see Mr. Ponds slap Ms. Adams. * * * I begin to prepare the papers and I ask Ms. Adams to return in two days, so that she can review and sign them.

"Two days later, Ms. Adams calls to say that she has decided not to go through with any legal action. Mr. Ponds has told her that he loves her, and has been especially nice to her. * * * She says that he really has not hurt her all that much * * *. * * *

"I have recognized, after reflection on these experiences * * * the following layers of inconsistent stories: the two different stories my client tells on different days, the discrepancies between my client's perceptions and those of her witness, the differences between what my client wants and what I think she needs, and the variation between my client's desire to stay and the oft-asked question, 'Why doesn't she leave?' Underlying these different stories include the stories my client tells me and what she tells herself. Once we file the papers, there will be another set of inconsistent stories: differences between my client's language and 'courtroom' language, dissimilarities between my client's story and her desired remedies, which differ from the judge's story and stock of remedies, which further differ from the definitions of what her 'case' actually is.

"The issues of whose story is told and of how the story will be related are complex. A lawyer envisions several tellings of the story; the client envisions several tellings as well. Each has (in)complete information about what will happen within the legal system, and about what 'actually happened.' Different approaches by lawyers and clients and a more fluid ethical system will allow for some better attorney-client relationships and some better retellings. Some stories will also 'seem' truer than others. But the conflicts will remain, conflicts between stories within the same 'case,' conflicts over what constitutes the 'case,' and conflicts between and within outsider groups seeking to tell their own stories. * * * So long as we have a legal system that values consistent stories, we must confront, and challenge, the possibility of constructing a true story of a case. Examining how inconsistent stories are left out of traditional legal ethics makes visible their presence and their significance, and provides an opportunity to accept and use them."[3]

b.   Bring these insights to bear on our problem. How do you know that Mary, the young daughter, told the social workers the truth about her mother's violence against her? How do you know the social workers accurately reported what Mary said? How do you know that Anderson's account of her husband's conduct is reliable? How should you as a lawyer go about determining the facts you need to know?

3.   Do you have sufficient skills to handle this case effectively?

a.   Is your law school training preparing you to be a social worker? Are you confident of your skills as a family therapist? May you simply say that you will limit your practice to giving legal advice and not worry about the context in which the client's legal problem arises?

b.   Can you deal effectively with the legal problems without addressing the context? Should you get a restraining order against John Anderson's domestic violence? Should you get an order requiring him to send a regular part of his paycheck to a bank account that only Mary cane access?

c.   In short, rather than being overwhelmed by what you don't know and can't fix, should you concentrate your efforts on steps that

---

[3]   Naomi R. Cahn, Inconsistent Stories, 81 Georgetown L.J. 2475 (1993). Used with permission.

only deal with some of the problem but that are steps that only a lawyer knows how to take?

4. What "styles" of client counseling should you adopt in your dealings with Anderson?

a.   Any categorization of counseling styles is obviously arbitrary, but that has not stopped commentators from trying to do it. Professors David Binder and Susan Price, for example, focus on "client-centered" counseling in which the lawyer's primary role is to help the client understand what the client wants and how to achieve it.[4]

b.   By contrast, Professor William Simon suggests taking a more directive view that urges lawyers to move clients toward results that are just, not simply favorable to one's own clients.[5]

c.   Professors Thomas Shaffer and Robert Cochran advocate a counseling of moral discourse and treating the client as one would treat a good friend, being supportive but willing to urge moral considerations as well as merely legal advice.[6]

d.   Does any one of those approaches seem intuitively better to you than the others? Whatever your initial view, keep these kinds of alternatives in mind as you think about what you would do in counseling Anderson and other clients you will meet in this chapter.

B.   LIMITS ON THE ADVICE A LAWYER MAY GIVE

1.   Look at Model Rule 1.2(d) and Comments 9 & 10. Do you agree that there should be no exceptions to the rule that a lawyer may not "counsel or assist" a client to commit a crime or fraud?

a.   People v. Chappell, 927 P.2d 829 (Colo.1996), involved a lawyer who represented the wife in a custody dispute. Court orders forbade both parents to take the child out of state. When the lawyer for the mother learned that the court-appointed evaluator was going to recommend giving the father custody of both her living and her unborn child, the lawyer "advised her [the client] as an attorney to stay, but as a mother to run" and told her of a network of safe houses that would take her in. At the lawyer's request, a friend of the client came into the client's home and moved her belongings into a storage locker to which the lawyer kept the key. When the lawyer came to the next hearing and the court asked where her client was, the lawyer told the court that the client's location was privileged. Only at a later hearing did the lawyer admit the client had fled the state. The court ruled that the lawyer violated Rule 1.2(d) by counseling the client to commit a crime, and what is now Rule 3.3(b) by not revealing the client's action to the trial judge. The court disbarred the lawyer.

---

[4]   Their leading book on the subject is David Binder & Susan Price, Legal Interviewing and Counseling: A Client–Centered Approach (1977).

[5]   See, e.g., William Simon, The Practice of Justice: A Theory of Lawyers' Ethics (1998). See also, Deborah L. Rhode, In the Interests of Justice: Reforming the Legal Profession (2000).

[6]   See, e.g., Thomas Shaffer & Robert F. Cochran, Jr., Lawyers, Clients and Moral Responsibility (1994). See also, Thomas D. Morgan, Thinking About Lawyers as Counselors, 42 Florida L. Rev. 429 (1990).

b.   Iowa Supreme Court Bd. of Professional Ethics & Conduct v. Hughes, 557 N.W.2d 890 (Iowa 1996), imposed a public reprimand on a lawyer who advised his client to ignore a court order to undergo substance abuse testing at the client's expense. The lawyer believed such an order was beyond the authority of the court. The client disregarded the advice and underwent the testing, but the trial judge referred the lawyer's conduct to the disciplinary committee. The Iowa Supreme Court assumed, without deciding, that a lawyer could counsel a client to ignore a void order, i.e., the order of a court with no jurisdiction over the matter, but in a case like this one, when the client's interests "conflict with a lawful court order, the lawyer's duty to uphold the law is paramount."

c.   Do you agree with the results in these cases? Can you imagine ever counseling a client to flee the jurisdiction or violate a court order? What if you believed your client's life would be in danger if she did not flee? What if she must violate the court order to make it ripe for appellate review?

2.   Is it obvious what it means to "counsel or assist" wrongdoing?

a.   Would you be "counseling" wrongdoing if you gave the client honest information about the likelihood the state would prosecute a particular violation of law? Does Model Rule 1.2, Comment 9, answer that question?

b.   Would you "assist" wrongdoing if you answered a murder defendant's question about which South American countries have no extradition treaties with the United States? Look at Model Rule 1.2, Comments 9 & 10.

c.   In Morganroth & Morganroth v. Norris, McLaughlin & Marcus, 331 F.3d 406 (3d Cir.2003), plaintiffs sued the Norris McLaughlin law firm for assisting a client's fraudulent conveyances that sought to evade a writ of execution to enforce plaintiffs' claim against the client. The firm's involvement consisted of preparing a deed purporting to confirm the conveyance of an interest in land, creating a purported life lease on certain land, and facilitating the delivering of shares the client owned in a Nevada corporation into his brother's control. Plaintiffs alleged that the law firm made these transfers with the intent to hinder, delay, and defraud the plaintiffs. The court found that plaintiffs "have alleged facts that, if proven, would establish that defendants went beyond the bounds of permissible advocacy; they allege that defendants were active participants and planners in the scheme to obstruct the plaintiffs' efforts to execute on their judgment."

d.   Should a lawyer in such cases offer such information and assistance as a way of providing the client full service? Must the lawyer refuse to answer questions that a dishonest client could use to avoid the consequences of past misconduct or plan future misdeeds? Must the lawyer ask a client for his passport and hold it lest the client try to flee?

3. **Assume that Anderson's mother owns her own house and a few stocks but has no other source of income. If she were to become ill, the house could be seized to reimburse Medicaid authorities for her care. What would you think of encouraging Anderson's mother to give her house to Anderson as a way of avoiding that result?**

a.   Assume that, as long as she did not make clear she had given her house to a relative, Anderson's mother could also qualify for welfare because she would be without assets and unable to work. She could even pay part of her benefits to Anderson as "rent."

b.   Would it be appropriate for you to suggest this approach to Anderson's mother and offer to draft the documents necessary to transfer the property to Anderson?[7] Would it be important for you to have Anderson promise to care for her mother or otherwise show some consideration for the transfer?

c.   The Bankruptcy Abuse Prevention and Consumer Protection Act of 2005 prohibits any "debt relief agency" from advising clients "to incur more debt in contemplation" of filing for bankruptcy. Lawyers argued that it would be unconstitutional to allow the provision to prevent them from giving truthful legal advice. Milavetz, Gallop & Milavetz, P.A. v. United States, 559 U.S. 229 (2010) read the law narrowly to avoid that constitutional problem. It held that lawyers are "debt relief agencies" but the law only prohibits them from "advising an assisted person to incur more debt when the impelling reason for the advice is the anticipation of bankruptcy." For example, a lawyer may advise a client to buy a car on credit when doing so will let the client work, even if the debtor later files for bankruptcy, because it was the hope of enhanced financial prospects, not the anticipated filing, that was the impelling cause of incurring further debt.

d.   Given the relative freedom these decisions suggest lawyers have to give advice, if you fail to give such asset-management advice, will you be violating Model Rule 1.1's obligation to act "competently"? Will you be committing malpractice? If you *do* give the advice, will you be violating Model Rule 1.2(d)? Which rule should control?

C.   THE CLIENT SUFFERING FROM DIMINISHED CAPACITY

1. **Would you follow Anderson's directions if you concluded that she had less than normal intelligence and was immature for her age?**

a.   Look at Model Rule 1.14 and Restatement Third, The Law Governing Lawyers § 24, which advised, in part:

> "(1) When a client's capacity to make adequately considered decisions in connection with the representation is diminished, whether because of minority, physical illness, mental disability, or other cause, the lawyer must, as far as reasonably possible, maintain a normal client-lawyer

---

[7]   Lest you think this proposal is hypothetical, the ethics of "asset management" of elderly clients is an everyday issue faced by "elder law" attorneys around the nation. See, e.g., Steven H. Hobbs & Fay Wilson Hobbs, The Ethical Management of Assets for Elder Clients: A Context, Role, and Law Approach, 62 Fordham L. Rev. 1411 (1994).

relationship with the client and act in the best interests of the client as stated in Subsection (2).

"(2) A lawyer representing a client with diminished capacity as described in Subsection (1) and for whom no guardian or other representative is available to act, must, with respect to a matter within the scope of the representation, pursue the lawyer's reasonable view of the client's objectives or interests as the client would define them if able to make adequately considered decisions on the matter, even if the client expresses no wishes or gives contrary instructions."

When should you conclude that your client has "diminished capacity"? Are you competent to determine a client's mental capacity? Does Model Rule 1.14, Comment 6 give you helpful guidance? Have you committed malpractice if you treat your client as entitled to make decisions when she really lacks the ability to do so?

b. If your client was not legally competent, did she have the capacity to retain you? Can she consent to your continuing to act as counsel? Does such a client have the capacity to fire you? Look at Model Rule 1.16, Comment 6. Many such clients have the capacity to make decisions to retain and terminate a lawyer without having the realistic capacity to make all decisions about the objectives and conduct of the representation.

2. May or must you ever seek to have a guardian appointed to act on an apparently incompetent client's behalf? What if the client objects to having a guardian?

a. Look at Model Rule 1.14, Comments 7 and 8. May you testify at the client's competency hearing? In doing so, may you reveal what the client told you in confidence? What if the incoherence of those confidential conversations is your best evidence of the client's need for the assistance of a guardian?

b. ABA Formal Opinion 96–404 (Aug. 2, 1996) acknowledges that if a client's "ability to communicate, to comprehend and assess information, and to make reasoned decisions is partially or completely diminished," Rule 1.14's admonition to "maintain a normal lawyer-client relationship" with the client "may be difficult or impossible." Indeed, in some states, the principal-client's incompetence automatically dissolves the agency relationship between lawyer and client, but the lawyer's withdrawal may have a significant adverse effect on the client's interests. The opinion counsels a lawyer to take the "least restrictive action under the circumstances." The lawyer should seek a guardianship only "if other, less drastic, solutions are [not] available." Further, even if the client needs a guardian for some purposes, the lawyer should seek something less than a general guardianship if possible. Although the lawyer may file the petition for guardianship, it must be because the lawyer concludes it is necessary, not because someone else (such as a family member) requests it. If the lawyer recommends a guardian, the lawyer must disclose to the appointing court any expectation of future employment by the guardian, and any preference the client may have expressed about whom the court should appoint as guardian.

c.   Matter of M.R., 638 A.2d 1274 (N.J.1994), involved a moderately-retarded 21-year-old woman with Down syndrome who was said to be "generally incompetent" and in need of a guardian. The question before the court was whether M.R. could decide whether she wanted her father or her mother to be that guardian. Part of the court's analysis involved whether appointed counsel should advocate M.R.'s preference to have her father as guardian or should make an independent report to the court about M.R.'s best interest. The court drew a distinction between a court-appointed lawyer and a court-appointed guardian ad litem. The latter is to make an investigation and report. Citing Model Rule 1.14, however, the court said that counsel appointed to represent M.R. must try to maintain "a normal client-lawyer relationship" with her. The lawyer must advocate what the client wants, short of things "patently absurd or that pose an undue risk of harm to the client." Do you agree?

3.   Should special rules apply if immediate action must be taken on behalf of a person—typically not a current client of the lawyer—who seems to lack the ability to make the necessary decisions to provide for his or her own welfare?

a.   In response to ABA Formal Opinion 96–404, supra, the ABA House of Delegates amended the Comments to Rule 1.14 in February 1997 to add Comments 9 & 10 on "Emergency Legal Assistance." The core idea of Comment 9 is that "where the health, safety or a financial interest of a person with seriously diminished capacity is threatened with imminent and irreparable harm, a lawyer may take legal action on behalf of such a person even though the person is unable to establish a client-lawyer relationship or make or express considered judgments about the matter, when the person or another acting in good faith on that person's behalf has consulted with the lawyer."

b.   Comment 10 goes on to say that the lawyer should protect the confidences of the person with seriously diminished capacity, should not provide assistance if the person has another lawyer, and normally should not charge a fee for the services rendered.

c.   How would you exercise the authority and responsibility given by these Comments? Should you seek to find and involve family members of the person? Should you see if she belongs to a church or other religious or social community whose members could help her? Might the lack of such a support network help explain why this person is now in crisis?

4.   If you reasonably believed that your client was about to make a fatal mistake, would you have an obligation to disregard the client's expressed preference and substitute your own judgment of what was best for the client?

a.   Convicted killer Gary Gilmore said that he "had to" die for a crime he had committed two centuries ago in England, and that he would still be in existence after his death. His attorneys thought that Gilmore's references to eighteenth century England would have made a difference to psychiatrists if they had heard it. The lawyers said, "we feel duty bound to go ahead with the appeal." Gilmore sent a letter to the attorneys saying: "butt out" and "you're fired." The attorneys then filed a notice of appeal in their own names saying that it was "in the best interest" of Gilmore, who was eventually executed.[8]

Were the lawyers right to ignore the client's call for his own death? One commentator has argued: "If the client expresses ends which, due to imprudence or excessive moralism, seem self-destructive, * * * [i]t is the lawyer's job to question the client's competence where it may need questioning * * *. When, on the other hand, the client is able to make his or her ends plausible to the lawyer, the check which he means to provide must give way."[9]

Do you agree? Should the client have to convince the lawyer before the lawyer has to give the client his own way?

b.   Massachusetts Bar Association Opinion 01–2 (2001) discusses whether the lawyer should reveal a client's intention to commit suicide. Because neither suicide nor attempted suicide is a crime in Massachusetts, its Rule 1.6 did not authorize disclosure. Relying upon Rule 1.14, the Opinion says that if a lawyer reasonably believes the client's suicide threat is real and that the client is suffering from a mental disorder or disability that prevents him from making a rational decision about whether to continue living, the lawyer may notify family members, adult protective agencies, the police, or the client's doctors in an attempt to prevent the suicide. The opinion does not give the lawyer a blanket authority to disclose a client's wish to die. It suggests that if the client were in great pain from a terminal disease, but not mentally depressed or otherwise mentally impaired, Rule 1.14 would not authorize the lawyer to disclose the client's plans.

Do you agree? Under Restatement, § 24, supra, or the Massachusetts Opinion, what should you do if the client tells you that she intends to take her own life?

D.   THE CLIENT WHO IS LIKELY TO ENDANGER OTHERS

1.   Should the interest of your client be the only interest relevant to you? Suppose you discover in the course of the representation that your client is guilty of child abuse?

a.   Association of the Bar of the City of New York, Formal Opinion 1997–2, 52 Record of the Association of the Bar of the City of New York 430 (1997), written in the context of a lawyer for a social services agency, acknowledges that children ordinarily have the right to have their communications with a lawyer kept confidential. The opinion even suggests that a lawyer may not be able to disclose the intention of the child to kill or maim himself. If the lawyer observes physical evidence of child abuse, however, the visual observations are not privileged. The lawyer may disclose the child's communications if: (1) disclosure is "required by law," (2) necessary to save the life of the child, or (3) the child is too young to have the capacity to make decisions.

b.   Utah Bar Opinion 97–12 (Jan.1998) addressed the situation where a client tells his lawyer that he is a child abuser. The opinion says that a state law requiring "any person" who suspects child abuse to report it does not apply to such cases. Under Rule 1.6(b)(1), the lawyer

---

8   Norman Mailer, The Executioner's Song 490, 513–14 (1979).

9   David Luban, Paternalism and the Legal Profession, 1981 Wisconsin L. Rev. 454, 493.

may disclose the client's intent to commit *future* abuse, but a client's confession to a lawyer about past conduct is privileged and the lawyer may not disclose it.

c.   L.A. County Bar Association, Formal Opinion 504 (2000) discusses an attorney's duty with regard to confidential information of a minor client's being a victim of ongoing sexual abuse. The opinion says the attorney has a duty to keep such information confidential if, after discussing the matter with the minor, the attorney reasonably believes that the client is competent to make a decision on the matter. What the attorney thinks is in the best interest of the client is not controlling. Indeed, even if the attorney feels that the minor is not competent to make such a decision, the attorney may not substitute her own decision for that of the client but may seek other appropriate measures such as having a guardian ad litem appointed and disclosing the information to that guardian.

2.   Is your duty different now that you have taken the case than it would have been had you not yet decided to represent Anderson?

a.   In re Pressly, 628 A.2d 927 (Vt.1993), involved a client who had obtained a restraining order against her husband and had custody of the children, subject to the husband's visitation rights. Later, she told the lawyer she wanted the husband to have only supervised visitation. When asked why, she said she thought he had sexually abused their daughter but she explicitly told the lawyer not to tell her husband of her suspicions. When the lawyer told opposing counsel the wife wanted supervised visitation, however, opposing counsel asked if it was because of suspected sexual abuse. The lawyer confirmed that the mother suspected abuse and asked opposing counsel not to tell the husband. Opposing counsel did tell the husband, and the wife was shocked and furious at her lawyer. The Vermont Supreme Court said the lawyer's confirmation that the mother suspected abuse—contrary to the client's express direction not to reveal it—justified a public reprimand of the lawyer.

b.   How would you have responded to opposing counsel's question in *Pressly*? Was the lawyer's mistake accepting the client's original direction without discussion or qualification? A client can always fire her lawyer, of course, so the client necessarily has the last word. Should the lawyer take the client's direction as the beginning of a conversation with the client, not as an order that the lawyer must carry out blindly?

3.   Can you identify any creative approaches to deal with Anderson's situation?

a.   Think back to Anderson's mother. What would you think of having Anderson and the children move in with her? Anderson's mother could watch the children while Anderson went back to work. In exchange, Anderson would make sure her mother was in good health. She could start proceedings to divorce John and request child support. Do you have some better ideas?

b.   Suppose that at the custody hearing the social worker from the Department of Children and Family Services appears without counsel. You still represent Anderson, but no one represents Anderson's children. May you suggest that the court appoint counsel for the children even though you surmise that, if the court does so that will substantially reduce your chances of winning?

c. Do you have an ethical obligation to Anderson to oppose appointment of such counsel? Does Model Rule 4.3 provide a good analogy that helps you decide what to do?[10] If the court appoints counsel, does that lessen your own ethical burden and allow you to use all the tricks in your bag on Anderson's behalf?

———

PROBLEM 18

ADVISING THE BUSINESS CORPORATION

This is a second problem that focuses on your duty to give candid advice to a client. It is one thing to advise an individual whom the lawyer can address face to face. When the client is a business corporation, the lawyer can only counsel the client's agents. Those agents, in turn, are likely to believe themselves limited by the authority of others, so the lawyer's task of giving wise counsel becomes immeasurably more complex. This problem explores who the lawyer's ultimate client is when the lawyer represents an organization and from whom the lawyer is to accept direction. Next, it asks when a lawyer may or must disclose wrongdoing either inside or outside the organization. It then examines whether a lawyer may personally be liable to persons hurt by client conduct that the lawyer did not prevent, and finally, it considers whether the role of inside counsel as to these issues differs from that of a lawyer in an outside firm.

FACTS

You have long been outside counsel to Sleepware, Inc., a clothing manufacturer. The company makes a line of children's pajamas that is a big seller. Recent tests have shown, however, that the pajama fabric can catch fire if a lit match is held against it for a few seconds.

Sleepware's vice president for pajamas wants to keep selling the pajamas until the company can reformulate the fabric in this product line. Regulations of the Consumer Product Safety Commission (CPSC) prohibit sale of products known to cause burns to children, but the vice president believes that the CPSC is unlikely to discover the flammability defect in the pajamas.

Further, the vice president points out that, although children wearing pajamas sometimes play with matches, experts he has consulted say that not more than one in 50,000 children would hold the matches on their pajamas long enough for it to catch fire. The experts admit that if the pajamas burn, the child's injuries could be severe, but a management-consulting firm has estimated that civil damages would not

———

[10] D.C. Bar Legal Ethics Committee Opinion 326 (2004) expressly affirms that it is not a conflict of interest for a lawyer to help even an unrepresented opposing party get legal counsel. It follows that it would be proper to help the child get counsel in the circumstances described.

exceed $250,000 per victim. Sleepware sells 200,000 of these pajamas each year, the vice president tells you proudly, and it makes a profit of $4,000,000 on this product. Thus, even under a worst-case scenario, he has calculated that it will be $3 million more profitable to sell the pajamas than not to sell them.

The client has not asked you for advice about whether to market this product; you only learned about the flammability while working on an unrelated matter. Indeed, the vice president is annoyed that you have raised the issue with him. "The president will retire soon," he tells you, "and I am his natural successor. My enemies in the company would love to embarrass me with this."

QUESTIONS

A. THE CLIENT TO WHOM A CORPORATE LAWYER OWES PRIMARY LOYALTY

1. Is your client in this problem Sleepware's vice president for pajamas?

a. Describing the corporate lawyer's client has proved harder for lawyers than for rule drafters. It is tempting to think that the "clients" are the individual human beings to whom the lawyer gives her advice and from whom she receives confidential information. Other lawyers sometimes think of their clients as shareholders generally, or perhaps the largest shareholder—the one who influences decisions the corporate managers will make.

b. To try to deal with this issue, Model Code of Professional Responsibility, Ethical Consideration 5–18 simply said:

"A lawyer employed or retained by a corporation or similar entity owes his allegiance to the entity and not to a stockholder, director, officer, employee, representative, or other person connected with the entity."

c. That statement of the rule was and is accurate, but to point out that corporations and other organizations only act through living people, Model Rule 1.13(a) now says:

"A lawyer employed or retained by an organization represents the organization acting through its duly authorized constituents."

d. The Restatement Third, The Law Governing Lawyers § 96(1)(a) refines this principle:

"When a lawyer is employed or retained to represent an organization, the lawyer represents the interests of the organization as defined by its responsible agents acting pursuant to the organization's decision making procedures."

2. How do these definitions apply in real life? Do they all point the same way in particular cases?

a. Is the interest of the entity always self-evident? For example, the employees may want higher pay and secure jobs, while some

refused to disqualify counsel. This is an old case; do you think a court should be as restrained about enforcing Rule 4.3 today?

c.   ABA Standards Relating to the Administration of Criminal Justice, The Defense Function, Standard 4–4.3(c) says: "It is not necessary for defense counsel or defense counsel's investigator, in interviewing a prospective witness, to caution the witness concerning possible self-incrimination and the need for counsel." Do you agree? Does a lawyer's duty of loyalty to her client require that she take advantage of the ignorance of the employee she is interviewing?

d.   How does Model Rule 1.13(f) deal with the issue? Does it give the lawyer any latitude to take advantage of an unrepresented person's ignorance? Do Comments 10 and 11 to Model Rule 1.13 give ambiguous direction? See also Model Rule 1.13(g).

DO STATE ETHICS RULES APPLY TO FEDERAL PROSECUTORS

State prosecutors, of course, are subject to the rules of professional conduct. Model Rule 3.8 focuses specifically on prosecutor ethics, and Standard 3–2.7 of the ABA Standard Relating to the Prosecution Function encourages prosecutors not to permit misconduct by the police.

Particularly in the prosecution of terrorism and organized crime activity, however, federal prosecutors have argued that they need more latitude than Model Rule 4.2 permits.[25] When a low-level criminal defendant wishes to talk to an Assistant U.S. Attorney directly, the argument goes, even the latitude Rule 4.2 gives to seek a court order authorizing the conversation is not sufficient to meet the government's needs to investigate criminal activity. That position was taken by both Attorney General Thornburgh under President George H.W. Bush and Attorney General Reno under President Clinton.

What do you think of the argument that federal needs trump the regulatory authority of state courts over the lawyers they license? The courts were not impressed by the argument. See United States v. Colorado Supreme Court, 87 F.3d 1161 (10th Cir.1996); Matter of Howes, 940 P.2d 159 (N.M.1997) (per curiam).

Congress has now resolved this issue by enacting a law that expressly makes federal lawyers subject to state ethics rules. Called the McDade Act, the law took effect in April 1999 and is found at 28 U.S.C.A. § 530B. Do you agree with this resolution of the issue?

———

PROBLEM 20

THE ETHICS OF NEGOTIATION

Negotiation may be the quintessential activity of a lawyer and the best example of the lawyer's contact with a third party on the client's behalf. Reaching agreement on a sale of an asset or formation of a

---

[25] Long before adoption of Model Rule 4.2, ABA Formal Opinion 95 (May 3, 1933) stated: "It would be unavailing to contend that the police officers or detectives are not under the supervision and control of the law officer * * *."

contractual relationship can provide protection for and benefits to the lawyer's client. Indeed, year in and year out, even where relationships sour and litigation ensues, over 90% of the parties to filed cases resolve their differences by negotiation before trial. Is negotiation an ethical wasteland where the lawyer has no standards of conduct? Is it a world where literally anything goes? This problem suggests that the answer is no. It considers first where the lawyer gets authority to negotiate and the boundaries of that authority. Next, it looks at the duty to tell the truth in negotiations and any limits to that duty. Then, it asks whether lawyers ever have to volunteer information in order to avoid a misapprehension by the other side. Finally, it examines limits on what negotiated results parties and their lawyers may reach.

FACTS

James Young, age 19, was in a traffic accident. The driver of the other car suffered personal injuries and has paid medical bills of $18,000. There was $7,000 in property damage to the other car. Young was unhurt, but his car suffered $5,000 damage.

At the scene of the accident, the investigating officer charged Young with drunken driving. Young denied it and told the officer that he had nothing alcoholic to drink the entire day. He told you, however, that he had three large drinks within an hour of the accident. By chance, the arresting officer failed to bring along his kit to test for blood alcohol, so there is no scientific evidence on that issue.

Young's criminal trial is coming up next week. Conviction of drunk driving would probably mean that Young would pay a large fine and lose his driving privileges for a year. You have plea negotiations scheduled with the prosecutor this afternoon. You expect that settlement discussions about the potential civil claims will begin soon.

You have not talked at all with Young about what kind of plea he might enter, but you have authority from his insurance company to pay up to a total of $20,000 for the combined personal injuries suffered by the other driver and the property damage incurred by the owner of the other car.

QUESTIONS

A.   AUTHORITY TO PARTICIPATE IN AND CONSUMMATE NEGOTIATIONS

1.   What gives you the authority to conduct negotiations on behalf of James Young? Is the authority to negotiate inherent in a lawyer's role as a client's representative?

a.   Restatement Third, The Law Governing Lawyers § 21, Comment *e*, says:

"A lawyer has authority to take any lawful measure within the scope of representation that is reasonably calculated to advance a client's objectives as defined by the client, unless there is a contrary agreement or instruction and unless a decision is reserved [by law] to the client."

b. Thoughtful lawyers acknowledge, however, that they have only as much authority to conduct negotiations as their client gives them. Remember what Model Rule 1.2(a) says about who ultimately has the legal authority to settle a matter?[26]

c. Restatement Third, The Law Governing Lawyers § 22 reinforces Rule 1.2(a):

"(1) As between client and lawyer, * * * the following and comparable decisions are reserved to the client except when the client has validly authorized the lawyer to make the particular decision: whether and on what terms to settle a claim; how a criminal defendant should plead; * * *

"(3) Regardless of any contrary contract with a lawyer, a client may revoke a lawyer's authority to make the decisions described in Subsection (1)."

2. Why is even the commencement of negotiations something the lawyer should not take lightly?

a. Is talking about settlement of a case a "means by which the client's objectives are to be accomplished" within the meaning of Model Rule 1.4(a)(2)?

b. Can a lawyer intelligently even make a first offer or respond to one from the other side without knowing what the client is currently prepared to accept? Negotiators often talk about trying to find ways to "create value," i.e., to identify ways to engage in sufficient "trade" of issues that both parties feel themselves better off because of the negotiations. In short, most negotiations involve a range of potential outcomes and the optimal result will vary with the personal values placed on them by the parties.

c. Is obtaining authority to negotiate and determining the range of acceptable settlement terms a one-time event? Does Model Rule 1.4 create a continuing obligation on the lawyer? Is negotiation often an evolving process in which settlement authority that seemed reasonable at one time may require revision as new opportunities for agreement open up while others seem less likely?

d. Imagine that in this problem the prosecutor is willing to forego most sanctions if Young will plead guilty to some misdemeanor. Young, in turn, would accept almost any offense that will not involve jail time or a fine in excess of $1,000. May you negotiate competently on your client's behalf without knowing the relative importance of such alternatives to your client? Can you know those objectives without communicating with your client as Model Rule 1.4 requires?

3. Must a lawyer inform the client about all settlement offers received from the other side?

a. Restatement § 20, Comment e, says:

"A lawyer must ordinarily report promptly to the client a settlement offer in a civil action or a proposed plea bargain in a criminal prosecution."

b. Model Rule 1.4, Comment 2, goes on:

---

[26] Problem 4, Issue D discusses the fact that a lawyer cannot bind a client to a settlement unless the client authorizes the lawyer or agrees to the settlement.

"[A] lawyer who receives from opposing counsel an offer of settlement in a civil controversy or a proffered plea bargain in a criminal case must promptly inform the client of its substance unless the client has previously indicated that the proposal will be acceptable or unacceptable or has authorized the lawyer to accept or reject the offer."

c.   Is this requirement realistic? May a lawyer ever say: "That offer is so bad I would not dignify it by taking it back to my client"? Do we want lawyers to make such statements without having learned what kinds of settlement offers are acceptable to the client?

d.   Think back to Problem 19. Is requiring a lawyer to convey all offers to his or her client a necessary corollary to Rule 4.2's prohibition of the other side's direct contact with that lawyer's client?

B.   THE DUTY OF HONESTY IN NEGOTIATIONS

1.   When you start to discuss this case with the prosecutor, or the opposing counsel in the civil case, may you assert that Young had nothing alcoholic to drink on the day of the accident?

a.   Remember that Young has told that story to everyone but you, and if you fail to take that position, you may undercut Young's credibility. May you confirm Young's story in response to a question from the prosecutor or opposing counsel? How would you answer the question: "Are you sure that your client had no alcohol to drink?"

b.   As you will see in Problem 27, you clearly cannot encourage Young to testify falsely in the upcoming criminal trial that he did not drink any alcoholic beverage. Does Model Rules 4.1 and 8.4(c) support any distinction between perjury in a trial and deception in negotiation? Should there be a distinction? Should the answer that governs the trial setting be controlling in a negotiation setting as well?

c.   May your negotiating position in the civil and criminal cases be that, whether or not your client drank anything alcoholic before the accident, he was not intoxicated at the time the accident occurred? Is that a different question than what he had to drink? Is it a representation that you *know* is untrue?

d.   May you claim that neither the police nor the plaintiff can prove that Young was intoxicated? Are statements about facts and statements about strength of the evidence different as a practical matter? Are they—should they be—different as a matter of ethics?

e.   May you tell the opposing lawyer that your client will testify that the other car was traveling at an excessive rate of speed and "came out of nowhere" to cause the accident? May you say that if you know that your client does not really remember the accident very well, but you hope that the other side will factor into its estimate of the worth of the case the risk that your client would tell such a story?

2.   Are all lies created equal? Do we tolerate some lies, even encourage some, while forbidding others?

a.   In Office of Disciplinary Counsel v. DiAngelus, 907 A.2d 452 (Pa.2006), during the course of plea bargaining a relatively serious motor vehicle violation down to a lesser one, DiAngelus told the prosecutor that the arresting officer had agreed to a reduction of the charges. Later, however, the arresting officer denied that he said that and he could prove he had been elsewhere when DiAngelus said the conversation had occurred. The court found the lawyer's misrepresentation was dishonest, violated Rule 8.4(c), and materially affected the outcome of the case in violation of Rule 8.4(d). The court suspended DiAngelus for 5 years.

b.   Rule 4.1(a) prohibits making a false statement of "material" fact or law. Does Rule 8.4(c) incorporate that restriction when it prohibits "dishonesty"? Now, look at Model Rule 4.1, Comment 2:

> "Under generally accepted conventions in negotiation, certain types of statements ordinarily are not taken as statements of material fact. Estimates of price or value placed on the subject of a transaction and a party's intentions as to an acceptable settlement of a claim are ordinarily in this category * * *."

What about misrepresenting one's attitude? Is it proper to fake anger during negotiations? May a lawyer lie about the client's alternatives? Is it proper to delay making or responding to an offer so as not to let the other side get the sense that your client is in a hurry to dispose of the case by settlement?

c.   ABA Formal Opinion 06–439 (Apr. 12, 2006) acknowledges that negotiators often make statements that are "less than entirely forthcoming." So long as the statements are of a kind "upon which parties to a negotiation ordinarily would not be expected justifiably to rely," they are acceptable of a form of "posturing" or "puffing," the opinion says. Negotiators, however, may not make false statements of material fact. Thus, even though a client has authorized a $100 settlement figure, a lawyer may say the client does not wish to settle for more than $50; what the lawyer may not say is that the client has not authorized a settlement for more than $50. Do you agree? Is the ABA Committee too willing to split ethical hairs?

3.   Do lawyers have a higher obligation to be truthful than nonlawyers?

a.   Look closely at Model Rule 4.1 and its Comments. Does it prohibit anything more than "false" statements of "material" fact? May the lawyer lie about where James Young was going on the day of the accident? May he say James was going to church services when he really was going to shoot pool? Is the issue of where he was going "material" to the legal issues in the case? Would it be disloyal to the client to suggest that he is other than a choir boy?

b.   If a nonlawyer knowingly made a false statement of material fact, wouldn't the nonlawyer be guilty of fraud? Does Model Rule 4.1 demand any more of lawyers? Put another way, if a statement would not constitute the tort of fraud or intentional misrepresentation, would it violate Model Rule 4.1? Look especially at Comment 2. Is there any statement that would subject a lawyer to professional discipline but not to liability for damages?

c.   Fire Ins. Exchange v. Bell by Bell, 643 N.E.2d 310 (Ind.1994), involved a lawyer's client who was burned in a fire at his grandfather's home. The homeowner's insurer retained one of the state's most prominent law firms. The insurer offered to pay policy limits, which the law firm represented to be $100,000. Although the injuries would justify a higher verdict against the plaintiff's grandfather, the plaintiff's lawyer recommended taking the settlement as the only money the plaintiff would be likely to collect. Only later did the lawyer learn that the policy limits were in fact $300,000, not $100,000. Plaintiff then sued the defense lawyers for misrepresentation. The lawyers argued that no one can reasonably rely on what a lawyer says in "adversarial settlement negotiations." But the court answered: "[t]he reliability and trustworthiness of attorney representations constitute an important component of the efficient administration of justice." Even though the plaintiff's counsel could have obtained discovery of the policy and learned the policy limits himself, he was entitled to rely on what opposing counsel told him about this material matter. Hence, plaintiff could seek damages for fraudulent misrepresentation.[27] The law firm may not lie.

d.   Restatement Third, The Law Governing Lawyers § 98, Comment c, suggests that Model Rule 4.1 has two functions. First, it shows that lawyers at least have the same obligations of truthfulness as do persons generally, i.e., lawyers have no special privilege to make material misstatements of fact. Second, to prove a violation of Model Rule 4.1, it is not necessary to show either reliance on the misstatement or actual damages as a tort suit would require.

e.   Should the law require lawyers to be more honest than it requires nonlawyers to be? Because people are more on their guard when dealing with a lawyer, should the lawyer's obligation to tell the truth be less?

4.   Is deception and withholding of information inevitably good negotiating strategy?

a.   Is negotiation inevitably a zero-sum game in which anything one side receives is at the expense of the other? Assume Ann has a candy bar and Bill has a pen. Ann needs something with which to write and Bill is hungry. Will Ann and Bill each be better off trying to figure out how to trick the other out of what the other has? Will the lot of both of them improve once they acknowledge the possibility of a fair trade?

b.   Some students of negotiating strategy have used computer simulations to explore approaches to negotiation and have evaluated them in terms of benefits to each negotiator. One successful strategy is known as tit-for-tat.[28] A wise negotiator breaks the process down into a series of small deals, not just one large one. For the first deal, you begin by being open and honest in your negotiating. If your opposing number responds in the same way, you reward her by continuing to be open and honest. If your opponent deceives you or takes advantage of your honesty, however, you punish her by noncooperative behavior as to the next issue. The point is that neither side needs to trust the other or sacrifice its own interests. It simply will turn out to be better for all sides to make honesty and cooperation pay.

---

[27] See also, Shafer v. Berger, Kahn, Shafton, Moss, Figler, Simon & Gladstone, 131 Cal.Rptr.2d 777 (Cal.Ct.App.2003) (cause of action for fraud because of false assertion that claim not covered by insurance); Siegel v. Williams, 818 N.E.2d 510 (Ind.Ct.App.2004) (cause of action for fraud for false assertion that paying more than $25,000 would force lawyer into bankruptcy).

[28] See Robert Axelrod, The Evolution of Cooperation (1984).

c.   However, is every negotiating situation one that has multiple steps? Is every situation one that both sides can win? Even negotiations that "increase the size of the pie" have a stage in which the parties must divide the pie. At that stage, what would good negotiators do? Should they agree on a solution that mimics the situation in which one party cuts the pie and the other chooses the first piece?[29]

C.   THE DUTY TO VOLUNTEER INFORMATION OR CORRECT A MISAPPREHENSION

1.   Should the law require a lawyer to disclose affirmatively adverse facts in a negotiation? Is it instead the duty of the adverse side to ask direct questions to the opposing lawyer to confirm its assumptions, and not that lawyer's obligation to volunteer harmful facts?

a.   *Virzi v. Grand Trunk Warehouse & Cold Storage Co.*, 571 F.Supp. 507 (E.D.Mich.1983), raises this question in a particularly interesting form. The plaintiff in a personal injury case died from causes unrelated to the lawsuit prior to a pretrial conference and settlement negotiation. Plaintiff's lawyer did not inform either opposing lawyer or the court of the plaintiff's death throughout negotiations. But defendant's lawyer at no time specifically asked plaintiff's lawyer if plaintiff was still alive and available for trial. The opposing lawyer did not lie, but he did fail to volunteer his client's death. When the probate appointed a personal representative to administer the plaintiff's estate, the plaintiff's lawyer did not move to substitute parties. When the defendant later learned what had happened, it moved to set aside the settlement. The court relied, inter alia, on what is now Model Rules 3.3 and 4.1, and on Judge Rubin's article, to grant that relief, saying that zealous representation

> "does not justify a withholding of essential information, such as the death of the client, when the settlement of the case is based largely upon the defense attorney's assessment of the impact the plaintiff would make upon a jury because of his appearance at depositions. Plaintiff's attorney clearly had a duty to disclose the death of his client both to the Court and to opposing counsel prior to negotiating the final agreement."

b.   ABA Formal Opinion 95–397 (Sept. 18, 1995) addressed the same question and explained why the lawyer must voluntarily disclose her client's death while the law does not normally require the lawyer to volunteer adverse facts in negotiation. The client's death is special because that death automatically terminates the agency relationship and the lawyer has no client. The failure to disclose is "tantamount to making a 'false statement of material fact'" to the opponent and to any tribunal. The lawyer "must inform her adversary of the death of her client in the first communication with the adversary after she has learned of that fact."

---

[29] Many observers remain unconvinced that honesty is the best policy if the only measure is "profit and effectiveness." See, e.g., Gerald B. Wetlaufer, The Ethics of Lying in Negotiations, 75 Iowa L. Rev. 1219, 1230 (1990): "In those bargaining situations which are at least in part distributive, a category which includes virtually all negotiations, lying is a coherent and often effective strategy." Professor Wetlaufer argues that "lying in negotiations is instrumentally effective and that most such lies are ethically impermissible."

c.   Most cases are consistent with this result. In Kentucky Bar Ass'n v. Geisler, 938 S.W.2d 578 (Ky.1997), the client was a pedestrian hit by a car. The lawyer told the defense lawyer that the client was too ill to be deposed. After the client's death, she wrote to defense counsel and asked for an offer of settlement. The defense first learned of the client's death when the plaintiff's administrator endorsed the settlement check. Citing ABA Opinion 95–397 and *Virzi*, the court condemned her silence about the client's death in the letter opening settlement talks and ordered a public reprimand.[30]

2.   Should each round of settlement discussions begin with questions by each side designed to trigger disclosure of unfavorable facts? Would a general obligation on lawyers to disclose relevant changes in circumstances be preferable? Can you see problems with both approaches?

a.   ABA Formal Opinion 94–387 (Sept. 26, 1994) narrowly interpreted the duty to disclose. It ruled that "where the lawyer knows that her client's claim may not be susceptible of judicial enforcement because the statute of limitations has run, * * * the ethics rules do not preclude a lawyer's nonetheless negotiating over the claim without informing the opposing party of this potentially fatal defect." However, the lawyer must "be careful not to make any affirmative misrepresentations about the facts showing that the claim is time-barred, or suggest that she plans to do something to enforce the claim (e.g., file suit) that she has no intention of doing. See Rule 4.1." According to the opinion, there is also no violation of Rule 3.1 (frivolous suits) or Rule 3.3 (candor to tribunal) to file a time-barred claim in court "so long as this does not violate the law of the relevant jurisdiction," such as would be the case if the limitations defect were jurisdictional. Normally, the opinion noted, the statute of limitations is an affirmative defense that the opposing party must assert. Finally, there is no basis in the ethical rules to hold a government lawyer to a higher or different standard.

Committee member Richard McFarlain filed a dissent. He regarded this opinion much "as Julia Child would regard a fly in her soup;" it is "unneeded, unwanted, and too much to swallow." In his view, Rule 8.4(c), prohibiting deceit, prohibits lawyers from engaging in this activity.

b.   With which of these views do you agree? If the opposing lawyer objects to your statute of limitations defense in his negotiations, but does not know of recent authority that helps his case by creating a laches defense to prevent the limitations from barring your client, do you have any obligation to volunteer that case to him? If you were in court and writing a brief on the issue, would you have to volunteer the case to the judge? Compare Rule 3.3(a)(2) with Rule 4.1(a).

---

[30] See also, Matter of Forrest, 730 A.2d 340 (N.J.1999) (discussing settlement while saying a deceased client was "unavailable" for an arbitration hearing and delaying court-ordered medical examination justified lawyer's six-month suspension); In re Warner, 851 So.2d 1029 (La.2003) (lawyer suspended for assisting client's daughter to negotiate settlement and forge her father's name after client's death).

3.   Should the rules about negotiation be different in criminal cases? How candid must a prosecutor be about the strength of the evidence?

a.   In People v. Jones, 375 N.E.2d 41 (N.Y.1978), cert. denied, 439 U.S. 846 (1978), the court held that there was no due process violation when the district attorney did not disclose, during plea negotiations, that the complaining witness had died. Under Brady v. Maryland, 373 U.S. 83 (1963), the prosecutor is under a constitutional duty to respond to defendant's request that he disclose material evidence favorable to the accused, either as to guilt or punishment. The death of the state's critical witness did not fit within *Brady,* the court reasoned, because while it affected the prosecutor's practical ability to prove the case, it did not cast doubt on the defendant's guilt.

b.   Do you agree? Should either Model Rule 3.8(d) or ABA Standard Relating to the Prosecution Function 3–3.11(c) change the result in this case? Do the cited provisions merely incorporate the *Brady* rule?

c.   United States v. Ruiz, 536 U.S. 622 (2002), made clear that, under *Brady*, in negotiating a plea bargain, the government need not tell a criminal defendant about impeachment information relevant to its witnesses even though it would have to disclose that information if the case went to trial. After immigration agents found 30 kilos of marijuana in Ruiz' luggage, the government offered a "fast track" plea bargain if Ruiz would waive trial in exchange for a two-level sentence reduction. The government agreed to tell Ruiz of any exculpatory information it had if she waived receiving exculpatory information about informants or information supporting affirmative defenses she might raise. The Ninth Circuit held that defendants are entitled to such information before entering a plea and the required waiver was thus unconstitutional, but the Supreme Court reversed. Justice Breyer, for the Court, said that this "impeachment" information might affect the fairness of a trial but not affect a guilty plea. Full disclosure of matters such as informant identity "could seriously interfere with the Government's interest in securing those guilty pleas that are factually justified, desired by defendants, and help to secure the efficient administration of justice." Does Model Rule 3.8(d) require more?

POSSIBLE LIMITS ON THE RESULTS THAT PARTIES CAN REACH
IN NEGOTIATIONS

Problem 20 dealt primarily with the manner in which one may negotiate. It turns out that there also may be substantive limits on what one may give or obtain in negotiation.

1.   Suppose a lawyer agrees, for example, that in exchange for a generous financial payment to the lawyer's client, neither the lawyer nor the client will file criminal charges against the opposing party for conduct that would justify such charges? ABA Model Code of Professional Responsibility, DR 7–105(A) implied that the lawyer could not do that:

> "A lawyer shall not present, participate in presenting, or threaten to present criminal charges solely to obtain an advantage in a civil matter."

California State Bar Rule 5–100(A) has the same restriction.

You will not find a comparable provision in the ABA Model Rules; therefore, ABA Formal Opinion 92–363 (July 6, 1992) concluded that a lawyer *may* use the possibility of bringing criminal charges in negotiations in a civil case if both the civil case and criminal violation are well founded in fact and law, the lawyer does not suggest improper influence over the criminal process, and the threat would not constitute extortion under state law. The lawyer may even agree not to file criminal charges as an element of settling a civil claim *if* that agreement would not violate a provision of law that required reporting of crimes.

2.   On the other hand, authorities still tend to say that a lawyer may not agree to refuse to file disciplinary charges against an opposing lawyer in order to induce settlement of a civil case. Recall that In re Himmel, 533 N.E.2d 790 (Ill.1988), cited in Problem 2, held that a lawyer may not bargain away a duty to report a lawyer's disciplinary violation in order to secure a better settlement for a client. See also ABA Formal Opinion 94–383 (July 5, 1994) (lawyer may not agree to fail to report anything that Model Rule 8.3(a) requires the lawyer to report).

3.   May you agree in exchange for a generous payment to your client that you the lawyer will never take another case of the same kind against the same defendant? Look at Model Rule 5.6(b). What rationale justifies that rule? Why should a rule require a lawyer to sacrifice the interests of a current client, to protect the interests of a hypothetical future client?

See ABA Formal Opinion 93–371 (Apr. 16, 1993) ("While the Model Rules generally require that the client's interests be put first, forcing a lawyer to give up future representations may be asking too much, particularly in light of the strong countervailing policy favoring the public's unfettered choice of counsel.").

4.   May you settle a case on the condition that you will not use any information learned against the defendant in the future. ABA Formal Opinion 00–417 (Apr. 7, 2000) said that a settlement term that prohibits a lawyer from, for example, using the same expert witness or subpoenaing certain records on behalf of the new client that the lawyer

had previously subpoenaed on behalf of the former client would, "[a]s a practical matter" effectively bar the lawyer from future representations, and that would violate Rule 5.6(b), because the lawyer's inability to use that information would materially limit her representation of a future client. "On the other hand," the opinion noted, "it is generally accepted that offering or agreeing to a bar on the lawyer's disclosure of particular information is not a violation of the Rule 5.6(b) proscription." The information is "information relating to the representation" and protected by Rule 1.6. Thus, if the client agrees to a restriction on the lawyer's use of the information, for the lawyer to abide by that agreement violates no ethical standard.

5.   May you negotiate a settlement that gives you the right to apportion the total received among the clients you represent in the case? For example, suppose you settle an automobile case for $20,000. May you tell the personal injury victim that he will receive an $18,000 offer and tell the car owner that there is only $2,000 left to cover the property damages?

Take a look at ABA Model Rule 1.8(g). Why should the result be different when a single lawyer represents both plaintiffs? Should a lawyer who represents two clients be able to settle on behalf of the most deserving first, without giving the less deserving client a right to veto that settlement? Restatement Third, The Law Governing Lawyers § 128, Comment *d(i)*, suggests that any such situation presents a conflict of interest and that Model Rule 1.8(g) should be seen as a requirement of informed consent that simply takes a particular form in the context of an aggregate settlement. See also, Model Rule 1.8, Comment 13. Does that make sense to you? What is the justification for requiring a "writing signed by the client" in this context given that consent "confirmed in writing" is sufficient for most conflicts?

ABA Formal Opinion 06–438 (Feb. 10, 2006) considered these issues and said two problems with "aggregate settlements" are that the lawyer might be tempted not to investigate the cases individually and might be tempted to close the cases too early. What Rule 1.8(g) requires is that the lawyer disclose to all the clients the entire deal, what each plaintiff will be getting, the total fee paid to the lawyer, how costs are to be allocated, and the like. The Rule also requires consent in writing from each of the clients. Because making that kind of disclosure could violate the Rule 1.6 interests of the individual clients, however, lawyers should get a waiver of such Rule 1.6 protection from each of the clients prior to undertaking the representation. If the lawyer cannot secure the waivers, she should not be representing all the clients in the first place.

————

PROBLEM 21

THE LAWYER AS EVALUATOR

A lawyer has duties of confidentiality and loyalty to a client's interest. The lawyer also has a duty of honesty when making representations to third persons. The lawyer's role as an evaluator involves each of those obligations. When the lawyer acts as an evaluator, the lawyer undertakes to vouch for facts or legal conclusions in an effort to assist the client to complete a transaction or resolve a disagreement. This problem looks first at the traditional legal opinion a lawyer addresses to a client. It then examines what, if anything, changes when the lawyer drafts that opinion to give comfort to a third party whom the lawyer does not represent. Next, it looks at reports the lawyer makes to a client's auditor, and then it asks what consequences flow from an inaccurate opinion.

FACTS

Luther Klose is president of the Klose Corporation, a privately-held family enterprise. All of the stockholders are also officers of the corporation and receive benefits from the corporation both in the form of dividends and in the form of salary. In order to keep the overall tax liability at a minimum, the shareholders would prefer that as much money as possible be paid as salary that is deductible to the corporation, rather than as dividends that are not. Mr. Klose would like you, the corporation's outside attorney, to write him an opinion letter explaining that the company's new salary schedule properly represents greater responsibilities of the shareholder officers and thus is bona fide and not adopted with intent to circumvent the tax laws.

Klose Corporation is also seeking a large loan from the local bank. Given the Klose Corporation's local reputation for taking aggressive tax positions, the bank wants to be aware of any foreseen tax difficulties that could materially affect the Klose Corporation's ability to repay its loan. At the request of the bank, Mr. Klose has asked you to write a letter to the bank giving your legal opinion that all of the major tax deductions taken by the Klose Corporation in the last three years are reasonable under the tax laws and that, if the Internal Revenue Service disallows any of these deductions, the taxpayer is likely to prevail in litigation.

Now, the company's auditor has asked for information on "all actual or potential legal problems that might materially affect the Klose Corporation." You know that Klose Corporation has sold a large stock of defective goods, but no customer has yet discovered the defects. When a final purchaser does discover the defect, it may be difficult to trace it back to your client, but if the purchaser does trace the chain of custody, the company may be liable for up to half its net worth in damages.

QUESTIONS

A.   DUTIES TO A CLIENT WHO ASKS FOR A LEGAL OPINION

1.   Does Mr. Klose have a right to "purchase" the opinion letter he wants from you concerning the reasonableness of his salary?

a.   Think back to Model Rule 2.1. What obligation do you have to tell a client something the client does not want to hear? To what extent, if any, must you "audit" the client to assure yourself that the duties of the officers are what your opinion will assume them to be?

b.   To whom does your duty run in this situation? Even when your client is a privately-held corporation, does your professional duty of loyalty run solely to Mr. Klose? Remember Model Rule 1.13(a).

2.   Would you let a client purchase your ratification of its officials' socially beneficial objectives in the guise of a legal opinion?

a.   Suppose the president of the corporate client wants the company to make a significant charitable contribution to engender goodwill or for other positive reasons, but also wants to nip in the bud a shareholder suit second-guessing the president's judgment.

b.   May you advise the client that certain legal considerations make it proper for the company contribute to the charity, even though nonlegal considerations are your real reason? Assume that the legal justification is at least arguable but that you need to be less than candid about the client's primary motivation. Medical doctors, some people claim, are sometimes justified in lying to their patients. May juris doctors ever lie to the clients for the clients' own good? How about to make the lawyer feel good?

3.   Does the fact that this problem involves a tax opinion increase or decrease the lawyer's responsibilities? Can one say that anything is fair where avoiding taxes is concerned?

a.   ABA Formal Opinion 314 (Apr. 27, 1965), concerning the lawyer's duty of candor in dealing with the IRS, said:

> "The Internal Revenue Service is neither a true tribunal, nor even a quasi-judicial institution. * * * [F]ew will contend that the service provides any truly dispassionate and unbiased consideration to the taxpayer. * * *
>
> "It by no means follows that a lawyer is relieved of all ethical responsibility when he practices before this agency. * * *
>
> "[A] lawyer who is asked to advise his client in the course of the preparation of the client's tax returns may freely urge the statement of positions most favorable to the client just as long as there is reasonable basis for those positions. Thus where the lawyer believes there is a reasonable basis for a position that a particular transaction does not result in taxable income, or that certain expenditures are properly deductible as expenses, the lawyer has no duty to advise that riders be attached to the client's tax return explaining the circumstances surrounding the transaction or the expenditures."

b.   However, in Formal Opinion 85–352 (July 7, 1985), the ABA modified Opinion 314. The ABA Standing Committee on Ethics and Professional Responsibility reported that it learned that many lawyers interpreted "reasonable basis" to mean they could they could use "any colorable claim on a tax return to justify exploitation of the lottery of the tax return audit selection process." To correct the record, the Standing Committee offered this guidance:

> "[A] lawyer may advise reporting a position on a return even where the lawyer believes the position probably will not prevail, there is no 'substantial authority' in support of the

position, and there will be no disclosure of the position in the return. However, the position to be asserted must be one which the lawyer in good faith believes is warranted in existing law or can be supported by a good faith argument for an extension, modification or reversal of existing law. This requires that there is some realistic possibility of success if the matter is litigated. In addition, in his role as advisor, the lawyer should refer to potential penalties and other legal consequences should the client take the position advised."

Does that help? Now is your responsibility clear?

c. Shortly after the ABA released Opinion 85–352, the ABA Section on Taxation published a Report of the Special Task Force on Formal Opinion 85–352, 39 Tax Lawyer 635, 638–39 (1985). The Report stated:

"More important to differentiating between 'reasonable basis' and the standard articulated by Opinion 85–352 is that the new standard requires not only that there be some possibility of success, if litigated, rather than merely a construction that can be argued or that seems reasonable, but also that there be more than just any possibility of success. The possibility of success, if litigated, must be 'realistic.' A possibility of success cannot be 'realistic' if it is only theoretical or impracticable. This clearly implies that there must be a substantial possibility of success, which when taken together with the assumption that the matter will be litigated, measurably elevates what had come to be widely known as the minimum ethical standard.

"A position having only a 5% or 10% likelihood of success, if litigated, should not meet the new standard. A position having a likelihood of success closely approaching one-third should meet the standard. * * * "

Does this report clarify the lawyer's obligation?

d. Lawyers who practice in the tax area also are subject to regulation by the Treasury and the IRS. The Treasury has authorized the Internal Revenue Service to regulate all professionals who practice in the federal tax area through Circular 230, 31 C.F.R. §§10.0-10.97 (2012) at http://www.irs.gov/pub/irs-pdf/pcir230.pdf. Circular 230 implements stringent requirements for lawyers who prepare "covered opinions" for clients. 31 C.F.R. §10.35 (2012). Tax opinions fall under this category if the IRS has identified them as involving listed transactions for tax avoidance, any arrangements whose primary purpose is the avoidance of taxation, and any opinions that are marketed or subject to conditions of confidentiality. A "marketed opinion" is one the lawyer knows the client will used to sell a plan to one or more taxpayers.

Practitioners must use "reasonable efforts" to identify and ascertain all relevant facts regarding the transactions. They may not rely on facts, assumptions, or statements they know or should know are unreasonable, and each opinion must contain a section that details all factual assumptions, representations, statements, or findings relied upon. Opinions must relate applicable law to the relevant facts in the case and must evaluate all significant federal tax issues, giving reasoned conclusions and the likelihood of success on the merits. If a practitioner cannot reach such a conclusion, the opinion must clearly say the lawyer cannot make the evaluation.

Any opinion must "prominently disclose[ ]" any referral or compensation arrangements between the practitioner and any promoter, marketer, or anyone else who referred the matter to the attorney, and practitioners may not give advice "contrary to or inconsistent with the required disclosure." To ensure proper implementation, the IRS requires practitioners to take "reasonable steps" to guarantee their firm has "adequate procedures" in place for associates, employees, and other firm members to comply with new requirements. Practitioners who fail to take such steps or who themselves fail to comply with the rules through willfulness, recklessness, or "gross incompetence" may be censured, suspended, or disbarred from practice before the IRS.

4.   Suppose you conclude in your opinion that the ultimate tax liability will depend largely on the intent of the taxpayer. May you help Klose "manufacture" intent? Does your answer depend on whether you personally believe that Klose has the proper legal intent and you are merely helping him preserve and articulate it?

a.   How may you properly counsel creation of proof of intent? May you prepare minutes of meetings that never occurred in which the participants recite their intent? Does it matter whether the participants eventually approve ("ratify") these minutes?

b.   One might argue that the lawyer is not justified in "drawing a misleading minute" in order to develop intent for tax consideration, but that "having made the decision in his own mind that the action the client proposes is justified under the law, he is entitled to set out in the minutes the considerations that led him to that conclusion, and when he has done that he probably has gone as far as he can."[31] Do you agree?

B. DUTIES IN PREPARATION OF A LEGAL OPINION FOR DELIVERY TO A THIRD PARTY

1.   Look at Model Rule 2.3. The Model Code did not contain any specific guidance for lawyers who prepared opinions. Was this provision an important addition? Do you suppose lawyers were "evaluators" even before adoption of the Rule?

a.   Restatement Third, The Law Governing Lawyers § 95, Comment b, suggests that the role is familiar and reasonable.

> "For example, a lawyer for a corporation entering into a contract with a third person may address an opinion letter to the third person as to the authority of the officers of the corporate client to bind the corporation to the contract. In a real-estate transaction, a title opinion rendered by the lawyer for the seller may be addressed to the purchaser or a financial institution lending funds to the purchaser to be secured by the

[31] Business Planning and Professional Responsibility—Problem 1, 8 The Practical Lawyer 18, 33 (1962).

property. In such instances, the * * * client's interest is advanced by making it possible for the third person to proceed with the transaction on the basis of the evaluation."

b.   In connection with the bank loan described in this problem, what does Rule 2.3 require of you? Why must you "consult" with the client before agreeing to give the opinion? Why isn't the fact the client asked you to prepare the evaluation enough?

2.   What circumstances would ever make you conclude that an evaluation was incompatible with other aspects of your relationship with the client?

a.   Does the attorney-client privilege apply when one is conducting an internal investigation, the results of which may be available to others? Look again at Upjohn Co. v. United States, 449 U.S. 383 (1981), in Problem 8. The privilege applies to communications with inside and outside corporate counsel if the company does not plan to publicly disclose it. However, the result may be different where the client intends to make lawyer's conclusions available outside of the corporation. See also, Model Rule 2.3(c).

b.   Suppose you learn something in the course of your investigation that is harmful to your client, e.g., that its factory is too close to the property line under applicable zoning regulations. Might it be more prudent for the client not to seek the loan rather than publicly to reveal its problem? May the lawyer who discovers the zoning issue simply include a line in the opinion that states, the opinion does not address any issues other than the tax consequences of the transaction for the client?

c.   Both such possibilities should suggest to you that, while rendering third-party opinions is a significant part of many transactional lawyers' work, a lawyer should not routinely decide that it is wise to render such an opinion.

3.   May you cover up or ignore embarrassing facts in your opinion? What relationship do you assume vis-a-vis the nonclients to whom you address your opinion?

a.   Restatement Third, The Law Governing Lawyers § 95, Comment c, says:

> "* * *Unless otherwise required or permitted by the terms under which the evaluation is given, the lawyer's duty is to provide a fair and objective opinion. * * * By statements in the evaluation, the lawyer may undertake to exercise a higher or lesser standard of care. * * *

> "* * * [However, t]he third-person recipient of a lawyer's evaluation does not thereby become the client of the lawyer, and the lawyer does not thereby undertake all duties owed to a client, such as confidentiality or avoidance of conflicting interests * * *."

b.   Is your obligation of factual accuracy greater, less, or the same as one you would assume in giving an opinion to your own client? Do you have a duty to conduct to investigate the facts given to you by the client? Restatement § 95, Comment c, continues:

"In all events, unless stated or agreed otherwise, a lawyer's evaluation does not entail a guarantee by the lawyer that facts stated in it are accurate. In some circumstances, such as when the lawyer purports to be making a report of a factual investigation undertaken by the lawyer, a reasonable reader of the report would assume that the lawyer is reporting facts known by the lawyer to be accurate. A lawyer normally may rely on facts provided by corporate officers and other agents of a client that the lawyer reasonably believes to be appropriate sources for such facts without further investigation or specific disclosure, unless the recipient of the opinion objects or the version of the facts provided or other circumstances indicate that further verification is required."

c.   May you simply base your opinion on an *assumed* set of facts? Comment *c* responds:

"A lawyer may not without express disclosure rely for purposes of a legal opinion or other evaluation report on a fact or factual assumption that the lawyer knows to be inaccurate or, in the case of a factual representation, to have been provided under circumstances making reliance unwarranted."

d.   May the client limit the lawyer's scope of investigation in preparing the opinion? Clients should have the right to tailor the opinion to the third party's needs and to minimize costs, but some limitations may be unduly limit the lawyer's ability to render a reliable opinion. Of course, the opinion will expressly state any limitations upon the scope that the lawyer followed. But, in some cases, a prudent lawyer should decline to perform an evaluation at all if the client will not let the lawyer investigate sufficiently to know what the facts really are.

e.   In 1998, the ABA Business Law Section's Committee on Legal Opinions published its own "Legal Opinion Principles" that summarize the emerging consensus in this area. Among the principles declared are:

(i) "The matters usually addressed in opinion letters, the meaning of the language normally used, and the scope and nature of the work counsel is expected to perform are based (whether or not so stated) on the customary practice of lawyers who regularly give * * * opinions of the kind involved." An opinion giver may vary any of the customary practice, but must do so expressly.

(ii) "The opinions contained in an opinion letter are expressions of professional judgment regarding the legal matters addressed and not guarantees that a court will reach any particular result."

(iii) "* * *[A]n opinion recipient ordinarily need not take any action to verify the opinions it contains."

(iv) Opinions may and customarily do "specify the jurisdiction(s) whose law they are intended to cover and sometimes limit their coverage to specified * * * [laws] of the named jurisdiction(s)."

(v) "Customary practice permits [an opinion author to rely 'in large measure on factual information obtained from others, particularly company officials'] * * * unless the factual information * * * appears irregular on its face or has been provided by an inappropriate source."

(vi) "An opinion should not be based on a factual representation that is tantamount to the legal conclusion being expressed."

(vii) "An opinion letter speaks as of its date. An opinion giver has no obligation to update an opinion letter for subsequent events or legal developments."[32]

e.   Because these so-called "third-party opinions," i.e., opinions to be relied upon by persons other than the lawyer's client, have become such a central part of commercial dealing, several groups have developed standard definitions for the usual representations that lawyers make.[33]

C.   LAWYER LIABILITY FOR AN INACCURATE OPINION

1.   Mr. Klose wants you to write him a letter that will make him feel good about his decision to raise the salaries of his family members. Might you be liable to your client, the Klose Corporation, for the opinion that Mr. Klose wanted you to render but that turned out to be inaccurate?

a.   It is tempting for lawyers to tell their clients what they want to hear. In a world in which clients can fire lawyers at will and a dozen new lawyers stand ready to pursue the client's business, a naive person might assume that lawyers could not behave otherwise. Remember, however, that the lawyer's corporate client is not Mr. Klose; it is the Klose Corporation. If the company should go into bankruptcy or if a third party buys it, do you suppose the bankruptcy trustee or the new owner will be impressed that you wrote your opinion to please Mr. Klose rather than based it on your independent professional judgment?

b.   If the law firm did not use reasonable care in rendering an opinion, even one solicited by the client's management, the client will very likely have a malpractice claim against the lawyer. See, e.g., FDIC v. O'Melveny & Myers, 969 F.2d 744 (9th Cir.1992), rev'd on other grounds, 512 U.S. 79 (1994), aff'd on remand, 61 F.3d 17 (9th Cir.1995) (firm held liable for failing to discover that its client was in poor financial health); FDIC v. Clark, 978 F.2d 1541 (10th Cir.1992) (firm failed to discover that bank officers were diverting bank funds to their own use), both discussed in Problem 18.

2.   If you write an opinion for your client, knowing that it will give your opinion to the bank, will you be liable to the bank (a non-client) if your report is inaccurate or misleading?

a.   Restatement Third, The Law Governing Lawyers § 51(2) makes clear that lawyers may be held liable to a nonclient "when and to the extent that: (a) the lawyer or (with the lawyer's acquiescence) the lawyer's client invites the nonclient to rely on the lawyer's opinion or

---

[32] For background and more detail about these principles, see Donald W. Glazer, It's Time to Streamline Opinion Letters, Business Lawyer Today, Nov/Dec 1999, at pp. 32, 35.

[33] These definitions are collected and analyzed in Scott FitzGibbon & Donald W. Glazer, Legal Opinions: What Opinions in Financial Transactions Say and What They Mean (1992).

provision of other legal services, and the nonclient so relies * * *." Numerous cases confirm that basis for lawyer liability.

b. In Greycas, Inc. v. Proud, 826 F.2d 1560 (7th Cir.1987), cert. denied, 484 U.S. 1043 (1988), a borrower sought to raise money from a finance company on the strength of a security interest in certain farm machinery. The lender, Greycas, agreed to put up the money if the borrower would supply the borrower's lawyer's opinion that there were no prior liens on the assets. Lawyer Proud, who was the borrower's brother-in-law, wrote a letter saying that he had "conducted a U.C.C., tax, and judgment search" and that Greycas had the only perfected security interest. In fact, Proud made no such inquiry, the assets were encumbered, and when the borrower defaulted, Greycas had no security.

Under these circumstances, the court held, the lawyer was liable to Greycas for the amount of the loan. The lawyer argued that he owed no duty to someone who was not his client. The court agreed with that general proposition, and indeed called it "an undesirable novelty to hold that every bit of sharp dealing by a lawyer gives rise to prima facie tort liability to the opposing party in the lawsuit or negotiation." The court also assumed that Greycas did not become Proud's client. However, the court said that Proud supplied information to Greycas knowing that Greycas would rely on it. Whether the suit was for negligent misrepresentation or for professional malpractice, it stated a cause of action and the lawyer was liable.[34]

c. In Vega v. Jones, Day, Reavis & Pogue, 17 Cal.Rptr.3d 26 (Cal.Ct.App.2004), a shareholder in an acquired corporation sued the acquiring corporation's lawyers, Jones Day, for fraud. The acquirer provided a disclosure schedule to the lawyers for the company it was buying; the schedule indicated that the acquiring company would raise the $10 million price for the deal through third-party financing. Both Jones Day and the acquiring corporation knew the financing included "toxic" stock, i.e., restricted stock that seriously dilutes the value of all the company's shares. Plaintiff alleged that Jones Day knew that "toxic" stock financing is a "desperate and last resort of financing for a struggling company," and 95% of companies who engage in such financing end up in bankruptcy. Jones Day prepared the disclosure schedule; it properly characterized the transaction but gave it only to their client; they gave a sanitized version to acquired company's lawyers and it made no mention of "toxic" stock and called the financing "standard." The plaintiff shareholder learned the true nature of the financing eight months after the deal closed and after losing nearly $3.5 million. Jones, Day responded that it had not made affirmative misstatements and had no duty to disclose the terms of the third party investment to an adverse party in the merger transaction. The court held that the complaint stated a fraud claim based on nondisclosure. "The complaint alleged the law firm, while expressly undertaking to disclose the financing transaction, provided disclosure schedules that did not include material terms of the transaction."

---

[34] Accord, Vanguard Production, Inc. v. Martin, 894 F.2d 375 (10th Cir.1990) (title opinion used in selling oil and gas leases); Vereins–Und Westbank, AG v. Carter, 691 F.Supp. 704 (S.D.N.Y.1988) (lawyer's letter to support issuance of surety bond).

The California Court of Appeals agreed that a lawyer ordinarily owes a professional duty of care only to his client and intended beneficiaries of his work, but fraud claims are different: a lawyer may be liable to a nonclient if he knowingly makes false statements of material fact. The fact that Jones, Day filed documents revealing the true nature of the financing across the country in Delaware before the closing was no defense. The court found that in writing the disclosure schedule, telling a "half-truth calculated to deceive" was the equivalent of "active concealment or suppression of facts." A half-truth is a whole lie. Jones Day had a duty not to engage in fraudulent activity, "even if . . . negotiating at arm's length," so the court allowed the case to go to trial.

PROBLEM 22

OBLIGATIONS WHEN THE CLIENT MAY BE ENGAGED IN FRAUD

A series of financial collapses at major companies greeted the 21st century. Each of the companies that collapsed had many lawyers, and at first glance, each of the companies engaged in transactions and practices that many people said the lawyers could have prevented. A decade earlier, in the context of a widespread savings and loan scandal, District Judge Stanley Sporkin asked, "where . . . were the outside accountants and attorneys when these transactions were effectuated?"[35] On the other hand, circumstances may not be as they initially appear. To the lawyers, individual steps in the company's decline might have seemed innocent, even mundane. As you work through this problem, ask yourself when a client has crossed the line from risk taking to dishonesty, from brash optimism to fraud. We look at the lawyer's general duty not to assist a client's crime or fraud, and then at the special world of securities lawyers. We also examine special duties that the SEC has imposed on lawyers for publicly traded companies. Finally, we consider analogous issues faced by government employees.

FACTS

International Energy, Inc., a publicly held company listed on the New York Stock Exchange, has done most of its recent financing through bank loans. It is about to sell a new issue of securities and obtain a new line of credit from the banks. The company, to induce the bank to lend and the public to invest, has written a glowing account of its prospects.

The strength of the company is its reputation for vigorous research, which thus far has resulted in a series of patents for energy-saving devices. The loan will finance production of a new product, which is another patented device. All of the company reports suggest glowing prospects for its performance. The company's auditors have declared International Energy to be in outstanding financial health. The current draft of your firm's opinion letter indicates no knowledge of material facts inconsistent with that optimism.

---

[35] See Lincoln Sav. & Loan Ass'n v. Wall, 743 F.Supp. 901, 920 (D.D.C. 1990).

You had lunch today with your good friend, the director of research and development at International Energy, Inc. "A great company is in real trouble," he told you. "When our former president retired, a sense of integrity retired as well." Your friend and his scientist colleagues have great concern that the company has not sufficiently tested the device described in the documents and that the company has overrated its reliability and performance.

In addition, the engineer told you that the company recently purchased the production facility for the new product from a shell corporation that the company's new president owned. He said the price paid by the company was outrageously high. The auditors did not catch the problem and thus their audit did not footnote the fact that the purchase was from a corporate officer. As a result, the balance sheet of the corporation looks significantly better than it would if the books carried the facility at its true value.

QUESTIONS

A.   DISCLOSURE OF A CLIENT'S INTENDED CRIME OR FRAUD

1.   Has your lunch given you indigestion? What will you do with the information you now possess?

a.   May your firm's opinion letter that will accompany the new issue of securities reflect what the director of research and development has told you? Must it do so?

b.   How sure are you that what your friend has told you is true? Do you really *know* that the new product is unreliable? Perhaps your friend, the engineer, is simply depressed. Is that possibility enough to let you ignore what he has told you?

c.   How will you go about finding out what is really going on at International Energy, Inc.? Will you ask questions in any event as part of your due diligence before completing your opinion letter?

d.   What kinds of questions will you now ask? If your client's officers are dishonest, will you be confident they will give you reliable answers? Could you give the information that you have to the client's auditors and rely on those auditors to ask the necessary questions?

2.   What is the legal status of what you have learned from the director of research and development? What legal right or obligation do you have to reveal it to others?

a.   Is the information protected by the attorney-client privilege? If so, whose privilege would it be? Did the director communicate this information in confidence? Did the director communicate it for the purpose of seeking legal advice? Did it involve the client's possible crime or fraud?

b.   Does the information "relate to the representation" within the meaning of ABA Model Rule 1.6(a)? Would disclosure of the information to other members of corporate management violate Model Rule 1.6(b)? Does Model Rule 1.13(b) require the disclosure?

c.   May you disclose the information to persons or entities outside the corporation? Look at Model Rules 1.6(b)(2) & (3) and 1.13(c).[36] Do any of them permit disclosure outside the corporation in a situation like the one in this problem?

3.   Is confidentiality the only relevant issue that you face? What other obligations do you have under the Model Rules that you need to take into account?

a.   Look at ABA Model Rule 1.2(d): "A lawyer shall not counsel a client to engage, or assist a client, in conduct that the lawyer knows is criminal or fraudulent."

b.   Model Rule 4.1(b) continues: "In the course of representing a client a lawyer shall not knowingly fail to disclose a material fact when disclosure is necessary to avoid assisting a criminal or fraudulent act by a client, unless disclosure is prohibited by Rule 1.6."

c.   Where does this combination of obligations leave you? Remember Model Rule 1.16(a): "[A] lawyer shall not represent a client or, where representation has commenced, shall withdraw from the representation of a client if: (1) the representation will result in violation of the rules of professional conduct or other law."

d.   ABA Formal Opinion 463 (May 23, 2013) examines the *Good Practices Guidance for Lawyers to Detect and Combat Money Laundering and Terrorist Financing*, adopted by the ABA House of Delegates in August 2010, in light of a lawyer's duty not to counsel or assist a crime or fraud. The *Guidance* is an American document but part of an international effort to combat illegal money transfers and adopts what it calls a "risk based" approach consisting of considering the legal work being done, where the alleged business is being done, whether people on a Treasury Department "specially designated nationals" list are involved, and other similar factors. The Opinion does not view lawyers as having a "gatekeeper" role, and it forbids reporting mere suspicion of a client's wrongdoing, or reporting at all without advising the client, two items that are required under EU regulations. But the Opinion finds the idea of paying attention to the possibly illegal activities in which a client may be engaged is consistent with Rules 1.2(d) and 1.16(b)(2) and it endorses use of the *Guidance* as one of the kinds of "moral and ethical considerations that should inform a lawyer," citing Model Rules, Scope, Comment 16.

4.   What is the significance of the fact that the information you have relates in part to the security of bank loans the company has already received? Are a lawyer's rights and responsibilities different when dealing with a client's (and perhaps the lawyer's) past statements?

a.   Think of the opinions your firm has transmitted to the bank. In them, you have opined that corporation adopted the appropriate resolutions granted the relevant powers. You may even have opined that you know of no material facts that have been misstated or omitted from the documents that the bank has received. If preparing those

---

[36]   See also, Restatement Third, The Law Governing Lawyers § 67. It was the source for most of the ideas incorporated into Model Rules 1.6(b)(2) & (3).

opinions was part of your role, what should you do now after your lunch with the chief engineer?

b.   ABA Formal Opinion 92–366 (Aug. 8, 1992) assumes that a lawyer for a small manufacturing firm issues an opinion that its client's accounts receivable represent legal obligations of the purchasers of the goods. Later, the lawyer finds that many of the accounts are fictional and that the client is in financial trouble. The opinion says that under Model Rule 1.6, the lawyer must withdraw from all future dealings involving this loan, and may or, in some cases, must disavow the prior opinion. Otherwise, the lawyer would be "assisting" the client to get future extensions of credit. The ABA issued this opinion before the 2002 and 2003 revisions to the Model Rules; those revisions eliminated the "notice of withdrawal" provisions of Rule 1.6 and replaced them with the permissive disclosure of Rule 1.6(b).

c.   ABA Formal Opinion 92–366 was controversial, and there was a vigorous dissent, but Model Rule 1.2, Comment 10 now provides:

> "* * * A lawyer may not continue assisting a client in conduct that the lawyer originally supposed was legally proper but then discovers is criminal or fraudulent. The lawyer must, therefore, withdraw from the representation of the client in the matter. See Rule 1.16(a). In some cases, withdrawal alone might be insufficient. It may be necessary for the lawyer to give notice of the fact of withdrawal and to disaffirm any opinion, document, affirmation or the like. See Rule 4.1."

d.   Suppose, instead, that you gave advice to the company about how to structure the financing transaction but did not render an opinion to any third parties. May you assume that therefore the bank will not rely on anything you did? Does it mean you need do nothing to correct what you now believe were misstatements?

e.   Is withdrawal the best approach to the situation you face? Even if withdrawal were to get you off the hook, will it help either your corporate client or its past lenders and potential investors?

5.   Should a lawyer have the same duties outside of the financing transaction context?

a.   Suppose your firm is doing work with the Department of Energy (DOE) to get the client's new device approved for sale. Suppose further that if the DOE had the device tested at an independent laboratory, it would be likely to find the device unreliable and thus ruin the likelihood that the bank would issue the loan. May you argue to DOE officials that it should not require such outside testing?

b.   Look at Model Rule 3.9, "Advocate in Nonadjudicative Proceedings." Does it require representations to the DOE to have the same level of integrity and candor as representations to a court? Does it mean only that you may not help the company invent records of nonexistent outside tests to persuade the DOE to approve the product?

c.   What is the significance of Model Rule 3.9, Comment 3, which says that the Rule does not "apply to the representation of a client in connection with an investigation or examination of the client's affairs"? If the rule does not apply in that setting, to what matters does it apply?

d.   In re American Continental Corp./Lincoln Savings and Loan Securities Litigation, 794 F.Supp. 1424, 1450–52 (D.Ariz.1992), involved a regulatory investigation of a savings and loan association in which the court, refusing to grant summary judgment approving the conduct of the law firm, observed:

> "During the regulatory compliance audit * * * the law firm found multiple regulatory violations. There is evidence that Jones Day knew that Lincoln had backdated files, destroyed appraisals, removed appraisals from files, told appraisers not to issue written reports when their oral valuations were too low, and violated affiliated transaction regulations. * * *

> "There is evidence that Jones Day instructed ACC in how to rectify deficiencies so that they would not be apparent to FHLBB examiners. * * *

> * * *

> "Jones Day contends that it may not be held liable for counseling its client. The line between maintaining a client's confidence and violating the securities law is brighter than Jones Day suggests, however. Attorneys must inform a client in a clear and direct manner when its conduct violates the law. If the client continues the objectionable activity, the lawyer must withdraw 'if the representation will result in violation of the rules of professional conduct or other law.' Ethical Rule 1.16. * * * An attorney may not continue to provide services to corporate clients when the attorney knows the client is engaged in a course of conduct designed to deceive others, and where it is obvious that the attorney's compliant legal services may be a substantial factor in permitting the deceit to continue. * * *"

e.   ABA Formal Opinion 93–375 (Aug. 6, 1993) was the ABA's reflection on a lawyer's duty to disclose adverse information in the context of a bank examination. The opinion says that while the lawyer may not lie to the examiners, the lawyer is not affirmatively obliged to warn about problems at the bank or otherwise reveal confidential client information. The bank itself may have disclosure obligations, however, and if the lawyer reasonably believes the bank is engaged in fraud, the lawyer *must* take steps to avoid assisting it to do so, including, in some cases, withdrawing from the representation.

6.   Should you be liable to investors in an offering of securities if your investigation is inadequate or if you fail to prevent fraudulent conduct by your client?

a.   Central Bank of Denver, N.A. v. First Interstate Bank of Denver, N.A., 511 U.S. 164 (1994), is the leading securities case limiting lawyers' financial exposure under § 10(b) of the Securities Exchange Act of 1934. In 1986, the city issued municipal bonds to finance public improvements related to a residential and commercial project near Colorado Springs. The bonds required that the appraised value of the land exceed 160% of the amount of the bonds. Central Bank, the indenture trustee, delayed getting an independent 1988 appraisal, allegedly because it might show land values were declining. When the bonds went into default, plaintiff-investors sued the issuer and underwriter claiming that they were primarily liable under § 10(b), and that Central Bank was secondarily liable for aiding and abetting the violation. The Supreme Court held that there is no "aiding and abetting" liability under § 10(b). Before this decision, many securities plaintiffs sued lawyers, accountants, and other professionals under an "aiding and abetting" theory. Does this rule give lawyers more protection than they should have?

 b. In re Enron Corp. Securities, Derivative & ERISA Litigation, 235 F.Supp.2d 549 (S.D.Tex.2002), held that "professionals, including lawyers and accountants, when they take the affirmative step of speaking out, whether individually or as essentially an author or co-author in a statement or report, whether identified or not, about their client's financial condition, do have a duty to third parties not in privity not to knowingly or with severe recklessness issue materially misleading statements on which they intend or have reason to expect that those third parties will rely." The court worried, however, about "opening the professional liability floodgates to any and every potential investor or foreseeable user of the allegedly misleading information who might obtain and rely on the statement." Thus, the court limited the class of plaintiffs to persons "the attorneys or accountants allegedly intended, or might reasonably have expected, to rely on their material misrepresentations."

 In considering potential liability of the Vinson & Elkins law firm, the court found that the pending "complaint goes into great detail to demonstrate that Vinson & Elkins did not remain silent, but chose not once, but frequently, to make statements to the public about Enron's business and financial situation. * * * Moreover in light of its alleged voluntary, essential, material, and deep involvement as a primary violator in the ongoing Ponzi scheme, Vinson & Elkins was not merely a drafter, but essentially a co-author of the documents it created for public consumption concealing its own and other participants' actions."[37]

 c. The Supreme Court revisited these issues in Stoneridge Investment Partners v. Scientific–Atlanta, Inc., 552 U.S. 148 (2008). Investors in Charter Communications, Inc., filed suit against vendors and customers that had entered into sham or mislabeled transactions with Charter. Those transactions allowed Charter to issue financial statements showing its condition to be much better than it really was. The Court held (5 to 3) that the allegations against the vendors and customers were charges of aiding and abetting, and thus not actionable under *Central Bank*. The vendors and customers dealt with Charter "in

---

 [37] The National Law Journal, June 5, 2006, p. 3, col. 1, reported that Vinson & Elkins agreed to pay $30 million in settlement of claims against it arising out of its representation of Enron, although the firm continues to maintain that it did nothing wrong. Later, in In re Enron Corporation Securities, Derivative and "ERISA" Litigation, 2007 WL 209923 (S.D.Tex.2007), Judge Harmon approved the dismissal of class action plaintiffs' claims against Vinson & Elkins and the Enron directors. The opinion acknowledges: "Defendants have argued that by dismissing those most directly responsible for Enron's business and instead pursuing secondary-actor banks, Lead Plaintiff is 'taking the Enron out of Enron.'" But the court based its decision on the Lead Plaintiff's statement that the dismissal was "based on [V & E's] relative financial status, not on the merits of the claims against them," and the fact that, at least in theory, class members could pursue individual claims against the lawyers and directors.

the marketplace for goods and services, not in the investment sphere," so they could not be held liable as primary actors under § 10(b). Congress had the chance to reverse *Central Bank*, the Court said, and it expressly did not do so.

SEC REGULATIONS THAT ARE COUNTERPARTS TO MODEL RULE 1.13

Ever since SEC v. Frank, 388 F.2d 486 (2d Cir 1968), the SEC has claimed authority to regulate lawyers who appear before it. For many years, however, that authority went largely unexercised. But the collapse of the Enron Corporation and the accounting corrections at WorldCom and other high-profile companies led Congress to adopt the Sarbanes-Oxley Act of 2002, Pub. L. 107–204. Section 307 of that act required the SEC to "establish rules, in the public interest, setting forth minimum standards of professional conduct for attorneys appearing and practicing before the Commission in any way in the representation of public companies. . . . " On January 29, 2003, the SEC issued the Final Rule mandated by Section 307. It is contained in 17 C.F.R. Part 205, and is reproduced in the Standards Supplement of this book.

The SEC regulations apply to lawyers "appearing and practicing before the Commission," which the SEC defines to include anyone "providing advice * * * regarding any document that the attorney has notice will be filed with * * * the Commission" or even providing advice that information need not be filed with the Commission. Notice that this definition reaches many lawyers who would not ordinarily self-identify as securities lawyers.

The attorney's duty to act is triggered when he or she "becomes aware" of "evidence" of a client's "material violation" of federal or state securities law, a material breach of fiduciary duty by an officer or agent of the client, or a "similar" violation of any other federal or state law. 17 CFR §§ 205.2(i). That class of cases is larger than the class of cases where Model Rule 1.13(b) requires the lawyer to take action.

The "evidence" required is "credible evidence, based upon which it would be unreasonable, under the circumstances, for a prudent and competent attorney not to conclude that it is reasonably likely that a material violation has occurred, is ongoing, or is about to occur."

The attorney who becomes aware of "evidence of a material violation" must "report such evidence to the [client's] chief legal officer" (CLO). If you are a "subordinate attorney," for example, one who works "under the supervision or direction of another attorney," it is sufficient to report the evidence to your superior. It then becomes the supervisor's responsibility to report the information to the client's CLO. 17 CFR §§ 205.3(b)(1), 205.4 & 205.5.

Upon getting the report, the CLO must "cause such inquiry into the evidence of a material violation as he or she reasonably believes is appropriate to determine" whether there has been or will be such a violation. Whether the CLO concludes that no such violation has or will occur, or concludes that the reporting attorney was right and takes steps to correct the violation, the CLO must report the conclusion back to the reporting attorney "and advise the reporting attorney of the basis for such determination," 17 CFR § 205.3(b)(2).

Unless the reporting attorney "reasonably believes" that the [CLO] has provided an appropriate response within a reasonable time, the attorney must report the evidence of a material violation to the "audit committee of the [client's] board of directors," a different committee composed solely of independent directors, or the full board of directors. 17 CFR § 205.3(b)(3).

There is an alternative if the client has established a qualified legal compliance committee (QLCC) composed solely of independent directors and given that QLCC the authority to investigate and report to the full board about evidence of the client's possible material violations of the law. The lawyer may make the initial report directly to that QLCC and have no further obligation to evaluate what the QLCC does to investigate or correct the situation. 17 CFR § 205.3(c).

Do you find this process clear and logical? How, if at all, does it differ from the steps required by Model Rule 1.13(b)? Which approach do you prefer to protect the corporate client? Have the Sarbanes-Oxley regulations increased the level of protection for corporate clients? Have they instead primarily created inflexible procedures that may increase costs for clients but provide little more protection.[38]

At the same time, it published the regulations that the Sarbanes-Oxley Act required, the SEC issued a proposed rule that would provide that, if the response from the CLO is insufficient or not received within a reasonable time, the lawyer must withdraw from the representation and inform the SEC of that action. Under one alternative, the rule would require the client, not the lawyer, to notify the SEC of the lawyer's action. The report would then presumably trigger an SEC investigation and would likely be disclosed to the securities markets.

Would this obligation give leverage with which to require clients to do what the lawyers believe they should do? If lawyers were required to withdraw and report that withdrawal to the SEC, do you suppose most clients would change their conduct so as to avoid reaching that point?

---

[38] These issues are explored in Thomas D. Morgan, Sarbanes-Oxley: A Complication, Not a Contribution in the Effort to Improve Corporate Lawyers' Professional Conduct, 17 Georgetown J. Legal Ethics 1 (2003).

CHAPTER VI

ETHICAL PROBLEMS IN LITIGATION

The classic role of the lawyer is to act as an advocate. Our legal system embraces the model of an impartial judge presiding over two parties represented by lawyers who present their clients' cases to the judge and jury. Canon 7 of the former ABA Model Code (which went into effect in 1970) imposed upon all lawyers a duty of zealous representation within the bounds of the law. The Model Rules no longer use the term "zeal" within any rule, but the preamble does note that: "As advocate, a lawyer zealously asserts the client's position under the rules of the adversary system."

Civil and criminal litigation present dramatic problems of legal ethics that attract a great deal of public attention. The lawyers who face these issues do not always think of themselves as litigators. Because the issues that any lawyer confronts ultimately may be resolved in a courtroom, a lawyer may face many problems presented in this chapter no matter what the nature of her practice. As you think about these problems, ask yourself such questions as:

a. How far may an attorney go to suppress the truth in representing a client in litigation? How far *must* he or she go? For example, may (or must) the lawyer refrain from disclosing relevant information to the trier of fact? May or must she allow her client to offer perjured testimony to further the client's interest?

b. To what extent must a lawyer adopt the client's values and objectives? Is the lawyer solely the client's advocate and never a judge of the client's position?

c. How is the role of the lawyer as litigator different from the role of the lawyer as counselor? May a lawyer defend what she could not recommend?

Remember as well that the reputation of a lawyer is his or her most important asset. A litigator may appear before the same judge or agency with some frequency. If hindsight shows that she was too clever by half in one case, she may develop a reputation that will haunt her and her clients in other cases. The extent to which a lawyer should take into consideration the effect on her future clients of the way she represents the current client is a recurring issue of professional responsibility.

———

PROBLEM 23

THE DECISION TO FILE A CIVIL SUIT

It may seem that the decision to file a civil suit is an easy one. Your client feels wronged and knows that the courts are available to vindicate him. A moment's reflection, however, suggests how simplistic that view is. Litigation is expensive; although one side may prevail on paper, there may be no real winner. Sometimes, parties may use litigation as a tactic, perhaps a delaying tactic, rather than as an instrument for reaching a particular result. This problem looks first at the minimum standards governing the filing of a civil action. Next, it examines the tactical use of litigation as an instrument of delay. It then considers sanctions for abusive use of the litigation process and concludes with issues raised by alternative forms of dispute resolution.

FACTS

Your client is a producer of a large assortment of California wines. Many of its wines do not "travel well" from California to their destination and have a short bottle life. In order to enable the wines to travel better and maintain their quality for a longer period of time, your client uses a unique process that places a small amount of a chemical substance into each bottle. Recent testing of that substance suggests that when rats consume large amounts of the substance, a statistically significant number of rats contract cancer of the throat. Assume that under an applicable provision of the Food and Drug Act, if the Food and Drug Administration (FDA) determines that any substance consumed in any amount by man or animal causes cancer, the FDA must ban the substance.

Some reputable scientists fully support the conservative approach taken by the Food and Drug Act; others do not. Your client tells you that it is essential that the FDA delay banning his wines, because he believes he would likely go bankrupt if he could not sell the thousands of cases he has already shipped out. The food and drug laws do not provide for any compensation for your client, and the chances of Congress passing a private bill for your client are remote. Moreover, he tells you that the shelf life of his wine is only six months (that is, within six months, stores will sell consumers over 95% of the wine he has shipped). The new wines that he is producing will not contain substances that the FDA has found to be carcinogenic.

You plan to file suit attacking the factual basis for the FDA order in this case and the constitutionality of the Food and Drug Act provision. You know that court dockets are so crowded that such a suit is likely to delay the implementation of the FDA's order banning the wines. Several years ago, however, your circuit upheld the law against just such a constitutional attack.

QUESTIONS

A.   ETHICAL STANDARDS GOVERNING THE FILING OF A CIVIL ACTION

1.   Do the Model Rules tell you whether you may file suit in this case? Is the fact that the delay obtained by such a suit might serve to save the client from bankruptcy the only relevant concern?

a.   Look at Model Rule 3.1. Is there any proposition of law that cannot be the subject of a good faith proposal for at least a change in the law?

b.   In re Capoccia, 709 N.Y.S.2d 640 (N.Y.App.Div.2000) (per curiam), involved a lawyer who represented debtors in consumer collection cases. The lawyer assembled a list of defenses and counterclaims that courts in over 70 prior cases had uniformly rejected, but the lawyer continued to assert them anyway. "A common finding in many of these decisions sanctioning or warning respondent was that he had intentionally engaged in a course of conduct whereby he barraged the court system with meritless and 'canned' defenses and counterclaims as a tactic to force settlements," the court said. The court found, first, that the prior judicial determinations that this lawyer engaged in frivolous conduct had a collateral estoppel effect. Second, that the lawyer's conduct violated various disciplinary rules, including "knowingly advancing a claim or defense that is unwarranted under existing law which could not be supported by a good-faith argument for an extension, modification or reversal of existing law."

Does *Capoccia* confirm for you that Model Rule 3.1 has teeth? Does it suggest instead that it takes so much to violate the rule that it is not a significant deterrent to frivolous suits?

c.   Why should anyone care that a lawyer files frivolous litigation? Is the burden that frivolous litigation imposes on the court sufficient justification for the prohibition? If the litigation is truly frivolous, does it really impose much of a burden on the court? Does the cost of defense that the plaintiff involuntarily imposes on the defendant provide a sufficient explanation? Is frivolous litigation a form of economic mugging? See Restatement Third, The Law Governing Lawyers § 110 (frivolous advocacy).

d.   Should the law prohibit some nonfrivolous filings? Why should the law allow a lawyer to file a claim that the court rejected before? Is the answer that if one could not file suit seeking legal change, there never would have been a Brown v. Board of Education?

2.   What other rules impose discipline for the filing of frivolous litigation?

a.   In federal court, Rule 11 of the Federal Rules of Civil Procedure has a much greater impact on the filing of civil actions than Model Rule 3.1 does. Many states have adopted a similar rule to govern state proceedings.

b.   Rule 11, as amended in 1993, is not a traditional standard of professional discipline because courts enforce it in the course of litigation, while disciplinary authorities enforce their state versions of Model Rule 3.1. Federal Rule 11 certainly offers the most important practical sanction if a lawyer fails to verify the factual basis of a representation made to a federal court. Rule 11 provides:

Rule 11. Signing of Pleadings, Motions, and Other Papers; Representations to Court; Sanctions

(a) Signature. Every pleading, written motion, and other paper shall be signed by at least one attorney of record in the attorney's individual name, or, if the party is not represented by an attorney, shall be signed by the party. * * *

(b) Representations to Court. By presenting to the court (whether by signing, filing, submitting, or later advocating) a pleading, written motion or other paper, an attorney or unrepresented party is certifying that to the best of the person's knowledge, information, and belief, formed after an inquiry reasonable under the circumstances,—

(1) it is not being presented for any improper purpose, such as to harass or to cause unnecessary delay or needless increase in the cost of litigation;

(2) the claims, defenses, and other legal contentions therein are warranted by existing law or by a nonfrivolous argument for the extension, modification, or reversal of existing law or the establishment of new law;

(3) the allegations and other factual contentions have evidentiary support or, if specifically so identified, are likely to have evidentiary support after a reasonable opportunity for further investigation or discovery; and

(4) the denials of factual contentions are warranted on the evidence or, if specifically so identified, are reasonably based on a lack of information or belief.

(c) Sanctions. If, after notice and a reasonable opportunity to respond, the court determines that subdivision (b) has been violated, the court may, subject to the conditions stated below, impose an appropriate sanction upon the attorneys, law firms, or parties that have violated subdivision (b) or are responsible for the violation.

(1) How Initiated.

(A) By Motion. A motion for sanctions under this rule * * * shall not be filed with or presented to the court unless, within 21 days after service of the motion * * *, the challenged paper, claim, defense, contention, allegation, or denial is not withdrawn or appropriately corrected. If warranted, the court may award to the party prevailing on the motion the reasonable expenses and attorney's fees incurred in presenting or opposing the motion. Absent exceptional circumstances, a law firm shall be held jointly responsible for violations committed by its partners, associates, and employees.

(B) On Court's Initiative. On its own initiative, the court may enter an order describing the specific conduct that appears to violate subdivision (b) and directing an attorney, law firm, or party to show cause why it has not violated subdivision (b) with respect thereto.

(2) Nature of sanction: Limitations. A sanction imposed for violation of this rule shall be limited to what is sufficient to deter repetition of such conduct or comparable conduct by others similarly situated. Subject to the limitations in subparagraphs (A) and (B), the sanction may consist of, or include, directives of a nonmonetary nature, an order to pay a penalty into court, or, if imposed on motion and warranted for effective deterrence, an order directing payment to the movant of some or all of the reasonable attorneys' fees and other expenses incurred as a direct result of the violation.[1]

c.   Before its amendment in 1993, Rule 11 had a Procrustean quality that neither gave lawyers a chance to correct a pleading prior to imposition of sanctions nor gave the trial court discretion to reject sanctions. Cross & Cross Props., Ltd. v. Everett Allied Co., 886 F.2d 497 (2d Cir.1989), for example, imposed Rule 11 sanctions for a single improper count in a complaint, although all other counts in the complaint were well pleaded. Cooter & Gell v. Hartmarx Corp., 496 U.S. 384 (1990), imposed sanctions even though the plaintiff had withdrawn the offending complaint.

d.   Some lawyers report that judges suggest or threaten them with Rule 11 sanctions as a way to affect conduct without creating an appealable issue. For example, the judge might say, with respect to a motion, "If I rule against you, I may decide to impose Rule 11 sanctions." The lawyer then may withdraw the motion. There is no appeal because judge decided nothing, but he affected the proceeding in a way that the appeals process cannot alter. Is that fair? Is it a good way for judges to manage unruly lawyers?

3.   Does the current version of Rule 11 appropriately balance the interests of forcing lawyers to do their homework before they file a document against the danger of turning sanctions issues into collateral litigation that ultimately delays justice in the case?

a.   Examine the language of Rule 11(b). A lawyer is required to certify to four aspects of each filing after an "inquiry reasonable under the circumstances." This language imposes upon a lawyer a duty to investigate before filing a complaint, answer, or other motion with the court. It may be reasonable to require a lawyer to investigate the law so

---

[1]   Consider also, 28 U.S.C.A. § 1927, which provides:

"Any attorney or other person * * * who so multiplies the proceedings in any case unreasonably and vexatiously may be required by the court to satisfy personally the excess costs, expenses, and attorneys' fees reasonably incurred because of such conduct."

California Bar Formal Opinion 1997–151 (July 1997), considered whether a motion for sanctions filed against both lawyer and client created a conflict of interest between them. The opinion says that a conflict clearly exists if they plan to file different answers to the charges, i.e., blame each other for the misconduct. Ordinarily, however, the lawyer will defend the client and herself without a problem. Who pays sanctions, in turn, should be addressed in the retainer agreement and applied accordingly unless the court orders one or the other to bear them alone.

as not to file a frivolous legal claim, but is it always equally easy to investigate the facts? Suppose that the statute of limitations is about to expire. What is the lawyer to do when the adversary possesses the relevant information? Does this rule unfairly punish plaintiffs' lawyers?

b.   In re Keegan Mgmt. Co., Securities Litigation, 78 F.3d 431 (9th Cir.1996), the plaintiffs alleged that sellers of Nutri/System weight loss centers did not disclose gall bladder problems that the system could cause. Ultimately, the district court found insufficient connection between weight loss and gall bladder damage and granted summary judgment for the defendant. At the same time, on its own motion, the court imposed Rule 11 sanctions on the plaintiff's lawyers for failure to do adequate inquiry into the facts. In evaluating the lawyers' conduct, the district court considered only what they knew when they filed their complaint, not the confirming evidence learned afterwards. The Ninth Circuit reversed and said that, if the facts turn out to be nonfrivolous, there is no Rule 11 violation, regardless of the quality of the lawyer's original investigation. It held that a court cannot sanction a lawyer for filing a well-founded complaint solely because the lawyer's failed to conduct a reasonable inquiry.

c.   Whitehead v. Food Max of Mississippi, Inc., 332 F.3d 796 (5th Cir.2003) (en banc), affirmed a Rule 11 sanction for attorney Minor's behavior in trying to execute a judgment against Kmart. After getting a $3.4 million judgment, Minor invited the media to accompany him to a local Kmart store where he attempted to execute the judgment by seizing currency in the cash registers and vault. News reports about the execution of the writ included "Minor's extremely hyperbolic, intemperate, and misleading comments." The Fifth Circuit upheld sanctions because Minor violated Rule 11(b)(1) ("improper purpose" in obtaining writ of execution). His improper purposes in obtaining the writ were "to embarrass Kmart and advance his personal position."[2]

4.   **Are the answers about what is frivolous the same when one is selecting which issues to raise on appeal? Should it matter whether the appeal involves a criminal conviction instead of a verdict in a civil case?**

a.   Anders v. California, 386 U.S. 738 (1967), held that appointed counsel in a criminal case may not withdraw a nonfrivolous appeal. The Court required counsel appointed in appeals of criminal cases of indigents to file what we now call an *Anders* brief. If the appointed lawyer, after conscientious examination, finds the criminal defendant's case to be wholly frivolous, the lawyer should advise the court and request permission to withdraw. However, the lawyer must then supply a brief referring to anything in the record that may arguably support an appeal. The lawyer should furnish the defendant with a copy of the brief

---

[2] In Cunningham v. Hamilton County, Ohio, 527 U.S. 198 (1999), the Court unanimously held that an order imposing sanctions on a lawyer for discovery abuse pursuant to the Federal Rule of Civil Procedure is not a "final" decision and not immediately appealable under either the final judgment rule or the collateral order doctrine, even if the court has disqualified the lawyer from representing the party in the case. The Court noted that if an immediate appeal were permitted, that would undermine the purpose of Rule 37(a), Federal Rules of Civil Procedure, which was designed to protect courts and opposing parties from delaying or harassing tactics during discovery. On the other hand, one could just as well argue that, if the sanctioned lawyer's conduct were that bad, an immediate appeal would not take the appellate court much time.

with enough time to raise any points that the defendant chooses. Then, the court (not counsel) should proceed, after full examination of all proceedings, to decide whether the case is wholly frivolous, grant the lawyer's request to withdraw if it finds the claims to be frivolous, and afford assistance of counsel to argue the appeal for the indigent if it finds some legal issues to be nonfrivolous.

b. Later, Jones v. Barnes, 463 U.S. 745 (1983), held that an indigent defendant has no constitutional right to compel appointed counsel to press all nonfrivolous issues requested by the client "if counsel, as a matter of professional judgment, decides not to present those points." Both the Court and the dissent in *Barnes* cited Model Rule 1.2(a) and Defense Function Standard 4–5.2.[3] Who has the better argument? Are most clients competent to specify errors worthy of appeal? Is giving the client the sense that he or she is in control as important as the inherent force of the arguments raised? If a client who can afford a lawyer can insist on focusing on a particular nonfrivolous issue (although it may not be wise to do so), should an indigent defendant have fewer rights?[4]

c. Smith v. Robbins, 528 U.S. 259 (2000), considered how much appointed counsel must do to comply with *Anders*. Robbins defended himself at trial. On appeal, his appointed counsel filed a no-merits brief, which briefly outlined the facts surrounding the trial and presented no possible grounds for appeal. Robbins then filed a brief of his own, which the California courts rejected. In a federal habeas corpus proceeding, the district court held that, in these circumstances, the *Anders* brief amounted to ineffective assistance of counsel. The Court of Appeals affirmed, but the U.S. Supreme Court reversed (5 to 4), holding that the California procedure adequately protects a defendant's rights. Justice Thomas, writing for the Court, said that although California's procedure does not comply in all respects with *Anders*, under the procedure, appellate counsel allows the defendant to file a supplemental brief and the lawyer remains available to brief any issue requested by the appellate court. The *Anders* reference to the lawyer's noting any points that might support an appeal was an example of acceptable procedure, the Court said, not the minimum procedure tolerable. The California procedure allows "adequate and effective" appellate review, and the Supreme Court should not impose a single procedure on the states.

Justices Stevens, Souter, Ginsburg, and Breyer dissented, arguing that the Court had effectively overruled *Anders* and that, while frivolous litigation is a problem, denying defendants an appeal by a "committed representative" who will engage in a "partisan scrutiny of the record" is much more serious. "Without the assurance that assigned counsel has done his best as a partisan, his substantial equality to a

---

[3] Each Circuit is required to have a "criminal justice plan" for providing counsel to indigent defendants. The Fourth Circuit plan required counsel to file petitions for certiorari on behalf of indigent defendants regardless of whether there were any nonfrivolous claims to raise. In Austin v. United States, 513 U.S. 5 (1994), the Supreme Court required that the plan be amended to not require filing frivolous claims.

[4] On sanctions for a frivolous civil appeal, see Cooter & Gell v. Hartmarx Corp., 496 U.S. 384 (1990), and Hilmon Co. (V.I.) Inc. v. Hyatt International, 899 F.2d 250 (3d Cir.1990).

lawyer retained at a defendant's expense cannot be assumed." Do you agree with the dissenters? Can *Anders* and *Robbins* both be right?

B.   THE ETHICAL STATUS OF DELAY AS A LITIGATION TACTIC

1.   Does Model Rule 3.2 establish a different ethical standard for the use of litigation to resolve differences? Its key principle is that a lawyer must "expedite" resolution of the dispute. Why should the Rule require a lawyer to do that? Does this Rule focus only on the inefficient use of court time that delay engenders?

a.   What does Rule 3.2 mean when it says that a lawyer need only expedite litigation when "consistent with the interests of the client"? Look at the last sentence of the Comment. If one cannot use delay to "realize financial or other benefit," what other "interests of the client" would justify it? If the reason for a delay is "nonfrivolous" and thus not subject to Rule 11 sanctions, does that mean the lawyer has complied with the requirements of Model Rule 3.2? Should the prohibition on realizing financial benefit be in the Rule itself rather than in the Comment?

b.   Must a motion be justified only in terms of its probability of success? May you ever consider the benefits of delay that arise from filing the motion? May a lawyer consider the benefits of delay if there is *some* possibility of success, i.e., he does not file the motion *solely* for purposes of delay? Because the Comment refers to "otherwise improper delay," may the lawyer file a nonfrivolous motion with delay as its dominant purpose? Is it significant that in the Model Rules revisions of 2002, the ABA removed from Rule 3.1, Comment 2, the statement that an action is frivolous if the "client desires to have the action taken primarily for the purpose of harassing or maliciously injuring a person"?

c.   If your motion is not baseless, and if your client desires delay, *must* you file a motion that will delay resolution of the matter? In short, are you required to use every tool in your bag to further your client's interest? Suppose you conclude that if you pull your punches in this case, the FDA may be pleased and more likely to give the benefit of the doubt to your *other* clients, and to this one on other cases.

d.   One book on trial practice states that the "duty of supporting the client's cause is sometimes so forcefully stated as to support the argument that as a trial lawyer you are obliged to assert every legal claim or defense available, except those you reject on tactical grounds relating to the immediate case. But the aim of the trial system to achieve justice, the interests of future clients, and your legitimate interest in your own reputation and future effectiveness at the bar compel moderation of that extreme view." Robert Keeton, Trial Tactics and Methods § 1.3 (2d ed. 1973). See also, Ronald D. Rotunda, Book Review, 89 Harvard L. Rev. 622, 628–29 (1976). Do you agree?

2.   What obligation do you have to make witnesses available for trial and for deposition by the opposing party?

a.   Assume that prior to any FDA hearing to determine whether to issue a ban against your client's wine additive, you knew that the first and most important witness that the FDA would seek to call would be the chief research chemist for your client. The chemist prefers not to testify because his testimony would greatly damage his employer, your client. May you recommend that the chemist be hospitalized for tests and possible surgery on his recently discovered knee injury that, although not life threatening or terribly painful, limits his workday? Are you off the ethical hook if the company doctor initiated the suggestion that the knee needs treatment? Is it a rationalization to think that creating delay eliminates the possibility that the zealously loyal chemist might commit perjury?

b.   In Chevron Chemical Co. v. Deloitte & Touche, 501 N.W.2d 15 (Wis.1993), the lawyer represented that a witness would be unavailable for six weeks due to surgery; in fact, he had hernia surgery and would be available in two days. For this and other misconduct, the court granted a judgment against the defendant notwithstanding the verdict and remanded the case to assess damages. The court said, "The unprofessional misconduct of counsel in using misleading, if not outright false, statements to the circuit court and in the presence of the jury is conduct that this court will not tolerate." Do you agree that this misconduct justified such a severe sanction? Could the professional discipline process produce a sanction that was nearly this quick and sure?

c.   May you advise a witness who is not your client not to talk to the other party? Suppose that the witness does not want to "become involved." Look at Model Rules 3.4(a) and (f).

In People v. Kenelly, 648 P.2d 1065 (Colo.1982), the Colorado courts suspended an attorney because he drew up a contract under which his client settled a civil case against *X,* and, in exchange, agreed to evade a subpoena in *X*'s upcoming criminal trial. Accord, In the Matter of Lutz, 607 P.2d 1078 (Idaho 1980).[5]

d.   To cope with the knee problem, should you simply ask the FDA staff for a delay in the hearings? Remember, in six months the case will be moot as far as your client is concerned, although it would still be a real issue to the FDA and possibly other wine producers. Is the only ethical issue your motive for delaying the expected testimony of the research chemist?

e.   Should the appropriateness of delay in litigation vary depending on the type of legal proceeding involved? Consider Ronald D. Rotunda, Law, Lawyers, and Managers, in Clarence Walton, ed., The Ethics of Corporate Conduct 142–43 (1977):

> "[D]elay is a knife that cuts both ways. Some corporate lawyers have charged that environmentalists and other public-interest litigants have used delay to bog down the regulatory system, to prevent needed rate increases, to prohibit or delay power plant expansion, to obstruct programs for highway construction, and to delay or modify housing developments."

---

[5]   See also, Snyder v. State Bar, 555 P.2d 1104 (Cal.1976) (attorney disbarred, inter alia, for advising clients not to be available for depositions); Florida Bar v. Machin, 635 So.2d 938 (Fla.1994) (lawyer suspended for offering to establish a trust fund for the child of a murder victim if the victim's family agreed not to testify at the client's sentencing hearing). Cf. Taylor v. Commonwealth, 233 S.W. 895 (Ky.1921) (attorney disbarred when he was party to an arrangement under which a witness was paid to leave the jurisdiction and not return).

Is delay permissible when invoked in service of the public interest?

f.   May a lawyer use delay in criminal cases? Is filing appeals and habeas corpus petitions for purposes of delay a permissible strategy in a death penalty case? Is it often the *only* strategy?

3.   In the dispute with the FDA, are you representing your client in your capacity as a lawyer giving advice in litigation or your capacity as a lawyer advising a client more generally?

a.   Look at Model Rule 2.1 governing the lawyer as advisor. Now look again at Model Rule 3.1. If the lawyer may advance any nonfrivolous claim without facing professional discipline, does if follow that the lawyer acting under Rule 2.1 should advise the client to take any position that is not utterly frivolous?

b.   Does it trouble you that, under the assumptions in this problem, your delay will allow the client to sell tainted wine *in the future?* That is, what you do here may expose consumers to the risk of getting cancer, not simply help allocate losses after an event has occurred.

c.   Will selling the wine expose your client to unwanted publicity or litigation if the additive in the wine becomes public knowledge? Would you then be liable to your client for a failure to warn it about the adverse consequences of pressing its litigation right to the limit? See, e.g., Restatement Third, The Law Governing Lawyers § 94 (Advising and Assisting a Client—In General).

d.   Rather than seek delay, should you suggest that your client— before the FDA's expected order becomes effective—immediately sell his stock of tainted wine to a foreign wholesaler, assuming foreign law and scientific understanding are different and that the wholesaler can resell the wine abroad? Will you sleep better knowing that only people you are unlikely to meet will have their cancer risk increased?

C.   OTHER SANCTIONS FOR LITIGATION MISCONDUCT

1.   Do courts have authority to sanction lawyers beyond Rule 11 and its state-law equivalents?

a.   Earlier in this problem, we saw that courts may sanction lawyers for violations of Model Rule 3.1 and Rule 11 of the Federal Rules of Civil Procedure. Other sources of sanction authority are available as well.

b.   Chambers v. NASCO, Inc., 501 U.S. 32 (1991), held that a federal court has inherent power to award attorneys' fees to a party whom the court concludes has engaged in harassing litigation. Chambers agreed to sell his television station to NASCO, but then changed his mind. The Court found that he tried to prevent the sale by fraudulently trying to deprive the federal court of jurisdiction and by other tactics of "delay, oppression and harassment." Rule 11 allowed sanctions for frivolous pleadings, of which there were several, but not for the other wrongs. The Supreme Court held that a district judge has inherent power to manage the proceedings and may award attorneys' fees to sanction bad faith and oppressive conduct, even if Rule 11 does not cover the conduct.

Chief Justice Rehnquist and Justices Kennedy, Scalia, and Souter dissented, suggesting the Court granted *carte blanche* to judges to sanction lawyers. Are you equally concerned?

c. United States v. Eisen, 974 F.2d 246 (2d Cir.1992), found lawyers guilty of criminal and tortious conduct—here, mail fraud and RICO violations—for what they did in their role as lawyers. The government convicted the lawyers of conspiring with private investigators and others in a scheme of contriving phony traffic accidents and then filing claims with insurance companies. The opinion looked at several issues. For example, the "fortuity" that a witness' testimony as "influenced turned out to be truthful" is not a defense to the bribery of the witness because: "The essence of bribery is the intent to influence improperly the conduct of another by bestowing a benefit, [so] there is no requirement that the intended result be accomplished." The lawyers' "misrepresentations in pleadings and pretrial submissions were made in the hope of fraudulently inducing a settlement before trial. And in cases that went to trial, fraudulent representations concerning the claims were directed at the civil defendants and their insurers in an effort to induce settlement before verdict. In fact, several of the lawsuits listed in the indictment were settled. Even in cases decided by a jury, defendants' misconduct was intended to defraud their adversaries."

d. Zamos v. Stroud, 87 P.3d 802 (Cal.2004), held that the tort of malicious prosecution covers situations where a lawyer who had probable cause to initiate a lawsuit continues to prosecute the case after discovering that the probable cause no longer exists. Citing the Restatement of Torts § 674 and "every other state that has addressed the question," the California Supreme Court held the traditional standard—that malicious prosecution is actionable in instances where "any reasonable attorney" would find the claims are "totally and completely without merit"—applies to both initiation and continuation of a suit. Extending the tort to continuation of the lawsuit improves the efficiency of the court system by encouraging early dismissals, and serves the clients' best interests by saving them from unnecessary legal fees. The bottom line is that Rule 11 and the Model Rules may be the least of a lawyer's worries in some cases.

2. Should courts have the power to sanction a lawyer for filing a lawsuit that is nonfrivolous, but is a case that he would not have filed but for the plaintiff's desire to hurt or impose costs on the defendant? Should litigants have a Constitutional right to impose burdens on their enemies?

a. Dove Audio, Inc. v. Rosenfeld, Meyer & Susman, 54 Cal.Rptr.2d 830 (Cal.Ct.App.1996), involved statements that Audrey Hepburn's lawyer made in a letter seeking to get celebrities to join in a complaint against a recording company that allegedly reneged on its promises to make gifts to the celebrities' favorite charities. The recording company sued the lawyer's firm for defamation, but the court dismissed the suit, finding that statements relating to litigation were privileged against a defamation charge. More interesting, the court held that the lawyer had his own claim for damages (over $27,000) from the recording company filing the action. California has an anti-SLAPP (strategic lawsuit against public participation) statute that permits the award of attorney's fees against someone who uses litigation to try to prevent someone else from asserting First Amendment rights.

b.   These SLAPP statutes can raise their own First Amendment problems. The First Amendment guarantees a right to petition the government for redress of grievances. A lawsuit is a classic petition, and if it is not frivolous, i.e., not "baseless," ordinarily it would be protected conduct. The plaintiff may harbor ill will towards the defendant, but the law does not require litigants to like each other; indeed, they often grow to dislike each other immensely.[6]

c.   The First Amendment protection even applies if the lawsuits are ultimately unsuccessful. In BE & K Constr. Co. v. National Labor Relations Board, 536 U.S. 516 (2002), unions lobbied and filed health and safety charges against a nonunion contractor who secured a large contract. The contractor retaliated by filing secondary boycott and antitrust claims against the unions; a court dismissed all the claims or the party voluntarily withdrew with prejudice. Then, the unions complained to the National Labor Relations Board (NLRB), which found that the contractor's suits were "unmeritorious" and the employer had a bad motive: it filed the suits in order to retaliate against union members who were engaged in conduct that the National Labor Relations Act protects. The NLRB and the Sixth Circuit agreed that the employer engaged in an unfair labor practice, but the Supreme Court reversed.

Justice O'Connor wrote for the Court that lawsuits could not constitute an unfair labor practice unless they were "sham litigation," that is, both (1) subjectively brought with a bad motive and (2) "objectively baseless," which these were not. The NLRB may not "burden an unsuccessful but reasonably based suit" even though it "was brought with a retaliatory purpose." Mere ill will is not enough because "ill will is not uncommon in litigation." The right to petition, said the Court, is one of "the most precious of the liberties safeguarded by the Bill of Rights," and the "right of access to the courts" is "one aspect of the right of petition. * * * As long as a plaintiff's *purpose* is to stop conduct he reasonably believes is illegal, petitioning is genuine both objectively and subjectively." (emphasis added). The Court made clear, however, that it was not undercutting the right of lower courts to impose "common litigation sanctions," e.g., Rule 11.

3.   Should there be a remedy against the government for a wrongful or vexatious criminal prosecution?

a.   United States v. Gilbert, 198 F.3d 1293 (11th Cir.1999), considered the criminal law counterpart to Rule 11. The jury convicted Gilbert of fraudulently concealing assets in bankruptcy, but the court reversed his conviction because the statute of limitations had run. The defendant then sued for attorneys' fees under the 1997 Hyde Amendment, 18 U.S.C. § 3006A, which allows such fees if the prosecution was "vexatious, frivolous or in bad faith." The court determined that the decision as to when the statute of limitations began

---

[6]   See, e.g., Bill Johnson's Restaurants, Inc. v. N.L.R.B., 461 U.S. 731, 742–43 (1983), where the Court said that, in light of "the First Amendment right of access to the courts," the "filing and prosecution of a well-founded lawsuit may not be enjoined as an unfair labor practice, even if it would not have been commenced but for plaintiff's desire to retaliate against the defendant for exercising rights protected by the [National Labor Relations] Act."

to run was a matter of first impression in the circuit and that the government was entitled to take the position it did. Thus, the statute did not justify any fee award.

b.   United States v. Adkinson, 247 F.3d 1289 (11th Cir.2001), on the other hand, found that the government, with full knowledge, asserted a position that recent and controlling precedent foreclosed. That conduct constituted "vexatious," "frivolous," and "bad faith" prosecution that entitled the defendant to Hyde Amendment fees.

c.   Should the fact the government fails to prove its case be enough to demonstrate that the proceeding was vexatious? In United States v. Sherburne, 249 F.3d 1121 (9th Cir.2001), the government prosecuted thirteen defendants for alleged abuses in the funding and construction of a housing development. The prosecution charged over fifty offenses, and the court failed to convict on any of them. In a subsequent related hearing, the trial court awarded attorney's fees pursuant to the Hyde Amendment to some, but not all, of the defendants. The Ninth Circuit found that the use of a solely objective standard to measure "vexatiousness" was incorrect, and that the correct standard involved both subjective and objective characteristics. The test should be whether "the prosecution was unwarranted because it was intended to harass and [was] without sufficient foundation." The court stated that to use a solely objective standard would put too much of a burden on the prosecution and would lead to judicial second-guessing. Do you agree?

D.   CONSIDERATION OF ADR ALTERNATIVES

1.   What is your obligation to propose nonlitigation alternatives to your client, the wine producer?

a.   The buzzword in modern times is Alternative Dispute Resolution, or ADR. In the 2002 revisions to the Model Rules of Professional Conduct, the ABA added a sentence to Model Rule 2.1, Comment 5, which now provides: "[W]hen a matter is likely to involve litigation, it may be necessary under Rule 1.4 to inform the client of forms of dispute resolution that might constitute reasonable alternatives to litigation." What alternatives to litigation does the Comment have in mind? Is negotiation an alternative to litigation, or is negotiation always done in the shadow of litigation, i.e., whether or not a party actually files litigation, does the right to litigate make the alternative of negotiation more compelling?

b.   Many federal and state courts require that parties mediate their cases before a trial date will be set.[7] In addition, federal and state agencies have established mediation procedures to settle adjudicative disputes involving a government agency and a private party. The growth in the use of ADR and the increasing costs of litigation have combined to form a trend called the vanishing trial. See Marc Galanter, The Vanishing Trial: An Examination of Trials and Related Matters in Federal and State Courts, 1 J. Empirical Legal Studies 459 (2004).

---

[7]   See, e.g., Ettie Ward, Mandatory Court Annexed Alternative Dispute Resolution in the United States Federal Courts: Panacea or Pandemic?, 81 St. John's L. Rev. 77 (2007).

c.   The Model Rules explicitly give their approval to ADR in particular instances. Rule 1.5, Comment 9, for example, requires lawyers to comply with any system of mandatory arbitration or mediation of fee disputes. Another clause in that same sentence urges lawyers to submit to arbitration or mediation "even when it is voluntary." Further, if the lawyer and client have a dispute as who owns funds in the lawyer's trust fund account, Rule 1.15, Comment 3, advises the lawyer to suggest means, "such as arbitration," for resolving the dispute promptly.

d.   Will mediation or arbitration work in the case of the wine producer? At least to date, the alternative seems unlikely. In disputes with the government, the FDA and similar agencies do not have a reputation of favoring mediation or arbitration over litigation, although there is some evidence that policy could be changing.

2.   Why are there special rules restricting lawyers who act as third party neutrals that do not apply to nonlawyers who occupy the same role?

a.   In the 2002 amendments, the ABA added a new provision dealing specifically with ADR. Model Rule 2.4, "Lawyer Serving as Third–Party Neutral," defines a "third-party neutral" as a person who acts as a "mediator, arbitrator, conciliator or evaluator," to assist two or more persons who are not the lawyer's clients. See Model Rule 2.4(a) and Comment 1.

b.   At the same time the ABA created Model Rule 2.4, it eliminated Model Rule 2.2, which had governed the lawyer as "intermediary." Model Rule 2.2 had defined an intermediary as a lawyer who represented two or more clients with "potentially conflicting interests," typically a dispute between them. In contrast, under Rule 2.4, the lawyer explicitly does not represent any clients.

c.   Model Rule 2.4 does not, of course, regulate the conduct of third-party neutrals who are not lawyers. Why are people who use a third-party neutral more likely to be confused by the neutral's role if the neutral is a lawyer? Look at Model Rule 2.4, Comment 3. Are you convinced?

d.   Should Rule 2.4(b) require more than a warning that the lawyer does not represent either of the disputing parties? Does the suggestion in Comment 3, that the lawyer inform the parties about the inapplicability of the attorney-client privilege, sound suspiciously like the giving of legal advice? Is anything wrong with that? The ABA Ethics 2000 Commission rejected a proposal that would have prohibited third-party neutrals from giving legal advice to the parties.[8] Does that mean the third-party neutral may not help the parties draft a settlement agreement?

e.   Should the ABA leave the rules governing third-party neutrals to standards-setting bodies more focused on current thinking about ADR processes? Model Rule 2.4, Comment 2 suggests that a great deal of regulation of ADR neutrals will come from such other sources.

---

[8]   Margaret Colgate Love, The Revised ABA Model Rules of Professional Conduct: Summary of the Work of Ethics 2000, 15 Georgetown J. Legal Ethics 441, 462 (2002).

3.   If a lawyer was a third-party neutral in a matter, may that lawyer or one of his partners later represent a client in a related matter?

a.   Assume that after the FDA required the recall of wine from retailers' shelves, one of the retailers wanted your client to reimburse it for its loss. Alpha was the arbitrator who decided that dispute. Now, your client has another dispute with the retailer that is tangentially related to the earlier one. In the new dispute, the retailer has hired Beta, who has recently become Alpha's law partner. Your client did not give any information to Alpha during the arbitration that you expected he would keep secret from the retailer. Do you have any grounds to object to Beta's representing the wine retailer in the controversy?

b.   Look at Model Rule 1.12(a) and (c). How related should two disputes be before Rule 1.12(a) would prohibit Alpha's own representation of the retailer in the second dispute? Remember that Alpha did not represent either party to the arbitration so Model Rules 1.9 and 1.10 are not controlling. What is the rationale for excluding Alpha from involvement in later stages of the same "matter"? If a court disqualifies Alpha, what must the Alpha Beta firm do to screen Alpha so that Beta may continue to represent the retailer?

c.   If Beta represented the retailer on various other matters over the years, although not this one, should Alpha (Beta's partner) be ineligible to serve as arbitrator? Does either Rule 1.12 or Comment 4 to Rule 2.4 authoritatively answer the question? How would you answer it? How would you explain your answer?

d.   Rule 1.12(d) expressly permits a partisan arbitrator on a multimember panel to represent the party in subsequent matters. Parties to domestic and international agreements often use the tripartite method of selecting a three-member panel for the arbitration of disputes. Each party selects a partisan arbitrator and the two select a third neutral arbitrator. Notice that the limitations of Rule 1.12 do not apply to partisan arbitrators.

Problem 24

LITIGATION TACTICS

Some of the public's favorite stories involve lawyers uncovering deception or acting as deceivers in order to uncover deception. Early television lawyer Perry Mason was adept at goading the guilty party into confessing in open court (with Mason sometimes suggesting that he knew more than he did) just before Mason's client was about to be bound over for trial at the end of each episode. This problem explores when we should admire a lawyer's imagination and when we should condemn it. We first look at the line between creative lawyering and deception, wonder if the line is bright or equivocal, and then explore the role of deception in the search for truth. Next, we ask when a lawyer may use confidential information inadvertently disclosed by an opponent, and whether and how judges should enforce standards of civility among litigators.

FACTS

Hugh Martin, one of the most famous insurance defense lawyers in San Francisco, defends clients of many of the largest insurance companies in the United States. His firm's office overlooks the bay and occupies an entire floor of the Transamerica building. Yet despite his luxurious office and income to match, Martin cuts a different figure in court. He dresses in baggy tweed jackets with elbow patches, his shirts have badly frayed sleeves, and his unpolished shoes have very worn heels and soles. While he is a dapper figure outside of the courtroom with his custom suits and handmade cigars, he justifies his shabby attire and country lawyer act in the halls of justice as an effort to win sympathy from the juries while helping insurance companies avoid large tort judgments.

Martin confides to his young associates that they should avoid choosing younger jurors because of their "social worker, do-gooder mentality." He also advises: "Try to pick a jury with racial and class differences; by exploiting and encouraging dissension you create disunity; a disunified jury rarely grants large awards."

In one lecture to new associates in his firm, he explained:

> "You have to use your ingenuity and use all the tricks of the trade to win for the defense in a large tort claim. If you see that you can exploit an opposing witness' emotional weakness to make him seem uncertain about a fact, don't hesitate to do so even if the fact is true. The client doesn't pay for justice. It pays for victory."

Martin also trains his associates to impose costs upon opposing parties and counsel. "Be sure to schedule depositions at the most unfavorable times and in remote places. We can teach opponents a lesson that we will go to all ends to prevail in litigation."

In a case that Martin likes to brag about, he defended a manufacturing concern charged with the negligent death of the wife of a middle-aged worker. All during the trial Martin had his attractive secretary sit in the courtroom. Then, according to plan, Martin had this secretary—just before closing arguments, during a short break in the proceedings when the plaintiff's lawyer's back was turned—ask the plaintiff-widower the time; she smiled at his response, patted him on the head, and then left. The three older members of the jury looked with icy stares at the plaintiff and five hours later, the jury returned a verdict for the defense. One or more of the jurors mistakenly assumed that Martin's secretary was the plaintiff's new wife.

Martin justifies these and similar practices (he calls them "tricks") as necessary to counteract what he considers the unfair advantage of the plaintiff's lawyer in winning verdicts because of sympathy and other reasons not connected with the merits of the case.[9]

QUESTIONS

A. THE AMBIGUOUS LINE BETWEEN CREATIVE LAWYERING AND DECEPTION

1. Which of Hugh Martin's litigating "tricks" are proper, if any? Are some in a gray area? Should Martin be subject to criticism for wearing different clothes in court than he wears to the office, for example?

a. Should regulation of Martin's wardrobe be the responsibility of the judges before whom he appears? Courts sometimes do try to regulate the clothing of lawyers who appear before them. In State v. Cherryhomes, 840 P.2d 1261 (N.M.App.1992), for example, the lawyer appeared in a dress shirt with a bandanna at his neck. A local court rule required that he wear a necktie. He argued that a bandanna was a form of tie, but the court fined him for contempt. The Court of Appeals affirmed. A lawyer's dress is not a form of "speech," the court ruled, and the judge's interpretation of the local rule controlled. Do you agree?

b. In Berner v. Delahanty, 129 F.3d 20 (1st Cir.1997), a court required a lawyer to take off a political advocacy button when he was in the courtroom. The button said "No on 1" and referred to an upcoming referendum issue. The First Circuit held that the prohibition of all advocacy buttons did not discriminate on the basis of content and was appropriate to preserving an atmosphere of impartiality in the courtroom.

2. Is there anything improper about Martin's approach to jury selection? When, if ever, does a lawyer have a duty to the justice system to pick only jurors who will be fair to both sides?

a. Georgia v. McCollum, 505 U.S. 42 (1992), held that it is unconstitutional for either prosecutor or defense counsel to exercise peremptory challenges based on race. J.E.B. v. Alabama ex rel. T.B., 511 U.S. 127 (1994), reached the same result as to sex-based challenges; Edmonson v. Leesville Concrete Co., Inc., 500 U.S. 614 (1991), came to the same conclusion in a civil case involving only private litigants.

b. United States v. Omoruyi, 7 F.3d 880 (9th Cir.1993), held that a prosecutor's statement indicating that he exercised peremptory challenges against two unmarried female prospective jurors because he was concerned they would be attracted to a "good-looking" male defendant was an admission of purposeful sex discrimination in violation of the defendant's right to equal protection.

c. What should the result be in a medical malpractice case if the defense lawyer exercises a peremptory challenge against a potential juror (a Jehovah's Witness or a Christian Scientist) for religious reasons? Assume that the lawyer believes that the juror may be prejudiced against the defendant medical doctor. See State v. Davis,

---

[9] This problem is adapted, with permission, from the discussion of a somewhat analogous situation in Ending Insult to Injury: No–Fault Insurance for Products and Services 4–6 (Univ. of Illinois Press 1975) by Professor Jeffrey O'Connell.

504 N.W.2d 767 (Minn.1993) (religiously-motivated peremptory challenge against Jehovah's Witness is constitutional).

d.   Given this authority, why do the Model Rules include the following sentence in Model Rule 8.4, Comment 3: "A trial judge's finding that peremptory challenges were exercised on a discriminatory basis does not alone establish a violation of this rule"? Shouldn't unconstitutional conduct by a litigator constitute a per se violation of Model Rule 8.4(d)? Is the Comment simply saying that the accused lawyer may try to persuade a disciplinary panel that he did not exercise the challenges on a discriminatory basis?

e.   In Virgin Islands v. Weatherwax, 77 F.3d 1425 (3d Cir.1996), the prosecutor accused the white defendant of killing a black man. Black persons made up a majority of potential jurors, and the jury selected included nine blacks and three whites. One day during the trial, defense counsel saw that a white juror took a newspaper with a story prejudicial to the defendant into the jury room in violation of a court order. Counsel failed to call it to the judge's attention, however, because he did not want the court to dismiss the white juror. Ultimately, the jury convicted the defendant of second degree murder and he appealed his lawyer's failure to challenge the juror misconduct. By a 2–1 vote, the Third Circuit refused to second guess the lawyer's decision. This was a tactical matter within the "exclusive province of the lawyer," the court held, and the failure to act did not constitute ineffective assistance of counsel. Do you agree? Did the lawyer who took race into account act properly in light of *McCollum*?

3.   When Martin cross examines a truthful witness, may he properly try to get that witness to express uncertainty about something that Martin knows to be true?

a.   Read Model Rule 3.3(a)(1). If a lawyer may not "make a false statement of fact or law to a tribunal," do the ethics rules permit Martin to try to impeach the reliability of testimony that he knows is accurate? What understanding of "justice" would warrant Martin's approach? Is Martin right that the client is not paying for justice? Should that end the ethical discussion?

b.   Read Model Rule 4.4(a). What seems to be its primary concern? Should the proper issue for a lawyer be whether the witness is "embarrassed" or "humiliated unnecessarily"? Should the issue instead be whether the lawyer is misleading the trier of fact?

c.   How would you draft a rule that prohibits vigorous cross-examination of a truthful witness and yet preserves the essence of the adversary system? If lawyers were required to go easy on witnesses who were telling the truth, would that send the jury too clear a signal about whom they should believe? Would that be a bad thing? Are there times when the adversary system is too adversarial for its own good?

d.   Restatement Third, The Law Governing Lawyers § 106, Comment *c*, defends the present rule by arguing:

> "A particularly difficult problem is presented when a lawyer has an opportunity to cross-examine a witness with respect to testimony that the lawyer knows to be truthful, including harsh implied criticism of the witness's testimony, character, or capacity for truth-telling. Even if legally

permissible, a lawyer would presumably do so only where that would not cause the lawyer to lose credibility with the tribunal or alienate the factfinder. Moreover, a lawyer is never required to conduct such examination, and the lawyer may withdraw if the lawyer's client insists on such a course of action in a setting in which the lawyer considers it imprudent or repugnant."

Is a lawyer "never required to conduct such examination" when the best hope for the client is to persuade the jury that the nervous witness with bad eyesight is wrong, even though the lawyer knows that the witness is accurate in this instance?

4.   Do any of Martin's other "tricks" raise ethical issues?

a.   Would it be proper for Martin to have a low-income employee sit at the counsel table instead of a company manager to make the company appear nearly broke? Look at Model Rule 3.4(e).

b.   Did it offend you when Martin's secretary implied that she had a relationship with the plaintiff? What, if anything, made the incident ethically improper? Should we worry about trial tactics at all? Is the point of the adversary system that a lawyer may rely on opposing counsel's guile to counterbalance his or her own?

c.   In deciding which of Martin's "tricks" are unethical, should the rules impose a bright line standard or should it vary depending on whether a case is before a jury, for example? Would one argue that wearing shabby clothes during a settlement conference is improper? Is the test whether the lawyer's *motive* was to mislead? Is the test whether in a given case a juror or lawyer was in fact misled?

B.   USING DECEPTION IN THE SEARCH FOR TRUTH

1.   May a lawyer ever use deception as a way of bringing out the truth in court?

a.   Model Rule 3.3(a)(1) provides that a lawyer shall not knowingly "make a false statement of fact or law to a tribunal." Model Rule 4.1(a), the rule as applied to third persons (not tribunals), is similar, except that it adds the word "material."

b.   Does "never" mean "never"? Is there a place for deception in the search for truth? What if the purpose of the deception is to uncover an honest, but significant, mistake in identification? Commentators tell us that some of the most persuasive testimony is eyewitness identification, but sometimes that testimony is simply mistaken. Witnesses "tend to incorporate post-identification feedback into their recollections of events," and "witnesses to a crime in which the perpetrator displays a weapon tend to focus their attention on the weapon, not the perpetrator."[10]

---

[10] Mark Hansen, Expertise on Trial: Testimony on Reliability of Eyewitness Identification Stalls on General Acceptance, ABA Journal, Dec. 2002, at 22.

Furthermore, what one remembers may not be true. For example, there were no television pictures of the first airplane hitting the World Trade Center on September 11, 2001, yet 77% of New Yorkers surveyed, and 73% of people nationwide recall that they saw such coverage. Memories "suffused with emotion are barely more likely to be true than memories of last Tuesday's lunch." The September 11 memory studies "confirm that eyewitness recall is

c.   Consider the lawyer's strategy in United States v. Thoreen, 653 F.2d 1332 (9th Cir.1981), cert. denied, 455 U.S. 938 (1982). The court tells us:

"In February 1980, Thoreen represented Sibbett, a commercial fisher, during Sibbett's nonjury trial * * * for criminal contempt for three violations of a preliminary injunction against salmon fishing. In preparing for trial, Thoreen hoped that the government agent who had cited Sibbett could not identify him. He decided to test the witness's identification.

"He placed next to him at counsel table Clark Mason, who resembled Sibbett and had Mason dressed in outdoor clothing—denims, heavy shoes, a plaid shirt, and a jacket-vest.

"Sibbett wore a business suit, large round glasses, and sat behind the rail in a row normally reserved for the press.

"Thoreen neither asked the court's permission for, nor notified it or government counsel of, the substitution.

"On Thoreen's motion at the start of the trial, the court ordered all witnesses excluded from the courtroom. Mason remained at the counsel table.

"Throughout the trial, Thoreen made and allowed to go uncorrected numerous misrepresentations. He gestured to Mason as though he was his client and gave Mason a yellow legal pad on which to take notes. The two conferred. Thoreen did not correct the court when it expressly referred to Mason as the defendant and caused the record to show identification of Mason as Sibbett.

"Because of the conduct, two government witnesses misidentified Mason as Sibbett. Following the government's case, Thoreen called Mason as a witness and disclosed the substitution. * * *

[The court let the government recall the government agent who then made the proper identification. Sibbett was convicted, and the Judge held Thoreen in contempt.]

"Thoreen's principal defense is that his conduct was a good faith tactic in aid of cross-examination and falls within the protected realm of zealous advocacy. He argues that as defense counsel he has no obligation to ascertain or present the truth and may seek to confuse witnesses with misleading questions, gestures, or appearances. * * *

"While we agree that defense counsel should represent his client vigorously, regardless of counsel's view of guilt or innocence, we conclude that Thoreen's conduct falls outside this protected behavior.

"Vigorous advocacy by defense counsel may properly entail impeaching or confusing a witness, even if counsel thinks the witness is truthful, and refraining from presenting evidence

fallible." Sharon Begley, The Memory of September 11 Is Seared in Your Mind: But Is It Really True?, Wall Street J., Sept. 13, 2002, at B1, col. 1.

even if he knows the truth. When we review this conduct and find that the line between vigorous advocacy and actual obstruction is close, our doubts should be resolved in favor of the former. * * *

"Thoreen's view of appropriate cross-examination, which encompasses his substitution, crossed over the line from zealous advocacy to actual obstruction because, as we discuss later, it impeded the court's search for truth, resulted in delays, and violated a court custom and rule. Moreover, this conduct harms rather than enhances an attorney's effectiveness as an advocate.

" 'It is fundamental that in relations with the court, defense counsel must be scrupulously candid and truthful in representation of any matter before the court. This is not only a basic ethical requirement, but it is essential if the lawyer is to be effective in the role of advocate, for if the lawyer's reputation for veracity is suspect, he or she will lack the confidence of the court when it is needed most to the serve the client."[11] * * *

"The record shows that Sibbett's identification was not an issue, contradicting the need to attack credibility."

The court upheld the finding of contempt but did not indicate what sanction was imposed.[12]

d. Do you agree that Thoreen's conduct crossed the line and was impermissible deception? How else was he to establish reasonable doubt about the government's identification? In a later portion of the opinion, the court suggests:

"If identification is at issue, an attorney could test a witness's credibility by notifying the court and counsel that it is [at issue] and by seeking the court's permission to (1) seat two or more persons at counsel table without identifying the defendant * * *; (2) have no one at counsel table; (3) hold an in-court lineup."

Would you as defense counsel choose any of those alternatives? Is the problem with Thoreen's conduct the fact that he designed it to mislead the trier of fact, not aid the search for truth? What if Thoreen did not trust the judge and did not seek the court's permission for that reason? Would that make his actions proper?

---

[11] The court was quoting American Bar Association Standards for Criminal Justice, The Defense Function 4.9 (1980).

[12] By a 4 to 3 vote, the Illinois Supreme Court followed *Thoreen* on similar facts. People v. Simac, 641 N.E.2d 416 (Ill.1994), as did the Massachusetts Supreme Judicial Court in Matter of Gross, 759 N.E.2d 288 (Mass.2001). Attorney Gross represented a woman on drunk driving charges. Even though his client had admitted at the accident scene that she had been driving the car, Gross chose to present an alibi witness to testify that the defendant had been at home watching television. Upon discovering that the alibi witness also looked like the defendant, and believing that the accident victim could probably not identify the driver, Gross had the alibi witness impersonate the defendant in court. A police investigator present in the courtroom realized that the alibi witness was not the real defendant and that the defendant was present as a spectator. Even after the court questioned Gross as to the identity of the woman he had presented as the defendant, Gross continued to contend that she was his client. The district attorney reported this conduct to the state Board of Bar Overseers, and the Massachusetts Supreme Judicial Court upheld an 18–month suspension of Gross.

e.   May the lawyer pretend to be reading from a document, or pretend to have one, when he does not? See Model Rule 8.4(c). Consider Cincinnati Bar Ass'n v. Statzer, 800 N.E.2d 1117 (Ohio 2003), which sanctioned a lawyer for conduct during a deposition. In a hearing on allegations that the lawyer induced her former legal assistant to execute a false affidavit and provide false testimony, Statzer deposed the legal assistant. During the deposition, Statzer conspicuously placed nine audio cassette tapes in front of her former legal assistant. "By suggestively labeling the tapes and referring to them during questioning, respondent implied that she had recorded conversations with the legal assistant that could impeach and personally embarrass the legal assistant." The cassettes were actually blank or irrelevant and never introduced into evidence. Statzer contended that the tactic she employed was necessary "to draw honest testimony from a theretofore untrustworthy witness." The Ohio Supreme Court acknowledged the importance of latitude in the discovery process, but that does not include "subterfuge that intimidates a witness." While this kind of "deception may induce truthful testimony, it is just as likely to elicit lies if a witness believes that lies will offer security from the false threat. Respondent's deceitful tactic intimidated her witness by creating the false impression that respondent possessed compromising personal information that she could offer as evidence." The court imposed a six-month suspension, stayed on the condition that Statzer employ no further "fraud, deceit, dishonesty, or misrepresentation."

2.   May a lawyer use deception as part of law enforcement or other investigatory functions?

a.   A different use of deception in a search for truth is found in In re Gatti, 8 P.3d 966 (Or.2000). Lawyer Gatti knew that a company, CMR, did reviews for State Farm Insurance of how badly hurt claimants were. He believed State Farm had CMR deny benefits using a formula rather than relying on doctors' professional judgment of the injuries. State Farm denied the claim of Gatti's client, and the lawyer suspected that State Farm based its denial on a CMR report. The lawyer then called both the doctor who conducted the review for CMR and the director of operations for CMR. He said—or at least wanted them to believe—that he was a chiropractor who wanted to work as a claim reviewer for CMR. He asked them detailed questions about their protocols and guidelines, hoping in fact to develop facts to support a lawsuit, which he later filed, alleging fraud by CMR and State Farm.

The Oregon Supreme Court found that lawyer Gatti violated DR 1–102(A)(3) and DR 7–102(A)(5) [Model Rules 8.4(c) and 4.1]. "A misrepresentation may be a lie, a half-truth, or even silence," the court said, and a "material fact consists of information that, if disclosed, would have influenced the recipient's conduct." This lawyer's conduct clearly met that definition. The court, in this attorney discipline case, imposed a public reprimand.

The lawyer defended his conduct by saying that government lawyers use deception all the time in undercover operations that seek to "root out evil." He, too, was trying to root out evil in the insurance industry. Even the U.S. attorney intervened in the case to assert the importance of the government's ability to do undercover work, as did the Oregon Fair Housing Council and other groups that use testers to develop discrimination cases. However, the court held that there were no exceptions (not even a law enforcement exception) to the rule against misrepresentation. Until the court formally amends the Rules, it said, the prohibition applies to all lawyers in all cases. As you might imagine, this case joined Rule 4.2 as Exhibit A in the Justice Department's campaign against states subjecting federal prosecutors to state ethics rules while they engage in customary law enforcement operations.

What do you think of Gatti's defense? Is Model Rule 4.1(a) too absolute? Gatti, after all, was trying to get people to talk honestly, and they would not talk at all if he told them the truth.

b.   In response to the public reaction to *Gatti*, the Oregon Supreme Court amended its Code of Professional Responsibility DR 1–102 to add a (D) that says:

> "Notwithstanding DR 1–102(A)(1), (A)(3) and (A)(4) and DR 7–102(A)(5), it shall not be professional misconduct for a lawyer to advise clients or others about or to supervise lawful covert activity in the investigation of violations of civil or criminal law or constitutional rights, provided the lawyer's conduct is otherwise in compliance with these disciplinary rules. 'Covert activity,' as used in this rule, means an effort to obtain information on unlawful activity through the use of misrepresentations or other subterfuge. 'Covert activity' may be commenced by a lawyer or involve a lawyer as an adviser or supervisor only when the lawyer in good faith believes there is a reasonable possibility that unlawful activity has taken place, is taking place or will take place in the foreseeable future."

c.   D.C. Ethics Opinion 323 (Mar. 29, 2004) discussed "whether attorneys who are employed by a national intelligence agency violate the Rules of Professional Conduct if they engage in fraud, deceit, or misrepresentation in the course of their non-representational official duties." The opinion acknowledged that the law sometimes requires intelligence officers acting in their official capacity to act deceitfully. For example, a lawyer working for the CIA in a clandestine capacity might be required to offer false information about her identity or employment. The opinion concludes that Rule 8.4 addresses deceitful conduct that "calls into question a lawyer's suitability to practice law." Understood in this light, "the category of conduct proscribed by the Rule does not include misrepresentations made in the course of official conduct as an employee of an agency of the United States if the attorney reasonably believes that the conduct in question is authorized by law."

d.   What about "friending" a witness or opposing party on the social networks, MySpace or Facebook, to discover "public information" about the person? Philadelphia Bar Ass'n Professional Guidance Committee Opinion 2009–02 (Mar. 2009) held that a lawyer could not use an agent to friend a target in order to find out information on the personal page because such conduct involved deception under Rule 8.4(c). The opinion claimed that was improper even when the agent used a real name, because the purpose for contacting the target was not for friendship, but for gaining access to personal information. On the other hand, a Facebook "friend" is not like a real friend. A person might have thousands of Facebook "friends," but none of them invites him to

Thanksgiving dinner. If the lawyer or agent makes no misrepresentation and only asks the person to link as a "friend," what is wrong with that? If the person on Facebook does not like the invitation, he or she can simply not accept it.

e.   New York County Lawyers' Ass'n Ethics Opinion 289 (May 2007) concluded that lawyers may supervise nonlawyer investigators who use "dissemblance," defined as "misstatements as to identity and purpose made solely for gathering evidence," but only if four conditions are present. First, the investigation must (1) involve civil rights violations or intellectual property rights or (2) be authorized by law. Second, the evidence may not be readily available by other means. Third, the conduct may not otherwise violate ethical standards, and fourth, the dissemblance must not unlawfully or unethically violate the rights of third persons.

Now are you clear what you may and may not do? How would you resolve the conflicting concerns inherent in the use of deception in the search for truth?

C.   USING AN OPPONENT'S INADVERTENTLY DISCLOSED CONFIDENTIAL INFORMATION

1.   May a lawyer take advantage of a confidential email that her adversary inadvertently sent to her?

a.   Remember from Problem 7 that, under the rules of evidence, some courts hold that the inadvertent disclosure of confidential information forfeits the attorney-client evidentiary privilege, even if the lawyer acted "reasonably." Other courts are more forgiving, finding that inadvertent disclosure (whether reasonable or not) does not necessarily result in loss of the evidentiary privilege. The question remains what a litigator who *receives* such documents should do with them. If the law of evidence says that the party loses the privilege when the lawyer sends a misdirected email or fax (or loses the privilege if the lawyer acted negligently), does the lawyer *receiving* the email or fax have any ethical obligation in Model Rule 1.6 to refrain from using the document? May she use the misdirected fax or email to argue that the opposing lawyer has "waived" the privilege? *Must* she use, or try to use, the information as part of her duty to fight zealously for her client? Should the lawyer receiving this information let her opponent off the hook while thinking, "there but for the grace of God go I," or should she press the advantage on behalf of her own client?

b.   ABA Formal Opinion 92–368 (Nov. 10, 1992), came down in favor of letting the lawyer who made the mistake off the hook. It held that as a matter of ethical responsibility, a lawyer who gets misdirected material from an opponent should refrain from reading it, notify the sending lawyer, and either return or destroy the material as the sending lawyer directs.

c.   The Model Rules were silent on these issues until 2002. Then, the ABA House of Delegates added subsection (b) to Model Rule 4.4. This Rule requires a lawyer who receives an inadvertently sent document to "promptly notify the sender" but does not require the receiving lawyer to avoid reading or using the document. Faced with this change in law and policy, the ABA Standing Committee on Ethics and Professional Responsibility "withdrew" (i.e., overruled) Formal Opinion 92–368. See ABA Formal Opinion 05–437 (Oct. 1, 2005)

d.   Although most of the early rules and authorities dealing with the inadvertent disclosure issue discussed faxes, many lawyers believed that the same analysis should govern emails and other electronic communication. In August 2012, the ABA amended Rule 4.4(b) to include "electronically stored information." It also amended Comment 2 to interpret how this rule applies inadvertent disclosure to electronically stored information: "A document or electronically stored information is inadvertently sent when it is accidentally transmitted, such as when an email or letter is misaddressed or a document or electronically stored information is accidentally included with information that was intentionally transmitted."[13]

The use of the word, "included" seems to encompass attachments and text that appears within the communication. Would this provision apply to include the email path that often appears at the bottom of back and forth communication? Would it encompass a link at the bottom of an email that reveals to the recipient that a law firm has a data folder holding confidential client files on a cloud? What if a lawyer negligently gives an opposing lawyer a memory stick, part of which includes privileged client information? What if one lawyer negligently responds to a request for hard copy documents by including documents that are privileged?

e.   Look at Model Rule 4.4, Comment 2. When the recipient notifies the sending lawyer about the inadvertent disclosure, what "protective measures" should the sender seek? Should the sending lawyer ask the receiving lawyer whether she has read the confidential information, and if not, direct the receiving lawyer not to do so? Should the sending lawyer assert the attorney-client privilege to prevent use of the information in any proceeding? If the court finds that the sending lawyer waived the privilege, may the receiving lawyer take advantage of his adversary's mistake? If the receiving lawyer is not sure how the court would rule, does it make the most sense to ask the court to rule whether the rules of evidence in that jurisdiction say that misdirecting the fax serves to waive the privilege?[14]

Is the issue really a legal ethics question, or is it a question of evidence law? If the sending lawyer's mistake results in loss of the privilege, why can't the receiving lawyer take advantage of it, just as if she would take advantage of the adversary's mistake in not objecting to a question or his mistake in missing the statute of limitation.

f.   Now, look at Comment 3. What "professional judgment" is involved in deciding whether to return the document unread? Is the citation in Comment 3 to Model Rules 1.2 and 1.4 an implicit acknowledgment that the lawyer must tell the client: "Using the document is very helpful to us, and the rules of evidence in this

---

[13]   For a critical analysis of the ABA amendments to Rule 4.4(b), see Ronald D. Rotunda, Applying the Revised ABA Model Rules in the Age of the Internet: The Problem of Metadata, 20 Hofstra L. Rev. (2013).

[14]   Of course, when a lawyer learns about an inadvertent disclosure, the lawyer must revisit the measures used to protect against inadvertent disclosure of confidential information in the law firm. See Model Rule 1.6(c) and Comments 18–19. The lawyer may need to change or increase those protective measures so that they meet the standard of reasonableness.

jurisdiction conclude that their mistake serves to waive the privilege. So, you tell me what to do." If so, why does Comment 3 seem to say just the reverse?

g.   Suppose an employer's lawyer receives a copy of an employee's confidential communication from her counsel. The communication is an email containing information about the plaintiff's employment discrimination claim against the employer, but because the lawyer sent it to the employee' work computer, the employer copied the computer hard drive for use in the litigation. Does the employer's lawyer have a duty to inform the opposing lawyer under Rule 4.4(b)? ABA Formal Opinion 11–460 (Aug. 4, 2011) states that Rule 4.4(b) only applies to inadvertently sent communications and this situation does not fall within this definition. And, it goes on to opine that the ABA has declined to read this provision more broadly to develop a more general duty of disclosure. Ultimately, Rule 1.6(b)(6) and other law govern the lawyer's obligation to inform the other side. Do you agree with this narrow reading of 4.4(b)?

2.   If the other side's word processing program leaves metadata in documents turned over in discovery, may a lawyer receiving the documents use that metadata to learn more about the document (e.g., who drafted it, when, what earlier drafts looked like)?

a.   Some word processing programs such as Microsoft Word include a feature that allows someone who receives an electronic version of the document to see when the document was created, what changes were made in the document during its preparation. This information can be very helpful in determining authenticity of the document and alternatives the preparers considered and rejected. Most lawyers would not want their opponents to have that information, and yet the receiving party can retrieve the information easily. The information can be "scrubbed" and rendered unavailable by creating a PDF version of the document, but not everyone remembers to transmit only scrubbed versions. Further, the act of scrubbing itself in some cases might constitute obstruction of justice or spoliation of evidence.

b.   ABA Formal Opinion 06–422 (Aug. 2006) considered whether a lawyer who receives an unscrubbed document may properly access the metadata. It concluded somewhat controversially that if Rule 4.4(b) intended to treat metadata as inadvertent disclosure it would have said so. Therefore, the opinion placed no limitation on a recipient's retrieving and using the concealed information and said that anyone who does not want an opponent to use such information must negotiate a special agreement to that effect, or only send the document in hard copy, or send only a version in which the metadata is not retrievable. What do you think of the result reached in Opinion 06–422?[15]

c.   The ABA's amendment of Model Rule 4.4 added one sentence to Comment 2 regarding metadata. "Metadata in electronic documents creates an obligation under this Rule only if the receiving lawyer knows or reasonably should know that the metadata was inadvertently sent to the receiving lawyer." How can a receiving lawyer know or reasonably

---

[15]   Some state ethics opinions have come out the other way. See, e.g., New York State Bar Ethics Opinion 749 (Dec. 14, 2001); Alabama State Bar Opinion 2007–2 (Mar.14, 2007).

suspect whether opposing counsel intentionally or inadvertently included metadata? What factors should a lawyer consider? If the opposing lawyer is from a large law firm, should the receiving lawyer assume that large law firms educate their lawyers about metadata, so this had to be included intentionally? Or, if the opposing lawyer is computer illiterate, should you presume all metadata that appears on sent documents was inadvertent? Does the new language in Comment 2 reverse Opinion 06–422 or does it largely confirm that Opinion?

3. May (must) the lawyer use the information that a whistleblower from the opposing party *intentionally* sent?

a.   ABA Formal Opinion 94–382 (July 5, 1994) (withdrawn in 2005) did not deal with the misdirected fax but with documents that the sender intended to send to the lawyer although the sender had no authority to send. The sender might be a whistleblower, a disgruntled employee (whether or not the discontent is justified), or someone seeking to rectify what he or she considered to be improper or unjust conduct, for example, the failure to disclose documents pursuant to a valid subpoena.

The ABA opinion first discussed In re Shell Oil Refinery, 143 F.R.D. 105 (E.D.La.1992). That case required that the party receiving the materials not make use of them. The court required that person to identify and return the materials and have no further contact with the disclosing persons. The opinion noted (but did not find convincing) a number of state ethics opinions that concluded that "the receiving lawyer has no obligation to disclose to a court or an adverse party that she possesses the adverse party's privileged or confidential information and that the receiving lawyer may use such materials." The opinion rejected an "absolute rule that would prohibit a receiving lawyer from reviewing or using such materials under all circumstances;" the receiving lawyer, for example, may have a legitimate claim that the documents should have been produced during discovery, or the person sending the documents may be acting under the authority of a whistleblowing statute. The opinion recommended that the lawyer's actions include:

> "(a) refraining from reviewing materials which are probably privileged or confidential, any further than is necessary to determine how appropriately to proceed; (b) notifying the adverse party or the party's lawyer that the receiving lawyer possesses the documents, (c) following the instructions of the adverse party's lawyer, or (d), in the case of a dispute, refraining from using the materials until a definitive resolution of the proper disposition of the materials is obtained from a court."

Does this advice make sense to you?[16]

b.   It made sense to the court in Maldonado v. State, 225 F.R.D. 120 (D.N.J.2004). Maldonado sued for employment discrimination, a hostile work environment, and retaliation. Someone unknown sent Maldonado a copy of a letter that his employers addressed to their

---

[16]   ABA Formal Opinion 06–440 (May 13, 2006) withdrew Opinion 94–382, not because the analysis was wrong, but because the Model Rules as amended in 2002 seemed not to answer the question.

lawyer containing their impressions as to the credibility of certain prospective witnesses. Maldonado turned the document over to his lawyers, who incorporated the information into their amended complaint. The lawyers, however, did not notify opposing lawyers that they had possession of the letter. Defense counsel realized that the plaintiff had the letter when they received the amended complaint, so they asked the lawyers to return it. When Maldonado's lawyers refused, defense counsel sought a protective order. After a hearing, the trial judge ruled that the document was privileged and that defendants were not "careless in their handling of the letter." Defense counsel moved to dismiss the case or to disqualify plaintiff's lawyers based on the substantial prejudice their knowledge would have on the defendants' case at trial. The judge refused to dismiss the case, but, relying on ABA Formal Opinion 94–382, he decided that the plaintiff's lawyers, after their reading showed that the information was privileged, should have notified opposing counsel and returned the document. Because plaintiff's lawyers were wrongly privy to what was "[e]ssentially . . . a blue print to [the] merits" of his case, their continued representation would have a "substantial taint" on future proceedings. So, the court disqualified the lawyers.[17]

c.   State Bar of California Standing Comm. On Professional Responsibility and Conduct, Formal Opinion 2013–188 holds that a lawyer may not read or use otherwise facially privileged documents sent by a whistleblower. Even if the cover letter suggests the documents might fall outside the privilege because of the crime or fraud exception, the lawyer must notify opposing counsel and try to work out a solution. Another option is to receive court permission to read or use the documents.[18]

d.   Do these "stolen papers" cases present different issues than those raised by the "inadvertent disclosure" cases? Does Model Rule 4.4(b)'s approach work in both situations?

---

[17] See also Lipin v. Bender, 644 N.E.2d 1300 (N.Y.1994) (plaintiff took privileged documents belonging to defense counsel that she found in a conference room while the lawyers were engaged in a heated exchange; court dismissed the plaintiff's complaint with prejudice).

[18] The opinion is consistent with Rico v. Mitsubishi Motors Corp., 171 P.3d 1092 (Cal.2007), where the defense lawyer made notes of a meeting with defense experts discussing litigation strategy and vulnerabilities. Later, the defense lawyer deposed the plaintiff's experts and left the notes in his briefcase while he went to the restroom. Somehow, the plaintiff's lawyer got the defense notes; the court could only say that it was "through inadvertence." Thereafter, the plaintiff's lawyer made copies of the notes and used them to impeach the defense experts at their deposition. When the defense realized what had happened, it moved to disqualify the plaintiff's lawyer and experts. The court agreed. The notes were attorney work product and absolutely protected against discovery, the court held. Where a lawyer "receives materials that obviously appear to be * * * confidential and privileged and where it is reasonably apparent that the materials were provided or made available through inadvertence, the lawyer receiving the materials should refrain from examining the materials any more than is essential to ascertain if the materials are privileged, and shall immediately notify the sender that he or she possesses material that appears to be privileged. The parties may then proceed to resolve the situation by agreement or may resort to the court for guidance * * *." The plaintiff's lawyer admitted that he had soon known the document was confidential and that he had not notified the defense, so the court affirmed the order of disqualification.

PROBLEM 25

DISCLOSURE OF LAW OR FACTS FAVORABLE TO THE OTHER SIDE

Confidentiality is the watchword for much of what a lawyer does. Litigators in particular assert work product immunity, as well as the attorney-client privilege and their ethical duty of confidentiality, as bases for nondisclosure. Some advocates are surprised to learn that the confidentiality obligation has important exceptions. Indeed, in some situations, the law requires lawyers to volunteer information they prefer to keep undisclosed. This problem begins by discussing the duty to reveal adverse legal authority. It then examines when the rules require the lawyer to disclose factual information. Next, it explores the lawyer's duty when discovery responses have been incomplete or inaccurate, and it examines the lawyer's duty where the court's mistake about publicly available information favors the lawyer's client.

FACTS

You have prepared your case fully, and you consider it a sure winner on the motion for summary judgment. However, hours before the argument on that motion, you discovered several cases with dicta directly against you. Two of the cases have holdings that by analogy are against you. You have concluded that the likelihood is great that the judge would rule against your client on the summary judgment motion if she knew of the cases you have discovered. Your opponent (perhaps because he is less prepared than you) has not referred to these cases.

Now, you have come across a witness who can supply a *factual* piece of evidence harmful to your client's case. You conclude that if you make a motion for summary judgment you would win because opposing counsel has not been able to present an affidavit on a vital point. However, your secretly-discovered witness could supply the essential link in the opposition's evidentiary chain. The opposing party has not contacted this witness, and you assume no one else knows of his existence.

You are in the midst of discovery. The other side has asked your client to produce emails and documents pertaining to the litigation. Your client has several mainframe computers full of information. Your client also automatically deletes emails daily that are over three months old. You are concerned that such data may be part of the discovery request. But as a lawyer, you are not computer savvy and will simply do your best to comply.

As you are reviewing the deposition testimony that you have attached to your motion for summary judgment, you realize that one of your best witnesses testified about a fact important to your case in a way that you know is false. You don't know whether she was lying or simply mistaken, and the other side clearly has not discovered the inaccuracy.

In another case, you represent a convicted client who stands before the judge in a sentencing hearing. The court clerk indicates to the court that the defendant has no record. The court thereupon says to the defendant—who stands silent—"Since you have no criminal record, I will only put you on probation." You know, either by independent investigation or from what your client has told you, that he in fact has a criminal record and the clerk's information is incorrect. The judge turns to you and says, "Anything to add, counsel?"

QUESTIONS

A.   CANDOR ABOUT ADVERSE LEGAL AUTHORITY

1.   Must you cite all relevant cases to the court, even those not favorable to your position? What are the limits, if any, on that obligation?

a.   Look at Model Rule 3.3(a)(2). What does this rule imply the courts expect of a lawyer? May you simply put contrary cases in a footnote in your brief without in any way explaining their relevance? Do you have to highlight the contrary authority?

b.   In Katris v. Immigration and Naturalization Service, 562 F.2d 866 (2d Cir.1977), the attorney for petitioner failed to cite a particular Second Circuit case and several cases from other circuits because, he said "these decisions were adverse to his position here and that he did not agree with them." The attorney had represented one of the parties in the adverse Second Circuit case. The court concluded the lawyer misled the court and taxed costs against the attorney personally.

c.   ABA Informal Opinion 84–1505 (Mar. 5, 1984) reaffirmed the disclosure obligation. A plaintiff's lawyer successfully defeated the defendant's motion to dismiss in a case of first impression interpreting a recently enacted statute. Based on earlier analogous cases, the trial court's ruling was correct. Later, however, during the pendency of the action, plaintiff's lawyer learned that an appellate court elsewhere in the state recently interpreted the statute in a way that was arguably contrary to the trial court's ruling. He asked the ABA Standing Committee on Ethics and Professional Responsibility whether he must disclose the new appellate opinion to the trial court. Even though one could interpret the appellate ruling in a way not "directly adverse to the position of the client," another reading was clearly adverse. The trial court would certainly benefit in this case of first impression by knowing about the appellate decision, so the ABA Committee concluded that the plaintiff's lawyer must reveal it to the court.

d.   In re Thonert, 733 N.E.2d 932 (Ind.2000), involved a client who wanted to withdraw his guilty plea. The lawyer argued that the trial judge had a duty to ask whether the client understood his rights at the time of the plea, in spite of the fact the client had seen a videotape explaining those rights. The lawyer's position was directly contrary to a decision made by the same Indiana Supreme Court a year earlier in a case argued by the same lawyer. He neither cited that decision nor argued that the result should be changed or distinguished. For the failure to do so—and for taking a fee from the client without disclosing

their names or role. See, e.g., Kansas Bar Association, Legal Ethics Opinion 09–01 (Nov. 2009). Other authorities do not require the lawyers to disclose anything. This is the view adopted by the ABA in ABA Formal Opinion 07–446 (May 5, 2007), which concludes that "there is no reasonable concern that a litigant appearing *pro se* will receive an unfair benefit from a tribunal as a result of behind-the-scenes legal assistance." If that is so, why are lawyers and their apparently *pro se* clients often reluctant to admit the lawyers' involvement?

C.   CANDOR ABOUT INCOMPLETE OR INACCURATE DISCOVERY RESPONSES

1.   What obligations do you have to comply with discovery requests by the opposing party?

a.   Model Rule 3.4(d) requires that a lawyer make a "reasonably diligent effort to comply with a legally proper discovery request." Of course, this brings into consideration the entire body of discovery law and procedure. In the 1970s, Federal Rule of Civil Procedure 26 implemented modern discovery governing depositions, written interrogatories, document production, physical examinations, and requests for admissions. The basic principle authorized lawyers to engage in a broad search reasonably calculated to lead to the discovery of admissible evidence. In the 1980s, judges began to use discovery conferences to manage discovery issues and abuse. In 1983, the Court amended the rules to authorize courts to provide for protective orders that limit discovery and impose some standards on lawyers to ensure that they only engage in legitimate discovery requests.

b.   Historically, lawyers treated discovery as a poker match. If the opposing party did not ask the question, the lawyer had no obligation to disclose adverse information. Over the years, scholars and judges sought to move the gaming of discovery to a more open and cooperative system. In the 1990s, the federal rules and several federal courts moved to a system of open discovery, which obligated both parties to share all information relating to the claims and defenses presented by the parties. Open discovery presented interesting ethical issues when it appeared to ask lawyers to self-disclose information relevant to the other side's case. Some questioned how such discovery methods could co-exist with an adversary system.

c.   Modern storage of data in computer files instead of file cabinets requires discovery rules that recognize electronic data as a major source of discoverable information necessary for litigation. Once a party files suit, what must a client do with electronic files and data? What are the lawyer's obligations to ask a client to preserve this information? If the client's IT (Information Technology] department claims that it is too costly to search for and provide this electronic information, may the client refuse to cooperate in discovery? And, if the lawyers and clients delay in preserving such information, what should a court do when such data if a party destroyed or altered electronic data?

In a prominent series of decisions that largely created the modern world of e-discovery, Judge Shira Scheindlin addressed the application of traditional discovery rules to electronic data in the context of a gender discrimination lawsuit against UBS Warburg. Zubulake v. UBS Warburg, LLC, 217 F.R.D. 309 (S.D.N.Y. 2003) (*Zubulake I*), held that a plaintiff has a right to electronically stored emails as documents within the scope of proper discovery.

The defendant refused to provide plaintiff with access to data on backup tapes because it was costly to make this data accessible. In response, Judge Scheindlin crafted a multifactor test to determine how the parties should share the costs. With respect to accessible data in a computer-readable format, the producing party must bear the costs of production. But with respect to restoring inaccessible data, the court must balance factors of need, the amounts at stake in the litigation, the importance of the issues in the case, and the benefit to the parties of obtaining the information. In *Zubulake III*, the judge held that the plaintiff should pay 25% of the costs of restoring the data. Zubulake v. UBS Warburg, 216 F.R.D. 280, 292 (S.D.N.Y. 2003).[21]

UBS Warburg was unable to produce some of the data because it had destroyed it, and Judge Scheindlin ruled: "Once a party reasonably anticipates litigation, it must suspend its routine document retention/destruction policy and put in place a 'litigation hold' to ensure the preservation of relevant documents." Zubulake v. UBS Warburg, 220 F.R.D. 212 (2003) (*Zubulake IV*).

In *Zubulake IV*, the court imposed no sanctions because the other party did not prove the value of the lost information. However, when subsequent depositions of the UBS Warburg witnesses disclosed that defendant had destroyed additional emails after receiving instructions from counsel to retain all emails, in *Zubulake V*, Judge Scheindlin found willful destruction of discoverable evidence and ordered an adverse inference instruction to the jury. Zubulake v. UBS Warburg, 229 F.R.D. 422 (S.D.N.Y. 2004). A jury awarded Ms. Zubulake $29 million at trial. Taken together, this series of decisions illustrated the need for lawyers to preserve electronic data and to instruct clients on the obligations under the discovery rules.

d. The 2006 amendments to the Federal Rules of Civil Procedure specifically address e-discovery. Under Rule 34, a party may request electronic data as part of its discovery request. The other party must produce this information in an accessible format. Parties may object to production of electronic data on the grounds of its cost or undue burden. See Fed.R.Civ.P. 26(b)(2)(B). Under Rule 26(c), a judge may limit or condition disclosure of electronic information after considering a series of factors. Rule 37 provides a safe harbor for electronic data that is lost "as a result of the routine, good-faith operation of an electronic information system."

e. What does the average litigator know about electronically-stored information in a client database? Given what may be a lack of knowledge, how can a lawyer comply with discovery rules? At a minimum, lawyers need to inform their clients about the litigation hold and duty to provide accessible data. But should lawyers have a duty to physically monitor compliance with these electronic discovery rules?

---

[21] Zubulake v. UBS Warburg, LLC, 230 F.R.D. 290 (S.D.N.Y.2003) (Zubulake II) involved the plaintiff's request to disclose the transcript of a UBS Manager's deposition to the SEC because it revealed that UBS had failed to follow SEC document retention policies. The court denied the motion because it found that the plaintiff had no duty to disclose such information to the SEC.

Should law firms have a computer specialist on staff to ensure client compliance with these rules?

2. What should a lawyer do if, as in this problem, she discovers that the client or a material witness has given false testimony in a deposition?

a.   Look at Rule 3.3(a)(1) and Rule 3.3(a)(3). Must a lawyer reveal the truth if doing so will injure the client? ABA Formal Opinion 93–376 (Aug. 6, 1993) made clear that a lie in response to a deposition question or a discovery request is "perjury" and the requirement of current Model Rule 3.3(a)(3) controls. As provided in Model Rule 3.3, Comment 1, the lawyer has an obligation to correct the record in spite of the usual operation of Model Rule 1.6.

b.   Jones v. Clinton, 36 F.Supp.2d 1118 (E.D.Ark.1999), confirms the client's duty not to dissemble in a deposition. Judge Wright held President Clinton in contempt for providing misleading answers in his deposition in a case filed by Paula Jones, an Arkansas state employee, alleging sexual harassment. Judge Wright noted she had ruled that Ms. Jones, in discovery, was entitled to "information regarding any individuals with whom the President had sexual relations * * * and who were during the relevant time frame state or federal employees." In spite of those rulings, Judge Wright found that "the President responded to plaintiff's questions by giving false, misleading and evasive answers that were designed to obstruct the judicial process." The two answers that Judge Wright found no reasonable person could believe were truthful were whether the president had ever been alone with Monica Lewinsky and whether he had ever had sexual relations with her. Judge Wright also referred the matter to the Arkansas Supreme Court for possible disciplinary action because President Clinton, the deponent, was also a lawyer. The Arkansas court suspended President Clinton from practice for five years and fined him $25,000.[22]

c.   Feld's Case, 815 A.2d 383 (N.H.2002), suspended attorney Feld for one year for violating Rules 3.4 and 8.4 during discovery. Feld's clients, who recently purchased a piece of property, filed an eviction claim against Bussiere. Prior to the purchase, Bussiere notified the clients that he had a leasehold interest and enclosed supporting documentation. When questioned during discovery, however, Feld's clients denied knowledge of Bussiere's documentation. Feld " 'orchestrated, assisted, counseled and tolerated the formulation of inaccurate and incomplete sworn responses that he knew were inaccurate' in violation of New Hampshire Rules of Professional Conduct 3.4 and 8.4." Feld was also present during his client's deposition where she gave numerous evasive answers. "Given the importance placed by Bussiere upon this line of inquiry, and Feld's repeated involvement with false answers, the record does not support

---

[22] Neal v. Clinton, 2001 WL 34355768 (Ark.Cir.2001). The United States Supreme Court suspended Mr. Clinton from practice before it and issued a rule to show cause, returnable in 40 days, why he should not be disbarred. In re Discipline of Clinton, 534 U.S. 806 (2001). On the 40th day, Mr. Clinton resigned from membership in the Supreme Court bar.

The president's counsel, Robert Bennett, later notified Judge Wright that he had, unknowingly, submitted false evidence during the course of the president's deposition. See 36 F.Supp.2d at 1130 n. 15.

Feld's claim that his assistance with the response to the request for admission was inadvertent." In another incident, the client answered evasively on the nature of his involvement with the financing of the property. "A pattern of evasive or non-responsive conduct, such as that demonstrated in the responses to the interrogatory," the court held, "demonstrates a lawyer's failure 'to make reasonably diligent effort to comply with a legally proper discovery request made by an opposing party.'" The one-year suspension imposed by the court was equivalent to similar sanctions it had imposed for intentional deceit during trial.

D.   CANDOR ABOUT FACTUAL MATTERS THAT ARE NOT EASILY VERIFIABLE

1.   Is the third item not disclosed to the court in this problem—the prior criminal record of your client—a factual matter or a legal matter, i.e., is it more analogous to the situation in Part A or Part B of the problem?

a.   Is a conviction legal authority? Does the defense counsel have an obligation to correct the court clerk who mistakenly informed the judge that the client had no previous record? In ABA Formal Opinion 287 (June 27, 1953), the ethics committee ruling on this question split three ways. The committee included Henry S. Drinker, later author of *Legal Ethics*, and William B. Jones, later a district judge in the District of Columbia. The majority concluded:

"If the court asks the lawyer whether the clerk's statement is correct, the lawyer is not bound by fidelity to the client to tell the court what he knows to be an untruth, and should ask the court to excuse him from answering the question, and retire from the case, though this would doubtless put the court on further inquiry as to the truth.

"Even, however, if the court does not directly ask the lawyer this question, such an inquiry may well be implied from the circumstances, including the lawyer's previous relations with the court. The situation is analogous to that discussed in our Opinion 280 where counsel knows of an essential decision not cited by his opponent and where his silence might reasonably be regarded by the Court as an implied representation by him that he knew of no such authority. If, under all the circumstances, the lawyer believes that the court relies on him as corroborating the correctness of the statement by the clerk or by the client that the client has no criminal record, the lawyer's duty of candor and fairness to the court requires him, in our opinion, to advise the court not to rely on counsel's personal knowledge as to the facts of the client's record. * * * The indignation of the court * * * on learning that the lawyer had deliberately permitted him, where no privileged communication is involved, to rely on what the lawyer knew to be a misapprehension of the true facts, would be something that the lawyer could not appease on the basis of loyalty to the client. No client may demand or expect of his lawyer, in the furtherance of his cause, disloyalty to the law whose minister he is (Canon 32) or 'any manner of fraud or chicane' (Canon 15).

"If the lawyer is quite clear that the court does not rely on him as corroborating, by his silence, the statement of the clerk or of his client, the lawyer is not, in our opinion, bound to speak out."

The dissenting opinion argued that the lawyer may in no event "stand idly by in open court and permit the court to be deceived at a time when the lawyer knows that the court is relying upon an untrue statement."[23]

b.   What is the law today, under Rule 3.3, if the court clerk mistakenly tells the court that the defendant has no criminal record? The lawyer did not make a false statement about the client's previous record; the client made no statement; the lawyer called no witness who misled. Will the lawyer be confirming a false statement (that the client has no criminal record) if she simply stands silent?

The ABA Committee on Ethics and Professional Responsibility revisited this issue after adoption of the Model Rules and concluded that, on the assumption that the client has engaged in no fraud or perjury, the ABA Committee "could offer no better guidance under the Model Rules" than that offered by the authors of Formal Opinion 287. ABA Formal Opinion 87–353 (Apr. 20, 1987). California Formal Opinion 1986–87 (undated) is to the same effect. Do you agree with this analysis? Is the proposed course of conduct workable? If the judge turns to you and asks, "Anything to add, counsel?" what do you say? Do you just hem and haw?

2.   In determining what to say about the criminal record, is it helpful to analyze the distinction between candor regarding adverse law and nondisclosure of adverse facts?

a.   Is the distinction best grounded in the law of confidential client information? Although one may correctly view disclosure of contrary legal authority as detrimental to the client, is such information part of as the client's confidential information? Is all "information relating to the representation" properly viewed as confidential? Cf., Model Rule 1.9, Comment 8 (lawyer can use information that is "generally known" in a later case on behalf of another client).

b.   ABA Formal Opinion 93–370 (Feb. 5, 1993) addressed whether a court should ask a lawyer to be candid about the limits of the lawyer's settlement authority. The opinion recognized that settlement discussions are an important part of modern trial management but concluded that a lawyer should not tell a judge the extent of his settlement authority. Further, because this authority is a "material fact" the lawyer cannot lie if asked, so the judge should not inquire into it.

Is asking about the client's criminal record the same as asking about the lawyer's settlement authority? If asked either question, should a lawyer tell the judge, "Don't ask me about that?" Or, "I am not permitted to answer that question?" Is there any way to deflect a judge's question gracefully?

---

[23] ABA Formal Opinion 287 also considered what the lawyer should do if the lawyer knows that the client will lie about his or her previous record or the lawyer later discovers that the client lied. Problem 27, *infra* considers these issues.

c.   ABA Formal Opinion 98–412 (Sept. 9, 1998) dealt with the obligation of a lawyer who learns that his client has violated a court order prohibiting the transfer of assets. The opinion says that the lawyer must disclose the fact to the court (1) if necessary to avoid or correct a misrepresentation made by the lawyer to the court, or (2) to avoid assisting the client in a fraud upon the court. If the lawyer has made misstatements to the court, Rule 3.3(a)(1) requires the lawyer to make a correction. If the client made the misstatement, what is now Rule 3.3(a)(3) requires the correction. If no one has made a misrepresentation, the opinion says, the lawyer does not have to report a violation of a court order if the violation is unlikely to have a material effect on the resolution of the case. However, if failure to report the violation would imply that all was well, a lawyer must correct that misapprehension.[24]

Are the governing principles all becoming clear to you? How, for example, is the lawyer supposed to know if failure to report the violation implies that all is well?

————

PROBLEM 26

HANDLING PHYSICAL EVIDENCE

Information "relating to the representation" comes in a variety of forms. Model Rule 1.6(a) requires a lawyer to hold most in confidence most information relating to the representation. Yet the lawyer *may* disclose some kinds of confidential material and *must* disclose other types of information. In this problem, we first examine the name of the client, normally something a lawyer discloses to anyone with whom the lawyer deals. Next, we look at physical evidence of a crime that has come into the lawyer's possession. Then, we ask whether there is a difference between concealing information and simply not disclosing it. Finally, we consider how a lawyer may advise a client on whether and when he or she may or should destroy documents or other potential evidence of misconduct.

FACTS

Neil Hammer, a person whom you have never advised before, has come into your office, set a gun and a bag of money on your desk, and said, "I have just used this gun to rob a bank, and I killed a guard in the process. Help me. I don't want to get caught. What should I do?"

Only yesterday, J.B. Wallace, president of the Wallace Corporation, came into your office. The *Wall Street Journal* had reported that the Justice Department is investigating a firm in Wallace's industry for possible price fixing. A *Wall Street Journal* reporter asked to interview Mr. Wallace about

———

[24] ABA Formal Opinion 98–412 also says that if the client discharges the lawyer before the client engages in misconduct, but the lawyer knows that client plans to engage in misconduct, the lawyer has neither the duty nor the right to disclose those plans, even to successor counsel, without the client's consent. Is that advice, written in 1998, consistent with the present version of Model Rule 3.3(b)?

industry pricing practices, and Mr. Wallace asked you to help him prepare for the interview. He told you that in order to help you evaluate any allegation involving him and price fixing, you could listen to the secret tape recordings of all discussions in his office for the last three years. He keeps these tapes at his home and plans to use them to help write his memoirs. You later learned that the department is about to file a criminal antitrust action against the corporation and perhaps Mr. Wallace personally.

The local police have contacted you about reports that a man with a gun was seen entering your office. You are thinking about how to respond.

QUESTIONS

A. CONFIDENTIALITY OF A CLIENT'S IDENTITY

1. What will you say when the police ask you who came to your office at the time a witness saw Hammer enter? Are the names of your clients confidential? How about the names of your prospective clients?

a.   Client identity is not normally confidential; it is something the lawyer is "impliedly authorized" to disclose. After all, if lawyers did not tell courts and other lawyers whom they represented, the lawyers could get little done for those clients. However, a client may ask an attorney to keep the client's identity confidential from third persons. A lawyer may act as an agent for an undisclosed principal in purchasing real estate. Or a lawyer may represent several confidential investors putting together a bid for a race track. The ethical duty of confidentiality governs the analysis of these questions.

Suppose the prosecutor calls the lawyer before the grand jury to disclose information about the client? The usual evidentiary rule is that the identity of the client, the amount of the fee, the identification of payment by case file name, and the general purpose of the work performed are not protected from disclosure by the attorney-client privilege, because such information ordinarily reveals no confidential professional communications between attorney and client.

On the other hand, what if there are situations in which the fact one had consulted a lawyer is itself incriminating or embarrassing? Suppose you are a divorce lawyer. During an Internal Revenue Service audit of your tax records, the investigator discovers a $25,000 cash deposit that you made into your client trust account marked "retainer." The client has not yet told his wife he is considering a divorce. If the investigator asks you to identify the source of the money, may you reply without obtaining the client's permission? In such cases, disclosing the identity of the husband may disclose that he is considering a divorce from his wife.

b.   Baird v. Koerner, 279 F.2d 623 (9th Cir.1960), is the leading case on the attorney-client privilege and client identity. The clients consulted a lawyer for legal advice as to what to do about unpaid taxes. Paying the taxes stops the accrual of interest, and there are clients who would like to clear their consciences by paying the money owed, but do not want to confess to tax fraud. The lawyer, on behalf of the undisclosed clients, paid the additional income tax. The IRS wanted to know the clients' identity, but the court concluded that the attorney-client privilege protected the clients' identity from disclosure.

If the unidentified clients in *Baird* hired a nonlawyer to deliver the money to the IRS, would there be any evidentiary privilege protecting the nonlawyer from disclosing the identity of the payer? Why should the fact that the money was transmitted by a lawyer change that result?

c. Restatement Third, The Law Governing Lawyers § 69, Comment *g*, concludes that the privileged character of client identity cannot be determined categorically but should be decided based on the extent to which the information sought would, "directly or by reasonable inference, reveal the *content* of a privileged communication" (emphasis added). The evidentiary privilege, the Restatement continues, does not protect clients or lawyers "against revealing a lawyer's knowledge about a client solely on the grounds that doing so would incriminate the client or otherwise prejudice the client's interests."

d. In a criminal setting, some cases have called the *Baird* rule the "last link" doctrine: if the fact of consultation would itself be sufficient to tie the client to a crime, the lawyer should not have to disclose the client's identity. See, e.g., In re Grand Jury Proceedings 88–9, Cherney, 899 F.2d 1039, 1043 (11th Cir.1990):

> "the 'last link' doctrine is only applicable to rare situations 'where the disclosure of fee information would give the identity of a previously undisclosed client/suspect.' In essence, the last link doctrine extends the protection of the attorney-client privilege to nonprivileged information—the identity of the client—when 'disclosure of that identity would disclose *other*, privileged communications (e.g., motive or strategy) and when the incriminating nature of the privileged communications has created in the client a reasonable expectation that the information would be kept confidential.' "

2. Would you rule the client identity privileged in the following cases?

a. Baltes v. Doe I, 57 U.S.L.W. 2268 (Fla.Cir.Ct.1988) (No. CL–88–1145–AD), was a celebrated case where a client told a lawyer that he was the driver in a highly publicized hit-and-run accident. Without disclosing the client's identity, the lawyer tried to plea bargain on his behalf. The victim's survivors filed a civil action against the unknown driver and tried to compel the lawyer to disclose his identity. The trial court held that, under these circumstances, the client's identity is privileged. The client ultimately turned himself in before a higher court heard the appeal.

b. Matter of Nackson, 555 A.2d 1101 (N.J.1989), considered whether an attorney may refuse to disclose the whereabouts of a client who jumped bail and consulted the lawyer about a fugitive warrant for his arrest. The client wanted to return to the jurisdiction only if his lawyer could work out a plea agreement in advance. Citing *Baltes*, the court held that the privilege applied. The lawyer may not disclose the client's whereabouts. The court relied on matrimonial cases, holding that the attorney need not disclose the whereabouts of a wife who feared injury from her husband. The privilege is not absolute, the court said, but prosecutors must first use all other reasonable ways of learning the defendant's whereabouts. Even then, before ordering disclosure, the lower court must "balance" the need to know against the client's right to confidentiality. However, the court did not calibrate the scales and tell us how to weigh the competing interests. The court did not refer to the last link doctrine.

Should the court deny the applicability of the privilege on the ground that the purpose of keeping the client's whereabouts secret was to assist the client to avoid lawful process in a proceeding pending at the time the lawyer gave his advice? See In re Doe, 456 N.Y.S.2d 312 (1982) (bail jumper's counsel required to reveal his client's whereabouts to a grand jury).

c.   In re Grand Jury Subpoena, 204 F.3d 516 (4th Cir.2000), was a successful effort to force a lawyer to reveal his client's identity. The government filed a petition for forfeiture of property used as an open-air drug market. The property was titled in the name "Daniel C. Quispehuman," a name likely to be a straw owner. The lawyer said that he would be representing the owner of the property whom he said was not Quispehuman, but he refused to reveal the client's real name because, he argued, its disclosure would reveal the client's confidential communication—his motive or purpose for seeking legal advice. The court agreed that a lawyer sometimes may avoid identifying a client who has not sought to get involved in a matter. However, once the client authorized the attorney to disclose the client's motives or purposes in retaining the attorney (to deal with the allegations of drug-trafficking on his property), those motives or purposes were no longer confidential, and thus the client's identity was not within the attorney-client evidentiary privilege. The court specifically rejected the "last link" doctrine as giving too much protection to clients.

d.   Levy v. Senate of Pennsylvania, 65 A.3d 361 (Pa. 2013), involved a media inquiry seeking bills paid by the state senate for representation of a senator facing a grand jury investigation. Should the press have access to such information? The Pennsylvania Supreme Court held that client identity and legal bills are privileged if they "would reveal information otherwise protected by the attorney-client privilege." The court expressly distinguished its analysis from the "last link" doctrine that focuses "on the potential negative consequences of the disclosure rather than on whether exposing the identity will divulge otherwise protectable information."

3.   Must you appeal a court order making you reveal your client's identity?

a.   Suppose you refuse to disclose the client's identity to the investigator. The IRS, in turn, asserts a claim against you for back taxes on the $25,000, asserting that it is unreported income. Are you still obliged not to disclose the name of the client? Look at Model Rule 1.6(b)(5).[25]

---

[25]   26 U.S.C.A. § 6050I, adopted as part of the war on drugs, requires cash transactions in excess of $10,000 to be reported to the Internal Revenue Service on its Form 8300. On its face, the requirement applies to everyone, but lawyers have argued that transactions with them

b.   Suppose, in order to test a lower court order, you must appeal it. Must you go to jail before revealing the client's identity? Does Model Rule 1.6(b)(6) adopt the position of two judges in People v. Kor, 277 P.2d 94 (Cal.Ct.App.1954), who stated that the attorney, rather than having testified, "should have chosen to go to jail and take his chances of release by a higher court"? Is such self-sacrifice necessary or realistic?

c.   The cases deal with the evidentiary privilege. The confidentiality protection of Model Rule 1.6 is broader. Assume that the court rules that the name of the client who owns property in your trust account is unprivileged and orders you to disclose the name to the grand jury. You do so. Then, you leave the grand jury room and a reporter asks you, "Did you disclose the name of your client?" You respond that you obeyed the court order. The reporter then says, "What is the name?" Can you answer that question, knowing that the court held that the evidentiary privilege did not to apply to the information and that you earlier disclosed the name to the grand jury?

B.   TAKING POSSESSION OF PHYSICAL EVIDENCE FOR TESTING OR SAFEKEEPING

1.   May you take Hammer's gun for safekeeping? If Hammer turns the gun over to you, does the attorney-client privilege protect the gun from discovery?

a.   The leading case on that issue is In re Richard R. Ryder, 263 F.Supp. 360 (E.D.Va.) (per curiam), aff'd per curiam, 381 F.2d 713 (4th Cir.1967). The issue before the district court was whether to remove Richard R. Ryder, a former assistant U.S. attorney, from practice before that court.

"On August 24, 1966 a man armed with a sawed-off shotgun robbed the Varina Branch of the Bank of Virginia of $7,583. Included in the currency taken were $10 bills known as 'bait money,' the serial numbers of which had been recorded.

"On August 26, 1966, [after a bank robbery], Charles Richard Cook rented safety deposit box 14 at a branch of the Richmond National Bank. Later in the day Cook was interviewed at his home by agents of the Federal Bureau of Investigation, who obtained $348 from him. Cook telephoned Ryder, who had represented him in civil litigation. * * *

"Later that afternoon Ryder telephoned one of the agents and asked whether any of the bills obtained from Cook had been identified as a part of the money taken in the bank robbery. The agent told him that some bills had been identified. * * *

"The next morning, * * * Ryder conferred with Cook again. He urged Cook to tell the truth, and Cook answered that a man, whose name he would not divulge, offered him $500 on the day of the robbery to put a package in a bank lockbox. Ryder did not believe this story. Ryder told Cook that if the

---

should be exempt from the requirement. The IRS considers lawyers subject to the law, but criminal defense lawyers complain that reporting will render Baird v. Koerner a nullity. Problem 29, *infra* also discusses this issue.

government could trace the money in the box to him, it would be almost conclusive evidence of his guilt. He knew that Cook was under surveillance and he suspected that Cook might try to dispose of the money.

"That afternoon Ryder telephoned a former officer of the Richmond Bar Association to discuss his course of action. * * *

"The lawyers discussed and rejected alternatives, including having a third party get the money. At the conclusion of the conversation Ryder was advised 'Don't do it surreptitiously and do be sure that you let your client know that it is going back to the rightful owners.' * * *

"Ryder did not follow the advice he had received on Saturday. He did not let his client know the money was going back to the rightful owners. He testified about his omission:

'I prepared [the power of attorney] myself and told Mr. Cook to sign it. In the power of attorney, I did not specifically say that Mr. Cook authorized me to deliver that money to the appropriate authorities at any time because for a number of reasons. One, in representing a man under these circumstances, you've got to keep the man's confidence, but I also put in that power of attorney that Mr. Cook authorized me to dispose of that money as I saw fit, and the reason for that being that I was going to turn the money over to the proper authorities at whatever time I deemed that it wouldn't hurt Mr. Cook.'

"Ryder took the power of attorney which Cook had signed to the Richmond National Bank. He rented box 13 in his name with his office address, presented the power of attorney, entered Cook's box, took both boxes into a booth, where he found a bag of money and a sawed-off shotgun in Cook's box. * * * He transferred the contents of Cook's box to his own and returned the boxes to the vault. He left the bank, and neither he nor Cook returned.

" * * * Within a half-hour after he left the bank, he talked to a retired judge and distinguished professor of law. * * * Ryder testified that he told about the shotgun. The judge also testified that Ryder certainly would not have been under the impression that he—the judge—thought that [Ryder] was guilty of unethical conduct. That same day Ryder talked with other prominent persons [and] was advised that a lawyer could not receive the property and if he had received it he could not retain possession of it. * * *

"On September 12, 1966, F.B.I. agents procured search warrants for Cook's and Ryder's safety deposit boxes in the Richmond National Bank. They found Cook's box empty. In Ryder's box they discovered $5,920 of the $7,583 taken in the bank robbery and the sawed-off shotgun used in the robbery. * * *

"We reject the argument that Ryder's conduct was no more than the exercise of the attorney-client privilege. * * *

"It was Ryder, not his client, who took the initiative in transferring the incriminating possession of the stolen money and the shotgun from Cook. Ryder's conduct went far beyond the receipt and retention of a confidential communication from his client. * * *

"The money in Cook's box belonged to the Bank of Virginia. The law did not authorize Cook to conceal this money or withhold it from the bank. His larceny was a continuing offense. Cook had no title or property interest in the money that he lawfully could pass to Ryder. * * * No canon of ethics or law permitted Ryder to conceal from the Bank of Virginia its money to gain his client's acquittal.

"Cook's possession of the sawed-off shotgun was illegal. Ryder could not lawfully receive the gun from Cook to assist Cook to avoid conviction of robbery. Cook had never mentioned the shotgun to Ryder. When Ryder discovered it in Cook's box, he took possession of it to hinder the government in the prosecution of its case, and he intended not to reveal it pending trial unless the government discovered it and a court compelled its production. No statute or canon of ethics authorized Ryder to take possession of the gun for this purpose. * * *

"Ryder's action is not justified because he thought he was acting in the best interests of his client. To allow the individual lawyer's belief to determine the standards of professional conduct will in time reduce the ethics of the profession to the practices of the most unscrupulous. Moreover, Ryder knew that the law against concealing stolen property and the law forbidding receipt and possession of a sawed-off shotgun contain no exemptions for a lawyer who takes possession with the intent of protecting a criminal from the consequences of his crime. * * *

"[However,] Ryder intended to return the bank's money after his client was tried. He consulted reputable persons before and after he placed the property in his lockbox, although he did not precisely follow their advice. Were it not for these facts, we would deem proper his permanent exclusion from practice before this court. In view of the mitigating circumstances, he will be suspended from practice in this court for eighteen months * * *."

The Fourth Circuit affirmed and called the suspension "lenient in the circumstances." It then "suspend[ed] Ryder from practice before * * * [the Court of Appeals] for the duration of his suspension from the District Court."

Does Mr. Ryder's conduct incense you? What, if anything, about his behavior troubles you?

b.   Compare State ex rel. Sowers v. Olwell, 394 P.2d 681 (Wash.1964). Olwell was a lawyer who refused to honor a coroner's subpoena for the knife allegedly used by his client in a murder. He asserted both the attorney-client privilege and the client's privilege against self-incrimination. The lower court held him in contempt and he appealed. The state supreme court reversed. It held that the attorney client privilege protected the lawyer from contempt. However, "by so holding," we do not "mean to imply that evidence can be permanently withheld by the attorney under the claim of the attorney-client privilege." The court elaborated:

> "The attorney should not be a depository for criminal evidence (such as a knife, other weapons, stolen property, etc.), which in itself has little, if any material value for the purposes of aiding counsel in the preparation of the defense of his client's case. Such evidence given the attorney during legal consultation for information purposes and used by the attorney in preparing the defense of his client's case, whether or not the case ever goes to trial, could clearly be withheld for a reasonable period of time. It follows that the attorney, after a reasonable period of time, should, as an officer of the court, on his own motion turn the same over to the prosecution.

> " * * * [T]he state [in order to protect the attorney-client privilege], when attempting to introduce such evidence at the trial, should take extreme precautions to make certain that the source of the evidence is not disclosed in the presence of the jury and prejudicial error is not committed."

The court also found the self-incrimination privilege inapplicable because it the client alone must assert it. Is the decision consistent with *Ryder*? Does the procedure the court suggests protect all the relevant interests?

2.   May you hold the bag of money for safekeeping? What if you are concerned that the client will spend the money instead of returning it to its rightful owners?

a.   The money belongs to the bank, while the gun presumably belongs to Hammer. In *Ryder*, the court noted that Ryder "knew that Cook was under surveillance and he suspected that Cook might try to dispose of the money." Does that make it more or less reprehensible for Ryder to hold the money? Compare Rule 1.4, Comment 7, with Rule 3.4, Comment 2.

b.   Consider In re January 1976 Grand Jury, 534 F.2d 719 (7th Cir.1976). The attorney refused to comply with a grand jury's subpoena *duces tecum* to turn over money received by him from clients suspected of bank robbery. The Court of Appeals affirmed the contempt order, and Judge Tone, joined by Judge Bauer, argued in a concurring opinion:

> "We must assume for purposes of this appeal that shortly after robbing a savings and loan association, the robbers delivered money stolen in the robbery to appellant. If that occurred, the money was delivered either for safekeeping, with or without appellant's knowledge that it was stolen, or as an attorney's fee.

> "If it was the latter, the robbers voluntarily relinquished the money and with it any arguable claim that might have arisen from their possession or constructive possession. As Judge Pell points out, the payment of a fee is not a privileged communication. The money itself is non-testimonial and no plausible argument is left for resisting the subpoena.

"If the money was not given as a fee but for safekeeping, the delivery of the money was an act in furtherance of the crime, regardless of whether appellant knew it was stolen. The delivery of the money was not assertive conduct and therefore was not a privileged communication, and, as we just observed, the money itself is non-testimonial. The attorney is simply a witness to a criminal act. The fact that he is also a participant in the act, presumably without knowledge of its criminal quality, is irrelevant since he is not asserting his own privilege against self incrimination. There is no authority or reason, based on any constitutional provision or the attorney-client privilege, for shielding from judicial inquiry either the fruits of the robbery or the fact of the later criminal act of turning over the money to appellant. Accordingly, it is immaterial that in responding to the subpoena appellant will be making an assertion about who turned over the money and when.

"Finally, the proceedings have not yet reached the point at which we must decide whether, when the robbers have chosen to make appellant a witness to their crime, they may invoke the Sixth Amendment [right to effective assistance of counsel] to bar his eyewitness testimony at trial, although, for me, to ask that question is almost to answer it."

3.   What principles can you derive from these cases? Is a client's statement to the lawyer linking the gun to the crime a privileged communication?

a.   Morrell v. State, 575 P.2d 1200 (Alaska 1978), upheld the decision of the trial court to admit incriminating evidence of a kidnapping plan that the defendant had allegedly written. A friend of the defendant turned the plan over to defense counsel, who aided the friend in turning the evidence over to the police. Defense counsel then withdrew from the case. After examining the cases discussed in the text, the Alaska Supreme Court held:

"From the foregoing cases emerges the rule that a criminal defense attorney must turn over to the prosecution real evidence that the attorney obtains from his client. Further, if the evidence is obtained from a non-client third party who is not acting for the client, then the privilege to refuse to testify concerning the manner in which the evidence was obtained is inapplicable. * * *

"We believe that [defense counsel] would have been obligated to see that the evidence reached the prosecutor in this case even if he had obtained the evidence from Morrell. His obligation was even clearer because he acquired the evidence from [a third party], who made the decision to turn the evidence over to [defense counsel] without consulting Morrell and therefore was not acting as Morrell's agent.

"[Defense counsel] could have properly turned the evidence over to the police himself and would have been obliged to do so if [the third party] had refused to accept the return of the evidence.

> "[Finally, while] statutes which address the concealing of evidence are generally construed to require an affirmative act of concealment in addition to the failure to disclose information to the authorities, taking possession of evidence from a non-client third party and holding the evidence in a place not accessible to investigating authorities would seem to fall within the statute's ambit. Thus, we have concluded that [defense counsel] breached no ethical obligation to his client which may have rendered his legal services to Morrell ineffective."

Do the earlier cases in this problem support the court's conclusion?

b.   Consider People v. Meredith, 631 P.2d 46 (Cal.1981). The defendant told his lawyer the location of the robbery-murder victim's wallet. The lawyer then had his investigator remove it. The court held that the client's disclosure was privileged and that telling the investigator the location did not destroy the privilege. On the other hand, removing the wallet did destroy it. When defense counsel removes or alters evidence, he necessarily deprives the prosecution of the opportunity to observe that evidence in its original condition or location. The lawyer's decision to remove evidence is therefore tactical; if he leaves the evidence where he discovered it, the privilege protects his observations derived from privileged communications. If he removes the evidence to examine or test it, "the original location and condition of that evidence loses the protection of the privilege." Do you agree that it makes sense to put defense counsel to such a choice?[26]

c.   Restatement Third, The Law Governing Lawyers, tries to sum up these cases in § 119, which says that with respect to physical evidence of a client crime, a lawyer

> "(1) may, when reasonably necessary for purposes of the representation, take possession of the evidence and retain it for the time reasonably necessary to examine it and subject it to tests that do not alter or destroy material characteristics of the evidence; but
>
> "(2) following possession under Subsection (1), the lawyer must notify prosecuting authorities of the lawyer's possession of the evidence or turn the evidence over to them."

Comment *a* to § 119 then provides that the rules on turning over physical evidence of client crime apply to "contraband, weapons, and similar implements used in an offense. It also includes such materials as documents and material in electronically-retrievable form used by

---

[26] See also, Commonwealth v. Stenhach, 514 A.2d 114 (Pa.Super.Ct.1986), leave to appeal denied 534 A.2d 769 (Pa.1987), where the court affirmed the rule that physical evidence of a crime in possession of criminal defense attorneys who acquired the evidence at client's direction was not protected against disclosure by the attorney-client privilege. The court reversed the criminal conviction of the lawyers for failure to turn over the physical evidence, however, on the ground that the statutes prohibiting hindering prosecution and tampering with evidence were unconstitutionally vague or overbroad as applied to lawyers engaged in representation of criminal defendants.

The good faith of an attorney who advises his client to invoke the Fifth Amendment in response to a subpoena in a civil case protects the lawyer from being held in contempt. Maness v. Meyers, 419 U.S. 449, 468 (1975). Should the same principle apply here?

the client to plan the offense, documents used in the course of a mail-fraud violation, or transaction documents evidencing a crime."

d.   Model Rule 3.4, Comment 2, also summarizes these principles. Do you agree that courts should sometimes require defense counsel to turn over evidence that will help convict their clients?

C.   NONDISCLOSURE OF PHYSICAL EVIDENCE

1.   Is failure to disclose facts different from affirmatively concealing them? Are there times a lawyer simply must keep quiet about information others would consider significant to them?

a.   A news story, highly publicized at the time, reported what became known as the "buried bodies" case:

> "An Onondaga County grand jury this afternoon [February 7, 1975] cleared a lawyer, Frank H. Armani, of criminal wrongdoing in failing to disclose that his client in a murder case had told him where he had hidden two bodies. * * *
>
> "Mr. [Francois] Belge and Mr. Armani were lawyers for Robert Garrow, who was found guilty of murder after a trial in Hamilton County last summer.
>
> "During the trial Mr. Belge revealed that he and Mr. Armani had discovered the two bodies after having been told of their whereabouts by Mr. Garrow, but that they did not tell authorities. * * *
>
> "Mr. Armani's attorney, Elliot A. Taikoff of New York City, said later that his client had been 'very troubled' over his role in the matter and had received advice from a 'very high-ranking judge in this state.' He refused to name the judge, but said he had testified before the grand jury."[27]

Was the grand jury's decision consistent with that of the *Ryder* court? Were the situations analytically different?

b.   In considering the *Belge* case, N.Y. State Bar Comm. on Prof'l Ethics Opinion No. 479 (Mar. 6, 1978), advised: "the lawyer was under an injunction not to disclose to the authorities his knowledge of the two prior murders, and was duty-bound not to reveal to the authorities the location of the bodies." The opinion also concluded that the attorney acted properly by using the information, with his client's consent, in engaging in plea bargaining and in destroying photographs the lawyer took of the bodies and records the lawyer made of his conversation with the client.

Do you agree with the opinion's analysis? Were the photographs that Belge took of the bodies privileged information? Would Belge's duties change if he had moved some of the body parts to get a better picture? Could Belge tell the police about the location of the bodies—so that they could receive a decent burial—by calling the police

---

[27] New York Times, Feb. 8, 1975, p. 54, col. 5. See also, People v. Belge, 372 N.Y.S.2d 798, 803 (Co.Ct.1975) (indictment on same facts dismissed on "grounds of a privileged communication and in the interests of justice * * * ").

anonymously and not revealing either his name or the name of his client?

c. In Clutchette v. Rushen, 770 F.2d 1469 (9th Cir.1985), cert. denied, 475 U.S. 1088 (1986), the government accused the defendant of shooting a man in the defendant's car. The police were having a hard time proving their case until the defendant's wife voluntarily turned over some receipts to them. She was acting as an investigator for her husband's defense lawyer, and the lawyer sent her to Los Angeles to get (and arguably to destroy) the receipts that showed that her husband had arranged for the car to be reupholstered shortly after the murder. With the help of the receipts, the police found the former seat covers and matched the blood type to the victim. The court held that the wife's surrender of the receipts was not a violation of the defendant's attorney-client privilege. If the attorney had not done anything to retrieve the receipts, he would not have had to tell the police about them. Having the wife-investigator take possession of the receipts, however, made them fair game for police discovery.

2.   Suppose you, like Belge, have a client who claims that he killed several women and buried their bodies in a secluded place. This time, however, when you check out his story, one of the victims is not yet dead. May you tell the police her location?

a.   Look at Model Rule 1.6(b)(1), a provision that was not in effect at the time of the *Belge* case. Do you agree with the disclosure authority given to you by that rule? Should you disguise your voice when you disclose the information about the victims to the police so they cannot connect you to your client?

b.   Under the auspices of the Roscoe Pound–American Trial Lawyers Foundation, a special commission prepared its own proposed ethics rules called The American Lawyer's Code of Conduct.[28] The commission applied its proposed Code to this hypothetical as follows:

> "[S]he is seriously injured and unable to help herself or to get help. The lawyer calls an ambulance for her, but takes care not to be personally identified. The lawyer has *committed a disciplinary violation * * *.*"[29]

Do you agree that loyalty to the client requires this result? What logic would lead otherwise sensible lawyers to such a conclusion?

c.   Such cases do arise in real life. In McClure v. Thompson, 323 F.3d 1233 (9th Cir.2003), McClure clubbed Jones to death with the butt of a gun, then murdered her two children and hid them in the woods. He was convicted of all three murders. In discussions with his original defense attorney, Mecca, days after the murder, McClure drew Mecca a map indicating where the children were located. McClure did not say whether the children were dead or alive, but he did say that Satan had killed Jones, while Jesus had saved the children. Mecca tried to bargain with the prosecutor for a lesser charge once he had the map, but the prosecutor refused, so Mecca arranged for his secretary to call the police

---

[28]   The drafters intended this proposal to compete with the ABA Model Rules. It provides interesting contrast to the Model Rules on several issues, but no state ever adopted it.

[29]   The American Lawyer's Code of Conduct, Illustrative Case 1(g) (Revised Draft, 1982) (emphasis added).

anonymously, telling them the location of the child victims in the belief that they might be alive. He then withdrew from the case.

McClure argued that Mecca did not provide "effective assistance of counsel" in that he (1) failed to obtain McClure's informed consent before disclosing what McClure had told him, and (2) failed to verify whether disclosure was necessary to prevent the children's deaths. McClure argued that Mecca's concern for the victims was a conflict of interest that rendered Mecca's representation constitutionally-ineffective. The court found Mecca's disclosure permissible because of his reasonable belief that it was necessary to prevent imminent deaths. Mecca's attempt to negotiate with the prosecution and his concern that McClure's kidnaping charges would be aggravated to murder if the children were found dead were sufficient evidence of his overall loyalty to the client, and the court denied habeas relief because McClure could not "demonstrate that his counsel 'actively represented a conflicting interest.' " Do you agree with the court's analysis?

D.   DESTROYING, OR FAILING TO RETAIN, PHYSICAL OR DOCUMENTARY EVIDENCE

1.   If Hammer's fingerprints were on the gun that he put on your desk, may you advise him to wipe off the fingerprints?

a.   Does Hammer's right not to incriminate himself allow him to wipe the gun clean? Would you, his lawyer, have a right to do it for him? Does even the privilege against self-incrimination give a client authority to try to cover up evidence of a crime?

b.   If Hammer does not wipe off his fingerprints, should you tell him the consequences of leaving his prints undisturbed? Should you send the gun to the police with the fingerprints on it?

c.   Cases have routinely held that a party may be charged with a "conspiracy to obstruct the due administration of justice in a proceeding which [is not pending but which] becomes pending in the future. * * *"[30] In general, it is an obstruction of justice "to stifle, suppress or destroy evidence knowing that it *may* be wanted in a judicial proceeding or is being sought by investigating officers. * * *"[31] How should this construction of the law affect the lawyer's ethical responsibilities in this problem? See also Rule 3.4, Comment 2.

d.   As individuals and entities have turned to social media to express views and opinions, lawyers have in turn sought to discover such postings to determine whether they are relevant to the legal matters at issue. New York County Lawyers Ass'n Ethics Opinion 745 (July 2, 2013) discusses the question whether lawyers may review client social media pages and advise the clients to remove the content. The opinion held that lawyers are permitted to advise clients on social media policies and may review posts in advance of publication. Lawyers must be mindful of laws and court rules requiring the preservation of evidence that may be subject to discovery. However, absent such

---

[30]   United States v. Perlstein, 126 F.2d 789, 796 (3d Cir.1942), cert. denied, 316 U.S. 678 (1942). See also, e.g., In re Williams, 23 N.W.2d 4, 9 (Minn.1946) (per curiam).

[31]   Rollin M. Perkins, Criminal Law 499 (2d ed.1969) (emphasis added).

restrictions, lawyers could advise clients to "take down" posts that may injure a client's legal position.

2. Turning to your second client, Mr. Wallace, may you properly counsel him to destroy the incriminating tape recordings? Does it matter whether or not anyone has already filed suit?[32]

a. No law compelled Wallace to make the tape recordings. Will Wallace be obstructing justice if he destroys these tapes to prevent a party from later subpoenaing them?

b. Assume that the Justice Department is not yet involved but that Wallace is afraid the *Wall Street Journal* reporter may come across information that indicates the secret taping device has been set up in the office. May you advise Wallace to destroy the tapes, using as your reason the embarrassment that would ensue if his business associates knew he had secretly taped and retained tapes of private conversations?[33] Look at Rule 3.4(a) and Comment 2. Remember our discussion in Problem 25 of the duty to preserve electronic evidence.

3. After Wallace has told you of his taping system and you have listened to the relevant conversations, should you tell Wallace that the tapes are damaging and the government is likely to subpoena them?

a. May you tell Wallace this bad news if you privately expect him to destroy the incriminating material, which is not yet subject to a subpoena? Can you do anything about that? How does Model Rule 1.2(d) require you to act? How about Model Rule 3.4(a)?

b. Could the attorney in *Belge*, supra, ethically destroy the photographs of the dead girls' bodies if his client had taken the photographs? If the client had given them to the attorney for safekeeping? What if the subpoena sought production of all client produced information given to the attorney? Does the work product immunity protect them from disclosure in any event?

---

[32] There is an important question presented whether you represent the corporation as an entity, the president of the corporation, or both, and whether representing both the president and the corporation involve a conflict of interest. For now, assume that you just represent Wallace, because that is the focus of this question.

[33] Cf. Wall Street J., Apr. 7, 1975, at 7, col. 1–2 ("Official at ITT Unit Destroyed Letters After Journal Questioned Some Practices"):

"A retired official of International Telephone & Telegraph Corp. subsidiary disclosed in testimony before a Senate subcommittee that last summer, while he was still with the company, he destroyed certain letters in his file after the Wall Street Journal began questioning the unit's competitive practices.

" 'I was scared,' John James told the Senate subcommittee on Antitrust and Monopoly, which is investigating the effectiveness of voluntary industry standards. 'I have been associated with code and standard-making activities for many years, and this was the first time in all of that experience that I had anybody question the propriety of the way I conducted myself in connection with this type of work,' he said. * * *

"After reviewing the testimony, an arm of the [American Society of Mechanical Engineers] came up with a conclusion that appears in the current issue of Mechanical Engineering. It commends Mr. James on this testimony and says the society's Professional Practice Committee 'finds no improper or unethical conduct in his action.' "

Would this conclusion have been the same if a lawyer had been the one who destroyed the letters?

c.   To prevent Wallace from destroying the evidence, may you refuse to tell him that the material in the files is damaging? Remember Rule 1.4, and Comment 7. Would you do this to protect Mr. Wallace? Would you do it to protect yourself?

4.   May you tell Mr. Wallace that if he destroys only the tapes, he may well be involved in an obstruction of justice but that the next time he engages in a regular housecleaning of his files he should destroy the tapes and any transcripts of them?

a.   Must a client keep all incriminating material even though businesses routinely dispose of countless other documents every day?

b.   If you suspect that the government may soon subpoena materials, may you send an email to your client's employees advising them that, if there is no business reason to keep the materials, they should destroy them? If the Wallace Corporation has a document retention policy but has not followed it on a regular basis (e.g., the policy says to destroy documents after they are four years old if no one has accessed them for two years, but the company just keeps the documents around). May you advise the corporation to destroy the documents now that newspapers report that the government may want to subpoena them?

c.   In 2002, when the Enron Corporation fell into bankruptcy after its stock collapsed amid charges of fraud, attention turned to Enron's auditors, Arthur Andersen. After an Andersen lawyer emailed Andersen employees reminding them of a policy that, after an audit, they should not keep documents that were not necessary to back up the audit, the employees engaged in extensive shredding of documents. Later, the federal government indicted Arthur Andersen for obstruction of justice. On June 15, 2002, the jury found Arthur Andersen guilty. "Soon afterward, Andersen informed the government that it would cease auditing public companies as soon as the end of August, effectively ending the life of the 89–year–old firm."[34]

d.   Did the lawyer serve her client well? The stakes associated with decisions to destroy potential evidence were increased by Congress in the wake of the Arthur Andersen scandal by passage of § 802 of the Sarbanes–Oxley Act of 2002, 18 U.S.C.A. § 1519. That provision increases to twenty years in prison and a fine of up to $10 million, the sanction for obstruction of justice by destruction of corporate and financial records.

e.   Ironically, after the public outcry and adoption of the new statute, in Arthur Andersen LLP v. United States, 544 U.S. 696 (2005), the Supreme Court unanimously reversed the firm's obstruction of justice conviction. The federal statute, 18 U.S.C.A. § 1512, requires the defendant to have acted "corruptly." Telling people to follow a records

---

[34]   Kurt Eichenwald, Andersen Guilty in Effort to Block Inquiry on Enron, New York Times, June 16, 2002 at § 1, pp. 1, 22. The story went on: "The jury verdict, reached in the 10th day of deliberations, reflected a narrow reading of the events last fall that led to Andersen's indictment. In interviews, jurors said that they reached their decision because an Andersen lawyer had ordered critical deletions to an internal memorandum, rather than because of the firm's wholesale destruction of Enron-related documents. At bottom, then, the guilty verdict against Andersen—on a charge brought because of the shredding of thousands of records and deletion of tens of thousands of email messages—was ultimately reached because of the removal of a few words from a single memorandum." Id.

destruction policy is not inevitably corrupt, the Court said. " 'Document retention policies,' which are created in part to keep certain information from getting into the hands of others, including the Government, are common in business." So, it is "not wrongful for a manager to instruct his employees to comply with a valid document retention policy under ordinary circumstances." Moreover, the trial judge told the jury too little about both the mental state required for a conviction and the nexus between the destruction and the particular government case thereby prejudiced. A knowingly corrupt persuader "cannot be someone who persuades others to shred documents under a document retention policy when he does not have in contemplation any particular official proceeding in which those documents might be material."

Arthur Andersen LLP was ultimately acquitted of wrongdoing, but the damage had already been done. And you thought practicing law was going to be easy!

———

PROBLEM 27

THE CLIENT WHO INTENDS TO COMMIT PERJURY

Now we turn to perhaps the classic, most-mooted problem in legal ethics. Surely every law student has been asked, "How can you defend someone you know is guilty?" It is one thing to answer that the prosecution must meet its proof of proof, but your client may want to present an affirmative defense. Indeed, he may want to take the witness stand to deny his guilt even though you and he knows he is guilty. This problem initially explores what it means to "know" a client plans to lie. What is a lawyer's duty when the client offers to produce a witness who will be willing to lie on the client's behalf? Does the criminal defendant have a right to testify in his or her own defense? Then, the problem asks what the lawyer is to do when the defendant actually gives false testimony.

FACTS

William Smith is a defendant in a robbery prosecution. Smith is also one of the many criminal defendants represented by M. Maynard Hawley. Smith said to Hawley that he would like to testify in order to present an alibi defense. After Hawley reminded him that he had never mentioned an alibi defense before, Smith said that his friend had now agreed to testify that he was at her house at the time of the robbery. Smith told Hawley that he would like to take the stand to confirm his friend's story.

Hawley told Smith, "I cannot be a party to perjured testimony." Smith retorted that he had a right to take the stand and testify, but Hawley was reluctant to let Smith do so. Smith assured Hawley: "The last thing I would want you to do is to be unethical. Put me on the stand; I will tell the truth."

Hawley put Smith on the stand. Contrary to Smith's pledge, he lied.

QUESTIONS

A.   KNOWING WHEN A LAWYER KNOWS SOMETHING

1.   How does an attorney ever really "know" that a witness will commit perjury?

a.   When the Model Rules talk about "knowing," do they mean "know pragmatically" or "know absolutely"? How does Model Rule 1.0(f) define what it means to "know" something? If you think that you only "reasonably believe"—Rule 1.0(i)—something, is there a risk that a disciplinary panel, or a judge or jury in a later malpractice case, will decide that you really did "know" the information?

b.   At some point, the lawyer cannot close her eyes to what she "knows." The client may confide in the lawyer that he intends to lie. Or, the lawyer may know because the client's testimony keeps changing in order to accommodate new evidence. The lawyer may know that the client seeks to deny the existence of a document that the lawyer (but not the opposing side) knows exists. At some point, in short, the lawyer does not "suspect" or "infer" but "knows" within the meaning of Rule 1.0(f). Rule 3.3, Comment 8, states "although a lawyer should resolve doubts about the veracity of testimony or other evidence in favor of the client, the lawyer cannot ignore an obvious falsehood."

c.   In Patsy's Brand, Inc. v. I.O.B. Realty, 2002 WL 59434 (S.D.N.Y.2002), the court introduced its opinion by stating this case "arises from this Court's *sua sponte* issuance of an order requiring Pennie & Edmonds, the attorneys for the principal defendants, to show cause why it should not be sanctioned for permitting its client to submit a false affidavit." The court did "not dispute counsel's assertion that they acted with subjective good faith." But the court concluded that, "rather than risk offending and possibly losing a client, counsel simply closed their eyes to the overwhelming evidence that statements in the client's affidavit were not true."

The underlying dispute involved the trademark rights to use of the name "Patsy's" in marketing spaghetti sauce. A principal of the defendant in an infringement suit submitted an affidavit stating that he created the Patsy's name before the plaintiff registered its mark. The man further stated that he took the mark to a printer at that time and submitted a sample jar label to the court. The plaintiff, however, showed that the label the defendant submitted was created long after the time that defendant asserted, based on a bar code on the label and the printer's own records. Defense counsel then withdrew from representation and Pennie & Edmonds, a firm specializing in trademark law, replaced them. Although the plaintiff already proved the falsity of the defendant's affidavit in court, Pennie & Edmonds allowed its client to submit a new affidavit that contained substantially the same statements as the first. The firm argued that it was required to rely on its clients' assertions about the date defendant created the mark. The court, however, found that no reasonable attorney ("a lawyer of even modest intelligence"), much less one knowledgeable in trademark law, could believe the statements in the affidavits.[35]

2. In preparing Smith's testimony, if Smith tells Hawley a story that appears untruthful, may Hawley explain to him the weaknesses that the prosecutor would see in his story?

a.   What, if anything, should give Hawley pause about engaging in such coaching? If Smith then revises his story to eliminate the weaknesses Hawley saw, may Hawley counsel him as to whether the new story is more plausible? May Hawley advise him that the new story would be even more plausible if Smith would change it slightly again? Might Hawley simply be helping Smith tell a true story more convincingly? At some point, might Hawley be suborning perjury? See Rule 1.2(d).

b.   In Resolution Trust Corp. v. Bright, 6 F.3d 336 (5th Cir.1993), the district judge disbarred two lawyers from practice in his court for trying to get a witness to sign an affidavit that described how certain events had occurred. The witness said she had no knowledge about some of the things they wanted her to say and she refused to sign the affidavit. The Fifth Circuit reversed the disbarments and described the conduct as follows:

> "With respect to some of the statements in the affidavit, the attorneys were not content to accept Erhart's initial refusal to revise her changes. In an effort to have Erhart see things their way, Lovato and Graber described their understanding of how certain events transpired at Bright Banc, presented Erhart with independent evidence to support this interpretation of events, and aggressively challenged some of Erhart's assumptions about Bright and Reeder. After making their case for further revisions, Lovato and Graber asked Erhart whether she believed them and whether she was now convinced that their version of certain events was correct. Erhart, unconvinced, declined to alter the initial changes she had made to the draft affidavit. When it was clear to the attorneys that Erhart would not sign a statement agreeing with the attorneys' version of some of the disputed events at Bright Banc, they incorporated Erhart's handwritten changes into a new draft affidavit. Erhart read this draft and made a few changes which were then included in a third draft. Erhart read and approved this version of the affidavit, signed it and left the offices of Hopkins & Sutter."

The witness, Erhart, initially described the lawyers' conduct as "almost like browbeating me" but later said that the lawyers "were doing their job, just like everybody else." The Fifth Circuit rejected the

---

[35] Ultimately, the court adopted what many consider a light sanction: "Given Pennie & Edmonds' reputation and its candor in these proceedings, the Court is persuaded that little sanction beyond the publication of this Opinion is required to prevent repetition of similar conduct. Thus all that the Court will require is that a partner of the firm submit to the Court an affidavit stating that a copy of this Opinion has been delivered to each of the lawyers in the firm with a memorandum that states that it is firm policy that its partners and associates adhere to the highest ethical standards and that if a lawyer's adherence to those standards results in the loss of a client, large or small, the lawyer will not suffer any adverse consequence."

District Court's conclusion that the lawyers were "making or urging the making of 'false' statements," and concluded: "The attorneys' sometimes laborious interviews with Erhart were conducted with the goal of eliciting an accurate and favorable affidavit from a key witness in the underlying case."

Are you convinced that account accurately describes what the lawyers were doing?

c.   State ex rel. Abner v. Elliott, 706 N.E.2d 765 (Ohio 1999) (per curiam), involved lawyers who gave instructions to asbestos workers about the answers to give in their depositions. Plaintiffs said the instructions were helpful advice; defendants said they were improper "coaching." The trial court found that a particular deposition preparation document constituted evidence of improper coaching of prospective deponents.

The document, entitled "Preparing For Your Deposition," started by telling plaintiffs what they will need to say to make the defendant "want to offer you a settlement." The document stated: "try to remember how close you were [to these products at the place where you worked]. The more often you were around [them], the better for your case." This witness preparation statement advised that the defendants and their attorneys "have NO RECORDS to tell them what products were used on a particular job." And, "never mention" the existence of this witness preparation document. It also instructed: "You will be asked if you ever saw any WARNING labels on containers of asbestos. It is important to maintain that you NEVER saw any labels on asbestos products that said WARNING or DANGER."[36] The court upheld the trial court's order that plaintiffs turn the "advice" documents over to the defendants in discovery or face adverse jury instructions about them.

d.   Philadelphia Bar Ass'n Prof'l Guidance Comm., Opinion 2013-5 (June 2013), addressed a situation in which a married couple involved in a car accident lied about who was driving the car to the police, their insurance company, and their lawyer. The lawyer filed an action against a defendant using the false information in the complaint. When the clients informed the lawyer about their misrepresentation, he sought guidance on what to do. The Opinion says that the lawyer may satisfy his duty to the tribunal either by dismissing the litigation with prejudice without disclosing the misrepresentation or by amending the complaint to reflect the accurate facts. However, the lawyer also owes a duty to the client's insurer under Rule 4.1(b) because the lawyer had transmitted papers containing the misrepresentation to the company. If the clients refuse to allow the lawyer to dismiss the case or correct the complaint and to disclose the misrepresentation to the insurer, the lawyer must withdraw. The lawyer must then inform the clients' new lawyer about the misrepresentations and if that lawyer does not rectify the fraud to the court and the insurer, the withdrawing lawyer would have an obligation to do so.

---

[36] Lester Brickman & Ronald D. Rotunda, When Witnesses Are Told What to Say, Washington Post, Jan. 13, 1998, at A–15. See also, G–I Holdings, Inc. v. Baron & Budd, 179 F.Supp.2d 233, 242 (S.D.N.Y.2001), which said that: "Baron & Budd conducted regular in-house training sessions concerning the giving of misleading and false deposition testimony and issued various memoranda instructing employees how to prepare clients for giving testimony without regard to its truth."

B. THE DECISION TO CALL A WITNESS WHO MAY TESTIFY FALSELY

1. Must the lawyer refuse to call Smith's friend if he knows she will commit perjury on his client's behalf?

a. The general rule is clear: Lawyers, like anyone else, have a duty not to aid and abet perjury, which is a criminal offense. See, e.g., Model Rule 3.3(a)(3), and Comments 5–8; Harris v. New York, 401 U.S. 222 (1971)(a criminal defendant's privilege to testify in his own behalf does not include a right to commit perjury). Complying with this rule, however, has been difficult for some litigators.

b. In Louisiana State Bar Ass'n v. Thierry, 366 So.2d 1305 (La.1978), a grand jury indicted Thierry (a lawyer) for having Henry Joshua testify falsely as an alibi witness for Thierry's client in a robbery prosecution. The jury found Thierry guilty of suborning the perjury of Joshua and the court sentenced him to three years. Thierry's main defense "appears to be that in his enthusiasm he acted zealously in the interest of his client as well as out of naiveté or ignorance * * *." He argued that "a more experienced lawyer would perhaps have considered the impropriety of his conduct and 'have seen [it] as a stop sign,' but respondent demonstrated a 'lack of caution.'" The state supreme court ordered Thierry disbarred. "So basic to the criminal justice system of this country is the sanctity of the oath of witnesses and the integrity of lawyers that these principles cannot be unknown to or violated by, the least learned or experienced in the profession of law."

c. In Breezevale Ltd. v. Dickinson, 759 A.2d 627 (D.C.2000), the night before a deposition in which Client's records custodian was going to be asked about key documents, the witness told the lawyer the documents were forged. The custodian said she did not want to lie, and the lawyer told her to tell the truth. Before her deposition testimony reached those issues, Client demanded that the lawyer and witness walk away from the deposition, but the lawyer said he had no basis for doing so. Thus, the fact of the forgery came out at the deposition, and the case consequently settled for a much lower amount. At that point, Client sued the firm for malpractice, arguing that the employee was lying and that the documents were real. The jury in the malpractice case found that the documents were forged but that it was malpractice to have let the witness testify truthfully without at least vigorously trying to prevent her from testifying at all.

The trial judge set aside the malpractice verdict, saying that if the documents were forged (as he too found they were), the plaintiff could not use the failure to introduce forged documents as the basis for the underlying claim. Thus, the lawyer's conduct could not have caused the plaintiff's loss. The trial judge also ordered plaintiff to pay defendant's attorneys' fees in the malpractice case, finding that plaintiff filed the case in bad faith and in knowing reliance on the forged documents. The D.C. Court of Appeals reversed, arguing that the jury could have found that the firm did not do enough to try to protect its dishonest client. The jury could have found that the law firm's failure to postpone the deposition of the employee and to settle the case before the defendants caught on to the fraud were the cause of the plaintiff's loss.

The en banc court of appeals then vacated that opinion, reheard the case, and reaffirmed the original appellate ruling. The en banc court said, 783 A.2d 573 (D.C.2001), that the former client's forging of documents in an attempt to bolster its underlying suit for breach of contract, did *not* bar Client from bringing a malpractice action against the lawyers, where Client's wrongdoing was not "central[ ]" to the damages it was seeking. The court was "unable to agree with the sweeping nature of an assertion that regardless of malpractice, a client who engages in wrongdoing in connection with any aspect of litigation thereby as a matter of law forfeits all rights of recovery against the attorney." The court still left the question of "sanctions in the discretionary hands of the trial court upon remand."

On remand, the trial court found by clear and convincing evidence that Client knowingly brought the malpractice litigation primarily relying upon documents that Client knew were forgeries. The judge assessed Client a total of over $4 million in attorneys' fees and costs, and $1 million in punitive damages, and dismissed the cause of action for legal malpractice (thus vacating a jury verdict of nearly $3.4 million). The Court of Appeals sustained the dismissal and the award of attorneys' fees. However, it vacated the separate $1 million award of punitive damages as excessive given that the attorneys' fees and dismissal also bore punitive elements. 879 A.2d 957 (D.C. 2005).

d.   In United States v. Lamplugh, 334 F.3d 294 (3d Cir.2003), a client fabricated documents that she wanted to use in defense of her prosecution for willfully failing to file tax returns. Her lawyer turned the documents over to the prosecution, not knowing that they were false but without fully investigating their authenticity. The district court found ineffective assistance of counsel because of the lawyer's failure to conduct an adequate examination of the documents and warn his client of the consequences of producing fabricated documents.

The Third Circuit reversed, holding that clients "forfeited" their right to effective assistance of counsel by certain "extremely serious misconduct." The client's conduct here met the "extremely serious misconduct" standard. Granting relief to a dishonest client would allow her "to manipulate the justice system by knowingly presenting fabricated written documents to her counsel in an attempt to deceive the court, the jury, and the Government into accepting her theory of defense." Do you agree? May a lawyer ever facilitate a client's fraudulent conduct?

2.   What do the Model Rules tell a lawyer to do when the client wants to call an alibi witness whom the lawyer knows will lie on the stand?

a.   Look at Model Rule 3.3(a)(3) and (c). Look also at Rule 3.3, Comments 5–13. How should the lawyer proceed?

b.   The Model Rules build on some of the prior case law. People v. Schultheis, 638 P.2d 8 (Colo.1981), examined the procedures a lawyer should follow when confronted with a client who insists that the lawyer call an alibi witness who will testify perjuriously. The court declared:

> "A lawyer who presents a witness knowing that the witness intends to commit perjury thereby engages in the subornation of perjury. We will not permit the truth-finding process to be deflected by the presentation of false evidence by an officer of the court. Therefore, we hold that a lawyer may

c.   In United States v. Litchfield, 959 F.2d 1514 (10th Cir.1992), defense counsel held an ex parte conference with the judge during the trial. He told the judge that he advised the client he should testify but the lawyer now feared the client would not be truthful. The judge told the lawyer it was for the jury to decide what was true and untrue, so the trial went on normally, the defendant took the stand, and the jury convicted him. The Court of Appeals held that the lawyer did not deny the defendant effective assistance of counsel by alerting the judge about his concerns. Under the Model Rules, is it correct to conclude that a lawyer must alert the judge if he has concerns the client will testify falsely?

d.   In United States v. Williams, 698 F.3d 374 (7th Cir. 2012), the client sent his lawyer an envelope marked, "legal mail" (to avoid authorities opening it) that contained another letter addressed to the client's cousin. The client asked the lawyer to send the letter to the cousin, but the lawyer opened it and read a request that the cousin support the client's false alibi. The lawyer received permission from the court to withdraw, sent the letter to the prosecutor, and testified at the now former client's trial. On appeal from a conviction, the defendant claimed ineffective assistance of counsel. Seventh Circuit Judge Posner, writing for the majority, disagreed. There was no violation of the privilege because the communication was in furtherance of a crime. There was effective assistance of counsel, because new counsel represented the defendant effectively. Further, although the lawyer's minimum duty to the court involved dissuading the client from creating the false alibi, withdrawal and testifying did not amount to going too far. "Lawyers enjoy a broad discretion in responding to litigation misconduct by their clients, and in the unusual circumstances of this case we do not think the lawyer acted unethically." A dissenting judge argued that this lawyer seriously overreacted to a client's ill-advised plan.

e.   In United States v. Midgett, 342 F.3d 321 (4th Cir.2003), the defendant repeatedly told his lawyer that he had not committed the crimes and wanted to testify that a third person with him on the night in question committed them. The lawyer refused to put Midgett on the stand, and in a private conference with the judge, the lawyer moved to withdraw. The court reported this to the defendant and gave him two choices: testify and proceed without counsel or not testify and keep his lawyer. Midgett said that he could not proceed without a lawyer, so he chose not to testify and was convicted of the crimes. On these facts, the Fourth Circuit reversed the convictions. Midgett never told his lawyer he was guilty; indeed, he always asserted his innocence. It was not for counsel to decide whether a client should testify based on his own beliefs about the defendant's truthfulness, nor was it proper for the district court to give the defendant an ultimatum that required him to choose between two constitutionally protected rights—the right to counsel and the right to testify.

4.   Should the lawyer advise a client who wants to testify falsely that he must give his testimony in the form of a narrative?

a.   Rule 3.3(b) of the D.C. Rules of Professional Conduct provides that a lawyer for an accused in a criminal case who plans to lie should first "make a good faith effort to dissuade the client from presenting the false evidence." If unsuccessful, "the lawyer shall seek leave of the tribunal to withdraw." However, if withdrawal is not permitted: "the lawyer may put the client on the stand to testify in a narrative fashion, but the lawyer shall not examine the client in such manner as to elicit testimony which the lawyer knows to be false, and shall not argue the probative value of the client's testimony in closing argument."

What do you think about the narrative approach? It was once the heart of Proposed Standard 4–7.7 of the ABA Standards Relating to the Defense Function, but no longer. Nor does the ABA embrace the "narrative approach" in Model Rule 3.3.[38]

b.   In its footnote 6, the majority opinion in Nix v. Whiteside expressly acknowledged the debate about the narrative approach:

> "In the evolution of the contemporary standards promulgated by the American Bar Association, an early draft reflects a compromise suggesting that when the disclosure of intended perjury is made during the course of trial, when withdrawal of counsel would raise difficult questions of a mistrial holding, counsel had the option to let the defendant take the stand but decline to affirmatively assist the presentation of perjury by traditional direct examination. Instead, counsel would stand mute while the defendant undertook to present the false version in narrative form in his own words unaided by any direct examination. This conduct was thought to be a signal at least to the presiding judge that the attorney considered the testimony to be false and was seeking to disassociate himself from that course. Additionally, counsel would not be permitted to discuss the known false testimony in closing arguments. * * * Most courts treating the subject rejected this approach and insisted on a more rigorous standard, [but t]he Eighth Circuit in this case and the Ninth Circuit have expressed approval of the 'free narrative' standards." * * *

The court was alluding to Lowery v. Cardwell, 575 F.2d 727 (9th Cir.1978), which approved narrative testimony in principle but found it inappropriate in a trial where the judge is the fact finder. In the midst of a trial, the court went on, if a client's perjury surprises defense counsel, counsel need not withdraw because that course is not feasible. Instead, the lawyer should not "advance" the perjury. Judge Hufstedler, concurring, said: "No matter how commendable may have been counsel's motives, his interest in saving himself from potential violation of the canons was adverse to his client, and the end product was his abandonment of a diligent defense." Is any of Lowery good law in light of Rule 3.3?

c.   State v. McDowell, 681 N.W.2d 500 (Wis.2004), held that defense counsel may not substitute narrative questioning for the traditional question-and-answer format unless counsel first knows that the client intends to testify falsely. "Absent the most extraordinary circumstances, such knowledge must be based on the client's expressed admission of intent to testify untruthfully." The court added that the

---

[38] Likewise, Florida Bar Rule 4–3.3(4) prohibits all false testimony, whether or not in narrative form.

lawyer must advise the client, opposing counsel, and the trial court of the change of questioning style prior to using the narrative. In this case, during a confidential interview, defendant said that he might testify falsely at trial. Defense counsel warned him that he would then have to use narrative questioning. Later, the defendant said that he would testify truthfully, so his counsel said he would use the traditional question-and-answer format. However, when the defendant took the stand, his lawyer employed narrative questioning without telling the defendant beforehand. In this case, the defense counsel's performance was defective for two reasons: (1) he failed to inform the defendant of his intentions to use narrative questioning beforehand; and (2) he employed the narrative questioning technique despite believing that the defendant intended to testify truthfully. Still, the court affirmed the conviction after finding that the defense counsel's actions did not prejudice defendant.

d.   Contrast People v. Andrades, 828 N.E.2d 599 (N.Y.2005), where the defense attorney sought to withdraw during the course of a murder trial, citing an ethical conflict upon which he could not elaborate. The trial court inferred that the defendant intended to perjure himself. It concluded that the attorney could continue to represent the defendant effectively and that he had complied with his ethical responsibilities. At a hearing on a motion to suppress the defendant's confession, the defendant testified mainly in narrative format and his attorney offered no closing argument. At trial, the defendant defended himself and the jury convicted him of second-degree murder.

On appeal, the New York Court of Appeals agreed that the lawyer must balance zealous representation of a client with the "truth-seeking function of the justice system." Yet, it made clear that counsel must refrain from participating in a client's committing perjury or presenting false evidence. It expressly rejected the idea that counsel should remain silent to protect a defendant who commits perjury because such an approach was incompatible with counsel's role as an officer of the court. The court said that a client's intent to commit the crime of perjury is not protected as attorney-client privilege and that counsel's ethical obligations are the same regardless whether a judge or jury is the fact-finder. Because defense counsel properly balanced his duties to his client and the court and did not breach any recognized professional duty, the court held that the defendant had a fair trial and the effective assistance of counsel.

e.   Should we be more troubled than some courts have been by the use of narrative testimony? What should the court do if the opposing counsel makes the obvious evidentiary objection? A lawyer is supposed to ask nonleading questions to which the other lawyer may object; the lawyer is not supposed to say, "tell us your side of the story."

D.   WHAT TO DO WHEN THE CLIENT DOES GIVE FALSE TESTIMONY

1.   When Smith takes the stand and breaks his promise to be truthful, what should Hawley do? Should Hawley try to withdraw from the representation in the middle of the trial?

a.   If the client knows that the lawyer will urge him not to testify if he plans to testify falsely, we can expect savvy, street-smart defendants (who are ready to lie under oath) to lie to their lawyers when they are not under oath.

b.   Did the ABA Model Code of Professional Responsibility provide helpful guidance on this point? Look at DR 7–102(B)(1), for example:

> "A lawyer who receives information clearly establishing that [h]is client has, in the course of the representation, perpetrated a fraud upon a person or tribunal shall promptly call upon his client to rectify the same, and if his client refuses or is unable to do so, he shall reveal the fraud to the affected person or tribunal, except when the information is protected as a privileged communication."

Did that rule give the lawyer clear guidance? Did it create as many questions as answers for the lawyer? Is a client's admission to past perjury privileged? What may the lawyer do if the client did not admit anything, but the lawyer knows (because on his earlier privileged discussions with the client) that the testimony is perjurious?

c.   After the adoption of the Model Rules and the Supreme Court's decision in Nix v. Whiteside, the ABA Standing Comm. on Ethics and Prof'l Responsibility issued Formal Opinion 87–353 (Apr. 20, 1987). The opinion reviewed and superseded Formal Opinion 287 (June 27, 1953) (discussed in Problem 25), and Formal Opinion 341 (Sept. 30, 1975). The committee wrote: "It is now mandatory * * * for a lawyer, who knows the client has committed perjury, to disclose this knowledge to the tribunal if the lawyer cannot persuade the client to rectify the perjury."

In 2002, the ABA amended Rule 3.3 to make the mandate clearer. What do Model Rules 3.3(a)(3) and 3.3(b) mean by the term "reasonable remedial measures"? Do Model Rule 3.3, Comments 10, 11, and 15, help you answer that question?[39]

2.   Could someone responsibly argue that the Model Rules approach to client perjury is wrong, i.e., that the right to testify is meaningless if the defendant cannot tell the story he wants to tell, even if that story is false?

a.   Professor Monroe Freedman has been a prime advocate of the argument that the lawyer's duty is to call the client, ask the relevant questions, let the client tell his own story even if the story is fabricated, and then rely on the client's story in his summation to the jury. He says that any other approach ignores what he calls the lawyer's "trilemma":[40]

> "[T]he attorney functions in an adversary system of justice which imposes three conflicting obligations upon the advocate. The difficulties presented by these obligations are particularly acute in the criminal defense area because of the presumption of innocence, the burden on the state to prove its case beyond reasonable doubt, and the right to put the prosecution to its proof.

---

[39]   See also, Restatement Third, The Law Governing Lawyers § 120, Comments h and i.

[40]   The version of the argument quoted here comes from Monroe H. Freedman, Perjury: The Lawyer's Trilemma, 1 Litigation 26 (Winter 1975).

"First, the ABA Standards Relating to the Defense Function requires the lawyer to determine all relevant facts known to the accused * * *. The lawyer who is ignorant of any potentially relevant fact 'incapacitates himself to serve his client effectively,' because 'an adequate defense cannot be framed if the lawyer does not know what is likely to develop at trial.'

"Second, the lawyer must hold in strictest confidence the disclosures made by the client in the course of the professional relationship. * * * [C]ounsel is required to establish a relationship of trust and confidence, to explain the necessity of full disclosure of all facts, and to explain to the client the obligation of confidentiality which makes privileged the accused's disclosures.

"Third, * * * the lawyer is an officer of the court, and his or her conduct before the court 'should be characterized by candor.'

"As soon as one begins to think about those responsibilities, it becomes apparent that the conscientious attorney is faced with what we may call a trilemma—that is, the lawyer is required to know everything, to keep it in confidence, and to reveal it to the court. * * *

"In my opinion, the attorney's obligation [when the client wants to lie] would be to advise the client that the proposed testimony is unlawful, but to proceed in the normal fashion in presenting the testimony and arguing the case to the jury if the client makes the decision to go forward. Any other course would be a betrayal of the assurances of confidentiality given by the attorney to induce the client to reveal everything, however damaging it might appear.

"A frequent objection to the position that the attorney must go along with the client's decision to commit perjury is that the lawyer would be guilty of subornation of perjury. Subornation, however, consists of willfully procuring perjury, which is not the case when the attorney indicates to the client that the client's proposed course of conduct would be unlawful, but then accepts the client's decision. Beyond that, there is a point of view which has been expressed to me by a number of experienced attorneys, that the criminal defendant has a 'right to tell his story.' What that suggests is that it is simply too much to expect of a human being, caught up in the criminal process and facing loss of liberty and the horrors of imprisonment, not to attempt to lie to avoid that penalty. * * *

"I agree that * * * the case involving collateral witnesses is not at all as clear as that involving the client alone. [However,] * * * a spouse or parent would be acting under the same human compulsion as a defendant, and I find it difficult to imagine myself denouncing my client's spouse or parent as a perjurer, and, thereby, denouncing my client as well. I do not know, however, how much wider that circle of close identity might be drawn."

b.   What do you think of Professor Freedman's position? Is any other position consistent with the desire to leave a convicted defendant with the sense that he had a fair trial? Is giving the defendant a sense that he did everything he could more important than giving the jury only honest evidence upon which to base its verdict?

c.   The implications of Professor Freedman's position are provocative. Professor Freedman was one of the reporters for the Proposed American Lawyer's Code of Conduct (Rev.Draft, 1982), prepared under the auspices of the Roscoe Pound–American Trial Lawyers Foundation. That Code proposed to solve the problem of client perjury by protecting client confidences completely. Consider some of its illustrative cases:

Illustrative Case 1(j). "A lawyer learns from a client during the trial of a civil or criminal case that the client intends to give testimony that the lawyer knows to be false. The lawyer reasonably believes that a request for leave to withdraw would be denied and/or would be understood by the judge and by opposing counsel as an indication that the testimony is false. The lawyer does not seek leave to withdraw, presents the client's testimony in the ordinary manner, and refers to it in summation as evidence of the case. The lawyer has not committed a disciplinary violation."

Illustrative Case 3(e). "A lawyer is conducting the defense of a criminal prosecution. The judge calls the lawyer to the bench and asks her whether the defendant is guilty. The lawyer knows that the defendant is guilty, and reasonably believes that an equivocal answer will be taken by the judge as an admission of guilt. The lawyer assures the judge that the defendant is innocent. The lawyer has not committed a disciplinary violation."

Illustrative Case 3(f): "The same facts as in 3(e), but the lawyer replies to the judge, 'I'm sorry, your Honor, but it would be improper for me to answer that question.' The lawyer has committed a disciplinary violation."

What do you think? Would you want to try cases in a system that was tolerant of the fact that defendants' testimony is untrue? What do you think juries believe about such testimony today?

d.   Does Professor Freedman convince you that the Supreme Court was wrong in *Nix*? Do you agree that a defendant's rights include the choice of what to say from the witness stand? Does the fact that a lawyer would be aiding and abetting perjury if he or she knowingly elicited false testimony from the client ultimately make the Freedman argument unsatisfying?

————

PROBLEM 28

THE VERDICT THAT MAY BE TAINTED

Lawyers don't like to lose, and win or lose, they like to know how jurors reacted to their presentation. Lawyers often ask jurors, after the verdict, why they voted the way they did. Jurors have no obligation to respond but they often do, and in this and other settings, lawyers sometimes want to preserve an accurate record of what was said. Hence, this problem first explores the propriety of a lawyer contacting jurors after trial to find out where a lawyer went wrong. It then moves to the rules restricting the contact of jurors before or during trial, and the restrictions relating to the payment of experts and fact witnesses. Following that, the problem explores the ethics of the lawyer secretly tape recording a conversation, and, finally, it looks at the rules governing when a lawyer may testify about what she has heard and observed.

FACTS

Marian Talley represented the defendant in a products liability case in which the jury returned an unexpectedly large verdict against her client. After the verdict, Talley sought to determine what went wrong. She asked a juror to come to her office and he did so. He was completely cooperative and said, "Most of the jurors initially voted to find no liability, or at least to set a much lower damage figure. One juror held out, however, and we finally came around to his position. That juror later confided to me, after the foreman announced the verdict, that he worked for a competitor of your client and the competitor would pay him handsomely for making the verdict come out as it did. It was too late to do anything, and I don't want to get involved, but it is good to get this off my chest."

This explanation of the verdict angered Talley and she asked the former juror to put the story in an affidavit. The juror said that he would prefer not to do so, but he told Talley where the supposed payoff would occur. The juror threatened to deny everything if Talley ever asked her about the incident in court. At that point, Talley activated a secret tape recording device that she always carried with her for occasions where she needed to preserve what was said in a conversation. Talley skillfully got the former juror to repeat most of the story, and Talley left satisfied that she had the information on tape.

Using the information supplied by the former juror, Talley went to the place established for the payoff and saw a fat envelope handed to the allegedly dishonest juror by an executive of the juror's employer. She has moved for a new trial and plans to authenticate the tape recording of the former juror's disclosures and testify about her own observations of the payoff at the hearing on her motion. She asked one of the firm's investigators to accompany her, but he never showed up (it turns out he got sick), so she is the only witness to the transfer of the envelope.

QUESTIONS

A.   THE ETHICS OF CONTACTING JURORS AFTER TRIAL

1.   Was it proper for Talley to talk to the juror and investigate the jury's deliberative process?

a.   Consider one report of how juries really work:

"In an unusual post-trial move, the lawyer for Eric Menendez invited seven sympathetic female jurors to her office where they told reporters on Saturday that a battle between men and women on Mr. Menendez's jury doomed the chances for a verdict.[41] * * *

" 'It was hostile in there,' said one juror * * *. 'There were insults, sexual comments. * * *

"Another juror * * * said, 'We were called ignorant asses and empty headed and those women.' " We had one juror who would put on his sunglasses and be balancing his checkbook and cutting out coupons when the women were talking.' * * *

"A vote on the first day of deliberations indicated the jury was split, the female jurors said, with six women for manslaughter convictions and six men for first-degree murder. Ultimately, five men voted for first-degree murder, one for second-degree. The women voted for voluntary manslaughter."[42]

b.   Look at Model Rule 3.5. Do any of the restrictions placed on contacting jurors surprise you? Do you think they unduly restrict lawyers' ability to get the kind of information Talley was seeking? Did the juror's reluctance to put the facts in an affidavit indicate a desire not to communicate with Talley?

c.   Rapp v. Disciplinary Bd. of Hawaii Supreme Court, 916 F.Supp. 1525 (D.Haw.1996), held that restrictions on post-trial contact with jurors violate free speech rights of the lawyers, the litigants and the jurors. Rapp, a lawyer, was a *pro se* plaintiff in a state case. The jurors voted in his favor and he wanted to thank the jurors and learn how they reacted to aspects of his advocacy. Alleging a fear of discipline if he contacted jurors, he filed this federal court action to have Rule 3.5 held unconstitutional. The court held that by allowing only contact with jurors that was "permitted by law," Rule 3.5(c) placed a vague and overbroad limitation on First Amendment rights. Do you agree with this decision? Does the court seem to have been "solving" a nonexistent problem?

d.   In Commission for Lawyer Discipline v. Benton, 980 S.W.2d 425 (Tex.1998), the plaintiff's lawyer in a personal injury action where the jury awarded no damages wrote to all the jurors: "I was so angry

---

[41] The state prosecuted Eric and Lyle Menendez for killing their parents in order to inherit a substantial fortune. They ultimately admitted the killing but claimed self-defense, asserting that their father had molested them for many years and they were afraid he would kill them to prevent them from disclosing his acts. The first trial deadlocked. The second resulted in conviction for first degree murder and conspiracy. The sentence was life without parole.

[42] New York Times, Jan. 13, 1994, sec. A. p. 13, col. 1.

with your verdict that I could not talk with you after the trial. I could not believe that 12 allegedly good people from Cameron County, who swore to return a verdict based on the evidence, could find [as you did]. * * * Your cold and unfair conduct does not matter now. Judge Hester * * * decided that your verdict was obviously unjust and granted * * * a new trial." The Texas Commission for Lawyer Discipline found that by sending this letter, the lawyer violated the Texas version of Rule 3.5. It put the lawyer on probation. The Court of Appeals reversed, finding the Rule itself unconstitutional, but a badly split Texas Supreme Court found the Rule did not violate the lawyer's right of free speech, was not unconstitutionally overbroad, and was not unconstitutionally vague in prohibiting communications calculated to influence a juror's actions in future jury service. The court remanded for a new hearing.

Does the lawyer's letter in *Benton* violate Model Rule 3.5(c)(3)? If a lawyer wrote such a letter to the judge after a trial, could the judge hold the lawyer in contempt of court?

e.   The ethics rules regulate lawyers, not representatives of the press. Yet, some people believe that the risk that the news media will harass jurors is no less serious than the concern that lawyers will harass them. Others object that some jurors try to sell stories about their deliberations to the highest bidder.[43] Are there significant constitutional issues raised if a court tried to impose restrictions on reporters that are similar to the restrictions that Model Rule 3.5 imposes on lawyers?

2.   Now that Talley believes that a juror violated his oath, what should she do?

a.   Rule 606(b) of the Federal Rules of Evidence provides that "a juror may testify on the question whether extraneous prejudicial information was improperly brought to the jury's attention or whether any outside influence was improperly brought to bear upon any juror." Many state laws similarly make it possible to impeach a jury's verdict by showing that one or more of the jurors were corrupt and that the integrity of the verdict is in doubt. Does that possibility, in turn, create a duty on a lawyer to bring the issue to the attention of the court?

b.   Do the Model Rules give Talley such a professional obligation? Look at Rule 3.3(b) and Comment 12. Do you have any doubt about what Talley is required to do?

c.   Talley is undoubtedly glad she did not learn that her client tried to bribe a juror. Suppose her client committed that crime. What would Talley's obligation be? Is she required to reveal information that clearly relates to the representation and thus would be confidential under Model Rule 1.6(a)? Look at Model Rule 3.3(c).

B.   CONTACTING JURORS BEFORE TRIAL; COMPENSATION OF WITNESSES

1.   Was it unethical for Talley's opponent to try to bribe one or more of the jurors before the trial?

a.   Do not ponder long whether or not a lawyer may bribe a juror. That is clearly illegal under the law of all jurisdictions.

---

43   See, e.g., Mark Hansen, Post–Trial Interview Limits Criticized, ABA J., Apr. 1994, at p. 26 (limits imposed on interviews of "Crazy Eddie" fraud trial jurors).

b.   Do the Model Rules also prohibit this conduct? Look at Rule 3.5(a). Remember also Rules 8.4(b), 8.4(c), and 8.4(d). Everywhere Talley's opponent turns, it is clear that he or she is in big trouble.

2.   Does the complex mix of people in a modern society mean that the trial lawyer should investigate the characteristics of individual members of the jury pool?

a.   Would Talley or any other lawyer be violating the Model Rules if she interviewed members of the jury pool before the trial outside the presence of the judge? May a lawyer hire private investigators to perform background checks on potential jurors? Should prosecutors be able to use police officers to investigate the jurors?

b.   Given the fact that the Supreme Court has limited the use of peremptory challenges to strike jurors based on general categories of race and sex,[44] do lawyers need more freedom to investigate to challenge for cause and to defend their peremptory strikes? Should judges give lawyers less information in order to limit the lawyers' ability to exclude jurors for reasons that do not relate to impartiality?

3.   If there is to be a prohibition on pretrial communication or contact with jurors, how broadly should the rule apply?

a.   Restatement Third, The Law Governing Lawyers § 115(1) says that, "except as allowed by law," a lawyer may not "communicate with * * * a person known by the lawyer to be a member of a jury pool from which the jury will be drawn." Comment *b* to § 115 explains: "The rules concerning jury trial undertake to ensure that no juror will have a predisposition toward either party. Prohibition of pre-trial communication with prospective jurors both prevents improper influence and avoids the necessity of inquiry concerning such contacts."

Are you convinced that the entire jury pool should be off-limits to lawyer contact? Would a prohibition directed at any smaller group of jurors adequately protect the interest in seeing that none of the jurors is tainted?

b.   Is part of the justification for restrictions on lawyers pre-trial contact of jurors the desire to protect their privacy? In the O.J. Simpson murder case, the court forced prospective jurors to answer a court questionnaire over 50 pages in length about their religion, political attitudes, and life experiences. Should we be concerned about lawyers intruding into the jurors' personal lives?

4.   Is it proper for the lawyer to pay a witness for the time it takes to prepare and give testimony?

a.   Look at Model Rule 3.4(b) and Comment 3. A lawyer clearly may not pay a witness for the content of his or her testimony, i.e., only pay the witness if he or she testifies in a particular way.[45] It is routine,

---

[44] Georgia v. McCollum, 505 U.S. 42 (1992) (unconstitutional for either prosecutor or defense counsel to exercise peremptory challenges based on racial stereotypes); J.E.B. v. Alabama ex rel. T.B., 511 U.S. 127 (1994) (same result regarding sex-based challenges). We discussed these issues earlier in Problem 24.

[45] E.g., Florida Bar v. Wohl, 842 So.2d 811 (Fla.2003). Wohl represented Bruce Winston, son of jeweler Harry Winston, in a dispute with his brother over his mother's estate. Wohl solicited the help of Kerr, a former employee of the Winston jewelry business, and offered compensation of $25,000 for her first 50 hours of service, and up to a one million dollar "bonus"

however, to pay expert witnesses for the time they spend preparing and testifying in a case.[46]

b.   In re Hingle, 717 So.2d 636 (La.1998), disbarred a lawyer for arranging to have his clients assume debts owed by an employee in exchange for the employee's favorable testimony. The lawyer told the district attorney "[i]f you as prosecutors can offer immunity to a witness to get him to cooperate, why can't I offer him money?" Do you find the lawyer's analogy persuasive?[47]

c.   Should it be proper for Martin to pay a fact witness (not an expert) for his time when he testifies and prepares for the testimony? ABA Formal Opinion 96–402 (Aug. 2, 1996) concluded that it is proper to pay fact witnesses who have to devote substantial time to a case. Comment 3 to Model Rule 3.4 does not literally permit such payments, the opinion conceded, but ABA Model Code of Professional Responsibility DR 7–109 did allow paying fact witnesses for the "loss of time in attending or testifying." The amount of any compensation paid must be reasonable, the opinion says, so as not to suggest payment for the content of the testimony. Moreover, the lawyers may pay even retired people: while they do not forego salary while they are testifying, lawyers may pay them for the value of their time in testifying and in preparing for their testimony.

What do you think of this opinion? Do you think the distinction between paying for time and paying for testimony is valid? On the other hand, could a company pay a current employee her regular salary for time spent working on and testifying in the case? Is the payment to a former employee or other outside witness significantly different?

C.   SECRET TAPE RECORDING

1.   Was it professionally responsible for Talley to tape record the conversation when it became clear that the juror would not commit his testimony to paper or repeat it to any other person? How should Talley be able to preserve accurate evidence of what was said?

a.   Talley's secret recording may or may not be a violation of state civil or criminal law. However, it is not a violation of federal law. Section 2511 of the Omnibus Crime Control and Safe Streets Act of 1968, 18 U.S.C.A. § 2511(2)(d), reads: "It shall not be unlawful under

---

depending on the "usefulness" of the information. The Florida Supreme Court held that this agreement violated Rule 3.4(b), because it was an unlawful inducement to a witness. The court suspended Wohl for 90 days, imposed one year probation, and required that he successfully complete a practice and professional enhancement program.

[46] However, expert witnesses may not be paid fees contingent on their testimony or the success of the client in the matters. See, e.g., Person v. Association of the Bar of the City of New York, 554 F.2d 534 (2d Cir.), cert. denied, 434 U.S. 924 (1977), discussed in Problem 36, *infra*.

[47] We will look at prosecutors' practice of granting immunity in Problem 29. Note that statutes authorize the immunity, the courts technically grant it on application of the prosecutor, and the court fully discloses to the jury that the prosecutor's witness has immunity from prosecution. ABA Standards Relating to the Administration of Justice, The Prosecution Function, Standard 3–3.2(b) states explicitly that there must be "no attempt to conceal the fact of reimbursement." The court said in Kastigar v. United States, 406 U.S. 441, 446 (1972): "many offenses are of such a character that the only persons capable of giving useful testimony are those implicated in the crime."

this Chapter for a person not acting under color of law to intercept a wire or oral communication where such person is a party to the communication * * * unless such communication is intercepted for the purpose of committing any criminal or tortious act * * *."[48]

b.   Federal Communications Commission (FCC) regulations apply only if telephones are used. These regulations require that the telephone company install and maintain an automatic tone warning device before a party can record telephone conversations. A person's failure to use this device is not criminal, although it can subject one to loss of phone service. The law of evidence does not prohibit the introduction of tapes obtained in violation of these FCC tariffs. Battaglia v. United States, 349 F.2d 556 (9th Cir.1965), cert. denied, 382 U.S. 955 (1965).

c.   State laws vary, but some states allow what is called "consensual" recording, i.e., one party to the conversation knows that it is being taped and does not object.

2.   If Talley's tape recording did violate state law, would her conduct also make her subject to professional discipline or other remedies?

a.   Whatever the answer where the recording is legal, what if the recording is not legal? Look at Model Rule 4.4(a). In this context, is tape recording a method of "obtaining evidence that violate[s] the legal rights" of the person being recorded?

b.   Whether or not a crime has been committed, however, there may be a violation of Model Rule 8.4(c) if circumstances indicate the lawyer deceived the person into believing there would be no taping. For example, in Committee on Professional Ethics and Conduct of the Iowa State Bar Ass'n v. Mollman, 488 N.W.2d 168 (Iowa 1992), the lawyer agreed to wear a concealed microphone to a meeting with his drug client in exchange for leniency in his own prosecution for drug possession. The court held that for the lawyer to mislead his client in this way justified a 30–day suspension.

3.   Should the ethical principle be that it is always unprofessional for a lawyer to engage in tape recording, whether of a client or a third party?

a.   This is more than a theoretical inquiry. ABA Formal Opinion 337 (Aug. 10, 1974), advised lawyers: "With the exception noted in the last paragraph [about use in law enforcement], the Committee concludes that no lawyer should record any conversation whether by tapes or other electronic device, without the consent or prior knowledge of all parties to the conversation."

b.   Was the ABA Committee too sweeping in its conclusion? Does our society have a common moral revulsion against secret tape recording? Notice the date of the opinion. The ABA issued it the same year that President Nixon (a lawyer) resigned from the presidency. During the Watergate investigation, it became public knowledge that he had secretly taped conversations to which he was a party. Many people

---

[48] See also, United States v. White, 401 U.S. 745 (1971) (Sections 2510–2520 of the Omnibus Crime Control Act permit a participant to record a conversation secretly).

objected to the secret taping along with other things President Nixon had done.

4.   Is the Opinion 337 position on tape recording now outdated?

a.   Does the text of the Model Rules justify the ABA opinion? The rules at the time, and the rules today, forbid deceitful conduct. Is it deceitful to secretly record a conversation to which you are a party, if you do not make any representation about whether you are recording it?

b.   Opinion No. 80–95 (1982) of the Association of the Bar of the City of New York partly rejected ABA Formal Opinion No. 337 on the ground that prosecutors may surreptitiously record a conversation by placing a tape recorder on one of the parties to the conversation with only the consent of that party. Therefore, criminal defense lawyers should be able to record their conversations with witnesses as well. Recording of conversations with the lawyer's own clients and recording in commercial or civil contexts remained prohibited.

c.   In Opinion No. 515 (1979), the New York State Bar Association added that a lawyer should be able to respond to a question initiated by a client and advise that client that the client himself may surreptitiously record a conversation where that recording is lawful. Counsel, however, may not do the recording. See also, Texas Prof'l Ethics Comm. Opinion No. 514 (Dec. 27, 1995), to the same effect.

Does that distinction make sense to you?

d.   Restatement Third, The Law Governing Lawyers § 106, Comment *b*, says:

> "When secret recording is not prohibited by law, doing so is permissible for lawyers conducting investigations on behalf of their clients, but should be done only when a compelling need exists to obtain evidence otherwise unavailable in an equally reliable form. Such a need may exist more readily in a criminal-defense representation."

Do you agree that there should be a "compelling need" requirement to engage in secret tape recording? Why might criminal defense lawyers have a greater such need than other lawyers?

e.   The ABA explicitly overruled ABA Formal Opinion 337 in ABA Formal Opinion 01–422 (June 24, 2001). The new opinion continues to prohibit recording in violation of state law. In addition, a lawyer may not falsely represent that there is no recording of a conversation. However, the opinion concluded that: (1) it is no longer universally accepted that nonconsensual taping of conversations is inherently deceitful, (2) there are circumstances in which disclosure would defeat a legitimate and necessary activity, and (3) Opinion 337 is no longer consistent with the Model Rules. However, the opinion said that it is inadvisable for a lawyer to record a conversation with his own client concerning the subject matter of the representation without the client's knowledge.

Has the opinion decided all the relevant issues to your satisfaction?

D. THE LAWYER AS A WITNESS AT THE CLIENT'S TRIAL

1.   Are any ethical issue presented if Talley testifies at the hearing on her motion for a new trial? Does Talley's testimony fall within any recognized exceptions?

a.   Look at Model Rule 3.7(a). Why is there a rule restricting the advocate also acting as a witness? Whom does this rule protect? The court? The opposing party? The client?

b.   Do you think that a jury is not able to distinguish between a lawyer's argument and her testimony? Does that mean the rule should not apply when the advocate testifies in a bench trial? A hearing on a motion for new trial? A *pro se* litigant may both represent himself and testify even if he has a law license, so how can one argue that the two roles are inherently inconsistent?

c.   Lawyers may become witnesses for a client in many different ways. Transactional lawyers are present when parties draft documents and when they negotiate agreements. A client may ask a lawyer to witness a testamentary document for a client. And, criminal defense lawyers may be present at police lineups and other interrogations. When lawyers work in a large firm, litigation and nonlitigation functions are often separated into different departments, so the advocate-witness rule may not affect current practice. However, in small law firms and smaller communities, the advocate-witness rule may more severely impact practice.

d.   The prohibition against a lawyer acting as an advocate and a witness does not apply if the testimony involves (1) an uncontested issue, (2) a dispute over the value of legal services in the case, or (3) if the disqualification of the lawyer would impose substantial hardship on the client. Rule 3.7(a). Would Talley's testimony fall within any of these exceptions? The first two exceptions do not involve situations that would confuse the finder of fact about the lawyer's role in the matter, but if courts interpret the third exception too broadly, it will eradicate the rule.

e.   In Zurich Insurance Co. v. Knotts, 52 S.W.3d 555 (Ky.2001), the plaintiff sued an insurance company to obtain payment of a personal injury award against the insured. Plaintiff's lawyer handled the claim throughout initial settlement negotiations and jury trial, and the plaintiff now says the insurance company acted in bad faith by not acting reasonably and promptly during the course of negotiations. The plaintiff's attorney filed a personal affidavit attesting to some of the practices of the defense counsel, although the attorney indicated no intention to testify at trial. The court held that filing the affidavit did not disqualify the attorney from continuing to represent the plaintiff. The court found it would be unduly prejudicial to disqualify counsel and opposing counsel could mitigate any potential prejudice to the defendant by effective cross-examination. Disqualification is an extreme measure, and factors such as the attorney's level of expertise, familiarity with the claim, and the level of trust and confidence of the client in the attorney were all relevant considerations.

Do you agree with this result? Is it consistent with Model Rule 3.7(a) and (b)?

2. Should a party be able to "waive" the protections of Model Rule 3.7?

a.   If the lawyer expects his testimony to be adverse to the client, the situation presents a conflict of interest under Model Rule 1.7(a) that would itself disqualify the lawyer. Unless prohibited by Model Rule 1.7(b), however, the client can waive this particular conflict.

b.   On the other hand, notice that Model Rule 3.7 does not provide for a waiver. Why not? Is the purpose of the rule to protect the parties or to protect the court and the fact-finding process?

c.   California does allow the client to "waive" the disqualification. The rule grew out of the decision in Comden v. Superior Court, 576 P.2d 971 (Cal.1978), cert. denied, 439 U.S. 981 (1978). Plaintiff argued that disqualification of the firm created a "substantial hardship" because of the distinctive value of the services of the law firm. The lawyer argued that, although he could transfer some of his work product to new counsel, he could not transfer his "impressions and rapport with the people involved." The court rejected these arguments and held that loss of expertise, interviews, research, and preliminary discussions of trial strategy do not constitute enough to support the substantial hardship exception also found in Model Rule 3.7(a)(3).

California responded to *Comden* by amending its Rule [now Rule 5–210] to allow a lawyer to let the client decide how to balance the need for the lawyer against the possible problems created by the dual role. A lawyer could be both advocate and witness if the lawyer secures the "informed, written consent of the client" after fully advising the client and after giving the client a reasonable opportunity to seek the advice of independent counsel.

Do you agree with the California approach? Is this a case in which, where California leads, the nation should follow?

3. When should the court disqualify the lawyer from participating in the representation? Is it at the moment when the lawyer is put on a witness list? Is it at some earlier time?

a.   In Comden v. Superior Court, supra, the California Supreme Court upheld a trial court decision disqualifying a lawyer who could testify as to what was said in certain meetings involving the litigants. The plaintiffs argued that the disqualification order was premature because later discovery might make the attorney's testimony unnecessary. However, the court concluded that withdrawal is required whenever the attorney "ought" to testify. Contra, e.g., Connell v. Clairol, Inc., 440 F.Supp. 17, 19 n.1 (N.D.Ga.1977) (the attorney's testimony must be "in fact, genuinely needed"). Which rule do you think is better?

b.   Chappell v. Cosgrove, 916 P.2d 836 (N.M.1996), involved a lawyer who was one of five persons at a meeting where the defendants allegedly agreed to construct a park. The plaintiff residents moved to disqualify him, alleging he was a potential witness. The court said that the test for disqualification is materiality of the testimony, the need for the lawyer to give it, and the prejudice if the lawyer does testify. Because there were several people at the meeting, the court concluded that the lawyer's testimony would be cumulative, not necessary, and it did not order disqualification.

c.   Restatement Third, The Law Governing Lawyers § 108, Comment *e*, however, says that the advocate-witness prohibition "is not affected by the character of the testimony as cumulative." Even cumulative testimony may be important, the Comment says, so the issue is whether "a reasonable lawyer, viewing the circumstances objectively, would conclude that failure of the lawyer to testify would have a substantially adverse effect on the client's cause."

d.   If an attorney is disqualified from representing a client because the attorney will be a witness and the client then hires another law firm to handle the litigation, may the lawyer/witness help prepare the new lawyers? Why or why not, given the rationale that animates the Rule?

4.   If the lawyer-witness is not herself the trial lawyer, are there any justifications for imputing the advocate-witness rules to other members of her firm who are trial counsel?

a.   Look at ABA Model Rule 3.7(b) and Comments 1 and 5 that discuss the rationale for the Rule. The ABA Model Code of Professional Responsibility drew no distinction between trial counsel and other members of the lawyer's firm acting as witnesses. It imputed disqualification of the advocate-witness to all lawyers in the same firm.

b.   Does Model Rule 3.7(b) represent more realism or simply a decline in ethical standards? If Talley's investigator in this problem had not gotten sick at the last minute, could Talley have avoided the problem by having the investigator act as the witness? If so, why should any question arise about allowing other lawyers in the same law firm to conduct the trial while Talley is the one who testifies?

c.   Rule 3.7(b) notes that a law firm may not be able to represent the client because of obligations under Rule 1.7 or 1.9. How may these two rules come into play when a lawyer in the firm is likely to be a necessary witness? One possible scenario involves a lawyer who will testify adversely to the client's position. That would create a concurrent conflict of interest. Another possible situation arises when a lawyer in the firm committed potential malpractice and those acts are now subject of this litigation. The conflict between the firm's interests and the client's interests may prevent the law firm from representing the client when a lawyer in the firm may be a witness.

5.   What should be defense counsel's response if the prosecutor in a criminal case tries to testify against the defendant? How can the prosecutor avoid the problem if it becomes necessary for her to testify?

a.   People v. Donaldson, 113 Cal.Rptr.2d 548 (Cal.Ct.App.2001), granted a new trial based on ineffective assistance of counsel in a case of child endangerment. The prosecution had only one witness to the defendant's alleged acts; that witness testified at the preliminary hearing that she actually saw the defendant holding a pillow over the defendant's daughter's face, but at trial, the witness seemed confused and said that she had never actually seen anything occur. The witness also said that the prosecutor had intimidated her and made her feel as though if she did not testify, the prosecutor would under arrest her. Then, the prosecutor called herself as a witness to impeach the credibility of this witness by giving a narrative account of the conversations she had with the witness before the witness testified. The court held that by calling herself as a witness, she violated the professional conduct rule generally prohibiting a lawyer from acting as both advocate and witness. The defense counsel also rendered ineffective assistance by failing to object when the prosecutor took the witness stand.

b.   Did the prosecutor in *Donaldson* violate any other rules? Look at Model Rule 3.4(e). Did the prosecutor "state a personal opinion as to * * * the credibility of a witness," for example? The court found that in her closing argument, the prosecutor improperly expressed personal belief in defendant's guilt.

———————

PROBLEM 29

THE CRUSADING PROSECUTOR

The prosecutor, as a representative of the state, is a lawyer with special authority and special responsibilities. It should not be surprising, then, that some ethical standards of prosecutors are also *sui generis*. This problem first considers the use of the media and other publicity as a tool in modern litigation in the context of a prosecutor's work. Next, it looks at the prosecutor's decision what to charge. Third, it asks when a prosecutor may subpoena the files or otherwise investigate a criminal defense lawyer. The problem then examines restrictions on the leverage available to a modern prosecutor and broader questions about the ethical responsibilities of government lawyers.

FACTS

"Clean Gene" White is the crusading young state's attorney of Springfield County, the home of the state legislature. He says he sees a public interest (and his detractors say a personal political benefit) in uncovering what he publicly has called a "lot of skeletons under the beds of some state legislators." Gene has started a "special prosecutions" branch of his office responsible for discovering the misdeeds of legislators. Each week, on Monday, Gene holds a press conference to assert his belief in ethics, report on indictments just issued, allude to possible indictments, and answer questions put to him by the reporters covering his office.

Newspapers have begun to report rumors and rumors of rumors as to which persons are likely to be indicted; Gene has denied publicly that he or anyone in his office is responsible for the leaks and has said that he "denounces the rumor mill."

The special unit has successfully prosecuted three cases: one consisting of forty-six unpaid parking tickets received by the chairman of the motor vehicle committee (a "callous breach of the public trust," according to Gene); a second for failure to report a sale of race track stock on a legislator's ethics form; and a third against a House committee chairman for taking a $5,000 bribe to kill a bill.

Though his office normally exercises discretion not to prosecute persons found with minor amounts of marijuana, the office recently indicted a state official found with one marijuana cigarette in his car. This particular legislator is widely suspected of being in league with organized crime, although no admissible evidence supports such a charge. Gene privately told one of his assistants to follow this legislator in an effort to uncover some wrongdoing. When the assistant reported the discovery of the marijuana cigarette, Gene said: "Prosecute. I know we normally don't in such cases, but I want to make it hot for this fellow."

QUESTIONS

A. MEDIA RELATIONS IN MODERN LITIGATION

1. Why do the Model Rules place limits on White's use of press conferences and other public statements to tell the public about his office's work?

a. ABA Model Rule 3.8(f) imposes specific trial publicity rules on the prosecutor, while Model Rule 3.6 imposes other publicity restrictions equally on both prosecutors and private lawyers. The history of the development of the modern day rules reflect the ABA responses to Supreme Court rulings in both free speech and fair trial cases. Canon 20 of the Canons of Professional Ethics (1908), in the Standards Supplement, provided:

> "Newspaper publications by a lawyer as to a pending or anticipated litigation * * * [g]enerally * * * are to be condemned. * * * An ex parte reference to the facts should not go beyond quotation from the records and papers on file in the court; but even in extreme cases it is better to avoid any ex parte statement."

b. Sheppard v. Maxwell, 384 U.S. 333 (1966), made clear that excessive pretrial and trial publicity could constitute a denial of due process of law. Marilyn Sheppard, wife of prominent Dr. Samuel Sheppard, was bludgeoned to death in their home. The authorities accused Dr. Sheppard of the crime even though he said there was an intruder in the home. From shortly after the murder, repeated news stories criticized Dr. Sheppard's alleged failure to cooperate with the police and accused prosecutors of letting Sheppard "get away with murder." The stories continued through jury selection and the trial, and the jurors saw much of it. The Court put primary blame for the "carnival atmosphere" on the trial judge. It said, "the trial court might well have proscribed extrajudicial statements by any lawyer, party, witness, or court official which divulged prejudicial matters."

2. Is the current version of Model Rule 3.6 consistent with the First Amendment?

a. Gentile v. Nevada State Bar, 501 U.S. 1030 (1991), was the first Supreme Court case in many years to test the rules on pretrial statements to the press. In *Gentile,* drug evidence disappeared from a safe deposit box that undercover police officers had rented. The state charged Gentile's client with taking the drugs. Gentile held a press conference on the day of the arraignment at which he said that a police officer had likely taken them and that the police were using his client as a scapegoat. The jury later acquitted his client and then the Nevada State Bar sought to discipline Gentile for creating a "substantial likelihood of material prejudice" by influencing the potential jury pool against the state. The Nevada Supreme Court affirmed a private reprimand.

The U.S. Supreme Court reversed in two separate opinions authored by Chief Justice Rehnquist and Justice Kennedy. The Chief Justice persuaded a slim majority (Justices White, O'Connor, Scalia, and Souter) that states may regulate lawyers' speech by less than a "clear and present danger" standard, and that the "substantial likelihood of material prejudice" standard used by Nevada balanced relevant interests permissibly. However, Justice Kennedy persuaded an equally slim majority (Justices Marshall, Blackmun, Stevens, and O'Connor) that the specific Nevada rule was void for vagueness. The rule permitted a lawyer to announce the "general nature of the defense" but only to do so "without elaboration." That, said the Kennedy majority, was too vague to let Gentile know what he could and could not say. Instead of creating a safe harbor, Rule 3.6(c) created a "trap for the wary as well as the unwary." The ABA amended Rule 3.6 in response to *Gentile*.

b. In Attorney Grievance Comm'n of Maryland v. Gansler, 835 A.2d 548 (Md.2003), the respondent was the state's attorney for one of Maryland's largest counties. He held press conferences about highly publicized cases; reported evidentiary details, prior criminal records, and alleged confessions; and offered plea deals. The Maryland Supreme Court agreed with Gansler that "information contained in a public record" includes all information made public from any source, including the media. Thus, publicly revealing a defendant's criminal record is permissible, even if prejudicial to the defendant, if the speaker can show that a private citizen could discover the record from public documents. The public, however, could not discover confessions, however or information about plea discussions, so Gansler's reference to them was improper. The fact Gansler was a public official was important, because "Prosecutors are held to even higher standards of conduct than other attorneys due to their unique role as both advocate and minister of justice." In addition, "a prosecutor's opinion of guilt is much more likely to create prejudice, given that his or her words carry the authority of government and are especially persuasive in the public eye." The court concluded that a formal reprimand, issued publicly, would adequately deter future violations of professional standards.

c. Maldonado v. Ford Company, 719 N.W.2d 809 (Mich.2006), upheld the dismissal of a sexual harassment case because of the plaintiff's lawyer's release of pretrial publicity. A Ford employee was convicted of sexual harassment, but the conviction was subsequently expunged. The trial judge ruled the fact of the conviction was inadmissible in the current case, so plaintiff's counsel went to the media to disclose both the conviction and the judge's ruling. When later rulings similarly would have kept information from the jury that the lawyer wanted them to know, he went to the media "definitely over ten" times to be sure the jury pool would be informed. After several such incidents, the trial judge dismissed the case and the Michigan Supreme Court affirmed, two judges dissenting. "The trial court has a gate-keeping obligation," the court said, "when such misconduct occurs, to impose sanctions that will not only deter the misconduct but also serve as a deterrent to other litigants."

3.   Assuming that some restrictions on pretrial comment are constitutional, on whom should state ethics codes impose such restrictions?

a.   Did you notice that in most of the above cases, it was defense counsel, not prosecutors, who were accused of prejudicial publicity? Do you suppose the incidence of excessive publicity is as one-sided as these numbers suggest?

A notable exception was the disciplinary case against Durham, North Carolina, district attorney Mike Nifong in connection with his prosecution of members of the Duke lacrosse team.[49] One of the key issues was Nifong's going on television to announce on several occasions that Duke lacrosse players were guilty of raping an exotic dancer at a team party, a charge later found to be baseless.

b.   Robert Shapiro, a well-known criminal defense attorney, has argued that prosecutors have a significant advantage in the publicity battle.[50] The media reports details about the crime and the arrest. Police officers often calm the public with statements such as "We have found the person responsible for these crimes." Shapiro argues that if a defense attorney refuses to comment, that very fact sends a message to the potential jury pool that the defendant must be guilty. Thus, Shapiro believes that defense attorneys have a duty to monitor press accounts and respond appropriately. Does Model Rule 3.6(c) respond effectively to Mr. Shapiro's concerns?

4.   Did "Clean Gene" White violate Model Rule 3.6? If so, when?

a.   Did White violate Rule 3.6 when he said that there are "a lot of skeletons under the beds of some state legislators"? When he held press conferences to report on indictments just issued? When he alluded to possible indictments? Should White not give any press conferences but let his press secretary perform that function? Look at Model Rule 3.6(d). Would it help if his press secretary were not a lawyer? See Model Rule 3.8(f).

b.   Would White violate Rule 3.6 if he truthfully stated, "We have just filed a motion to force Judge Smith to recuse himself, because, as our motion states, 'the judge's actions in this case show that he is soft on public corruption' "? Why or why not? Cf. Model Rule 8.2(a).

c.   Would White violate Rule 3.6 if he truthfully said, "We have just indicted Kyle Jones, who often calls himself 'Kyle the Killer.' He was last seen heading south on Route 66. If you see him, call police, but do not try to apprehend, for he is considered armed and dangerous"? Should prosecutors have the latitude to make such statements?

---

[49] See The Duke Lacrosse Case, Innocence and False Identifications: A Fundamental Failure to "Do Justice," 76 Fordham L. Rev. 1337 (2007).

[50] See Robert L. Shapiro, Using the Media to Your Advantage, Champion Magazine, Jan.–Feb. 1993, at 6 (Journal of the National Association of Criminal Defense Lawyers).

d.   Was Gene White acting properly in denouncing "the rumor mill"? If a commentator claims that a trial court ruled, in an unpublished opinion, that one of White's assistants is "an overzealous prosecutor," may White respond truthfully: "The commentator is simply repeating a false charge that one of the suspects has made several times. The suspect is lying; the commentator should check his facts before he opens his mouth." Does Model Rule 3.6(c) protect such responses from prosecutors or only the responses of defense counsel?

5.   If a lawyer's statements fall within one of the exceptions contained in Rule 3.6(b) and (c), does this preclude other remedies against the lawyer who has created trial publicity?

a.   In Buckley v. Fitzsimmons, 509 U.S. 259 (1993), plaintiff filed a damage suit against a prosecutor for allegedly fabricating evidence of defendant's guilt and for announcing the defendant's arrest at a press conference that may have prejudiced the later trial. The defendant spent about three years in jail and went through one mistrial before a third party confessed to the crime and the defendant was released. The Seventh Circuit held the conduct of the prosecutor subject to an absolute privilege because it was all part of normal preparation of a case. The Supreme Court reversed and instead applied a "functional test" looking to the function being performed rather than the role of the actor. "Comments to the media have no functional tie to the judicial process," the Court said. In some cases, such comments may serve an important public function, but that is not enough to cloak them in the absolute immunity that applies to statements made in the course of a trial. Do you agree?

b.   In Seidl v. Greentree Mortgage Co., 30 F.Supp.2d 1292 (D.Colo.1998), plaintiff's counsel in a suit charging Internet "spamming" (i.e., bulk email advertising) issued a press release about the case and published it on her web page. She argued that an attorney's absolute privilege against defamation liability for statements connected with the case protected her against the defendant's claim of libel. The court disagreed. It is one thing to say a lawyer cannot be sued for libel for what is in a complaint, but in this case, the recipients of the press release had nothing to do with the case, so the release did not bear "some relation to the proceeding" and the lawyer could be found liable for defamation.[51]

c.   Helena Co. v. Uribe, 281 P.3d 237 (N.M. 2012), however, involved an attorney's public statements made before litigation to prospective clients in a mass tort case. The court held the lawyer had an absolute privilege against defamation to explain the allegations of the complaint because "(1) the speaker is seriously and in good faith contemplating class action or mass-tort litigation at the time the statement is made, (2) the statement is reasonably related to the proposed litigation, the attorney has a client or identifiable client at the time the statement is made, and the statement is made while the attorney is acting in the capacity of counsel or prospective counsel."

---

[51] See also Bochetto v. Gibson, 860 A.2d 67 (Pa.2004) (lawyer transmittal of complaint to freelance reporter was extrajudicial act that did not provide absolute immunity in a defamation action). For more on a lawyer's privilege against defamation for statements made in litigation, see Restatement Third, The Law Governing Lawyers § 57, Comment *c*.

6.   Suppose White prosecutes the state legislator with a marijuana cigarette in his car. If publicity will help the legislator beat the charge, may the legislator's lawyer advise him of that? Does it make any difference whether the state legislator is a lawyer?

a.   May the legislator himself call a press conference to give his side of the story? Cf. Rule 8.4(a). If the legislator does give a press conference, may his lawyer answer questions that reporters pose and that relate to the upcoming trial?

b.   In the background of all of these cases is the reluctance of state and federal courts to allow discovery of print and broadcast media. United States v. Cutler, 6 F.3d 67 (2d Cir.1993), involved John Gotti's lawyer, Bruce Cutler, who was quoted in several news stories commenting on the lack of merit of the government's case, all in apparent violation of a gag order imposed by the trial judge. When charged with a violation of the order, Cutler sought the notes of all the reporters who had quoted him, including their notes of statements made by others than Cutler. The court held that Cutler was entitled to notes relating to his own statements, including portions of televised interviews that were not used, but that he was not entitled to notes of the reporters' conversations with government officials or others. Later, United States v. Cutler, 58 F.3d 825 (2d Cir.1995), affirmed the lower court, holding that Cutler willfully violated the trial court's valid gag order and that his statements were reasonably likely to prejudice prospective jurors in the case. The court upheld Cutler's three-year suspension from practice in the Eastern District of New York.

c.   Also lurking in all of these cases are state and federal constitutional restrictions on the breadth of gag orders. Twohig v. Blackmer, 918 P.2d 332 (N.M.1996), for example, vacated a gag order at the request of defense counsel for a Native American charged with vehicular homicide in the deaths of an Anglo mother and her three daughters. The case got unprecedented media attention, most of it favorable to the prosecution. Two trials ended in hung juries, but the prosecutor promised to try again. Defense counsel appeared on radio talk shows and wrote a newspaper article saying enough was enough. At that point, the trial judge imposed the gag order, but the state supreme court vacated the order because it did not lay out a factual foundation for finding "substantial likelihood of prejudice or clear and present danger to fair and impartial trial." It contained no analysis of facts supporting the trial court's conclusion that a gag order was necessary, and it did not indicate that the court considered alternatives less restrictive of free speech than an outright ban on all communication with the media.

B. STANDARDS GOVERNING A PROSECUTOR'S DECISION WHETHER
    AND WHAT TO CHARGE

1.   May prosecutors file a charge that they do not believe they can prove beyond a reasonable doubt? What if the prosecutor reasonably believes that overcharging will encourage the defendant to enter a plea to a lesser offense the defendant clearly committed?

a.   Look at Model Rule 3.8(a). Is a probable cause standard too restrictive on prosecutors? Not restrictive enough? Compare this requirement to Model Rule 3.1's obligation placed upon lawyers who file civil cases. Does such a standard belong in a code of professional standards rather than simply in a code of criminal procedure? If the grand jury is willing to indict, has the prosecutor necessarily complied with Rule 3.8(a)?

b.   In United States v. Goodwin, 457 U.S. 368 (1982), the government originally filed several misdemeanor charges against the defendant, but after he asked for a jury trial, the government obtained an indictment that included a felony count. The defendant alleged prosecutorial vindictiveness and retaliatory intent that he argued should void the conviction. The Supreme Court disagreed. "Just as a prosecutor may forego legitimate charges * * *, a prosecutor may file additional charges if an initial expectation that a defendant would plead guilty to lesser charges proves unfounded." Thus, a presumption of vindictiveness was inappropriate and it found no actual vindictiveness in the circumstances of the case. See also, Bordenkircher v. Hayes, 434 U.S. 357 (1978) (prosecutor, without violating due process, may threaten defendant with more severe charges to which he is plainly subject, if defendant does not plead guilty to lesser charges).

2.   Do any of the Model Rules require the prosecutor to give exculpatory information to the grand jury when seeking an indictment?

a.   In United States v. Williams, 504 U.S. 36 (1992), the government charged the defendant with giving willfully false financial statements to a bank in order to get a large loan. At the time the prosecutor obtained the indictment, he allegedly had exculpatory information in his possession that he did not reveal to the grand jury. The Supreme Court rejected a claim that therefore it should dismiss the indictment. A grand jury sits to determine whether there is enough evidence to charge, Justice Scalia wrote for the Court; it does not sit to weigh conflicting evidence. Justices Stevens, Blackmun, O'Connor, and Thomas dissented.

b.   Even assuming that the Constitution does not require disclosure at the pre-indictment stage, what should the prosecutor's ethical duty be? May the prosecutor who has a lot of exculpatory evidence still have probable cause to charge within the meaning of Model Rule 3.8(a)? Can the prosecutor properly ignore portions of the evidence in his or her possession in making that determination?

c.   Is it wise for the prosecutor to withhold exculpatory information from the grand jury? If the grand jury believes that the information significantly undercuts the prosecution's case, does it make more sense for the prosecutor to know that before the trial? Will Model Rule 3.8(d) necessarily mandate its eventual disclosure to the defense?

3. May a prosecutor let a criminal defendant go free in exchange for testimony against someone the prosecutor believes poses a greater danger to society? Should anyone have a basis to complain about such conduct?

a.   United States v. Singleton, 165 F.3d 1297 (10th Cir.1999) (en banc), cert. denied, 527 U.S. 1024 (1999), reversed an earlier panel decision that garnered a great deal of national publicity when it prohibited the government in a criminal case from offering immunity and leniency to a witness in exchange for his or her testimony. The three-judge panel ruled that this exchange constituted payment for testimony, i.e., bribery. The en banc Tenth Circuit rejected that result because the antibribery statute refers to an individual offering the bribe. By contrast, an assistant United States attorney who offers a plea bargain is acting as the United States, not as an individual. Moreover, the court, not the prosecutor, actually grants the immunity. The court should not interpret the statute to restrict the sovereign's prosecutorial powers and to prohibit that which other federal statutes authorize, the court said. Further, to so hold would upset generations of prosecutorial practice. Congress acts against a background of such practice; the statute could not have the meaning the panel found. Judges Kelly, Seymour, and Ebel dissented, saying the statute is simple and means what it says. United States v. Lowery, 166 F.3d 1119 (11th Cir.1999), disagreed with the panel decision in *Singleton* and agreed with the en banc majority.

b.   Prosecutors do not ask the court to grant immunity to a witness in exchange for testimony in the dark of night. It occurs in court and requires the judge's approval. On the other hand, in In re Disciplinary Proceedings Against Charles O. Bonet, 29 P.3d 1242 (Wash.2001), the agreement was not so open. The respondent (the county deputy prosecuting attorney) prosecuted a defendant on drug-related charges. That defendant named one of his co-conspirators to testify on his behalf at trial, though this witness had made conflicting statements as to whether or not he actually planned to testify. The respondent told the potential witness that he would dismiss the criminal charges against him if he agreed to assert the Fifth Amendment and refrain from testifying for the defense. The court found a violation of Rules 3.4(b) and 8.4(d): "a public or private attorney may not offer an inducement to a witness in order to influence that person to not testify at a trial * * * regardless of whether the offer or inducement influenced the witness's decision to testify or not testify." The witness' prior subjective intent not to testify was irrelevant because the inducement itself was improper.[52]

c.   May the prosecutor accept a plea to a reduced charge when she believes the defendant is guilty of a more serious charge, but that the jury might acquit on that charge, thus hurting the prosecutor's batting

---

[52] Cf. North Carolina State Bar v. Graves, 274 S.E.2d 396 (N.C.Ct.App.1981), disciplining a lawyer who attempted to influence a witness (not his client) to not testify or to plead the Fifth Amendment. The witness could plead the Fifth, but it is still a criminal act for someone "with corrupt motive to induce a witness to exercise that privilege."

average?[53] May a prosecutor negotiate the defendant's agreement to perform charitable work for a certain time in exchange for dropping all charges if the negotiated disposition conforms to rough justice?[54]

d. If an assistant prosecutor personally believes that the defendant is innocent and does not want to prosecute the case, may the chief prosecutor (who believes the defendant is guilty) order her to prosecute anyway? How does Model Rule 5.2 affect your answer?

C. LIMITS ON PROSECUTORS INVESTIGATING DEFENSE ATTORNEYS

1. Do the ethics rules permit a prosecutor to subpoena office records of lawyers known to do criminal defense work? May prosecutors require defense counsel to appear before a grand jury? What if there is a reasonable concern that the defense lawyer may also be involved in the criminal conduct?

a. On October 1, 1985, the Massachusetts Supreme Judicial Court adopted a new disciplinary rule, Prosecution Function 15, which stated:

> "It is unprofessional conduct for a prosecutor to subpoena an attorney to a grand jury without prior judicial approval in circumstances where the prosecutor seeks to compel the attorney-witness to provide evidence concerning a person who is represented by the attorney-witness."

United States v. Klubock, 639 F.Supp. 117 (D.Mass.1986), affirmed by an equally divided court 832 F.2d 664 (1st Cir.1987) (en banc), rejected a supremacy clause challenge to this Massachusetts rule as applied to federal prosecutors. Whitehouse v. U.S. District Court for Dist. of Rhode Island, 53 F.3d 1349 (1st Cir.1995), also upheld a rule requiring federal prosecutors to get advance judicial approval before issuing a subpoena to a lawyer. Model Rule 3.8(e) is the ABA version of the Massachusetts rule.

b. Is Rule 3.8(e) really a rule of procedure dressed up to look like an ethics rule? Critics of such rules often argue that the ABA and organized bars of defense lawyers have little success in getting courts to adopt particular evidence rules so they dress them up as rules governing lawyers. But see, Stern v. Supreme Judicial Court, 184 F.R.D. 10 (D.Mass.1999), holding that the Massachusetts federal court had the power to adopt what is now Rule 3.8(e).

---

[53] For a discussion of the prosecutor and selective prosecution, prejudgment of credibility, and conflict of interest in the light of the ABA Standards Relating to the Prosecution Function, see H. Richard Uviller, The Virtuous Prosecutor in Quest of an Ethical Standard: Guidance from the ABA, 71 Michigan L. Rev. 1145 (1973). For a different view, see Monroe H. Freedman, The Professional Responsibility of the Prosecuting Attorney, 55 Georgetown L.J. 1030 (1967).

[54] Iowa Supreme Court Disciplinary Board v. Barry, 762 N.W.2d 129 (Iowa 2009), suspended a prosecutor for various ethical lapses, including a practice of reducing criminal charges or excusing public service elements of sentences if the defendants would contribute to the sheriff's "drug fund." The court found that this practice gave the "appearance to the public that justice was for sale," and was prejudicial to the administration of justice.

2.   Should lawyers have any more right than nonlawyers to resist a subpoena to produce records or appear for questioning?[55]

a.   Two lawyers who specialize in the defense of white collar criminal cases argue that government subpoenas of attorneys are a serious interference with the attorney-client relationship and prosecutors should not issue them without prior judicial approval:

> "Regardless of the type of information sought, * * * an attorney-subpoena has an obvious, unavoidable, and substantial impact on the attorney-client relationship. The fragile relationship of trust, built upon the understanding that what is said to the attorney is confidential and that the attorney's sole function is to serve as a zealous advocate for the client within the bounds of the law, is seriously strained whenever the government even attempts to have the attorney act as a witness against his client. As a practical matter, most clients simply do not understand the fine distinctions the courts have drawn between what is a privileged communication and what is not. [A client may] hold back critical information for fear that a future subpoena might be enforced. Nor can the client be absolutely sure that the attorney has actually invoked the privilege in response to all of the substantive questions asked in the secrecy of the grand jury room. The attorney, too, may decide to skimp on eliciting certain information from the client for fear he may have to divulge it in the future. * * * [O]nce the subpoena is served on the attorney, the attorney's own philosophical, emotional and financial concerns may color his professional judgment. Any advice he gives in this situation, whether it be to fight, to comply, or to compromise, may reasonably be seen by the client, or by others, as having been affected by those concerns. The resulting peril to the attorney-client relationship, and to the adversary system, is apparent. * * *

> "Finally, and perhaps most importantly, by using the subpoena the prosecutor can effectively exercise a veto power over the defendant's choice of counsel. Disciplinary Rule 5–102(B) of the Code of Professional Responsibility requires that an attorney withdraw from a case if 'it is apparent that [the attorney's] testimony is or may be prejudicial to his client.' The unrestrained power to issue a grand jury or trial subpoena, therefore, may substantially skew the adversary system—defendant's counsel serves at the pleasure of the prosecution. * * * "

David S. Rudolph & Thomas K. Maher, The Attorney Subpoena: You Are Hereby Commanded to Betray Your Client, 1 Crim. Justice 15 (Spring 1986).

---

[55] Lawyers should understand that, contrary to the wishful thinking of some, neither the work product doctrine, the attorney-client privilege, nor the Constitution absolutely prohibits a police search of a lawyer's office if there is probable cause to believe that the lawyer may be aiding in commission of a crime. See, e.g., Law Offices of Bernard D. Morley, P. C. v. MacFarlane, 647 P.2d 1215 (Colo.1982); Lackland H. Bloom, Jr., The Law Office Search: An Emerging Problem and Some Suggested Solutions, 69 Georgetown L.J. 1 (1980).

b. In re Grand Jury Subpoena Served Upon Doe, 781 F.2d 238 (2d Cir.1986) (en banc), cert. denied sub nom. Roe v. United States, 475 U.S. 1108 (1986), involved a defendant who asserted that if the government required his attorney to testify before the grand jury, the attorney would be disqualified from representing him in the later criminal case. The government was investigating the "Colombo organized crime family and a faction of that enterprise known as the 'Anthony Colombo crew.'" The grand jury sought "to determine whether Colombo paid for, or otherwise arranged for, the legal representation of members of his crew. Evidence of such benefactor payments made to [Attorney] Slotnick might establish Colombo as the head of 'an enterprise' as that term is defined in the Racketeer Influenced and Corrupt Organizations Act (RICO)," 18 U.S.C.A. § 1961(4). The government did not attempt to show a compelling or reasonable "need" for the lawyer's information. In fact, it expressly asserted that there was no requirement that it demonstrate need, i.e., that it could not obtain the information from alternative sources.

The en banc court agreed and held that in the "preindictment context" a requirement of such a showing of need "would unjustifiably impede the grand jury process." The possibility that the lawyer's testimony would disqualify him from later representing the defendant under the lawyer/witness rule was not sufficient to change the result. The majority said: "Before disqualification can ever be contemplated, the attorney's testimony must incriminate his client; the grand jury must indict; the government must go forward with the prosecution of the indictment; and ultimately, the attorney must be advised that he will be called as a trial witness against his client." After all, the attorney's grand jury testimony "may be exculpatory or neutral," or be otherwise inadmissible, or come within one of the exceptions to DR 5–102(B) or Model Rule 3.7. "The pretrial stage, not the grand jury stage, is the appropriate time to balance Colombo's interest in his right to counsel against the public interest in obtaining benefactor payment information, should the issue of disqualification arise."

c. In 1990, the ABA amended Rule 3.8(e) to require prosecutors to obtain prior judicial approval before subpoenaing defense counsel. In 1995, the ABA again amended Rule 3.8(e) so that it no longer requires prior judicial approval of subpoenas directed to lawyers but does place some roadblocks in a prosecutor's path. Is the current version of the rule likely to reduce the concerns that defendants and defense counsel raise?[56]

---

[56] Cf. United States v. Mittelman, 999 F.2d 440 (9th Cir.1993), that involved a motion to suppress evidence seized in the search of a lawyer's office. The affidavit for the search warrant said the office was believed to contain evidence of conspiracy to commit bankruptcy fraud. The prosecutor subsequently charged the lawyer (and the lawyer's client) with that crime. The court found the search exceeded the terms of the warrant, but it would only suppress evidence seized in "flagrant disregard" of those terms.

D.   PROSECUTORIAL OBLIGATIONS TO DEFENDANTS

1.   What are the obligations of a prosecutor to provide favorable evidence to the defense? Should a prosecutor disclose all favorable evidence to the defense or just material exculpatory evidence? May a prosecutor ask a defendant to waive the rights provided by Rule 3.8(d)?

a.   The Supreme Court, in Brady v. Maryland, 373 U.S. 83 (1963), held that the Constitution requires prosecutors to disclose material exculpatory evidence relating to the question of guilt or punishment to the defendant. United States v. Bagley, 473 U.S. 667 (1985) linked the definition of materiality to the standard in Strickland v. Washington, 466 U.S. 668 (1984). The prosecutor must disclose this information only "if there is a reasonable probability that, had the evidence been disclosed to the defense, the result of the proceeding would have been different." The narrow definition of exculpatory evidence that is "material" and the practices of some prosecutors to delay disclosure until the last possible moment raise questions about the relationship between Rule 3.8(d) and the constitutional requirement under *Brady*.

b.   Read Rule 3.8(d). Does this rule incorporate the constitutional requirement described above in *Brady* and *Bagley*? Or does it propose a broader standard of conduct for prosecutors?

c.   ABA Formal Opinion 09–454 (July 2009), analyzed the scope of the Model Rule 3.8(d) through a hypothetical involving a purse-snatching where the victim and a bystander both identified the defendant, but the prosecutor was aware that two other bystanders had not identified the defendant in a line-up, and a confidential informant had named another suspect. The prosecutor pursued these alternate leads and found that they were not credible. The questions posed were whether the prosecutor must disclose this information, when the prosecutor must disclose it, and whether the defendant could consent to the prosecutor's non-disclosure.

The Committee first traced the history of Rule 3.8(d) and determined that it created an ethical obligation to disclose that is independent from the constitutional requirement established in Brady v. Maryland, 373 U.S. 83 (1963). The constitutional standard requires the disclosure of favorable information that is "material," or likely to lead to acquittal. The Committee said Rule 3.8(d) did not incorporate the materiality element. Therefore, the scope of Rule 3.8(d) is more demanding than the constitutional standard, and a prosecutor must disclose all favorable evidence and let the defendant determine its utility. The information includes all that tends to negate guilt or mitigate the offense. It also includes information that is favorable when viewed independently or when viewed in conjunction with other information or evidence. Information or evidence does not need to be admissible at trial for disclosure to be required, and there is no *de minimis* exception to the duty. Therefore, under the hypothetical, the Committee determined that the prosecutor would be obligated under Rule 3.8(d) to disclose the information about the alternate identifications to the defendant.

A prosecutor only needs to disclose information or evidence of which he has knowledge. A prosecutor need not conduct independent investigations for exculpatory evidence, unless the prosecutor was willfully ignoring the likely existence of such evidence. The prosecutor also need not search a voluminous case file or police report, unless the prosecutor knows that or it is obvious that the file or report contains exculpatory information.

As for the requirement that the disclosure be timely, the Committee defined timely as "early enough that the information can be used effectively." The disclosure should be early enough to allow the defendant to use the information to conduct investigations, decide whether to plead guilty, decide whether to raise an affirmative defense, or to determine trial strategy. The Committee recommended that a prosecutor seek a protective order from the court if he believes disclosure would jeopardize a witness or undermine an investigation.[57]

d.   Federal judges have taken federal prosecutors to task for failing to disclose exculpatory evidence. A court overturned the corruption conviction of the late Alaska Senator Ted Stevens, for example, because the government did not disclose exculpatory evidence. In Re Special Proceedings, 825 F.Supp.2d 203 (D.D.C. 2011), 842 F.Supp.2d 232 (D.D.C. 2012), 840 F.Supp.2d 370 (D.D.C. 2012), appeal dismissed, 2012 WL 1473327 (D.C. Cir. 2012). In Massachusetts, Chief District Judge Wolf, "listed at least nine major cases he presided over during the last two decades in which prosecutors . . . withheld important evidence." Jonathan Saltzman, Judge Chastises Federal Attorney: Says Prosecutor Failed to Disclose Crucial Evidence, Boston Globe, Jan. 27, 2009.

2.   Should government lawyers have greater ethical obligations to do justice than lawyers in general have?

a.   Model Rule 3.8 places special rules on government lawyers who are prosecutors. Do these rules apply to other government lawyers who represent the government in civil cases? Do the Model Rules place any stricter obligations on them than on lawyers who represent private clients in civil cases?

b.   Freeport–McMoRan Oil & Gas Co. v. F.E.R.C., 962 F.2d 45 (D.C.Cir.1992) argued that government lawyers have a special duty to be fair in *civil* litigation. The government knew certain orders were superseded, but instead of conceding the point, it made the plaintiff challenge them in court.

Do you agree that courts should condemn such conduct? Do you believe that the government should press every advantage? If private lawyers, instead of government lawyers, refused to concede the obvious point, would that not be just as wrong? If so, does that suggest that the government lawyers in civil cases do not have a special duty, but have the same duty as private lawyers?

---

[57] The Committee also addressed whether a defendant could consent to non-disclosure and answered that question in the negative. Allowing a defendant to consent to non-disclosure would impede a defense attorney's ability to advise and defend the defendant. It would also undermine the "public's interest in the fairness and reliability of the criminal justice system."

The Committee also explained that the disclosure duty is slightly different in the context of sentencing. The prosecutor must disclose mitigating information that could lead to a lesser sentence, and the prosecutor must disclose the information to the tribunal as well as the defendant. When a defendant pleads guilty, mitigating information that normally would be disclosed in the course of a trial otherwise might not come to the court's attention.

3. Does the former or current prosecuting attorney have an obligation to take a second look at the case?

a. Do the obligations of Model Rule 3.8 extend beyond the end of a case? ABA Standard Relating to the Prosecution Function 3–1.2(c) says only what many cases say, that the "duty of the prosecutor is to seek justice, not merely to convict." How do we give meaning to that platitude?

b. Imbler v. Pachtman, 424 U.S. 409 (1976), was a damages action under 42 U.S.C. § 1983. Plaintiff alleged that a prosecutor knowingly suppressed favorable evidence and knowingly used false evidence against him. The Court held that an absolute privilege protected the prosecutor from liability in this damage action. The Supreme Court said it did not want to discourage a prosecutor from reporting evidence of an unjust conviction. "[A]fter a conviction," the Court said, "the prosecutor is * * * bound by the ethics of his office to inform the appropriate authorities of after-acquired or other information that casts doubt upon the correctness of the conviction."

c. In 2008, the ABA House of Delegates added new paragraphs (g) and (h) to Model Rule 3.8. They require that when "a prosecutor knows of new, credible and material evidence creating a reasonable likelihood that a convicted defendant did not commit an offense of which the defendant was convicted," the prosecutor must tell the defendant of the evidence and begin an investigation to determine whether the defendant had been wrongly convicted. The rule goes on: "When a prosecutor knows of clear and convincing evidence establishing that a defendant in the prosecutor's jurisdiction was convicted of an offense that the defendant did not commit, the prosecutor shall seek to remedy the conviction." Are you convinced that defendants can now be confident that the criminal justice system will not promptly correct any mistakes?

d. As of November 2013, only one state (Idaho) has adopted ABA Model Rule 3.8(g) and (h) and eight states (Arizona, Colorado, Delaware, New York, North Dakota, Tennessee, Washington, and Wisconsin) have modified the ABA language to soften the duty on prosecutors in light of limited resources to investigate allegations of erroneous convictions in closed cases. Does the ABA rule place too high a burden on prosecutors to investigate closed cases? Is this a burden that society *must* bear in light of the number of wrongfully convicted defendants?

PROBLEM 30

THE DUTY TO SEE JUSTICE DONE

OMITTED IN CONCISE EDITION

CHAPTER VII

THE DELIVERY OF LEGAL SERVICES

As discussed in Chapter 1, the world of practicing lawyers has changed dramatically over the last forty years. The changes profoundly impact the delivery of legal services in the United States and around the world. This chapter considers many of those changes.

Before 1977, for example, ethics rules said that making legal services broadly available to people who need them was the essence of professional activity. Yet those same rules prohibited lawyers from advertising or seeking clients through other communications. Today, all lawyers and law firms are concerned with getting their names before a desired group of prospective clients. Lawyers talk openly and aggressively about "marketing" services, stimulating client demand for those services, and seeking to take away clients currently served by other lawyers.

Over the same forty years, law firms, corporate legal departments, and government legal offices have become important institutions for training and supervising lawyers. It is no longer sufficient to require that each lawyer follow the rules of ethics. Partners who profit from their organization and supervisory lawyers who direct and monitor groups of lawyers and nonlawyers each must play an important role in the implementation of ethical standards. Lawyers often switch firms or employers several times during their careers, and this increased mobility accentuates these problems.

Changes in the manner in which lawyers offer legal services to clients continue to challenge the development of ethical standards. Referrals from one law firm to another are commonplace today, and traditional litigation has given way to class actions and other complex litigation to provide clients with redress. As litigation has become more complex and expensive, lawyers continue to look for new ways of funding and securing their fees.

The complexity of laws in today's society also means a continued need for legal services that the market does not meet. Many citizens cannot afford to hire lawyers to represent them in criminal and civil cases. As law becomes more of a business, the tradition of providing pro bono legal service to the poor and middle class presents an important challenge for the legal profession.

In the most recent two decades, the legal profession has also faced challenges to its monopoly of the delivery of legal services and receiving legal fees. American lawyers have resisted efforts to allow nonlawyer investors to own all of part of law firms. We have resisted accounting firms' attempts to introduce multidisciplinary practices. However, pressures from different rules in the United Kingdom, Australia, and elsewhere have pushed the American legal profession to consider alternative forms of practice. Lawyers talk of making their firms into "one-stop shopping" resources for both legal services and ancillary activities such as accounting, business consulting, investment banking, lobbying, and real estate development. In a global economy with instant telecommunications, international pressures become more real when clients can use law firms and non-lawyer services outside the United States to serve their global needs.

This chapter provides several windows on current issues in the delivery of legal services. As you examine the materials in this chapter, ask yourself such questions as:

a.   Has law become a "commercial" activity? Is that inevitable? Desirable for lawyers? Desirable for clients? Does such a change make law less of a "profession"? Is there a difference between practicing a "profession" and working in a "trade or business"?

b.   What role are the federal courts—as distinguished from state supreme courts—playing in transforming the profession? At whose expense are the rules being changed?

c.   What is the nature of a law firm today? How does it come into being? How does it break up? What are the duties of its members to each other?

d.   How can we make legal services more widely available? Should the law require lawyers to volunteer their services to persons unable to pay for assistance? Should the law give lawyers an incentive to bring cases in the public interest by requiring defendants to pay the plaintiffs' legal fees?

e.   Do alternatives to traditional law firms better provide legal services to persons not now receiving them? To what standards of conduct should these providers adhere?

––––––––

PROBLEM 31

MARKETING PROFESSIONAL SERVICES

Most lawyers enjoy practicing law and obtaining good results for their clients. However, for many lawyers, the problem is finding clients to consult them in the first place. A lawyer without clients finds it hard to pay the bills, but for many years the organized bar, and state courts in their regulation of lawyers, forbade lawyer advertising. Canon 27 of the ABA Canons of Professional Ethics (1937) said simply: "It is unprofessional to solicit professional employment by circulars, advertisements, through touters or by personal communications or interviews not warranted by personal relations."[1] Much has changed since the 1977 Supreme Court decision in Bates v. State Bar of Arizona, 433 U.S. 350 (1977), found such state bar efforts unconstitutional under the First Amendment. Advertising is everywhere, and skill at "marketing" is now a requirement for promotion to partner at many law firms. This problem first traces the constitutional analysis that led to the current rules about lawyer advertising. Next, it considers the

––––––––

[1]   The 1908 Canons originally permitted lawyer advertising, but a 1937 revision imposed substantial restrictions on lawyer efforts to communicate with prospective clients. See ABA Formal Opinion 276 (Sept. 20, 1947).

distinction between advertising and solicitation, and then it looks at limits the rules may and should impose on both advertising and solicitation.

FACTS

Jerry Harrold spent five years working for a large law firm in general litigation and then decided to open his own firm. On his first day at his new office, he called people he represented at the large law firm to let them know where he was and offer them a free "legal checkup," but none of them accepted his offer. Then, Jerry took several other steps to communicate his availability to potential clients.

First, Harrold put a quarter page advertisement in the local newspaper describing his credentials, the types of law that he practices, and how prospective clients can reach him. The ad said that "Jerry is willing to represent all clients in civil litigation—you choose the legal fee—either a 33% contingent fee or an hourly fee of $125 per hour."

Harrold then developed a website for his firm. At www. harroldlawfirm.com, one can find a general page with the same kinds of information he provided in the newspaper ad. The website tells visitors they can call the firm, come by Harrold's office, or send an email detailing their situation. The link for the email brings up a page with a large space in which to type facts and provide information. Another page contains links to several articles that Jerry has written about employment law, personal injury, and tenants' rights. It also contains a description of the cases that Jerry worked on while at the large firm and the outcomes he achieved. This page advises readers to "See if Jerry can get the same results for you in your litigation!"

Jerry Harrold also hired a public relations firm to publicize his litigation practice. The firm contacted newspapers and offered to provide quotes from Jerry about recent cases in the news. The firm also developed a brochure and mailed it to doctors, asking them to display it in their office waiting rooms. It also sent the brochure to all individuals who were involved in a car accident in the county. The firm even created a classy poster to place in the restrooms in area hospital emergency rooms. It arranged for Jerry to participate in a coupon offer of $50 prepaid for one hour of consultation. At first, Jerry paid the public relations firm a monthly fee of $500, but recently they have asked Jerry to pay them 1% of firm billings instead.

Finally, whenever a major accident occurs in the state, Jerry logs onto the internet and looks for blogs, chatrooms, twitter, and Facebook discussions about the accident. Jerry's screen name is HarroldLawyer and he posts information about his legal services. He tries to engage victims and their families and get them to contact him at his office for potential representation. He also plans to offer webinars (online conferences that individuals can log into), where he will discuss the legal consequences of an accident for a larger internet audience.

QUESTIONS

A. THE CONSTITUTIONAL CONTEXT OF THE REGULATION OF LAWYER MARKETING

1. What makes state-regulated lawyer advertising a matter of federal court concern?

a. The legal profession takes pride in regulating itself, but even lawyers live under the authority of the Constitution. For many years, the Constitution carefully protected political speech, but "commercial speech" was fair game for regulation. The leading case was Valentine v. Chrestensen, 316 U.S. 52 (1942), which held that New York could regulate distribution of leaflets advertising a tour of a submarine even though regulating the distribution of political leaflets would have raised constitutional concerns.

b. By the mid–1970s, however, that distinction was breaking down. In Bigelow v. Virginia, 421 U.S. 809 (1975), the Supreme Court said that Virginia could not punish a newspaper that published an advertisement for a New York abortion referral service. Similarly, Virginia Pharmacy Bd. v. Virginia Citizens Consumer Council, 425 U.S. 748 (1976), held that a pharmacist's advertising of prescription drug prices was entitled to First Amendment protection, in part because of consumers' interest in receiving the information.

c. Thus, when John Bates and Van O'Steen left the Maricopa County Legal Aid Society to open what they called a "legal clinic" and sought to advertise their "very reasonable fees," the time was right for the Court to say that prohibition of such advertising violated constitutional standards. A low cost legal clinic needed a high volume of clients to survive, so Bates and O'Steen believed they had no choice but to place a newspaper ad listing their services and fees. In Bates v. State Bar of Arizona, 433 U.S. 350 (1977), Justice Blackmun, writing for the Court, expressed doubt about the alleged state interest in maintenance of the prohibition:

> "* * * [W]e find the postulated connection between advertising and the erosion of true professionalism to be severely strained. At its core, the argument presumes that attorneys must conceal from themselves and from their clients the real-life fact that lawyers earn their livelihood at the bar. We suspect that few attorneys engage in such self-deception. And rare is the client, moreover, even one of modest means, who enlists the aid of an attorney with the expectation that his services will be rendered free of charge. * * * If the commercial basis of the relationship is to be promptly disclosed on ethical grounds, once the client is in the office, it seems inconsistent to condemn the candid revelation of the same information before he arrives at that office.

> "Moreover, the assertion that advertising will diminish the attorney's reputation in the community is open to question. Bankers and engineers advertise, and yet these professions are

"We need not discuss or evaluate each of these interests in detail as appellant has conceded that the State has a legitimate and indeed 'compelling' interest in preventing those aspects of solicitation that involve fraud, undue influence, intimidation, overreaching, and other forms of 'vexatious conduct.' * * *

"* * * But appellant errs in assuming that the constitutional validity of the judgment below depends on proof that his conduct constituted actual overreaching or inflicted some specific injury on Wanda Holbert or Carol McClintock. * * *

"The Rules prohibiting solicitation are prophylactic measures whose objective is the prevention of harm before it occurs. * * *

"The State's perception of the potential for harm in circumstances such as those presented in this case is well-founded. The detrimental aspects of face-to-face selling even of ordinary consumer products have been recognized and addressed by the Federal Trade Commission, and it hardly need be said that the potential for overreaching is significantly greater when a lawyer, a professional trained in the art of persuasion, personally solicits an unsophisticated, injured, or distressed lay person. * * * Although it is argued that personal solicitation is valuable because it may apprise a victim of misfortune of his or her legal rights, the very plight of that person not only makes him or her more vulnerable to influence but also may make advice all the more intrusive. Thus, under these adverse conditions the overtures of an uninvited lawyer may distress the solicited individual simply because of their obtrusiveness and the invasion of the individual's privacy, even when no other harm materializes. Under such circumstances, it is not unreasonable for the State to presume that in-person solicitation by lawyers more often than not will be injurious to the person solicited.

"The efficacy of the State's effort to prevent such harm to prospective clients would be substantially diminished if, having proved a solicitation in circumstances like those of this case, the State were required in addition to prove actual injury. * * * It therefore is not unreasonable, or violative of the Constitution, for a State to respond with what in effect is a prophylactic rule."[7]

c.   Justice Powell also wrote for the Court in a companion case, In re Primus, 436 U.S. 412 (1978). *Primus* gave constitutional protection to a lawyer addressed a gathering of pregnant mothers on public assistance. The county was sterilizing them or threatening them with sterilization as a condition of their continued receipt of medical

---

[7]   The opinion was for a six-member majority. Justice Marshall concurred in the judgment, but said that even unsolicited contact from a lawyer can often provide important information and help to an accident victim whom the defendant or its insurer is already free to contact and with whom they may negotiate a settlement. Justice Rehnquist, also concurring in the judgment, continued to argue that the Constitution does not protect lawyer marketing. Justice Brennan did not participate.

assistance under the Medicaid program. Later, she sent one of them a letter advising that the ACLU was offering free legal assistance to women who were involuntarily sterilized. The Court distinguished *Primus* from *Ohralik* on several grounds. First, it was important that the personal solicitation was in writing, which gave the recipient time for reflection. Second, the case had a political character and was a form of expression because it sought to redress an injustice done to many women. Third, the lawyer who sent the letter was cooperating with the local branch of a nonprofit organization. The Court thus had two extreme cases. In one, it protected in-person contact; in the other, it did not. It left open where other cases would fall along this continuum.

d.   Examine modern-day ABA Model Rule 7.3. What you see is the product of a long series of changes, most of which responded to litigation that invalidated various restrictions that the ABA tried to impose on advertising and solicitation, first in the Model Code and later in the Model Rules. Model Rule 7.3 now limits "direct contact" with prospective clients only when pecuniary gain is a "significant motive," but the definition of direct contact now extends to "in-person, live telephone or real-time electronic contact."

2. When does permitted lawyer advertising become prohibited in-person solicitation? May Harrold's public relations agency send his brochures to all individuals who have been involved in an injury car crash in the county?

a.   Contact with persons believed to have a specific current need for legal service is called "targeted direct mail." Is targeted mail more like advertising, protected by *Bates,* or subject to the greater regulation of in-person solicitation?

b.   Matter of Von Wiegen, 470 N.E.2d 838 (N.Y.1984), saw targeted mail as advertising. In-person solicitation "permits the exertion of subtle pressure and often demands an immediate response," the court said, while targeted direct mail gives the recipient time to reflect about—or indeed ignore—the offer of services and "the process of decision-making may actually be aided by information contained in the mailing."

c.   Not all states agreed, and the Court resolved the issue by invalidating a state rule that banned targeted direct mail. In Shapero v. Kentucky Bar Association, 486 U.S. 466 (1988), Mr. Shapero applied to the state attorney general's advertising commission for approval of a letter he planned to send to persons against whom he believed foreclosure suits had been filed. The commission did not find the letter false or misleading, but it cited a Kentucky Supreme Court rule that prohibited sending letters "precipitated by a specific event or occurrence involving or related to the addressee" rather than to the public generally.

The Supreme Court held that such a blanket ban was unconstitutional. The lawyer clearly could have published his truthful letter in a newspaper or mailed it in bulk throughout the community, the Court said. The Constitution does not require that lawyers distribute advertising in an inefficient manner. As for *Ohralik*'s concerns about "overwhelming" the targets of the letters, the Court said that whether or not letters are overwhelming has nothing to do with whether lawyers send them randomly or not. Furthermore, no form of written communication presents the dangers of overreaching that *Ohralik* illustrated. "A letter, like a printed advertisement (but unlike a lawyer), can readily be put in a drawer to be considered later, ignored, or discarded." The fact that some targeted direct mail might be abusive did not justify banning all such mail.[8]

3.   How do Internet communications fit into this analysis? After a major accident, Jerry plans to surf the web looking for blogs, chat rooms, twitter, and Facebook discussions about the accident and then seek to get participants to consult the lawyer for legal services. How does Model Rule 7.3 apply?

a.   In 2012, the ABA amended the comments to Model Rule 7.3 to clarify that passive advertisements, such as a website, internet banner, or the webpage results of an internet search do not constitute solicitation. Comment 1 to Model Rule 7.3.

b.   Does "real-time electronic contact" present the same concerns about solicitation that face-to-face contact presents? The lawyer providing truthful information in an electronic "chat room" is engaged in "real-time" contact, but no one has to respond. Quietly leaving a chat room is not impolite, like abruptly hanging up a phone. If anyone in a chat room says he does not want to be solicited, Rule 7.3(b)(1) requires the lawyer to stop.

Should the Rules seek to ban solicitation of prospective clients through this medium? Is "real-time electronic contact" more like a letter that one can throw away, like a prerecorded telephone call, or like a live telephone call that Rule 7.3 has long treated as direct contact?

c.   Philadelphia Bar Ass'n Prof. Guidance Comm. Opinion 2010–6 (June 2010) examined lawyer involvement in blogging, email, and chat room posts. It concluded that each of these forms of communication could occur in real-time, but the important test for whether each is solicitation is whether "it would be socially awkward or difficult for a recipient of a lawyer's overtures to not respond in real time." Thus, blogging, email, and posts in chat rooms are not prohibited solicitation. The opinion warned lawyers not to participate in real-time voice conversations in chat rooms and to abide by the prohibitions against false and misleading statements. Could Jerry Harrold operate a chat room on his web site where only those who chose to enter would interact with him?

d.   D.C. Bar Legal Ethics Opinion No. 316 (July 2002) discussed a variety of ways lawyers operate in chat rooms. It reports one chat room in which inquirers write questions and lawyers visiting the site write answers. The lawyers often invite the questioner to call for a brief, initially free, consultation. The opinion recommends that lawyers give "legal information" on such web sites, but not "legal advice." The former "involves a discussion of legal principles, trends and considerations [such as] * * * one might give in a speech or newspaper article." The latter "involves offering recommendations tailored to the unique facts of

---

[8]   Justice O'Connor, joined in dissent by Chief Justice Rehnquist and Justice Scalia, was willing to reconsider all of the attorney advertising cases. Justice O'Connor said that the cases were "built on defective premises and flawed reasoning." The entire analytical framework, she argued, "should be reexamined." She implicitly did so in Florida Bar v. Went For It, Inc., *infra*.

a particular person's circumstances." Giving advice, the opinion warns, may involve the lawyer in an attorney-client relationship with someone the lawyer does not know and create obligations greater than the lawyer means to assume. Do you agree?

e.   If Harrold obtains the cell phone numbers of individuals involved in accidents from public sources, may he text these potential clients and give them information about his legal services? Ohio Supreme Court Ethics Opinion 2013–2 (Apr. 5, 2013) holds that lawyers may use text messages as long as they comply with the advertising rules. It held that text messages are not live communications, and not prohibited solicitation, but texts must contain accurate information and the lawyer much honor recipients' indicated desire not to receive future texts. The Opinion states that the texts may not (1) impose costs upon the recipients, (2) target minors, and (3) violate any federal or state laws on such communications. It also says that innovations in video chatting may change the analysis.

C.   CONTINUING ISSUES IN THE FIELD OF LAWYER ADVERTISING

1.   Is it proper for a state to regulate advertising out of concern that it will increase litigation by encouraging people to sue who otherwise would not do so?

a.   The Court gave added content to the constitutional standards in *Bates* when it decided in Zauderer v. Office of Disciplinary Counsel, 471 U.S. 626 (1985). Philip Zauderer put an advertisement in 36 Ohio newspapers offering to represent women injured by use of the Dalkon Shield Intrauterine Device (IUD). The ad included a drawing of the device and a question "Did you use this IUD?" Zauderer's ad said that his firm was representing other women in such cases and that the cases "are handled on a contingent fee basis of the amount recovered. If there is no recovery, no legal fees are owed by our clients."

b.   Ohio disciplinary counsel raised concern that such advertising constituted "stirring up litigation," but the Supreme Court answered:

> "That our citizens have access to their civil courts is not an evil to be regretted; rather, it is an attribute of our system of justice in which we ought to take pride. The State is not entitled to interfere with that access by denying its citizens accurate information about their legal rights. Accordingly, it is not sufficient justification for the discipline imposed on appellant that his truthful and nondeceptive advertising had a tendency to or did in fact encourage others to file lawsuits."

2.   Do illustrations in a lawyer's advertisement have the same constitutional protection as the text message? May the state regulate illustrations if they are "undignified"? Some might view Harrold's posters in the restrooms of emergency rooms as undignified.

a.   The *Zauderer* Court held the illustrations were protected speech.

> "The use of illustrations or pictures in advertisements serves important communicative functions: it attracts the attention of the audience to the advertiser's message, and it

may also serve to impart information directly. Accordingly, commercial illustrations are entitled to the First Amendment protections afforded verbal commercial speech: restrictions on the use of visual media of expression in advertising must survive scrutiny under the *Central Hudson* test."[9]

b.   It also found that the state has no valid regulatory interest in preserving the dignity of the legal profession's image.

> "[A]lthough the State undoubtedly has a substantial interest in ensuring that its attorneys behave with dignity and decorum in the courtroom, we are unsure that the State's desire that attorneys maintain their dignity in their communications with the public is an interest substantial enough to justify the abridgment of their First Amendment rights. * * * [T]he mere possibility that some members of the population might find advertising embarrassing or offensive cannot justify suppressing it. The same must hold true for advertising that some members of the bar might find beneath their dignity. * * * "

3.   Should a lawyer be entitled to make claims as to her quality? Her won-lost record? May a lawyer include client testimonials in an advertisement?

a.   In Matter of Zang, 741 P.2d 267 (Ariz.1987), cert. denied, 484 U.S. 1067 (1988), two lawyers claimed to have "a personal injury law firm" with the capability to discover facts "essential to victory in the courtroom." Each of their advertisements emphasized their thorough preparation and use of investigators. The television ads showed Mr. Zang arguing before a jury. In fact, Mr. Zang had very little trial experience and "scrupulously avoided" taking a case to trial. If a trial were ever necessary, he would refer the case to another firm. He personally had never tried a personal injury case, and he conceded in the discipline proceeding that he did not feel competent to try one. He argued that the advertisements did not say that the lawyers were good at trial; they only said the lawyers were good at *preparing for* trial. The court rejected the distinction and suspended the lawyers for 30 days. The court found the advertisement "flattering beyond the point of deception."

b.   In re Keller, 792 N.E.2d 865 (Ind.2003), involved a lawyer whose television commercial showed insurance adjusters planning to delay payments to an accident victim. One of them asks who is representing the defendant, and when he learns it is Keller & Keller, he responds, "Let's settle this one." Actor Robert Vaughn then appears and says, "The insurance companies know the name Keller & Keller." The Indiana Supreme Court held that this advertisement and others that the firm used falsely implied that Keller & Keller usually obtained a favorable outcome for their clients. The court imposed a public reprimand.

---

[9]   The Court's reference was to Central Hudson Gas & Elec. Corp. v. Public Service Comm'n of New York, 447 U.S. 557 (1980), which held that commercial speech could only be regulated in pursuit of a substantial government interest and by means narrowly tailored to protect that interest.

c.   In re Anonymous Member of the S.C. Bar, 684 S.E.2d 560 (S.C. 2009), involved a disciplinary proceeding against a lawyer who practiced primarily in the area of personal injury and worker's compensation. In 2003, he produced and began airing a television commercial to promote his practice. The commercial said:

> "It's not your fault you were hurt on the job, but I know you're afraid to file a job injury claim. You're afraid your boss won't believe you're really hurt—or worse, that you'll be fired. We'll protect you against these threats—these accusations— and work to protect your job. I'm not an actor, I'm a lawyer. I'm [Anonymous]. Call me and we'll get you the benefits you deserve. The [Law] Firm."

The Supreme Court of South Carolina held that the Office of Disciplinary Counsel failed to prove a violation of the state version of Model Rule 7.1. First, no evidence showed that the ad misled any member of the public. Further, the text of the advertisement did not contain material misrepresentations and did not create any unjustified expectations. The respondent attorney truthfully said that he would work to protect the client's job, and that the statement simply demonstrated his intention to act as an advocate for the client and utilize all means to protect the job, including statutory provisions which provide liability for employers who retaliate against employees who file worker's compensation claims.

d.   Comment 3 to Model Rule 7.1 notes that accurate statements about a lawyer's successes for other clients "may be misleading if presented so as to lead a reasonable person to form an unjustified expectation that the same results could be obtained for other clients in similar matters without reference to the specific factual and legal circumstances of each client's case." Jerry Harrold included a list of cases (and outcomes) worked on while at his large firm and said "See if Jerry can get you the same results for you in your litigation." May he make this statement?

e.   What problem would a lawyer encounter with an advertisement presenting a client testimonial?

Office of Disciplinary Counsel v. Shane, 692 N.E.2d 571 (Ohio 1998), publicly reprimanded lawyers who used "not inaccurate" but self-laudatory claims of success in their television advertising. Former clients of the lawyers appeared before the camera saying such things as: "They really fought for me. * * * I never expected the large settlement they won for me," and "They fought for me and got me a very good judgment. * * * Take my word for it, they're the best." Do such testimonials "create unjustified expectations of similar outcomes in the future"?

4. Would requiring a disclaimer excessively "chill" protected speech?

a.   The Court in *Zauderer* distinguished requiring disclaimers from prohibiting speech altogether. It said:

> "[There are] material differences between disclosure requirements and outright prohibitions on speech. In requiring attorneys who advertise their willingness to represent clients on a contingent-fee basis to state that the client may have to

bear certain expenses even if he loses, Ohio has not attempted to prevent attorneys from conveying information to the public; it has only required them to provide somewhat more information than they might otherwise be inclined to present. * * *

"We do not suggest that disclosure requirements do not implicate the advertiser's First Amendment rights at all. We recognize that unjustified or unduly burdensome disclosure requirements might offend the First Amendment by chilling protected commercial speech. But we hold that an advertiser's rights are adequately protected as long as disclosure requirements are reasonably related to the State's interest in preventing deception of consumers."

b. Tillman v. Miller, 133 F.3d 1402 (11th Cir.1998), held the Georgia Workers' Compensation Truth in Advertising Act of 1995 unconstitutional. The Act required all lawyers and others involved in filing workers' compensation claims to put a large legend in their television ads saying that "willfully making a false * * * representation to obtain * * * benefits is a crime * * *." The court acknowledged that Zauderer permits a state to require disclaimers necessary to render an advertisement not false or misleading, but these ads were truthful. A state may not impose on a lawyer "the burden of the cost of educating the public about the criminal penalties for filing fraudulent claims."

c. In Mason v. The Florida Bar, 208 F.3d 952 (11th Cir.2000), the state bar sought to discipline a lawyer who publicly advertised his rating in the Martindale–Hubbell Legal Directory. The bar notified Mason that his advertisement must include a full explanation as to what the Martindale–Hubbell ratings mean and how the publication chooses the participating attorneys. This explanation must state "that the ratings and participation are based 'exclusively on * * * opinions expressed by * * * confidential sources' and that these publications do not undertake to rate all Florida attorneys." The lawyer's advertisement said that he was " 'AV' Rated, the Highest Rating Martindale–Hubbell National Law Directory." Specifically, the bar objected to the phrase "highest rating." The court held that the bar could not prove that Mason's truthful advertisement would mislead anyone. Moreover, "the Bar is not relieved of its burden to identify a genuine threat of danger simply because it requires a disclaimer, rather than a complete ban on Mason's speech."

d. In many states, magazine publishers have seized upon the idea of publishing the ratings of the best lawyers in the locality by practice area. The lawyers then use such designations in their own advertising. New Jersey Supreme Court Committee on Lawyer Advertising Opinion 39 (2006) examined the use of the designation "Super Lawyer" or "Best Lawyers in America." It found that, in contrast to Martindale–Hubbell ratings, the "Super" and "Best" designations are directed to the public and do convey misleading comparative information. The publisher allegedly grants the designations after a minimal system of peer review, and the program makes its money by firms buying ads in the publication congratulating lawyers who have received the designation. Do you agree that states should be able to prohibit use of the "Super

Lawyer" designation? Do you believe the court can or should suppress the apparently insatiable public desire for comparative information?

Later, the New Jersey Supreme Court vacated Opinion 39 and adopted twelve standards for determining whether lawyers may advertise such designations. In re Opinion 39 of the Committee on Attorney Advertising, 961 A.2d 722 (N.J. 2008). In 2009, the New Jersey Supreme Court amended its version of Model Rule 7.1 to make clear that lawyers may advertise information listing the designation of a "Super Lawyer" or "Best Lawyers in America." The new rule requires that "(i) the name of the comparing organization is stated, (ii) the basis for the comparison can be substantiated, and (iii) the communication includes the following disclaimer in a readily discernible manner: 'No aspect of this advertisement has been approved by the Supreme Court of New Jersey'." Does the required disclaimer go too far by casting doubt on the validity of the designation? Is the disclaimer necessary to inform potential lay clients about the source of the rating authority? In New Jersey Supreme Court Comm. on Attorney Advertising, Opinion 42 (Dec. 27, 2010), the committee further limited such advertising to prohibit statements such as "super," "best," "leading," "top," or "elite."

5.   May a lawyer use a memorable trade name or Internet web address such as "The Winning Team" or "<u>www.suethebums. com</u>"? Under what circumstances may a firm name be false or misleading?

a.   DR 2–102(B) of the ABA Model Code of Professional Responsibility provided:

> "A lawyer in private practice shall not practice under a trade name * * * or a name containing names other than those of one or more of the lawyers [currently or formerly] in the firm * * *."

What justification does Model Rule 7.5, Comment 1, offer for elimination of the broad prohibition? What should be the relevant concerns with respect to the names law firms use? Do you agree that even firms whose names are those of former partners in effect are using a trade name?

b.   Model Rule 7.5 is largely an elaboration of Model Rule 7.1's prohibition against false and misleading statements as applied to firm names and letterhead. For example, a law firm that used the name Official Texas Child Support Enforcement Firm might confuse potential users that in some way they were contacting the division of the State Attorney General's Office that handles child support enforcement.

c.   In Gibson v. Texas Department of Insurance–Division of Workers' Compensation, 700 F.3d 227 (5th Cir. 2012), the Fifth Circuit reinstated a lawyer's First Amendment claim to be entitled to use the domain name texasworkerscomplaw.com to publish information about Texas workers' compensation law and advertise his law practice. The defendant, a public agency, issued a cease and desist letter, citing a Texas statute forbidding the use of such a name to advertise a business "regarding workers' compensation coverage or benefits." The court rejected the idea that use of the domain name was entitled to a higher level of Constitutional scrutiny than that accorded commercial speech, but it also found the name was not "inherently deceptive." It thus remanded for a determination under the *Central Hudson* test whether prohibiting use of the name advances a substantial state interest and is no more extensive than necessary to serve that interest.

d.   Now that lawyers can form law firms as general partnerships, limited liability partnerships, and professional corporations, all references to the firm must accurately describe the organizational status. Similarly, when a law firm creates business cards or letterhead with the names of individual lawyers, the presumption is that all lawyers are licensed to practice in the jurisdiction listed. If some lawyers are not, the business card or letterhead must so indicate in order to avoid the false and misleading prohibition. When a firm lawyer accepts a government position, the firm must stop using the lawyer's name during any period where the person is not "actively and regularly practicing with the firm." Model Rule 7.5(c).

e.   Although Model Rule 7.5 is titled "Firm Names and Letterhead," it covers all professional designations of a law firm including internet domain names. Thus, under Maryland State Bar Ethics Opinion 2004–15 (Apr. 15, 2004), the internet domain, www. marylandadoptions.us, would imply a connection with a governmental entity and thus be false and misleading. Would it be appropriate to prohibit domain names like the ones suggested in this question?

6.   Does television advertising justify special regulation?

a.   Remember that *Bates* itself acknowledged that "the special problems of advertising on the electronic broadcast media will warrant special consideration." The issue became significant after Committee on Professional Ethics and Conduct of Iowa State Bar Ass'n v. Humphrey, 377 N.W.2d 643 (Iowa 1985). The Iowa Supreme Court adopted strict limits on television advertising. The Iowa rules forbade background, visible displays, more than a single nondramatic voice, and any self-laudatory statements. The U.S. Supreme Court remanded *Humphrey* to see if Iowa believed its rules could still stand in light of *Zauderer*, and on remand, the Iowa Supreme Court again said that they could. The problems with television advertising, the Iowa court believed, are that:

> "Both sight and sound are immediate and can be elusive because, for the listener or viewer at least, in a flash they are gone without a trace. Lost is the opportunity accorded to the reader of printed advertisements to pause, to restudy, and to thoughtfully consider."

Once again there was an appeal to the U.S. Supreme Court, which surprised almost everyone by dismissing the appeal for lack of a substantial federal question, 475 U.S. 1114 (1986). Do you agree that there was no substantial question?[10] Had the Iowa court simply articulated concerns the U.S. Supreme Court had raised as early as *Bates* and *Ohralik*?

b.   Should the rules allow Jerry Harrold to hire someone from the cast of *Law and Order* to say they wished they had someone like Jerry on their team? Should a lawyer be allowed to buy an ad on reruns of *Boston Legal* if she wanted to emphasize her sophisticated, tough trial

---

[10]   The Court was divided on this issue. Justices White, Blackmun, and Stevens would have set the case for oral argument.

style, or on *Entertainment Tonight* if she wanted to imply that she had high-profile celebrity clients? The court in *Humphrey* did not think so, saying: "Electronically conveyed image-building was not a part of the information package which has been described [by the U.S. Supreme Court] as needed by the public."

Is that correct? Are most lawyer ads that you see any more than image building? Cf. Alexander v. Cahill, 598 F.3d 79 (2d Cir. 2010) (several New York advertising regulations found insufficiently related to advancing substantial state interests.)

D.   CONTINUING ISSUES OF SOLICITATION BY LAWYERS

1.   Jerry Harrold plans to launch a major internet initiative after major accidents. Are his plans likely to raise any concern? Is the concern that Jerry will be too assertive in this context? Is the concern that a lawyer will make potential clients do something they would rather not do?

a.   Some Supreme Court authority on solicitation of clients by professionals involved accountants. Edenfield v. Fane, 507 U.S. 761 (1993), arose because Florida tried to regulate CPAs' personal solicitation of business clients. The plaintiff sued for the right to make unsolicited calls to such clients and to arrange appointments to explain his expertise and lower fees. The state said that the purpose of the rule against such contacts is to protect consumers of accounting services against overreaching and to assure the independence of financial audits. Justice Kennedy, speaking for the Court, found the state interests "substantial in the abstract" but concluded that business clients were able to protect themselves against overreaching. In addition, the concern about a lack of audit independence is greater if businesses *cannot* turn to newcomers like Fane because incumbent firms could get too close to management.

b.   The state expressly relied on *Ohralik*, and the Court expressly distinguished it. The *Ohralik* "holding was narrow and depended upon certain 'unique features of in-person solicitation by lawyers' that were present in the circumstances of that case." CPAs, the Court observed, are not "trained in the art of persuasion" and clients being solicited for accounting work "are sophisticated and experienced business executives who understand well the services that a CPA offers."

c.   Do you agree with the Court's concern that lawyers have qualities of intimidation against which clients need protection? Do you consider yourself intimidating? Are there any of your classmates against whom you think potential clients need protection?

2.   May a law firm send "investigators" to the victims' homes to leave the attorney's business cards and encourage the signing of retainers?[11]

a.   In Falanga v. State Bar of Georgia, 150 F.3d 1333 (11th Cir.1998), two lawyers challenged state restrictions on in-person,

---

[11] Several courts have suspended attorneys who used such nonlawyer agents. Koden v. United States Department of Justice, 564 F.2d 228 (7th Cir.1977), and Goldman v. State Bar, 570 P.2d 463 (Cal.1977) (both decided before *Ohralik* and *Primus*), and In re Arnoff, 586 P.2d 960 (Cal.1978), and In re Teichner, 387 N.E.2d 265 (Ill.1979) (both decided later).

uninvited solicitation of professional employment. The lawyers tended to represent poor, uneducated persons in personal injury cases. The lawyers obtained names of potential clients by having law firm "public relations agents" contact doctors and chiropractors while other employees sifted through police reports. The lawyers then visited the potential clients and tried to persuade them to sign a retainer. The court found this conduct much more like that in *Ohralik* than that in *Edenfield*. The conduct fell "squarely within [the] category of 'ambulance chasing,'" and the bar had anecdotal evidence the public did not like unsolicited, intrusive contact from these lawyers. Thus, the court held the state had sufficiently justified its prohibitions on in-person solicitation, at least as applied to lawyers who approach "unsophisticated, injured, or distressed lay person[s]."

    b.   May your law firm ask real estate agents to recommend your law firm to their customers? The New York Court of Appeals said no, because the lawyer might have an incentive to find good title to assure that the referring agent received his fee. Greene v. Grievance Comm. for Ninth Judicial Dist., 429 N.E.2d 390, 395 (N.Y.1981). Do you agree? Why does the lawyer care if the real estate agent gets his fee? Wouldn't the real estate agent want his client to know about problems now rather than sue the agent later?

    c.   ABA Model Rule 7.2(b)(4) now permits lawyers to refer clients to particular real estate agents pursuant to an understanding that the real estate agents will refer customers to the lawyers, so long as the agreement is not exclusive and the lawyers fully disclose the details of the agreement to the client. If the rule permits reciprocal referral arrangements, why should lawyers not be able to ask real estate agents to make the referrals unilaterally? Note that the rule allows lawyers to make such agreements only with another lawyer or nonlawyer professional. Could a lawyer make a reciprocal referral agreement with a tow truck driver?

    3.   Other circumstances in which lawyers engage in face-to-face solicitation of accident victims continue to amaze, but are all of them equally appropriate for discipline?

    a.   In The Florida Bar v. Weinstein, 624 So.2d 261 (Fla.1993), the lawyer tried to solicit a brain injury victim who was still in the hospital. In Texas State Bar v. Kilpatrick, 874 S.W.2d 656 (Tex.1994), the lawyer waited until the brain-damaged victim had been transported to a nursing home, but otherwise the solicitation—and the disbarment sanction—were the same.

    b.   In Norris v. Alabama State Bar, 582 So.2d 1034 (Ala.1991), a young child died after being left in a closed van in the hot sun by a day care center. Someone called the lawyer's office and told the receptionist that the family was "broke" and too poor to buy flowers for the funeral. The lawyer sent a wreath to the funeral home with his firm brochure attached and a letter inviting the family to contact him if he could be of any help. The story of his gesture got into the news and a disciplinary hearing followed. The Alabama Supreme Court acknowledged that DR 2–103 of its Code of Professional Responsibility did not precisely cover this situation, but said that Norris showed "indifference to the purpose and spirit of the rule." The court rejected Norris' reliance on *Shapero* (the flowers did not go through the mail) and suspended him for two years. Does Model Rule 7.3 require this result?

c.   Matter of Ravich, Koster, Tobin, Oleckna, Reitman & Greenstein, 715 A.2d 216 (N.J.1998), reprimanded members of a law firm a/k/a TEAMLAW who showed up outside a Red Cross shelter on the morning after at a gas line explosion that displaced many apartment residents. TEAMLAW rented an RV, taped copies of their newspaper ad to the RV's windows, and distributed toiletries to the victims after the lawyers interviewed them. The New Jersey Committee on Attorney Advertising said this conduct went too far. The New Jersey Supreme Court agreed. That close to the time of the explosion, victims were "in a state of mind not conducive to making reasoned judgment about such a weighty matter as legal representation." The court recognized that insurance agents were not similarly prevented from contacting the victims while they were confused and distraught, but it said the lawyers should have contented themselves with warning victims not to sign away their rights and not gone on to solicit future employment.

d.   Maracich v. Spears, 133 S. Ct. 2191 (2013), examined whether lawyers may access state drivers' license records in order to pursue a class action. The 1994 federal Driver's Privacy Protection Act limits most access to such records. It allows lawyers to get the information in "anticipation of litigation" but not to solicit particular clients. The case in question involved trial lawyers who wanted access to the records in order to file a class action against local car dealers that allegedly charged excessive administrative fees. In a 5–4 decision, the Supreme Court held that finding clients does not fall within the anticipation of litigation exception. A dissent, authored by Justice Ginsburg and joined by Justices Scalia, Sotomayor and Kagan, argued that the lawyers had sought personal information on a "specific concrete proceeding, imminent or ongoing, with identified parties on both sides of the controversy" and said that should be sufficient to fall within the anticipation of litigation exception.

4.   Shapero v Kentucky Bar Association, 486 U.S. 466 (1988) held that targeted mail was not solicitation. The ABA responded to *Shapero* by revising Model Rule 7.3. In contrast, Florida prohibits lawyers for potential plaintiffs from sending any targeted direct mail within 30 days of an accident. Does the Florida rule go too far? Is it constitutional?

a.   The U.S. Supreme Court considered the Florida rule in Florida Bar v. Went For It, Inc., 515 U.S. 618 (1995). The rule prohibited plaintiffs' lawyers from using targeted direct mail to contact victims and their families within 30 days following an accident or disaster, but it did not regulate similar contact by defense lawyers or insurance adjusters. The lawyers challenging the regulation relied on *Shapero*, but Justice O'Connor, the longtime dissenter in lawyer advertising cases, spoke for the Court and upheld the Florida rule. Chief Justice Rehnquist, and Justices Scalia, Thomas and Breyer joined her opinion.

First, in this case, the state's "substantial interest" justifying the regulation was "the protection of potential clients' privacy." Second, the state showed that its regulation advanced that interest "in a direct and material way" by citing a collection of newspaper editorials and a survey the bar commissioned to study citizen attitudes. "Significantly, 27% of direct-mail recipients reported that their regard for the legal profession and for the judicial process as a whole was 'lower' as a result of receiving the direct mail." The Court concluded that this factual basis justified regulation of post-accident contact.

The Court distinguished *Shapero* as a case that dealt with a broad ban on targeted direct mail. That case did not justify striking down a narrower ban directed at protecting the privacy of persons who have recently suffered a traumatic event. It was not sufficient to respond that recipients of mailings could just dispose of them because mailings sent to bereaved persons inflict their pain when they were first seen, i.e., before recipients could throw them away. The majority also argued that the Florida regulation was a "reasonable fit" for the problem that the bar had identified. It was "narrowly tailored to achieve the desired objective," even if not the "least restrictive means" of addressing the concern. Other ways remain for lawyers to make themselves known to potential clients, e.g., television, newspapers, billboards, the Yellow Pages, or even non-targeted direct mail.

b.   Justice Kennedy led Justices Stevens, Souter and Ginsburg in an indignant dissent. The fact that advertising is "offensive" or "undignified" has not been enough before to justify state regulation, the dissent noted, so to say that this result followed the earlier precedents was disingenuous. The dissenters found the bar's "proof" that a problem existed to be methodologically flawed and largely anecdotal. Finally, they found the "flat ban" on direct mail contact too broad because it applied no matter how serious the accident or disaster. They found the bar's regulation self-serving and the Court's decision a "retreat" from constitutional guarantees. "[T]he State is doing nothing more * * * than manipulating the public's opinion [of lawyers] by suppressing speech that informs us how the legal system works. * * * This, of course, is censorship pure and simple."

c.   With which opinion do you agree? Note that the ABA has not added the Florida restriction to the Model Rules. Do you think it should do so?[12]

PROBLEM 32

THE ETHICS OF REFERRAL TO A SPECIALIST

Your directory listing will say "lawyer." Your business card will call you a "member of the bar" of one or more jurisdictions. You will know, however, that you cannot competently provide all of the services that those titles suggest. No lawyer and few law firms stand ready to practice all the substantive areas of law that the modern world

----

[12] The New York Rules of Professional Conduct (2009) include the Florida 30–day limit. The Second Circuit upheld it in Alexander v. Cahill, 598 F.3d 79 (2d Cir. 2010). The court found that, while contact with potential clients was protected speech, the state had a substantial interest in protecting the privacy and tranquility of accident victims and their families. A 30–day prohibition of contact with victims materially advanced this interest in a narrowly tailored way, so the moratorium was a constitutionally permissible restriction on commercial speech.

demands. Indeed, as a practical matter, most lawyers find it a full time job to keep their skills honed in enough areas to be able to sustain a satisfying practice. This problem asks you to think about how lawyers should be able to describe the fields in which they practice and their level of expertise in those fields. It also explores when lawyers may take a case in a different field, and how they may distribute the financial rewards from the cases that come into their office so as to provide incentives to refer cases to practitioners better able to handle an unfamiliar matter.

FACTS

Hector Ramirez has represented the Peron family for several years in minor matters for which he has charged minimal fees. Young Joseph Peron recently suffered seriously injuries when a telephone company truck went out of control and into a schoolyard. The Peron family wants to file suit and has come to Ramirez for help.

Ramirez realizes that he is a competent attorney and could handle this case without making any obvious errors. However, he also knows that he is not experienced in personal injury work, that the medical evidence necessary to prove the case correctly will be complex and that he may not be able to cross-examine the defense doctors effectively. Ramirez can see, on the other hand, that the fee this case would justify would be the largest he has ever earned and would support him while he did other, less remunerative work.

Ramirez also knows that Joe Castro is a very successful "Certified Trial Specialist," And experienced at handling personal injury cases. He will take the Peron case very seriously. Best of all, Castro has offered to pay Ramirez one-third of his own one-third fee, or $10,000, whichever is less, as a "finder's fee" for sending the case to him. If Ramirez prefers, he and Castro will "jointly" handle the case on the same financial basis. Ramirez also has met another personal injury lawyer who might do an even better job than Castro but who is so ethical that he would be shocked at being asked to share his fee with Ramirez.

QUESTIONS

A. A LAWYER'S DUTY WHEN A MATTER REQUIRES NEW SKILLS OR RAISES UNFAMILIAR ISSUES

1. Does Ramirez have an ethical obligation not to handle this case entirely by himself?

a. What are the elements of "competence" identified in ABA Model Rule of Professional Conduct 1.1? Assume that Ramirez will work hard on the matter and prepare to the best of his ability. Does Model Rule 1.1 require any more?

b. Look at Model Rule 1.1, Comments 1–4. Do they help you understand the level of legal knowledge and skill Ramirez must have before he decides not to send the Peron family to a different lawyer? Is

must assume joint responsibility for the representation. A disqualified lawyer may not assume responsibility for the representation and so may not collect a fee. However, the opinion says, if the client consents to the conflict of interest, the lawyer could collect the referral fee.

4. In order to make the referral proper, must the lawyers tell the client what percentage of the fee the referring lawyer will receive?

a. Model Rule 1.5, prior to 2002, did not require such disclosures. Was the former approach parallel to what a client would know in dealing with a private firm? Does a law firm client usually know the intra-firm division of the fee?

b. In contrast, the Restatement Third, The Law Governing Lawyers § 47(2) said that clients must consent to "the terms of the [fee] division." The present version of Model Rule 1.5(e)(2) now also requires that the client agree to "the share each lawyer will receive." What might be the reason for this change? Do you agree with the additional requirement?

D. ALTERNATIVES TO REFERRAL FEES DESIGNED TO ACHIEVE SIMILAR BENEFITS

1. Could Ramirez avoid the referral issue by "associating" with Castro in handling the case, i.e., by creating a joint venture in which each lawyer would contribute some services?

a. Would Ramirez retain significant obligations in an association that he could avoid by referral? May the fee allocation in an association relationship be different in amount from a traditional "finder's fee"?

b. Would such an arrangement inevitably be a sham? To the contrary, could Ramirez serve an important function by remaining involved in the case as an active co-counsel or even by acting as lead counsel and hiring help for the trial itself? Do we sometimes overemphasize trial experience, given that only 5% or so of cases go to trial? May the Peron family's confidence in Ramirez and his own desire to see them well served be among the most important factors in assuring that the Perons will get a satisfactory resolution of their case?

2. Could Ramirez avoid all referral fee problems by saying to Castro, "I'll send you this big case if you'll refer some good clients my way"? Suppose Ramirez was the Peron family physician. Could he refer the case to Castro on the condition that Castro referred his clients to the doctor for medical care?

a. New Jersey Supreme Court Advisory Opinion No. 681 (July 17, 1995), considered a proposed affiliation between a New Jersey and a London firm whereby each would refer clients to the other and share fees in those cases. The opinion condemned the arrangement. Even though it made business sense and might help clients of each firm find qualified counsel in the other country, the opinion said it would violate what is now Model Rule 7.2(b). Do you agree that the arrangement would be "giving * * * value to a person for recommending the lawyer's services"? Do you see any other reasonable objections to such an arrangement?

b.   Look at ABA Model Rule 7.2(b)(4) and Comment 8. The ABA adopted this provision to allow informal "networks" among solo practitioners and small firms. Is the development of such networks a positive one for both lawyers and clients? Is it likely to allow lawyers to deliver "full service" to their clients without being absorbed into a larger law firm? How should authorities interpret the requirement that such referral agreements not be exclusive? Should this hinge on whether the lawyers offer clients more than one referral option or should we examine whether all business referrals flow exclusively between two firms?

c.   Model Rule 7.2(b)(4) permits reciprocal referral agreements between lawyers and nonlawyers. No money can change hands, the agreements cannot be exclusive, and the lawyer and nonlawyer must inform the client of the existence of the agreement. Only nonlawyers who are members of a profession can qualify for this exception, which otherwise prohibits referral arrangements between lawyers and nonlawyers. Could the Peron family doctor expect a high volume of referrals from Castro if the Peron case generated significant fees? Why should the rule ban the exchange of money, yet permit quid pro quo referral of clients and business?

3.   May lawyers make payments analogous to referral fees to nonlawyers, assuming that the client does not object? Are such arrangements always corrupt or are they simply another way to offer a range of services to clients?

a.   In Florida Bar v. Barrett, 897 So.2d 1269 (Fla.2005), attorney Barrett hired Cooper, an ordained pastor, to find clients for Barrett. To secure Cooper's access to hospital emergency rooms, Barrett paid for his training as a hospital chaplain. In one instance, Cooper dressed in pastoral clothing and "counseled" a family whose son was in intensive care to retain Barrett. For such referrals, Barrett paid Cooper large bonuses purportedly for "pastoral services" to clients. The court acknowledged that solicitation cases often no longer result in significant sanctions, but this case involved both solicitation and lying to hospital staff. The court disbarred Barrett. Does this case help you understand the bar's traditional condemnation of such practices?

b.   In "We the People" Paralegal Services, L.L.C. v. Watley, 766 So.2d 744 (La.App.2000), a firm of paralegals orally contracted with a law firm to perform paralegal services for a percentage of any legal fee recovered in the cases. When the law firm accepted the services but refused to pay, the paralegals sued. The court held that a contract to share fees with a nonlawyer is null and void, but the services performed in this case were not those of a "runner" or someone engaged in unauthorized practice. Thus, the court permitted the paralegals to proceed on a theory of unjust enrichment, not for a percentage of the fees, but for the fair value of their services.

If a law firm employs the paralegals instead of the paralegals being part of a different firm composed entirely of nonlawyers, does Model Rule 5.4(a) allow the lawyers to share fees with them? Model Rule 5.4(a)(3) permits law firms to include its nonlawyer employees in a compensation plan based on profit sharing. Is there any reason to treat fee sharing and profit sharing differently in this context?

4. Should the Rules prohibit sharing legal fees with a recognized lawyer referral service?

a.   In ACLU/Eastern Missouri Fund v. Miller, 803 S.W.2d 592 (Mo.1991), an ACLU staff attorney agreed that he would turn over to the ACLU any attorney's fees he recovered in actions filed while the ACLU employed him as a staff member. On behalf of two clients, Miller and a volunteer lawyer pursued and won a civil rights action against the city of St. Louis. The court awarded the client fees totaling $8,090 for the work done by Miller, who by this time had resigned from the ACLU. The defendant paid the fees to Miller, who then refused to turn the fee over to the ACLU, asserting that to do so would violate the Missouri version of Model Rule 5.4(a). The court agreed with Miller, although there was a strong dissent arguing that the ACLU already paid Miller for his work and he was now getting paid twice.

Do you agree with the court that the ACLU is the functional equivalent of an ambulance driver who puts a copy of the lawyer's card on a stretcher and wants to be paid for doing so? If the court required Miller to keep the promise he made to the ACLU, would there be any violation of any significant principle of ethical conduct? The ABA Standing Committee on Ethics and Professional Responsibility rejected the court's reading of Model Rule 5.4(a) and agreed with the ACLU, in ABA Formal Opinion 93–374 (June 7, 1993).

b.   Richards v. SSM Health Care, 724 N.E.2d 975 (Ill.App.2000), involved sharing fees with a bar-sponsored nonprofit lawyer referral service. The West Suburban Bar Association near Chicago charged potential clients $25 for a referral to a lawyer but demanded that lawyers remit to it up to 25% of the fee they receive from referred clients. Lawyer Dahlgren refused to pay, citing the Illinois versions of Model Rules 1.5(e) and 5.4(a). He added that the referral service did not agree to assume joint responsibility for the matter. The court rejected the argument. The controlling rule is what is now Model Rule 7.2(b)(2). The court noted that percentage referral fees support 117 state and local bar associations. Referral services help potential clients make informed decisions, the court said, and public policy favors continuing financial support of their existence.

c.   Examine Model Rule 5.4(a)(4). The ABA has clearly come down in favor of sharing fees with the organizations involved in the cases described in the two previous notes. Do you agree that approach is the wisest one to take?

d.   If a law firm may share court-awarded legal fees with a nonprofit organization, why do the rules prohibit sharing a percentage of the fees with a for-profit firm of nonlawyers? Do lawyers usually view making a profit as a bad thing?

———

PROBLEM 33

ROLES AND RESPONSIBILITIES IN A MODERN LAW FIRM

Although a majority of American lawyers do not work for large law firms, working for them has been a way that young lawyers learn how the best lawyers practice and earn high starting salaries to pay off student loans. Increasingly, however, lawyers are coming to question both ideas. This problem examines some issues about practice in modern firms. First, it considers the obligations of supervisory lawyers and those that they supervise. Next, it examines the rights of a lawyer who reports an ethical violation of someone else in the practice organization. Third, it asks whether lawyers are entitled to the same statutory and other legal rights to fair treatment in employment as are employees generally. Finally, it considers concerns expressed about life in many large law firms and some ideas about overcoming those concerns.

FACTS

Smart & Howe is one of the most successful new firms in its region of the country. The *American Lawyer*'s annual survey regularly reports that, among firms under 300 lawyers, Smart & Howe has the highest earnings per partner. In addition, its starting salary of $150,000 per year is among the region's highest. So is its minimum annual billing requirement for associates of 2,500 hours per year.

Sarah Smart is co-managing partner of Smart & Howe, and she is in charge of the firm's real estate group. Smart assigns work to the sixteen associates who work with her, evaluates their work, and signs all legal opinions and other documents prepared by her group in the name of the firm.

One of her associates, Arnie Able, has billed over 3,500 hours in each of his first two years, over 30% more than any other associate in the real estate group. Smart was surprised that Able could report such billings, because he seemed to leave at five o'clock most days and did not appear in the office on weekends. Clients had not complained, however, and Smart had appreciated the boost in her own compensation she got because she supervised such a productive associate. Indeed, when a middle-aged partner, Ted Truthful, confronted Smart with concrete evidence that Able was billing fictitious hours, Smart's only response was to try to force Truthful to retire and to deny him a promised pension.

QUESTIONS

A. THE OBLIGATIONS OF SUPERVISORY LAWYERS AND THOSE THEY SUPERVISE

1. Is there any doubt that Arnie Able is subject to discipline for billing hours he never worked?

a.   How would you characterize his conduct for purposes of imposing discipline? Is billing more than on the basis agreed per se "unreasonable" under Model Rule 1.5(a)? Does it constitute "dishonesty" under Model Rule 8.4(c)?

b.   In Matter of Disciplinary Proceeding Against Haskell, 962 P.2d 813 (Wash.1998), the evidence showed that a lawyer had billed at his own hourly rate for work done by lower paid associates. He traveled first class in violation of his client's direction and billed for the higher fares, but he had his travel agent give him bills showing the tickets were for coach class. Finally, while he was having a cabin built for himself in Idaho, he had his secretary "bury" phone and blueprint charges for the work in bills sent to clients. The court suspended the lawyer for two years.

2.   What was Smart's responsibility to assure that Able did not engage in dishonest billing?

a.   Did Smart meet her responsibilities under Model Rule 5.1 in this case? Do her responsibilities flow from her role as co-managing partner or as head of the real estate group? Are her duties as a "supervisor" different from those she has as a firm manager? As far as we know, Smart did not "order" the overbilling or directly "ratify" it, but does that mean she is off the hook? Did she "know of the conduct at a time when its consequences [could] be avoided" but fail "to take reasonable remedial action"? Should she be deemed to have known of the overbilling even if she asserts now that she lacked actual knowledge of it? What remedial action should she take? Is it ever too late to return overbilled fees to a present or former client?

b.   Attorney Grievance Comm. of Maryland v. Ficker, 706 A.2d 1045 (Md.1998), imposed an indefinite suspension on a lawyer, in part for a failure to supervise associates. The respondent had a high-volume practice—750 to 850 cases per year—including many serious drunk driving cases. He had virtually no case management system and associates rarely stayed with him long enough to have any experience in his field of practice. The court found that he regularly assigned cases to associates the day before trial. The lawyers typically would not have met the clients and they often had not even read the file. "Ficker essentially operated his practice like a taxicab company," the court found. "What he apparently, and inexcusably, failed to realize is that * * * legal services cannot routinely be dispensed on that basis with an acceptable degree of competence." The court found violations of the state version of Model Rules 1.1, 5.1, 5.3 and 8.4(d). The facts are extreme, but they show that the duty to supervise can have teeth.

c.   Matter of Kristan Peters, 941 F.Supp.2d 359 (S.D.N.Y. 2013), illustrates Rule 5.1 discipline for ordering the improper conduct of a subordinate. It imposed a seven-year suspension from practice before the federal court on a lawyer who conceded that she ordered a first-year associate to make handwritten comments in the margins of deposition transcripts. Peters seems to have wanted to claim they were protected as work product and thus not turn them over to the court. She also sent the transcripts to a Massachusetts court in violation of a confidentiality order in the S.D.N.Y. case. Ms. Peters' "most serious failing," the court said, "involves the corruption of a young and inexperienced lawyer over whom she had power and authority," thus putting that lawyer's career at risk.

d.   Notice that Model Rule 5.3 imposes similar obligations on all lawyers—potentially even new lawyers—who supervise nonlawyer assistants. In re Bailey, 821 A.2d 851 (Del.2003) (per curiam), suspended Bailey, the managing partner of Bailey & Wetzel, for six months and one day. He was the partner responsible for maintaining firm books and records and paying taxes. When an auditor for the

Lawyers' Fund for Client Protection audited the firm's books and records, he discovered, inter alia, that the firm had taken money from client trust accounts to pay personal debts, failed to timely file and pay certain taxes, and overdrawn firm accounts. Bailey conceded that these acts violated Rules 1.15 and 8.4, but he testified that the firm's bookkeeper had made the transfers without Bailey's consent or knowledge. Bailey expressed remorse, but the court held that Bailey, as managing partner, had a duty to properly supervise his employees, including his bookkeeper. "A lawyer who accepts responsibility for the administrative operations of a law firm stands in a position of trust vis-à-vis other lawyers and employees of the firm. The managing partner must discharge those responsibilities faithfully and diligently." Bailey breached this duty by failing to exercise "even a modicum of diligence."

e.   In re Wilkinson, 805 So.2d 142 (La.2002), involved Wilkinson's employment of a law school graduate, Paul Stewart, who took the bar examination but was not yet admitted. When a client approached Wilkinson about handling an estate matter, Wilkinson referred her to Stewart. Wilkinson explained that Stewart was not yet licensed, but said he could handle preliminary aspects of the case before his admission to the bar. Wilkinson also instructed Stewart not to give any legal advice to the client, but when the client needed to know what to do, Stewart offered legal advice that resulted in significant losses to the estate. Moreover, when Stewart left the firm, Wilkinson did not even look at the file for several months. The court held that Wilkinson violated both Rules 5.1(b) and 5.3(b) because of his failure to supervise Stewart. He received a 60–day suspension from practice.

3.   Is Andy Howe, Sarah Smart's co-managing partner, equally responsible for Able's overbilling?

a.   What does Model Rule 5.1(a) mean when it requires each partner in a law firm—and each lawyer with "comparable managerial authority"—to "make reasonable efforts to ensure that the firm has in effect measures giving reasonable assurance" that each lawyer in the firm is living up to applicable professional standards. Are law firms required to hire "time sheet police" to prevent what Able did?

b.   In re Fonte, 905 N.Y.S.2d 173 (N.Y.App.Div. 2010), relied upon Rule 5.1 to suspend a partner for three years for failing to discover and prevent another partner's fraud that resulted in a theft of over $17 million from firm accounts. The grievance committee charged the partner with (1) failing to supervise the accounts and failing to discover the fraud at a time when the loss could be prevented or mitigated, (2) failing to promptly pay third parties amounts owed to them when the law firm checks bounced, and (3) failing adequately to supervise his partner's conduct to be sure that he complied with the ethics rules. The court agreed with the grievance committee that the respondent "ignored multiple warning signs and blatantly apparent indicators of criminality which could have forestalled such a massive escrow fraud."

c.   Does the duty to supervise a lawyer extend to lawyers outside one's own law firm? Whalen v. DeGraff, Foy, Conway, 863 N.Y.S.2d 100 (N.Y.App.Div. 2008), found that a New York firm that had secured a $1.2 million judgment against a Florida defendant was responsible in malpractice for the conduct of the Florida law firm hired to obtain a satisfaction of the judgment. The New York law firm, not the client, hired the Florida law firm; thus, it was responsible for assuring that the Florida lawyers filed the appropriate claims to protect the judgment.

d.   In some situations, a client hires two law firms to perform different legal work on the same transaction. When two law firms are involved in a single representation, the lawyers "should consult with each other and the client about the scope of their respective representations and the allocation of responsibility among them." Model Rule 1.2, Comment 7 (added in 2012).

e.   Would it be enough for Howe to show that the firm's orientation video contains a two-minute section in which Howe tells the new lawyers that the firm expects them to bill honestly? What more, if anything, should Model Rule 5.1(a) require? Would failure to put such a statement in the orientation program constitute a per se violation of Model Rule 5.1(a)?

4.   Would Able's liability be different if overbilling was not his idea; he was just following orders?

a.   Suppose Sarah Smart had said to Able, "That checklist that you took 40 hours to prepare lets you do complex real estate transactions in half the time it takes lawyers at other firms. There is no reason our current clients should pay less for our superior work; bill every client an extra 40 hours for preparation of the checklist as if we had prepared it just for them." Would following Smart's direction give Able a defense to discipline?

b.   Does Model Rule 5.2(a) give a clear answer? Does billing clients for valuable work, but work that the firm has previously done, raise an "arguable question of professional duty" under Model Rules 1.5 and 8.4 and make Able immune from discipline under Model Rule 5.2(b)?

c.   ABA Formal Opinion 93–379 (Dec. 6, 1993) opines that billing for recycled work as if the lawyer had done anew violates Model Rule 1.5. Should the disciplinary authorities assume that young associates know the substance of all ABA ethics opinions? Should the ethics rules require young associates to investigate the propriety of directions from superiors, even if violating those directions could get them fired?

d.   Texas Comm. on Prof'l Ethics, Opinion 523 (1997), examined the extent to which the partners have a duty to inform a former associate that they have complied with the ethics rules. An associate working on a client tax matter discovered that in a prior year a lawyer in the firm had negligently advised the client, which resulted in the filing of inaccurate tax returns. The associate resigned from the firm but asked the partners to inform him that they told the client about the negligent advice. The partners refused and the associate filed a request for an ethics opinion. The Committee concluded that the associate had a right to receive written confirmation that the firm informed the client of the firm's negligent advice. "If the partners or shareholders refuse to give a written assurance, the former associate is obligated to inform the client about the negligent representation."

e.   What is the principled basis for Model Rule 5.2(b), if any? Once a lawyer takes an oath to live up to professional standards, why should he or she be able to defend by saying "the devil made me do it"?

5.   Regardless of individual discipline that the law may impose, should Smart & Howe be subject to professional discipline as a law firm for the conduct of Arnie Able?

a.   Will Smart & Howe be liable if the clients who were overbilled sue the firm? Wasn't the firm the principal beneficiary of Able's misconduct? If the law requires firms qua firms to bear civil liability, why shouldn't we subject firms to professional discipline as well?

b.   As you may remember from Problem 2, New York was the first jurisdiction to subject a law firm itself to professional discipline. See N.Y. Rules of Prof'l Conduct, Rule 8.4. New York Rule 5.1(a) imposes a duty upon law firms "to ensure that other lawyers in the law firm conform to these Rules." What form should discipline of a law firm take in a case like this? Could the disciplinary authorities disbar a law firm, i.e., put it out of business, for example? Could the authorities publicly censure it?

6.   In recent years, law firms have begun to outsource legal work to law firms and nonlawyer entities outside of the United States. What are a law firm's responsibilities with respect to supervising the employees of the outside entity?

a.   The perceived benefits of outsourcing include lower labor costs and, in the case of work sent to Asia, the ability to work on client matters 24 hours a day given the time differences. Some law firms have formed subsidiaries often referred to as captive outsourcing centers that only work on one law firm's cases. But other law firms use entities that perform work for many different law firms and in-house legal departments. At first, the outsourced work was a kind normally done by paralegals and other nonlawyers, such as document review. However, more recently, outsourcing firms are offering traditional legal services.

b.   Ass'n of the Bar of the City of New York, Committee on Professional and Judicial Ethics, Formal Opinion 2006–3 (Aug. 2006), advised about outsourcing. It said that New York law firms may outsource work to a firm in India as long as the New York law firm (1) assumes responsibility for the work and assures its quality, (2) supervises the Indian nonlawyers in "vigilant and creative" ways such as interviewing them and conducting reference checks, (3) sees that confidential information of the client is protected, (4) checks for conflicts the Indian firm might have, (5) bills only the direct cost to the client, and (6) obtains advance consent from the client to outsource, particularly if the role of the Indian firm is likely to be substantial.

c.   ABA Formal Opinion 08–451 (Aug. 5, 2008) offers similar guidance. Lawyers who outsource legal work must "ensure that tasks are delegated to individuals who are competent to perform them, and then to oversee the execution of the project adequately and appropriately." The opinion requires that lawyers perform background checks on the lawyers doing the work. If the outsourced work is of a sensitive nature, the lawyers should investigate the security of the entity performing the work. If the firm releases confidential information to individuals outside of the law firm, it must obtain the clients' consent to the disclosure. But the ABA opinion does not seem to require client consent in every outsourcing situation.

d.   The ABA Ethics 20/20 Commission studied American law firm outsourcing and in 2012, the ABA added Comments 6 and 7 to Model Rule 1.1 to deal with retaining or contracting with other lawyers. When do you now have to inform your client about the involvement of another lawyer? How do these comments change the obligations of lawyers who outsource work to a law firm in another country? In 2012, the ABA also changed the title of Model Rule 5.3 from Responsibilities Regarding "Nonlawyer Assistants" to "Nonlawyer Assistance" and added Comments 3 and 4 dealing with lawyer supervision of nonlawyers outside of the law firm. What should a lawyer do if the client asks the law firm to hire a particular firm of nonlawyers to help with the representation?

e.   Today, law firms have turned to outsourcing in order to add efficiency to the delivery of legal services. And, that in turn, has led to significant growth in law-related service providers. For example, Novus Law, www.novuslaw.com, is a firm of lawyers and nonlawyers that does document review and production for law firms and corporate legal departments. Using technology and process management techniques developed as part of PricewaterhouseCoopers' Business Process Outsourcing organization, Novus Law offers its clients an alternative to work previously done within law firms.

B.   THE RIGHTS OF A LAWYER WHO REFUSES TO VIOLATE THE LAW

1.   If a lawyer refuses a direction to do something illegal, does that lawyer have any protection if the client or law firm fires him or her for that courage?

a.   The issue first arose in a setting involving an in-house corporate counsel who sued for wrongful discharge in Herbster v. North American Co. for Life and Health Insurance, 501 N.E.2d 343 (Ill.App.1986), cert. denied, 484 U.S. 850 (1987). The chief legal officer of North American Insurance alleged that the company fired him for refusing to destroy or remove documents that tended to show the company's fraud in its sale of flexible annuities. He said that he would commit a fraud on the Federal court and violate the ethics rules if he complied with company's order. The Illinois court assumed these allegations were true but still held the lawyer had no recourse for his discharge. The court conceded that "at will" employees typically can sue for retaliatory discharge if the discharge contravenes a clearly mandated public policy, but it said that lawyers are different. "The attorney is placed in the unique position of maintaining a close relationship with a client where the attorney receives * * * information that otherwise would not be divulged to intimate friends," the court said. Because of the sensitive nature of this relationship, a private client always has the right to change lawyers for any reason. The court was unwilling to create an exception to that principle, even where the client wanted the lawyer to violate the law.

b.   In Balla v. Gambro, Inc., 584 N.E.2d 104 (Ill.1991), the Illinois Supreme Court extended this holding. The former house counsel, Balla, threatened to reveal that his employer's kidney dialysis devices did not comply with FDA regulations and presented a danger to patients' lives. When the company fired him for his insubordination, the Illinois Supreme Court reached the same result as it had in *Herbster*. Its reasoning was ingenious. The ethics rules already *require* the lawyer to report the employer's wrongdoing, the court said. Thus, to say the employer could not fire him for doing so would discourage the employer from consulting the lawyer about the issue in the first place and impose the cost of ethical compliance on the client instead of the lawyer. "Since the relationship between the plaintiff and the defendant company required an atmosphere of continued mutual trust, the breakdown of that trust allowed the defendant to discharge the plaintiff without liability."[18]

2.   Do these results make sense to you? Should saying that a client may fire a lawyer for no reason be the same as saying that the client may fire the lawyer for a wrong reason, i.e., for a failure to violate the law?

a.   Even if the lawyer's actions would rupture the trust relationship between the lawyer and the officers of the client, does it follow that the entity itself would not benefit from the lawyer's action? Would the relief for wrongful discharge have to be reinstatement? How about damages?

b.   The California Supreme Court refused to follow the Illinois approach in General Dynamics Corp. v. Superior Court, 876 P.2d 487 (Cal.1994). This time, the in-house lawyer allegedly gave his employer advice it did not want to hear about violations of the Fair Labor Standards Act and the alleged bugging of the office of the chief of security. Although it reaffirmed the general rule that a private client in a single case may fire its lawyer for any reason, the court believed that a lawyer working for a corporate employer was in a different position. The private lawyer with many clients can lose one without being unemployed; a fired in-house counsel, by contrast, loses everything. By "providing the employee with a remedy in tort damages for resisting socially damaging organizational conduct, the courts mitigate the otherwise considerable economic and cultural pressures on the individual employee to silently conform." The court upheld the retaliatory discharge remedy. The court offered two qualifications. First, the values the lawyer is protecting must be grounded in the Rules of Professional Conduct or specific statutes. Second, "the in-house attorney who publicly exposes the client's secrets will usually find no sanctuary in the courts."

c.   In Kachmar v. SunGard Data Systems, Inc., 109 F.3d 173 (3d Cir.1997), the in-house lawyer objected to the company's handling of Equal Employment Opportunity (EEO) matters and alleged her dismissal was based on her "campaigning on women's issues." The Third Circuit reinstated her complaint, agreeing that the fact she was a lawyer did not cause her to lose the right to sue for retaliatory discharge. The company argued such a suit would require disclosure of confidential information beyond that permitted by Model Rule 1.6(b)(5).

---

[18] See also, Ausman v. Arthur Andersen, LLP, 810 N.E.2d 566 (Ill.App.2004). In-house counsel for an accounting firm sued the firm for retaliatory discharge and breach of contract, alleging that it fired her for insisting that it subject proposed business transactions to independent review to assure compliance with SEC regulations. Following *Balla*, the court held that in-house counsel could not bring a retaliatory discharge claim, because allowing such a claim would have a "chilling effect" on the communications between the employer/client and the lawyer. The Illinois Supreme Court declined to review the case. 823 N.E.2d 962 (Ill.2004).

The court agreed that protection of material protected by the attorney-client privilege was an important consideration, but it left it up to the district judge to use protective orders, in camera review, and similar devices to protect such privileged material from public disclosure.

d.   ABA Formal Opinion 01–424 (Sept. 22, 2001) affirms that the Model Rules do not prohibit in-house lawyers from filing a suit for retaliatory discharge if the lawyers were discharged for complying with ethical obligations. The opinion requires that in doing so, the lawyer not use information relating to the former representation that is protected by Model Rule 1.9(c) except as permitted by Model Rules 1.6(b)(5) and 3.3. The opinion advised that a suit for retaliatory discharge is a "claim" within the meaning of Model Rule 1.6(b)(5). However, it reminded lawyers that Comment 14 to Model Rule 1.6 requires that disclosures be "no greater than the lawyer reasonably believes necessary to accomplish the purpose" and that "appropriate protective orders or other arrangements should be sought by the lawyer to the fullest extent practicable." See also, Van Asdale v. International Game Tech, 577 F.3d 603 (9th Cir. 2009) (confidentiality and privilege do not bar a lawyer's suit for retaliatory discharge under Sarbanes-Oxley).

3.   The important question for most young lawyers is how all this should apply to an associate's discharge by a law firm for reporting an ethical violation. Is discharge by a law firm subject to the same principles as discharge by a corporate client?

a.   The courts have not reached consensus on these issues. In Wieder v. Skala, 609 N.E.2d 105 (N.Y.1992), Wieder asked his own law firm to represent him in the purchase of an apartment. The associate the firm assigned to do the work did little or nothing, and when Wieder inquired, he found that the firm knew that the associate was a "pathological liar" who had neglected several other clients' matters as well. Wieder insisted that the firm report the associate to the discipline commission, and for so insisting, the firm fired Wieder. The New York Court of Appeals held that a law firm does not have the same freedom to dismiss a lawyer that a private client would have. "Associates are, to be sure, employees of the firm but they remain independent officers of the court responsible in a broader public sense for their professional obligations." The contract between an associate and the firm contains an implied term that the firm will not impair the associate's obligations to obey the "prevailing rules of conduct and ethical standards of the profession." Wieder's suit for breach of contract thus stated a cause of action.

b.   Yet other cases come out the other way. Jacobson v. Knepper & Moga, P.C., 706 N.E.2d 491 (Ill.1998), involved a lawyer who concluded that some of his firm's practices violated venue provisions of the Fair Debt Collection Agency Act. He pointed that out to one of the firm's principal partners who promised things would change. They did not, so he protested a second and third time, after which the firm fired him. The Illinois Supreme Court agreed that the conduct discovered by the lawyer violated duties under the Rules of Professional Conduct but it said the lawyer should have reported it to disciplinary authorities. Such a report would have adequately protected "the public policy established by the collection statutes," and the court found it unnecessary to create a tort of retaliatory discharge to protect that policy. Chief Justice

Freeman dissented, saying the opinion sent a clear message that it was more "economically advantageous to a lawyer to keep quiet" than to try to get his law firm to conform to proper professional conduct.

c.   Bohatch v. Butler & Binion, 977 S.W.2d 543 (Tex.1998), involved the discharge of a partner and held that she had no cause of action when the law firm expelled her from the partnership for, in good faith, accusing another partner of overbilling a major client. Such an accusation "may have a profound effect on the personal confidence and trust essential to the partner relationship," the court said. "Once such charges are made, partners may find it impossible to continue to work together to the * * * benefit of their clients."

Justice Spector and Chief Justice Phillips dissented, saying that "retaliation against a partner who tries in good faith to correct or report perceived misconduct virtually assures that others will not take these appropriate steps in the future." That result "sends an inappropriate signal to lawyers and to the public that the rules of professional responsibility are subordinate to a law firm's other interests."

d.   Should a law firm be able to fire or expel a lawyer for insisting that the firm's lawyers comply with their professional obligations? Is there any good explanation why courts have come out so differently on this question? Are the competing values too absolute for the courts to treat them in a nuanced way?

PROBLEM 34

LEAVING ONE LAW FIRM AND FORMING ANOTHER

Lawyers once pictured themselves as wedded to their law firms for life. In recent years, however, those bonds have weakened. Whether because of unhappiness with pay, work assignments, hours at the office, or insensitive treatment by superiors, lawyers are leaving one firm to move to another setting. When they go, they often like to take as much familiar work with them as they can. Doing so usually increases their financial rewards at the new firm and reduces their dependence upon cases assigned by that firm. In this problem, we look first at the law and ethics of departure from a law firm—what Professor Robert Hillman calls the "law and ethics of grabbing and leaving."[19] Second, we examine firms' efforts to limit such departures by restrictive agreements with their partners and associates. Third, we consider when lawyers handle a departure by actually buying all or part of a law practice. Finally, we ask whether lawyers should be able to agree, for a fixed fee, to deliver legal services to all members of a defined group.

FACTS

Several years ago, Bill Bright and Larry Learned started the firm of Bright & Learned. It prospered and has grown to 425 lawyers. The two female partners and eight female associates who make up Bright & Learned's estate planning

----

[19] Robert W. Hillman, Hillman on Lawyer Mobility: The Law and Ethics of Partner Withdrawals and Law Firm Breakups § 1.3 (1994).

group, however, view the firm as singularly unenlightened. The firm has not allowed any female lawyers to move into the litigation section of the firm, and the firm holds many of its partnership meetings at the all-male Thomas Jefferson Club. Although estate planning brings the firm substantial, steady revenue, the lawyers in the group believe they have not been paid as well as they would be in a firm of their own.

The group's lawyers believe that, if they leave together, they can bring with them most of the client families on whose estate plans they have worked during the past several years. Each lawyer will write a letter to the clients she knows best before she leaves Bright & Learned. The lawyers then plan to use these clients' expressions of willingness to follow them to the new firm as a basis for getting loans to finance the new firm's start-up costs.

When Bill Bright and Larry Learned came in one morning and found that their entire estate-planning group had disappeared, they were hurt and angry. In an effort to avoid a lawsuit, however, Learned suggests selling its former estate planning practice to the departing lawyers for an amount equal to the group's prior two years' billings. Bright is so angry that he wants to sell the practice to another law firm in the city with a large existing estate planning practice.

QUESTIONS

A.   THE LAW AND ETHICS OF DEPARTING FROM A LAW FIRM

1.   What duties do law firm partners owe to each other? May some decide they would like to practice law somewhere else without violating their duties to the others?

a.   Partners traditionally owe each other the fiduciary duties of loyalty and care. Revised Uniform Partnership Act § 404. That includes the duty "to refrain from competing with the partnership and the other partners in the conduct of the partnership business before the dissolution of the partnership." Id. § 404(b)(3). The usual complaint of the original firm when partners leave with little warning is that the departing lawyers have breached their fiduciary duties.

b.   How should courts approach that claim? Are partners yoked together for life? Does the quoted prohibition imply that at all? Indeed, Revised Uniform Partnership Act § 601(1) recognizes that a partner becomes "dissociated" from the partnership upon "the partnership's having notice of the partner's express will to withdraw as a partner or on a later date specified by the partner." The critical issues on departure, then, are likely to be openness and fairness. Once the partners disclose their desire to depart, the issues are (1) how much money (the withdrawing partner's equity, payment of unbilled fees) the firm owes the departing partners and (2) who will have ongoing relationship with the firm's clients.

c.   In Dowd & Dowd, Ltd. v. Gleason, 693 N.E.2d 358 (Ill.1998), 58% of the firm's business was for a single client, a subsidiary of Allstate Insurance. The two departing lawyers contacted that client on

December 31, the same day they notified the firm. That same day, the client sent a letter to the old firm requesting that it send the client's files to the new firm. The departing lawyers then hired others from the old firm to help work on the cases.

Lawyers who plan to leave a firm, the court recognized, "face a dilemma, caught between the fiduciary obligations they owe the other members of their firm * * * and the duty of being able to adequately represent clients who choose to follow them to their new place of employment * * *." As a way of accommodating these competing pressures, the court said, lawyers "may make arrangements, prior to their departure, to obtain new office space * * * and other materials necessary for the practice of law." However, "pretermination solicitation of clients by members of an existing firm for the benefit of a new firm rises to a breach of fiduciary duty." Determining both the actual facts and what fiduciary duties partners owe each other under those circumstances, however, is not the stuff of summary judgment motions, so the court remanded the case for trial.

2.   Who owns a law firm's clients? Do departing partners and associates have a right to persuade clients to follow them to their new firm?

a.   Are clients an "asset" of a law firm? Should it matter whether the clients originally came to Bright & Learned because of the firm's reputation, not that of the individual departing lawyers? Should it be relevant whether the clients now consider the individual women, not the firm, as their lawyers?

b.   Koehler v. Wales, 556 P.2d 233 (Wash.App.1976), adopted the traditional view that a client's exercise of the power to hire or fire a lawyer at any time does not give rise to a cause of action by their lawyer. In this case, one lawyer agreed to handle another's cases while the latter was out of the country; they based their fee division on work performed. When the absent lawyer returned, some of her clients stayed with the "interim" lawyer, but the court refused to allow the formerly-absent lawyer to sue for damages for business interference. "The attorney-client relationship is personal and confidential, and the client's choice of attorneys in civil cases is near absolute. * * * [W]e decline to recognize that plaintiff had any proprietary interest in her former law practice."

c.   In Fred Siegel Co., L.P.A. v. Arter & Hadden, 707 N.E.2d 853 (Ohio 1999), KB worked for Fred Siegel Co. for ten years and then she resigned to join Arter & Hadden. Her expertise involved real estate property assessments. She told Arter & Hadden who Fred Siegel's clients were and that she thought several would follow her. When she left, she took the cards she had in her Rolodex, and wrote letters to Siegel clients notifying them of her new association and closing, "When you need assistance or have questions, please contact me." Siegel responded, and wrote to the same clients telling them that it was still fully capable of serving them. Then Siegel filed suit against Arter & Hadden, claiming tortious interference with business relationships, and against KB for breach of fiduciary duty. The court rejected the tortious interference claim, saying that the right of fair competition in Restatement of Torts § 768 trumps that theory when a contract is terminable at will. However, the court remanded the case to determine

influence over his fees and often controls the disposition of cases. Furthermore, from 1930 to at least 1959, the union had required these approved attorneys to pay to it a portion of their fees, usually 25%. * * * This state of affairs degrades the profession, proselytes the approved attorneys to certain required attitudes and contravenes both the accepted ethics of the profession and the statutory and judicial rules of acceptable conduct. * * *"[23]

Do you share Justices Clark and Harlan's concern? Do clients participate in a group legal services plan every time they buy auto insurance? Under most policies, the insurance company promises to select and provide a lawyer to defend the insured and to pay any judgments within policy limits. Should it be important as a matter of legal ethics that in the insurance situation, the insurance company is obliged to pay the judgment?

The Model Rules now address group legal services somewhat indirectly. Look at ABA Model Rule 7.3(d). Does the exception for an "organization not owned or directed by the lawyer" suggest a prohibition on a law firm's organizing such a plan? Look at Model Rule 7.3, Comment 6. Doesn't it clearly speak of a "plan or arrangement which the * * * lawyer's firm is willing to offer"?

Is Model Rule 7.2(b)(2) addressing the same issue? Does a group legal services plan have some of the characteristics of a lawyer referral service? From the standpoint of the law firm, for example, will the organization that runs a group legal services plan send clients to the firm?

Should a professionally proper plan be required to have an "opt-out" provision allowing a client to reject an attorney assigned by the plan? For many years, the ABA required such plans to include an ability to change lawyers. See ABA Model Code of Professional Responsibility DR 2–103(D)(4)(e). Why would plan advocates resist that feature? Is it enough to say that the union member can always hire his or her own attorney?

———

[23] Editors' note: Following this case, United Mine Workers of America, Dist. 12 v. Illinois State Bar Ass'n, 389 U.S. 217 (1967), upheld as constitutionally protected the practice of the United Mine Workers in employing a licensed attorney on a salaried basis to represent any of its members who wished to prosecute workmen's compensation claims before the Illinois Industrial Commission. Next, in United Transportation Union v. State Bar of Michigan, 401 U.S. 576 (1971), the union recommended selected attorneys to its members and their families in connection with suits for damages under the Federal Employers' Liability Act. It secured a commitment from those attorneys that the maximum fee charged would not exceed 25% of the recovery. In this case, it recommended Chicago lawyers to represent Michigan claimants. The Court found the practice constitutionally protected and concluded that the "common thread running through our decisions in *NAACP v. Button, Trainmen,* and *United Mine Workers* is that collective activity undertaken to obtain meaningful access to the courts is a fundamental right within the protection of the First Amendment."

PROBLEM 35

THE DUTY TO WORK FOR NO COMPENSATION

Although earlier problems have introduced some issues about pro bono work, for the most part we have thus far assumed that lawyers provide legal services to people who agree to pay for them. In this problem, we acknowledge the obvious reality that many people in our society cannot afford the kinds of bills you will send your other clients. If such people are to get help on what are often significant matters to them, they will require that lawyers provide their services free, or at much reduced cost. This problem first explores whether lawyers have a moral obligation to provide such services. Next, it asks whether there is any basis for putting legal force behind the obligations. Third, it examines the appointment of lawyers as defense counsel in criminal cases and considers whether the legal obligation to serve should be so limited. Finally, it presents some more general efforts to fund delivery of legal services to the poor.

FACTS

Assume that all lawyers practicing in the State of George must belong to the State Bar.[24] Assume also that the State Bar has proposed a requirement that each lawyer in the state devote a minimum of 100 hours per year to uncompensated legal assistance in legal aid clinics that the State Bar would establish. The attorneys could schedule their time insofar as possible to suit their convenience, and the Bar would not require any attorney to take an individual case in which there was a conflict of interest. An attorney could begin a case at the legal aid office but credit work done on the case in his or her own office against the 100 hours.

Not pursuant to any formal plan, the court appointed J.R. Wright to represent a defendant in a murder case after the defendant refused representation by the public defender. The statutory compensation in such a case is a maximum of $750. Wright believed his client was guilty, but the defendant protested his innocence and the case ultimately required 300 hours of the attorney's time. Wright sued the state for a fee of $30,000 based on his regular hourly fee of $100 per hour. The state's defense was, in part, that the work was part of the inherent duty of an attorney.

---

[24] As described in this problem, the State Bar of Georgia is an "integrated" or "unified" bar. The introduction to Chapter II discusses this concept and the limits on how such a bar may use income from member dues.

QUESTIONS

A. THE MORAL OBLIGATION TO PROVIDE PRO BONO LEGAL SERVICES

1. Do lawyers have any moral obligation to provide free or reduced-price legal services?

a. In 1958, the Joint Committee on Professional Responsibility of the ABA and the Association of American Law Schools (AALS) set out a rationale for pro bono services in clear tones:

> "The moral position of the advocate is here at stake. Partisan advocacy finds its justification in the contribution it makes to a sound and informed disposition of controversies. Where this contribution is lacking, the partisan position permitted to the advocate loses its reason for being. The legal profession has, therefore, a clear moral obligation to see to it that those already handicapped do not suffer the cumulative disadvantage of being without proper legal representation, for it is obvious that adjudication can neither be effective nor fair where only one side is represented by counsel.

> "In discharging this obligation, the legal profession can help to bring about a better understanding of the role of the advocate in our system of government. Popular misconceptions of the advocate's function disappear when the lawyer pleads without a fee, and the true value of his service to society is immediately perceived. The insight thus obtained by the public promotes a deeper understanding of the work of the legal profession as a whole.

> "The obligation to provide legal services for those actually caught up in litigation carries with it the obligation to make preventive legal advice accessible to all. It is among those unaccustomed to business affairs and fearful of the ways of the law that such advice is often most needed. If it is not received in time, the most valiant and skillful representation in court may come too late."[25]

b. Raymond Marks and colleagues at the American Bar Foundation articulated the source of such an obligation this way:

> "Given the function that the lawyer has to perform—structuring the conflicts of society so that they are capable of peaceful resolution—we feel that even without a monopoly grant of power the legal profession is a public utility. The law is a calling which by definition deals with public interest, not self-interest. The monopoly grant simply makes the need for regulation by self or state more urgent.

> "In many ways the legal profession is like that sensitive area of the field of radio and television in which licensees control access to public discussion. In the communications field, the announced public policy—the Communications Act—requires that a commitment be made when a license is

---

[25] 44 A.B.A.J. 1159, 1216 (1958).

granted, that the licensee affirmatively undertake to 'operate its license in the public interest.' * * *

" * * * The absence of controls over the lawyer with respect to what he turns away is socially dangerous. It is more dangerous than the risk involved in drafting or socializing a percentage of a lawyer's time."[26]

c.   Should the obligation to provide pro bono legal services fall on all lawyers, including those in government, law teaching, and the judiciary? Should the obligation vary based upon the income the lawyer receives from the practice of law? Is the likely inability to craft a fair allocation of the burden of pro bono services relevant to the issue of whether there should be an obligation in the first place?

2.   Do these arguments persuade you that members of the bar have a moral obligation to see that all have access to their services?

a.   Can you derive the obligation, if any, from the lawyer's role as advocate? Is it because only lawyers are authorized to provide legal services?

b.   Is there such a shortage of available legal help that the law must allocate part of it to poor people as one might allocate food after a hurricane? Is Marks right that the number of lawyers is as limited as the number of broadcast licenses, for example?

c.   Is there a "market failure" in the provision of legal services? That is, while there are certainly some lawyers who serve poor people, do we see a commercial market to serve them analogous to the marketplace of doctors willing to serve Medicaid patients? Does this kind of market failure require a response from lawyers or does it suggest the need for a publicly funded system such as the one adopted for medical care?

d.   Should lawyers see a moral obligation that flows from the number of persons who had to sacrifice to see that they obtained a legal education? Are any of us truly self-made? Do all members of the bar have a talent that others badly need and only some can afford?

B.   EFFORTS TO TRANSLATE A MORAL OBLIGATION INTO A LEGAL REQUIREMENT

1.   Assuming that lawyers have some moral obligation to use their legally protected license to practice on behalf of those who cannot afford to pay, do we see that obligation reflected anywhere in the Model Rules?

a.   Does Model Rule 6.1 impose such a requirement? Why should a rule be specific—i.e., set a standard of 50 hours per year and prescribe how that standard should be met—if it is not to be made mandatory?

b.   Some explanation—if not justification—for the voluntary rule we §have comes from an ABA Report on the lawyer's public interest obligation that said in part:

---

[26] F. Raymond Marks, et al., The Lawyer, the Public and Professional Responsibility 288–92 (1972).

"In August, 1975, in Montreal, the American Bar Association House of Delegates confirmed 'the basic responsibility of each lawyer engaged in the practice of law to provide public interest legal services' without fee, or at a substantially reduced fee, in one or more of the following areas: poverty law, civil rights law, public rights law, charitable organization representation, and administration of justice. * * * We suggest * * * that the ABA encourage each state and local bar association to adopt *specific guidelines* for members of the bar who wish to budget their public interest legal service. * * *

"In this connection, it is important to note that a practicing lawyer may spend from 1,000 to 2,000 hours or more each year on billable client matters (as distinguished from non-client matters such as law firm administration, continuing legal education, bar association activity, and professional writing and speaking). Without focusing on this wide range of legal practice, some commentators have urged every lawyer to budget a flat 5% of client-related time for public interest legal service, yielding 50 to 100 hours per year; others have called for 10% of a lawyer's time, or 100 to 200 hours per year. Still others have suggested that a more realistic and manageable approach would be for the bar to settle on a fixed minimum number of hours, without reference to the time a lawyer spends on fee-producing matters. * * * "[27]

c.   To the argument that poverty law is largely its own specialty, unknown to most private practitioners, the committee responded:

"In our committee's judgment, the professional responsibility to contribute public interest legal service is inherently an obligation to contribute one's time—one's abilities. Given the breadth of the 1975 definition, few lawyers, if any, can responsibly argue that they are unable to make a useful, personal contribution. * * *

Do you agree?

d.   In the last decade, several law schools have imposed pro bono requirements upon their students. In 2012, the New York Court of Appeals adopted a mandatory 50-hour pro bono requirement before new lawyers can be admitted to the bars that will take effect in 2015. 22 N.Y. Comp. Codes Rules & Regs § 520.16. The requirement does not apply to those seeking admission without examination. If the prospective lawyer performs this pro bono work outside of New York, he or she must do it under the supervision of a lawyer, professor, or judge. Student work in a clinic or during a summer clerkships, whether for credit or compensation, may count toward the 50 hours. However, it must involve law-related work for government, indigent individuals, nonprofit organizations that promote access to justice.

e.   In 2013, a task force of the California State Bar proposed that all applicants to its bar must complete 50 hours of pro bono either before or within the first year of bar admission. State Bar of California,

---

[27] A.B.A. Special Committee on Public Interest Practice, Implementing the Lawyer's Public Interest Obligation 1–7 (June 1977).

Task Force on Admissions Regulation Reform: Phase I Final Report 16-17 (June 14, 2013).

2. What legal authority supports a requirement to deliver free legal services?

a.   Is the duty to take cases without compensation "inherent" in being a lawyer? Is the same duty inherent in being a plumber, a funeral director, or some other licensed professional? Do we require landowners to devote their land to public uses without compensation? Do the moral arguments made in the earlier questions translate easily into legal duties?

b.   Schwarz v. Kogan, 132 F.3d 1387 (11th Cir.1998), was an action under 42 U.S.C.A. § 1983 challenging the Florida Bar rule that required its members to report the number of pro bono hours they worked each year. It encouraged them to donate at least 20 hours of such work each year or to pay $350 to a legal aid organization if they did not want to do the work themselves. In upholding the requirement, the Eleventh Circuit said that Florida "undoubtedly has a legitimate interest" in encouraging pro bono service and that "[d]ue to the unique and important role of the legal profession in this country, the free provision of legal services to the poor has long been recognized as an essential component of the practice of law." Indeed, the court said, "one of the traditions of the legal profession is that a lawyer, as an officer of the Court, is 'obligated to represent indigents for little or no compensation upon court order'." The Florida program was a rational way for the Florida Bar to learn how much pro bono service lawyers were doing and where in the state more services may be needed. Only reporting, not service, was mandatory, but "even assuming that the reporting requirement may have some implicit coercive effect, and thereby motivates otherwise reluctant lawyers to honor their professional responsibility, this result justifiably furthers the Rule's legitimate purpose."

c.   Is *Kogan* precedent for upholding a requirement of providing free legal services to the poor? Does a reporting requirement raise quite different issues? Would you favor adoption of such a reporting requirement in your own state?

3. Rule 6.1 is directed at individual lawyers. Should law firms as organizations profiting from the practice of law bear some burden to encourage their lawyers to deliver pro bono legal services?

a.   In the thirty-five year period of law firm growth from 1970–2005, the competition for law students grew at a fierce pace. In 1971, the placement directors from 36 law schools founded the National Association of Legal Placement, NALP, to facilitate legal career counseling and planning. At some point, NALP began to ask law firms for information about their pro bono programs. This information included whether the firm had a commitment to pro bono, whether the firm counted pro bono hours as billable hours, and whether the firm had a pro bono coordinator. These questionnaires, along with the competition for law students, led many large firms to implement formal pro bono programs for their lawyers.

b.   Partners at big law firms have many motivations to embrace an organized pro bono program. Pro bono work (1) gives junior attorneys control over cases, thus enhancing and diversifying their skills, (2) exemplifies noblesse oblige, (3) may arise from a major event such as Hurricane Katrina or 9/11, (4) gives firms points on external ranking systems, (5) can generate positive publicity, (6) may generate funds from attorneys' fees award to fund future pro bono work, and (7) may enable partners to advance political causes. See, e.g., Scott Cummings & Deborah Rhode, Managing Pro Bono: Doing Well by Doing Better, 78 Fordham L. Rev. 2357 (2010). If pro bono work is so advantageous to law firms, why do courts see a need to impose a pro bono requirement?

C.   THE   TRADITION   OF   ACCEPTING   COURT   APPOINTMENT   IN   A CRIMINAL CASE

1.   What is the basis, if any, of the distinction between the "should [do pro bono service]" in Model Rule 6.1 and the "shall [accept court appointments]" in Model Rule 6.2? Do cases holding that defendants have a constitutional right to counsel necessarily imply that attorneys must bear the uncompensated burden of such representation?

a.   Some lawyers have not taken low pay in assigned cases without protest. Matter of Hunoval, 247 S.E.2d 230 (N.C.1977), for example, concerned an appointed attorney who had seen his client convicted and sentenced to death. The state supreme court affirmed the conviction, but it then granted a stay of execution for the attorney to seek certiorari in the U.S. Supreme Court. At that point, the attorney refused to file the petition for certiorari until the state court approved paying him more money, saying "I cannot justify working for * * * a rate less than that received by a garage mechanic." The court turned down the demand for money, and the lawyer failed to file the petition for certiorari on behalf of the condemned man. The court was not sympathetic. It suspended the attorney from practice in the state's appellate courts and barred him from receiving appointments in criminal cases for one year.[28]

b.   Some attorneys have had greater success protesting low pay in assigned cases. DeLisio v. Alaska Superior Court, 740 P.2d 437 (Alaska 1987), for example, reversed the contempt conviction of a lawyer who refused to accept a trial court's order to serve as appointed counsel. Quoting a case from 1854, the court said that a lawyer's "professional services are no more at the mercy of the public, as to remuneration, than are the goods of the merchant, or the crops of the farmer, or the wares of the mechanic." The court reasoned that "requiring an attorney to   represent   an   indigent   criminal   defendant   for   only   nominal compensation unfairly burdens the attorney by disproportionately placing the cost of a program intended to benefit the public upon the

---

[28]   See also, State v. Richardson, 631 P.2d 221 (Kan.1981) (lawyer indefinitely suspended for failing to take steps to represent defendant for whom he was appointed counsel); Federal Trade Comm'n v. Superior Court Trial Lawyers Ass'n, 493 U.S. 411 (1990) (lawyers who were not employees of the same law firm or other entity and who regularly volunteered to take assigned cases committed a per se violation of the antitrust laws when they agreed among themselves to withhold services until the D.C. government raised their rates of compensation).

attorney rather than upon the citizenry as a whole." An attorney should receive "just compensation," the court said, defined as the rate reflecting compensation received by the average competent attorney operating in the open market.

c.   Olive v. Maas, 811 So.2d 644 (Fla.2002), involved an attorney regularly appointed as counsel for death row inmates in post-conviction proceedings. In one case, however, he refused to sign the usual engagement contract that contained a cap on the fee he could receive. By a 4 to 3 vote, the Florida Supreme Court agreed that a mandatory cap on an attorney's fee in post-conviction review of a capital case interferes with the prisoner's right to counsel. Such a fee cap discourages an attorney from expending extra time and effort on the defendant's case, the court said, and risks reducing the effectiveness of a defendant's representation. Thus, attorneys may petition the court for additional compensation in appropriate capital cases.[29]

d.   Are these results persuasive to you? The timing of the protest in *Hunoval* was clearly inexcusable, but do you agree that courts should listen sympathetically to a lawyer's complaint about being forced to work for little or no compensation? Look at Model Rule 6.2(b). Should the lawyer's right to payment be the principal focus of the court, or should the real question be the effect on the clients' representation?[30]

e.   Should we see the right to reimbursement of expenses as an issue separate from, or as part of, the fee question? Compare State v. Lynch, 796 P.2d 1150 (Okla.1990) (lawyers for indigent defendants must be paid expenses, plus same hourly rate that state pays public defenders), with Williamson v. Vardeman, 674 F.2d 1211 (8th Cir.1982) (state may compel lawyer's services without compensation but may not deny reimbursement of litigation expenses).

2.   Should the court excuse an appointed counsel in a criminal case if the defendant's conduct puts him in a difficult ethical position?

a.   In Chaleff v. Superior Court, 138 Cal.Rptr. 735 (Cal.Ct.App.1977), the defendant was trying to represent himself and the court appointed a deputy public defender as "advisory counsel." This counsel asked to withdraw because the defendant's conduct allegedly put him in an "untenable ethical position." He said he could not explain further, but it later came out that the client's self-destructive urges caused him to reject the lawyer's suggestions of defenses and to seek imposition of the death penalty. Should the lawyer be relieved in such a case? The court said yes, citing California Rule 2–111 [comparable to Model Rule 1.16]. It noted that "while the attorney's duty is to his client, he cannot be placed in the position where discharging that duty impinges upon his ethical responsibilities as a member of the bar."

b.   Should the court excuse counsel if he can show he lacks the skill to represent the client competently? United States v. Wendy, 575

---

[29] See also, People ex rel. Conn v. Randolph, 219 N.E.2d 337 (Ill.1966) (reimbursement in excess of statutory maximum required where "extraordinary" time and financial burden is required to defend case).

[30] See, e.g., Sheppard & White, P.A. v. City of Jacksonville, 827 So.2d 925 (Fla.2002), saying rate of pay lawyer entitled to receive must be a rate "that ensures the provision of effective assistance to his client," not the rate lawyers earn for other kinds of work.

F.2d 1025 (2d Cir.1978), said that it should. The trial court had held a lawyer in contempt for refusing to accept an assignment to defend a felony tax case carrying a potential five-year prison term. The lawyer's expertise was in tax and accounting, but he had never tried a case "civil or criminal, state or federal." The Second Circuit said that the court may not require a lawyer to do what he is incapable of doing.

c.   Zarabia v. Bradshaw, 912 P.2d 5 (Ariz.1996), held the entire Yuma County system for appointing counsel unconstitutional. When there were not enough experienced lawyers who wanted court appointments, the plan required appointments on a "rotational basis" from a pool that included lawyers with no experience in either criminal law or trial work. The inexperienced lawyers could consult with "mentors," but the county assumed that any lawyer who worked hard could become competent to conduct a defense occasionally. The court said it did "not share [the county's] optimism that an attorney * * *, who has no trial or criminal experience, can become reasonably competent to represent a defendant * * * charged with a very serious crime." The court held that a county has a duty to appoint only competent counsel and then to pay them a reasonable fee.

d.   Do you agree with these results? Look at Model Rule 6.2(a) and Comment 2. Are courts too willing to accept an "ethics" rationale when a lawyer is unwilling to accept an assigned case? Don't we normally presume that every lawyer can become competent with sufficient study and preparation?

PAYING THE COSTS OF LITIGATION AND THE PROBLEM OF LITIGATION FUNDING

Whether in a pro bono context, a personal injury practice, or commercial litigation, problems of financing a case from the initial investigation through possible appear can be central to a lawyer's practice. The Model Rules place some surprising controls on such financing.

1.   Look at ABA Model Rule 1.8(e). What could possibly be the rationale for preventing a lawyer from providing help to a client in need? Restatement Third, The Law Governing Lawyers § 36(2), Comment c, says that advancing funds to a client "gives the lawyer the conflicting role of a creditor and could induce the lawyer to conduct the litigation so as to protect the lawyer's interests rather than the client's." See also, Model Rule 1.8, Comment 10. Are you convinced?

2.   The reporters for the Restatement Third, The Law Governing Lawyers originally suggested in § 36(2), Comment c, that the law should permit payment of living expenses, at least where the loan would permit the client "to withstand delay in litigation that otherwise might unjustly induce the client to settle or dismiss a case because of financial hardship rather than on the merits." The American Law Institute membership voted down that proposal, however, after an impassioned appeal that the lawyers who would offer such support would likely those who were less than scrupulous, thus putting honorable lawyers at a competitive disadvantage. What do you think of that argument?

3.   May a lawyer lend the client money at a market rate of interest? Would that also be "financial assistance?" Would it be a financial transaction with a client subject to Rule 1.8(a)? Must the lawyer require each client to repay any such loans? If a lawyer may waive payment of fees even if the case is successfully resolved, should the law allow a lawyer to waive repayment of expenses? Does Model Rule 1.8, Comment 10, persuade you that Model Rule 1.8(e) properly resolves these issues?

4.   Are the same issues raised if the case needs the aid of an expert witness and the client is too poor to hire one? Should a lawyer be able to hire the expert witness and make his or her fee contingent on the outcome of the case?

What does Model Rule 3.4(b) tell you?. The prohibition against paying contingent fees to expert witnesses was attacked in Person v. Association of the Bar of the City of New York, 554 F.2d 534 (2d Cir.1977), cert. denied, 434 U.S. 924 (1977).

5.   In recent years, litigation costs have risen at astonishing rates so that only the largest firms may have the resources to fund major complex litigation. Plaintiffs and law firms have not been able to obtain traditional bank financing for these expenses. These financial pressures have led to an emergence of a "litigation funding" or "third party financing" industry abroad and now in the United States.[31] Essentially, litigation-funding companies provide plaintiffs with cash advances to fund the litigation expenses in exchange for a share of the litigation proceeds.

Such litigation financing by third parties raises ethical issues.

First, may a lawyer refer a client to a third party financing company? New Jersey Advisory Committee on Professional Ethics, Opinion 691 (2001) approved of referrals "provided the lawyer has no financial interest in the entity securing or providing the funding, the entity will not be funding any portion of the unrealized legal fees, and the lawyer will be independent of and will not profit from the business of the entity."

Second, because third parties will not provide financing unless they can evaluate the strengths and weaknesses of the litigation, the client will need to authorize the lawyer to disclose confidential information to the third party. Before the client can consent to such disclosure, the lawyer needs to discuss the risks of revealing confidential information to a third person, including the possible loss of attorney-client privilege. See Connecticut Opinion 99–42 (1999).

Finally, some litigation financing agreements may give the third party companies too much control over the client's litigation and thus

---

[31] "[I]n order to keep the courthouse doors open in legal systems where losers pay winners' legal costs and lawyers generally charge hourly rather than contingent fees, many countries including the UK, Australia, the Netherlands, Belgium, Germany, and South Africa have become more amenable to third parties financing lawsuits, typically on a contingency basis." Susan Lorde Martin, Litigation Financing: Another Subprime Industry That Has a Place in the United States Market, 53 Villanova L. Rev. 83, 107–08 (2008). Burford Capital reports total net income of over $54 million in 2012 on its litigation finance activities. www.burfordcapital.com.

interfere with the lawyer's independent professional judgment in violation of Model Rule 5.4(c).

See also, Ohio Supreme Court Bd. Of Commissioners on Grievances & Discipline, Opinion 2012-3 (Dec. 7, 2012) (examining the lawyer's obligation to inform the client about the risks and benefits of third party nonrecourse funding).

6. Before the codification of crimes into a Model Penal Code, three common law crimes prohibited third party involvement in litigation. (1) *Champerty* prohibited a third party from becoming an investor in another person's litigation. (2) *Maintenance* prohibited third party support for another person's lawsuit. (3) *Barratry* prohibited stirring up litigation. Although in most jurisdictions, these common law crimes do not exist in the criminal codes, courts and state bar organizations could still view such behavior as violating state public policy. One author concludes that 29 states, including Texas, prohibit some forms of champertous agreements.[32] Third party financing would need to take into account these restrictions, but why impose the restrictions at all?

7. Does third party financing help to increase plaintiff access to the justice system or does it simply reduce the lawyer's cost of funding litigation? Are the arrangements inherently exploitive and unconscionable? Do the concepts of champerty and maintenance add anything to the analysis or are they just archaic words thrown in to justify a predetermined conclusion? Do third party financing arrangements create unresolvable conflicts of interest? See Model Rule 1.7(a)(2). Should the ABA allow lawyers to take alternative litigation funding inside the law firm by removing the Rule 1.8(e) restriction on providing loans to clients and advancing monies for living expenses? These and other questions all remain to be resolved in this quickly-evolving field.

POSSIBLE OTHER WAYS TO FINANCE LEGAL SERVICES TO THE POOR

Requiring individual lawyers to provide uncompensated legal services is, of course, only one possible way to provide assistance to the poor.

1. The Legal Services Corporation (LSC), for example, is a federal agency that provides funding to over 175 local affiliates around the country that hire lawyers to provide a wide variety of legal services. Annual funding for LSC activities was as high as $400 million in 1994–95. It dropped to $278 million in 1996, but is up to $365 million for FY 2014.[33] Congress imposed statutory restrictions on the LSC's expenditure of funds in the agency's 1996 and 1997 appropriations acts. Congress forbade use of LSC funds to aid entities in lobbying, class actions, giving aid to certain aliens, supporting advocacy training, litigating on behalf of prisoners, and suing to reform welfare. The law

---

[32] Christy B. Bushnell, Champerty is Still No Excuse in Texas: Why Texas Courts (and the Legislature) Should Uphold Litigation Funding Agreements, 7 Houston Bus. & Tax J. 358, 369 (2007).

[33] You can find this and other information about the LSC at its website, www.lsc.gov.

also imposed these restrictions on non-federal funds raised by the LSC and its local entities.[34]

Legal Services Corp. v. Velazquez, 531 U.S. 533 (2001), involved a challenge to the congressional prohibition on the use of LSC appropriations to seek to amend or otherwise challenge the existing welfare law. The Second Circuit held that was an unconstitutional content-based restriction on speech and the Supreme Court agreed (5 to 4). In an opinion by Justice Kennedy, the Court acknowledged that Congress has excluded several kinds of cases from LSC jurisdiction, e.g., most criminal cases. However, restricting the kinds of arguments LSC lawyers can make in cases they may take is another story. That "distorts the legal system by altering the traditional role of attorneys * * * [and] threatens severe impairment of the judicial function. * * * The statute is an attempt to draw lines around the LSC program to exclude from litigation those arguments and theories Congress finds unacceptable but which by their nature are within the province of the courts to consider." Justice Scalia, joined by Chief Justice Rehnquist and Justices O'Connor and Thomas, argued that the statute did not regulate speech; it defined the scope of a program. Congress routinely says that federal dollars may be used for some things but not others, they observed. Poor people are free to seek welfare reform; they simply may not use LSC dollars to do it.

2.   Well before creation of the public Legal Services Corporation, charitable legal services agencies provided free services to the poor. In this country, legal aid is often traced back to 1876 and the formation of a legal aid society for German immigrants living in New York. By 1916, there were legal aid societies in 37 American cities. One common form of those agencies today are law school clinics. They, too, sometimes come under fire from those who oppose their activities on behalf of poor clients.

Southern Christian Leadership Conference v. Supreme Court of Louisiana, 252 F.3d 781 (5th Cir.2001), involved an effort by law professors, law students, and community organizations, to challenge an amendment to the student practice rules of the Louisiana Supreme Court adopting a more restrictive definition for the "indigence" of clients whom students could represent. Those who opposed this amendment argued that it was payback because Tulane Law School clinic took environmental cases that angered business interests. The Fifth Circuit rejected all constitutional challenges to the new rule, concluding that the new legal requirement of detailed financial disclosures before clients could obtain representation did not deny equal protection: the wealth classification was rationally related to the purpose of the law to help poor people. Second, although the new rule effectively limited certain kinds of representation by student clinics, it did not implicate the constitutional right of free speech. Even *Velazquez* did not require a different result. A restriction based on client wealth was content-neutral, the court reasoned, unlike the restrictions in *Velazquez*.

---

[34] Data on the LSC website suggests that those sums amount to another $250 million annually.

Do you agree with the court? Should the political purpose behind legislation be relevant to its constitutionality if on its face the legislation is content-neutral? Do we want courts trying to discern whether legislators had appropriate motives when they voted for or against a law?

3. Another technique widely used to avoid the problems of pleasing outside funding sources has been to try to find "free" money associated with lawyer trust accounts. For many years, lawyers were forbidden to deposit client funds that are small in amount or held only for a very short time in an interest-bearing account. IOLTA (Interest on Lawyer Trust Accounts) programs are in existence in most jurisdictions today, however, even though the plans rarely require the lawyers to notify the client or seek client consent.

As you saw in Problem 6, interest on a client's funds normally belong to the client. However, Formal Opinion 348 said:

> "[N]o ethical rule proscribes placing client funds at interest for the benefit of an individual client, [but] administrative costs and practical considerations often will make it self-defeating for the lawyer to attempt to obtain interest on small sums or even on large amounts of clients' funds held for short periods of time. * * *

> "* * * The Committee perceives no intention by the drafters of the Model Code to relax in any manner the long-standing restrictions on a lawyer's [own] use of client funds. * * *

> "[However, s]uccessful programs using the interest on lawyers' trust accounts for law-related public service projects in Canadian provinces and several British Commonwealth countries have inspired bar groups in the United States to consider the creation of similar programs. * * *

> "* * * The practical effect of implementing these programs is to shift a part of the economic benefit from depository institutions to tax-exempt organizations. There is no economic injury to any client. The program creates income where there was none before. For these reasons, the interest is not client funds in the ethical sense any more than the interest is client property in the constitutional sense or client income in the tax law sense." * * *

Do you agree with this analysis? Have lawyers instead created a special exception for themselves from normal fiduciary standards so they can divert clients' money to fund services that lawyers would otherwise be morally obliged to provide?

Phillips v. Washington Legal Foundation, 524 U.S. 156 (1998), brought the constitutionality of state IOLTA plans to the Supreme Court. The issue before the Court was very specific. The Court assumed that a lawyer was required to put funds into an IOLTA account only if the interest generated on the funds would not be sufficient to offset bank service charges and accounting for the interest. The issue thus was whether the interest was nevertheless "property" of the client so that the takings clause could apply.

Chief Justice Rehnquist, for the Court (5 to 4), held that even that little bit of interest on a client's funds in a lawyer's account is property of the client for purposes of the takings clause. The amount at stake is not the issue, the Court said. "[P]roperty is more than economic value; it also consists of 'the group of rights which the so-called owner exercises in his dominion of the physical thing.'" Rental income would be the property of the owner of a building, for example, even if the cost of collecting the rent cost more than the tenant owed. Because the lower court did not decide other issues, the Court left for another day whether, given this view of property, the IOLTA program constituted an unconstitutional taking and what, if any, compensation might be due.

Washington Legal Foundation v. Texas Equal Access to Justice Foundation, 270 F.3d 180 (5th Cir.2001), was the remand of *Phillips*. A Fifth Circuit panel held (2 to 1) that the confiscation of interest income was a taking of property, because it was not in exchange for any services performed by the state. In addition, the statutory scheme did not allow a client to withdraw any of the interest that his account generated. Thus, the program permanently appropriated the client's income, and the use of the funds constituted a per se taking even if not a measurable award. The Supreme Court, however, rejected a "just compensation" challenge to IOLTA programs in Brown v. Legal Foundation of Washington, 538 U.S. 216 (2003). When the Washington Supreme Court set up its IOLTA program it required that: (a) *all* client funds be deposited in interest-bearing trust accounts, (b) funds that cannot earn net interest for the client be deposited in an IOLTA account, (c) lawyers direct banks to pay the net interest on the IOLTA accounts to the Legal Foundation of Washington (Foundation), and (d) the Foundation use all such funds for tax-exempt, law-related charitable and educational purposes.

The Supreme Court agreed that a law requiring that the interest on IOLTA accounts be transferred to a different owner for a legitimate public use could be a per se taking requiring the payment of "just compensation" to the client. However, it viewed the amount of interest generated for any individual client-owner of the principle to be so small that the net benefits to the client-owner after paying the bank fees was, in essence, zero. Moreover, the use of this interest to benefit "millions of needy Americans" satisfied the "public use" requirement of the just compensation clause. [35]

Unfortunately, since 2008, low interest rates on bank deposits have significantly reduced interest in IOLTA programs as a way to generate funds to support legal services for the poor.

PROBLEM 36

PROBLEMS IN CLASS ACTION AND MULTIPARTY REPRESENTATIONS

OMITTED IN CONCISE EDITION

---

[35] The case is discussed in Ronald D. Rotunda, Found Money: IOLTA, Brown v. Legal Foundation of Washington, and the Taking of Property without the Payment of Compensation, 2002–2003 Cato Supreme Court Rev. 245 (2003).

people to put all their property into "living trusts." The book contained 310 pages of forms "perforated for easy removal from the book," and the book told readers the forms "will be suitable for use" to achieve the desired results. "The giving of legal advice * * * including instructions and advice as to the preparation and use of legal instruments, constitutes the practice of law which is forbidden * * * to all but duly licensed New York attorneys," the appellate division said. "It is immaterial that Dacey has no face-to-face dealings nor a confidential relationship with particular clients."

But the Court of Appeals reversed, saying: "It cannot be claimed that the publication of a legal text which purports to say what the law is amounts to legal practice. And the mere fact that the principles or rules stated in the text may be accepted by a particular reader * * * does not affect this. * * * This is the essential of a legal practice—the representation and the advising of a particular person in a particular situation."

5.   **Traditionally, if a lay advisor goes beyond writing books and starts giving personalized legal advice, unauthorized practice issues arise. Should filling in the blanks on prepared forms constitute the practice of law?**

a.   The leading case on this issue, State Bar of Arizona v. Arizona Land Title and Trust Co., 366 P.2d 1 (Ariz.1961), supplemented 371 P.2d 1020 (Ariz.1962), held that real estate agents engaged in the unauthorized practice of law when they helped buyers and sellers fill in the blanks on preprinted real estate contract forms. Arizona citizens responded with a ballot initiative that amended the state constitution and reversed the decision. See Arizona Constitution, Art. 26, § 1.[38]

b.   In Fifteenth Judicial Dist. Unified Bar Ass'n v. Glasgow, 1999 WL 1128847 (Tenn.App.1999), Glasgow (a non-lawyer) filled in the blanks on divorce forms for low-income clients who would then represent themselves in court. She charged them a fee of from $99 to $148 and suggested where and "approximately" when the clients should file the papers. She even prepared some quitclaim deeds if they were necessary to divide real property. Ever vigilant, the Tennessee Bar sued to enjoin Glasgow's services, and the court complied. The applicable statute defines drafting "any paper, document or instrument affecting or relating to secular rights" as the practice of law that can be only performed by lawyers. The statute is constitutional because "the practice of law by untrained persons endangers the public's personal and property rights, as well as the orderly administration of the judicial system."

Suppose Glasgow offers competent legal services? Is the public required to have only first-class legal services? Should we be concerned whether Glasgow's clients can afford superior services?

---

[38] See also, Countrywide Home Loans, Inc. v. Kentucky Bar Ass'n, 113 S.W.3d 105 (Ky.2003) (lay persons may conduct real estate closings, but they may not answer legal questions that arise at the closing or offer any legal advice to the parties); Real Estate Bar Ass'n for Massachusetts, Inc. v. National Real Estate Information Services, 946 N.E.2d 665 (Mass. 2011) (clearing title defects and drafting deeds are the practice of law, but preparation of most mortgage documents is not); Crawford v. Central Mortgage Co. 744 S.E.2d 538 (S.C. 2013) (loan modification may be done by bank without attorney involvement).

THE DELIVERY OF LEGAL SERVICES

c.   Admission to Practice Rule 28: Limited Practice Rule for Legal Technicians, is a new rule from the Washington Supreme Court that authorizes the licensing of paralegals to provide limited services to pro se clients in particular practice areas. Among things these Legal Technicians may do is "select and complete forms * * * prepared by a [Washington state] lawyer" and "advise the client of the significance of the selected forms to the client's case." The development is one long-advocated as a way to extend legal services to more low- and middle-class clients. Its requirement that Washington lawyers develop the forms will complicate efforts to create nationally applicable forms, but one can imagine "legal technicians" operating out of kiosks in shopping malls as a way to bring services to currently under-served clients.

d.   Since 2007, the province of Ontario in Canada has authorized paralegals to offer limited legal services to clients including representation before small claims court and in minor matters under the Criminal Code. The Law Society of Upper Canada, the lawyer regulatory authority, regulates the licensing and rules governing paralegal practice. In a five year study of paralegal practice, the Law Society generally concluded that "Consumer protection has been balanced with maintaining access to justice and the public interest has thereby been protected." Report to the Attorney General of Ontario, Pursuant to Section 63.1 of the Law Society Act 3 (2012).

6.   Where should computer-assisted drafting programs fit into our unauthorized practice analysis?

a.   In Unauthorized Practice of Law Comm. v. Parsons Technology, Inc., 1999 WL 47235 (N.D.Tex.1999), a federal district court held that the creators of Quicken Family Lawyer were guilty of unauthorized practice. The "Family Lawyer" software package contains over 100 legal forms that Quicken represented were "valid in 49 states." The program asks questions about the user and, based on the responses, generates forms to deal with the user's problem in the user's jurisdiction, all the while expressly disclaiming providing "specific information for your exact situation." The court held that both the preparation of legal forms and the selection of which form to use constitute the practice of law in Texas. The court also argued that the state had a justifiable interest in not letting people who are not lawyers give legal advice that might harm Texas citizens. Thus, the court said, the prohibition in this case did not burden commercial speech more than was necessary, and it enjoined the sale of the software.[39]

Shortly after the Quicken decision, the Texas legislature enacted a law specifically providing that "the 'practice of law' does not include the design, creation, publication, distribution, display, or sale . . . [of] computer software, or similar products if the products clearly and conspicuously state that the products are not a substitute for the advice of an attorney." The law was effective immediately. The Fifth Circuit vacated the lower court injunction and judgment, 179 F.3d 956 (5th Cir.1999) (per curiam), and remanded in light of the statute.

---

[39] See also, Frankfort Digital Services v. Kistler, 477 F.3d 1117 (9th Cir.2007) ("expert system" elicited client information, purported to take into consideration multiple facts about the client and select the best approach, provided clients with information about "loopholes" and "stealth techniques," and generated bankruptcy forms completely filled-in).

Does the outcome tell you whom lay people tend to think unauthorized practice rules are protecting? Do you agree with their view?

b.   Janson v. LegalZoom.com, Inc., 802 F.Supp.2d 1053 (W.D. Mo. 2011), asked whether LegalZoom.com's activities constitute the unauthorized practice of law.[40] The service in question provides complete, fully-executable documents based on information provided by the customer over the company's website. LegalZoom's "decision tree" program then turns customer-provided information into a legal document. The court said "[t]here is little or no difference between this and a lawyer in Missouri asking a client a series of questions and then preparing a legal document based on the answers provided and applicable Missouri law." The court cited LegalZoom's ads that say "we'll prepare your legal documents" and brag that LegalZoom "takes over" once the customer "answer(s) a few simple online questions."

Further, the court cited the company's quality-control review process as proof that LegalZoom crossed the line from merely providing forms to providing legal advice. First, a non-lawyer employee reviews each document to see that the client information appears where it should in the document, and second, a person applying Missouri law created the decision-tree system itself. To the court, LegalZoom's distinction between providing advice in a face-to-face setting versus the impersonal medium of the internet was unpersuasive because the ultimate character of the transaction was the same, i.e. a client paying money for a ready-to-sign legal document.

Do you believe companies like LegalZoom.com will provide competition for traditional lawyers in the future?[41]

c.   In 2000, a former Davis, Polk attorney founded Axiom, Global, Inc., a Delaware corporation, that operates as www.axiomlaw.com. AxiomLaw has over 1000 employees in 11 states and, although it claims it is not a law firm, it defines itself as the modern interpretation of a law firm. AxiomLaw represents large and mid-sized corporate clients by offering relatively low-cost insourcing, outsourcing, and project staffing of law-related work. By having its lawyers work under the direct supervision of corporate general counsel rather than AxiomLaw itself, AxiomLaw seeks to avoid classification as a law firm or legal services provider. In 2013, AxiomLaw received $28 million from private investors. Can this nonlaw firm model pose a threat to the business of large law firms? Will its business model avoid issues of imputed conflicts of interest?

---

[40] LegalZoom.com, Inc. says that it has had two million customers during the last decade, sold almost 500,000 documents in 2011, and had $156 million in 2011 revenue and $12 million in 2011 profits.

[41] LegalZoom itself has seen that some customers want a mix of computer-aided and in-person help. It has begun to suggest that customers consult a local attorney if they have questions about how to complete its forms.

B.   THE MULTIJURISDICTIONAL PRACTICE OF LAW

1.   In what jurisdictions may a licensed lawyer regularly practice?

a.   To many people, admission to the bar of one state should guarantee the right to practice in every other. But that is not the law today. Each individual jurisdiction licenses the lawyers who may practice there.

b.   As a practical matter, many states automatically admit experienced lawyers that other states have licensed if the state of licensing will do the same for other states' lawyers. That tit-for-tat system is called "reciprocity." However, states typically require an examination of lawyers from states that do not grant reciprocity or grant it only on certain conditions. So far, the courts have rejected most challenges to the constitutionality of lawyer reciprocity requirements.[42]

Schumacher v. Nix, 965 F.2d 1262 (3d Cir.1992), for example, upheld the Pennsylvania rule preventing California graduates of non-ABA accredited law schools from sitting for the Pennsylvania bar exam. California does not admit Pennsylvania lawyers without taking the California exam and thus it is not a "reciprocal state" under Pennsylvania law. The court agreed that it was hard to see any rational basis for the Pennsylvania rule, but it found one by saying that Pennsylvania may have hoped to "entice states to enter into reciprocal agreements with it and thereby promote its interest in securing similar treatment for its attorneys who are graduates of accredited law schools."[43]

c.   Does restricting admission of lawyers from other states make sense to you? Is it anything more than an effort by lawyers who already have licenses to make it harder for out-of-state lawyers to compete with them?

---

[42] In other contexts, the Supreme Court, using the dormant commerce clause, has invalidated reciprocal barriers to the transfer of goods and services across state lines. Great Atlantic & Pacific Tea Co., Inc. v. Cottrell, 424 U.S. 366 (1976), unanimously invalidated a Mississippi law providing that milk from another state may not be sold in Mississippi unless that other state accepts milk processed in Mississippi. If a state concludes that another state's rules on milk imports are unfair, the Court said, it should file a lawsuit, not impose a trade barrier. Mississippi could require that all milk (including milk imported from other states) meet its standards, but it could not exclude milk that met those standards simply because that other state did not sign a reciprocal trade agreement with Mississippi.

[43] The Supreme Court has made clear that states do not have unlimited ability to condition admitting lawyers licensed in other states to practice in their own state. E.g., Supreme Court of Virginia v. Friedman, 487 U.S. 59 (1988) (Maryland resident successfully challenged Virginia Requirement that, in order to be admitted to the Virginia bar without taking the bar exam, a lawyer had to be a resident of Virginia); Barnard v. Thorstenn, 489 U.S. 546 (1989) (same result; the Virgin Islands bar required a one-year residency and an intent-to-remain rule). But see Scariano v. Justices of the Supreme Court of the State of Indiana, 38 F.3d 920 (7th Cir.1994), cert. denied, 515 U.S. 1144 (1995), upholding a rule granting admission only to lawyers who have "practiced predominantly" in Indiana for five years under a conditional license; the court said that this rule related to familiarity with Indiana law and was not a residency requirement per se.

2.   Litigators' clients often find themselves sued in states where the lawyers are not licensed. Should there be a way for them to continue to represent their clients in those cases?

a.   In general, if a litigator is not a member of the bar where the litigation is filed, she will file an appearance in court and ask to be admitted pro hac vice, i.e., for that particular case. Typically, local court rules require that the lawyer admitted pro hac vice, must associate in the litigation with a lawyer who is admitted to practice in that state.[44]

b.   Paciulan v. George, 229 F.3d 1226 (9th Cir.2000), challenged California's rule that permits nonresident lawyers to appear pro hac vice, but does not permit lawyers without California licenses who reside in California to so appear. The Ninth Circuit upheld the rule. A state has a significant interest in not letting its residents secure a license elsewhere, the court said, and then regularly practice in California. Limiting occasional pro hac vice status to nonresidents is consistent with that interest. Do you agree?

3.   Should transactional lawyers, i.e., those doing deals or other kinds of commercial activity, have a similar way to follow their clients to other jurisdictions?

a.   For transactional lawyers giving advice to clients with interests around the country or around the world, the practical problems of state-by-state admission are different. There is no "proceeding" where one can ask a court to be admitted for purposes of a particular negotiation or closing. Even in litigation, prelitigation activities such as interviewing witnesses and other investigation may occur before the lawyer files a case, or the parties may resolve their disagreement in alternative dispute resolution proceedings before a judge ever enters the picture.

b.   Birbrower, Montalbano, Condon & Frank, P.C. v. Superior Court, 949 P.2d 1 (Cal.1998), struck terror in the management committees of many "national" law firms. Birbrower, a New York law firm, represented ESQ, a California corporation, in claims it had against Tandem Computers, Inc., relating to a software and marketing contract. California law governed the contract and New York firm partners traveled to California on several occasions. The case was going to arbitration, but the parties ultimately settled the dispute. The firm asked for its fee, which was to be over a million dollars. At that point, the client refused to pay.

The California Supreme Court upheld the refusal. First, it found the New York lawyers "practiced" in California. While the lawyers did much of their work in the New York office, they were physically present in California when they advised the California company about the California arbitration, which California law governed. Second, the court said, even nonphysical presence in California can constitute unauthorized practice of law. One may practice in California "although not physically present here [such as] by advising a California client on

---

[44] Some states try to limit the number of pro hac vice appearances to prevent lawyers from avoiding their obligation to become admitted to the bar. However, such limits can have significant adverse effects on the availability of counsel in civil rights cases, so Sanders v. Russell, 401 F.2d 241 (5th Cir.1968), struck down a district court rule limiting pro hac vice appearances by out-of-state lawyers to one case per year.

California law in connection with a California legal dispute by telephone, fax, computer, or other modern technological means." However, the court did "reject the notion that a person automatically practices law 'in California' whenever that person practices California law anywhere, or 'virtually' enters the state by telephone, fax, email, or satellite." The court allowed the firm to collect payment for services rendered to the client in New York, but only for services that the court could sever from those performed in California.[45]

c.   Not all cases construed unauthorized practice this restrictively. Fought & Co., Inc. v. Steel Engineering and Erection, Inc., 951 P.2d 487 (Haw. 1998), for example, involved an Oregon firm acting as general counsel to an international client that built an airport on Maui. The client won a judgment against the state of Hawaii in a case handled by lawyers licensed there, but the Oregon firm sought a portion of the statutory attorneys' fees for work it did helping prepare for the litigation. Many clients do work that is interstate and international, the court said. These clients, whether or not based in Hawaii, get important help from law firms who are familiar with their operations, wherever the firms are based. Making it impossible for firms to collect fees for work relating to Hawaii would make it hard for all clients to get high quality, efficiently delivered legal services. Even applying the standards set forth in *Birbrower,* the court said, the Oregon firm retained local counsel for work done in Hawaii. It was simply assisting the Hawaiian counsel and thus the law did not bar it from collecting a fee.[46]

d.   The European Union has sought to remove obstacles to the free movement of capital, persons, and services among the member states. Under the Treaty, a qualified European Community (EC) lawyer may provide legal services in another member state either by visiting on an occasional basis or by setting up a permanent office. He or she may provide this legal service using the qualifications of his or her original home (home title), or by obtaining additional qualifications as an "integrated lawyer" from the place where he or she is setting up the permanent office. A lawyer from one country in the European Community relying on his or her home title while practicing in another country in the EC may give legal advice, "including advice in local law." Do we have something to learn from the "United States of Europe"?

e.   The cases and international model provide the context for Model Rule 5.5(c). Its first three subparts authorize an out-of-state lawyer to practice temporarily (1) in association with a local lawyer who is admitted and who "actively participates in the matter," (2) in preparation for litigation where the lawyer reasonably expects that the court will admit him *pro hac vice*, and (3) in an ADR process if the services reasonably relate to a jurisdiction where the lawyer is a member of the bar.

---

[45] The California legislature reversed *Birbrower* as applied to arbitration cases for work *before* January 1, 2007. Code of Civil Procedure § 1282.4 and Rule 983.4 of the Rules of Court.

[46] See also, Estate of Condon, 76 Cal.Rptr.2d 922 (Cal.Ct.App.1998) (California court allows fees to Colorado lawyer probating a Colorado will who had to come to California to sell assets located there); Matter of Opinion 33 of the Comm. on Unauthorized Practice of Law, 733 A.2d 478 (N.J.1999) (out-of-state bond lawyers may advise public entities issuing state and municipal bonds).

But look at Model Rule 5.5(c)(4): provide legal services that "arise out of or are reasonably related to the lawyer's practice" where the lawyer is licensed. How broadly should we read that language? The standard derives from Restatement Third, The Law Governing Lawyers § 3, Comment e, which explained that several factors help determine whether a matter is "reasonably related" to the lawyer's home state practice, including:

> "whether the lawyer's client is a regular client of the lawyer or, if a new client, is from the lawyer's home state, has extensive contacts with that state, or contacted the lawyer there; whether a multistate transaction has other significant connections with the lawyer's home state; whether significant aspects of the lawyer's activities are conducted in the lawyer's home state; whether a significant aspect of the matter involves the law of the lawyer's home state; and whether either the activities of the client involve multiple jurisdictions or the legal issues involved are primarily either multistate or federal in nature."[47]

How easy is it to decide when that definition authorizes work on an out-of-state matter?

4.   If a transactional lawyer works exclusively on questions of federal law, what definitions of the practice of law should control?

a.   Look at Model Rule 5.5(d)(2). Sometimes federal law will provide that some activity is not the unauthorized practice of law. The leading case is Sperry v. Florida Bar, 373 U.S. 379 (1963), where the Supreme Court held that Florida could not enjoin a nonlawyer registered to practice before the United States Patent Office from preparing and prosecuting patent applications in Florida, notwithstanding that such activity, under state law, constituted the "practice of law." The court noted that both a federal statute and patent office regulations specifically authorized practice before the patent office by nonlawyers. Thus, the supremacy clause overrode the state restriction because no state law "can hinder or obstruct the free use of a license granted under an act of Congress."[48]

b.   In re Desilets, 291 F.3d 925 (6th Cir.2002), is a modern application of the *Sperry* doctrine. Attorney Rittenhouse, was licensed in Texas, moved to Wisconsin and opened an office in Michigan to handle only bankruptcy cases. He was not admitted to practice in either Wisconsin or Michigan, but he was admitted in the federal court for the

---

[47] Remember that because of a parallel change in ABA Model Rule 8.5, a lawyer who travels to another jurisdiction in handling a matter will be subject to the disciplinary jurisdiction of the state to which she travels. See, e.g., In re Harper, 785 A.2d 311 (D.C.2001) (reciprocal discipline after D.C. lawyer who had never been licensed in Maryland was formally "disbarred" from practicing there in the future because of misconduct during his unauthorized practice).There may be other consequences of a lawyer's unauthorized practice. In re Jackman, 761 A.2d 1103 (N.J.2000), involved a Massachusetts lawyer who practiced as a senior associate in New Jersey for seven years without a license to practice there. The court found that he had engaged in the unauthorized practice of law for those seven years and thus withheld his admission to the New Jersey bar for an unlimited period.

[48] Note however, that federal courts often make a part of their own rules for admission to practice before them, a requirement that the lawyers also be admitted in the state where the federal court sits. See "Sample Federal Court Rules" in the Supplement.

Western District of Michigan. The state bar of Michigan accused him of the unauthorized practice of law, and the federal bankruptcy court refused to award him fees because he was not an "attorney" where he practiced law. Rittenhouse relied on the fact he only practiced federal law and the federal district court admitted him. Judge Boggs, speaking for the Sixth Circuit, agreed. Citing *Sperry*, the court held that states may not decide who may practice federal law in federal court. Dissenting, Judge Merritt said that federal court admission does not preclude separate state regulation of a lawyer who opens an office to practice in that state.[49]

c.   Schindler v. Finnerty, 74 F.Supp.2d 253 (E.D.N.Y.1999), however, held that lawyers who did federal patent work were not exempt from jurisdiction of the New York lawyer discipline system when their clients complained of neglect and similar misconduct. The district court acknowledged *Sperry*, but it said that state law governs all lawyers to the extent state law does not hinder operation of the patent system. Keeping practitioners honest is consistent with federal objectives, so the lawyers had to respond to their clients' complaints in the discipline proceedings.

5.   May lawyers form a virtual law firm that has no physical location but has only a centralized referral system that sends work to lawyers who work out of their home to provide the clients with legal services all over the country?

a.   One possible evolution of the traditional law firm may be towards a virtual law practice, a group of lawyers practicing together with modern technology. As you think about a number of lawyers who provide legal services to clients from locations physically separated from each other and from their clients, what problems might arise?

b.   Such practices promise the delivery of high quality legal services at low prices because of low overhead costs. Do you think that e-lawyers can deliver quality legal services to clients without face-to-face meetings with the clients or with other lawyers? How can the owners of such firms supervise the delivery of legal services? What issues should the virtual law firm raise with clients before commencing the representation? Could a virtual law firm hire a first-year associate who has no experience? Might such practices offer document-based or unbundled legal services to clients who want to save money?

c.   North Carolina State Bar, 2005 Formal Ethics Opinion 10 (Jan. 20, 2006), addressed whether a lawyer may maintain an exclusively virtual law firm (VLF). The opinion approved such a practice—and even approved providing unbundled services to clients, subject to the requirements of Rule 1.2(c). However, it identified five pitfalls such a virtual practice must avoid. First, it must avoid unauthorized practice in jurisdictions in which the lawyers are not licensed, a problem that is endemic to virtual practice. Second, the firm must comply with local advertising rules, ironically including the

---

[49]   Gallo v. United States Dist. Ct. for the Dist. of Arizona, 349 F.3d 1169 (9th Cir.2003), challenged an amendment to the rules of the local district court admitting to practice only lawyers who were also members of the Arizona state bar. The court held that the rule change does not violate either substantive or procedural due process. An out-of-state lawyer simply must apply for *pro hac vice* admission in order to appear in the federal district court in Arizona.

requirement that the firm's website display a physical office address. Third, the firm must provide competent client representation in spite of the limited client contact. Fourth, it must not create lawyer-client relationships with people the firm does not mean to represent. And fifth, the firm must preserve client confidences.

Do you disagree with any of the requirement?[50] Given these conditions, are virtual law firms likely to be a large part of the legal services world you are about to enter?

c.   In 2009, lawyers in Washington, D.C. formed Clearspire, a law firm built upon a $5 million computer platform that connects lawyers and clients through virtual offices: www.clearspire.com. The firm has grown to include offices in most major cities to serve Fortune 500 clients, but it continues to allow lawyers to work from a home environment. Clearspire also owns a related business-services entity that offers nonlaw services to its clients.

C.   PROHIBITION OF THE CORPORATE PRACTICE OF LAW

1.   Should courts be concerned if Dowd, a licensed lawyer, does general estate planning work for the customers of an insurance company?

a.   Traditionally, lawyers view the lawyer-client relationship as a personal relationship between a lawyer and a client. Is that still true? Do clients today often engage firms to represent them instead of retaining individual lawyers?

b.   Consistent with the individual-service and lawyer-service models, laws typically prohibit corporations from providing legal services. In-house legal departments clearly may handle the company's own legal matters, see Model Rule 5.5(d)(1), but they may not let those lawyers represent customers or other third parties. This is the reason, for example, that a bank trust department ordinarily may not draft a will for a client of the bank, even if the trust officer is a lawyer.

Take a look at Model Rule 5.4(d) and the concern expressed in Model Rule 5.4, Comment 2. Do you agree that the concern is justified?

c.   In spite of the concern and traditional prohibition, some cases have upheld the corporate delivery of legal services. Perkins v. CTX Mortgage Co., 969 P.2d 93 (Wash.1999), held that a mortgage company that prepared documents for loan closings was not engaged in the unauthorized practice of law. Only licensed lawyers selected the legal documents and only lawyers exercised legal judgment. Nonlawyers filled in some blanks, and the court held the company to the same standard of practice as a lawyer.

---

[50] Ohio Supreme Court Board of Commissioners on Grievances & Discipline, Opinion 2011–2 (Oct. 7, 2011) advised out-of-state lawyers that they may not provide debt settlement legal services in Ohio, even on a temporary basis, if (1) the matter is not connected with the lawyer's home jurisdiction, (2) there is no pre-existing relationship between the lawyer and the client, or the lawyer has no "recognized expertise" in a particular body of federal or nationally-uniform law. The opinion explained that Ohio clients could likely only find such lawyers on the internet but the internet's convenience and low prices are not enough to overcome the state's preference for Ohio lawyers. See also, State ex rel. Commission on Unauthorized Practice of Law v. Hansen, 834 N.W.2d 793 (Neb. 2013) (enjoins non-lawyer from holding himself out on website as authorized to practice "eviction" and "common law lien" law in Nebraska).

d.   The lawyer in State ex rel. Oklahoma Bar Ass'n v. Israel, 25 P.3d 909 (Okla.2001), specialized in obtaining child support orders. He also created a corporation that helped clients collect court-ordered payments. He received 25% of each child support payment for his legal fees and his corporation received another 25% of each payment for its own work. The court held that the lawyer's involvement with the company was not an impermissible conflict of interest. The corporation's interest and the client's interest in collecting the money were the same. Also, the respondent adequately disclosed his interest in the company through his oral statements to his client and in the fee stipulation in the client's contract.

e.   Is the increasing liberality toward corporate legal services justified? Are the courts overlooking some protection the law previously thought was worth providing?

2.   How should unauthorized practice of law principles apply to insurance companies who hire licensed lawyers as full-time employees to represent the company's policyholders as counsel of record in actions brought by third parties for incidents covered by the terms of the policy? Is that a conflict of interest or simply a more efficient way to buy legal services?

a.   Gardner v. North Carolina State Bar, 341 S.E.2d 517 (N.C.1986), was a relatively early case holding that insurance companies may not employ lawyer-employees to represent the insured. Nor may the attorney appear as counsel of record for the insured in the prosecution of a subrogation claim for property damage. "Since a corporation cannot practice law directly," the court said, "it cannot do so indirectly by employing lawyers to practice for it."

b.   In re Allstate Insurance Co., 722 S.W.2d 947 (Mo.1987) (en banc), specifically refused to follow *Gardner* and concluded that the insurance company may either hire independent lawyers or use its own employees instead. "An insurer has a very substantial interest in litigation involving its insured, and is entitled to retain counsel of its own choosing to protect its interest." If an insurer can hire an independent contractor, it may act through its employee. Any danger of conflict of interest is minimal because the company uses its employee-lawyers "only when there is no question of coverage, and when the claim is within policy limits."

c.   In Cincinnati Insurance Co. v. Wills, 717 N.E.2d 151 (Ind.1999), the insurance company provided the lawyers through a "captive" firm called "Berlon & Timmel" whose only practice was on behalf of policyholders of the insurer. The court agreed that Indiana corporations could not practice law. However, they could hire lawyers to represent themselves. Thus, the only question was whether they could hire lawyers to represent others. Conflicts could arise and the lawyers must address them, the court said, but that reason does not support a blanket prohibition. However, the court found it misleading to use a traditional law firm name for a group of lawyers who do all their work for a single company. Change that and the practice may continue.

d.   Insurance companies are trying to expand the use of in-house lawyers. With which of these cases do you agree? Is what the insurance companies are doing significantly different from the system of prepaid legal insurance discussed in Problem 34?

3. How do these principles apply to the practice of accounting firms hiring lawyers full-time to give corporate and transactional advice to the firms' business clients?

a.   By far the most controversial issues of practice by nonlawyer organizations—as well as the most important multidisciplinary practice issues—were raised by the fact that the largest firms offering legal services in Europe at the turn of the millennium were American accounting firms. What Model Rules impose the greatest barriers to these firms expanding their practice to the representation of clients in the United States?

b.   Does Model Rule 5.4 stand as a barrier to the delivery of "one-stop business services" by accounting firms? What interests of clients— as distinct from interests of lawyers in traditional law firms—do you believe justify prohibiting the phenomenon?

c.   The ABA Commission on Multidisciplinary Practice (MDP) issued a report in 1999 acknowledging the development of one-stop business services by accounting firms and concluded that it inevitably represented a useful new way to deliver legal services to some clients. The Commission proposed a new Model Rule 5.8 to regulate such firms, but in February 2000, the ABA summarily rejected the proposal and efforts to revisit MDPs by the Ethics 20/20 Commission in 2012 did not lead to any proposed changes.

d.   Wouters v. Algemene Raad van de Nederlandse Orde van Advocaten (C309/99), 2002 WL 29971, [2002] All E.R. (EC) 193, [2002] 4 C.M.L.R. 27, even undercut the growth of MDPs in Europe where the phenomenon began. The case held that, under European Union law, whether MDPs may include lawyers is a matter for national law. Arthur Andersen and other large accounting firms were providing legal services throughout Europe, and the Netherlands Bar, a national entity, adopted rules prohibiting such partnerships from operating there. Plaintiffs challenged those rules as the product of a cartel, which the EU Treaty prohibited, but the European Court of Justice found that the Treaty did not limit proper exercise of power by national authorities. The decision itself did not outlaw European MDPs, but it did deter their presence, and when the Arthur Andersen accounting firm (one of those most responsible for the MDP phenomenon) imploded as part of the Enron bankruptcy, the future of the organizations became doubtful.

e.   But significantly, in 2007, England enacted the Legal Services Act, which represents a significant transformation of the British legal services industry. First, the Act created a new regulatory structure for supervising the regulation and delivery of legal services in the United Kingdom. This included the creation of the Legal Services Board as the key policy and oversight regulatory agency and an Office for Legal Complaints to serve as the independent source for redress of consumer complaints. Second, the Act authorized lawyers in the United Kingdom to associate with nonlawyers (up to a limit of 25% ownership) for the purposes of delivering legal disciplinary practices (LDPs) to consumers. England has permitted such LDPs to operate since March 2009. Finally, the Act expressly allows the creation of alternative business structures (ABS) to deliver legal and nonlegal services. The basic concept of an ABS is that the regulations will permit nonlawyers to practice together with lawyers to deliver legal and nonlegal services. Moreover, the law allows such entities to have nonlawyer owners and managers. Commentators expect that law firms will be able to attract investment and capital from nonlawyers to operate an ABS. The British regulators have studied the challenges presented by ABSs since 2007 and authorized the first ABSs in October 2011. These developments have the potential to have a profound impact on legal professions around the world.[51]

4. Are these issues all about big firms and corporate clients? Do you see a place for multidisciplinary organizations to deliver legal services to low- and middle-income clients?

a. An early draft of the Model Rules recommended that they should allow nonlawyers to form partnerships with lawyers if (1) there would be no interference with the lawyers' independent professional judgment or with the lawyer-client relationship, (2) the multidisciplinary organizations would keep client confidentiality, and (3) the advising and fee arrangements did not otherwise violate the Rules governing lawyers. During the ABA floor debates an ABA delegate asked: "Does this rule mean Sears & Roebuck will be able to open a law office?" Professor Geoffrey C. Hazard, Jr., the Reporter for the Model Rules, answered "Yes." The proposal failed.[52]

b. Think of an office that serves clients like Mrs. Andrews, whom we met in Problem 17. She was the woman in an abusive relationship who had lost custody of her children. Are there any circumstances where a social services agency with a lawyer on its staff would serve her needs better than a traditional private law firm?

c. New Jersey Supreme Court Advisory Committee on Professional Ethics, Opinion 711 (July 2007) considered a "center for divorce mediation," established by a lawyer, that referred parties to experienced accountants, therapists and mediators to try to achieve relatively noncontentious divorce settlements. The opinion found that the arrangement constituted the practice of law. Thus, the requirement that affiliated attorneys refer clients only to center-approved professionals violated Rule 5.4(c). In addition, Rule 7.5 (governing trade names) prohibited the center's name and Rule 5.4(b) prohibited the center from sharing its fees with the nonlawyer professionals. Do you think that lawyers who are adversaries will better serve New Jersey citizens seeking divorces than mediation services such as the center?

d. Suppose a firm in a Model Rules jurisdiction works on a case with a D.C. or United Kingdom firm that has non-lawyer partners. May the firms share fees without violating Model Rule 5.4(a)? ABA Formal Opinion 464 (Aug. 19, 2013) says "yes." A lawyer in a Model Rules

---

[51] In 2002, the ABA amended Model Rule 7.2 to authorize reciprocal referral agreements between lawyers and nonlawyer professionals. The ABA viewed reciprocal referral agreements as an alternative to the prohibited integrated law and non-law entities sought by the advocates of the MDP movement. Rule 7.2(b)(4) permits such arrangements as long as they are not exclusive and the lawyer informs the client of their existence.

[52] See Rita Henley Jensen, Ethics Row Looms on [Law Firm] Affiliates, National L. J., Feb. 20, 1989, at 1, 28.

jurisdiction may share fees with "another lawyer" pursuant to Model Rule 1.5(e) and "any concerns of the lawyer subject to the Model Rules regarding inter-firm division of legal fees should end at that point." The fact the firm receiving part of the fee may share it with nonlawyers "should not expose the lawyer in the Model Rules jurisdiction to discipline" as long as the lawyer does "not permit a nonlawyer in the other firm to interfere with the lawyer's own independent professional judgment." Now is all becoming clear?

e.   How about it? Should we let Dowd work with the insurance company? Should we let banks help their clients prepare wills and trusts? Dowd's organization is clearly nontraditional, but is it as crazy as it might have sounded when you first thought about it? Until lawyers figure out a way to deliver legal services relatively noncontentiously and at a price most people can afford, do lawyers have the moral authority to stand in the way of people who can deliver such services?

D.   LAW FIRM DELIVERY OF ANCILLARY, NOT-TRADITIONALLY-LEGAL SERVICES

1.   Could Dowd eliminate all problems with his multidisciplinary organization if he simply ran it out of his law firm?

a.   Subsidiaries or law firm "affiliates" are becoming more common today as law firms have gone into the publishing business, financial consulting, and even forms of investment banking. Are these positive developments or do they constitute a threat to the independence and professionalism of lawyers?[53] The debate as to whether law firms should be able to operate nonlaw entities has become more heated over the years.

b.   Washington, D.C. firms initially founded many of the first wave of law firm affiliates. A partner in Arnold & Porter explained a typical reason for creating the subsidiary. The firm wished to hire a departing government official who was not a lawyer; the firm would hire this official to engage in lobbying activities for clients but "[w]e would have to call him or her a paralegal."

c.   The arguments in favor of such affiliates seem to be threefold. First, they make the law firm more convenient for the client. When the client has a problem that requires the services of several professionals, as is often the case, it is beneficial and useful for the client be able to engage in one-stop shopping. Second, these entities might not be as constrained in the manner of calculating fees as lawyers may be. Third, having the affiliates may retain existing clients, bring in new clients, and thus offer new sources of revenue.

d.   The arguments against creating such affiliates are both ethical and pragmatic. Ethically, a lawyer who advises a client in dealings with the lawyer's affiliate may not have the independent judgment needed to give sound advice, such as the advice to fire the affiliate. Also, such

---

[53] There is no ethical restriction on a lawyer owning a business that is not ancillary to the practice of law. Two lawyers in a law partnership may buy a restaurant, for example, and they presumably may take clients there to dine without the restaurant's becoming law-related.

arrangements inevitably involve the lawyer in business transactions with the client, raising separate problems under Rule 1.8(a).

Pragmatically, law firms must be concerned about the partners' being jointly and severally liable for the acts of the affiliates, ranging from simple negligence to dishonesty of the nonlawyers. When the affiliate is making large sums of money brokering substantial transactions, potential malpractice exposure may look small by comparison, but liability can be enormous. Further, the affiliate may expand the number of situations disqualifying the law firm, e.g., the affiliate may work on behalf of a client who has an interest that conflicts with a different client of the law firm.

Finally, to the extent that law firms become one-stop shopping centers instead of dispensers of a unique service, some see a danger that lawyers will lose their power of self-regulation and that the state supreme courts, which usually claim an inherent power to regulate the practice of law, will lose that claim of authority.

2.   Look at Model Rule 5.7 and its Comments. The ABA adopted a similar rule in 1992, repealed it in 1993, and adopted the present version in 1994. What should constitute "law-related services" within the meaning of the rule?

a.   Is "financial planning" a law-related service, for example? Is the test whether a service is one that some lawyers might offer to some clients? By that definition, is every service performed by any lawyer potentially law-related?

b.   What is the significance of calling something "law-related"? Is a lawyer's title insurance business subject to different in-person solicitation rules than would govern sale of the usual insurance policy, for example? What is the rationale for holding lawyers to a more restrictive standard?

c.   Is there any reason not to call every service a lawyer provides a legal service? Should the Rules prohibit a lawyer's ancillary business to do environmental consulting for a customer that may disadvantage one of the lawyer's clients, without the consent of that client?

3.   If the law allows law firms to provide nonlaw services, should law firms be able to admit nonlawyers as partners to perform those services?

a.   One jurisdiction permits nonlawyers to be partners of law firms. District of Columbia Court of Appeals Rule 5.4 provides:

"(b) A lawyer may practice law in a partnership or other form of organization in which a financial interest is held or managerial authority is exercised by an individual nonlawyer who performs professional services which assist the organization in providing legal services to clients, but only if:

"(1) The partnership or organization has as its sole purpose providing legal services to clients;

"(2) All persons having such managerial authority or holding a financial interest undertake to abide by these rules of professional conduct;

"(3) The lawyers who have a financial interest or managerial authority in the partnership or organization undertake to be responsible for the nonlawyer participants to the same extent as if nonlawyer participants were lawyers under Rule 5.1;

"(4) The foregoing conditions are set forth in writing."

b.   Comment 5 to this Rule explains that nonlawyer participants "ought not to be confused with nonlawyer assistants under Rule 5.3. Nonlawyer participants are persons having managerial authority or financial interests in organizations which provide legal services."

4.   If the jurisdiction permits non-lawyer partners, does it follow that non-lawyer investors should be able to invest in those law firms?

a.   Comment 8 adds that the D.C. Rule "does not permit an individual or entity to acquire all or any part of the ownership of a law practice organization for investment or other purposes" because "such an investor would not be an individual performing professional services within the law firm or other organization."[54]

b.   Why not? If a firm can pay a lawyer with a well-known name to meet with potential clients but do little else, why shouldn't the firm be able to pay a passive investor to provide the firm with operating capital?

c.   In 2007, the Australian law firm Slater & Gordon raised several million dollars selling shares in itself on the Australian Stock Exchange. Does this development shock you? Do you see any reason not to permit the same practice in the United States?[55]

d.   ABA Formal Opinion 01–423 (Sept. 22, 2001), advised that U.S. lawyers may form partnerships with lawyers not licensed in the United States, so long as the foreign lawyers are members of a recognized legal profession in a foreign jurisdiction and the arrangement complies with the law of all jurisdictions where the firm practices. If the foreign country would not recognize these lawyers as a legal profession, they would be "nonlawyers" and making them partners would violate Rule 5.4. The purpose of Rule 5.4 is to protect a lawyer's independence in exercising professional judgment on the client's behalf, the opinion says. As long as a foreign lawyer is a member of a recognized legal profession, this objective would be realized.[56]

---

[54] The ABA Commission on Ethics 20/20 announced that it would not recommend even modest changes to Rule 5.4 to permit a minority of non-lawyer firm partners, which D.C. allows. See also, New York State Bar Ass'n Comm. on Professional Ethics, Opinion 911 (Mar. 14, 2012) (British firms with non-lawyer owners may not have a New York office even if they employ only New York licensed lawyers).

[55] One result of this prohibition is that it "can forestall attempts to form the capital structures necessary to make law practice a true consumer product for a mass market. It also prevents competition from banks, insurance companies, title insurance companies and other potential competitors. The prohibition presented a momentary embarrassment when, for tax reasons, it made economic sense for a lawyers to practice in the corporate form. That was gotten around by obtaining state legislation permitting lawyers to form 'professional corporations.' " Charles W. Wolfram, Modern Legal Ethics 840 (1986).

[56] New York law has been to this effect for several years. See Rules of the Court of Appeals for the Licensing of Legal Consultants, 22 N.Y.C.R.R. Part 521.

e.   Jacoby & Meyers v. Presiding Justices, 847 F.Supp.2d 590 (S.D.N.Y. 2012), was a direct challenge to Rule 5.4's prohibition of non-lawyer investment in law firms. Jacoby & Meyers said that it wanted to fund its program of "legal services for the masses" and that private equity capital represented its most attractive source of funds. The court dismissed the case for lack of standing. New York Judiciary Law § 495 does not allow corporations to practice law, the court said, so the relief the plaintiffs seek under Rule 5.4 could not provide them concrete benefit. In addition, Jacoby & Meyers does not fit under the exception for a pre-paid legal services plan for the indigent. Thus, the court did not reach the merits of the Rule 5.4 prohibition of non-lawyer investment, but the policy question underlying the Jacoby & Meyers challenge remains.

f.   What kinds of legal delivery organizations do you see in your future? Is the prospect of using your legal skills to work for many different kinds of organizations a cause for celebration or a cause for apprehension?

CHAPTER VIII

ETHICAL CONDUCT OF JUDGES

Not all lawyers will be judges, but almost all lawyers will appear before them. In addition, public and professional confidence in the integrity of the judiciary is close to the heart of the respect for law. Thus, judicial ethics is of central importance to any lawyer, whether or not he or she aspires to be on the bench.

Judges are usually lawyers and so the state's version of the ABA Model Rules of Professional Conduct (particularly Rule 8.4) continues to govern them. The conduct of lawyers who deal with judges—or who want to become judges—is also the concern of the Model Rules.

However, for the issues in this chapter—judicial conduct—the state's version of the ABA Model Code of Judicial Conduct controls. The Judicial Conference of the United States has also adopted a Code of Judicial Conduct, which it derived from the ABA Model Code. These federal rules explicitly do not apply to the U.S. Supreme Court, an exception that some commentators criticize. In addition, the federal recusal statute is found in 28 U.S.C.A. § 455. By this time, it should be clear to you that ethical standards do not draw simple lines between honest persons and crooks. The Model Code of Judicial Conduct is no exception.[1]

As you work through these materials, ask yourself questions such as:

a.   Which of the principles of judicial ethics help assure "correct" or at least disinterested decisions?

b.   Which principles prevent judges from abusing the unusual influence they have over lawyers and in the community?

c.   How do issues of judicial misconduct reach official attention and what is the role of lawyers in that process?

d.   To what extent would the Model Code of Judicial Conduct be unnecessary if judges were appointed and not elected?

e.   Are any aspects of the Model Code unnecessarily restrictive on judges? Do any ethics rules discourage able people from seeking judicial office?

f.   Rule 1.2 of the 2007 Model Code requires judges to avoid "the appearance of impropriety." Is that standard too vague to use as a basis for judicial discipline?

------

[1]   In February 2007, the ABA approved a new Model Code of Judicial Conduct that changed the format of the 1990 Model Code and substantially reorganized the standards. Unless described otherwise, all references in this chapter are to the 2007 Model Code.

PROBLEM 38

JUDGES' DISQUALIFYING CONFLICTS OF INTEREST

Grounds for disqualifying judges are probably the judicial ethics issues of most interest to practicing litigators. Judges, like everyone else, have financial dealings. They get a mortgage to buy a house, borrow money to purchase a car, and try to take advantage of investment opportunities. Their family members lead their own lives and have their own financial relationships and careers, but the judge is not likely indifferent to their welfare. Judges also often have strongly held views on public questions, some of which may come before their courts. This problem first asks what financial relationships create a conflict of interest that requires the judge's disqualification. Next, it asks when interests of the judge's family may create similar problems for the judge. It then examines whether views about policy issues constitute a similarly disqualifying bias, and it closes by exploring when and how a judge should secure a waiver of the judge's conflict of interest.

FACTS

Harold Baxter and Martha Anderson met in law school and have been good friends ever since. Baxter has now become a state trial judge and Anderson practices in the same city. Recently, Baxter sought to buy a new house, but the required down payment was higher than he had expected. Anderson, who was an attorney for the bank from which Baxter planned to borrow, personally lent Baxter $25,000, evidenced by a demand note that Anderson assured Baxter would not be "called under any conditions I can foresee." Judge Baxter then got his mortgage from the bank.

Anderson is now representing the same bank, which is the plaintiff in a case assigned to Judge Baxter. The case involves a close question of lien priorities and both sides expect the case to go to the state supreme court. Judge Baxter orally informed counsel about the loans in an early pretrial conference and asked, "Do you have any problems with my presiding in this case?" Both Anderson and the defense counsel, who frequently appears before Judge Baxter, replied, "No, sir."

Judge Baxter's niece is 19 and lives with the Baxters while going to college. She has some money of her own that she has invested. She owns ten shares, a 1/100,000 interest, in the insurance company that is defendant in the lien priorities case before Judge Baxter. The judge does not know of her interest. "I don't ask my relatives about their business dealings nor tell them about mine," he says.

Before going on the bench, Judge Baxter served as local chair of the "Committee for Responsible Assessment Policy," a committee of citizens who favor correction of what they see as an inequitable method of making local tax assessments. He is no longer a member of that committee. The computer randomly assigns cases to judges in this district, so Judge Baxter will hear a case in which a local taxpayer is challenging the validity of her own assessment. Judge Baxter has taken no steps either to recuse himself from the matter or to determine whether either party believes he should do so.

QUESTIONS

A. FINANCIAL INTERESTS THAT MAY CREATE DISQUALIFYING BIAS

1. Was it improper for Anderson to lend money to Judge Baxter to help him buy a house, or for Judge Baxter to accept the loan?

a.   Look at Model Rules 3.5(a) and 8.4(f). Do they tell you that Martha Anderson has to take a good look at the Model Code of Judicial Conduct to know the status of her own conduct under the Model Rules of Professional Conduct?

b.   What will Anderson find when she turns to the Code of Judicial Conduct? Does Rule 3.11(C)(3) provide an unambiguous answer to the propriety of the loan? Does Rule 3.15 require Judge Baxter to publicly report the loan? Does the loan require automatic disqualification under Rule 2.11? Was Judge Baxter required to disclose the loan to opposing counsel as the problem says he did?

c.   In Lisi v. Several Attorneys, 596 A.2d 313 (R.I.1991), a judge called twenty-one lawyers at various times, pleading that he desperately needed money to cover some urgent needs. Some of the lawyers had appeared before the judge in family court but several had known him in other settings. Each lent him the money he requested, not knowing others were doing so as well. There was no reported quid pro quo treatment, but some lawyers did have matters pending before the judge while the loans were outstanding. The judge resigned; the court suspended four of the lawyers for a year and imposed public reprimands on seventeen others.

d.   Operation Wrinkled Robe was a federal investigation that videotaped Judge Alan Green soliciting and accepting a campaign contribution for his niece who was running for the Louisiana House of Representatives. One lawyer making a donation had just won a large verdict before Judge Green. For his conduct, a federal jury convicted Judge Green of mail fraud and the court sentenced him to 51 months in prison. He also resigned as a judge and the court permanently disbarred him. In re Green, 913 So.2d 113 (La.2005) and 920 So.2d 861 (La.2006). The state suspended from practice the lawyer who made the contribution for a year and a day. In re LeBlanc, 972 So.2d 315 (La.2007).

2. Was it improper for Judge Baxter to finance his home mortgage at a bank that regularly appears before him?

a.   Look generally at Rule 3.13 of the ABA Model Code of Judicial Conduct, and particularly at Rule 3.13(B)(4) & Comment 3. Do you agree that borrowing from a bank—even a litigious bank—should be treated differently from borrowing from the bank's attorney? Why?

b.   In Ausherman v. Bank of America, 216 F.Supp.2d 530 (D.Md.2002), the plaintiffs claimed that a bank improperly accessed their credit reports. They sought to disqualify the federal magistrate judge because the defendant bank held his home mortgage, but the judge refused to step down. Citing 28 U.S.C. § 455,[2] the federal law counterpart to Rule 2.11 of the Model Code of Judicial Conduct, the judge observed, "A loss for the bank, even if ruinous, would not extinguish or reduce the obligation of the mortgagor to repay * * *. Similarly, a victory for the bank, regardless of how substantial, affords no possible benefit to the mortgagor." Do you agree that the issue of how having the loan might influence the judge is that simple?

c.   In re United States, 158 F.3d 26 (1st Cir.1998), involved a government motion to recuse a federal judge who was presiding in a criminal trial of a bank's officers. The judge and her husband had overdrawn their account at this bank and had a delinquent commercial loan during the period when the defendants were bank officers. When the trial judge refused to recuse herself, the government filed a mandamus action. The First Circuit held that the judge's decision not to recuse herself was not an abuse of discretion. The government could not show that the officials on trial were in any way involved with the bank's decision to grant the judge's loan or that the bank treated the judge differently from other borrowers.

3.   How large must the judge's financial interest be before it becomes a disqualifying financial interest in litigation where the judge is presiding?

a.   Look at Rule 2.11(A)(3), and the definition of "economic interest" in the Terminology section of the ABA Model Code of Judicial Conduct.[3] What makes an interest "more than de minimis"? The 1972 version of the ABA Model Code of Judicial Conduct defined "financial interest" as any interest "however small."

b.   Should the Rules disqualify a judge from hearing a case involving IBM if he or she owns ten shares of IBM stock? Does the process for determining when an interest is "de minimis" intrude on the privacy of the judge? After all, what may seem like a large amount to a judge of modest means may be de minimis to a very rich judge, and thus litigants might have to inquire into the judge's overall financial position in order to determine whether the interest is de minimis. The Reporter's Notes to the 1972 Judicial Code explain that, to avoid such inquiries, the 1972 Code adopted an absolute prohibition and then mitigated it by allowing the parties to waive it pursuant to Rule 2.11(C), discussed below.

Was the 1972 approach preferable to the current provision? Did that approach give parties too much opportunity to disqualify a judge they did not like for reasons unrelated to the issue of financial interest?

c.   Virginia Electric & Power Co. v. Sun Shipbuilding & Dry Dock Co., 539 F.2d 357 (4th Cir.1976), extensively analyzed both 28 U.S.C. § 455 and what is now Rule 2.11. The electric utility sued for damages caused by the defendant's fabrication of pump supports. At least in

---

[2]   The text of 28 U.S.C. § 455 is in the Standards Supplement to this book.

[3]   The Terminology section of the 2007 Model Code adds several terms that were not in the 1990 Code (such as, "domestic partner," and "impending matter"). And it removes some definitions as unnecessary. Other than that, definitions in the 1990 Model Code are the same as the 2007 Model Code. The Reporter's Explanation of Changes explains, "any differences are intended to be purely stylistic."

principle, if the utility won the case, the state regulatory commission could require it to lower the electric bills of everyone in Virginia, including the trial judge's bills. The total reduction could have been $100, payable in small amounts over 40 years. The Fourth Circuit refused to disqualify the trial judge because he had no "financial" interest in the outcome of the case. Any rate relief was speculative and wholly within the discretion of the Virginia Corporation Commission, which sets utility rates. That possibility did constitute an "other interest" that is a basis for disqualification within the meaning of that section, but the interest was too speculative and remote to require the judge's recusal.

     d.   Should placing the judge's assets into a blind trust satisfy the Code of Judicial Conduct? Why or why not? Does a blind trust satisfy the requirements of Rule 2.11(B)? If a judge puts property into a blind trust, is she keeping informed about her financial holdings?

     4.   Is a judge disqualified from ruling on a court challenge to the judge's own compensation, or does the "Rule of Necessity" allow the judge to hear the case? Should it matter that the reason for disqualifying this judge extends to all judges, so that no one could decide the case in a wholly impartial manner?

     a.   In 1976, 140 federal judges filed a lawsuit arguing that since their last pay increase, inflation had reduced the purchasing power of their salaries by over 34%. They argued that Congress' failure to grant them cost-of-living pay increases constituted an unconstitutional reduction of their salaries. Then, as now, 28 U.S.C. § 455(e) provided that federal judges could not accept a waiver of recusal in a case involving the judge's personal financial interest. The Court of Claims applied the "rule of necessity" and held that, under that rule, its judges could hear the case. Otherwise, no judge would be available to decide some important legal questions. The court then turned to the judges' substantive claim and denied it. Atkins v. United States, 556 F.2d 1028 (Ct.Cl.1977) (per curiam), cert. denied, 434 U.S. 1009 (1978).

     b.   After losing *Atkins*, 13 judges filed new suits in a federal district court. The Supreme Court also held that the rule of necessity allowed both the lower courts and the Supreme Court to hear the case, notwithstanding 28 U.S.C.A. § 455. United States v. Will, 449 U.S. 200 (1980). The *Will* Court explained: "The Rule of Necessity had its genesis at least five-and-a-half centuries ago. Its earliest recorded invocation was in 1430, when it was held that the Chancellor of Oxford could act as judge of a case in which he was a party when there was no provision for appointment of another judge." The rule of necessity is a "well-settled principle at common law that, as Pollack put it, 'although a judge had better not, if it can be avoided, take part in the decision of a case in which he has any personal interest, yet he not only may but must do so if the case cannot be heard otherwise.' F. Pollack, A First Book of Jurisprudence 270 (6th ed. 1929)." *Will* concluded that Congress did not intend § 455 to change the rule of necessity, "a doctrine that had not been questioned under prior judicial disqualification statutes." *Will* then held that Congress had unconstitutionally diminished salaries of Article III judges and justices for two of the four years in dispute.

c.   Beer v. United States, 696 F.3d 1174 (Fed.Cir. 2012) (en banc), revisited the issue of cost-of-living pay increases. Congress voted to grant increases in the Ethics Reform Act of 1989, but for several years, it did not follow that up with funding for these increases. The Federal Circuit held that Congress must keep its promise. It remanded to the Court of Claims to determine the damages.

d.   Does the "rule of necessity" exception to required recusal make sense to you? Note that Model Code of Judicial Conduct, Rule 2.11, Comment 3, expressly acknowledges it.

5.   What other "personal interests" might bias a judge?

a.   Is a Supreme Court justice biased in favor of the incumbent administration because he accepts the invitation of the Vice President to go hunting together? That issue arose in 2004 when Justice Scalia and Vice President Cheney, who had known each other for many years, were among a group of nine who participated in a hunting trip in Louisiana. At the time of the trip, the Supreme Court had granted certiorari in a case involving the Vice President's handling of an energy task force. Justice Scalia refused to recuse himself from the pending case, saying that informal relationships between government officers are common and do not normally affect the exercise of their official duties. Cheney v. U.S. District Court for the District of Columbia, 541 U.S. 913 (2004). Are you comfortable about such associations? Should it matter that plaintiffs were suing the Vice President in his official capacity?

b.   Is a judge biased in one case because he took a bribe in a completely different case? Bracy v. Gramley, 520 U.S. 899 (1997), a habeas corpus case, allowed discovery to show judicial bias during habeas review after a judge sentenced the defendant to death. The defendant wanted to show that the judge at his state court trial, Judge Thomas J. Maloney, had accepted bribes in other murder cases and had a compensatory bias against defendants who did not bribe him in order to avoid appearing "soft" on criminal defendants. A unanimous Court concluded that the defendant stated a claim and may try to prove his point. Defendant did more than charge the judge's bias in general; he specifically alleged that he did not get a fair trial. The Court remanded the case for further discovery.

c.   Is a judge biased against a defendant if the defendant threatens to kill the judge? Should we be worried that a defendant might engage in judge shopping by threatening to kill each judge assigned to his case? Does the risk of criminal prosecution for uttering such threats prevent that? In United States v. Greenspan, 26 F.3d 1001 (10th Cir.1994), the FBI reported that the defendant had taken steps to hire a hit man to kill the trial judge and his family. The trial judge knew of the threats and expedited the sentencing hearing to get the defendant off the streets "immediately." The Court of Appeals held that a defendant may not force a judge's recusal simply by uttering a threat, but in this case—where the facts suggested this was more than a ruse to disqualify the judge—a reasonable person would think the judge's impartiality would be affected. The court held that § 455(a) required that another judge impose the defendant's sentence.

B. FINANCIAL INTERESTS OF THE JUDGE'S FAMILY

1. What obligation does Judge Baxter have to know his niece's financial holdings?

a.   Should a judge be able to take an "I don't ask" attitude about his or her relatives' financial affairs? Look carefully at Rules 2.11(A)(2) & (3) and Rule 2.11(B). Is Judge Baxter's 19-year-old niece a "member of the judge's family residing in the judge's household"? Is she a minor child? Is she "within the third degree of relationship" to Judge Baxter? The 2007 Model Code defines the "third degree of relationship" in its Terminology section.

b.   If Judge Baxter knew of the niece's holdings, must he recuse himself in this case? Should his "don't ask, don't tell" approach to others' financial interests subject him to discipline no matter what an appropriate inquiry would reveal?[4]

c.   May a judge "cure" a financial conflict of a relative by having the relative sell the stock? During the discovery period in Union Carbide Corporation v. United States Cutting Service, Inc., 782 F.2d 710 (7th Cir.1986), an antitrust class action, Judge Susan Getzendanner got married. Her husband had a self-managed retirement account that contained stock in IBM and Kodak. At the time, there was no list of class members. When the judge disclosed her husband's holdings in her annual financial disclosure statements, the defendant moved to disqualify her because it knew that IBM and Kodak had bought products from the defendant. Instead, the judge immediately ceased ruling on motions in the case while her husband sold his interest in the two companies. The Court of Appeals upheld that procedure. After the sale, the husband no longer had an interest in the stock, the court reasoned. The majority said "we do not mean to endorse sale as a cure for disqualification in all cases," but in this case no basis existed for saying that one could reasonably question the judge's impartiality.

Judge Flaum's dissent argued that nothing in 28 U.S.C. § 455(b)(4)—which corresponds to Rule 2.11(A)(3)—permits a judge to "cure" a disqualifying situation in this way. "Congress desired to rid the statute of flexibility where financial interests are concerned." After the case, Congress added 28 U.S.C.A. § 455(f), which largely codified the Seventh Circuit ruling.

---

[4]   You can find out the financial holdings of a federal judge and his or her close relatives. See P.L. 95–521, Title III, Judicial Personnel Financial Disclosure Requirements § 305, in the Standards Supplement. The Fifth Circuit summarily rejected a challenge to these disclosure requirements. Duplantier v. United States, 606 F.2d 654 (5th Cir.1979), cert. denied, 449 U.S. 1076 (1981).

Federal judges do not always disqualify themselves when their ethics rules require them to do so. "A number of federal appellate judges have ruled on cases involving companies in which they own stock, despite a federal law designed to prevent judges from taking part in any case in which they have a financial interest." When interviewed, the judges, "who include some of the nation's best-known jurists, attributed their participation in the cases to innocent mistakes or memory lapses about their financial portfolios." As one judge remarked, "It's embarrassing." See Joe Stephens, Taking Stock On the Bench: Federal Appeals Court Judges With Conflicts of Interest, Washington Post, Sept. 13, 1999, at p. A1.

2. If Judge Baxter has a daughter who practices federal tax law in a local firm, must he recuse himself whenever his daughter's firm enters an appearance in a case?

a. Does Rule 2.11(A)(2)(b) provide the answer? The daughter's direct involvement in the case would disqualify Judge Baxter; do the 2007 Rules also require disqualification whenever any member of the daughter's law firm is before him? Does Rule 2.11, Comment 4, provide a clear answer? Should the answer be the same in a large city (with many available judges) as in a small town (with no other available judges within 50 miles)?

b. In Bernard v. Coyne, 31 F.3d 842 (9th Cir.1994), Judge Kozinski had to decide when he must disqualify himself in bankruptcy cases arising out of the district in which his wife was the United States bankruptcy trustee. Most of the trustee's actual duties are administrative, but she has the right to become involved in any case and some of the cases establish precedents that are important to her office. Judge Kozinski referred the issue to the Judicial Conference's Committee on the Code of Conduct, which concluded that unless a case involved the trustee as a party or was of such high profile that it would affect her career, he did not have to recuse himself. He took that advice and heard this case.

c. If there is any question about the issue, how should Judge Baxter determine whether his daughter has "more than a de minimis interest" that will be "substantially affected" by the outcome of a case? May he call his daughter on the telephone and ask her how her firm divides income from such cases? Should the parties have right to contact the relative to make a similar inquiry? Must the judge hold a public hearing?[5]

d. Would the analysis of recusal change if the firm took the case on a contingent fee basis so that its fee would depend upon the outcome of the proceedings? Suppose the daughter were "of counsel" to the firm, i.e., she did not automatically share all fees?

e. Might Rule 2.11(A)(2)(b) encourage litigants to use its limitations as a way of disqualifying judges or justices? Several justices of the U.S. Supreme Court have spouses, children, or other relatives who practice law and whose law firms may work on matters that will come before the Court. On November 1, 1993, seven justices[6] announced that, absent "some special factor," they would not recuse themselves solely because one of their relatives had personally worked on a matter at an earlier stage before it reached the Supreme Court. One "special factor" requiring recusal would be that the relative acted as "lead counsel below," because then the outcome of the case "might reasonably be thought capable of enhancing or damaging his or her professional reputation." 112 S.Ct. at *CX* (Dec. 1, 1993) (unbound). See also, 80 A.B.A.J. 18 (Feb. 1994). If the relative is a law firm partner, the justices' voluntary practice mandates recusal unless the relative's firm

---

[5] One federal case that seems to read 28 U.S.C.A. § 455(a) and (b)(5) to disqualify the judge when anyone in his brother's firm appears before him was SCA Services, Inc. v. Morgan, 557 F.2d 110 (7th Cir.1977).

[6] Justice Blackmun, who was about to retire, and Justice Souter, a bachelor, did not sign the statement. 112 S.Ct. at CIX (1993).

gives "written assurance that income from Supreme Court litigation is, on a permanent basis, excluded from our relative's partnership shares." 112 S.Ct. at *CXI*.

Have the justices appropriately balanced the competing interests in establishing these standards? Were they properly concerned that recusing themselves in more cases would create opportunities for " 'strategizing' recusals, that is, [clients] selecting law firms with an eye to producing the recusal of particular Justices." Id. at *CX*.[7]

3. Should a judge disqualify herself when someone from the judge's former firm (or the judge's former law clerk) appears before the judge?

a. In National Auto Brokers Corp. v. General Motors Corp., 572 F.2d 953 (2d Cir.1978), four years into an antitrust case, the plaintiffs moved to recuse the judge because the judge's former law firm represented the defendant. The Second Circuit held that, although the defendant was a client of the firm while the judge was there, he had never represented the defendant and the specific case did not come to the firm until after the judge had left. Would the case come out the same under Rule 2.11(A)(6)(a)?

b. Is the judge–clerk relationship likely to have been more or less close than the judge's relationship with her former law partners? Should the law bar a judge's former law clerk from appearing before the judge?

Monument Builders of Pennsylvania, Inc. v. Catholic Cemeteries Association, Inc., 190 F.R.D. 164 (E.D.Pa.1999), involved a lawyer who served as the judge's clerk in 1984 when the federal district court considered a class action against various cemetery associations. Indeed, she had clerked for the judge until his retirement in 1998. The parties brought a new case in 1999 to enforce a settlement agreement that the parties had entered into with the judge's approval in 1989. The former clerk was with the firm representing the plaintiff and had been involved in working on the enforcement action. The court held that the enforcement action was the same matter as the case that began in 1984 so it disqualified the lawyer pursuant to Rule 1.12 of the ABA Model Rules of Professional Conduct and Canon 2 of the federal Code of Conduct for Law Clerks. However, the court did not disqualify her law firm because she telecommuted and the firm could easily screen her from further involvement in the matter.

c. In Bradley v. State of Alaska, 16 P.3d 187 (Alaska App.2001), the state moved to allow a former appellate court law clerk to represent the state in the appeal. The proposed lawyer served as a law clerk while the appeal was pending, but by the time the appeal was assigned to a judge within the court, the clerk had finished his clerkship and was working for the state. The state appellate rule seemed to impose an inflexible ban on participation in a case that had been pending in the court during the period in which he served as a law clerk. The court turned to the state's later adoption of Model Rule of Professional Conduct 1.12(a), allowing a law clerk to participate in a case that was previously pending in the court in which the clerk served unless he "participated personally and substantially" in the matter during his

---

7   See Ronald D. Rotunda, Rubbish About Recusal, Wall Street J., Dec. 13, 2000, at A26.

time as a clerk. The court held that Rule 1.12(a) is "inconsistent" with the earlier rule, and that Rule 1.12(a) is now the law. The former clerk submitted an affidavit declaring that he had no contact with any of the pleadings in this appeal and that he did not discuss any aspect of this case with any judge, secretary, law clerk, or other court system employee. The court granted the state's motion to let him handle the appeal.

d.   Should we suspect bias if the judge's personal lawyer appears before her in a different matter? ABA Formal Opinion 07–449 (Aug. 9, 2007) said this situation presents a conflict for the lawyer under Model Rule 1.7(a)(2). If the lawyer concludes she can provide competent and diligent representation to both the judge and to the client before the judge, and if the lawyer secures the informed consent of both the litigant and the judge confirmed in writing, then the lawyer may handle both cases. If the judge, in turn, would have a personal bias for or against the lawyer or the lawyer's firm because of the representation, the judge must disqualify herself under Code of Judicial Conduct Rule 2.11(A) and may not seek a waiver under Rule 2.11(C). Because this bias is not inevitable, however, if the judge concludes she has no bias, she may put the issue of waiver before the parties and accept a Rule 2.11(C) waiver.

If the judge refuses to recuse herself or seek a waiver, the opinion says that the lawyer must withdraw under Model Rule 1.16(a) from one or both representations. Otherwise, the opinion concludes, the lawyer would be in violation of Model Rule 8.4(f), *i.e.*, assisting the judge to violate the CJC. To try to avoid the need for withdrawal, the opinion says the lawyer may talk to the judge about her obligations without violating the Model Rule 3.5 or the CJC Rule 2.9(A) prohibitions of ex parte contact.

e.   ABA Formal Opinion 462 (Feb. 21, 2013) discusses judges' use of "electronic social media" (ESM). The opinion recognizes that the Rules do not require judges to be "isolated or out of touch," but they must "be sensitive to the appearance of relationships with others." They must assume comments they post on ESM sites will not remain within the circle of the judge's connections. The simple act of being someone's internet "friend" is not disqualifying, but "context is significant" and the judge may have to disclose ESM connections with witnesses or parties to a case. The opinion goes on to say that, if the judge visits a political website, the judge must not "like" a candidate or otherwise advocate his or her election. "When used with proper care," the fact that judge use ESM "does not necessarily compromise their duties under the Model Code any more than use of traditional and less public forms of social connection such as U.S. Mail, telephone, email or texting." One might add that ESM is different from the U.S. Mail, texting, etc. because those communications are from one person to another; an ESM is a posting on the internet to a group of people who are "friends" only because some ESM sites use that term.

C. BIAS ARISING FROM PERSONAL VIEWS RATHER THAN FINANCIAL INTEREST

1. Does Judge Baxter's prior involvement in the Committee for Responsible Assessment Policy require his recusal from the case challenging the plaintiff's assessment?

a.   Do Rule 1.2 and Rule 2.11(A) provide an answer or only suggest more questions? Look at the definitions of "impartiality" and "impropriety" in 2007 Model Code, Terminology. The 1990 Model Code did not define these terms. Do the new definitions help? Look at Rule 1.2, Comment 5, which elaborates on the prohibition against an "appearance of impropriety." Does 2007 Model Code give any examples of something that is not an impropriety but *appears* to be an impropriety to "reasonable minds" who know the facts? Can you think of any?[8]

b.   Justice Rehnquist (before he became Chief Justice) weighed in on the question of issue bias shortly after he joined the Supreme Court:

> "Though the Canons of Ethics are extraordinarily detailed and specific about what shall constitute a 'financial interest,' they have virtually nothing to say about what constitutes 'bias.' The Canons state that: 'A judge should disqualify himself in a proceeding in which his impartiality might reasonably be questioned * * *.' [Webster's Dictionary defines 'impartiality' as] 'freedom from bias or favoritism'; one of the definitions of 'bias' in that same volume is 'an inclination of temperament or outlook.' In that broad definition of 'bias,' one can scarcely escape the conclusion that all judges, to a greater or lesser extent, are biased. * * * The late Justice Black was, in this sense of the word, 'biased' in favor of a literal construction of the First Amendment to the United States Constitution, and made no bones about saying so. But it cannot be this sort of 'bias' which would disqualify a judge, else it would be the rare case in which a quorum of a court could be mustered for decision.

> "[The] true distinction is between the concept of attitude or outlook, which is not disqualifying, and the concept of 'favoritism,' which is disqualifying. Favoritism to me means a tendency or inclination to treat a particular litigant more or less generously than a different litigant raising the identical legal issue."[9]

---

[8]   For criticism of the ABA's decision to elevate "appearance of impropriety" to a standard of discipline, see, e.g., Ronald D. Rotunda, Judicial Ethics, the Appearance of Impropriety, and the Proposed New ABA Judicial Code, 34 Hofstra L. Rev. 1337 (2006). The ABA Commission that drafted the 2007 Model Code of Judicial Conduct was concerned that "a duty to avoid the appearance of impropriety was too vague to be independently enforceable." However, lobbying "from legal organizations and the judiciary led the Commission to accept an amendment (during debate in the House of Delegates) that reinstated the obligation of a judge to avoid impropriety and the appearance of impropriety as black letter Rule 1.2." 2007 Model Code, Reporter's Explanations of Changes, at 8.

[9]   William H. Rehnquist, Sense and Nonsense About Judicial Ethics, 28 Record of Assoc. of the Bar of the City of New York 694, 708–13 (1973). This article elaborates on his opinion in Laird v. Tatum, 409 U.S. 824 (1972), where he refused to disqualify himself.

c.   Do you agree with Justice Rehnquist's approach to policy bias? Will his attempt to distinguish "bias" from "favoritism" help Judge Baxter know what he should do? Is any thoughtful person old enough to become a judge likely to have well-formed views on many questions of public policy?

2.   Should it be harder to disqualify a judge for a bias based on policy preferences than for bias based on financial or other personal grounds?

a.   Sometimes, the line between financial grounds for disqualification and the judge's policy preferences grounds is less clear than one might expect.

In Aetna Life Insurance Co. v. Lavoie, 475 U.S. 813 (1986), appellees submitted a health insurance claim to Aetna, which paid about half of the amount requested. It failed to pay the rest, about $1,375, on the ground that the length of the hospitalization was unnecessary. Appellant sought punitive damages for the alleged bad faith refusal to pay the claim and the jury awarded $3.5 million in punitive damages. The Alabama Supreme Court affirmed (5 to 4) in an opinion written by Justice Embry. While the case was pending before the Alabama Supreme Court, Justice Embry filed for himself two actions against other insurance companies making similar allegations and seeking punitive damages. The U.S. Supreme Court held that "only in the most extreme of cases would disqualification [for bias or prejudice] be constitutionally required, and appellant's arguments [based on the judge's general hostility toward insurance companies] here fall well below that level." However, the Court held, much more than Justice Embry's general hostility was at stake. This was the first case in which the Alabama Supreme Court clearly established the right of action upon which Justice Embry was seeking to rely in his own simultaneous litigation. The Supreme Court held that a decision rendered under these circumstances violated due process. "Justice Embry's opinion for the Alabama Supreme Court had the clear and immediate effect of enhancing both the legal status and the settlement value of his own case," it said. "We hold simply that when Justice Embry made that judgment, he acted as 'a judge in his own case.'" Three justices concurred but made the point that they would have found Justice Embry's participation improper even if his had not been the deciding vote in the case and even if he had not written the majority opinion.

b.   Interests the judge may have forgotten may still constitute an impermissible "bias" in a judge.

In Liljeberg v. Health Services Acquisition Corp., 486 U.S. 847 (1988), after a bench trial about who owned a hospital corporation, the loser learned that the trial judge was a trustee of Loyola University. During the time the case was pending, the ultimate winner, Liljeberg, was negotiating with Loyola to buy some land for a hospital and prevailing in the litigation was central to Liljeberg's ability to buy Loyola's land. The judge ruled for Liljeberg, which thereby benefitted Loyola. Health Services then moved to vacate the judgment, alleging that the trial judge should have disqualified himself under § 455(a). At a hearing to determine what the trial judge knew, he testified that he knew about the land dealings before the plaintiff filed the case, but that he forgot all about them during the pendency of the matter. He learned again of Loyola's interest after his decision, but before the expiration of the ten days in which the loser could move for a new trial. Even then, the judge did not recuse himself or tell the parties what he knew.

The Court of Appeals reversed the judgment in favor of Liljeberg in the underlying case and the Supreme Court affirmed by a 5 to 4 vote. The Court held that "[s]cienter is not an element of a violation of § 455(a)." While the trial judge could not have disqualified himself over something about which he was unaware, he was "called upon to rectify an oversight and to take the steps necessary to maintain public confidence in the impartiality of the judiciary." Moreover, while § 455 does not, on its own, authorize the reopening of closed litigation, "Congress has wisely delegated to the judiciary the task of fashioning the remedies that will best serve the purpose of the litigation." The Court recognized that while harmless error could justify failing to reverse a judgment in some cases, in this instance the appearance of impropriety required reversal of the judgment because there was "ample basis in the record for concluding that an objective observer would have questioned" the trial judge's impartiality. Moreover, the trial judge's failure to stay informed of his fiduciary interest in Loyola University "may well constitute a separate violation of § 455. See § 455(c)." Chief Justice Rehnquist, joined by Justices White and Scalia, dissented, saying that § 455(a) required an "actual knowledge" standard. Justice O'Connor agreed and would have remanded as well to determine whether "extraordinary circumstances" justified a reversal of the underlying case. With which of these opinions do you agree?

c.   Does a judge's religious beliefs constitute "bias" under Rule 2.11(A)(1) or 28 U.S.C. § 455? Look at the definitions of "impartiality" and "independence" in the Terminology section of the 2007 Model Code.

Idaho v. Freeman, 507 F.Supp. 706 (D.Idaho 1981), involved a judge hearing a case concerning the constitutionality of Congress' extension of the deadline for ratification of the equal rights amendment (ERA). The principal leaders of the Church of Jesus Christ of Latter-day Saints (popularly called the "Mormons") had publicly opposed both the ERA and extension of the deadline. The judge was a Mormon; indeed, he was a lay regional representative of that church. However, the church was not a party to the case, the judge was neither required nor requested to promote the church's position as a judge, and his duties as a church officer did not relate to the ERA. The judge concluded that his religious affiliation did not require him to disqualify himself. Do you agree with the judge's conclusion?

3.   Would the analysis change if the judge formed her views based on information learned in the courtroom rather than information learned in other settings?

a.   The "extrajudicial source doctrine," that views formed in the course of trying a case should not normally be disqualifying, is usually traced to United States v. Grinnell Corp., 384 U.S. 563 (1966): "The alleged bias and prejudice to be disqualifying must stem from an extrajudicial source." The challenge for later courts has been defining when that doctrine should apply and when it should not.

b.   In Liteky v. United States, 510 U.S. 540 (1994), for example, the government charged three defendants with spilling human blood on walls and objects at Fort Benning, GA. The judge assigned to preside at their trial tried and convicted one of the defendants, Father Bourgeois, for similar conduct eight years earlier. During that first trial, the judge repeatedly admonished the defense to limit its evidence and argument to the issues in the case, not on the motivations for the protest. On the basis of those admonitions, defendants alleged that the judge's "impartiality might reasonably be questioned" and that 28 U.S.C.A. § 455(a) required his recusal. The judge refused to recuse himself, and the jury convicted the defendants.

Justice Scalia, writing for the Court, observed that a "judge who presides at a trial may, upon completion of the evidence, be exceedingly ill disposed towards the defendant, who has been shown to be a thoroughly reprehensible person. But the judge is not thereby recusable for bias or prejudice, since his knowledge and the opinion it produced were properly and necessarily acquired in the course of the proceedings, and are indeed sometimes (as in a bench trial) necessary to completion of the judge's task." However, extrajudicial sources are "not the *exclusive* reason a predisposition can be wrongful or inappropriate." A point of view can also constitute "bias or prejudice" even if it comes from a judicial source, if "it is so extreme as to display clear inability to render fair judgment." The Court concluded that judicial rulings alone almost never constitute valid basis for a disqualification motion; "they are proper grounds for appeal, not recusal." In addition, "opinions formed by the judge on the basis of facts introduced or events occurring in the course of the current proceedings, or of prior proceedings, do not constitute a basis for a bias or partiality motion unless they display a deep–seated favoritism or antagonism that would make a fair judgment impossible." Clearly, "expressions of impatience, dissatisfaction, annoyance, and even anger" such as shown by this judge at the first trial, do not constitute bias.

Justice Kennedy, concurring in the judgment joined by Justices Blackmun, Stevens and Souter, believed that Congress intended § 455(a) to reach any case where "an objective observer [would] conclude that a fair and impartial hearing is unlikely." In this case, however, they concluded that the judge's prior conduct did not require recusal.

c.   Just two years before *Liteky*, Haines v. Liggett Group, 975 F.2d 81 (3d Cir.1992), ordered a change in trial judges. Judge Lee Sarokin conducted the first trial of, and would retry, the nation's major cigarette companies. Plaintiffs accused them of producing a product that caused cancer. In a ruling applying the crime-fraud exception to allegedly privileged documents, he said, "Who are these persons who knowingly and secretly decide to put the buying public at risk solely for the purpose of making profits and who believe that illness and death of consumers is an appropriate cost of their own prosperity! * * * [T]he tobacco industry may be the king of concealment and disinformation." The Court of Appeals acknowledged that they believed Judge Sarokin could try the case "free from bias or prejudice," but "that is not the test."

Instead, the "polestar is 'impartiality and the appearance of impartiality.'" The court ordered a change of judge. [10]

d.   In Floyd v. City of New York, 959 F.Supp.2d 668 (S.D.N.Y. 2013), African American and Latino residents filed § 1983 class actions alleging that New York City's police department's stop and frisk policy violated their constitutional rights. Judge Shira A. Scheindlin granted the motion for injunctive relief, imposed sweeping changes on the police department, appointed a monitor, and then later denied the city's motion for a stay pending appeal.

In re Reassignment of Cases, 736 F.3d 118 (2d Cir. 2013)(per curiam), the Second Circuit, sua sponte, disqualified Judge Scheindlin. Without reaching the merits of the case, the Second Circuit said it was making "no findings of misconduct, actual bias, or actual partiality on the part of Judge Scheindlin." However, the court's review of the record indicated that she appeared to encourage the plaintiffs to file these lawsuits and then directed them to herself for decision. In addition, "her statements to the media and the resulting stories published while a decision on the merits was pending," "might cause a reasonable observer to question her impartiality," so 28 U.S.C.A. § 455(a) required her disqualification.[11]

e.   If you were Judge Baxter, would these authorities tell you whether you should sit when issues concerning real estate assessments were before the court? Would you be more confused than ever? What would you do?

D.   WAIVING JUDICIAL DISQUALIFICATION

1.   May the parties waive any circumstance requiring a judge's disqualification? How about the issues that this problem raises?

a.   May the parties waive the conflict created by Martha Anderson's loan to Judge Baxter? Look at Model Code of Judicial Conduct, Rule 2.11(C). Compare 28 U.S.C. § 455(e). Why does the federal statute allow the parties to waive fewer conflicts than the Judicial Code does?

b.   Would conflicts created by financial interests of the judge's relatives be subject to waiver by the parties? Is there any justification for treating state and federal judges differently as to this issue?

c.   If Judge Baxter's possible bias against current assessment practices is disqualifying, is it subject to waiver? Would his views

---

[10] Compare United States v. Microsoft Corporation, 253 F.3d 34, 116 (D.C.Cir.2001) (district judge disqualified as to future proceedings in the case). See also, In re International Business Machines Corp., 45 F.3d 641 (2d Cir.1995) (mandamus issued to recuse judge who was critical of government decision to dismiss case); United States v. Microsoft Corp., 56 F.3d 1448 (D.C.Cir.1995) (new judge required to hear remand of case in which judge had set aside consent decree agreed to by the Antitrust Division); Hathcock v. Navistar International, 53 F.3d 36 (4th Cir.1995) (judge showed bias against tort defendants in speech before Trial Lawyers' Association).

[11] Judge Scheindlin then filed a motion protesting the Second Circuit's decision, which that Court rejected, holding, inter alia, that the trial judge had no standing to protest the reassignment of cases. In re Motion of District Judge, 736 F.3d 166 (2d Cir. 2013). The court said that she had no legal interest in these cases or their outcome, and, consequently, suffered no legal injury by reassignment.

constitute "personal bias or prejudice concerning a party"? If so, would his recusal be subject to waiver in either the state or federal system?

2. How should the judge secure a valid waiver?

a.   Compare Model Code of Judicial Conduct, Rule 2.11(C), with 28 U.S.C. § 455(e). What must the judge "disclose" about the grounds for required recusal? Must consent to waive a judge's recusal be as "informed" as consent to waive a lawyer's conflict of interest? See Model Rule of Professional Conduct 1.0(e).

b.   May counsel make the waiver orally on the record in the manner defense counsel did in this problem? Look at Rule 2.11(C). Is there any comparable requirement in § 455(e)? May lawyers waive a disqualifying circumstance on behalf of their clients or must the clients specifically approve of the waiver?

c.   Are you satisfied that the procedure specified in the Code of Judicial Conduct will guarantee anonymity to an objector? Is this anonymity important in a setting where the parties and their counsel may have to appear again before the judge in the future?

Problem 39

THE JUDGE AS A POLITICAL CANDIDATE AND PUBLIC FIGURE

Many states choose their judges by popular election. Judges who run for office have to raise campaign funds, engage in political speeches and participate in other forms of political campaigns, and the rules relating to political activity have been among the most controversial aspects of judicial ethics. Some people think that it is unseemly for judges to campaign for office; others support election of judges but believe that ethical rules should limit what a judge can say or do in a political campaign. Further, if judges are limited in what they can say about themselves, then arguably others should also be limited in what they may say about judges. This problem first looks at what judges may say and do in a political campaign. Next, it examines how a judge may raise the funds necessary to participate in electoral politics. Third, it asks what limits lawyers face in making critical comments about a judge. Fourth, it considers what limits are imposed on what a judge may say about others.

FACTS

J.R. Kraft, a local lawyer, was a declared candidate for a vacancy on the trial court at a recent election. Shortly before the primary, the following advertisement appeared in the newspaper in his judicial district:

J. R. KRAFT

(A Working Man's Son)

— The Next Best Thing to Being a Judge Yourself —

I, J. R. Kraft, am a local boy. My Dad died when I was eight, and I worked in a foundry for ten years to earn enough money to go to law school. I have never lost a jury trial in all my time in practice and I have never been a member of a political party. If elected, I will do my best to stop inflation, give the benefit of the doubt to any working man who comes before me, and throw the book at every weirdo and pervert I can find.

Permissiveness is the issue in this campaign. My opponent stupidly gave bail to a 45-year-old low-life who everybody knew had raped a 12-year-old child, but then he slapped a $500 fine on a working man who had been laid off. You can count on me never to do those things!

VOTE FOR J. R. KRAFT

[C2592]

To most people's surprise, Kraft won the primary. To everyone's surprise, the "nonpolitician" became a party stalwart. He made the rounds of political meetings and gave a five-minute speech at each about how good it was for a working man's son to be on the ticket with the likes of Governor Ford, Senator Barker, and Mayor Black. He called upon "all working people" to support the entire ticket "from the top down to little me at the bottom."

At several meetings, listeners called him aside and pressed $1, $5, $10, or even $20 into his hand to help him meet his campaign expenses. He turned most of the money over to his campaign committee, but he used $389.95 of it to buy a second suit.

Kraft's style appealed to the voters. He won the general election as well and became a judge. He still had some campaign expenses left unpaid, so two weeks after the election he asked his campaign committee to solicit members of the bar to make up the deficit.

After Kraft was on the bench for less than a year, he presided over a major murder trial, which the defense won after Kraft approved unusual jury instructions. Ellen Embers, the state's attorney, was quite upset. She had no right of appeal, of course, so she called a press conference and said, "Judge Kraft is the most biased, incompetent judge that I have ever seen. He ruled against the people throughout the recent murder trial, and he alone is responsible for letting a maniacal killer out to prey on the citizens of this county."

Two weeks later, state's attorney Embers issued a statement from her office. "The rumors around the court house have been intense the past several weeks that Judge Kraft tilts his decisions toward Anthony Roberts, the city's leading slum landlord and a regular litigant before Judge Kraft, because Roberts was a major contributor to Kraft's election campaign. I have filed a grievance with the Judicial Inquiry Board to have Judge Kraft investigated and, if the rumors are true, to have him removed from the bench."

In the meantime, one of Kraft's close friends, who was also a major contributor to Kraft's campaign, is now on trial for perjury and bribery in connection with allegedly corrupt labor practices. His defense is that he engaged in an innocent, if careless, oversight. He has asked Judge Kraft to be a character witness. Kraft, who would disqualify himself anyway if the case came before him, said, "Of course, but it would be better if you would subpoena me."

QUESTIONS

A. THE CONTENT OF JUDICIAL CAMPAIGN SPEECH AND ACTIVITIES

1. What does the Model Code of Judicial Conduct say about Kraft's advertisement in his campaign to become a state judge?

a. Should it matter that Kraft was not yet a judge at the time he ran the advertisement? Look at ABA Model Rules of Professional Conduct, Rule 8.2(b). Is such a rule required to assure that no candidate can impair the dignity of a judicial campaign? Does it necessarily favor incumbent judges by making it harder for newcomers to unseat them?

b. Under the 2007 ABA Model Code of Judicial Conduct, does the content of Kraft's advertisement subject him to discipline? Look at Rule 4.1(A)(13) and Rule 4.1, Comments 11–15. Consider also Rule 4.2(A)(1). If Kraft's advertisement had extolled his credentials for sheriff, would it violate ethical standards for him to make these charges and promises? Why is the standard different when a lawyer is running for judge? See Rule 4.1, Comment 11.

c. In Judicial Campaign Complaint Against Burick, 705 N.E.2d 422 (Ohio Comm'n of Judges 1999), a judicial candidate said: (1) "political bosses" appointed the incumbent judge the previous year, (2) she (the candidate) "supports the death penalty and isn't afraid to use it," and (3) the incumbent judge gave a lenient sentence to a convicted rapist when in fact the judge gave the defendant the maximum sentence for a lesser offense to which the defendant had pled guilty. The special commission appointed to hear the case held that a judicial candidate could only say things about the appointment process that would "further, not obscure, the public's understanding of the law and legal system." It then concluded that the governor, not political bosses, appointed the incumbent judge. Further, while a nonjudicial candidate could express views about the death penalty, a judicial candidate must refrain from making statements "that adversely reflect on their impartiality." It concluded that the comment about the alleged rape sentence was improper because the case was still pending on appeal. Then, it publicly reprimanded the candidate, fined her $7,500, and ordered her to pay the complainant $5,000 for attorneys' fees and expenses. Do you agree that the candidate's statements justified this result?

2. Does the First Amendment protect J. R. Kraft's campaign speech even if the speech violates the Model Code of Judicial Conduct?

a. Courts are looking more carefully at restrictions imposed on judicial campaign speech. In Republican Party of Minnesota v. White, 536 U.S. 765 (2002), the U.S. Supreme Court held that state ethics rules that unduly restrict political campaign speech of judicial candidates violate the First Amendment. The parties did not challenge the Minnesota rule that prohibits a judicial candidate or judge from making "pledges or promises" as to how he or she will rule in a particular case. However, the Court declared unconstitutional the rule prohibiting a candidate for judicial office from "announcing" a view on a "disputed legal or political" issue, even as interpreted to apply to matters likely to come before the candidate's court.

Speaking through Justice Scalia, the five-person majority said that the announce clause must not "unnecessarily circumscrib[e] protected expression," and the Minnesota rule failed this test. One common view of "impartiality" is an absence of bias toward any party to the proceeding, the Court said, but the announce clause is not tailored to serve that interest because "it does not restrict speech for or against particular parties, but rather speech for or against particular issues." A lack of preconception for or against a particular legal view is not a compelling state interest, "since it is virtually impossible, and hardly desirable, to find a judge who does not have preconceptions about the law."[12]

Nor does the prohibition promote impartiality in the sense of "openmindedness" because the announce clause is "woefully underinclusive." For example, a judge may confront a legal issue on which he has expressed an opinion, whether on or off the bench. "Judges often state their views on disputed legal issues outside the context of adjudication, in classes that they conduct, and in books and speeches." The Minnesota rule allows a judicial candidate to say, "I think it is constitutional for the legislature to prohibit same-sex marriage" up until "the very day before he declares himself a candidate, and [he] may say it repeatedly (until litigation is pending) after he is elected. As a means of pursuing the objective of open-mindedness that respondents now articulate, the announce clause is so woefully underinclusive as to render belief in that purpose a challenge to the credulous." [13]

---

[12] The Court acknowledged the views of then-Justice Rehnquist described in Problem 38, supra. See Ronald D. Rotunda Judicial Campaigns in the Shadow of Republican Party v. White, 14 The Professional Lawyer 2 (2002); Ronald D. Rotunda, A Preliminary Empirical Inquiry into the Connection between Judicial Decision Making and Campaign Contributions to Judicial Candidates, 14 The Professional Lawyer 16 (2003).

[13] Compare Rule 2.2, Comment 1. The Reporters' Explanation of Changes to the 2007 Model Rules says: "This new Comment defines impartiality with reference to the two

Justice Kennedy, concurring, added, "Minnesota may not * * * censor what the people hear as they undertake to decide for themselves which candidate is most likely to be an exemplary judicial officer. Deciding the relevance of candidate speech is the right of the voters, not the State." Justices Stevens and Ginsburg filed dissenting opinions joined by Justices Souter and Breyer. They argued that the office of judge is significantly different from a legislative or executive office. Judges, they argued, should be elected because they have integrity, not because their views are popular. Thus, they argued, the government can restrict the speech of judges, and those seeking to be judges, in ways it cannot regulate the speech of others.

With which of these positions do you agree? Given the logic of these cases, do you believe that other provisions of Rule 4.1 and Rule 4.2 of the ABA Model Code of Judicial Conduct are likely to be at risk if a judge challenges them?

b.   In response to Republican Party of Minnesota v. White, there is pressure to ban judges from answering questions that political interest groups (e.g., organizations that favor or oppose abortion rules) may pose to them. Does the Code of Judicial Conduct prohibit judges from responding to such questionnaires? Look at Rule 4.1, Comment 15. Should it do so? Would it be constitutional, in light of *White*, for state judicial authorities to forbid judges from answering?

3.   Does the Code of Judicial Conduct place any additional limits on political activities of judges?

a.   May judges make speeches on behalf of candidates for nonjudicial public office? Look at ABA Model Code of Judicial Conduct, Rule 4.1(A)(2) & (3) & Comment 4. May they contribute money to a political party or to other candidates? Compare Rules 4.1(A)(4) & (5), with Rule 4.2(B)(4) & (6).

b.   May a judicial candidate run as part of a party team? See Rule 4.2(B)(5) & (6), Rule 4.2(C) & Rule 4.2, Comment 7. In Republican Party of Minnesota v. White, 416 F.3d 738 (8th Cir.2005) (en banc), cert. denied sub. nom., Dimick v. Republican Party of Minnesota, 546 U.S. 1157 (2006), the court examined the constitutionality of restrictions on partisan activities in light of the Supreme Court's decision discussed above. The state defended the restrictions by saying that identification with a party label is "nothing more than shorthand for the views a judicial candidate holds." In light of the Supreme Court's analysis of the "announce" clause, however, the court said that requiring judges to conceal their party affiliation during the course of a judicial campaign "can hardly be expected to open the mind of a candidate who has engaged in years of prior political activity." The court held the restrictions unconstitutionally violated judges' rights of free association.

c.   Siefert v. Alexander, 608 F.3d 974 (7th Cir. 2010), challenged the Wisconsin Code of Judicial Conduct rules prohibiting judges and judicial candidates from asserting their membership in a political party, endorsing partisan candidates for office, and personally soliciting campaign contributions. The plaintiff was an active Democrat before becoming a judge; he wanted to join the party again and to endorse

---

definitions of impartiality accepted by the Supreme Court in Republican Party of Minnesota v. White, lack of bias toward a participant in the judicial process, and open-mindedness."

President Obama. The district court declared the rules prohibiting such conduct unconstitutional. The Seventh Circuit agreed that the ban on joining a political party was unconstitutional, citing Republican Party v. White. The policy behind such a ban was to avoid indicating the judge's possible views on policy issues, but "that is the purported compelling state interest that *White* squarely rejected." If party membership were somehow relevant to issues in a particular case, the court believed, then recusal could solve the problem. There is no need for a blanket ban.

The court held that it would evaluate the ban on endorsement of political candidates by using balancing test, not strict scrutiny. The Court upheld the ban. Persons the judge has endorsed might appear in the judge's court, and a judge might trade his or her endorsement of political figures for reciprocal support by the officials. Moreover, the prohibition against endorsements does not inform the electorate of the judge's qualifications and beliefs," so the public interest in allowing judges unregulated speech is less.

d.   If Judge Kraft enters a race for Congress, must he resign from the bench? Look at Rule 4.5(A). If a state senator runs for Congress, must he or she resign the old office before running for the new one? Why do we treat judges differently? See Rule 4.5, Comment 1 and Rule 4.1, Comment 11.

e.   Should the rules be different if the judicial candidate is campaigning in a nonpartisan election? The 1990 Judicial Code did not distinguish between these different types of elections, and allowed judicial candidates to solicit endorsements—"publicly stated support"—through campaign committees. Rule 4.2(B)(5) of the 2007 Model Code, by contrast, permits candidates in a non-partisan election to solicit such support on their own from persons or organizations, but not from partisan political organizations. Are the rules wise to make such a distinction?

B.   JUDGES SOLICITING AND RECEIVING CAMPAIGN CONTRIBUTIONS

1.   Are you troubled if judges receive endorsements and campaign contributions from the lawyers who appear before them?

a.   Think back to Problem 38 and the cases condemning lawyers' payments to judges. Why should the law distinguish campaign contributions from any other gifts made to a judge?

b.   The multibillion-dollar Pennzoil v. Texaco litigation was primarily in the Texas state courts. The trial judge received a $10,000 campaign contribution from Pennzoil's chief trial lawyer "[w]ithin days of being assigned the Pennzoil case," a sum the trial judge described as "princely." Wall Street J., Nov. 4, 1987, at 1, 20, col. 2. In the three-and-one-half years prior to their decision in *Pennzoil*, all nine members of the Texas Supreme Court, consistent with Texas law, "openly accepted campaign contributions from lawyers with cases pending before them." Forbes, Sept. 7, 1987, at 8.

c.   If lawyers may contribute to judges deciding their clients' cases, do the lawyers have any choice but to make those contributions? Is a large campaign contribution from a litigant or lawyer a basis for questioning the judge's impartiality? See Rule 2.11(A)(4).

2. In this problem, J.R. Kraft accepted campaign contributions pressed into his hand. Was it proper for him to do so?

a.   Look at Rule 4.1(A)(8). Is there any doubt that J.R. Kraft has violated the ABA Model Code of Judicial Conduct?

b.   The present Model Code prescribes the proper method of handling campaign contributions in Rules 4.2(B) and 4.4. Do you think establishment of a campaign committee will prevent the judge from learning which lawyers support his or her candidacy and the generosity of that support? Are there other reasons to require creating such a committee?

c.   Does the requirement of a campaign committee impair free speech? Weaver v. Bonner, 309 F.3d 1312 (11th Cir.2002), held Georgia's version unconstitutional.

Whose free speech is limited if the law requires an intermediary between the judge and those who want to give the judge money?[14]

3. May a judge's campaign committee solicit funds from lawyers *after* the election when everyone knows who the winner is?

a.   Look at Rule 4.4(B)(2). Do you agree that a judicial campaign committee should be permitted to solicit campaign contributions until an "[insert number]" of days after the election?

b.   What arguments support this position? Do we want to avoid having judges start out a new term of judicial service in substantial debt because of the campaign? Might that put them under financial pressures that others could later exploit?

c.   Commentary 2 following Canon 5C(2) of the 1990 Model Code advised that campaign committees "should manage campaign finances responsibly, avoiding deficits that might necessitate post-election fund-raising, to the extent possible." That provision was not included in the 2007 Model Code of Judicial Conduct. Did the provision have any teeth? Was its suggestion of good budgeting and self-restraint just a way to assuage our collective embarrassment at permitting the practice of post-election fund raising?

4. Should we be concerned when a third party expends funds to praise the judge publicly or to criticize the judge's opponent?

a.   In Caperton v. A.T. Massey Coal Co., 556 U.S. 868 (2009), a state jury found the Massey company liable for $50 million. After the verdict, but before the appeal, West Virginia held its 2004 judicial election. Don Blankenship, Massey's chairman and principal officer, supported candidate Brent Benjamin rather than the incumbent justice seeking reelection. Blankenship gave $1,000—the statutory

---

[14] The Eighth Circuit joined the Eleventh Circuit in Republican Party of Minnesota v. White, 416 F.3d 738 (8th Cir.2005), in upholding the ban on personal solicitation of campaign funds as a way of limiting corruption, citing Buckley v. Valeo, 424 U.S. 1 (1976). "A direct solicitation closely links the quid—avoiding the judge's future disfavor—to the quo—the contribution." While the ban was not perfectly tailored—judges could serve on their own finance committees and know who had contributed, for example—it was sufficient to be constitutional.

maximum—to Benjamin's campaign committee. That contribution raised no issue of bias. Blankenship also donated $3 million of his own money, however, to an organization that made *independent* expenditures that opposed the incumbent judge against whom Benjamin was running. Benjamin won the election and when the *Massey* case came before the court, Benjamin refused to disqualify himself. He cast the deciding vote to reverse the judgment against Massey. The U.S. Supreme Court held (5 to 4) that the due process clause required Justice Benjamin not to participate in the decision of a case after having received the benefit of such a large campaign expenditure by an individual interested in the result.

Is this case is unique or will it lead to routine motions seeking to disqualify judges because of what the Court called a "debt of gratitude" to people who donate to other groups who oppose the judge's opponent? In this case, Justice Benjamin did not know Blankenship and Blankenship owned less than 0.5% of Massey, the company that prevailed in the case. The Court said that a party who seeks a judge's recusal need not prove actual bias. Instead, the Court cited the need for an "objective standard," i.e., "whether, under a realistic appraisal of psychological tendencies and human weaknesses, the interest poses such a risk of actual bias or prejudgment that the practice must be forbidden if the guarantee of due process is to be adequately implemented." Do you think that is an objective standard? The dissents predicted that a "flood of recusal motions" would follow this decision. Chief Justice Roberts, for example, listed 40 open questions including how a court is to tell when a contributor's influence in putting the judge on the bench was "disproportionate."[15]

b.   The issues raised in *Caperton* became even more interesting after Citizens United v. Federal Election Commission, 558 U.S. 310 (2010). *Citizens United* held that entities such as corporations or unions have a constitutional right to make independent expenditures to favor or oppose candidates for elective office. Facing the requirement imposed by *Caperton*, must a judge recuse herself if one of the parties spent money to support the judge or her opponent without the judge's consent? How will the judge know which parties made *independent* expenditures to support particular judicial candidates? May the judge leave the detective work to the parties? May the judge simply assume that anyone who thinks there may be a problem will call it to the judge's attention? See Rule 2.11(A)(4).

5.   Would a "merit system" of judicial selection—i.e., appointing judges as in the federal system—remove ethical issues from the selection process?

a.   If all judges were appointed, would "political activity" take other forms? Should it be proper for an attorney to work in a senator's election campaign, for example, in the hope of being rewarded with a federal judicial appointment? Look at Rule 4.3.

---

[15] See Ronald D. Rotunda, Judicial Disqualification in the Aftermath of Caperton v. A.T. Massey Coal Co., 60 Syracuse L. Rev. 247 (2009). *Caperton* remanded the case was to the West Virginia Supreme Court and a retired justice was appointed to join the court to hear the case in the absence of Justice Benjamin. The court reached the same result it had reached the first time. Caperton v. A.T. Massey Coal Co., 690 S.E.2d 322 (2009). See also, Ronald D. Rotunda, Codifying Caperton v. A.T. Massey Coal Co., 42 McGeorge L. Rev. 95 (2010).

b.   Would it be proper for a governor's aide to question a prospective judge about his or her attitudes on bail for "low-lifes"? Look at Rule 4.3 & Comment 1.

C.   LAWYER CRITICISM OF JUDGES

1.   Should Ellen Embers, the state's attorney in this problem, be subject to discipline for making critical remarks about Judge Kraft at her press conference?

a.   In re Holtzman, 577 N.E.2d 30 (N.Y.1991) (per curiam), upheld a letter of reprimand that the Grievance Committee issued to a district attorney who publicly released a letter charging a trial judge with misconduct. Someone erroneously told the district attorney that the judge in a sexual assault trial made the complainant get down on the floor and in effect reenact the crime before the judge and counsel. The district attorney repeated these charges in her letter, which also said that the incident made the complainant feel degraded and humiliated. The district attorney made no effort to speak with court officers, the court reporter, defense counsel or any other person present during the alleged misconduct. A later investigation determined the charge was false.

New York Times v. Sullivan, 376 U.S. 254 (1964), held that a public official cannot recover damages for a defamatory falsehood relating to his official conduct unless he proves that the defendant made the statement with "actual malice," which the Court defined as *scienter*; that is, that the statement was made "with knowledge that it was false or with reckless disregard of whether it was false or not." The N.Y. Court of Appeals, however, refused to apply the *Sullivan* standard to lawyer discipline cases. To do so, it said, "would immunize all accusations, however reckless or irresponsible, from censure as long as the attorney uttering them did not actually entertain serious doubts as to their truth. * * * It is the reasonableness of the belief, not the state of mind of the attorney, that is determinative"

b.   Does Model Rule 8.2(a) reach the same result? United States District Court v. Sandlin, 12 F.3d 861 (9th Cir.1993), affirmed a lawyer's six-month suspension from practice before the district court for falsely charging that the district judge had ordered important passages deleted from the transcript of a recusal hearing. The lawyer made the statements in a hearing on the lawyer's charges and in a statement to an assistant U.S. attorney. That, in turn, led to FBI scientific tests and a grand jury investigation that cleared the judge. The court agreed that Rule 8.2(a) does not prohibit all criticism of judges, but it refused to read an "actual malice" standard into the "reckless disregard as to its truth or falsity" language of the rule. The test should be "what the reasonable attorney, considered in light of all his professional functions, would do in the same or similar circumstances."

Do you agree with this reading of Model Rule 8.2(a)? See Restatement Third, The Law Governing Lawyers § 114, Comment *b* (*New York Times* rule should apply to charges by lawyers about conduct of judges).

c.   Should questions regarding criticism of judges depend on whether or not judges are elected? Consider Model Rule 8.2, Comment

1. Does the public have an interest in knowing about the characteristics of the judges who run for election? Would it matter how long it was until the next election? On the other hand, are you concerned that elected judges may suffer unjust vilification and may find themselves limited in their ability to respond to criticism? Should lawyers have more latitude to criticize judges with life tenure?

2.   If another judge believed that Embers' charges against Judge Kraft were true, would that judge have an obligation to report Judge Kraft?

a.   Look at Model Code of Judicial Conduct, Rule 2.15(A). Does Rule 8.3(b) of the Model Rules of Professional Conduct also give state's attorney Embers an obligation to file a disciplinary complaint against Judge Kraft?

b.   Should the law impose more limits on a lawyer who publicly announces that he has filed charges against a judge than if the lawyer files charges against another public official? Is there a public interest in preserving confidence in the judiciary that may distinguish these from ordinary cases? Does the argument cut the other way, i.e., that public confidence in judges is instilled by making it known that the system aggressively roots out corruption?

c.   If a judge makes reckless comments accusing a fellow judge of misconduct, is the judge civilly liable for a tort? The 1990 Model Code of Judicial Conduct, Canon 3D(3), said that a judge is "absolutely privileged" for filing a disciplinary charge against another judge or lawyer, "and no civil action predicated thereon may be instituted against the judge." The 2007 Model Code deleted this provision. The Reporters' Explanation said that neither "the ABA nor any adopting court is in the position to grant or deny immunity in the context of judicial conduct standards."

d.   Would it be proper for a judge to punish a lawyer who filed a disciplinary charge against the judge, such as by denying the lawyer a routine continuance? Look at Rule 2.16(B), which forbids retaliation, "directly or indirectly." This Rule also had no counterpart in the 1990 Model Code.

3.   Would state's attorney Embers be subject to any different form of discipline if she made her remarks about Judge Kraft to the judge's face or in a letter to the judge?

a.   In re Snyder, 472 U.S. 634 (1985), involved a lawyer appointed to handle a case under the Criminal Justice Act. He submitted a claim for fees, which the court returned with a request for additional information. Because the lawyer had technical problems with his computer software, he did not provide the information in the form that the chief judge requested. The lawyer did provide a supplemental application, which the secretary to the chief judge also returned. The lawyer then wrote the judge's secretary complaining of the "extreme gymnastics" required of him to get paid "puny amounts," which he said did not even cover overhead. He added that he was "extremely disgusted" by the Eighth Circuit's treatment and asked to be taken off the list of counsel willing to accept appointment. For these "disrespectful remarks," and because he refused to apologize "for what I consider to be telling the truth, albeit in harsh terms," the court suspended the lawyer from practice before federal courts for six months, 734 F.2d 334 (8th Cir.1984).

A unanimous Supreme Court reversed. One intemperate letter does not justify such a sanction, the Court said. The Court did not reach the First Amendment issue but rather relied on its interpretation of Federal Rule of Appellate Procedure 46, which authorizes a court to suspend or disbar an attorney "guilty of conduct unbecoming a member of the bar of the court * * *." The Supreme Court noted that the lawyer's criticisms of the administration of the Criminal Justice Act had merit (a point the Eighth Circuit had conceded) and that such criticism cannot be a cause for discipline or suspension. The Court of Appeals' testy opinion on remand is at 770 F.2d 743 (8th Cir.1985).

b.   Williams v. Williams, 721 A.2d 1072 (Pa.1998), involved a lawyer frustrated with a judge's conduct who, after an unfavorable ruling on an objection to a question, said under his breath, "He's such a [f—a—]." The opposing lawyer, always concerned about protecting the court's dignity, repeated the remark in a much louder voice to get it on the record. The Pennsylvania Supreme Court said the remark was ill mannered but caused no significant disruption in the proceeding and therefore did not rise to the level of criminal contempt.

D.   THE JUDGE REWARDING HIS FRIENDS

1.   May Judge Kraft testify as a character witness on behalf of his friend?

a.   Judges often have friends. Some of those friends are in politics. The politicians may wish to have the judge vouch for them. What is the point of Model Code of Judicial Conduct, Rule 3.3? When Kraft said, "it would be better if you would subpoena me," did he satisfy his obligation not to testify "voluntarily"?

b.   One state bar committee proposed that what is now Rule 3.3 should read:

> "He should not appear as a character witness unless he appears pursuant to compulsory process of law * * * and unless the judge or other official presiding in the proceeding determines that his testimony is needed to protect the constitutional rights of a party or to provide a fair hearing."[16]

Do you see the reason for the different language? Would such an approach make the subpoena more than a formality? Do you agree with the proposed change? How would you have a court make the determination of which witnesses a "fair hearing" requires?

c.   May a judge publicly support a friend's nomination to a public position? In re Honorable Nathan Hecht, 213 S.W.3d 547 (Tex.Spec.Ct.Rev.2006), held that it was not improper for a Texas Supreme Court justice and close personal friend of Harriet Miers to tell the U.S. Senate Judiciary Committee and several reporters that she would make a wonderful U.S. Supreme Court justice. This special court of review rejected those contentions: "we interpret 'endorsing' under the circumstances of this case to mean more than support, that is, more

---

[16] Report and Recommendations of the Joint Illinois State Bar Association–Chicago Bar Association Committee on Rules of Judicial Conduct, Apr. 1974, at 5.

than spoken praise." If there were a hearing, the Senate Judiciary Committee could have subpoenaed Hecht who would have said the same thing.

2. Should the law limit the power of a judge who appoints friends to a position that is within the power of the judge to fill, for example, naming a friend as a special master?

a. Look at ABA Model Rules of Professional Conduct, Rule 7.6. What is that Rule trying to regulate? Does it apply to seeking a senator's recommendation for a judgeship? Does Rule 7.6 relate to appointments to a position that a judge makes?

b. Suppose lawyer Mary contributed substantial amounts to Kraft's campaign because she and Kraft went to high school together and she wanted her old friend to win the election. May Judge Kraft appoint Mary as a special master in a case in which the fee would be substantial? Mary if asked, could truthfully say that she did not contribute any money "for the purpose of obtaining or being considered" for that appointment by Judge Kraft. May Mary accept the appointment from Judge Kraft under Model Rule 7.6 of the ABA Model Rules of Professional Conduct? May Judge Kraft appoint Mary if Mary has contributed more than the amount the state inserts into its version of Rule 2.13(B)?

c. Lawyer Harry has given no money to Judge Kraft's campaign, but he has contributed substantial amounts of time. He distributed leaflets, visited various newspapers and urged the editorial departments to endorse Kraft for election as judge. Now, Judge Kraft would like to appoint Harry to become an associate judge of the court. Does Model Rule 7.6 limit Harry's ability to accept this appointment? Look particularly at Comment 2. Why should the rule distinguish between cash and in-kind contributions to the judge?

———

A JUDGE'S PARTICIPATION IN NON-JUDICIAL ACTIVITIES

Judges are not hermits, and several were probably active in community life before going on the bench. A sitting judge may still participate in several—but not all—kinds of nonjudicial groups.

1. What kinds of nonjudicial groups may a judge participate? Is the organization "concerned with the law, the legal system, or the administration of justice," within the meaning of Rule 3.7(A)? What qualifies as a "civic organization" not conducted for profit? If an organization is not one that Rule 3.7 authorizes, may the judge remain a member?

Should the analysis depend upon whether the organization is frequently involved in litigation that may come before the court? Look at Rule 3.7(A)(6). May the judge hear a case filed by an organization of which the judge is a member? Remember Rule 2.11(A)(1).

2. If the governor appoints Judge Richardson to a new commission to examine problems of the homeless, may the judge accept that appointment? Look at Rule 3.4. Does it make sense that such commissions should not have judicial participation? May the governor

appoint the judge a trustee of State Law School? Does the answer change if the governor appoints the judge a trustee of State Medical School or State University? Do such distinctions make any sense to you?

3.   May a judge testify before a public body about the need for public funds to provide homeless shelters around the state? Look at Rule 3.2. May a judge, either alone or with others, ask local businesses to donate money to help the homeless? Look at Rule 3.7(A)(2) and Comments 2 & 3.

4.   May a judge work as a part-time law professor?

Rule 3.1 Comment 1 "encourage[s]" judges' "speaking, writing, teaching, or participating in scholarly research projects." Rule 3.10, on the other hand, provides that (subject to a few exceptions) a "judge shall not practice law." Why distinguish between the two activities?

Should a judge be obliged not to take positions in class on unsettled questions of law? Look at Rule 3.1(C). Could opinions expressed in class be a basis for disqualifying the judge in later cases? Would you as an advocate before the judge believe you should know the opinions he or she has expressed?

PROBLEM 40

THE ACTIVE FEDERAL JUDGE

OMITTED IN CONCISE EDITION

———

INDEX

References are to Pages

489

INTIMATE RELATIONSHIPS
Conflicts of interest, relationships
    between lawyers and clients, 163

INVESTIGATIONS
Discipline, conduct prejudicial to
    administration of justice, 35
Litigation tactics, use of deception in
    search for truth, 294
Marketing legal services, solicitation, 392
Prosecuting attorneys, 365

JOINT REPRESENTATION
Attorney-client privilege, 102
Specialists, 403

JOINT VENTURES
Specialists, 403

JUDGES
    Generally, 461 et seq.
Campaign contributions, solicitation and
    receipt of, 481
Campaign speech and activities, 478
Conflicts of interest
        Generally, 462 et seq.
    Family of judge, financial interests,
        467
    Financial interests, 463, 467
    Former judges, 206
    Personal views of judge, 471
    Remedies for conflict of interest
        violation, 208
    Waiver of judicial disqualification,
        475
Criticism of judges by lawyers, 484
Discipline, this index
Evidence, rewards to friends, 486
Family of judge, conflicts of interest based
    on financial interests of, 467
Financial interests, conflicts of interest,
    463, 467
Firm practice, conflicts of interest based
    on financial interests of family
    members, 468
Nonjudicial activities, participation in,
    487
Personal views of judge, conflicts of
    interest, 471
Political candidate and public figure,
    status as
        Generally, 475 et seq.
    Campaign speech and activities, 478
    Criticism of judges by lawyers, 484
    Rewards to friends, 486
    Solicitation and receipt of campaign
        contributions, 481
Public figure, status as. Political
    candidate and public figure, status
    as, above
Rewards to friends, 486
Solicitation and receipt of campaign
    contributions, 481
Waiver of judicial disqualification, 475

JURY SELECTION
Litigation tactics, creative lawyering vs.
    deception, 287

KUTAK COMMISSION
Model Code of Professional Responsibility,
    16

LABOR UNIONS
Generally, 11

LAST LINK DOCTRINE
Litigation, confidentiality of identity of
    client, 314

LAW ENFORCEMENT
Litigation tactics, use of deception in
    search for truth, 294

LAW SCHOOLS
Judges, participation in non-judicial
    activities, 487

LAW STUDENTS
Confidentiality, 108
Conflicts of interest, imputed
    disqualification, 188

LAWYER-TEMPORARIES
Conflicts of interest, imputed
    disqualification, 189

LEGAL ASSISTANTS
Conflicts of interest, imputed
    disqualification, 187

LEGAL SERVICE ORGANIZATIONS
Conflicts of interest
        Imputed disqualification, 181
        Positional conflicts, 151
Imputed disqualification, 181
Positional conflicts, 151

LEMON LAW
Conflicts of interest regarding former
    clients, automobiles, 173

LIBEL
Billing for services, contingent fees, 84

LIENS
Withdrawal from representation,
    attorneys' liens, 97, 98

LIMITATION OF ACTIONS
Admission to practice, character and
    fitness, 25

LIMITED LIABILITY COMPANIES
Malpractice, shielding lawyers from
    vicarious liability, 56

**LIMITED LIABILITY
    PARTNERSHIPS**
Malpractice, shielding lawyers from
    vicarious liability, 56

LITIGATION
    Generally, 273 et seq.
ADR alternatives, 285
Adverse facts, disclosure obligations, 304